Fodor's

P9-EGM-630

THAILAND

10th Edition

Where to Stay and Eat
for All Budgets

Must-See Sights
and Local Secrets

Ratings You Can Trust

Fodor's Travel Publications   New York, Toronto, London, Sydney, Auckland
www.fodors.com

FODOR'S THAILAND

Editors: Carissa Bluestone (lead project editor), Alexis Kelly

Editorial Production: Tom Holton
Editorial Contributors: Karen Coates, Mick Elmore, Robin Goldstein, Alexis Herschkowitsch, Trevor Ranges, Robert Tilley
Maps: Henry Columb and Mark Stroud, Moon Street Cartography; David Lindroth, *cartographer*; Rebecca Baer and Bob Blake, *map editors*
Design: Fabrizio La Rocca, *creative director*; Guido Caroti, *art director*; Ann McBride, *designer*; Moon Sun Kim, *cover designer*; Melanie Marin, *senior picture editor*
Production/Manufacturing: Robert B. Shields
Cover Photo (Wat Si Chum Temple, Sukhothai): Angelo Cavalli/The Image Bank/Getty Images

Tenth Edition

ISBN 978–1–4000–1744–7

ISSN 1064–0993

SPECIAL SALES

This book is available at special discounts for bulk purchases for sales promotions or premiums. Special editions, including personalized covers, excerpts of existing books, and corporate imprints, can be created in large quantities for special needs. For more information, write to Special Markets/Premium Sales, 1745 Broadway, MD 6-2, New York, New York 10019, or e-mail specialmarkets@randomhouse.com.

AN IMPORTANT TIP & AN INVITATION

Although all prices, opening times, and other details in this book are based on information supplied to us at press time, changes occur all the time in the travel world, and Fodor's cannot accept responsibility for facts that become outdated or for inadvertent errors or omissions. So **always confirm information when it matters,** especially if you're making a detour to visit a specific place. Your experiences—positive and negative—matter to us. If we have missed or misstated something, **please write to us.** We follow up on all suggestions. Contact the Thailand editor at editors@fodors.com or c/o Fodor's at 1745 Broadway, New York, NY 10019.

PRINTED IN THE UNITED STATES OF AMERICA

10 9 8 7 6 5 4 3 2 1

Be a Fodor's Correspondent

Your opinion matters. It matters to us. It matters to your fellow Fodor's travelers, too. And we'd like to hear it. In fact, we *need* to hear it.

When you share your experiences and opinions, you become an active member of the Fodor's community. That means we'll not only use your feedback to make our books better, but we'll publish your names and comments whenever possible. Throughout our guides, look for "Word of Mouth," excerpts of your unvarnished feedback.

Here's how you can help improve Fodor's for all of us.

Tell us when we're right. We rely on local writers to give you an insider's perspective. But our writers and staff editors—who are the best in the business—depend on you. Your positive feedback is a vote to renew our recommendations for the next edition.

Tell us when we're wrong. We're proud that we update most of our guides every year. But we're not perfect. Things change. Hotels cut services. Museums change hours. Charming cafés lose charm. If our writer didn't quite capture the essence of a place, tell us how you'd do it differently. If any of our descriptions are inaccurate or inadequate, we'll incorporate your changes in the next edition and will correct factual errors at fodors.com *immediately.*

Tell us what to include. You probably have had fantastic travel experiences that aren't yet in Fodor's. Why not share them with a community of like-minded travelers? Maybe you chanced upon a beach or bistro or bed-and-breakfast that you don't want to keep to yourself. Tell us why we should include it. And share your discoveries and experiences with everyone directly at fodors.com. Your input may lead us to add a new listing or highlight a place we cover with a "Highly Recommended" star or with our highest rating, "Fodor's Choice."

Give us your opinion instantly at our feedback center at www.fodors.com/feedback. You may also e-mail editors@fodors.com with the subject line "Thailand Editor." Or send your nominations, comments, and complaints by mail to Thailand Editor, Fodor's, 1745 Broadway, New York, NY 10019.

You and travelers like you are the heart of the Fodor's community. Make our community richer by sharing your experiences. Be a Fodor's correspondent.

Happy traveling!

Tim Jarrell, Publisher

CONTENTS

ABOUT THIS BOOK

Our Ratings

Sometimes you find terrific travel experiences and sometimes they just find you. But usually the burden is on you to select the right combination of experiences. That's where our ratings come in.

As travelers we've all discovered a place so wonderful that its worthiness is obvious. And sometimes that place is so unique that superlatives don't do it justice: you just have to be there to know. These sights, properties, and experiences get our highest rating, **Fodor's Choice,** indicated by orange stars throughout this book.

Black stars highlight sights and properties we deem **Highly Recommended,** places that our writers, editors, and readers praise again and again for consistency and excellence.

By default, there's another category: any place we include in this book is by definition worth your time, unless we say otherwise. And we will.

Disagree with any of our choices? Care to nominate a place or suggest that we rate one more highly? Visit our feedback center at www.fodors.com/feedback.

Budget Well

Hotel and restaurant price categories from ¢ to $$$$ are defined in the opening pages of each chapter. For attractions, we always give standard adult admission fees; reductions are usually available for children, students, and senior citizens. Want to pay with plastic? **AE, D, DC, MC, V** following restaurant and hotel listings indicate whether American Express, Discover, Diners Club, MasterCard, and Visa are accepted.

Restaurants

Unless we state otherwise, restaurants are open for lunch and dinner daily. We mention dress only when there's a specific requirement and reservations only when they're essential or not accepted—it's always best to book ahead.

Hotels

Hotels have private bath, phone, TV, and air-conditioning and operate on the European Plan (aka EP, meaning without meals), unless we specify that they use the Continental Plan (CP, with a Continental breakfast), Breakfast Plan (BP, with a full breakfast), or Modified American Plan (MAP, with breakfast and dinner) or are all-inclusive (including all meals and most activities). We always list facilities but not whether you'll be charged an extra fee to use them, so when pricing accommodations, find out what's included.

Many Listings

★	Fodor's Choice
★	Highly recommended
✉	Physical address
✛	Directions
✆	Mailing address
☎	Telephone
🖷	Fax
⊕	On the Web
✒	E-mail
🖾	Admission fee
☉	Open/closed times
►	Start of walk/itinerary
Ⓜ	Metro stations
🖃	Credit cards

Hotels & Restaurants

🏨	Hotel
🛏	Number of rooms
⚴	Facilities
⍾⍾⍾	Meal plans
✕	Restaurant
⚑	Reservations
🏛	Dress code
↘	Smoking
🍸	BYOB
✕🏨	Hotel with restaurant that warrants a visit

Outdoors

🏌	Golf
⚠	Camping

Other

☮	Family-friendly
🛈	Contact information
⇨	See also
✉	Branch address
☞	Take note

WHAT'S WHERE

BANGKOK	Bangkok is undoubtedly a 21st-century boomtown, characterized both by developing-nation squalor and futuristic luxury, by old-world charm and grotesquely unchecked development. You can dine at street stalls or hobnob at famous foreign eateries and shop for local handicrafts at the congested JJ weekend market, haggle over knickknacks within the maze of Chinatown's alleys, or find label after international label in Sukhumvit's upscale malls. As for nightlife, the "scene" includes everything from megaclubs to red-light districts. Don't skip town without visiting the Old City, home to the Grand Palace, Temple of Dawn, and National Museum—a more amazing trio of sights you won't find.
AROUND BANGKOK	Petchaburi, to the south, features ancient temples, a royal retreat, and roving gangs of macaque monkeys. To the west, Nakhon Pathom, Thailand's oldest city, is home to Phra Pathom Chedi, the largest Buddhist structure in the world. A couple of hours north of Bangkok is the floating market at Damnoen Saduak. Kanchanaburi Province, to the west of Bangkok, is a destination in its own right. The region features the seven-tiered waterfall of the magnificent Erawan National Park, a tiger temple where you can pet "wild" tigers, and the World War II Death Railway, which crosses the River Kwai and continues toward Myanmar (Burma), a path you may follow to Sangklaburi, the multiethnic border town.
THE CENTRAL PLAINS	Beyond temple tours, the Central Plains has plenty to offer in terms of solitude and natural beauty. From Bangkok, take a train or riverboat up to Ayutthaya, the famous remains of the ancient capital sacked by the Burmese in 1767. History and architecture enthusiasts will want to swing by Lopburi to examine Khmer, Thai, and French buildings. The ancient capital of Sukhothai has amazingly intact ruins dating to the birth of Thailand as a unified nation. If you're traveling in autumn, you must attend the romantic Loi Krathong festival here. Sukhothai's sister city, Si Satchanalai, has hilltop temples where you can meditate for hours without seeing another soul. Tak Province, still off the beaten path, has vast teak forests and river gorges that provide thrilling white-water rafting adventures.

WHAT'S WHERE

THE SOUTHERN BEACHES	Thailand is blessed with two amazing shores (one facing the Gulf of Thailand, the other facing the Andaman Ocean), which have alternating monsoon seasons, so there is great beach weather year-round. The Eastern Gulf features Pattaya, famous for its raucous (most would say raunchy) nightlife; Koh Samet, a quiet national park on weekdays and Bangkokian hot spot on weekends; and Koh Chang, a once pristine, but rapidly developing island. The Western Gulf showcases Hua Hin, the host of an annual, international jazz festival; and the three neighboring islands of Koh Samui (jewel of the gulf), Koh Phangan (world famous for its Full Moon parties), and Koh Tao (a top scuba spot). The Andaman Coast is best known for the oft-mispronounced Phuket Island and the spectacular Phan Nga Bay. Krabi is ideal for adventure enthusiasts: snorkeling, diving, kayaking, and rock-climbing are some of the most popular activities, while Phan Nga Province relies on the relatively unspoiled beaches of Khao Lak, Koh Similan, and Koh Surin to attract a more laid-back crowd.
NORTHERN THAILAND	The "capital" of Northern Thailand, Chiang Mai, is easily accessible from Bangkok by rail or by air. The city has a lovely moat-encircled Old City and dozens of temples; tasty regional cuisine and great restaurants that serve it; and a number of markets selling beautiful cloth and crafts. Outside the city, there's much for the adventurer, including the towering peaks of "The Loop" road and the hot springs near Pai. The smaller capital city of Chiang Rai is a chilled-out regional center for less touristy hill tribe treks and gateway to the so-called Golden Triangle. Remote Chiang Khong, on the Laos border, is a launching point for really adventurous multiday Mekong River trips to Luang Prabang. The region also has a handful of the country's most luxurious resorts, some of which are far from civilization.
ISAN	Isan is Thailand's heartland, as well as Thailand's most populous region and largest agricultural center. Among Thais, Isan is known for its distinctive contributions to Thai cuisine, music, and national character. If you are interested in immersing yourself in Thai culture and going where you'll see few fellow tourists, Isan is *the* region for you. In the east, Cambodian influences are noticeable in towns such as Phimai and some of the Khmer ruins in the area are superb. Closer to Laos, Laotian influences on culture and food are apparent, especially along

the Mekong River. Accessible via budget carrier Air Asia, the city of Nong Khai, on the Mekong River border with Laos, hosts tens of thousands of visitors for the mystical naga fireballs that rise out of the river around the end of Buddhist Lent every fall. Outdoor enthusiasts enjoy trekking or biking in Khao Yai National Park, home to wild elephants and even a few tigers.

CAMBODIA

No trip to Southeast Asia is truly complete without a visit to the spectacular ruins outside the Cambodian city of Siem Reap; the carving adorned walls of Angkor Wat, giant stone faces of Bayon, and tree-topped ruins of Ta Prohm. The capital of Phnom Penh is poised to become one of Asia's hippest cities. It's an imperative stop for those who wish to gain a greater understanding of Cambodia's civil war and the genocide that killed 1.7 million people. More adventurous travelers can try a combination of boat travel across Lake Tonle Sap to witness entire communities living upon floating houses. If Thailand's less developed beaches are still too touristy for your tastes, check out Cambodia's as-yet unspoiled coastline, which is very slowly being discovered and now has a small range of accommodations, including the occasional luxury resort.

LAOS

In recent years Laos has become an increasingly popular destination for both backpackers and spendthrift tourists. All visitors agree that the sincerity and hospitality of the predominantly rural Lao population and the photogenic rivers and mountainous countryside are major reasons to make the trip across the border. World Heritage sites Luang Prabang and Champasak both feature beautiful temples and exude centuries-old charm. Participating in morning alms for Buddhist monks in Luang Prabang and river-rafting on an inner tube in Vang Vieng are two of the many activities available to those looking for more than sightseeing.

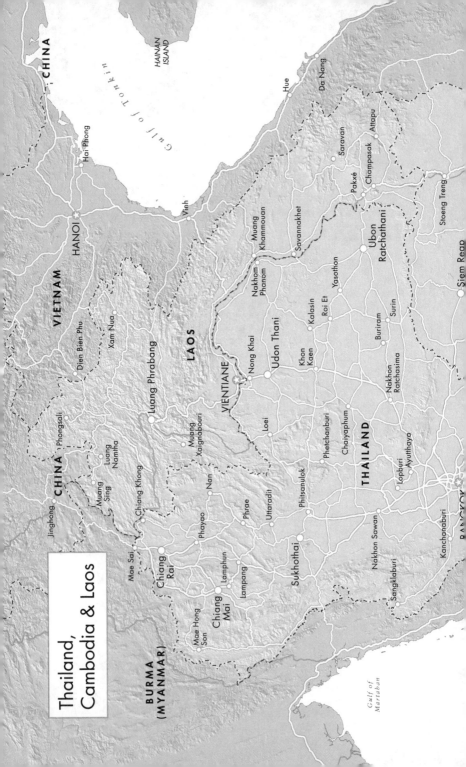

QUINTESSENTIAL THAILAND

Street Food

Thai people *love* to eat, evident by the sheer number of food stalls and sidewalk vendors in every town and city. Tropical fruits, miniature pancakes, barbecued bananas, virtually any type of meat on a stick, and even deep-fried insects are available 24-7 from pushcart vendors. With some of these items costing as little as B10 (25¢) per item, a random sampling is one of the best dining deals you'll find anywhere in the world. What's more, you're bound to identify a few tasty treats that you'll be able to hunt down on street corners throughout the country. Thai people don't just snack on the street however, they dine there, and to truly experience Thai cuisine (and culture), you must have a few meals at a sidewalk food stall. *Kau mun gai* (chicken with rice) is a staple at these simple eateries, but noodles are the primary attraction: *ba mee* (egg noodles), *sen lek* (thin rice noodles), and *sen yai* (large rice

noodles) are a few variations available, served with *mu daeng* (barbecue red pork) or *jay* (vegetarian). Many Thai meals are family style, so round up some Thai friends (they're not difficult to make), the more the merrier (and the more dishes you can sample), and sit back while they order a dizzying array of food for everyone to share. It's tasty, it's healthful, it's fast, and it's cheap. Don't worry too much about getting sick— "real" restaurants aren't necessarily safer. If you are particularly wary, just wipe down wet dishes and utensils with a tissue before piling your food on them and drink bottled water.

Thai Massage

Thailand is world renowned for its style of massage, and massage parlors are omnipresent wherever tourists can be found, from curtained-off, mattresses on the floor, holes in the wall to world-famous destination spa resorts. Bangkok's Wat Po has a

If you want to get a sense of contemporary Thai culture, start by familiarizing yourself with the rituals of daily life. These are a few highlights—things you can take part in with relative ease.

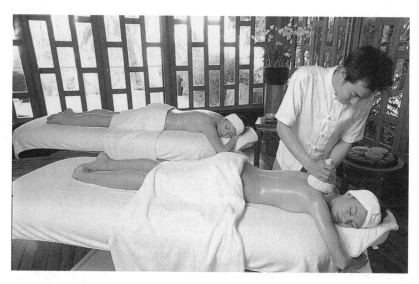

massage school for those looking for a unique and authentic experience in Thai traditional massage, called *nuat boran*. In the south, you'll often find licensed masseurs roaming the beaches offering traditional massages right on the sand, which isn't as scandalous as it may sound since traditional Thai massage is done with the recipient fully clothed.

Although Thai people don't make elaborate Wat Po–style massages a daily habit, you will find a number of Thais popping in to more casual places for a quick foot massage, which employs the principles of reflexology, believed to have full-body benefits. Many a foreigner expecting a soothing foot rub has received a painful surprise during the precise prodding required for optimal health benefits. Unfortunately, the same is often true for traditional Thai massage, which focuses on vigorous stretching, strong kneading, and the application of deep-tissue reflexology, all of which are often synonymous with torture for many a delicate foreigner.

Softies can opt for a fusion Thai-Swedish massage, usually called an "oil massage," which is a particularly nice experience at spas that use aromatic oils, such as lemongrass, Kaffir lime, and jasmine. Be advised that "special massage" and "body massage" at many massage parlors and "soapy massages" at Turkish bathhouses provide additional services that may be commonly offered, but aren't legal in Thailand. To avoid embarrassing misunderstandings, stick to well-established massage institutes or hotel spas or ask your hotel for recommendations of reputable local massage parlors.

Chiang Mai has several good massage schools and has become a very popular place of learning for those who want to bring the joys (and there are joys, once you get used to it) of nuat boran home to their friends and family.

QUINTESSENTIAL THAILAND

Songkran Festival

The Thai New Year is celebrated over a three- to five-day span in mid-April (April 13–15, plus adjoining weekend days). Traditionally, this celebration, which occurs on the cusp of the hot and rainy season, is centered around a type of spring-cleaning theme, whereby Thais congregate at their local temple to splash water on the Buddha and receive a blessing from a lotus blossom dipped in water.

Over the ages, this playful splashing of water has grown into one heck of a celebration; Songkran is now a multiday national party, akin to Brazil's Carnivale, featuring full-fledged water fights, blaring music, and conspicuous alcohol consumption. Critics decry these new festivities, citing battles with high-powered water guns and buckets of ice water, as well as soaring drunk-driving death rates, as indicators that things have gotten out of hand. Politicians have even attempted to impose a dress code on women and prohibit shotgun-style water guns, but have had very little success.

Funny enough, other than around the red-light districts and Banglamphu, Bangkok becomes a ghost town during Songkran, with migrant workers returning to their villages for the celebration and locals going abroad for holiday. Outside of experiencing a more subdued Songkran in a small Thai village, Chiang Mai's Old City is undoubtedly the most interesting and certainly most exciting place to celebrate. Any way you celebrate it, Songkran is the liveliest of Thai holidays.

Bangkok

Some people will wince at this quintessential choice, especially if they're not partial to big cities. But the capital deserves this honor because it is the epicenter of something that is very Thai: multiculturalism. Sure, Thailand's name may imply "land of the Thais," but the country has a long and rich multicultural history. Bangkok in particular has welcomed foreigners from around the world as they participated in the city's development as an economic hub. The world's largest Chinatown is practically a city in itself, with myriad markets, shops, and restaurants hidden throughout its winding alleys. Between Sukhumvit Soi 3 and Sukhumvit Soi 5 are thriving Middle Eastern and African communities. Near the Emporium shopping mall are a number of authentic Japanese bars and restaurants catering to expatriate Japanese and visitors alike, and parallel to Patpong Road there is even a Japanese red-light district off-limits to any other foreigners. Indians are one of Thailand's largest ethnic minorities, and Indian restaurants and tailors are found throughout the city. European, Russian, and American migrants also run businesses that cater to their expatriates and foreign visitors, longing for a taste of home or an atmosphere reminiscent of their homelands. If you've got a very specific picture of what Thailand is, Bangkok will surely turn that on its head.

IF YOU LIKE

Ancient Cities and Ruins

Prior to unifying in its current incarnation as a modern state, Thailand existed as a series of smaller kingdoms. Invasions by neighboring armies led to the demise of some kingdoms and the destruction of their structures, while others lost influence as they merged with other Siamese cities and remained beautifully intact.

Ayutthaya. After a number of unsuccessful attempts, the Burmese sacked the Siamese capital and brutally destroyed the city. The redbrick foundations of the Old City and its remaining stupas and wats are now beautiful ruins to explore, particularly around sunset.

Sukhothai. The first capital of "modern" Thailand was established in 1238 and saw over 100 years of prosperity and artistic development known as Thailand's Golden Age. Khmer and Hindi influences in sculpture and architecture are relatively unspoiled by the ages.

Chiang Mai. The Old City of Chiang Mai has continued to develop so that today its streets include bars and minimarts. Regardless, a stroll through the back alleys of the current city, both inside and outside the Old City walls, reveals centuries-old masterpieces of Thai art and architecture.

Beach Activities

With 3,200 km (2,000 mi) of coastline, Thailand is a beach lover's paradise. And many of those miles offer a lot more than just sunbathing or sunset strolls.

Above the water: Krabi's Railay Beach has world-class climbing, and even novices can take single or multiday climbing courses. Phang Nga Bay has spectacular kayak tours, while Railay Beach and Koh Tao are great for exploring with a hired boat. At the busier beaches of Patong, Pattaya, and Chawaeng jet-skiers buzz the waters while parasailers float above them.

Below the water: Koh Tao, with its fixed-rate diving courses, is the top destination for introductory dives. Koh Phi Phi is another great place for beginners (and snorkelers), as well as advanced divers looking to mingle with turtles and leopard sharks. From Phuket or Khao Lak, more experienced divers head to the Similan and Surin islands in search of the elusive whale shark.

Shopping

The first time you set foot in one of Thailand's ubiquitous markets you'll be absolutely mesmerized by the variety of goods, from hand-carved figurines to polo shirts with the alligator slightly askew. The prices, after negotiation, are tantalizingly low. In larger cities, you can find department stores and malls with prices significantly lower than in shopping meccas like Singapore or Hong Kong.

Chatuchak Weekend Market. JJ market, in northern Bangkok, is one of the world's largest markets. Every weekend, thousands of locals and tourists navigate the mazes of stalls shopping for pets, clothing, souvenirs, and almost anything else imaginable.

Siam Paragon. Are Gucci, Prada, and Armani more to your taste? Join throngs of Japanese tourists, Thai celebrities, and wide-eyed college coeds at this upscale Bangkok megamall. This palatial complex even has an aquarium you can scuba dive in.

Night Markets. Put on your best bargaining face and hit the streets of Silom, Patpong, Sukhumvit, and Khao San for the best night-market shopping in Thailand. Chiang Mai and Hua Hin also have great souvenirs and foods available after dark.

Trekking

The forests in Thailand would make for good trekking just for their rugged beauty. But these misty hills are also home to various hill tribes—Karen, Hmong, Yao, and many others—who have held on to ancient customs. Reaching the villages is often a challenging task, but the more remote, the more authentic the experience.

Chiang Mai and Chiang Rai. These two northernmost provinces are the focal points for both easygoing and adventurous tours to various hill tribe villages. Multiday treks include hikes through pristine forest, overnight stays in simple huts, elephant rides, and bamboo rafting. The farther from the cities you go, the better—some of the closer villages, accessible by day trips, are a bit over-visited after 25 years of tourism.

Luang Prabang. Treks in northern Laos practically transport you back in time. In some villages, the only apparent connections to the outside world are discharged Vietnam War–era bombs used as water troughs.

GREAT ITINERARIES

HIGHLIGHTS OF THAILAND: BANGKOK, BEACHES & THE NORTH

10 days

The best way to get the most out of your Thailand vacation is to decide what it is you'd like to do the most—party in the big city, lie on the beach, go trekking, etc.—and arrange your trip around the region best suited for that activity. Every region has so much to offer, you won't even scratch the surface in two weeks. However, if you don't know where to start, the following itinerary will allow you see a little piece of three very different areas of the country without requiring too many marathon travel days.

Almost every trip to Thailand begins in Bangkok. Don't be afraid to linger there for a day or two, because some of the country's most astounding sights can be found in and around the Old City. You'll probably be exhausted by the pace in a few days, so head down to explore the islands of the Gulf Coast, where you can swim in clear seas and sip cocktails on white sands. After lying on the beach for a few days, you'll be ready for more adventures, so head to Thailand's second city, Chiang Mai. The surrounding countryside is beautiful and even a short stay will give you a chance to visit the Elephant Conservation Center, a must-see.

Days 1 & 2: Bangkok

Experience the more traditional Thailand that resides within this modern megalopolis by beginning your first day with a tour of Bangkok's Old City. You may want to take a ferry across the Chao Phraya to its western bank to visit Wat Arun, one of Bangkok's most spectacular temples. In the late afternoon, head back to the eastern shore; there are street performers in the park on Phra Athit Road, which is a nice place to watch the sun set beside the river. Afterward, there are a number of small restaurants along the road to dine at, many of which feature local bands in the evenings.

On the second day, head to one of the city's most beautiful temples, Wat Benjamabophit. Nearby is Dusit Park, a refuge from the heat and dust. Here you can find the Vimanmek Mansion, the largest teak structure in the world. Head over to Jim Thompson's House for lunch at the outdoor terrace restaurant beside this beautifully adorned residence. In the evening, if you've got any energy left, head over to Lumphini Stadium for a Thai boxing match.

Days 3 to 5: The Beaches

Get an early start and head down to the beaches regions. Your choices are too numerous to list here, but Koh Samui and Krabi are good options because of their beauty and the daily direct flights that connect them with Bangkok. But if you have at least three days to spare, you can go almost anywhere that peaks your interest, as long as getting there doesn't involve long ferry rides (a definite mood-killer).

Koh Samui and Krabi are also good choices because of the variety of activities each offers. Things to do on Koh Samui include booking a treatment at Tamarind Springs, a spa retreat built literally into and around the jungle terrain; hiking to a waterfall; careening down a treetop zip line; taking a side trip to Angthong National Marine Park, where you can swim with a kaleido-

GREAT ITINERARIES

scope of colorful fishes; and having a tiki-torch-lighted dinner on the beach (a particularly romantic Samui experience). On Krabi, you can enjoy a relaxing afternoon at gorgeous Phra Nang Beach, where you can get a cheap beachside massage; rock-climbing on limestone cliffs; kayaking from beach to beach; and watching the sun set on Railay Beach, just to name a few options.

Day 6: Chiang Mai

Though it shouldn't be a terribly taxing day, getting to Chiang Mai requires some travel time, so you should get an early start. Wherever you are, you'll have to make a connecting flight in Bangkok; if you're pinching pennies, this actually works in your favor because it's cheaper to book two separate flights on a low-cost airline than to book one ticket from a more expensive airline "directly" from one of the beaches airports to Chiang Mai—you'll have to stop in Bangkok anyway. If you play your cards right, you should be in Chiang Mai in time to check into your hotel and grab a late lunch. Afterwards, stroll around the Old City, and in the evening visit the famous night market.

Day 7: Chiang Mai

Spend the day exploring the city and visiting the dazzling hilltop wat, Doi Suthep. Ring the dozens of bells surrounding the main building for good luck. On the way back to Chiang Mai, visit the seven-spired temple called Wat Chedi Yot or visit the pandas at the zoo. Chiang Mai is famous for its massage and cooking schools, so if you're interested in trying a class in ei-

ther—or just getting a massage—this is the place to do it.

Day 8: Lampang

Head out to the Elephant Conservation Center in Lampang to see these amazing creatures up close—in an environment that is safe and healthful for them (as opposed to some of the elephant shows you'll encounter in the south). Be sure to check the center's schedule, so you don't miss the performance by the elephant orchestra. This is an easy side trip from Chiang Mai.

Day 9: Around Chiang Mai

Your last day in the region can be spent in a variety of ways. Shoppers can takes taxis to the many nearby crafts villages and to Lamphun, which also has a few impressive wats to view. Active types can head to Doi Inthanon National Park to take any number of hikes, many of them leading to waterfalls.

Day 10: Bangkok

Head back to Bangkok. If you're not flying home the moment you step off the plane from Chiang Mai, spend your last day in the city doing some last-minute shopping around the boutiques of Siam Square or just relaxing in Lumphini Park.

TIPS

❶ Wats attractions such as Bangkok's Grand Palace, require modest dress.

❷ A taxi can take you to the Grand Palace, where you can walk south to Wat Po and then across the street to Tha Thien Pier, where a ferry will take you to Wat Arun. From the National Gallery, it's a short walk north to Phra Athit road.

❸ Book flights to Koh Samui online, directly from Bangkok Airways, and you'll get reduced airfare on the first and last flight of the day. Nok Air also has extremely low rates. Flight times both south and north are short, so it's not worth paying a lot for a little extra comfort.

❹ November through April is the best time to explore the Andaman Coast. For the Gulf Coast it's January through September.

❺ Hotels in the south are frequently booked during high season and Thai holidays, so book in advance.

❻ A great alternative to heading north to Chiang Mai is to use Bangkok as a base to explore the Central Plains. Sukhothai Historical Park isn't as famous as Ayutthaya, but it is even more spectacular and it and the surrounding region would make an excellent two- to three-day side trip from Bangkok.

Bangkok

WORD OF MOUTH

"Definitely stay on the river. The first time in Bangkok, we stayed at a perfectly nice hotel but had to take taxis everywhere and wasted hours stuck in traffic."

—laurieco

"The Puppet Theatre is superb—appropriate for anyone interested in Thai dance, music, and mythology. I never saw a performance engage children (young and old) as thoroughly and skillfully."

—jmf314159

www.fodors.com/forums

WELCOME TO BANGKOK

TOP REASONS TO GO

★ **The Canals** They don't call it "Venice of the East" for nothing. Sure, boat tours are touristy, but the sights, from Khmer wats to bizarre riverside dwellings, are truly unique.

★ **Street Food** Bangkok may have the best street food in the world. Don't be afraid to try the weird stuff—it's often fresher than the food you'd get at a hotel restaurant.

★ **Shopping Bargains** Forget Hong Kong and Singapore: Bangkok has the same range of high-end designer goods at much lower prices.

★ **Sky-High Sipping** "Bar with a view" is taken to the extreme when you sip martinis in open-air spaces that are 70 stories high.

★ **Temple-Gazing** From the venerable Wat Po to the little wats that don't make it into the guidebooks, Bangkok's collection of temples is hard to top.

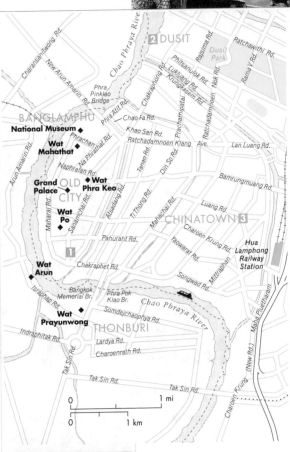

Khao San Road backpacker area

1 The Old City, Thonburi & Banglamphu. The Old City is home to opulent temples like Wat Po. Across the river is Thonburi, a mostly residential neighborhood, where you can find Wat Arun. Banglamphu, north of the Old City, is mostly residential; it's known for famous backpacker street Khao San Road, but it has much more to offer.

2 Dusit. North of Banglamphu is Dusit, the royal district since the days of Rama V. Dusit Park, one of the city's most appealing green spaces, is a highlight of this neighborhood, where wide avenues are lined by elegant buildings.

Central station, Bangkok.

GETTING ORIENTED

Bangkok's endless maze of streets is part of its fascination and its complexity—getting around a labyrinth is never easy. Although the *S* curve of the Chao Phraya River can throw you off base, it's actually a good landmark. Most of the popular sights are close to the river, and you can use it to get swiftly from one place to another. Also look to the Skytrain and subway to help you navigate and get around quickly.

3 Chinatown East of the Old City is Chinatown, a labyrinth of streets with restaurants, shops, and warehouses. Within its legendary bustle, you'll find an impressive array of Buddhas for sale, spice boutiques, and open-air fruit and vegetable markets that are amongst Bangkok's most vibrant.

4 Downtown Bangkok. "Downtown Bangkok" is actually several neighborhoods in one, and it's truly a mixed bag. In this busy area you'll find red-light districts; Lumphini Park, Bangkok's largest park; Sukhumvit Road, a bustling district filled with restaurants, hotels, and shops; and the riverbank that's home to some of the city's leading hotels.

BANGKOK PLANNER

When to Go

Late October to late March is the best time to visit. The city is at its coolest (85°) and driest. In April the humidity and heat build up to create a sticky stew until the rains begin in late May.

Hot Tickets

If you plan to hit Bangkok's hottest clubs, namely Q Bar, 87 Plus, or Bed Supperclub, it's a good idea to call ahead to be put on the guest list. That said, *farang* (foreigners) can generally walk right into most establishments, even those that have long, velvet-rope queues for Thais. Book cooking classes ahead of time—this is one activity that definitely requires advance planning. Spa treatments at top hotels tend to fill up at least a day in advance, so think ahead.

More Information

The **Tourist Authority of Thailand** (⊠ 1600 New Phetchaburi Rd., Sukhumvit ☎ 02/250–5500 Ⓜ Subway: Sukhumvit; Skytrain: Asok), open daily 8:30 to 4:30, has more colorful brochures than hard information, but it can supply material on national parks and out-of-the-way destinations. A 24-hour hotline provides information on destinations, festivals, and the arts. You can use the hotline to register complaints or request assistance from the Tourist Police.

Getting Around

Bangkok is large; it can take more than a half hour to walk between sights that look close together on the map. Pace yourself. Begin your sightseeing early in the day when it's cooler, take a break to escape the midday heat, and end by midafternoon, if possible.

Knowing your exact destination, its direction, and its approximate distance are all important in planning your day and negotiating taxi or *tuk-tuk* (three-wheeled open-air taxi) fares.

Taxis generally charge less, and get you there faster and safer; however, sometimes a tuk-tuk is all you can find, especially in less touristy areas. When getting in a taxi, be sure that the driver turns on the meter (if not, point to it emphatically), otherwise you're at his mercy when you arrive.

Note that many sights have no precise written address and the spelling of road names changes from map to map and even block to block, thus Ratchadamri is often spelled *Rajdamri*, Ratchadamnoen is sometimes seen as *Rajdamnern*, and Charoen Krung can be *Charoenkrung* or even *New Road*. Regardless, your hotel should be able to assist in writing the names of places in Thai on cards that you can then hand to taxi drivers; it is important to do this.

Crossing and recrossing the city is time-consuming, and you can lose many hours stuck in traffic jams. Remember that Bangkok is enormous, and distances are great; it can take a half hour or more to walk between two seemingly adjacent sights. Relying on the Skytrain and subway will make a huge difference, and knowing their routes will help you understand the city's layout. Don't forget to use the Chao Phraya River to ger around: there's no faster way to get from Thonburi to Chinatown, for example, than by boat.

How Much Can You Do?

You could spend weeks in Bangkok and not get bored, but chances are you'll only be in the City of Angels for a few days before departing for points north or south. If the jet lag and heat don't slow you down too much, you can cover a good number of Bangkok's attractions in three days. In another two days you can see more of the city or take short trips outside it. Between the Skytrain, subway, and express boats on the Chao Phraya River, you should be able to get to most places with relative ease. Planning around Bangkok's traffic is a must, so look for sights near public transportation or close enough to one another to visit on the same day. And never assume that taxis will be faster than the Skytrain.

If You Have 2 Days Start your first day with the most famous of all Bangkok sights, the Grand Palace. In the same complex is the gorgeously ornate Wat Phra Keo. Not far south of the Grand Palace is Bangkok's oldest and largest temple, Wat Po, famous for its enormous Reclining Buddha and for being the home of the traditional Thai massage. Don't miss the chance to try at least a 45-minute massage, which will probably leave you a bit sore. Later, head toward Banglamphu to take the river walk from Pinklao Bridge to Santichaiprakarn Park. That will put you on Phra Athit Road, where you can find many good restaurants and bars. If you feel up for more after that take a tuk-tuk the short distance to Khao San Road for some shopping and more strolling.

The next day, start out in Chinatown, where you can spend hours browsing the food and spice markets, peeking into temples and shops, and just absorbing the atmosphere. Next, work your way to the Chao Phraya River and take a *klong* (canal) tour, which will give you a glimpse of the fascinating canal life in Bangkok. Then, if it's a weekend head to Kukrit Pramoj Heritage House; if it's a weekday, visit Jim Thompson's House. Take the Skytrain in the evening to Sukhumvit Road, where there are many good restaurants.

Safety

For a city of its size, Bangkok is relatively safe; however, you still need to practice common sense.

Don't walk alone at night down poorly lighted streets.

Guard your valuables against theft by stashing them in an inside zipper pocket or in a hotel safe.

Don't accept food or drinks from strangers, as there have been reports of men and women being drugged and robbed or worse.

If you have a massage in your hotel room, be sure to put your valuables in a safe; likewise, don't take anything but a bit of cash with you when visiting massage parlors.

Avoid tour guides, taxis, canal tour operators, and tuk-tuk vehicles that actively solicit you, and choose those that don't.

Bangkok is no more dangerous for women than any other major city, but women should still take precautions not to walk the streets alone at night (take a taxi back to your hotel if you're out late).

WHAT IT COSTS In Baht

	$$$$	$$$	$$	$	¢
RESTAURANTS	Over 400	301–400	201–300	100–200	under 100
HOTELS	over 6,000	4,001–6,000	2,001–4,000	1,000–2,000	under 1,000

EXPLORING BANGKOK

Updated by
Mick Elmore
and Robin
Goldstein

The Old City is the most popular destination for travelers, as it's home to opulent temples like Wat Po and Wat Phra Keo. Across the river is Thonburi, a mostly residential neighborhood, where you can find Wat Arun. At the northern tip of the Old City is Banglamphu, one of Bangkok's older residential neighborhoods. It's mostly known now for Khao San Road, a world-renowned backpacker street, though the neighborhood has much more to offer. North of Banglamphu is Dusit, the royal district since the days of Rama V.

East of the Old City is Chinatown, a labyrinth of streets with restaurants, shops, and warehouses. Patpong, the city's most famous of several red-light districts, is also here, as are some of the city's leading hotels: the Oriental, the Peninsula, the Royal Orchid Sheraton, and the Shangri-La. To the north of Rama IV Road is Bangkok's largest green area, Lumphini Park. Continue north and you reach Sukhumvit Road, once a residential area. More recently, Thonglor, farther east along Sukhumvit, has become the "in" neighborhood for those want to see and be seen.

The Old City, Thonburi & Banglamphu

The Old City, which also includes Banglamphu on the north and Thonburi across the Chao Phraya River on the west, is the historical heart of Bangkok, where you can find most of the ancient buildings and the major tourist attractions. Because of the city's decision to preserve this historic area, it's the largest part of Bangkok to escape constant transformation. Much of the residential sections look run-down, but the whole area is safe and it's one of the best in the city for a stroll.

The Grand Palace and other major sights are within a short distance of the river and close to where express boats stop. There is a Skytrain station next to a boat pier downriver from the Old City as well, making the Chao Phraya convenient no matter where you're staying.

Of course, the magnificence of the sights, and the ease in reaching them, make them rather crowded. During rainstorms is about the only time you find few people at the sights. ■ TIP→ **The palace and the temples are busy every day, but you might have better luck earlier in the morning, when it's also cooler, and before some of the tour buses arrive.**

Thonburi is largely residential, including areas where people still live on the klongs, which are worth a day trip if you have the time. Most of Thonburi beyond the riverbank is of little interest to visitors. Many locals claim it retains more "Thai-ness" than Bangkok, but you have to live there, or visit for a long time, to appreciate that.

Banglamphu in the north part of Old City offers pleasant walks, markets, and the famous Khao San Road, one of the world's best-known backpacker hubs. The block-long Khao San has become a truly international street with visitors from dozens of countries populating the scene year-round. During the high season up to 10,000 people a day call the area home.

What to See

OLD CITY **Democracy Monument and October 14 Monument.** Democracy Monument is one of Bangkok's biggest and best-known landmarks. It was built after the military overthrew the absolute monarchy in 1932 and Thailand became a constitutional monarchy. Just to the south of the road that circles the Democracy Monument is the October 14 Monument, honoring the Thais killed during the student-led uprising against the military government that started on October 14, 1973, and left dozens dead. Tributes to those killed in October 1976 and May 1992, in other protests against military rule, are also part of the monument. Although mostly written in Thai, it's a sobering sight, especially so close to the Democracy Monument. The gate is often closed,

> **LOOK OUT!**
>
> The other downside to the surge of tourism in this area is the presence of phony tour guides, who will most likely approach you by offering tips about undiscovered or off-the-beaten-path places. Some will even tell you that the place you're going to is closed, and that you should join them for a tour instead. Often their "tours" (offered at too-good-to-be true prices) include a "short" visit to a gem shop for a bit of arm-twisting. The situation got bad enough in the mid-1990s that the government stepped in and distributed fliers to passengers on inbound flights warning of these gem scams.

and there seem to be no regular hours, but there are painting exhibitions on display at times. ⊠ *Ratchdamnoen Rd. at Thanon Din So.*

★ ❶ **Grand Palace.** This is Thailand's most revered spot and one of its most visited. King Rama I built this walled city in 1782, when he moved the capital across the river from Thonburi. The palace and adjoining structures only got more opulent as subsequent monarchs added their own touches. The grounds are open to visitors, but none of the buildings are—they're used only for state occasions and royal ceremonies. On rare occasions, rooms in the Chakri Maha Prasat palace—considered the official residence of the king, even though he actually lives at Chitlada Palace in north Bangkok—are sometimes open to visitors. The Dusit Maha Prasat is a classic example of palace architecture, and Amarin Vinichai Hall, the original audience hall, is now used for the presentation of ambassadors' credentials. If the door to the hall is open, you might glimpse the glittering gold throne inside. Just east of the Grand Palace compound is the **City Pillar Shrine,** containing the foundation stone (Lak Muang) from which all distances in Thailand are measured. The stone is believed to be inhabited by a spirit that guards the well-being of Bangkok. ■ TIP→ **Proper attire (no flip-flops, no shorts, shoulders and midriffs must be covered) is required, but if you forget, they loan unflattering but more demure shirts and shoes at the entrance.** ⊠ *Sana Chai Rd., Old City* ☎ *02/224–1833* 🎫 *B200, includes admission to Wat Phra Keo and to Vimanmek grounds for 1 wk* ☉ *Daily 8:30–3:30.*

NEED A BREAK?

Taking in all the sights can be exhausting, especially on a hot-and-muggy day. Fortunately two parks by the Grand Palace provide some respite from the heat. **Sanam Luang** is north of the palace and Wat Phra Keo. Trees offer shade and

Greater Bangkok

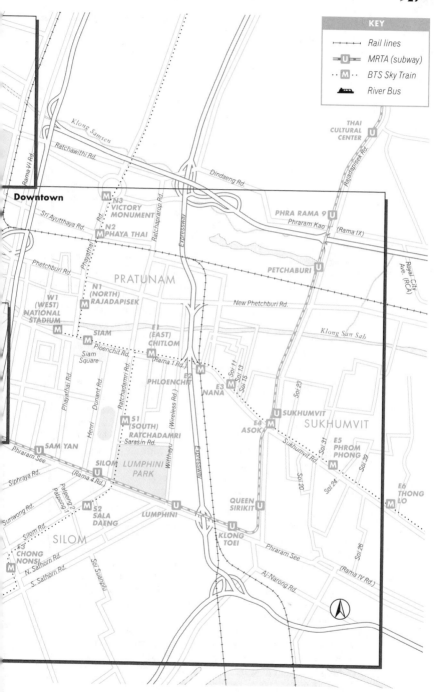

KEY

├─┼─┼─┤ Rail lines

▭Ⓤ▭ MRTA (subway)

···Ⓜ··· BTS Sky Train

River Bus

Klong Samsen

Ratchawithi Rd.

Rama VI Rd.

Dindaeng Rd.

THAI CULTURAL CENTER Ⓤ

Downtown

Sri Ayutthaya Rd.

Ⓜ**N3 VICTORY MONUMENT**

Ⓜ **N2 PHAYA THAI**

Ratchaprarop Rd.

Expressway

PHRA RAMA 9 Ⓤ
Phraram Kao (Rama IX)

Phetchburi Rd.

Phayathai Rd.

PRATUNAM

N1 (NORTH) RAJADAPISEK Ⓜ

PETCHABURI Ⓤ

Rajadapisek Rd.

Royal City Ave. (RCA)

W1 (WEST) NATIONAL STADIUM Ⓜ

New Phetchburi Rd.

SIAM Ⓜ

Siam Square

Ploenchit Rd. (Rama 1 Rd.)

E1 (EAST) CHITLOM Ⓜ

Klong San Sab

Ratchadamri Rd.

Ⓜ **E2 PHLOENCHIT**

Dunant Rd.

Henri

(Wireless Rd.)

E3 NANA Ⓜ

Soi 11

Soi 13

Soi 15

Soi 23

Phayathai Rd.

Ⓜ **S1 (SOUTH) RATCHADAMRI**

Sarasin Rd.

Withayu

Expressway

E4 ASOK Ⓜ

Ⓤ **SUKHUMVIT**

SUKHUMVIT

Sukhumvit Rd.

Soi 31

E5 PHROM PHONG Ⓜ

Soi 39

Ⓤ **SAM YAN**

Phraram See

Siphraya Rd.

(Rama 4 Rd.)

SILOM Ⓤ

LUMPHINI PARK

Soi 20

Soi 24

E6 THONG LO Ⓜ

Suriwong Rd.

Patpong 2

Patpong

Ⓜ **S2 SALA DAENG**

LUMPHINI Ⓤ

QUEEN SIRIKIT Ⓤ

Silom Rd.

SILOM

S3 CHONG NONSI Ⓜ

N. Sathorn Rd.

Soi Suanplu

Ⓤ **KLONG TOEI**

Phraram See

Soi 26

Soi 20

S. Sathorn Rd.

Ai-Narong Rd.

(Rama IV Rd.)

benches offer a place to sit with a cold drink and a snack from one of the vendors. You can also buy bread if you want to feed the numerous pigeons. **Suan Saranrom,** across from the southeast corner of the palace, is smaller but just as pleasant. It's surrounded by well-kept old government buildings. In the late afternoon you can join the free community aerobics sessions.

➐ National Gallery. Though it doesn't get nearly as much attention as the National Museum, the gallery's permanent collection (modern and traditional Thai art) is worth taking the time to see; there are also frequent temporary shows from around the country and abroad. The easiest way to find out what's showing is to ask your hotel's concierge to call, as you're not likely to get an English-speaker on the phone. To get to the gallery, walk down Na Phra That Road, past the National Theater and toward the river. Go under the bridge, then turn right and walk about 100 yards; it's on your left. The building used to house the royal mint. ⊠ *Chao Fa Rd., Old City* ☎ *02/281–2224* 🎫 *B30* ☉ *Wed.–Sun. 9–4.*

★ ➏ National Museum. There's no better place to acquaint yourself with Thai history than the National Museum, which also holds one of the world's best collections of Southeast Asian art. Most of the masterpieces from the northern provinces have been transported here, leaving up-country museums looking a little bare. You have a good opportunity to trace Thailand's long history, beginning with the ceramic utensils and bronze ware of the Ban Chiang people (4000–3000 BC). ■ TIP→ **There are free guided tours in English on Wednesday and Thursday; they're usually given at 9:30 AM, though sometimes the time changes.** ⊠ *Na Phra That Rd., Old City* ☎ *02/ 224–1333* ⊕ *www.thailandmuseum.net* 🎫 *B50* ☉ *Wed.–Sun. 9:30–4.*

➋ Wat Phra Keo (Temple of the Emerald Buddha). No single structure within the Grand Palace elicits such awe as this, the most sacred temple in the kingdom. You may prefer the simplicity of some other wats, but you'll never quite get over Wat Phra Keo's opulence—no other wat in Thailand is so ornate or so embellished with glittering gold. As you enter the compound, take note of the 20-foot-tall statues of fearsome creatures in traditional battle attire standing guard. Turn right as you enter the compound, because on the inner walls are lively murals depicting the whole epic tale of the *Ramakien*.

Several *aponsis* (mythical half-woman, half-lion creatures) stand guard outside the main chapel, which has a gilded three-tier roof. Inside sits the Emerald Buddha. This most venerated image of Lord Buddha is carved from one piece of jade 31 inches high. No one knows its origin, but history places it in Chiang Rai in 1464. From there it traveled first to Chiang Mai, then to Lamphun, and finally back to Chiang Rai, where as the story goes the Laotians stole it and took it home with them. The Thais sent an army to get it back; it reached its final resting place when King Rama I built this temple. The statue is high above the altar, so you can see it only from afar. Behind the altar and above the window frames are murals depicting the life and eventual enlightenment of the Buddha. At the back of the royal chapel you can find a detailed scale model of Cambodia's Angkor Wat. ⊠ *Sana Chai Rd., Old City* ☎ *02/224–1833* 🎫 *B200, included with admission to Grand Palace* ☉ *Daily 8:30–3:30.*

FodorśChoice
★

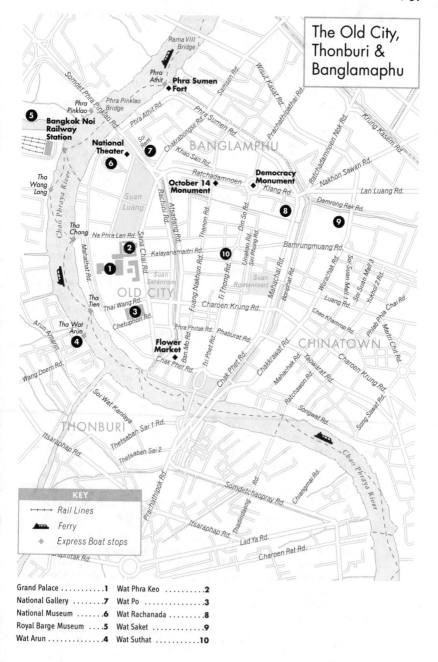

The Old City, Thonburi & Banglamaphu

Rama VIII Bridge

Phra Athit

Phra Sumen ♦ Fort

Somdet Phra Pinklao Rd.

Wisut Kasat Rd.

Samsen Rd.

Phra Pinklao

Phra Pinklao Bridge

Phra Pinklao Rd.

Phra Athit Rd.

Phra Sumen Rd.

Prachathipathai Rd.

Krung Kasem Rd.

5 **Bangkok Noi Railway Station**

Soi Ram

Chakrabongse Rd.

BANGLAMPHU

Ratchadamnoen Nok Rd.

National Theater 6

7

Khao San Rd.

Nakhon Sawan Rd.

Tha Wang Lang

Chaó Phraya River

Suan Luang

Ratchadamnoen

October 14 Monument ♦

Democracy Monument

Klang Rd.

Lan Luang Rd.

Damrong Rak Rd.

Tha Chang

Na Phra Lan Rd.

Sana Chai Rd.

Ratchini Rd.

Atsadang Rd.

Thanon Rd.

Din So Rd.

8

Bamrungmuang Rd.

9

Mahathat Rd.

Kalayanamaitri Rd.

Suan Saranrom

Fuang Nakhon Rd.

Ti Thong Rd.

Unakan Rd.

Siri Phong Rd.

10

Suan Romaninart

Mahachai Rd.

Boriphat Rd.

Worachak Rd.

Soi Suan Mali 1

Soi Suan Mali 3

Yukhol 2 Rd.

1

2

OLD CITY

Tha Tien

Thai Wang Rd.

3

Chetuphon Rd.

Charoen Krung Rd.

Luang Rd.

Chao Khamrop Rd.

Phlab Phla Chai Rd.

Maitri Chit Rd.

Tha Wat Arun

4

Arun Amarin

Phra Phitak Rd.

Phaburat Rd.

Flower Market

Ban Mo Rd.

Tri Phet Rd.

Chak Phet Rd.

CHINATOWN

Chakkrawat Rd.

Yaowarat Rd.

Ratchawong Rd.

Charoen Krung Rd.

Wang Doem Rd.

Soi Wat Kanlaya

THONBURI

Itsaraphap Rd.

Thetsaban Sai 1 Rd.

Thetsaban Sai 2

Mahachak Rd.

Songwat Rd.

Chao Phraya River

Prachathipok Rd.

Somdetchaopray Rd.

Chiangmai Rd.

Thadindaeng

Itsaraphap Rd.

Lad Ya Rd.

Charoen Rat Rd.

raphritak Rd.

KEY	
┝━━┿━┥	*Rail Lines*
🛳	*Ferry*
♦	*Express Boat stops*

★ ❸ **Wat Po** (Temple of the Reclining Buddha). The city's largest wat has what is perhaps the most unusual representation of the Buddha in Bangkok. The 150-foot sculpture, covered with gold, is so large it fills an entire viharn. Especially noteworthy are the mammoth statue's 10-foot feet, with the 108 auspicious signs of the Buddha inlaid in mother-of-pearl. Many people ring the bells surrounding the image for good luck.

Behind the viharn holding the Reclining Buddha is Bangkok's oldest open university. A century before Bangkok was established as the capital, a monastery was founded here to teach traditional medicine. Around the walls are marble plaques inscribed with formulas for herbal cures, and stone sculptures squat in various postures demonstrating techniques for relieving pain. The monks still practice ancient cures, and the **massage school** is now famous. A massage lasts one hour and costs less than B200 (you should also tip B100) Appointments aren't necessary—you usually won't have to wait long if you just show up. Massage courses of up to 10 days are also available.

At the northeastern quarter of the compound there's a pleasant three-tier temple containing 394 seated Buddhas. Usually a monk sits cross-legged at one side of the altar, making himself available to answer questions (in Thai, of course). On the walls, bas-relief plaques salvaged from Ayutthaya depict stories from the *Ramakien,* a traditional tale of the human incarnation of Vishnu. Around the temple area are four tall chedis decorated with brightly colored porcelain. Each chedi represents one of the first four kings of the Chakri Dynasty. Don't be perturbed by the statues that guard the compound's entrance and poke good-natured fun at farang. These towering figures, some of whom wear farcical top hats, are supposed to scare away evil spirits—they were modeled after the Europeans who plundered China during the Opium Wars. ✉ *Chetuphon Rd., Old City* 🎫 *B50* ⊙ *Daily 8–6.*

❽ **Wat Rachanada** (Temple of the Metal Castle). This wat was built to resemble a mythical castle of the gods. According to legend, a wealthy and pious man built a fabulous castle, Loha Prasat, from the design laid down in Hindu mythology for the disciples of the Buddha. Wat Rachanada, meant to duplicate that castle, is the only one of its kind remaining. Outside there are stalls selling amulets that protect you from harm or increase your chances of finding love. These souvenirs tend to be expensive, but that's the price of good fortune. ✉ *Mahachai Rd. near Ratchadamnoen Rd., Old City* 🎫 *Free* ⊙ *Daily 8–5.*

❾ **Wat Saket.** A well-known landmark, the towering gold chedi of Wat Saket, which is also known as the Golden Mount, was once the highest point in the city. King Rama III began construction of this temple, but it wasn't completed until the reign of Rama V. ⚠ **To reach the gilded chedi you must ascend an exhausting 318 steps, so don't attempt the climb on a hot afternoon.** On a clear day the view from the top is magnificent. Every November, at the time of the Loi Krathong festival, the temple hosts a popular fair with food stalls and performances. ✉ *Chakkaphatdi Phong Rd., Old City* 🎫 *B20* ⊙ *Daily 8–5.*

⑩ Wat Suthat & the Giant Swing. Wat Suthat is known for the 19th-century murals in the main chapel, but the numerous statues around the spacious tiled grounds are quite striking, too. There are rows of statue horses along one side of the wat. The Giant Swing (Sao Ching Cha) just outside Wat Suthat (but not part of it) was replaced to great fanfare in late 2006 for the first time in a generation. But it will not be used as it was in ancient times for Brahmanic ceremonies. Apparently, several people were killed in an swing-related accident in the early 20th century and it has not been used since. It is in a public area that is free to visit. ⊠ *Bamrung Muang Rd., Old City* ⬚ *B20* ☾ *Daily 8:30–9.*

THONBURI **Royal Barge Museum.** These splendid ceremonial barges are berthed on
★ ⑤ the Thonburi side of the Chao Phraya River. The boats, carved in the early part of the 19th century, take the form of mythical creatures in the *Ramakien*. The most impressive is the red-and-gold royal vessel called *Suphannahongse* (Golden Swan), used by the king on special occasions. Carved from a single piece of teak, it measures about 150 feet and weighs more than 15 tons. Fifty oarsmen propel it along the river, accompanied by two coxswains, flag wavers, and a rhythm-keeper. ⊠ *Khlong Bangkok Noi, Thonburi* ☏ *02/424–0004* ⬚ *B30* ☾ *Daily 9–5.*

④ Wat Arun (Temple of Dawn). If this riverside spot is inspiring at sunrise,
Fodor'sChoice it's even more marvelous toward dusk when the setting sun throws amber
★ tones over the entire area. The temple's design is symmetrical, with a square courtyard containing five Khmer-style prangs. The central prang, which reaches 282 feet, is surrounded by four attendant prangs at each of the corners. All five are covered in mosaics made from broken pieces of Chinese porcelain. Energetic visitors can climb the steep steps to the top of the lower level for the view over the Chao Phraya; the less ambitious can linger in the small park by the river, a peaceful spot to gaze across at the city. Festivals are held here occasionally; check the Web site for upcoming events. ⊠ *Arun Amarin Rd., Thonburi* ☏ *02/466–3167* ⊕ *www.watarunfestival.com* ⬚ *B20* ☾ *Daily 8:30–5:30.*

BANGLAMPHU **Khao San Road.** Khao San, which means "Shining Rice," has been the heart of the international backpacking scene for decades. In the past few years it's made an attempt at trendiness with new outdoor bars, restaurants, and hotels sharing the space with the ubiquitous low-budget guesthouses, some of which are no longer very budget. ■ TIP➔ **The road is closed to traffic at night, making early evening the best time to stroll or sit back and people-watch.** It has become popular with Thais as well, who frequent the bars and watch the foreigners. Nightfall also marks the start of a busy street market, where you can find clothing, Thai goods, bootleg CDs, fake IDs, used Western books, cheap street food, and more. The frenetic activity can, depending on your perspective, be infectious or overwhelming. During Songkran, the Thai New Year in mid-April, Khao San turns into one huge wet-and-wild water fight. Only join the fun if you don't mind being soaked to the bone.

Phra Athit Road. A more leisurely neighborhood stroll is the river walk off Phra Athit, which runs between Pinklao Bridge, near the National Museum, and Santichaiprakarn Park. The concrete walkway along the

The Monarchy

THAILAND BECAME A constitutional monarchy after a bloodless coup in 1932. The current king, His Majesty King Bhumibol Adulyadej, ascended to the throne 14 years later, following the death of his elder brother King Ananda Mahidol (Rama VIII). He is the world's longest reigning sovereign.

Thais *love* the king, and are devoted to him in the most imaginable sense. Any criticism of the monarchy will cause deep offense, and possibly worse. Is it is forbidden by law to speak ill of royalty, with a maximum penalty of seven years' imprisonment (though deportation is a more likely sentence for foreigners).

Many families have photos of kings, past and present, displayed in their homes, and thousands of people gather in Sanam Luang Park each December for the king's birthday celebrations. The king's birthday speech is eagerly anticipated—in recent years his criticism of government excesses has been especially pointed. During the nonviolent coup of 2006, in which former Prime Minister Thaksin was deposed and replaced by a military junta, the king's diplomacy helped restore the country to a state of calm.

Official symbols of the monarchy's importance are seen in its representation by the blue bar on the Thai flag and photographs of royal figures in government buildings and public spaces. Even Buddhist temples usually display a king's shrine next to the Buddha. The national anthem is played daily throughout Thailand at 8 AM and 6 PM, broadcast by radio and TV stations and piped into railway and bus stations. People stand respectfully for the duration.

King Bhumibol is the ninth monarch of the Chakri dynasty, which has ruled Thailand since 1782. Two of his most illustrious ancestors, King Rama IV and his son King Rama V, are also particularly revered. They were largely responsible for the modernization of Thailand in the late 19th and early 20th centuries. Both engaged in diplomacy with Western powers and have placed great value on having foreign educators for their children. One of Rama IV's hired tutors was Anna Leonowens, who penned her memoirs *The English Governess at the Siamese Court*, on which several books and two films, including *The King & I*, are based. It's widely accepted that Leonowens exaggerated her position at the court, and Thais are extremely offended that she misrepresented the monarchy. The books and films are banned in Thailand.

During his reign, King Bhumibol has been a figure of stability for his people through some turbulent times, including coups d'état, popular uprisings, and a bewildering number of civilian and military leaders. His public works—notably The King's Project, which supports small agricultural communities—further enhance the public's devotion. Even the younger generations love him.

Another notable thing about King Bhumibol is that he's an accomplished jazz musician. As a saxophonist and clarinet player he has jammed with the likes of Benny Goodman and Stan Getz, and Thailand often holds jazz festivals in December to coincide with his birthday.

–Mag Ramsay

Chao Phraya is cooled by the river breeze and offers views of the life along the water. **Phra Sumen Fort,** one of the two remaining forts of the original 14 built under King Rama I, is in Santichaiprakarn Park. The park is a fine place to sit and watch the river. Phra Athit Road itself is an interesting street with buildings dating back more than 100 years. It has some good cafés, and at night the street comes alive with little bars and restaurants with live music. It's a favorite among university students.

Dusit

More than any other neighborhood in the city, Dusit—north of Banglamphu—seems calm and orderly. Its tree-shaded boulevards and elegant buildings truly befit the district that holds Chitlada Palace, the official residence of the king and queen. The neighborhood's layout was the work of King Rama V, the first of the country's monarchs to visit Europe. He returned with a grand plan to remake his capital after the great cities he had visited. Dusit is a rather big area, but luckily the major attractions, the Dusit Zoo and the numerous museums on the grounds of the Vimanmek Mansion, are close together.

What to See

⑭ **Chitlada Palace.** When in Bangkok, the king resides here, an area that takes up an entire block across from Dusit Park. Although the palace is closed to the public, the outside walls are a lovely sight, especially when lighted up to celebrate the king's birthday on December 5. The extensive grounds are also home to a herd of royal white elephants, but it's difficult to arrange to see them. ⊠ *Ratchawith Rd. and Rama V Rd., Dusit* Ⓜ *Skytrain: Victory Monument (take a taxi from the station).*

🄲 ⑬ **Dusit Zoo.** Komodo dragons and other rarely seen creatures, such as the Sumatran rhinoceros, are on display at this charming little zoo. There are also the usual suspects like giraffes and hippos from Africa. (If you've heard about the pandas China gave Thailand, they are in Chiang Mai, not Bangkok.) While adults sip coffee at the cafés, children can ride elephants. ⊠ *Ratchawith Rd. and Rama V Rd., Dusit* ☎ *02/ 281–0000* 🎟 *B30* ☉ *Daily 8–6* Ⓜ *Skytrain: Victory Monument (take a taxi from the station).*

★ ⑫ **Vimanmek Palace.** The spacious grounds within Dusit Park include 20 buildings you can visit, but Vimanmek, considered the largest golden teak structure in the world, is truly the highlight. The mansion's original foundation remains on Koh Si Chang two hours south of Bangkok in the Gulf of Thailand, where it was built in 1868. In 1910 King Rama V had the rest of the structure moved to its present location and it served as his residence for five years while the Grand Palace was being fixed up. The building itself is extensive, with more than 80 rooms. The exterior was spruced up in 2006. The other 19 buildings include the **Royal Family Museum,** with portraits of the royal family, and the **Royal Carriage Museum,** with carriages and other vehicles used by the country's monarchs through the ages. There are several small air-conditioned restaurants offering a limited menu of Thai food. Admission includes everything on the grounds and the classical Thai dancing shows that take

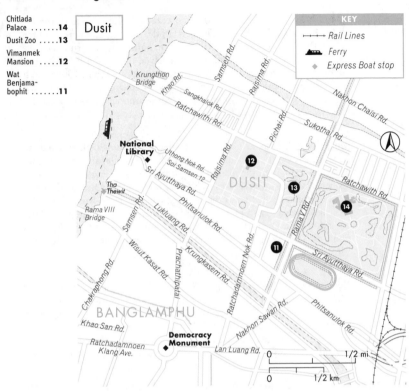

place mid-morning and mid-afternoon (10:30 AM and 2 PM, but these times are subject to change). English-language tours are available every half hour starting at 9:15. ■ TIP→ **Admission is free if you have a ticket less than one week old from the Grand Palace.** ☒ *Ratchawith Rd., Dusit* ☎ *02/ 281–1569* ☒ *B50* ☉ *Daily 9:30–4* Ⓜ *Skytrain: Victory Monument (take a taxi from the station).*

★ ⑪ **Wat Benjamabophit** (Marble Temple). This is a favorite with photographers because of its open spaces and light, shining marble. The wat was built in 1899. Statues of the Buddha line the courtyard, and the magnificent interior has crossbeams of lacquer and gold. But Wat Benjamabophit is more than a splendid temple—the monastery is a seat of learning that appeals to Buddhist monks with intellectual yearnings. ☒ *Nakhon Pathom Rd., Dusit* ☒ *B20* ☉ *Daily 8–5:30* Ⓜ *Skytrain: Victory Monument (take a taxi from the station).*

Chinatown

The neighborhood is an old and integral part of the city—almost as soon as Bangkok was founded, Chinatown started to form; it's the city's oldest residential area. Today it's a bustling area with many little markets (and a few big ones), teahouses, little restaurants tucked here and there,

CLOSE UP

Bangkok Spas

VENUES OFFERING TRADITIONAL MASSAGE are quite common in Bangkok—you can even pamper yourself while sightseeing at Wat Po. The staff at your hotel can recommend reputable therapists. If you have the time, pull out all the stops with a two-hour massage.

The new **I. Sawan Spa** (⊠ Grand Hyatt Erawan, 494 Ratchadamri Rd., Pratunam ☎ 02/254-6274 Ⓜ Skytrain: Ratchadamri) offers massage rooms and other facilities that are among the city's most cutting-edge, relaxing, and beautiful. Day passes cost B500, not including any treatments. There are also "residential spa cottages," suites clustered around a courtyard adjacent to the spa with their own treatment spaces; reasonably priced spa packages are available. The Conrad Hotel's **Seasons Spa** (⊠ Conrad Hotel, All Seasons Place, 87 Wittayu [Wireless Rd.], Sukhumvit ☎ 02/690-9999 Ⓜ Skytrain: Ploenchit) has 12 treatment rooms with views that are among the city's finest. A more low-key, inexpensive, but excellent option for traditional Thai massage is **Ruen Nuad** (⊠ Soi Convent, Silom ☎ 02/632-2662). A 90-minute massage will cost B700. Be aware that the place closes by 8 PM—another sign that it's legitimate and not a front for other activities like so many massage parlors.

The treatments at **Being Spa** (⊠ 88 Sukhumvit Soi 51, Sukhumvit ☎ 02/662-6171 Ⓜ Skytrain: Thong Lo) take place in a Thai-style house. Among the inventive treatments are a coffee-bean body scrub and detoxifying algae and green-tea body wraps.

If you're homesick for your yoga classes, **Bikram and Power Yoga Bangkok** (⊠ 14th fl., Unico House, 29/1 Soi Langsuan, Sukhumvit ☎ 02/652-1333 Ⓜ Skytrain: Chitlom) is the answer, for a drop-in rate of B500. Beginner classes, Power Vinyasa yoga, and yoga for kids are offered.

COMO Shambhala (⊠ Metropolitan Hotel, 27 S. Sathorn, Silom ☎ 02/625-3355 Ⓜ Subway: Lumphini; Skytrain: Sala Daeng) is the ultimate urban escape. The Metropolitan Bath starts with an invigorating salt scrub, followed by a bath and relaxing massage. In the heart of the city, **Divana Massage & Spa** (⊠ 7 Sukhumvit Soi 25, Sukhumvit ☎ 02/661-6784 Ⓜ Skytrain: Asok) has a cozy interior to make you feel right at home. All of the products used are designed by the spa and made mostly from Thai herbs.

A relaxing massage with deliciously warm oils is available at the **Four Seasons Hotel Bangkok** (⊠ 155 Ratchadamri Rd., Siam Square ☎ 02/251-6127 Ⓜ Skytrain: Ratchadamri). The small **Jivita Spa House** (⊠ 57/155 Silom Terrace Bldg., Saladaeng Soi 2, Silom ☎ 02/635-5422 Ⓜ Subway: Silom) is an oasis of calm and regeneration. There is a variety of treatments here, but the most unusual is the Japanese Healing Stone (using crystals, not stones).

A gentle massage in genteel surroundings is what you'll get at **Oriental Spa** (⊠ Oriental Hotel, 48 Oriental Ave., Silom ☎ 02/236-0400 Ⓜ Skytrain: Saphan Taksin). Amid the wood-panel sophistication you can treat yourself to facials, wraps, and even a "jet-lag solution." The Oriental's ayurvedic center is a major addition to the Bangkok spa scene, with ayurvedic massage treatments, that focus on holistic treatment.

and endless traffic. Like much of the Old City, Chinatown is a great place to wander around in, too. Meandering through the maze of alleys, ducking into herb shops and temples along the way, can be a great way to pass an afternoon, though the constant crowd, especially on hot days, does wear on some people.

Yaowarat Road is the main thoroughfare and it's crowded with gold shops and excellent restaurants. Pahuraht Road, which is Bangkok's "Little India," is full of textile shops; many of the Indian merchant families on this street have been here for generations.

■ TIP→ **Getting to Chinatown is easiest by boat—simply get off at one of the nearby piers and walk into the morass. But you can also start at the Hua Lamphong subway station and head west to the river.** The amount of traffic in this area cannot be overemphasized: avoid taking a taxi into the neighborhood if you can help it.

Another worthy stop is the Flower Market, but it is a bit of a distance, and more in between Chinatown and the Old City.

What to See

⑱ Flower Market. Like Yaowarat Road in Chinatown, the flower market is more of a street full of flower shops than one destination. It's open 24/7, but it's most interesting at night when more deliveries are heading in and out. This is where restaurants, hotels, other businesses, and individuals come to buy their flowers. Just stroll into the warehouse areas and watch the action. Many vendors only sell flowers in bulk, but others sell small bundles or even individual flowers. As everywhere else where Thais do business, there are plenty of street stalls selling a vast array of food. Though the area is not as busy as Chinatown proper, the traffic here can still be overbearing. Then again, one can say that about everywhere in Bangkok. ⊠ *Chakraphet Rd. between Pripatt and Yod Fa Rds., Chinatown and Old City* Ⓜ *Subway: Hua Lamphong.*

⑰ Thieves Market (Nakorn Kasem). The Thieves Market was once known for its reasonable prices for antiques, but stolen goods are no longer the order of the day. It's not worth a visit on its own, but as part of a greater Chinatown walk having a look in the covered lanes of stalls is interesting—like a rabbit warren of little shops. Mostly electronic goods are sold and it really starts slowing down about 5 in the afternoon. For shopping, Chatuchak weekend market is much better. ⊠ *Yaowarat Rd. and Chakraphet Rd., Chinatown* Ⓜ *Subway: Hua Lamphong.*

⑯ Wat Mangkorn (Neng Noi Yee). Unlike most temples in Bangkok, Neng Noi Yee has a glazed ceramic roof topped with fearsome dragons. Although it's a Buddhist shrine, its statues and paintings incorporate elements of Confucianism and Taoism as well. It's open daily from early to very late. ⊠ *Charoen Krung (New Rd.), Chinatown* Ⓜ *Subway: Hua Lamphong.*

★ **⑮ Wat Traimit** (Temple of the Golden Buddha). The actual temple has little architectural merit, but off to its side is a small chapel containing the world's largest solid-gold Buddha, cast about nine centuries ago in the Sukhothai style. Weighing 5½ tons and standing 10 feet high, the statue

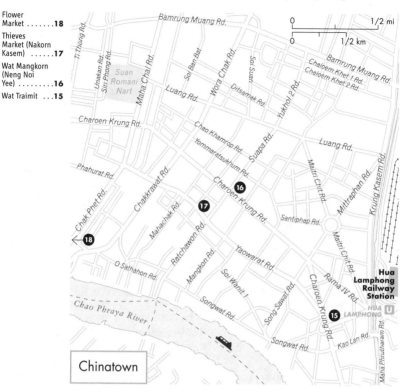

Chinatown

is a symbol of strength and power that can inspire even the most jaded person. It's believed that the statue was brought first to Ayutthaya. When the Burmese were about to sack the city, it was covered in plaster. Two centuries later, still in plaster, it was thought to be worth very little; when it was being moved to a new Bangkok temple in the 1950s it slipped from a crane and was simply left in the mud by the workmen. In the morning, a temple monk who had dreamed that the statue was divinely inspired went to see the Buddha image. Through a crack in the plaster he saw a glint of yellow, and soon discovered that the statue was pure gold. ⊠ *Tri Mit Rd., Chinatown* ☎ *B20* ⊙ *Daily 8–5* Ⓜ *Subway: Hua Lamphong.*

Downtown Bangkok

Bangkok has many downtowns that blend into each other—even residents have a hard time agreeing on a definitive city center—and so the large collective area considered "downtown" is actually seven neighborhoods. Most of the tourist attractions are in the adjacent neighborhoods of Silom and Pratunam. The Silom area, with a mix of tall buildings, residential streets, and entertainment areas, is the busiest business hub. Some of the city's finest hotels and restaurants are in this neighborhood, but it still retains some charm despite being so developed and so chock-full of concrete. Pratunam, north of Silom, is a large neighborhood that competes with Chinatown for the worst traffic in the city. There are numerous markets here, including those in the garment district (generally north of the Amari Watergate Hotel on Phetchaburi Road). Pratunam's Panthip Plaza is Thailand's biggest computer center, with five floors of computer stores.

The other neighborhoods— Lumphini Park, Siam Square, Victory Monument, Sukhumvit, and Rajadapisek—are residential areas, business centers, shopping districts, or all the above. The Lumphini Park area, north of Silom, has many green spaces behind its numerous embassy compounds and is home

GETTING AROUND DOWNTOWN

The sights in this part of the city are spread out, but most are near Skytrain stations. Stations are generally a half mile (and less than 3 minutes) from platform to platform, so Chong Nonsi to National Stadium, which is four stations, will take less than 12 minutes. Though working your way through the sights in this area will keep you busy, keep in mind that the options here are many, with shopping in Siam Square and many good restaurants throughout Downtown.

to the Bangkok Royal Sports Club. East of Lumphini is Siam Square, home to Thailand's most prestigious university, Chulalongkorn. Siam Square is also one of Bangkok's biggest shopping areas, with hundreds of stores north of the university and more in several shopping centers around the square. The central Skytrain station is here, making the action in this neighborhood even more frenetic.

North of Pratunam is Victory Monument, which remains predominately residential except for Phayathai Road, which is home to many businesses. Sukhumvit, east of Pratunam, is a mixed bag, with countless hotels and restaurants (many expat Westerners and Japanese live in the area, so restaurant pickings tend to be better than average), as well as many entertainment spots. Traffic is often gridlocked, but, fortunately, the neighborhood has good Skytrain service. Bangkok's newest high-society or yuppie area, called Thonglor (often spelled Thong Lo), is a bit east. For upmarket nightlife this is the current hotspot.

Rajadapisek, north of Sukhumvit, an up-and-coming neighborhood little explored by tourists, though that may change with the subway. Numerous clubs, restaurants, and hotels are being built for the expected influx of foot traffic. It is also home to multistory massage parlors.

What to See

PRATUNAM **Erawan Shrine** (San Phra Phrom). Completed in 1956, this is not a particularly old shrine by Bangkok standards, but it's one of the more active ones, with many people stopping by on their way home to pray to Brahma. Thai dancers and a small traditional orchestra perform for a fee to increase the likelihood that your wish will be granted. It's at one of Bangkok's most congested intersections, next to the Grand Hyatt Erawan and near the Chitlom Skytrain station. It was built by the Thai Hotel and Tourism Co. when they built the Erawan Hotel, which was replaced by the Grand Hyatt Erawan in 1991. Even with a traffic jam

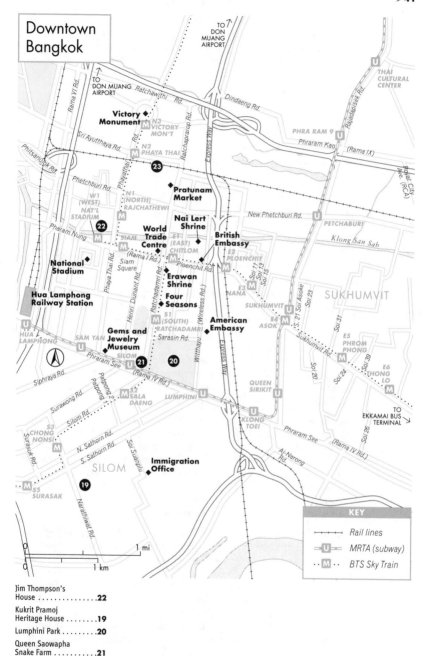

Downtown Bangkok

TO↑
DON
MUANG
AIRPORT

TO↑
DON MUANG
AIRPORT

THAI CULTURAL CENTER

Ratchawithi Rd.

Dindaeng Rd.

Rama VI Rd.

Sri Ayutthaya Rd.

Victory Monument

N3 VICTORY MON'T

N2 PHAYA THAI

Phitsanulok Rd.

Phetchburi Rd.

Phayathai Rd.

Ratchaprarop Rd.

Express Way

PHRA RAM 9

Phraram Kao (Rama IX)

Royal City Ave. (RCA)

Rajadapisek Rd.

23

Pratunam Market

N1 (NORTH) RAJCHATHEWI

New Phetchburi Rd.

PETCHABURI

Nai Lert Shrine

British Embassy

Klong San Sab

Pharam Nung

W1 (WEST) NAT'L STADIUM

22

SIAM

World Trade Centre

E1 (EAST) CHITLOM

E2 PLOENCHIT

SUKHUMVIT

National Stadium

Siam Square

Phaya Thai Rd.

Ratchadamri Rd. (Rama I Rd.)

Ploenchit Rd.

E3 NANA

Soi 11
Soi 13
Soi 15

S. 21 Soi Asoke

Soi 23

Erawan Shrine

Hua Lamphong Railway Station

Henri Dunant Rd.

Four Seasons

American Embassy

SUKHUMVIT

E4 ASOK

Soi 31

HUA LAMPHONG

SAM YAN

Gems and Jewelry Museum

S1 (SOUTH) RATCHADAMRI

Sarasin Rd.

Witthayu (Wireless Rd.)

E5 PHROM PHONG

Sukhumvit Rd.

U

SILOM

21

20

Express Way

Soi 20

Soi 24

Soi 39

E6 THONG LO

M

Siphraya Rd.

Patpong 2

(Rama IV Rd.)

QUEEN SIRIKIT

Surawong Rd.

Patpong

S2 SALA DAENG

LUMPHINI

Phraram See

TO EKKAMAI BUS TERMINAL

Silom Rd.

Soi 26

Surasak Rd.

S3 CHONG NONSI

N. Sathorn Rd.

S. Sathorn Rd.

Soi Suanplu

KLONG TOEI

At Narong Rd.

(Rama IV Rd.)

S5 SURASAK

SILOM

Immigration Office

19

Narathiwat Rd.

0 —————— 1 mi
0 —————— 1 km

KEY

+++++	*Rail lines*
U	*MRTA (subway)*
M	*BTS Sky Train*

right outside the gates, the mix of burning incense, dancers in traditional dress, and many people praying can be quite an experience. Entry is free, but many people leave small donations. A crazed man smashed the main statue in early 2006, then was beaten to death by people outside the shrine. It has since been repaired and is more popular than ever. ⊠ *At Ratchadamri and Ploenchit Rds., Pratunam* Ⓜ *Skytrain: Chitlom.*

㉒ Jim Thompson's House. Formerly an architect in New York City, Jim Thompson ended up in Thailand at the end of World War II, after a stint as an officer of the OSS (an organization that preceded the CIA). After a couple of other business ventures, he moved into silk and is credited with revitalizing Thailand's moribund silk industry. The success of this project alone would have made him a legend, but the house he left behind is also a national treasure. Thompson imported parts of several up-country buildings, some as old as 150 years, to construct his compound of six Thai houses (three are still exactly the same as their originals, including details of the interior layout). With true appreciation and a connoisseur's eye, Thompson then furnished them with what are now priceless pieces of Southeast Asian art. Adding to Thompson's notoriety is his disappearance: in 1967 he went to the Malaysian Cameron Highlands for a quiet holiday and was never heard from again. The entrance to the house is easy to miss—it's at the end of an unprepossessing lane, leading north off Rama I Road, west of Phayathai Road (the house is on your left). A good landmark is the National Stadium Skytrain station—the house is north of the station, just down the street from it. An informative 30-minute guided tour starts every 15 minutes and is included in the admission fee. ■ TIP→ **The grounds also include a two-story silk and souvenir shop and a restaurant in the reception building that is great for a coffee or cold-drink break.** ⊠ *Soi Kasemsong 2, Pratunam* ☎ *02/216–7368* ☜ *B100* ⊙ *Daily 9–5:30* Ⓜ *Skytrain: National Stadium.*

Fodor$Choice
★

㉒ Lumphini Park. Two lakes enhance this popular park, one of the few and the biggest in the center of the city. You can watch children feed bread to the turtles, or see teenagers taking a rowboat to more secluded shores. During the dry season (November through February) keep an eye (and ear) out for Music in the Park, which starts around 5 PM each Sunday on the Singha stage; there are different bands each week playing classical and Thai oldies. ⊠ *Rama IV Rd., Pratunam* Ⓜ *Subway: Silom and Lumphini stations; Skytrain: Sala Daeng.*

★ **㉓ Suan Pakkard Palace.** A collection of antique teak houses, built high on columns, complement undulating lawns and shimmering lotus pools at this compound. Inside the Lacquer Pavilion, which sits serenely at the back of the garden, there's gold-covered paneling with scenes from the life of the Buddha. Academics and history continue to debate just how old the murals are—whether they're from the reign of King Narai (1656–88) or from the first reign of the current Chakri Dynasty, founded by King Rama I (1782–1809). Whenever they originated, they are worth a look. Other houses display porcelain, stone heads, traditional paintings, and Buddha statues. ⊠ *352 Sri Ayutthaya Rd., Pratunam* ☎ *02/ 245–4934* ☜ *B100* ⊙ *Daily 9–4* Ⓜ *Skytrain: Phaya Thai (10-min walk from station).*

Roaming the Waterways

KRUNG THEP used to be known as the Venice of the East, but many of the *klongs* (canals) that once distinguished this area have been paved over. Several klongs remain, though, and traveling along these waterways is one of the delights of Bangkok. They have been cleaned up in the last decade, and the water is no longer so black and smelly, especially on the Thonburi side. In the longtail boats and ferries that ply the Chao Phraya River, not only do you beat the stalled traffic, but you get to see houses on stilts, women washing clothing, and kids jumping in with a splash. A popular trip to the Royal Barge Museum, and the Khoo Wiang Floating Market, starts at the Chang Pier on the Chao Phraya River and travels along Klong Bangkok Noi and Klong Bangkok Yai.

A fun introduction to the river—and Bangkok for that matter—can be bought with a Chao Phraya Tourist Boat day pass. They are a bargain at B70 and good for the whole day. One advantage of the tourist boat is while traveling from place to place there's a running commentary in English about the historical sights along the river and how to visit them. Included with the tour is a map of the river with its piers marked, along with the Skytrain route. A small booklet of river-area tourist sights attached to the map is also very helpful. The tourist boat starts at the pier under Saphan Taksin Skytrain station, but you can pick it up at any of the piers where it stops, and you can get on and off as many times and places as you want.

A pricier option is hiring a private boat to take you through the canals; tours usually run about two hours, stop at Wat Arun and/or other wats along the canal as well as the snake farm, and cost about B600 per boat.

SILOM

★ ⑲ **Kukrit Pramoj Heritage House.** Former Prime Minister Kukrit Pramoj's house reflects his long, influential life. After Thailand became a constitutional monarchy in 1932, he formed the country's first political party and was prime minister in 1974 and 1975. (Perhaps he practiced for that role 12 years earlier when he appeared with Marlon Brando as a Southeast Asian prime minister in *The Ugly American.*) He died in 1995 and much of his living quarters—five interconnected teak houses—has been preserved as he left it. Throughout his life, Kukrit was dedicated to preserving Thai culture, and his house and grounds are monuments to a bygone era; the place is full of Thai and Khmer art and furniture from different periods. The landscaped garden with its Khmer stonework is also a highlight. It took Pramoj 30 years to build the house, so it's no wonder that you can spend the better part of a day wandering around here. ⊠ *19 Soi Phra Pinit, S. Sathorn Rd., Silom* ☎ *02/ 286–8185* ⌧ *B50* ☉ *Weekends and official holidays 10–5* Ⓜ *Skytrain: Chong Nonsi (10-min walk from station).*

🄲 ㉑ **Queen Saowapha Snake Farm.** The Thai Red Cross established this unusual snake farm in 1923. Venom from cobras, pit vipers, and some of the other 56 types of deadly snakes found in Thailand is collected and used to make antidotes for snakebite victims. There are milking sessions at 10:30 AM on weekends and 10:30 AM and 2 PM weekdays, where you can watch the staff fearlessly handle these deadly creatures. They sometimes change the milking times, so you might want to have your hotel call and ask when it is. There are a few displays that can be viewed any time, but the milking sessions are the big reason to come here. ⊠ *1871 Rama IV Rd., Silom* ☎ *02/252–0161* 💲 *B70* 🕙 *Weekdays 8:30–4, weekends 8:30–noon* Ⓜ *Subway: Silom; Skytrain: Sala Daeng.*

WHERE TO EAT

Food is passion in Bangkok: Thais are obsessed with finding the out-of-the-way shop that prepares some specialty better than any other, then dragging a group of friends to share the discovery, and nowhere is this more true than in Bangkok. The city's residents always seem to be eating, so the tastes and smells of Thailand's cuisine surround you day and night. Food isn't confined to mealtimes, and noodle stalls are never far away. If you want a midnight snack, it's likely that there's a night market nearby serving up delicious dishes into the wee hours.

That said, Bangkok's restaurant scene is also a minefield, largely because the relationship between price and quality at times seems almost inverse. For every hole-in-the-wall gem serving, for pennies, the best *laab*, sticky rice, and *som tam* (the hot-and-sour green papaya salad that is the ultimate Thai staple) you've ever had, there's an overdressed, overpriced hotel restaurant that hawks touristy, toned-down fare at high prices. The best Thai food in the city is served not at places that are famous, expensive, or lauded by the media, but in the most bare-bones, even run-down restaurants. A good general rule: any place where you spot groups of office workers enjoying lunch or an after-work bite has to be good, as only a worthy restaurant would be chosen for such an important social outing.

If you want a break from Thai food, plenty of other world cuisines are well represented. Best among them is Chinese, although there's decent Japanese and Korean food in Bangkok as well. The city's ubiquitous noodle shops, though by all means Thai, also have their roots in China, as do roast-meat purveyors, whose historical inspiration was Cantonese. In general, Western fare tends to suffer from the distance.

As with anything in Bangkok, travel time is a major consideration when choosing a restaurant. If you're short on time or patience, choose a place with Skytrain and subway access—many great restaurants are within easy walking distance from the stations. Note that often the easiest way to reach a riverside eatery is by taking the Skytrain to the Saphan Taksin station (where the line ends on the river next to the Shangri-La Hotel). From there you can take an express boat upriver to many restaurants, including a dozen or so listed below.

Dinner Cruises

Though they're definitely very touristy, lunch or dinner cruises on the Chao Phraya River are worth considering. They're a great way to see the city at night, although the food is often subpar. So skip the dinner, just have drinks, and dine at a real Thai restaurant afterward. Two-hour cruises on modern boats or refurbished rice barges include a buffet or set-menu dinner and often feature live music and sometimes a traditional dance show. Many companies also offer a less expensive lunch cruise. Reservations are a must for some of the more popular cruises; in general, it's wise to reserve a few days in advance for all dinner cruises.

The **Horizon** (⊠ Shangri-La Hotel, 89 Soi Wat Suan Phu, Charoen Krung [New Rd.], Silom ☎ 02/236–7777) departs each evening at 7:30 PM and costs B2,200 per person. There's also a daylong lunch cruise to Ayutthaya and back for B1,800. It departs at 8 AM and returns around 5 PM. The **Manohra Song** (⊠ Marriott Royal Garden Riverside Hotel, 257/1–3 Charoen Krung [New Rd.], Thonburi ☎ 02/476–0021 ⊕ www. manohracruises.com) has both lunch and dinner cruises. It is the most beautiful dinner boat on the river, but it's smaller than most of the others, with less space to walk around. An incredibly mediocre set-price dinner is B1,500 per person. The **Yok Yor** (⊠ Wisutikasat Rd. at Yok Yor Pier, across from River City Shopping Complex, Thonburi ☎ 02/863–0565) departs each evening at 8 PM. The boat ticket costs B140; food is ordered à la carte, which in this case is a plus.

Cooking Classes

Culinary tourism is all the rage, and Bangkok is keeping up with the times. A Thai cooking class can be a great way to spend a half day—or longer. You won't be an expert, but you can learn a few fundamentals and some of the history of Thai cuisine. You can also find specialty classes that focus on things like fruit carving (where the first lesson learned is that it's more difficult than it looks) or hot-and-spicy soups. All cooking schools concentrate on practical dishes that students will be able to make at home, usually with spices that are internationally available, and all revolve around the fun of eating something you cooked (at least partly) yourself. Most classes are small enough to allow individual attention and time for questions. Prices vary from B2,000 to more than B10,000.

The **Blue Elephant Cooking School** (⊠ 233 S. Sathorn Rd., Silom ☎ 02/673–9353 ⊕ www.blueelephant.com Ⓜ Skytrain: Surasak) is a long-standing favorite, connected with the restaurant of the same name, but the Thai dishes here are heavily Westernized. However, it's cheaper than the others (about US$50), and the staff is very friendly. The **Landmark Hotel Cooking School** (⊠ 138 Sukhumvit Rd., Sukhumvit ☎ 02/254–0404, Ext. 4823 ⊕ www.landmarkbangkok.com) is also good. Both daylong and weeklong courses are offered. The **Oriental Cooking School** (⊠ 48 Oriental Ave., across from Oriental Hotel, Thonburi ☎ 02/659–9000) is the most established and expensive school (about US$100 for a half day), but far from being stuffy, it's fun and informative, and its dishes tend to be more interesting and authentic than those at other schools. Classes are taught in a beautiful century-old house.

West Bangkok: Dusit to Chinatown

Dusit & Northern Bangkok

Northern Bangkok is worth dining in only if you happen to be in the neighborhood for sightseeing, or really want to get to a part of the river that's off the beaten track.

CHINESE   ✕ **Dynasty.** This restaurant has long been a favorite among government
$$$$ ministers and corporate executives for its outstanding Cantonese cuisine and 11 private areas that are good for business lunches or romantic dinners. The main dining room is elegant with crimson carpeting,
carved screens, lacquer furniture, and porcelain objets d'art. The Peking
duck is among the draws, but the seasonal specialties include everything
from hairy crabs (October and November) to Taiwanese eels (March).
The service is efficient and friendly without being obtrusive. The restaurant is in Chatuchak, north of Pratunam. ⊠ *Sofitel Central Plaza
Bangkok, 1695 Phaholyothin Rd., Chatuchak, Northern Bangkok*
☎ *02/541–1234* ⌲ *Reservations essential* ▭ *AE, DC, MC, V* Ⓜ *Subway: Phahon Yothin.*

THAI   ✕ **Kaloang Seafood.** An alley near the National Library leads to this off-
¢–$$ the-beaten-track restaurant on the Chao Phraya. Kaloang might not look
like much, with its plastic chairs and simple tables on a ramshackle pier,
but it's a local favorite and worth the effort—and leap in imagina-
tion—for fantastic seafood on the river. Breezes coming off the water
keep things comfortably cool most evenings. The generous grilled
seafood platter is a bargain, as is the plate of grilled giant river prawns.
Try the *yam pla duk foo,* a grilled fish salad that's rather spicy, but goes
great with a cold beer. Also notable is the *laab goong,* spicy-and-sour
shrimp salad with banana blossoms. ⊠ *2 Sri Ayutthaya Rd., Dusit*
☎ *02/281–9228 or 02/282–7581* ▭ *AE, DC, MC, V.*

The Old City & Banglamphu

The Old City has every type of restaurant, including a huge prolifera-
tion of holes-in-the-wall, many with excellent food. Don't limit your-
self to the listings here, and don't be afraid to eat the street food—it often
makes for some of your most memorable meals in Bangkok.

INDIAN   ✕ **Roti-Mataba.** This little restaurant is the kind of place that earns
¢   Bangkok its reputation for excellent food. Roti (an unleavened, whole-
Fodor'sChoice   wheat flatbread), filled with your choice of vegetables, chicken, beef,
★   fish, seafood, or just sweetened with thick condensed milk, are cooked
near the door of the restaurant; all versions are recommended. The curry
chicken is another standout. Roti-Mataba is in a century-old building
across from Santichaiprakarn Park on the Chao Phraya; the downstairs
is narrow, hot, and usually crowded, but there's a more comfortable air-
conditioned dining room upstairs. ⊠ *136 Pra Artit Rd., Banglamphu*
☎ *02/282–2119* ▭ *No credit cards* ⊘ *Closed Mon.*

THAI   ✕ **Raan Jay Fai.** "Cult following" would be putting it mildly: it is said
★ $$ that there are people that come to Thailand just for a serving of the *pad
khee mao* at this little green room, which features nothing other than
cafeteria-style tables, green bare lightbulbs, and the culinary wizard with
her charcoal-fired wok. The dish, which is all anyone gets here, is a rice
noodle preparation with seafood including basil, crabmeat, shrimp,
and hearts of palm. The price for the dish—around B250—is sky-high
by Bangkok noodle prices, and the deal of the century for visiting food-
ies. ⊠ *327 Maha Chai Rd., Old City* ☎ *02/223–9384* ▭ *No credit cards.*

$–$$ ✕ **Ton Pho.** This eatery doesn't look special—it resembles a small, open-
air warehouse—but it's done a good trade since opening nearly two

Where to Eat in West Bangkok

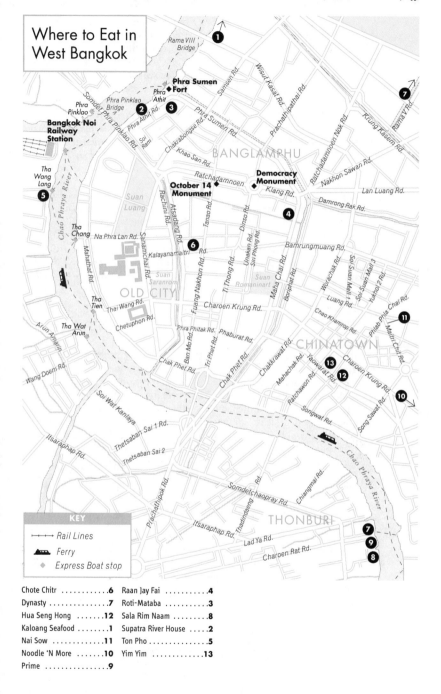

decades ago, well before the Phra Athit area became trendy. A board-walk along the river runs past the restaurant, and a pier where the express boats stop is off to one corner, so there's plenty of activity to watch as you eat. Try to secure a waterfront table where the breezes and views are better. The *tom khlong pla salid bai makham awn*, a hot-and-sour soup made from local dried fish, chili, lime juice, lemongrass, young tamarind leaves, and mushrooms, is a full frontal attack of seasonings, and is delicious. Less potent, but equally good, are the *gai hor bai toey* (deep-fried chicken in pandanus leaves) and *hoa mook pla* (a curried fish custard thickened with coconut cream and steamed in banana leaves). ⊠ *43 Phra Athit Rd., Banglamphu* ☎ *02/280–0452* ⌂ *Reservations not accepted* ▭ *MC, V.*

¢–$$ ✕ **Chote Chitr.** A favorite of legendary Bangkok food writer Bob Halli-
Fodor's Choice day, this simple, diminutive restaurant near Wat Suthat specializes in
★ seafood. Notable in a constellation of superstar dishes are banana-blos-som salad (here it's made with shrimp, chicken, tamarind pulp, chili, and coconut cream); perfectly balanced red curry shrimp; and *makheua yao* (a smoky green eggplant salad with shrimp, shallots, palm sugar, fermented shrimp, and lime juice). Come here for the food, not the atmosphere, and you'll be blown away. ⊠ *146 Phraeng Phuton, Old City* ☎ *02/221–4082* ▭ *No credit cards.*

Thonburi

Thonburi has restaurants boasting unparalleled river views, along with dinner cruises (⇨ *above*).

STEAK HOUSE   ✕ **Prime.** Though it's just a toddler in restaurant years, this spot in the
★ **$$$$** gleaming new Hilton Millennium has already attained the title of best steak house in Bangkok. It all begins with the groundbreaking interior architecture, which skillfully blends sweeping river and city views with the restaurant's open kitchen while still managing to feel intimate—an almost alchemical feat. Start with one of the signature martinis, and move on to the exemplary Caesar salad prepared table-side and perhaps a magnificent shellfish platter with fresh, briny oysters and lobster tails. Then there is the meat—whether it's Wagyu beef flown in from Australia or USDA Prime, no expense is spared in the kitchen (nor on the bill). The grilling is done over an extremely hot open flame. The wine list is also one of the best in the city, with lower than normal markups. ⊠ *Hilton Millennium Hotel, 123 Charoennakorn Rd., Thonburi* ☎ *02/442–2000* ⊕ *www.hilton.com* ▭ *AE, DC, MC, V.*

THAI   ✕ **Supatra River House.** Its location on the Chao Phraya River—and
$$$$ across from the Grand Palace—makes this restaurant worth a visit. A free ferry from Maharaj Pier shuttles diners back and forth. In the former home of Khunying Supatra, founder of the city's express boat business, the restaurant has a small museum dedicated to the art she collected. Try the steamed sea bass in soy or spicy lemon; on the other hand, the set menus (B750–B1,200) make for easy ordering. There's dinner theater on Friday and Saturday evening. ⊠ *266 Soi Wat Rakhang, Aruna-marin Rd., Thonburi* ☎ *02/411–0305 or 02/4110874* ⌂ *Reservations essential* ▭ *MC, V.*

$$–$$$$ ✕ **Sala Rim Naam.** To reach this elegant dining room you must take a boat across the Chao Phraya River from the Oriental Hotel. The restaurant is unbelievably touristy, with food designed exclusively for Westerners. Demand your food spicy if you want it to even resemble anything authentic. Still, the place is worth a mention for the unique Thai dancing show and the dimly lighted, almost magical ambience; make reservations for 7:30 PM if you want to see the show. ⊠ *48 Oriental Ave., across from Oriental Hotel, Thonburi* ☎ *02/437–3080* ⌔ *Reservations essential* ▤ *AE, DC, MC, V* Ⓜ *Skytrain: Saphan Taksin.*

Chinatown

Bangkok's Chinatown is impressive, to say the least, in large part for its food; it draws huge crowds of Thais who spend big bucks on specialties like shark's fin and bird's nest (which you'll see advertised on almost every single restaurant's storefront). Most of the food is Cantonese; many of these restaurants are indistinguishable from what you'd find in Hong Kong. Don't overlook the delicious street food, the noodle and dumpling shops, and the fruit and spice markets.

CHINESE ✕ **Hua Seng Hong Restaurant.** This expensive but worthwhile Chinatown
$$$–$$$$ classic takes you straight to China, or more specifically, to Hong Kong, with excellent Cantonese roast meats—try the duck—and soft, delicious goose foot–and–abalone stew. The restaurant is crowded and bustling and the service authentically brusque. Like many of the neighboring Chinatown restaurants, the place hawks the inexplicably prized shark's fin and bird's nest dishes, but here as elsewhere, they're not worth the sky-high prices—both taste essentially like slightly more resilient glass noodles. ⊠ *371–373 Yaowarat Rd., Chinatown* ☎ *02/222–0635* ▤ *MC, V.*

$$ ✕ **Yim Yim Restaurant.** This second-floor restaurant has been serving Chinese cuisine for more than 70 years. Though it lacks the elegance of the hotel restaurants in the area—the dining room is simple and you have to walk through the dish-washing room to reach the bathroom—it's a solid option in the heart of Chinatown. It's a favorite for family gatherings, but much smaller groups will still feel welcome. Try the sweet-and-sour fish, or if you're up for it, the chicken soup, which includes a whole bird in the bowl. ⊠ *89 Passai Rd., off Yaowarat Rd. near intersection with Ratchawong Rd., Chinatown* ☎ *02/224–2203 or 02/224–2205* ▤ *No credit cards* Ⓜ *Subway: Hua Lamphong.*

¢–$ ✕ **Noodle 'N More.** This narrow restaurant would be at home in Tokyo or Hong Kong, with its three small floors, the top one a no-shoes-allowed tearoom with sofas and floor seating. The second floor has regular table seating and a counter with benches along the window that offer great people-watching on the street below. It's a little more chic than your average noodle stand and its location near the Hua Lamphong subway station makes it a good place to refuel before exploring the neighborhood or while waiting for your train. As the name implies, you can find plenty of noodle dishes here, but the rice dishes are equally good. ⊠ *513–514 Rong Muang Rd., at Rama IV, Chinatown* ☎ *02/613–1992* ▤ *No credit cards* Ⓜ *Subway: Hua Lamphong.*

Eat Like a Local

THAILAND'S BORDERS HAVE AT times included parts of Malaysia, Myanmar (Burma), and Laos, and all these peoples, along with Chinese, Indians, Indonesians, ethnic Mon and Khmer, Persians, Europeans, and the Thai themselves, have added ingredients to an extraordinarily diverse cuisine.

Thailand has four regional food styles—northern, northeastern, southern, and central—and in cosmopolitan Bangkok you get a chance to try them all. The city itself is in the central region (the country's fertile "Rice Bowl"), where many of the dishes most familiar to foreigners, such as *tom yum goong* (spicy shrimp soup), *tom kha gai* (coconut soup with chicken), and the red and green curries, originate. Central food owes much to the influence of the royal kitchens, where coconut was first added and a fondness for sweeter tones was developed.

The other famous dishes *som tam* (spicy green papaya salad) and *laab* (minced meat or fish with chili and lime) are from the northeastern region of Isan, where spicy food is served with sticky rice and raw vegetables to cool the palate. (Both are ubiquitous in Bangkok and elsewhere in the country.) Traditionally, you eat sticky rice by making a small flat disc of the rice, which you wrap around some food. Other Isan specialties are insects gathered from the rice paddies. The black water beetles (*maeng da* or "pimps") are a particular favorite, with those-in-the-know choosing the females bearing tasty orange eggs.

Bangkok has a huge variety of both Western and Thai food in air-conditioned comfort, but many Thais still prefer to eat at food stalls, and not just because they're cheap. Vendors specialize in one or two dishes, and bad ones quickly go out of business, so the food quality is astonishingly consistent. You'll find different specialties in each neighborhood: Chinatown has *kway tio* and *ba mee* (noodles), Dusit is known for northern dishes, Phra Athit Road in Banglamphu has southern-style curries as well as the Indian staple roti. Ubiquitous are *gai yang* (grilled chicken), *yum* (spicy salads), *joke* (rice porridge), and *pad Thai* (thin noodles with shrimp, bamboo shoots, and peanuts). Food-poisoning scares are hugely exaggerated—if you see a crowd of healthy diners, join them. And remember: the super-sweet Thai iced tea should be avoided from vendors working off a block of ice—even frozen local water can make you sick.

Utensils: Many Thais are baffled by foreigners' repeated requests for chopsticks. Thais only use chopsticks for Chinese or noodle dishes—everything else is eaten with a fork and spoon (the fork is used to push food onto the spoon).

Tipping: Outside of posh restaurants, there is no need to leave a tip, save for any loose change left over from your bill.

Mouth on fire?: First-timers might have some difficulty with the liberal use of chili in most Thai dishes. Water won't extinguish that fire; eat rice or something sweet instead. Give chili a chance, even if it stings at first, because it lends balance to the dishes. Once you get used to it, make sure that restaurants don't assume you want your dish mild just because you're *farang (a foreigner)*.

—Howard Richardson

THAI
¢–$
× **Nai Sow.** Many regulars say this Chinese-Thai restaurant has the city's best *tom yam goong* (spicy shrimp soup). Chefs may come and go, but the owner somehow manages to keep the recipe to this signature dish a secret. The food here is consistently excellent; try the *naw mai thalay* (sea asparagus in oyster sauce), the curried beef, or the sweet-and-sour mushrooms. The fried taro is an unusual and delicious dessert. Wat Plaplachai is next door. ⊠ *3/1 Maitrichit Rd., Chinatown* ☎ *02/222–1539* ⌾ *Reservations not accepted* ▤ *MC, V* Ⓜ *Subway: Hua Lamphong.*

Downtown Bangkok

Pratunam & Siam Square

Unimaginably busy Pratunam and Siam Square have a little bit of everything, although many of the restaurants cater to the business crowd. These can range from humble lunch stops to power-dining extravaganzas.

JAPANESE
$$$–$$$$
× **Genji.** Bangkok has plenty of good Japanese restaurants, but many can be a bit chilly toward newcomers. Genji is the happy exception, and the staff is always pleasant. There's an excellent sushi bar and several small private rooms where you can enjoy succulent grilled eel or grilled Kobe beef roll with asparagus and fried bean curd. Set menus for lunch and dinner are well conceived, and are a nice change from typical Thai fare. Lunch seats fill up quickly and dinner sometimes requires a wait. ⊠ *Nai Lert Park Hotel Bangkok, 2 Wittayu [Wireless Rd.], Pratunam* ☎ *02/253–0123* ▤ *AE, DC, MC, V* Ⓜ *Skytrain: Ploenchit.*

THAI
$$–$$$$
× **Spice Market.** This casual hotel restaurant re-creates the interior of a well-stocked spice shop during a time when the only way to get to Bangkok was by steamer. Jars of spices line wooden shelves and sacks of garlic, piles of dried chilies, and heavy earthenware jars of fish sauce are lined up on the floor amid the tables, creating an interesting atmosphere, which is unfortunately lessened somewhat by overly bright lighting. The dishes are tempered to suit the tender mouths of Westerners, but you may ask for your curry to be prepared Thai-style. Set tasting menus are a good way to sample many different dishes. Dessert selections are particularly strong here, from mango sticky rice to the various Thai confections. ⊠ *Four Seasons Hotel Bangkok, 155 Ratchadamri Rd., Pratunam* ☎ *02/251–6127* ▤ *AE, DC, MC, V.*

$–$$$
FodorsChoice
★
× **Ban Khun Mae.** This casually upmarket Siam Square restaurant is where the locals go if they want to enjoy skillful, authentic Thai cuisine in an atmosphere that's a couple of notches above that of the simple family restaurants. The room is dark, comfortable, and inviting, filled with big round tables. Start with the sensational *khung sa oug* (a plate of sweet and silky raw shrimp delightfully balanced with chili and garlic), and continue with *pla rad pig* (deep-fried grouper with sweet-and-sour hot sauce) and *hoa muk ta ray* (a mixed seafood casserole steamed in banana leaf). Finish with the unique *tum tim krob* (water chestnut dumpling in coconut syrup with tapioca). ⊠ *458/7–9 Siam Sq. Soi 8, Pratunam* ☎ *02/658–4112 up to 13* ▤ *MC, V.*

$–$$
× **Once Upon a Time.** Period photos of the royal family, movie stars, and beauty queens cover the pink walls of this restaurant, which is really

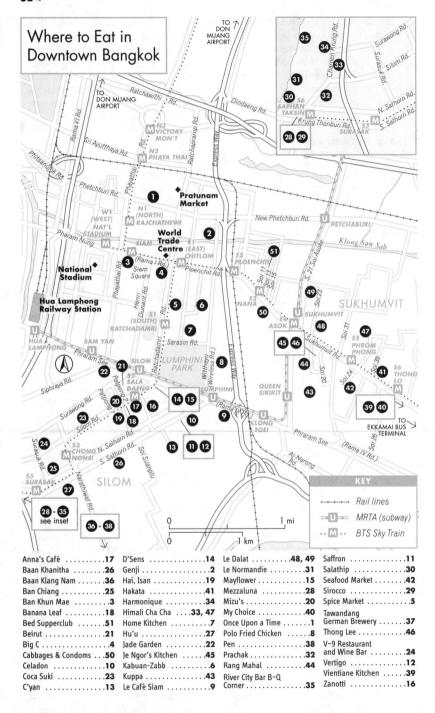

Where to Eat in Downtown Bangkok

KEY

+++++ Rail lines

==U== MRTA (subway)

···M··· BTS Sky Train

Anna's Café **17**	D'Sens **14**	Le Dalat **48, 49**
Baan Khanitha **26**	Genji **2**	Le Normandie **31**
Baan Klang Nam **36**	Hai, Isan **19**	Mayflower **15**
Ban Chiang **25**	Hakata **41**	Mezzaluna **28**
Ban Khun Mae **3**	Harmonique **34**	Mizu's **20**
Banana Leaf **18**	Himali Cha Cha ...**33, 47**	My Choice **40**
Bed Supperclub **51**	Home Kitchen **7**	Once Upon a Time **1**
Beirut **21**	Hu'u **27**	Polo Fried Chicken **8**
Big C **4**	Jade Garden **22**	Pen **38**
Cabbages & Condoms ..**50**	Je Ngor's Kitchen **45**	Prachak **32**
Celadon **10**	Kabuan-Zabb **6**	Rang Mahal **44**
Coca Suki **23**	Kuppa **43**	River City Bar B-Q
C'yan **13**	Le Café Siam **9**	Corner **35**
		Saffron **11**
		Salathip **30**
		Seafood Market **42**
		Sirocco **29**
		Spice Market **5**
		Tawandang
		German Brewery **37**
		Thong Lee **46**
		V-9 Restaurant
		and Wine Bar **24**
		Vertigo **12**
		Vientiane Kitchen **39**
		Zanotti **16**

two old teak houses. The dining rooms are filled with delightful antiques; there are also tables in the garden between the houses. *Mieng khum*, a traditional snack of dried shrimp, dried coconut, peanuts, pineapple, chili pepper, and sweet tamarind sauce rolled together in a green leaf, makes an excellent appetizer. Afterward move on to the chopped pork with chili sauce or the beef fillet with pickled garlic. The restaurant is about 100 yards down Soi 17, across the street from Panthip Plaza (a 15-minute walk from the Skytrain). ⊠ *Soi 17, Phetchburi Rd., Pratunam* ☎ *02/ 252–8629 or 02/653–7857* ⊟ *AE, DC, MC, V* Ⓜ *Skytrain: Rajchathewi.*

¢–$ ✕ **Polo Fried Chicken.** After offering only a lunch menu for decades, Polo Fried Chicken finally responded to its un-waning popularity by expanding its hours until 10 PM. The addition of an air-conditioned dining room is also a recent concession to its loyal clientele. Here you'll get world-class fried chicken, flavored with black pepper and plenty of golden-brown garlic; the best way to sample it is with sticky rice and a plate of som tam. The place is a bit hard to find—as you enter Soi Polo, it's about 50 yards in on your left. At lunchtime, you need to get here before noon to snag a table before the office workers descend. The restaurant will deliver to your hotel (if you're reasonably close to Lumphini Park) for B30. ⊠ *137/1–2 Soi Polo, off Wittayu [Wireless Rd.], Pratunam* ☎ *02/251–2772 or 02/252–0856* ⌕ *Reservations not accepted* ⊟ *No credit cards* Ⓜ *Subway: Lumphini.*

Fodor'sChoice
★

¢ ✕ **Big C.** The food court on the fifth floor of the Big C shopping mall offers a staggering selection of authentic Thai dishes at rock-bottom prices, with virtually nothing exceeding B35 (US$1). Service is cafeteria-style: you choose, point, and then bring your tray to one of the tables in the middle of the bustling mall. You'll need to pay for a charge card at the cashier station before ordering, which you fill up with an amount of your choosing (B200 should be plenty for two); the prices of the dishes at the many food counters are then deducted as you order. Don't worry about overfilling the card—you can get the remaining balance back after you're done. Highlights, if you can find them, include a good version of som tam, chicken with very spicy julienned ginger, Cantonese-style honey-roasted pork with delicious ribbons of fat and a crackly skin, and excellent sweetened Thai iced tea with milk. ⊠ *97/11 Ratchadamri Rd., opposite Central World Plaza, Pratunam* ☎ *02/250–4888* ⊟ *AE, MC, V* Ⓜ *Skytrain: Chitlom.*

¢ ✕ **Kabuan-Zabb.** There are so very many open-air holes-in-the-wall in Bangkok serving outstanding versions of local staples: spicy som tam, laab (a delicious Isan-style salad of minced pork with cilantro, mint, lime juice, fish sauce, and ground toasted rice), and of course, sticky rice. But there are few that, like Kabuan-Zabb, have English-language menus and a staff that has a basic facility with English, so that makes this one a find. It caters to the local lunch crowd and prices are unbelievably low. ⊠ *Wittayu (Wireless Rd.), across from U.S. Embassy, Pratunam* ☎ *02/ 253–5243 or 02/253–5244* ⊟ *No credit cards* ⊗ *No dinner.*

Silom

Silom has Bangkok's greatest proliferation of restaurants, period. Many of them are in hotels, on the upper floors of skyscrapers, or around Patpong. You can find a vast variety of ethnic cuisines and restaurant styles in this district, from authentic, humble Northern Thai to elaborate, wallet-busting preparations of foie gras.

CHINESE ✕ **Jade Garden.** You won't find a better dim sum brunch than the one
$$$$ at Jade Garden. The decor is more understated than at many expensive Chinese restaurants, with a remarkable wood-beam ceiling and softly lighted Chinese-print screens. Private dining rooms are available with advance notice. Two good dinner specials are fried Hong Kong noodles and pressed duck with tea leaves. Look for the monthly "special promotion" dish featuring seasonal ingredients. ⊠ *Montien Hotel, 54 Surawong Rd., Silom* ☎ *02/233–7060* ⊟ *AE, MC, V* Ⓜ *Skytrain: Sala Daeng.*

$$$$ ✕ **Mayflower.** Regulars at this top Cantonese restaurant include members of the Thai royal family, heads of state, and business tycoons. They favor the five opulent private rooms (two- to three-day advance notice required), but the main dining room is equally stylish, with carved wood screens and porcelain vases that lend an air of refinement that complements the outstanding Cantonese food. Two of the best items on the menu are the interesting abalone-and-jellyfish salad and the drunken chicken, which is made with steamed, skinned, and deboned chicken doused with Chinese liquor and served with two sauces, one sweet and one spicy. The excellent wine list assumes that price is no object. ⊠ *Dusit Thani Hotel, Rama IV Rd., Silom* ☎ *02/236–0450* ⟨ *Reservations essential* ⊟ *AE* Ⓜ *Subway: Silom; Skytrain: Sala Daeng.*

★ ¢–$ ✕ **Prachak.** This little place with bare walls and tile floor serves superb *ped* (roast duck) and *moo daeng* (red pork) and is a favorite of many locals. Wealthy Thai families will send their maids here to bring dinner home; you may want to follow their lead, as it can get crowded. Whether you eat in or take out, get here early—by 6 PM there's often no duck or pork left, and by 9 PM the place has closed for the night. Finding Prachak is a bit challenging. It's on busy Charoen Krung (New Road), across the street from the big Robinson shopping center near the Shangri-La Hotel. ⊠ *1415 Charoen Krung (New Rd.), Silom Bansak, Silom* ☎ *02/234–3755* ⊟ *No credit cards* Ⓜ *Skytrain: Saphan Taksin.*

ECLECTIC ✕ **C'yan.** The Metropolitan Hotel's new restaurant has become the
$$$$ trendy toast of the town, with pricey cuisine complementing an ultramodern look that draws in the see-and-be-seen crowd. Luckily, the food is up to the task. Whether you choose to sit out by the pool or in the minimalist dining room, you'll enjoy such creations as roast Australian crayfish with fried garlic, chili, and marjoram or ricotta, lemon, and mint tortellini with seared tiger prawns. Don't miss having a drink at the hotel's beautiful bar while you're there. ⊠ *27 S. Sathorn Rd., Silom* ☎ *02/625–3388* ⊕ *www.metropolitan.como.bz/bangkok* ⊟ *AE, DC, MC, V* Ⓜ *Subway: Lumphini; Skytrain: Sala Daeng.*

$$$$ ✕ **Sirocco.** The most memorable, impressive atmosphere of any restaurant in Bangkok—perhaps in all of Asia—is unfortunately diminished by the terrible food coming out of its kitchen. On the 63rd floor of one of Bangkok's tallest buildings, this is said to be the tallest open-air restaurant in the world. Its shockingly expensive, haphazard fusion menu boasts of imported prestige ingredients, but it stumbles from lamb to lobster with scarcely any success. If you don't want to put up

with the bad food, you can come just for a drink at the apocalyptic Sky Bar, which juts out at a gravity-defying angle; however, keep in mind that the bar doesn't offer seating. Perhaps the best strategy is to sit in the restaurant and just order something small. Be forewarned that the whole rooftop closes for windy weather from time to time. ⊠ *63rd fl., State Tower, 1055 Silom Rd., Silom* ☎ *02/624–9555* ⊟ *AE, DC, MC, V* Ⓜ *Skytrain: Saphan Taksin* ☺ *No lunch.*

$$$$ ✕ **V-9 Restaurant and Wine Bar.** On the 37th floor of the Sofitel Silom Bangkok, V-9 has great views through its ceiling-to-floor windows. Skip the pricey, underwhelming steaks; the Australian lamb is a solid pick, though, and the pièce de résistance is the sleek oyster bar, where fresh-tasting mollusks are shipped in from all over the world. If you want to pick just one wine, good luck to you—long rows of crates with more than 60 vintages of French, Italian, Australian, Californian, and South African wines line the entrance. ⊠ *Sofitel Silom Bangkok, 188 Silom Rd., Silom* ☎*02/238–1991* ⊟*AE, DC, MC, V* Ⓜ*Skytrain: Chong Nonsi.*

$$$$ ✕ **Vertigo.** You'll dine on top of it all at this classy lounge, bar, and eatery— it's one of the tallest open-air restaurants on the planet. Tables are set near the roof's edge for maximum effect; there are also comfy white couches and low-lying tables at the adjacent Moon Bar, if you prefer to come just for drinks. In spite of its name, Vertigo doesn't induce quite as much acrophobia as its competitor Sirocco atop the State Tower, and the international menu here, which focuses on barbecued seafood, is better, and the service is less pompous. Due to its altitude, the restaurant frequently closes when there are high winds, so you should have a backup plan in mind. ⊠*Banyan Tree Hotel, 21/100 S. Sathorn Rd., Silom* ☎*02/679–1200* ⊟*AE, MC, V* ☺*No lunch* Ⓜ*Subway: Lumphini; Skytrain: Sala Daeng.*

$$$–$$$$ ✕ **Le Café Siam.** This quiet restaurant, in a pleasant old house far from traffic noise, offers a successful mix of spicy Thai and subtle French cuisines. It's really like two restaurants in one, perfect for a group with disparate tastes. Some might find the portions small, but the quality of the food more than makes up for this, and, at any rate, it's worth saving room for the magnificent desserts. Many of the objects and artwork that decorate the house are for sale, so do some browsing while you eat. It's best to arrive by taxi as this place can be difficult to find on your own; if you call the restaurant, they will help arrange transportation for you. ⊠ *4 Soi Sri Akson, Silom* ☎ *02/671–0030* ⊕ *www.lecafesiam.com* ⊟ *AE, MC, V* ☺ *No lunch* Ⓜ *Subway: Klong Toei.*

$$–$$$ ✕ **Hu'u.** One of Bangkok's hippest new spots to eat and drink is worth checking out for dinner as well. The menu is all over the place, hopping from sashimi to cheeseburgers to fried wontons, but the best choices are the pasta dishes, such as homemade ravioli. Seared foie gras atop a toasted brioche is good, too. The place is dark, trendy, and modern; for a better atmosphere, you might choose to dine in the bar area downstairs, where many patrons come just for delicious pre- or post-dinner cocktails. ⊠ *The Ascott, Levels 1–2, 187 S. Sathorn Rd., Silom* ☎ *02/676–6677* ⊕ *www. huuinasia.com* ⊟ *AE, DC, MC, V* Ⓜ *Skytrain: Chong Nonsi.*

$ ✕ **Mizu's.** Opened by a Japanese man in the mid-1950s, Mizu's remains an institution. Considered Japanese by many, the menu actually offers an eclectic selection of dishes, including a range of spicy curries. Try the sizzling charcoal-broiled steaks from cattle raised in the north. The decor is a bit dated—some of the travel posters have been on the walls since the '70s—but the food is good and it's a good place for a bite before exploring the Patpong night market. ⊠ *32 Patpong Rd., Silom* 🕾 *02/ 233–6447* ▭ *AE, MC, V* Ⓜ *Subway: Silom; Skytrain: Sala Daeng.*

FRENCH   ✕ **D'Sens.** Bangkok's first Michelin three-star chefs arrived in 2004 in
$$$$ the form of brothers Jacques and Laurent Pourcel, executive chefs of Le Jardin des Sens in Montpellier, France. Granted, they only came to set things up, but they also installed a veteran of their restaurant to stay in Bangkok, and the results are delicious. Skip the dishes with prestige ingredients like foie gras and lobster, and choose instead to appreciate the subtlety of the kitchen in such dishes as mussel soup with saffron, Parmesan crisps, and orange cream or a delicate preparation of roast turbot. The prices and the views from the 22nd floor are both sky-high. ⊠ *Dusit Thani Hotel, 946 Rama IV Rd., Silom* 🕾 *02/200–9000 Ext. 2499* ⊕ *www.dusit.com* ▭ *AE, DC, MC, V* Ⓜ *Subway: Lumphini; Skytrain: Sala Daeng* ⊗ *Closed Sun. No lunch Sat.*

$$$$ ✕ **Le Normandie.** Perched atop the Oriental Hotel, this legendary restaurant commands a peerless view of the Chao Phraya. France's most highly esteemed chefs periodically take over the kitchen and often import ingredients from the old country to use in their creations. Even when no superstar is on the scene, the food is remarkable; the pricey menu (it's hard to get away with spending less than B5,000 on a meal) often includes classic dishes like slow-cooked shoulder of lamb. ⊠ *48 Oriental Ave., Silom* 🕾 *02/659–9000* ⚐ *Reservations essential* 🏛 *Jacket and tie* ▭ *AE, DC, MC, V* ⊗ *No lunch Sun.* Ⓜ *Skytrain: Saphan Taksin.*

GERMAN   ✕ **Tawandang German Brewery.** You can't miss Tawandang—it resem-
$–$$ bles a big barrel. Food may be an afterthought to the 40,000 liters of lager and other beers brewed here each month, but the kitchen turns out decent Thai food, with some German and Chinese fare thrown in for good measure. The taproom is especially boisterous when Bruce Gaston's Fong Nam Band is performing its fusion of Thai and Western music. On nights that the band's not playing, local singers perform Thai and Western favorites. You have to take a taxi from the Skytrain station. ⊠ *462/61 Rama III Rd., Yannawa, south of Silom* 🕾 *02/678–1114 up to 16* ⊕ *www.tawandang1999.com* ▭ *AE, DC, MC, V* Ⓜ *Skytrain: Chong Nonsi.*

INDIAN   ✕ **Himali Cha Cha.** Cha Cha, who cooked for Indian Prime Minister Jawa-
$ harlal Nehru, died in 1996, but his recipes live on and are prepared with equal ability by his son Kovit. The tandoori chicken is locally famous, but the daily specials, precisely explained by the staff, are usually too intriguing to pass up. The breads and the mango *lassi* (yogurt drinks) are delicious. The northern Indian cuisine is served in a pleasantly informal setting with the usual Mogul decor. A branch on Convent Road in Silom serves the same food in a more spacious dining area. ⊠ *1229/ 11 Charoen Krung (New Rd.), Silom* 🕾 *02/235–1569* ▭ *AE, DC, MC, V* Ⓜ *Skytrain: Saphan Taksin.*

ITALIAN ✕ **Mezzaluna.** The blockbuster restaurant in the State Tower's Dome
$$$$ (which until recently housed a champagne-and-caviar lounge) towers
above the rest of Bangkok—even above the adjacent Sky Bar and
Sirocco—in gaudy Italianate. Mezzaluna's faux-Roman columns are even
more shockingly ugly than the Bellagio's in Vegas, and its service is more
pretentious than even Alain Ducasse could manage. A string quartet ser-
enades you, members of Russian mafia, high-priced call girls, and
Bangkok's nouveau riche while you all dine on Italian-influenced preparations of foie gras, lobster, caviar, and so on. The food is good, if not
great, but more important, the view is unmatched anywhere else in the
city. Even if you don't come for the $25,000-a-head dinner (a visiting
chef's event recently staged at Mezzaluna), you should come here ready
to spend: this might be the most expensive restaurant in Bangkok.
✉ *65th fl., State Tower, 1055 Silom Rd., Silom* ☎ *02/624–9555* ▭ *AE,
DC, MC, V* ⊘ *No lunch* Ⓜ *Skytrain: Saphan Taksin.*

★ **$$–$$$$** ✕ **Zanotti.** Everything about this place is top-notch, from the attentive
service to the extensive menu focusing on the regional cuisines of Pied-
mont and Tuscany. You can find everything from pizza and pasta to fish
and steak, but the traditional osso buco served with gremolata and saf-
fron risotto is recommended. There's an unusually broad wine list, all
Italian, with selections by the bottle, glass, or carafe. The prix-fixe
lunches are a bargain. The low ceilings and closely grouped tables give
the place some intimacy, but the vibe is more lively than romantic, es-
pecially during the lunch and dinner rushes. ✉ *Saladaeng Colonnade
Condominium, 21/2 Soi Saladaeng, off Silom Rd., Silom* ☎ *02/636–0002
or 02/636–0266* ⊕ *www.zanotti-ristorante.com* ▭ *AE, DC, MC, V*
Ⓜ *Skytrain: Sala Daeng.*

MIDDLE EASTERN ✕ **Beirut Restaurant.** This simple neighborhood joint is a good place to
$–$$ escape the craze of Patpong and enjoy an authentic Lebanese meal. The
Middle Eastern classics, including good falafel and well-prepared sal-
ads, are all represented. ✉ *J City Tower, Silom Rd., Silom* ☎ *02/632–
7448* ▭ *No credit cards.*

PAN-ASIAN ✕ **Coca Suki.** This is the original branch—opened in 1957—of the suc-
¢ cessful Coca Suki chain. The spacious ground-floor restaurant has big
round tables for families and groups, which might leave a lone diner feeling very alone indeed. It's best visited with at least four diners. It's popular with locals, and the restaurant founder often eats lunch here. Try
the sukiyaki: order from a vast selection of meats and vegetables and watch
as the waitress cooks it on the communal hot plate built into the center
of the table. ✉ *8 Soi Anumarnratchathon, Surawong Rd., Silom* ☎ *02/
238–1137 or 02/238–1138* ▭ *MC, V* Ⓜ *Skytrain: Sala Daeng.*

THAI ✕ **Celadon.** Lotus ponds reflect the city's beautiful evening lights at this
★ **$$$$** romantic restaurant. The food is good, upmarket Thai, with elegant
touches that cater to Thais, not just foreigners. The extensive menu includes preparations of enormous river prawns, excellent red duck curry,
stir-fried morning glory, and a good version of banana-blossom salad.
Ask for your dishes spicy if you want the more authentic Thai taste balance. ✉ *Sukhothai Hotel, 13/3 S. Sathorn Rd., Silom* ☎ *02/344–8888*

⊕ *www.sukhothai.com* ⊟ *AE, DC, MC, V* Ⓜ *Subway: Lumphini; Skytrain: Sala Daeng.*

$$$$ ✕ **Salathip.** On a veranda facing the Chao Phraya River, this restaurant's setting practically guarantees a romantic evening. Be sure to reserve an outside table so you can enjoy the breeze. Although the food may not have as many chilies as some would like, at least the Thai standards are represented on the menu, and not just Westernized dishes. Good among those are Phuket lobster dishes and curried river prawns. Set menus make sampling many different things easy. The live traditional music makes everything taste even better. ⊠ *Shangri-La Hotel, 89 Soi Wat Suan Phu, Charoen Krung (New Rd.), Silom* ☎ *02/236–7777* ⌕ *Reservations essential* ⊟ *AE, DC, MC, V* ⊘ *No lunch* Ⓜ *Skytrain: Saphan Taksin.*

$$$–$$$$ ✕ **Pen.** This big, mirrored restaurant on the river is where Thai people
FodorsChoice   go when they want to splurge on seafood. It may be expensive by local
★   Thai restaurant standards, but not by hotel-restaurant standards; in short, you'd be well advised to come here before you spend B1,500 a head at one of Bangkok's famous international Italian or French restaurants. After all, what you get in Pen, you can only find in Thailand: deep-fried parrot fish served with shallots, sliced green mango in tamarind sauce, unique and delectable mud crabs, enormous charcoal-grilled river prawns, and the list goes on. This temple to seafood is not to be missed. ⊠ *2068/4 Chan Rd., Chongnonsee, Yannawa, south of Silom* ☎ *02/287–2907* ⊟ *No credit cards.*

$$$–$$$$ ✕ **Saffron.** This creative modern Thai menu is even more exciting than the stunning views from the 52nd floor of the towering Banyan Tree Hotel. Start with a banana-blossom salad with chicken, which mixes chili paste, dried shrimp paste, and cilantro for brightness. Then try the *phad pak kana moo grib* (stir-fried crisp pork belly with kale), a Chinese-influenced gem, or braised rack of lamb in massaman curry. ⊠ *Banyan Tree Hotel, 21/100 S. Sathorn Rd., Silom* ☎ *02/679–1200* ⊟ *AE, MC, V* Ⓜ *Subway: Lumphini; Skytrain: Sala Daeng.*

$$–$$$$ ✕ **Baan Klang Nam.** This clapboard house is right on the Chao Phraya River, and if you cruise the river at night, you'll probably end up gazing upon it, wishing you were among the crowd dining at one of Bangkok's most romantic spots. Happily, the place is less touristy than other restaurants of this type, most of which are part of big hotels. Spicy fried crab with black pepper, steamed fish with soy sauce, and stir-fried crab with curry powder are excellent choices from the seafood-centric menu. ⊠ *288 Rama III Soi 14, Yannawa, south of Silom* ☎ *02/292–0175* ⊟ *AE, MC, V* Ⓜ *Skytrain: Chong Nonsi.*

$–$$$ ✕ **Baan Khanitha & Gallery.** This is one of the places—and they can be hard to find—that balances an upmarket feel with fairly authentic Thai cuisine. The basics are done well here, from *chu chee goong nang* (curried river shrimp) to mango with sticky rice. It's in a converted house with a pleasant outdoor garden. Local artwork adorns the walls, as you might have guessed from the restaurant's name. ⊠ *69 S. Sathorn Rd., Silom* ☎ *02/2675–4200* ⊕ *www.baan-khanitha.com* ⊟ *AE, MC, V* Ⓜ *Skytrain: Saphan Taksin.*

$–$$ ✕ **Harmonique.** Choose between tables on the terrace or in the dining rooms of this small house near the river. Inside, Thai antiques, chests scattered with bric-a-brac, and bouquets that seem to tumble out of their vases create the best kind of clutter—one that invites you to relax as if you're sitting down for a meal at a relative's house. The menu is small, but the entrées are carefully selected, and the staff is very good at assisting indecisive diners. Try the fish satay, the massaman pork spareribs, the mild crab curry, or the Chinese cabbage topped with salted fish—all are excellent. Over the years the crowd has become increasingly tourist-heavy, but there are still Thais and expats who eat here regularly. ⊠ *22 Charoen Krung (New Rd.), Soi 34, Silom* ☎ *02/237–8175* ⊟ *AE, DC, MC, V* Ⓜ *Skytrain: Saphan Taksin.*

¢–$$ ✕ **Anna's Café.** There are quite a few Anna's branches around town, but this is the original. With its sunny yellow walls and fans, this restaurant exudes good cheer. Dining areas are separated by potted plants, affording you some privacy from other diners, which include many expats. There's a smattering of European dishes here, but most of the menu is modern Thai. The green curry with chicken and eggplant is mild and served with a salted boiled egg to counter its sweetness. Try the tamarind soup with crispy dried fish. ⊠ *118 Soi Sala Daeng, at top of Silom Rd., Silom* ☎ *02/632–0619* ⊕ *www.annascafes.com* ⊟ *AE, DC, MC, V* Ⓜ *Subway: Silom; Skytrain: Sala Daeng.*

★ ¢–$$ ✕ **Home Kitchen.** A true hole-in-the-wall across the street from Langsuan Soi 6, this kitchen shines as one of the best places in the city for authentic local cuisine; it's where many local groups of friends go to celebrate the simple act of eating delicious food. Don't miss the *tom yum goong* (hot-and-sour soup with giant river prawns), which is redolent of lemongrass, Kaffir lime leaves, and galangal; a delicately crispy oyster omelet; crispy catfish salad with green mango; or the fried whole fish in chili and lime sauce. Such classics simply excel here, and you owe it to yourself to try all of them before leaving Bangkok. ⊠ *94 Langsuan Rd., Silom* ☎ *No phone* ⊟ *No credit cards* Ⓜ *Subway: Lumphini.*

$ ✕ **River City Bar B-Q Corner.** This is a place where you can be the chef—a waiter brings you a hot plate and a mound of different meats and vegetables that you can grill to your own taste. Order some appetizers to nibble on while dinner is cooking; the Northern Thai sausage is excellent. A live band entertains on Friday, Saturday, and Sunday evenings. There's an air-conditioned dining room, but you might prefer the tables on the roof of the River City Shopping Complex, which have views of the Chao Phraya. ⊠ *River City Shopping Complex, Captain Bush La., Silom* ☎ *02/237–0077* ⊟ *AE, MC, V* Ⓜ *Skytrain: Saphan Taksin.*

¢–$ ✕ **Ban Chiang.** This old wooden house is an oasis in the concrete city; the decor is turn-of-the-20th-century Bangkok, with antique prints and old photographs adorning the walls. The place is popular with the *farang* (foreigners) set, and the food is fine-tuned for Western tastes, so ask for it spicy if you want it to be more authentic. Try the salted prawns with garlic and white pepper, or dried whitefish with mango dip; and finish with banana fritters with coconut ice cream. ⊠ *14 Srivieng Rd., Silom* ☎ *02/236–7045 or 02/266–6994* ⊟ *AE, MC, V* Ⓜ *Skytrain: Surasak.*

¢–$ ✕ **Banana Leaf.** If you need a break from shopping on Silom Road, this is the place to try—the food is delicious and quite a bargain. Try the baked crab with glass noodles, grilled black band fish, or grilled pork with coconut milk dip. The menu also offers 11 equally scrumptious vegetarian selections. Note that there's a B400 minimum if you want to use a credit card. ⊠ *Silom Complex, Silom Rd., Silom* ☎ *02/231–3124* ⊟ *AE, MC, V* Ⓜ *Skytrain: Sala Daeng.*

★ ¢–$ ✕**Hai, Isan.** A sure sign of quality, Hai is packed with Thais sharing tables filled with northeast favorites like grilled chicken, spicy papaya salad, and spicy minced pork. The open-air dining area can be hot and is often crowded and noisy, but that's part of the fun. The staff doesn't speak English, so the best way to order is to point to things that look good on neighboring tables. ⊠ *2/4–5 Soi Covent, off Silom Rd., Silom* ☎ *02/631–0216* ⊟ *No credit cards* Ⓜ *Subway: Silom; Skytrain: Sala Daeng.*

Sukhumvit

Sukhumvit is Bangkok's hippest area for dining and going out, and as such, many of the restaurants are more style than substance, although there's good food to be had. Avoid the trendiest and touristy places at all costs.

ECLECTIC ✕**Bed Supperclub.** You have to be 20 years old to get in here, even for
$$$$ dinner. Don't wear sandals or shorts if you're a man; make sure to bring a picture ID with you, no matter what your age; and don't do drugs here, because police raids are frequent. And whatever you do, make a reservation well in advance. But don't let any of that scare you away—this unique modern restaurant is worth all the headaches. The "tables" consist of long beds with white sheets, lined up along the walls. The Mediterranean and Asian fusion menu changes every two weeks, and the haphazardly eclectic food can be hit-or-miss (salmon with Gorgonzola?), but the experience is still worthwhile for a taste of Bangkok's trendiest side, especially if you stick around after dinner, when the place turns into one of the city's hottest nightclubs. ▄ TIP→ **Coming for dinner is a much easier way to get in than trying to impress the velvet-rope bouncers later in the evening.** ⊠ *26 Sukhumvit Soi 11, Sukhumvit* ☎ *02/651–3537* ⊕ *www.bedsupperclub.com* ⊟ *AE, DC, MC, V* Ⓜ *Skytrain: Nana.*

$$–$$$$ ✕**Kuppa.** This light and airy space maintains the aura of its former life as a warehouse, but it's certainly more chic than shabby these days, with polished metal and blond wood adding a hip counterpoint to cement floors. An advantage to such a space is that, unlike many downtown eateries, each table has plenty of room around it. Kuppa offers traditional Thai fare as well as many international dishes, and it has a dedicated following because of its coffee (roasted on the premises) and its impressive desserts. The one drawback is that the portions are somewhat small for the price. ⊠ *39 Sukhumvit Soi 16, Sukhumvit* ☎ *02/663–0450 or 02/258–0194* ⊟ *AE, DC, MC, V* ⊘ *Closed Mon.* Ⓜ *Subway: Sukhumvit; Skytrain: Asok.*

INDIAN ✕**Rang Mahal.** Savory food in a pleasant setting with great views of the
$$$$ city brings people back to this upscale Indian restaurant. *Bindi do piaza* with okra is interesting, and the homemade naan breads are top-notch. The main dining room has Indian music, which can be loud to some ears, but there are smaller rooms for a quieter meal. Take a jacket—the air-conditioning can be overpowering—and ask for a window seat for a great view of the city. ⊠ *Rembrandt Hotel, 19 Sukhumvit Soi 18,*

Sukhumvit ☎ *02/261–7100* ⬥ *Reservations essential* ▭ *AE, DC, MC, V* Ⓜ *Subway: Sukhumvit; Skytrain: Asok.*

JAPANESE
$$–$$$$

✕ **Hakata.** Although there are many good Japanese restaurants in the Sukhumvit area near the Emporium shopping center, Hakata is a step above most. The main dining area and sushi bar are spacious and relaxing, and there are private rooms available as well. Expect to spend more to make a meal out of sushi, but the regular dishes like tempura and *katsu-don* (fried pork strips) are reasonably priced and tasty. ⊠ *4 Sukhumvit Soi 39, Sukhumvit* ☎ *02/259–9154* ▭ *AE, DC, MC, V* Ⓜ *Skytrain: Phrom Phong.*

LAOTIAN
★ ¢–$

✕ **Vientiane Kitchen.** This open-air restaurant named after the capital of Laos is set under thatched roofs; there's table seating or you can opt for traditional seating on floor mats. Laotian cuisine is similar to the Thai food found in the country's northeastern province of Isan. Among the Thai-style standards like grilled chicken, sticky rice, and *som tam* (spicy papaya salad) are a few riskier dishes like *Nam tok* (waterfall)—so called because it's so hot it makes your eyes run like a waterfall (however, it's actually toned down here, so don't think you can order it in Laos and still feel your tongue afterward). Other dishes like frog soup and grilled duck beak are actually quite good, despite the images they conjure up. It's best to go with a group so you can share several dishes. Live Laotian music and dance add to the experience. ⊠ *8 Sukhumvit Soi 36, Sukhumvit* ☎ *02/258–6171* ⊕ *www.vientiane-kitchen.com* ▭ *DC, MC, V* Ⓜ *Skytrain: Thong Lo.*

THAI
$$$$

✕ **Seafood Market.** Although it's miles from the ocean, the fish here are so fresh it feels like the boats must be somewhere nearby. Like at a supermarket, you take a cart and choose from an array of seafood—crabs, prawns, lobsters, clams, oysters, and fish. The waiter then takes it away and instructs the chef to cook it any way you like. Typically your eyes are bigger than your stomach, so select with prudence, not gusto. Unfortunately, the 1,500-seat setting and fluorescent lighting add to the supermarket feel, but it's a fun and unique dining experience. ⊠ *89 Sukhumvit Soi 24, Sukhumvit* ☎ *02/661–1255 up to 59* ⊕ *www. seafood.com.th* ⬥ *Reservations not accepted* ▭ *AE, DC, MC, V* Ⓜ *Skytrain: Phrom Phong.*

$$–$$$$

✕ **Je Ngor's Kitchen.** Stir-fried morning glory is truly glorious at this minichain, which is absolutely adored by locals. People also swear by the stir-fried crab in red curry and the deep-fried rock lobster. The decor is simple but attractive, with warm colors, yellow lanterns, and curtains. Other branches dot Bangkok, but the Sukhumvit location is the biggest. There are good set menus at lunch. ⊠ *68/2 Sukhumvit Soi 20, Sukhumvit* ☎ *02/258–8008* ⊕ *www.jengor-seafoods.com* ▭ *AE, MC, V* Ⓜ *Skytrain: Phrom Phong.*

$

✕ **Cabbages & Condoms.** Don't be misled by the restaurant's odd name or put off by the array of contraceptive devices for sale. This popular place raises funds for the Population & Community Development Association, the country's family-planning program. You'll find the food here excellently prepared; standouts are the chicken wrapped in pandanus leaves, crisp fried fish with chili sauce, and shrimp in a mild curry sauce. The eatery lost some of its charm when it expanded, but it's comfortable and still serves up good food for a good cause. ⊠ *10 Sukhumvit Soi 12, Sukhumvit* ☏ *02/229–4611* ▭ *AE, DC, MC, V* Ⓜ *Subway: Sukhumvit; Skytrain: Asok.*

$ ✕ **My Choice.** Thais with a taste for their grandmothers' traditional recipes have flocked to this restaurant off Sukhumvit Road since the mid-'80s. The *ped aob*, a thick soup made from beef stock, is particularly popular. The interior is plain, so when the weather is cool most people prefer to sit outside. ⊠ *Sukhumvit Soi 36, Sukhumvit* ☏ *02/258–6174 or 02/259–9470* ▭ *AE, DC, MC, V* Ⓜ *Skytrain: Thong Lo.*

¢ ✕ **Thong Lee.** This small but attractive restaurant draws a devoted crowd to its air-conditioned dining room on the second floor. The menu is not very adventurous, but every dish has a distinct personality—evidence of the cook's vivid imagination. Almost everyone orders the *muu phad kapi* (pork fried with shrimp paste). The spicy *yam hed sod* (hot-and-sour mushroom salad) is memorable. This place is for lunch or early dinners only—it closes around 8 PM. ⊠ *Sukhumvit Soi 20, Sukhumvit* ☏ *No phone* ⌕ *Reservations not accepted* ▭ *No credit cards* ⊘ *Closed Sun.* Ⓜ *Subway: Sukhumvit; Skytrain: Asok.*

VIETNAMESE ✕ **Le Dalat.** This classy restaurant, a favorite with Bangkok residents, con-
$$–$$$ sists of several intimate dining rooms in what was once a private home. Don't pass up the *naem neuang*, which requires you to place a garlicky grilled meatball on a piece of rice paper, then pile on bits of garlic, ginger, hot chili, star apple, and mango before you wrap the whole thing up in a lettuce leaf and pop it in your mouth. Seafood dishes include *cha ca thang long*, Hanoi-style fried fish with dill. ⊠ *47/1 Sukhumvit Soi 23, opposite Indian Embassy, Sukhumvit* ☏ *02/260–1849* ⌕ *Reservations essential* ▭ *AE, DC, MC, V* Ⓜ *Subway: Sukhumvit; Skytrain: Asok.*

WHERE TO STAY

Bangkok offers a staggering range of lodging choices, and some of the best rooms are affordable to travelers on a budget. The city has nearly 500 hotels and guesthouses, and the number is growing. In fact, the amount of competition has brought the prices down at many of the city's hotels; unfortunately, service has suffered at some as hotels as a result of cutting corners to lower prices.

For first-class lodging, few cities in the world rival Bangkok. In recent years the Oriental, Peninsula, Four Seasons (formerly the Regent), and a handful of others have been repeatedly rated among the best in the world. And if there were a similar comparison of the world's boutique hotels, Bangkok's selection would be near the top, too. These high-end hotels are surprisingly affordable, with rates comparable to standard hotels in New York or London. Business hotels also have fine service, excellent restaurants, and amenities like health clubs, and a growing number have spas. Even budget hotels have comfortable rooms and efficient staffs.

Wherever you stay, remember that prices fluctuate enormously and that huge discounts are the order of the day. ▪ TIP→ **Always ask for a better** price, even if you have already booked a room (you can inquire about a discount upon check-in). Deals may be more difficult to come by during the high season from November through February, but that doesn't mean they're impossible to find, and during low season they're certainly plentiful.

Hotels are concentrated in four areas: along Silom and Sathorn roads in Silom (where many of the riverfront hotels are located); clustered in Siam Square and on Petchaburi Road in Pratunam; along Sukhumvit Road, which has the greatest number of hotels and an abundance of restaurants; and in the Chinatown and the Old City neighborhoods, which have a smaller number of properties. Backpackers often head to Khao San Road and its surrounding streets and lanes. The area has a mix of cheap cafés, secondhand bookstalls, trendy bars, and small guesthouses. It's still possible to get a room in that area for B150; even the newer, more upmarket guesthouses charge only around B500.

> ### NEW AIRPORT DIGS
>
> Bangkok's spectacular new international airport has a stunning new hotel to go with it. The **Novotel Suvarnabhumi Airport** (☎ 02/131-1111 ⊕ www.novotel.com) is the only hotel at the new airport—only five minutes away with free shuttle service. The massive 612-room complex has four restaurants, a pool, a gym, and a spa. Although it's too far south of the city to be a logical base of operations, it's important given that so many flights in and out of Bangkok happen in the middle of the night. Rooms start at B4,000 and can get quite expensive; the hotel also rents rooms in four-hour blocks starting at B2,200.

WHAT IT COSTS In Baht					
	$$$$	**$$$**	**$$**	**$**	**¢**
FOR 2 PEOPLE	over 6,000	4,001–6,000	2,001–4,000	1,000–2,000	under 1,000

Price categories are assigned based on the range between the least and most expensive standard double rooms in high season based on the European Plan (EP, with no meals) unless otherwise noted. Tax (17%) is extra.

Northern Bangkok

$$$$ ⬜ **Sofitel Central Plaza Bangkok.** Though it's north of much of the city and closer to the former airport than other luxury properties, there are plenty of reasons to stay at the Sofitel: the staff is very attentive, the property is close to expressways and subway and Skytrain stations, and rooms are gracefully appointed—antique prints, bronze statues of mythological figures, and temple-dog lamp stands remind you that you're in Thailand. To the west is a view of the Railway Golf Course; the other side looks out onto the city's astounding vertical growth. The refreshingly cool lobby, with a cascading waterfall, is a welcome retreat from the city streets. Among the hotel's numerous restaurants and bars is Dynasty, a popular spot for Chinese cuisine, and Le Denang one of the better Vietnamese restaurants. ✉ *1695 Phaholyothin Rd., Chatuchak, Northern Bangkok, 10210* ☎ *02/541-1234* ⊕ *www.sofitel.com* ➪ *579*

Where to Stay in Bangkok

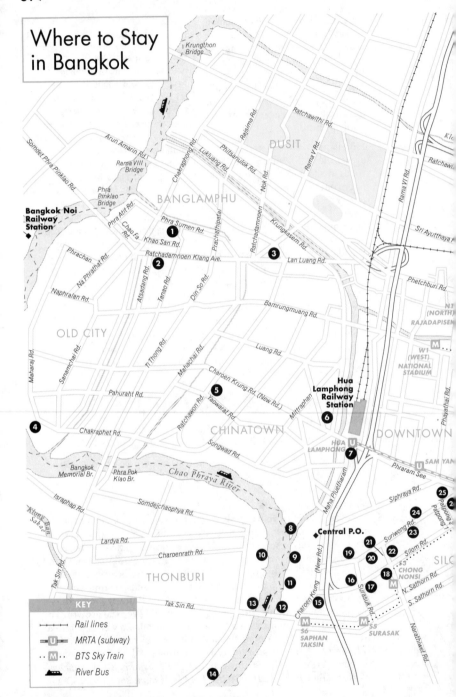

rooms, 6 suites ☖ In-room: safe, refrigerator, Wi-Fi. In-hotel: 6 restaurants, room service, bar, pool, gym, spa, laundry service, concierge ▭ AE, DC, MC, V Ⓜ Subway: Phahon Yothin.

★ **$$** ▧ **Reflections.** Although the purple facade and brightly colored rooms of this new boutique hotel are a bit campy for some, others will welcome the opportunity to stay in a place that's different from the sleek towers and tiny guesthouses that define the city's lodging choices. Each room has been individually decorated by different artists—styles range from art deco to romantic to quirkiness incarnate. All rooms have a lot of light, balconies that overlook the pool, minimal amounts of furniture. It's a bit north in Ari, a pleasant and well-established neighborhood; it's a five-minute walk to the Ari Skytrain station. The staff is very friendly and helpful. ✉ 81 Soi Ari, Phaholyothin, Phaya Thai, Northern Bangkok, 10400 ☎ 02/270–3344 ⊕ www.reflections-thai.com ⏎ 32 rooms ☖ In-room: safe, refrigerator, DVD, Wi-Fi. In-hotel: restaurant, room service, pool, spa ▭ AE, MC, V Ⓜ Skytrain: Ari.

The Old City, Banglamphu & Dusit

$$$$ ▧ **Chakrabongse Villas.** Perhaps the best three rooms in Bangkok are here
FodorśChoice in the gardens of Chakrabongse House. The problem is ⚠ there are only
★ three rooms, and the place is very popular, so you must book well in advance (at least a month). Located on the banks of the Chao Phraya River in an old part of the city, the rooms are in traditional Thai houses, originally built up-country and then brought to the grounds of the Chakrabongse House, which was built in 1908. The Riverside Villa and Garden Suite each offer more space and better views—the villa has a view of Wat Arun from the bedroom—but the Thai House is also unique and beautifully furnished. There's a sala next to the river for guests to enjoy, where Thai meals are served upon request. A minimum two-night stay is preferred. ✉ 396 Maharay Rd., Old City, 10200 ☎ 02/622–3356 ⊕ www.thaivillas.com ⏎ 3 rooms ☖ In-room: safe, refrigerator, Wi-Fi. In-hotel: restaurant, pool ▭ AE, DC, MC, V.

$$$ ▧ **Royal Princess Larn Luang.** This hotel is ideally located for exploring Dusit, the Old City, and Chinatown, but it's far from Skytrain and subway stations, and the neighborhood is virtually deserted in the evening. Fortunately, it's a short taxi ride to riverside restaurants, and the hotel offers Chinese, Italian, Japanese, and Thai cuisine. The tranquil lobby has gardens on two sides. The rooms are tastefully decorated in subdued colors that set off the dark-wood furnishings, but the bathrooms are on the small side. ✉ 269 Larn Luang Rd., Old City, 10100 ☎ 02/281–3088 ⊕ http://bangkok-larnluang.royalprincess.com ⏎ 167 rooms ☖ In-room: safe, refrigerator, Wi-Fi. In-hotel: 4 restaurants, 2 bars, pool, gym, laundry service ▭ AE, DC, MC, V.

$–$$ ▧ **Buddy Lodge.** Buddy Lodge has contributed greatly to Khao San Road's new trendiness by offering Bangkok's backpacker center its first boutique hotel. Standard rooms are very comfortable, but paying the extra B400 (roughly $12) for a deluxe room is worth it, considering the extra space and bigger balcony you get. You'll really appreciate the rooftop pool after trekking around the Old City sights all day. The lodge is also close to the river and many attractions like the Grand Palace. ✉ 265 Khao San Rd., Banglamphu, 10200 ☎ 02/629–4477 ⊕ www.buddylodge.

com ↻ *75 rooms* ♿ *In-room: safe, refrigerator. In-hotel: restaurant, 2 bars, pool, gym* ☰ *AE, DC, MC, V.*

$ ☷ **Royal Hotel.** Nearer to the Grand Palace and the Old City than any other of the city's lodgings, this hotel is a carefully kept secret of many frequent visitors. Its clean and comfortable rooms have homey touches like small writing tables. Several banquet rooms on the ground floor are popular with wedding parties. The lobby café is a good place to take a break from sightseeing. ✉ *2 Rajdamnoen Ave., Old City, 10200* ☎ *02/222–9111* ↻ *300 rooms* ♿ *In-room: refrigerator. In-hotel: 2 restaurants, room service, bar, pool, laundry service, public Internet* ☰ *AE, DC, MC, V.*

Chinatown

$$ ☷ **Grand China Princess.** One good reason for staying in Chinatown is the chance to experience the sights and sounds of the city's oldest neighborhood. Another reason is this hotel, which occupies the top two-thirds of a 25-story tower. The rooms are plain but have panoramic views of the city. The lobby has a bar, lounge, and coffee shop. ■ TIP➔ **Siang Ping Loh, serving Cantonese and Szechuan fare, is well worth a visit.** ✉ *215 Yaowarat Rd., at Ratchawongse Rd., Chinatown, 10100* ☎ *02/224–9977* ⊕ *www.royalprincess.com* ↻ *142 rooms, 13 suites* ♿ *In-room: safe, refrigerator, Wi-Fi. In-hotel: 2 restaurants, gym, concierge* ☰ *AE, DC, MC, V* Ⓜ *Subway: Hua Lamphong.*

$ ☷ **Bangkok Centre.** This hotel on the edge of Chinatown is near the Temple of the Golden Buddha and a couple of steps away from an entrance to Hua Lamphong station. Note that the hotel caters to tour groups from Singapore, Japan, China, and Europe, so the lobby can be chaotic at times, but service is attentive to the individual, too. The rooms are small, but clean and comfortable. It has a 24-hour coffee shop. ✉ *328 Rama 4, Chinatown, 10500* ☎ *02/238–4848* ⊕ *www.bangkokcentrehotel.com* ↻ *145 rooms* ♿ *In-room: safe (some), refrigerator. In-hotel: 2 restaurants, pool, laundry service, public Wi-Fi* ☰ *AE, DC, MC, V* Ⓜ *Subway: Hua Lamphong.*

¢ ☷ **Krung Kasem Srikrung Hotel.** This hotel, across a canal from Hua Lamphong station and near the Temple of the Golden Buddha, is in its fifth decade and a bit worse for wear. But it's ideally located if you arrive on a late train or are departing early in the morning. Basically, the sparsely furnished rooms are air-conditioned, the baths are clean, and the price is right—and that's about all you can say about it. ✉ *1860 Krung Kasem Rd., Chinatown, 10100* ☎ *02/225–0132 or 02/225–8900* ↻ *120 rooms* ♿ *In-hotel: restaurant* ☰ *No credit cards* Ⓜ *Subway: Hua Lamphong.*

¢ ☷ **River View Guest House.** ■ TIP➔ **This family-run hotel is one of the few budget accommodations that overlook the river,** and it's the view that sells it. The accommodations are a bit run-down and may remind you of college dorm rooms, but they're clean and comfortable. The staff will go out of its way for you, even staying up to accommodate late flights (someone sleeps downstairs during the night, in case you need something). One drawback is that tuk-tuk drivers sometimes have difficulty finding the place. The easiest way to find it is to head north from the Royal Orchid Sheraton; you can see the guesthouse's sign pointing down a side street. ✉ *768 Soi Panurangsri, Songvad Rd., Chinatown, 10100* ☎ *02/*

234–5429 🛏 *45 rooms* ⚒ *In-room: no a/c (some), refrigerator, no TV. In-hotel: restaurant, laundry service* ▤ *AE.*

Thonburi

$$$$
Fodor'sChoice
★

🏨 **Peninsula.** The rooms at the Peninsula have plenty of gadgets like bedside controls that dim the lights, turn on the sound system, and close the curtains; bathrooms with hands-free phones; and TVs with mist-free screens at the end of the tubs. Because the hotel is in Thonburi, its spacious rooms get a clear view of the Bangkok skyline; a free shuttle across the river to the nearest Skytrain station is provided. The restaurants include Cantonese and Pacific Rim cuisine and barbecue buffets are often held in the evening by the river. The hotel has a long swimming pool with private gazebos. ⊠ *333 Charoen Krung (New Rd.), Klonsan, Thonburi, 10600* ☎ *02/861–2888* ⊕ *www.peninsula.com* 🛏 *313 rooms, 67 suites* ⚒ *In-room: safe, refrigerator, Wi-Fi. In-hotel: 4 restaurants, room service, bar, pool, gym, spa, laundry service, concierge* ▤ *AE, DC, MC, V* Ⓜ *Skytrain: Saphan Taksin.*

★ **$$$–$$$$**

🏨 **Bangkok Marriott Resort & Spa.** Getting to the Marriott is a pleasant adventure in itself—free shuttle boats take you across the Chao Phraya from the Taksin bridge. This is more of a resort than a hotel, with many restaurants and a small mall connected. The big pool and garden area on the riverside make you feel a long way from the bustle of Downtown. All rooms are spacious and well furnished, but if you want a river view, remember to ask for it. The Manohra Song, an ancient rice barge converted into a floating restaurant, is berthed here. The only downside to the hotel is its distance from attractions—the shuttle boats are fun, but the trip takes some time, and traveling by road is even slower. ⊠ *257/ 1–3 Charoennakorn Rd., Thonburi, 10600* ☎ *02/476–0021* ⊕ *www. royal-garden.com* 🛏 *420 rooms* ⚒ *In-room: safe, refrigerator, ethernet. In-hotel: 8 restaurants, room service, 2 bars, pool, 2 tennis courts, gym, spa, laundry service, concierge* ▤ *AE, DC, MC, V.*

$$$–$$$$
Fodor'sChoice
★

🏨 **Hilton Millennium.** Lording over the Chao Phraya in postmillennial splendor, this flagship Hilton—which, like the Peninsula, is reached via hotel-operated ferry service from the downtown riverbank at the end of the Skytrain—boasts some of the most cutting-edge room design and hotel facilities in the city, competing successfully with Bangkok's longstanding hotel giants at considerably lower prices. The infinity pool hangs like a waterfall off the edge of the cleverly designed deck, an urban beach overlooking the entire city skyline. High above everything else, the 32nd-floor open-air roof deck, executive lounge, and chilled-out bar all have spectacular panoramas. Rooms (aside from suites) are on the small side, but their setups compensate well enough for that, and the bathrooms seem 22nd century. Every single room in the hotel has river and city views. ⊠ *123 Charoennakorn Rd., Thonburi, 10600* ☎ *02/442– 2000* ⊕ *www.hilton.com* 🛏 *465 rooms, 78 suites* ⚒ *In-room: safe, refrigerator, Wi-Fi. In-hotel: 5 restaurants, room service, 4 bars, pool, gym, spa, concierge, laundry service* ▤ *AE, DC, MC, V.*

Pratunam

$$$$
🏨 **The Conrad.** Though The Conrad is one of the city's biggest hotels, service doesn't suffer—the staff is attentive and the rooms and other facilities are well maintained. It's connected to All Seasons Place, which

has dozens of restaurants and shops. A hotel shuttle bus is available to and from the Skytrain. ☒ *All Seasons Place, 87 Wittayu (Wireless Rd.), Pratunam, 10330* ☎ *02/690–9999* ⊕ *www.conradhotels.com* ⟐ *381 rooms, 10 suites* ♿ *In-room: safe, refrigerator, ethernet (some). In-hotel: 5 restaurants, 2 bars, pool, spa, laundry service, concierge, public Wi-Fi* ☰ *AE, DC, MC, V* Ⓜ *Skytrain: Ploenchit.*

$$$$ 🏨 **Four Seasons Hotel Bangkok.** Formerly called the Regent, this hotel has long been one of Bangkok's leading hotels and arguably has the city's best pool. Local society meets for morning coffee and afternoon tea in the formal lobby where a string quartet plays most afternoons. Off the courtyard there are plenty of shops to browse. The large rooms are decorated with silk-upholstered furniture. The best rooms overlook the racetrack, but ask for a high floor so that the Skytrain doesn't block the view. The quartet of "cabana rooms," the private patios of which look onto a small garden with a lotus pond, are exquisite. Be sure to indulge yourself with the Four Season's signature fragrant-oil massage. ☒ *155 Ratchadamri Rd., Pratunam, 10330* ☎ *02/250-1000* ⊕ *www. fourseasons.com/bangkok* ⟐ *346 rooms, 10 suites* ♿ *In-room: safe, ethernet. In-hotel: 7 restaurants, bar, pool, gym, spa, concierge, public Wi-Fi* ☰ *AE, DC, MC, V* Ⓜ *Skytrain: Ratchadamri.*

$$$$ 🏨 **Grand Hyatt Erawan.** This stylish hotel hovers over the auspicious Erawan Shrine. The impressive atrium, with an extensive modern art collection, soars four stories high to a glass roof. Rooms are spacious; the wood floors are strewn with tasteful rugs, the walls are hung with original art, and a desk and a couple of chairs are positioned directly in front of bay windows. There are plenty of high-tech accoutrements, too. Baths have separate showers, oversize tubs, and private dressing areas. ■ TIP→ **The Italian fare at Spasso, created by a Milanese chef, is especially creative; lunch here is a must whether or not you stay in the hotel.** It is also a lively nightclub. A new Skytrain walkway system connects the hotel to many more places. ☒ *494 Ratchadamri Rd., Pratunam, 10330* ☎ *02/ 254–1234, 800/233–1234 in U.S.* ⊕ *www.bangkok.grand.hyatt.com* ⟐ *364 rooms, 38 suites* ♿ *In-room: safe, refrigerator, ethernet. In-hotel: 9 restaurants, bar, 2 tennis courts, pool, gym, laundry service, concierge, public Wi-Fi* ☰ *AE, DC, MC, V* Ⓜ *Skytrain: Ratchadamri.*

$$$$ 🏨 **Inter-Continental Bangkok.** This fine hotel, formerly Le Royal Meridian, is in one of the city's prime business districts and does a good job of catering to its corporate clientele. Club Inter-Continental rooms have 24-hour butler service. The lounge on the 37th floor has great city views to gaze at while sipping evening cocktails (complimentary for Club-floor guests). The rooftop pool is rather small, but feels cozy rather than cramped. The popular Summer Palace restaurant serves Cantonese cuisine. ☒ *973 Ploenchit Rd., Pratunam, 10330* ☎ *02/656–0444* ⊕ *www. intercontinental.com* ⟐ *344 rooms, 37 suites* ♿ *In-room: safe, refrigerator, DVD, ethernet. In-hotel: 3 restaurants, room service, pool, gym, spa, laundry service, concierge, executive floor, public Wi-Fi* ☰ *AE, DC, MC, V* Ⓜ *Skytrain: Chitlom.*

$$$–$$$$ 🏨 **Nai Lert Park Bangkok.** The best thing about this hotel, part of the Swissotel chain, is the garden, so ask for a room that faces it. The rooms are large, and the baths have showers and bathtubs. The on-site

Japanese restaurant, Genji, is excellent. Note that this is a popular hotel for weddings, conferences, and parties, so it may not be the most tranquil of retreats. ✉ *2 Wittayu (Wireless Rd.), Pratunam, 10330* 🕾 *02/253–0123* ⊕ *www.nailertpark.swissotel.com* ⇌ *303 rooms, 35 suites* ⌂ *In-room: safe, refrigerator, ethernet. In-hotel: 5 restaurants, 2 bars, pool, 2 tennis courts, spa, concierge, executive floor* ▭ *AE, DC, MC, V* Ⓜ *Skytrain: Ploenchit.*

$$$ ⊞ **Amari Watergate.** This huge flagship hotel has spacious and comfortable rooms, all decked out in silks and other rich fabrics. Baths are also quite large, although the separate showers are small. The executive floor has a lounge where complimentary cocktails are served in the afternoon. The restaurants serve up delicious Italian and Chinese fare, a Thai eatery offers specialties from the country's four major regions, and the coffee shop serves a tasty buffet. The swimming pool is one of the largest in the city. ✉ *847 Phetchburi Rd., Pratunam, 10400* 🕾 *02/653–9000* ⊕ *www.amari.com* ⇌ *540 rooms, 29 suites* ⌂ *In-room: safe, refrigerator, DVD (some), Wi-Fi. In-hotel: 4 restaurants, bar, pool, gym, laundry service, concierge, executive floor, public Wi-Fi* ▭ *AE, DC, MC, V* Ⓜ *Skytrain: Chitlom.*

$$–$$$ ⊞ **Novotel Bangkok on Siam Square.** This big hotel is convenient to shopping, dining, and entertainment. It's also a short walk from the Skytrain central station, which puts much of the city within reach. The rooms are comfortable and functional. Despite the size of the hotel, there are always plenty of staff members around to help you. One of Bangkok's top nightclubs, CM2, is in the basement. ✉ *Siam Sq. Soi 6, Pratunam, 10330* 🕾 *02/209–8888* ⊕ *www.accorhotels.com/asia* ⇌ *404 rooms, 25 suites* ⌂ *In-room: safe, refrigerator, Wi-Fi. In-hotel: 3 restaurants, room service, 3 bars, pool, gym, laundry service, concierge, public Wi-Fi* ▭ *AE, DC, MC, V* Ⓜ *Skytrain: Siam.*

$–$$ ⊞ **Ibis Siam Bangkok.** Ibis is a popular and well-respected chain in Asia, and this branch lives up to the global reputation—it's clean, efficiently run, and well managed. Rooms are kind of no-frills, though by using the warm browns, golds, and oranges that are so in vogue right now, they're slightly more attractive than most budget digs. The Ibis is a 10-minute walk from the Skytrain station. ✉ *97 Ratchaprarop Rd., Pratunam, 10110* 🕾 *02/209–3888* ⊕ *www.ibissiam.com* ⇌ *180 rooms* ⌂ *In-room: Wi-Fi. In-hotel: restaurant, bar, laundry service, public Wi-Fi* ▭ *AE, DC, MC, V* Ⓜ *Skytrain: Victory Monument.*

$ ⊞ **First House.** Tucked behind the Pratunam Market in the bustling garment district, the First House is an excellent value for a hotel in this price range. The compact rooms are nicely furnished, but rather dark. In the small lobby you can catch up on the latest with the complimentary newspapers. The 24-hour coffee shop serves Thai dishes. ✉ *14/20–29 Phetchburi Soi 19, Phaya Thai, Pratunam, 10400* 🕾 *02/254–0300* ⊕ *www.fiorsthosuebkk.com* ⇌ *100 rooms* ⌂ *In-room: refrigerator. In-hotel: restaurant, room service, laundry service* ▭ *AE, MC, V* Ⓜ *Skytrain: Rajchathewi.*

Silom

$$$$ ⊞ **Banyan Tree Bangkok.** After checking in on the ground floor, you soar up to your room at this 60-story hotel. The light-filled suites in the slender tower all have sweeping views of the city. The generous use of native woods in everything from the large desks to the walk-in closets gives each room a warm glow. A fully equipped spa offers the latest treatments, and a sundeck on the 53rd floor beckons with a relaxing whirlpool. For meals or a drink in the evening there's the rooftop Vertigo, which the hotel claims is Asia Pacific's highest alfresco eatery. In September you can test your fitness in the annual "vertical marathon" up the hotel's stairs. Note that about 80 rooms were being added (to be ready in late 2007) to the property in a refitted neighboring building—if you prefer to be in the main tower, be sure to specify. ✉ *21/100 S. Sathorn Rd., Silom, 10120* ☎ *02/679–1200* ⊕ *www.banyantree. com/bangkok/* ➷ *216 suites* ⚒ *In-room: safe, refrigerator, ethernet. In-hotel: 6 restaurants, room service, 2 bars, pool, gym, spa, laundry service, concierge, public Internet* ▤ *AE, DC, MC, V* Ⓜ *Subway: Lumphini.*

$$$$ 🏨 **Dusit Thani.** This high-rise hotel has a distinctive pyramid shape that makes it immediately identifiable. The reception area, where a sunken lounge overlooks a small garden, is one floor up. Rooms here are spacious, especially the high-price suites. The Dusit's proximity to the Skytrain and subway stations makes it a convenient base for exploring the city. It's also across the street from Lumphini Park, Bangkok's best public park. The pool is in a central courtyard filled with trees, making it a peaceful oasis from the heat and humidity. The Devarana Spa offers an impressive menu of treatments from herbal steam baths to body scrubs with unusual ingredients (coconut and turmeric or wolfberry and sesame) to a signature massage that combines several different styles including Thai massage. A popular Chinese restaurant, an elegant Thai restaurant, and a shopping arcade occupy the street level. ✉ *946 Rama IV Rd., Silom, 10500* ☎ *02/236–0450* ⊕ *www.dusit.com* ➷ *487 rooms, 30 suites* ⚒ *In-room: safe, refrigerator, ethernet. In-hotel: 7 restaurants, room service, bar, pool, gym, spa, laundry service, concierge* ▤ *AE, DC, MC, V* Ⓜ *Subway: Silom; Skytrain: Sala Daeng.*

$$$$ 🏨 **Lebua at State Tower.** The Lebua is a comfortable hotel with great restaurants, an beautiful rooftop bar, and more than a bit of flare. The rooms are spacious and have views of the city. The staff is efficient and helpful. It's at the end of Silom Road near the river, which makes it convenient to most attractions; it's a five-minute walk to the nearest Skytrain station. ✉ *1055 Silom Rd., Silom, 10500* ☎ *02/624–9999* ⊕ *www.lebua. com* ➷ *198 rooms* ⚒ *In-room: safe, refrigerator, Wi-Fi. In-hotel: 5 restaurants, 2 bars, pool, gym, laundry service* ▤ *AE, DC, MC, V* Ⓜ *Skytrain: Saphan Taksin.*

$$$$ 🏨 **Metropolitan Bangkok.** The Metropolitan has all the elements of hip: a crisp, modern esthetic; a pop-star clientele; a chic guests-and-members-only lounge; a sexy staff; and an ironic location in a refurbished YMCA. Some of the rooms are a bit small, but they're smartly turned out—dark woods and deep browns are offset by cream-color walls, pillows, and rugs. Though the rooms aren't dripping with high-tech gadgetry, they do have 25-inch flat-screen TVs with DVD players. ✉ *27 S. Sathorn, Silom, 10120* ☎ *02/625–3333* ⊕ *www.metropolitan.como.bz* ➷ *159 rooms, 12 suites* ⚒ *In-room: safe, refrigerator, DVD, Wi-Fi. In-hotel: 2 restaurants, room service, bar, pool, spa, laundry service,* *concierge, public Wi-Fi* ▣ *AE, DC, MC, V* Ⓜ *Subway: Lumphini; Skytrain: Sala Daeng or Chong Nonsi.*

$$$$ 🖼 **Oriental Hotel.** This opulent hotel on the Chao Phraya still sets the standard that other hotels try to match. Part of its fame stems from the celebrities who stayed here in the past, but the recent guest book reveals no-less-impressive names. The four suites in the original building, now called the Author's Residence, offer a unique experience, with superlative service in big historical rooms. In addition to its excellent restaurants, the hotel hosts a riverside barbecue every night. There are cooking classes that teach you the secrets of Thai cuisine, and a spa on the other side of the river that lets you indulge in all sorts of luxurious treatments from massage to facials to soothing herbal and milk baths in your own private suite. ✉ *48 Oriental Ave., Silom, 10500* ☎ *02/659–9000* ⊕ *www.mandarinoriental.com/bangkok* ⇲ *358 rooms, 35 suites* ♺ *In-room: safe, refrigerator, ethernet. In-hotel: 6 restaurants, room service, bar, pool, 2 tennis courts, gym, spa, laundry service, concierge, public Internet* ▣ *AE, DC, MC, V* Ⓜ *Skytrain: Saphan Taksin.*

Fodor'sChoice ★

$$$$ 🖼 **Royal Orchid Sheraton.** Of the luxury hotels along the riverfront, this 28-story palace is most popular with tour groups. All the well-appointed rooms face the river, but the color scheme of low-key peaches and creams is a little uninspired, and standard rooms tend to be long and narrow, making them feel cramped. The Thai Thara Thong restaurant is memorable, with subtle classical music accompanying your meal. You can also choose Indian or Italian cuisine. A glassed-in bridge leads to the adjacent River City Shopping Complex. The hotel runs a free shuttle bus service to the Skytrain every 30 minutes and free boat service to Saphan Taksin station. ✉ *2 Captain Bush La., Silom, 10500* ☎ *02/266–0123* ⊕ *www.sheraton.com/bangkok* ⇲ *714 rooms, 26 suites* ♺ *In-room: safe, refrigerator, ethernet. In-hotel: 4 restaurants, room service, 2 bars, 2 pools, tennis court, gym, spa, laundry service, concierge* ▣ *AE, DC, MC, V* Ⓜ *Skytrain: Chong Nonsi.*

★ **$$$$** 🖼 **Shangri-La Hotel.** Although it's one of Bangkok's best hotels, the Shangri-La has never managed to achieve the fame of the Oriental. That's a shame, because the marble lobby illuminated by crystal chandeliers is palatial, and the adjacent lounge, with its floor-to-ceiling windows, offers a marvelous view of the Chao Phraya River. The peace of the gardens is interrupted only by the puttering of passing boats. Many of the rooms, decorated in soothing pastels, are beginning to show their age, however. In the luxurious Krungthep Wing, a separate tower across the garden, the rooms are larger and quieter, with balconies overlooking the river, and cost a little more. Angelini's is considered one of city's finest Italian restaurants. ✉ *89 Soi Wat Suan Phu, Charoen Krung (New Rd.), Silom, 10500* ☎ *02/236–7777* ⊕ *www.shangri-la.com/bangkok* ⇲ *793 rooms, 6 suites* ♺ *In-room: safe, refrigerator, ethernet. In-hotel: 5 restaurants, 2 bars, 2 pools, 2 tennis courts, gym, spa, laundry service, concierge* ▣ *AE, DC, MC, V* Ⓜ *Skytrain: Saphan Taksin.*

$$$$ 🖼 **Sukhothai.** On 6 landscaped acres near Sathorn Road, the Sukhothai has numerous courtyards that make the hustle and bustle of Bangkok seem worlds away. Standard rooms are spacious, but not exceptionally well furnished. The one-bedroom suites, in contrast, are exquisite and have oversize baths paneled in teak and his and hers washbasins and

Fodor'sChoice ★

mirrors. The hotel's well-regarded restaurant is set in a pavilion on an artificial pond. The dining room serving continental fare is comfortable, but the prices are high. ✉ *13/3 S. Sathorn Rd., Silom, 10120* ☏ *02/344–8888* ⊕ *www.sukhothai.com* ✍ *140 rooms, 78 suites* ♿ *In-room: safe, refrigerator, ethernet. In-hotel: 3 restaurants, bar, pool, tennis court, gym, spa, concierge* ⊟ *AE, DC, MC, V* Ⓜ *Subway: Lumphini.*

$$$ ⌂ **Montien.** This hotel within stumbling distance of Patpong has been remarkably well maintained since it was constructed in 1970. The rooms are spacious, but the decor is not inspired. Prices are slightly higher than you would expect for the area, but the hotel often gives discounts. Perhaps a sign of the quirkiness that exists a few doors down in Patpong, there are in-house fortune-tellers who will read your palm for a small fee. ✉ *54 Surawong Rd., Silom, 10500* ☏ *02/233–7060 up to 69* ⊕ *www.montien.com* ✍ *475 rooms* ♿ *In-room: safe, ethernet. In-hotel: 2 restaurants, bar, pool, gym, public Internet* ⊟ *AE, DC, MC, V* Ⓜ *Subway: Silom; Skytrain: Sala Daeng.*

★ $$$ ⌂ **Siam Heritage.** The family that runs the Siam Heritage has created a classy boutique hotel with a purpose—to preserve and promote Thai heritage. Each room is individually furnished, mostly with pieces from Northern Thailand. The bedrooms have wood floors and the bathrooms have stonework in place of tiling. Much attention has been paid to small details from painted elevator doors to colorful weavings on the beds. ✉ *115/1 Surawong Rd., Silom, 10500* ☏ *02/353–6101* ⊕ *www.thesiamheritage.com* ✍ *51 rooms, 18 suites* ♿ *In-room: safe, refrigerator, Wi-Fi. In-hotel: restaurant, bar, pool, spa, laundry service, public Wi-Fi* ⊟ *AE, DC, MC, V* Ⓜ *Subway: Silom; Skytrain: Sala Daeng.*

$$$ ⌂ **Swiss Lodge.** This small hotel not far from Silom Road adds a friendly boutique option to the neighborhood. Nicely furnished rooms still feel fresh. Single rooms are really the size of doubles; doubles are large enough to hold king-size beds, and the suites added in 2006 by doubling up two rooms offer serious luxury. There's a very small pool and sundeck on the fifth floor. A good on-site restaurant has a daily breakfast buffet and a lunch buffet on weekdays; in the evening it specializes in fondue. ✉ *3 Convent Rd., Silom, 10500* ☏ *02/233–5345* ⊕ *www.swisslodge.com* ✍ *30 rooms, 12 suite* ♿ *In-room: safe, refrigerator, DVD (some), Wi-Fi. In-hotel: restaurant, room service, pool, public Internet* ⊟ *AE, DC, MC, V* Ⓜ *Skytrain: Sala Daeng.*

★ $$$ ⌂ **Triple Two Silom.** This trendy hotel is the sister property of the Narai Hotel next door; guests here can use the Narai's pool and fitness center. Spacious rooms have wood floors and modern fittings in what seem to be the standard colors of hip these days: deep brown, cream, black, and red. Unfortunately, the windows are small, so don't expect a lot of natural light. There's a courtyard in the center of the hotel, and a restaurant and bar with indoor and outdoor sections is at street level. ✉ *222 Silom Rd., Silom, 10500* ☏ *02/627–2222* ⊕ *www.tripletwosilom.com* ✍ *75 rooms* ♿ *In-room: safe, refrigerator, DVD, ethernet. In-hotel: restaurant, room service, bar, pool, gym, laundry service, public Internet* ⊟ *AE, DC, MC, V* Ⓜ *Skytrain: Chong Nonsi.*

$$–$$$ ⌂ **Holiday Inn Silom Bangkok.** With two towers of glass and steel, this former Crowne Plaza is impressive. It might be too big for some, however. The vast public areas make it seem like New York's Grand Central Station, especially with the clusters of airline employees and tour groups running to and fro. Less hectic are the two executive floors, which have their own concierge and lounge. Rooms are spacious, with lots of light streaming in. For meals, try the traditional fare at the Thai Pavilion, or the northern Indian cuisine at Tandoor. ⊠ *981 Silom Rd., Silom, 10500* ☎ *02/238–4300* ⊕ *www.bangkok-silom.holiday-inn.com* ⤳ *671 rooms, 25 suites* ♻ *In-room: safe, refrigerator, ethernet. In-hotel: 2 restaurants, bar, pool, tennis court, gym, laundry service, concierge, public Internet* ▭ *AE, DC, MC, V* Ⓜ *Skytrain: Surasak.*

$$ 🏨 **Narai Hotel.** Dating back to 1969, this is one of Bangkok's older hotels, but it's well kept up and conveniently located by the business district on Silom Road. It has basic but comfortable rooms and friendly service. This hotel's name refers to the god Vishnu (Narai is the Thai name for Vishnu), and an elegant bas-relief of the Hindu deity can be seen on the wall in front of the main staircase. Unfortunately, the hotel is a hike to the nearest Skytrain station. ⊠ *222 Silom Rd., Silom, 10500* ☎ *02/237–0100* ⊕ *www.naraihotel.co.th* ⤳ *455 rooms, 16 suites* ♻ *In-room: safe, refrigerator. In-hotel: 3 restaurants, bar, pool, gym, laundry service, public Wi-Fi* ▭ *AE, DC, MC, V* Ⓜ *Skytrain: Chong Nonsi.*

$$ 🏨 **Tawana Bangkok.** Most rooms here have wood floors and tasteful furnishings with a few details that call to mind the region's history. A few rooms have balconies overlooking the very modest pool, but they are not worth the extra cost. They added a few suites in 2005 that are two stories and go for B10,000. The hotel's location, in the heart of the Silom-Surawong district, gives you easy access to Bangkok's sights. The coffee shop stays open until 1 AM. ⊠ *80 Surawong Rd., Silom, 10500* ☎ *02/236–0361* ⊕ *www.tawanahotel.com* ⤳ *254 rooms, 3 suites* ♻ *In-room: safe, refrigerator, Wi-Fi. In-hotel: 3 restaurants, bar, pool, gym, spa* ▭ *AE, DC, MC, V* Ⓜ *Subway: Silom; Skytrain: Sala Daeng.*

$$ 🏨 **Tower Inn.** It's all going on at the top of this slender tower on Silom Road where there's a fitness center, a rooftop swimming pool with views of the skyline, and a sauna (for an extra B200). The rooms are spacious, with plenty of light from picture windows, though the furnishings are a bit utilitarian. There's also a pleasant rooftop restaurant serving international and Thai dishes from 6 PM to midnight. The coffee shop on the second floor is open 24 hours. ⊠ *533 Silom Rd., Silom, 10500* ☎ *02/237–8300* ⊕ *www.towerinnbangkok.com* ⤳ *205 rooms* ♻ *In-room: refrigerator. In-hotel: restaurant, bar, pool, gym, public Internet* ▭ *AE, DC, MC, V* Ⓜ *Skytrain: Chong Nonsi.*

★ **$** 🏨 **La Residence.** You'd expect to find this charming little hotel on the Left Bank of Paris. It's one of the few low-key lodgings in an area dominated by office towers. The rooms are small but comfortable and each is individually decorated; styles vary, so ask to look at a few rooms to decide which you like best. The seven suites are very big and have kitchenettes. A ground-floor restaurant serves Thai food and doubles as a sitting room for guests. The hotel entrance is just down Soi Anuman Rojdhon off Surawong. ⊠ *173/8–9 Surawong Rd., Silom, 10500* ☎ *02/233–3301* ⊕ *www.laresidencebangkok.com* ⤳ *16 rooms, 7 suites* ♻ *In-room: safe, refrigerator. In-hotel: laundry service, public Internet* ▭ *AE, MC, V* Ⓜ *Skytrain: Surasak.*

$ 🏨 **Manohra Hotel.** An expansive marble lobby is your first clue that this hotel is head and shoulders above others in its price range. Rooms have pleasant furnishings and spotless baths. There's a rooftop garden for sunbathing and a very small indoor pool next to the lobby. The best asset, though, may be the friendly staff. A lot of Asian tour groups stay here. The Skytrain is a 15-minute walk from the hotel. ✉ *412 Surawong Rd., Silom, 10500* ☎ *02/234–5070* ⊕ *www.manohrahotel.com* ➘ *200 rooms, 6 suites* ♿ *In-room: safe, refrigerator. In-hotel: restaurant, room service, pool, gym, public Internet* ▤ *AE, DC, MC, V* Ⓜ *Skytrain: Surasak.*

$ 🏨 **Silom Village Inn.** Reasonable rates are just one of the draws at this small hotel. It's also well run, with rooms that are as neat as a pin. The king-size beds leave just enough space for a desk and a couple of chairs, but the 20 new rooms added in 2005 are a little bigger and expensive. Ask for a room at the back of the hotel to avoid the ruckus on Silom Road. The staff at the reception desk is helpful and reliable at taking messages. A small restaurant serves Thai food, but many other choices are just outside your door. ✉ *Silom Village, 286 Silom Rd., Silom, 10500* ☎ *02/635–6810 up to 16* ➘ *80 rooms* ♿ *In-room: safe, refrigerator. In-hotel: restaurant, room service* ▤ *AE, DC, MC, V* Ⓜ *Skytrain: Surasak.*

$ 🏨 **Wall Street Inn.** Most of the guests at this hotel on Surawong Road are from Japan, perhaps because of the many Japanese businesses in the immediate area. But its location near Lumphini Park, Patpong's night market, and Silom Road makes it an appealing option for anyone. Standard rooms are small and windowless, so make sure to ask for one of the deluxe rooms. There's not much of a view, however. The hotel offers traditional Thai massage, and there is also a row of traditional massage centers on the soi. Sarika Cafe, at the mouth of the soi, is a good little restaurant if the hotel's coffee shop doesn't do it for you. ✉ *37/20–24 Soi Surawong Plaza, Surawong Rd., Silom, 10500* ☎ *02/233–4164* ➘ *63 rooms* ♿ *In-room: safe, refrigerator. In-hotel: restaurant, room service, public Internet* ▤ *AE, MC, V* Ⓜ *Subway: Silom; Skytrain: Sala Daeng.*

Sukhumvit

$$$$ 🏨 **Amari Boulevard.** This pyramid-shaped tower certainly has a dashing profile. Rooms in the newer glass tower are modern and airy, with plenty of amenities. The use of dark wood in the older rooms lends them a more traditional ambience. Particularly attractive are those rooms overlooking the pool in the older building. The ground-floor lobby is vast, with plenty of places to have a quiet conversation. The casual Peppermill restaurant serves a range of Thai and Japanese dishes. The hotel is on a one-way soi near Sukhumvit Road; it's convenient to shops and restaurants, but it can be noisy at night because there are also several bars on this street. ✉ *2 Sukhumvit Soi 5, Sukhumvit, 10110* ☎ *02/255–2930* ⊕ *www.amari.com* ➘ *315 rooms* ♿ *In-room: safe, refrigerator, ethernet. In-hotel: 2 restaurants, room service, bar, pool, gym, laundry service, concierge, public Internet* ▤ *AE, DC, MC, V* Ⓜ *Skytrain: Nana.*

$$$$ 🏨 **J. W. Marriott Hotel.** Sukhumvit's Marriott is conveniently located, with many restaurants and businesses nearby, but it's also around the corner from Nana Plaza, one of the city's biggest red-light districts, which might turn some people off as much as it turns others on. Rooms

have the standard amenities, although the firm beds make for a good night's sleep. It's worth a few extra baht to stay on the executive floors, which have a separate lounge where you are offered complimentary breakfast, afternoon tea, and evening cocktails. The fitness center is superb, with the latest equipment and saunas. Restaurants include Man Ho, serving Cantonese fare; the White Elephant, specializing in Thai favorites; and the New York Steakhouse. ☒ *4 Sukhumvit Soi 2, Sukhumvit, 10110* ☏ *02/ 656–7700* ⊕ *www.marriott.com* ↩ *441 rooms* ⚒ *In-room: safe, refrigerator. In-hotel: 5 restaurants, room service, bar, pool, gym, laundry service, concierge, executive floor* ⊟ *AE, DC, MC, V* Ⓜ *Skytrain: Nana.*

$$$$ 🏨 **Sheraton Grande Sukhumvit.** The Sheraton soars 33 floors above the noisy city streets, and the suites on the upper floors get tons of natural light. Standard rooms are a bit formulaic—you won't find any Thai-influenced accoutrements—but they're pleasant enough. You never go hungry here: on street level is Basu, serving sushi, while the Orchid Café on the second floor lays out an international buffet. In the afternoon you can enjoy tea in the lounge or cocktails in the rotunda. On the third floor, the health club and the serpentine swimming pool are laid out amid a lovely garden. Here you can also find a Thai restaurant and, during the dry months, a barbecue. The Skytrain is connected to the hotel via a covered walkway from the station to the lobby, and the subway station is next door (and below) the Skytrain station. ☒ *250 Sukhumvit Rd., Sukhumvit, 10110* ☏ *02/649–8888* ⊕ *www.starwoodhotels.com/ bangkok* ↩ *406 rooms, 23 suites* ⚒ *In-room: safe, refrigerator, DVD, Wi-Fi. In-hotel: 4 restaurants, room service, bar, pool, gym, spa, laundry service, concierge, public Wi-Fi* ⊟ *AE, DC, MC, V* Ⓜ *Subway: Sukhumvit; Skytrain: Asok.*

$$$–$$$$ 🏨 **Davis Bangkok.** This fine medium-size hotel is actually two buildings: the main one and The Corner wing, which is two doors down the street and has a separate reception and lobby. Rooms in both buildings have the same decor and amenities. The showpiece of the Davis is two Thai villas—separate modern houses built in traditional Thai style—both top-of-the-line two- and three-bedroom structures with all the amenities, their own pool, and a price tag of B25,000 to B30,000 per day to go with them (there are big discounts for monthly stays). But there are comfortable and classy rooms to fit more humble budgets in the main buildings. Rooms are individually decorated in styles that vary—from Bali and Bombay to Thai, and even Florida. ☒ *80 Sukhumvit Soi 24, Sukhumvit, 10110* ☏ *02/260–8000* ⊕ *www.davisbangkok.net* ↩ *238 rooms (164 in main hotel, 74 in The Corner wing), 10 villas* ⚒ *In-room: ethernet. In-hotel: 2 restaurants, bar, pool, spa, public Wi-Fi* ⊟ *AE, DC, MC, V* Ⓜ *Skytrain: Phrom Phong.*

$$$ 🏨 **Imperial Queen's Park.** Two gleaming white towers make up Bangkok's largest hotel. To help keep its numerous rooms filled, the hotel makes special arrangements with guests staying a month or more. Standard rooms are spacious and have large desks, but the junior suites have separate work areas and plenty of natural light. Many rooms have whirlpool tubs (although they're not the latest models). The penthouse suite on the top floor of one of the towers is one of the largest suites in Thailand. The hotel is off busy Sukhumvit Road, next to a small park that is ideal for jogging, and one of the city's premier malls, The Emporium, is on the other side of the park. ⊠ *199 Sukhumvit Soi 22, Sukhumvit, 10110* ☏ *02/ 261–9000* ⊕ *www.imperialhotels.com* ⟿ *1,082 rooms, 168 suites* ⚑ *In-room: safe, refrigerator, ethernet (some). In-hotel: 8 restaurants, room service, bar, 2 pools, gym, spa, laundry service, concierge, public Internet* ⊟ *AE, DC, MC, V* Ⓜ *Skytrain: Phrom Phong.*

$$$ ▥ **Imperial Tara Hotel.** This hotel is on a side street near Sukhumvit Road, which means restaurants and clubs are practically at your doorstep. While you check in, enjoy a cup of tea in the spacious lobby lined with teak carvings. Rooms, all of which are on the small side, have cool marble floors and nice views. Many overlook the eighth-floor terrace with a swimming pool. The Tara's sister property, the Imperial Impala, which was connected by a covered walkway, was closed in July 2006 for renovations, but the shared amenities between the two hotels remain unaffected. ⊠ *18/1 Sukhumvit Soi 26, Sukhumvit, 10110* ☏ *02/259– 2900* ⊕ *www.imperialtara.com* ⟿ *196 rooms* ⚑ *In-room: safe, refrigerator. In-hotel: 2 restaurants, pool, gym, spa* ⊟ *AE, DC, MC, V* Ⓜ *Skytrain: Phrom Phong.*

$$$ ▥ **Landmark Hotel.** The generous use of polished wood in the reception area may suggest a grand European hotel, but the Landmark actually prides itself on being thoroughly modern, and rooms, though elegant enough to satisfy the leisure traveler, are geared to corporate travelers, with good-size desks and business amenities. For a little extra, guests can stay on one of the Club floors, which have more business services and complimentary breakfast and cocktails. There's a staff of nearly 700, so it's no surprise that the service is attentive. There are shops and restaurants in the basement and first floors of the hotel building. ⊠ *138 Sukhumvit Rd., Sukhumvit, 10110* ☏ *02/254–0404* ⊕ *www.landmarkbangkok. com* ⟿ *386 rooms, 28 suites* ⚑ *In-room: safe, refrigerator, ethernet. In-hotel: 8 restaurants, bar, pool, gym, laundry service, concierge, executive floor* ⊟ *AE, DC, MC, V* Ⓜ *Skytrain: Nana.*

$$ ▥ **Bel-Aire Princess.** Part of the respected Dusit chain, the Bel-Aire Princess is a well-managed hotel steps from clamorous Sukhumvit Road—thankfully, it's on the quiet end of a bustling street, away from the bars. It gets its fair share of tour groups, but for the most part the lobby and lounge are peaceful retreats. The bowl of fruit on each floor is a thoughtful touch. Rooms at the back of the hotel look down on Soi 7, while those at the front have a view of the pool. ⊠ *16 Sukhumvit Soi 5, Sukhumvit, 10110* ☏ *02/253–4300* ⊕ *http://bangkok-sukhumvit. royalprincess.com* ⟿ *150 rooms* ⚑ *In-room: safe, refrigerator, Wi-Fi. In-hotel: restaurant, room service, bar, pool, gym, laundry service, concierge, public Wi-Fi* ⊟ *AE, DC, MC, V* Ⓜ *Skytrain: Nana.*

$$ ▥ **City Lodge.** There are two City Lodges off Sukhumvit, but this is the better choice because of a better location and a good restaurant in its lobby. The compact rooms are functional, designed to fit a lot into a small space, and each has a balcony with a view of Sukhumvit and the Skytrain. Business services here are minimal, but you can use those, along with other facilities like the pool, at its nearby sister hotel, the Amari Boulevard. Subway and Skytrain stations are nearby. The hotel's restaurant, La Gritta, specializes in Italian food. ⊠ *Sukhumvit Soi 19,*

Sukhumvit, 10110 ☎ *02/254–4783* ⊕ *www.amari.com/citylodge* ⤶ *34 rooms* ⅋ *In-room: safe, refrigerator, Wi-Fi (some). In-hotel: restaurant, room service, pool, gym, laundry service* ▤ *AE, DC, MC, V* Ⓜ *Subway: Sukhumvit; Skytrain: Asok.*

$–$$ ▦ **Ambassador Hotel.** The Ambassador has three wings, a dozen restaurants, and a shopping center with scores of stores. Its size makes it a bit impersonal, and the rooms are compact and decorated in standard-issue pastels. The Tower Wing is more comfortable, but more expensive. The Sukhumvit Wing overlooks a busy street and there is construction scheduled to continue through 2007 on two sides. But the noisy beer garden closed, so things are a bit quieter at night. ⊠ *171 Sukhumvit Soi 11–13, Sukhumvit, 10110* ☎ *02/254–0444* ⊕ *www.amtel.co.th* ⤶ *801 rooms, 31 suites* ⅋ *In-room: safe, refrigerator. In-hotel: 12 restaurants, room service, bar, 2 tennis courts, pool, gym, spa, laundry service, concierge, public Internet* ▤ *AE, DC, MC, V* Ⓜ *Skytrain: Nana.*

$ ▦ **Majestic Suites.** There are no actual suites here, but there is a wide selection of standard rooms. They range from studios barely big enough to fit a queen-size bed to larger deluxe rooms that have more amenities. There's a bar and coffee shop in the small lobby. ⊠ *110 Sukhumvit Rd., between Soi 4 and Soi 6, Sukhumvit, 10110* ☎ *02/656–8220* ⊕ *www.majesticsuites.com* ⤶ *55 rooms* ⅋ *In-room: safe, refrigerator, Wi-Fi. In-hotel: restaurant, bar, laundry service, public Wi-Fi* ▤ *AE, DC, MC, V* Ⓜ *Skytrain: Nana.*

$ ▦ **Stable Lodge.** On a residential street off Sukhumvit Road, this small hotel feels more like a guesthouse. The rooms are basic but clean and comfortable. Each has a private balcony where you can have your breakfast, and most have private bathrooms. The rooms at the back are the quietest. The pool in front is a delightful place to relax in the afternoon. Make sure to return in the evening, when there's a barbecue in the garden. The lobby restaurant serves Thai and Danish food. ⊠ *39 Sukhumvit Soi 8, Sukhumvit, 10110* ☎ *02/653–0017 up to 19* ⊕ *www. stablelodge.com* ⤶ *41 rooms* ⅋ *In-room: refrigerator. In-hotel: restaurant, pool* ▤ *AE, DC, MC, V* Ⓜ *Skytrain: Nana.*

NIGHTLIFE & THE ARTS

The English-language newspapers the *Bangkok Post* and the *Nation* have the latest information on current festivals, exhibitions, and nightlife. The Tourist Authority of Thailand's weekly *Where* also lists events. Monthly *Metro* magazine has extensive listings and offers reviews of new hot spots.

Nightlife

Bangkok's nightlife truly runs the gamut, from from beer bars doubling as brothels to velvet-rope hotel-club swankster scenes and everything in between. The curfew might be 2 AM, but this city never sleeps; after-hours clubs and restaurants stay open for late-night carousing until 5 AM or 6 AM. There are many great nightlife areas, but among the most notable are the area off Sukhumvit Soi 55 (also called Soi Thonglor), which is full of bars and nightclubs; Soi Sarasin, across from Lumphini Park, with friendly pubs and cafés that are popular with yuppie Thais

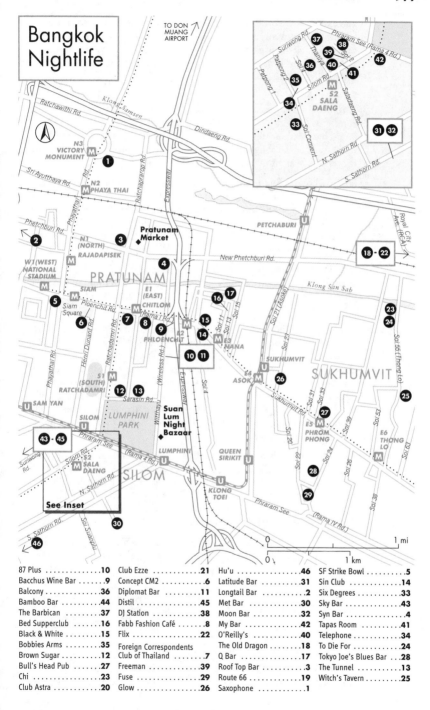

Bangkok Nightlife

and expats; and Narathiwat Road, which starts at Surawong, intersects Silom, then runs all the way to Rama III, with trendy bars and restaurants opening every month. RCA, which stands for Royal City Avenue, is where all the Thai youth go out; if you want to meet locals and avoid the red-light scene, that's your place.

Live sex shows, though officially banned, are still found in three areas. Patpong is the largest and most touristy, and it includes three streets that run between Surawong and Silom roads. Lining Patpong 1 and 2 are go-go bars with hostesses by the dozen. Shows are generally found one flight up. The Patpong area is well patrolled by police, so it is quite safe. It even has a night market patronized by Thais.

Soi Cowboy, off Sukhumvit Road at Soi 21, is a less raunchy, more easygoing version of Patpong, frequented more by locals. Some bars have go-go dancers, while others are good for a quiet beer (with or without a temporary companion, who is paid by the drink). Nana Plaza, at Soi 4, is popular with expats. The plaza is packed with three floors of hostess bars. The newest bars have spilled out along Soi 4.

Most gay bars and clubs happen to be located near Patpong on a pair of dead-end alleys off Silom Road. Soi 2 is filled with thumping discos. Other gay establishments are found near Sukhumvit Road.

Bars & Pubs

THONBURI   Though it's neither particularly authentic nor groundbreaking, the Marriott Resort's **Longtail Bar** (✉ Bangkok Marriott Resort & Spa, 257 Charoennakorn Rd., Samrae Thonburi, Thonburi ☎ 02/476–0022 ⊕ www.marriott.com) distinguishes itself with a tropical getaway feel that is elusive in the hubbub of Bangkok—this place will really make you want to sip a mai tai by the breezy river. In return, though, you'll have to sail about 30 minutes downriver from the Saphan Taksin Skytrain stop on one of the resort's dedicated boats, not an entirely unpleasant prospect on a nice night.

PRATUNAM   The glass-enclosed **Roof Top Bar** (✉ Baiyoke Sky Hotel, 222 Ratchaprarop Rd., Pratunam ☎ 02/2656–3000 ⊕ www.baiyokehotel.com Ⓜ Subway: Silom; Skytrain: Sala Daeng), in Thailand's tallest building, is kitschier and more Old Bangkok than its newer, hipper rooftop competitors, with lounge singers and neon Heineken signs. But it's still the highest in the city, on the 88th floor.

PATPONG AREA   The crowd of young Thais and expats at the **Barbican** (✉ Soi Thaniya off Silom Rd., Silom ☎ 02/234–3590 ⊕ http://greatbritishpub.com Ⓜ Subway: Silom; Skytrain: Sala Daeng), a split-level contemporary bar smack-dab in the middle of the Japanese soi, is a bit more stylish and hip than at other pubs. It's a great place to hang out with friends. You can get a decent pint of beer at the **Bobbies Arms** (✉ Patpong 2, Silom ☎ 02/233–6828 Ⓜ Subway: Silom; Skytrain: Sala Daeng), a rough approximation of an English pub. This longtime favorite remains popular even with the proliferation of new pubs.

The lively **O'Reillys** (✉ 62/1–4 Silom Rd., Silom ☎ 02/632–7515 Ⓜ Subway: Silom; Skytrain: Sala Daeng) sometimes has live music. Due to its convenient location to the Skytrain and the gateway to Patpong, this place is always jumping. If you're a Beatles fan, check out the Betters on Friday nights.

SILOM   Thai A-listers and entertainers have made **Distil** (⊠ State Tower, 1055 Silom Rd., Silom ☎ 02/624–9555 Ⓜ Skytrain: Surasak), on the 64th floor of one of Bangkok's tallest buildings, their stomping grounds. It's done in black, coffee, and slate tones, and a full-time sommelier is on staff to take care of your wine desires. **Hu'u** (⊠ The Ascott, Levels 1–2, 187 S. Sathorn Rd., Silom ☎ 02/676–6677 ⊕ www.huuinasia.com Ⓜ Skytrain: Chong Nonsi) is a great new restaurant, cocktail and wine bar that represents the hip new side of Bangkok. Famous for its inventive cocktails, this place is most popular for predinner drinks.

★ With a sister establishment in London, the exclusive **Met Bar** (⊠ 27 S. Sathorn Rd., Silom ☎ 02/625–3388 ⊕ www.metropolitan.como.bz/bangkok Ⓜ Subway: Lumphini; Skytrain: Sala Daeng) is supposed to be a private club limited to members and Metropolitan Hotel guests, but if you call ahead, you can usually get on the list. It's possibly the hottest lounge scene in town right now, done up in sleek dark red and black, with a glam crowd chilling out on comfortable couches.

My Bar (⊠ 946 Rama IV, Silom ☎ 02/200–9000 Ⓜ Subway: Lumphini), a minimalist lounge-style bar, is in the Dusit Thani hotel. It serves up signature drinks, hand-rolled Cuban cigars, and the finest single malt whiskey in town. **Moon Bar** (⊠ Banyan Tree Hotel, 21/100 S. Sathorn Rd., Silom ☎ 02/679–1200 Ⓜ Subway: Lumphini; Skytrain: Sala Daeng) at Vertigo restaurant is appropriately named—an open-air bar sitting high atop the Banyan Tree hotel. You can eat here, too, or just lounge around the sofas and low-lying tables. If the weather is clear, do some stargazing with the bar's telescope. As Moon Bar is often closed due to high winds or bad weather, you can also check out **Latitude Bar** (⊠ Banyan Tree Hotel, 21/100 S. Sathorn Rd., Silom Ⓜ Subway: Lumphini; Skytrain: Sala Daeng) on the 52nd floor of the same hotel, only a few floors down and also in open air, but it's not as impressive an experience because of the high railings and distracting sound system. A few blocks down, off Sathorn, **Six Degrees** (⊠ Soi Convent, Silom ☎ 02/632–2995 Ⓜ Skytrain: Sala Daeng) restaurant and bar has a simple, minimalist style offering a variety of smooth cocktails. The bar crowd starts to filter in after 10 PM.

Fodor'sChoice   There's nothing else quite like **Sky Bar** (⊠ State Tower, 1055 Silom Rd., ★ Silom ☎ 02/624–9555 Ⓜ Skytrain: Surasak), on the 65th floor of one of Bangkok's tallest buildings. Head toward the eerie blue light at the extreme end of the restaurant and check out the head-spinning views.

SUKHUMVIT   Wine bars are slowly popping up around the city, and one worth mentioning is **Bacchus Wine Bar & Cafe Lounge** (⊠ 20/6–7 Ruam Rudee Village, Soi Ruam Rudee, Sukhumvit ☎ 02/650–8986 Ⓜ Skytrain: Ploenchit). Here you'll find four floors of laid-back ambience and, well, wine. The popular **Bull's Head Pub** (⊠ Sukhumvit Soi 33, Sukhumvit ☎ 02/259–4444 Ⓜ Subway: Sukhumvit; Skytrain: Phrom Phong) is very British—it even has a Quiz Night on the third Wednesday of each month. This is a good place for serious beer drinkers.

Chi (✉ 998 Sukhumvit Soi 55, Sukhumvit ☎ 02/381–7587 Ⓜ Skytrain: Thong Lo), a Pan-Asian eatery with a bar and lounge, attracts a quirky mix of upscale diners and imbibers, including Thai designers, interior decorators, high-society folks, artists, and, of course, a few foreigners. Each room has a different theme—the living room has an eclectic range of chairs, cushions, and sofas to lounge about on. The Conrad Hotel's new **Diplomat Bar** (✉ All Seasons Pl., 87 Wittayu [Wireless Rd.], Sukhumvit ☎ 02/690–9999 Ⓜ Skytrain: Ploenchit) epitomizes the grown-up lounge: warm lighting, brown colors, smooth music, and a splendid selection of scotch and cigars—cigar makers are sometimes brought in from Cuba just to roll at the Diplomat. **Fuse** (✉ Camp Davis, Sukhumvit Soi 24, Sukhumvit ☎ 02/204–0970 Ⓜ Skytrain: Phrom Phong) is a low-ceilinged, wood-paneled cocktail bar that draws in Thais, expats, and models.

Celebrating the famous American highway, **Route 66** (✉ 29/37 Royal City Ave., Sukhumvit ☎ 02/203–0407) is often packed. It now features hip hop and R&B, and it's one of the best places in Bangkok for the latter. Hip **Syn Bar** (✉ Swissotel, Nai Lert Park, 2 Wittayu [Wireless Rd.], Sukhumvit ☎ 02/253–0123 Ext. 8147 Ⓜ Skytrain: Ploenchit), done in cool shades of gray and red, has some of the most creative seating you've ever seen—suspended inside floating hoops. DJs start spinning at 9 PM.

To Die For (✉ 998 Sukhumvit Soi 55, Sukhumvit ☎ 02/381–4714 Ⓜ Skytrain: Thong Lo) has an exquisitely manicured garden, perfect for sipping fancy drinks on brightly colored Moroccan seats. Situated in the midst of Japanese nightclubs, **Tokyo Joe's Blues Bar** (✉ 9–11 Sivaporn Plaza, Sukhumvit Soi 24, Sukhumvit ☎ 02/661–0359 Ⓜ Skytrain: Phrom Phong) stands out with its rustic interior and live music. Littered with blues mementos, vintage guitars, and stereos, this cozy bar has live music every night; Sunday brings jazz and blues jam sessions.

SIAM SQUARE If you're searching for something more than just a typical cocktail bar, look no farther than **SF Strike Bowl** (✉ MBK Shopping Center, Phayathai Rd., Victory Monument ☎ 02/611–4555 Ⓜ Skytrain: National Stadium). One of the city's hottest nightspots, this futuristic bowling alley, lounge, and bar has a sleek style that rivals most nightclubs in Asia. A DJ spins house tunes above the clatter of falling pins.

VICTORY MONUMENT The **Old Dragon** (✉ 29/78–81 Royal City Ave., Victory Monument ☎ 02/203–0972 Ⓜ Skytrain: Victory Monument) is filled with oddities, from wooden cinema seats to old mirrors etched with Chinese characters. The owner claims that little here besides the clientele is less than 50 years old. The snacks served are a mix of Chinese and Thai. **Saxophone** (✉ 3/8 Victory Monument, Phayathai Rd., Victory Monument ☎ 02/246–5472 Ⓜ Skytrain: Victory Monument) is popular with locals and expats. Live blues, R&B, jazz, rock, reggae, and even ska house bands perform seven nights a week.

LUMPHINI PARK **Suan Lum Night Bazaar** (✉ At Rama IV and Wittayu [Wireless] Rds., Lumphini Park Ⓜ Subway: Lumphini) has grown into one of Bangkok's most happening night markets, which is a big tourist draw. It offers an all-in-one experience: shopping, eating, massage, and drinking. There are three beer gardens, with good German beers on tap, and free nightly concerts performed by various bands from 6:30 PM to midnight.

Clubs

ROYAL CITY AVENUE   Since the enactment of the stricter curfew laws in Bangkok, **RCA** (Royal City Avenue), formerly just a hangout for teens, has turned into one of the city's hottest nightlife areas, staying open until 2 AM, sometimes later. It's north of Downtown; taxi is the only way to get there.

There are many clubs in the RCA pedestrian street, but **Club Astra** (✉ Royal City Ave., Rama IX Rd., Bangkapi, Huaykwang ☎ 02/622–2572) might be the best place to dance. Throbbing with good music, its dance floor fills up every night of the week. Get there before 11 PM if you want to secure a table space for your bottle, and bring your ID—they card to make sure you're over 20. **Club Ezze** (✉ Royal City Ave., Rama IX Rd., Bangkapi, Huaykwang ☎ No phone) is a different sort of choice in RCA: a smaller venue focusing exclusively on techno music. Like the other RCA venues, it packs them in nightly. Best of all the RCA ★ joints is the chandelier-heavy **Flix** (✉ Royal City Avenue, Rama IX Rd., Bangkapi, Huaykwang ☎ No phone), far and away the most popular, and deservedly so. Multiple rooms each have their own feel and different style of music. The size of Flix is staggering, the number of beautiful people equally so.

SUKHUMVIT & SIAM SQUARE   On the more grown-up and trendier side of things, **Bed Supperclub** (✉ 26 Sukhumvit Soi 11, Sukhumvit ☎ 02/651–3537 Ⓜ Skytrain: Nana) is Bangkok's answer to cool. The futuristic Jetsons-like bar and supper club has been the rage since its inception. You can take your drink and sprawl out on an enormous bed while listening to a mix of hip-hop, house, and a variety of other music.

Concept CM2 (✉ Novotel Siam, 392/44 Rama I, Soi 6, Siam Square ☎ 02/255–6888 Ⓜ Skytrain: Siam) is a flashy, energetic club with live pop bands every night. Be prepared to pay a B550 entrance fee on weekends (B220 on weekdays). For something sleek and groovy try the Conrad's **87 Plus** (✉ All Seasons Pl., 87 Wittayu [Wireless Rd.], Sukhumvit ☎ 02/690–9999 Ⓜ Skytrain: Ploenchit), where the dance floor meanders throughout the bar, instead of concentrating in front of the DJ booth. The crowd is super trendy and very well-to-do, although there is a fairly high concentration of working girls. There is now live music Tuesday through Sunday. Prices are through the roof. **Glow** (✉ 96/4–5 Sukhumvit Soi 23, Sukhumvit ☎ 02/261–3007), in a space formerly known as Faith Club, lights up Sukhumvit with an eternally trendy, beautiful crowd dancing to techno. It's got the biggest vodka selection in the city.

★ **Q Bar** (✉ 34 Sukhumvit Soi 11, Sukhumvit ☎ 02/252–3274 Ⓜ Skytrain: Nana) consistently plays quality music and regularly features international DJs. Upstairs there's a romantic lounge and a huge outdoor terrace perfect for any mood. Between the casually hip crowd, the selective but unpretentious door policy, and the effortlessly energetic scene here, this is perhaps the best and most balanced nightclub in town.

After-Hours Clubs

With Bangkok's harsh 2 AM curfew, after-hours bars are key to really making a night of it. Keep in mind that these parties can change from week to week, so always ask around before hitting them up—bartenders at upmarket bars and clubs are always a good resource.

Black and White (⊠ Sukhumvit Soi 1, Sukhumvit ☏ No phone Ⓜ Skytrain: Nana) is an exclusive, hard-to-find joint. Follow the noise up to the very top floor of the unmarked orange building on Sukhumvit Soi 1. **Sin Club** (⊠ Sukhumvit Soi 2, Sukhumvit ☏ No phone Ⓜ Skytrain: Nana) stays pumping as late as 5:30 AM on nights when the police don't shut it down. It's in the Rajah hotel complex, on the third floor—just follow the crowds. **The Tunnel** (⊠ Langsuan Soi 5, Sukhumvit ☏ No phone Ⓜ Skytrain: Nana) is a veritable who's who of the Bangkok scene these days. Expect to pay B1,000, which includes two drinks, to join the beautiful people. The place will stay open until 3 AM or 3:30 AM, depending on police activity week to week.

Gay Bars

Silom Soi 2 and Silom Soi 4 are the center of Bangkok's gay scene, with every establishment from restaurants to bars to clubs all catering to a gay clientele. **Balcony** (⊠ 86–88 Silom Soi 4, Silom ☏ 02/235–5891 Ⓜ Subway: Silom; Skytrain: Sala Daeng) does indeed look out over the street. It has one of the best happy hours on the soi. On crowded Silom Soi 2, **DJ Station** (⊠ 8/6–8 Silom Soi 2, Silom ☏ 02/266–4029 Ⓜ Subway: Silom; Skytrain: Sala Daeng) packs absolutely full with a young crowd. The cover charge is B200 on weekends and B100 on weekdays. Around the corner from DJ Station, **Freeman** (⊠ 60/18–21 Silom Rd., Silom ☏ 02/632–8033 Ⓜ Subway: Silom; Skytrain: Sala Daeng) has a famous drag show every night at midnight and a balcony where you can watch the dance floor.

Tapas Room (⊠ 114/17 Silom Soi 4, Silom ☏ 02/234–4737 Ⓜ Subway: Silom; Skytrain: Sala Daeng) gets crowded with a mixed gay-straight crowd on weekends. There's an intimate dance floor upstairs with couches and live percussion in a Balearic style.

The most venerable of Bangkok's gay bars, **Telephone** (⊠ 114/11–13 Silom Soi 4, Silom ☏ 02/234–3279 Ⓜ Subway: Silom; Skytrain: Sala Daeng) is hopping every night of the week. There are telephones on the table so you can chat up your neighbors.

Jazz Bars

To hear easy-on-the-ears jazz, try the Oriental Hotel's **Bamboo Bar** (⊠ Oriental La., Silom ☏ 02/236–0400 Ⓜ Skytrain: Saphan Taksin). This legendary bar features international jazz musicians. A good place to carouse over live jazz, and occasionally blues, is the smoky **Brown Sugar** (⊠ 231/19–20 Soi Sarasin, Silom ☏ 02/250–0103 Ⓜ Subway: Silom; Skytrain: Ratchadamri). **Fabb Fashion Café** (⊠ Mercury Tower, 540 Ploenchit Rd., Sukhumvit ☏ 02/843–4946 Ⓜ Skytrain: Ploenchit) is the place to go for live music early in the evening.

The **Foreign Correspondents Club of Thailand** (⊠ Maneeya Center, Ploenchit Rd., Sukhumvit ☏ 02/652–0580 Ⓜ Skytrain: Chitlom) has live music

Friday night, when it's open to the public. **Witch's Tavern** (⊠ Sukhumvit Soi 55, Sukhumvit ☎ 02/391–9791 Ⓜ Skytrain: Thong Lo) recently received a much-needed face-lift and has musicians on Friday, Saturday, and Sunday. The bar also serves hearty English fare.

The Arts

A contemporary arts scene is relatively new to Thailand, but the last decade has seen great changes in the fine arts: artists are branching out into all kinds of media, and modern sculpture and artwork can be increasingly found decorating office buildings, parks, and public spaces. Bangkok also offers an eclectic range of theater and dance performances such as traditional *khon* (drama dances), and masterful puppet shows. Music options range from piano concertos and symphonies to rock concerts and blues-and-jazz festivals.

Art Galleries

Today, artists use various media, often melding international art trends with distinctly Thai craftsmanship. To keep up with the pace of an emerging movement, galleries are popping up all over Bangkok. Exhibitions are now held in cafés, restaurants, shopping malls, foreign clubs, and even bars.

Eat Me (⊠ Soi Phi Phat 2, off Convent Rd., Silom ☎ 02/238–0931 Ⓜ Skytrain: Sala Daeng) is a restaurant-cum-art space. By day this split-level space features a variety of exhibitions from both Thai and foreign artists. In the evening it morphs into a fusion eatery.

The lovely courtyard at the **Four Seasons Hotel Bangkok** (⊠ 155 Ratchadamri Rd., Siam Square ☎ 02/251–6127 Ⓜ Skytrain: Ratchadamri) rotates their exhibits frequently and features paintings in different media, with a greater emphasis on photos. **H Gallery** (⊠ 201 Sathorn Rd., Silom ☎ 01/310–4428 Ⓜ Skytrain: Surasak) often shows solo exhibitions from renowned artists. They are open Thursday, Friday, and Saturday noon–6 PM; any other time is by appointment only.

Tadu Contemporary Art (⊠ Barcelona Motors Bldg., 99/2 Tiam Ruammit Rd., Northern Bangkok ☎ 02/645–2473 ⊕ www.tadu.net) exhibits an eclectic group of contemporary artists whose work is dynamic and powerful and comes in an array of media. **Tang Gallery** (⊠ B29, 919/1 Silom Rd., Silom ☎ 02/630–1114 Ⓜ Skytrain: Sala Daeng) features works by Chinese artists, including contemporary oil and watercolor paintings and ceramic sculptures.

Theater & Dance

For Thais, classical dance is more than graceful movements. The dances actually tell tales from the religious epic *Ramakien*. Performances are accompanied by a woodwind called the *piphat*, which sounds like an oboe, as well as a range of percussion instruments. Many restaurants also present classical dance performances.

The **Chalerm Krung Royal Theater** (⊠ 66 Charoen Krung [New Rd.], Wang Burapha, Phirom, Old City ☎ 02/222–0434) was designed in 1933 by a former student of the Ecole des Beaux-Arts in Paris. The design is Thai Deco, and it hosts traditional khon performances, a masked dance-drama based on tales from the *Ramakien*.

At the **National Theatre** (✉ Na Phra That Rd., Old City ☎ 02/224–1342), classical dance and drama can usually be seen here on the last Friday and Saturday of each month. Finding a schedule is a challenge though. If you're interested in seeing a show, the best bet is to ask your hotel whether they can call and ask for a schedule.

Across the river, **Patravadi** (✉ 69/1 Soi Wat Rakang, Thonburi ☎ 02/412–7287) offers a dance show during dinner. There's also a theater in the restaurant showing performances from classical to contemporary.

At the Oriental Hotel, **Sala Rim Naam** (✉ Oriental La., Silom ☎ 02/236–0400 Ⓜ Skytrain: Saphan Taksin) stages a beautiful show accompanied by a touristy dinner. **Silom Village** (✉ 286 Silom Rd., Silom ☎ 02/234–4448 Ⓜ Skytrain: Sala Daeng) appeals most to foreigners, but it also draws many Thais. The block-size complex, open daily 10 AM–10 PM, features performances of classical dance.

The **Thailand Cultural Center** (✉ Ratchadaphisek Rd., Huaykwang, Northern Bangkok ☎ 02/247–0028 Ⓜ Subway: Thai Cultural Center) hosts local and international cultural events, including opera, symphony orchestras, modern dance, and ballet. You can ask your concierge to find out what performance is showing while you're in town.

SHOPPING

Each Year, more and more tourists are drawn to the Thai capital for its silk, gems, and tailor-made items. But there are a slew of other goods worth discovering: quality silverware, furniture, fine porcelain, and handmade leather goods—all at prices that put Western shops to shame. Plus, already low prices can often be haggled down even further (haggling is mainly reserved for markets, but shopkeepers will let you know if they're willing to discount). ⚠ **A word to the wise: to avoid getting scammed when shopping for bigger-ticket items (namely jewelry), be sure to patronize reputable dealers only.** Don't be fooled by a tuk-tuk driver offering to take you to a shop. This is a popular con perpetrated by shop owners, who in turn pay drivers a commission to lure in unsuspecting tourists.

The city's most popular shopping areas are Silom Road and Surawong Road, where you can find quality silk; Sukhumvit Road, which is rich in leather goods; Yaowarat Road in Chinatown, where gold trinkets abound; and along Oriental Lane and Charoen Krung (New Road), where there are many antiques shops. The shops around Siam Square and at the World Trade Center attract both Thais and foreigners. Peninsula Plaza, across from the Four Seasons Hotel Bangkok in the embassy district, has very upscale shops. If you're knowledgeable about fabric, you can find bargains at the textile merchants who compete along Pahuraht Road in Chinatown and Pratunam Road off Phetchaburi Road. You can even take the raw material to a tailor and have something made.

You can reclaim the 10% V.A.T. (Value-Added Tax) at the airport if you have a receipt. Ask shopkeepers about the V.A.T. refund—you must fill out the proper forms at the time of purchase. If you still want the convenience of duty-free shopping, try **King Power International Group** (⊠ King Power Complex, Rangnam Rd. ☎ 02/205–8888 ⊠ Suvarnabhumi Airport, 2nd–4th fls. ☎ 02/134–8888). The branch at the airport is open 24 hours. You pay for the items at the shop, then pick them up at the airport (or simply take them with you) when you leave. You need your passport and an airline ticket, and you need to make your purchase at least eight hours before leaving the country.

Markets

FodorśChoice You can purchase virtually anything at the sprawling **Chatuchak Week-**
★ **end Market** (⊠ Phaholyothin Rd., Chatuchak, Northern Bangkok Ⓜ Subway: Chatuchak Park; Skytrain: Mo Chit), including silk items in a *mudmee* (tie-dyed before weaving) design that would sell for five times the price in the United States. Strategically placed food vendors mean you don't have to stop shopping to grab a bite. It's open on weekends from 9 AM to 7 PM, and the city's (some say the world's) largest market is best in the morning. It's easy to reach, across the street from the northern terminus of the Skytrain and near the Northern Bus Terminal. ⚠ Whatever you do, don't take a taxi here; it will literally add hours to your journey compared with the Skytrain trip.

An afternoon at JJ, as it is known by locals ("ch" is pronounced "jha" in Thai, so phonetically Chatuchak is Jatujak), is not for the faint of heart: up to 200,000 people visit each day and there are more than 8,000 vendors. But what's a little discomfort when there are such fantastic bargains to be had? Go prepared with bottles of water, comfortable shoes, and, if you can get a copy, Nancy Chandler's Map of Bangkok, which has a helpful, color-coded, stall-by-stall rendering of the market. You can order the map online at ⊕ www.nancychandler.net or call ☎ 02/266–6579.

The borders between the market's many sections can be a bit hazy (for example, the animal section spills into the silverware section), but you can keep your bearings by remembering that the outer ring of stalls has mainly new clothing and shoes, with some plants, garden supplies, and home decor thrown in for good measure. The next ring of stalls is primarily used clothing and shoes, as well as new clothing, shoes, and accessories. Farther in are pottery, antiques, furniture, dried goods, and live animals. Even with a map, it's easy to get turned around in the mind-boggling array of goods, but this is also part of the joy that Chatuchak has to offer—wandering through the maze of vendors and suddenly stumbling upon the beautiful teak table, handmade skirt, or colorful paper lamp you'd been seeking.

Pahuraht Market (⊠ Near Yaowarat Rd., Chinatown Ⓜ Subway: Hua Lamphong) is known for its bargain textiles. A man with a microphone announces when items at a particular stall will be sold at half price, and shoppers surge over to bid. It's best to come in the evening, when many

Bargaining for Bargains

EVEN IF YOU'VE HONED YOUR bargaining skills in other countries, you might still come up empty-handed in Thailand. The aggressive techniques that go far in say, Delhi, won't get you very far in Bangkok. One of the highest compliments you can pay for any activity in the Land of Smiles is calling it *sanuk* (fun), and haggling is no exception. Thais love to joke and tease, so approach each bargaining situation playfully. However, be aware that Thais are also sensitive to "losing face," so make sure you remain pleasant and respectful throughout the transaction.

As you enter a market stall, smile and acknowledge the proprietor. When something catches your eye, inquire politely about the price, but don't immediately counter. Keep your voice low—you're more likely to get a deal if it's not announced to the whole shop—then ask for a price just slightly below what you want. Don't get too cavalier with your counteroffer—Thai sellers generally price their wares in a range they view as fair, so asking to cut the initial price in half will most likely be seen as an insult and might end the discussion abruptly. In most cases, the best you can hope for is 20%–30% discount.

If the price the shopkeeper offers in return is still high, turn your smile up another watt and say something like, "Can discount more?" If the answer is no, your last recourse is to say thank you and walk away. If you are called back, the price is still negotiable; if you aren't, maybe B500 wasn't such a bad price after all.

–Molly Petersen

street vendors are out selling food. Hundreds of vendors jam the sidewalk each day at **Pratunam Market** (⊠ At Phetchaburi and Ratchaprarop Rds., Pathumwan Ⓜ Subway: Phetchaburi; Skytrain: Asok). The stacks of merchandise consist mainly of inexpensive clothing. It's a good place to meet Thais, who come in the evening to sample the inexpensive Thai and Chinese street food.

Soi Sampeng (⊠ Parallel to Yaowarat Rd., Chinatown Ⓜ Subway: Hua Lamphong) also has lots of fabrics—it's Bangkok's best-known and oldest textile center.

Khao San Road (⊠ Yaowarat Rd. and Charoen Krung [New Rd.], Banglamphu Ⓜ Subway: Hua Lamphong), in the middle of backpacker central in Banglamphu, is closed to cars, and has some of the finest and most fun street shopping in the city. If the hip clothes, Thai souvenirs, used books, and delicious B10 pad Thai doesn't make the trip to Khao San worth it, the people-watching and energy of the place will.

Asking a taxi driver to take you to **Patpong** (⊠ Silom Rd. at Soi 2, Silom Ⓜ Subway: Silom; Skytrain: Sala Daeng) may prompt a smirk, but for fake Rolex watches, imposter Louis Vuitton handbags, and Western-size clothing there's no better place than this notorious red light district street. You can easily make a night of Patpong's great shopping, good restaurants, and happening bars and clubs.

Shopping Centers

In stark contrast to the grit and overcrowding of the markets are Bangkok's glittering high-end shopping centers. For a whirlwind tour of these facilities, hop on the Skytrain. **Peninsula Plaza** (⊠ 153 Ratchadamri Rd., Sukhumvit Ⓜ Subway: Sukhumvit; Skytrain: Ratchadamri) is tucked between the Grand Hyatt Erawan and the Four Seasons Hotel Bangkok. Eerily quiet, but very elegant, it has quite a selection of imported labels, top local fashion designers, and jewelry shops.

The next stop on the line, Siam, is pay dirt for shoppers. **Gaysorn** (⊠ Ratchaprasong Intersection, Siam Square ⊕ www.gaysorn.com Ⓜ Subway: Sukhumvit; Skytrain: Siam) may outshine all the other posh centers with its white marble and chrome fixtures. Here you can find all the requisite European labels as well as many local designers, such as Somchai Songwatana. **Siam Discovery** (⊠ 989 Rama I Rd., Siam Square ⊕ www.siamdiscoverycenter.co.th Ⓜ Subway: Sukhumvit; Skytrain: Siam) is full of international labels, but has the added bonus of the most grandiose movie theater in Thailand, the Grand EGV. Across Sukhumvit, **Siam Centre** (⊠ At Phaya Thai and Rama I, Siam Square Ⓜ Subway: Sukhumvit; Skytrain: Siam) is the place to check out Bangkok's young hipsters searching for the latest fashion trends. With one-of-a-kind handmade clothing, shoes, and accessories, Siam Centre oozes style, but be forewarned that the clothes are all made to Thai proportions, and as such are often small. An overhead walkway connects Siam Centre with the massive shopping complex **Mah Boon Krong** (MBK; ⊠ At Phaya Thai and Rama I, Siam Square Ⓜ Subway: Sukhumvit; Skytrain: Siam). It's an impressive seven stories high, and though it's no longer the biggest shopping center in Bangkok, it's still one of the busiest. It's not as stylish as Siam Centre and about as hectic as shopping can get, but it does have an entertainment center complete with a movie theater and bowling alley, and you can find everything under the sun here.

One stop east of Siam on the Skytrain is **Central Chidlom** (⊠ 1027 Ploenchit Rd., Sukhumvit Ⓜ Subway: Sukhumvit; Skytrain: Chitlom). The flagship store of Thailand's largest department store chain is not as flashy as its neighbors, but it does have a Jim Thompson silk shop. Two more Skytrain stops beyond Chidlom is the **Emporium** (⊠ 622 Sukhumvit, between Sukhumvit Sois 24 and 26, Sukhumvit ⊕ www.emporiumthailand. com Ⓜ Subway: Sukhumvit; Skytrain: Phrom Phong). It's glitzy, but often has sales. There's a little area on the sixth floor full of beautiful Thai silks, incense, and glassware, which are all reasonably priced.

Specialty Stores

Antiques

Thai antiques and old images of the Buddha require a special export license; check out the Thai Board of Investment's Web site at ⊕ www. boi.go.th/english/ for rules on exporting, and applications to do so. Surawong Road, Charoen Krung (New Road), and the Oriental Plaza (across from Oriental Hotel) have many art and antiques shops, as does the River City Shopping Complex. Original and often illegal artifacts from Angkor Wat are sometimes sold there as well.

As you wander around the Old City, don't miss the small teak house that holds **123 Baan Dee** (✉ 123 Fuengnakorn Rd., Old City ☎ 02/221–2520 Ⓜ Subway: Hua Lamphong). Antique silks, ceramics, beads, and other fascinating artifacts fill two floors. If you need sustenance, there's a small ice-cream parlor at the back. **Peng Seng** (✉ 942 Rama IV, at Surawong Rd., Silom ☎ 02/234–1285 Ⓜ Subway: Sam Yan; Skytrain: Sala Daeng) is one of the city's most respected dealers of antiquities. Prices may be high, but articles will most likely be genuine. **Rasi Sayam** (✉ 32 Sukhumvit Soi 23, Sukhumvit ☎ 02/258–4195 Ⓜ Subway: Sukhumvit; Skytrain: Asok), in an old teak house in a garden, has a wonderful collection of fine Thai crafts.

Clothing & Fabrics

Thai silk gained its reputation only after World War II, when technical innovations made it less expensive. Two fabrics are worth seeking out: mudmee silk, produced in the northeastern part of the country, and Thai cotton, which is soft, durable, and easier on the wallet than silk.

Design Thai (✉ 304 Silom Rd., Silom ☎ 02/235–1553 Ⓜ Subway: Silom; Skytrain: Chong Nonsi) has a large selection of silk items in all price ranges. If you ask, you can usually manage a 20% discount. For factory-made clothing, visit the **Indra Garment Export Centre** (✉ Ratchaprarop Rd. behind Indra Regent Hotel, Pathumwan Ⓜ Skytrain: Phaya Thai), where hundreds of shops sell discounted items. This rabbit warren of a place is kind of fun to hunt around in, and bargains can be found. The heat and humidity can be oppressive during the hot and rainy seasons, though. There are a few little restaurants tucked here and there for when you need a break. The **Jim Thompson Thai Silk Company** (✉ 9 Surawong Rd., Silom ☎ 02/632–8100 ⊕ www.jimthompson.com Ⓜ Subway: Silom; Skytrain: Sala Daeng) is a prime place for silk by the yard and ready-made clothes. The prices are high, but the staff is knowledgeable. There are numerous other locations throughout the city, such as in the Oriental Hotel, Four Seasons Hotel, Peninsula Hotel, and Central Chidlom shopping center.

Napajaree Suanduenchai studied fashion design in Germany and more than two decades ago opened the **Prayer Textile Gallery** (✉ Phayathai Rd. near Siam Sq., Siam Square ☎ 02/251–7549 Ⓜ Subway: Sukhumvit; Skytrain: Siam) in her mother's former dress shop. She makes stunning items in naturally dyed silks and cottons and in antique fabrics from the farthest reaches of Thailand, Laos, and Cambodia.

Many people who visit Bangkok brag about a custom-made suit that was completed in just a day or two, but the finished product often looks like the rush job that it was. If you want an excellent cut, give the tailor the time he needs, which could be up to a week at a reputable place. One of the best custom tailor shops in Bangkok is **Marco Tailor** (✉ 430/33 Siam Sq., Soi 7, Siam Square ☎ 02/252–0689 Ⓜ Subway: Sukhumvit; Skytrain: Siam), which sews a suit equal to those on London's Savile Row. Check out photographs of both Presidents Bush modeling their new suits made by **Raja Fashions** (⊠ Sukhumvit Soi 4, Sukhumvit ☎ 02/ 253–8379 Ⓜ Subway: Sukhumvit; Skytrain: Nana). Raja has the reputation for tailoring some of the finest men and women's fashions in Bangkok. For women's apparel, **Stephanie Thai Silk** (⊠ 55 Soi Shangri-La, New Rd., Sukhumvit ☎ 02/233–0325 Ⓜ Subway: Sukhumvit; Skytrain: Nana) is among the city's finest shops. A skirt with blouse and jacket made of Thai silk starts at B5,000.

Jewelry

Thailand is known for its sparkling gems, so it's no surprise that the country exports more colored stones than anywhere in the world. There are countless jewelry stores on Silom and Surawong roads. Be wary of deals that are too good to be true, as they probably are. Scams are common, so it's best to stick with established businesses. If you decide to buy anything more than a few small items, stopping by the Gem and Jewelry Institute of Thailand (GIT) at Chulalongkorn University and their museum could be time well spent. The gem-testing service will let you know if your newly bought jewels are genuine. It's located on the southeast corner of Chulalongkorn University, Phaya Thai Road.

A long-established firm is **Johny's Gems** (⊠ 199 Fuengnakorn Rd., Old City ☎ 02/224–4065 Ⓜ Subway: Hua Lamphong). If you call first, they'll send a car (a frequent practice among the city's better stores) to take you to the shop near Wat Phra Keo. You can rest assured you are getting a genuine piece from **Lin Jewelers** (⊠ 9 Soi 38 Charoen Krung [New Rd.], Old City Ⓜ Subway: Hua Lamphong), though their prices are a bit more expensive than average. **Oriental Lapidary** (⊠ 116/1 Silom Rd., Silom ☎ 02/238–2718 Ⓜ Subway: Silom; Skytrain: Sala Daeng) has a long record of good service. **Than Shine** (⊠ Sukhumvit Soi 22, Sukhumvit ☎ 02/381–7337 Ⓜ Subway: Sukhumvit; Skytrain: Thong Lo), run by sisters Cho Cho and Mon Mon, offers classic and modern designs. With top-quality gems, reliable service, and hordes of repeat clients, it's no wonder you need an appointment to peruse the huge inventory at **Uthai's Gems** (⊠ 28/7 Soi Ruam Rudi, Sukhumvit ☎ 02/253–8582 Ⓜ Subway: Sukhumvit; Skytrain: Ploenchit).

Leather

It's easy to find good buys on leather goods in Bangkok, which has some of the lowest prices in the world for custom work. Crocodile leather is popular, but be sure to obtain a certificate that the skins came from a domestically raised reptile; otherwise, U.S. Customs may confiscate the goods. The River City Shopping Complex, next to the Royal Orchid Sheraton Hotel, has a number of leather shops.

The **Chaophraya Bootery** (⊠ 116 Silom Soi 4, Silom Ⓜ Subway: Silom; Skytrain: Sala Daeng) will custom-make cowboy boots in four or five days. This service is in addition to the already large inventory of ready-made leather shoes, boots, and accessories. For shoes and jackets, try 25-year-old **Siam Leather Goods** (⊠ River City Shopping Complex, 23 Trok Rongnamkhaeng, Silom ☎ 02/237–0077 Ⓜ Subway: Sam Yan; Skytrain: Saphan Taksin).

Porcelain, Ceramics & Celadon

The pale green ceramic that will remind you of Thailand for years to come can be found in abundance at the **Celadon House** (✉ 8/3 Ratchadaphisek Rd., Sukhumvit Ⓜ Subway: Sukhumvit; Skytrain: Asok). This retailer carries some of the finest celadon tableware found in Bangkok. **Damrongluck Benjarong** (✉ River City Shopping Complex, Yotha Rd., Thonburi) has a huge inventory, and will make to-order dining sets, bowls, and vases. The blue-and-white porcelain may look more Chinese than Thai, but a lovely selection of dishes and more can be found at **Siamese D'art** (✉ 264 Sukhumvit Rd., Sukhumvit Ⓜ Subway: Sukhumvit; Skytrain: Phrom Phong).

A UNIQUE SOUVENIR

One of the famous artisanal products of Bangkok is the steel **monk's bowl**, handmade by monks in the area of tiny alleyways around Soi Banbat (near Wat Suthat). The unique bowls, which resonate harmonically when tapped, are made out of eight strips of metal—one for each Buddhist stage—and are traditionally used by the monks to collect donations. At the shop at 14 Soi Banbat (☎ 02/621-2635), you can purchase one for around B500, which will also buy you a look at the workshop.

Precious Metals

Chinatown is the place to go for gold. There's no bargaining, but you're likely to get a good price anyway. Just around the corner from Lin Jewelers is its sister shop **Lin Silvercraft** (✉ 14 Soi Oriental, Charoen Krung [New Rd.], Silom Ⓜ Subway: Sam Yan; Skytrain: Saphan Taksin). Among all the knickknacks stacked from floor to ceiling, this shop has some of the most finely crafted silver cutlery in town. For bronze try **Siam Bronze Factory** (✉ 1250 Charoen Krung [New Rd.], Silom ☎ 02/234-9436 Ⓜ Subway: Sam Yan; Skytrain: Saphan Taksin). It's near the Oriental Hotel.

Souvenirs

For a one-stop souvenir shop, go to **Narayana Phand Pavilion** (✉ 127 Ratchadamri Rd., Sukhumvit Ⓜ Subway: Sukhumvit; Skytrain: Ratchadamri). Thai silk, ceramics, lacquerware, and hand-tooled leather are all under one roof. It was established by the Thai government in 1941; expect to find high-quality goods, low prices, and half the crowds of the packed markets.

SPORTS

Although Thailand is home to an abundance of adventure and water sports, trekking, and boat racing, it's often difficult to find outdoor activities within Bangkok. Due to elevated temperatures, Bangkok residents generally head to malls on weekends where they can cool off, but the city does have golfing, jogging, and cycling options.

Bangkok offers visitors one of the most intense spectator sports in the world, *muay thai* (thai kickboxing). This is the national sport of Thailand and a quintessential Bangkok experience.

Muay Thai, the Sport of Kings

THAIS ARE EVERY BIT AS passionate about their national sport as Americans are about baseball. Though it's often dismissed as a blood sport, muay thai is one of the world's oldest martial arts, and it was put to noble purposes long before it became a spectator sport.

Muay thai is believed to be over 2,000 years old. It's been practiced by kings and was used to defend the country. It's so important to Thai culture that until the 1920s, muay thai instruction was part of the country's public school curriculum.

Admittedly, some of the sport's brutal reputation is well-deserved. There were very few regulations until the 1930s. Before then, there were no rest periods between rounds. Protective gear was unheard of—the exception was a groin protector, an essential item when kicks to the groin were still legal. Boxing gloves were introduced to the sport in the late 1920s. Hand wraps did exist, but some fighters actually dipped their wrapped hands in resin and finely ground glass to inflict more damage on their opponent.

Techniques: Developed with the battlefield in mind, its moves mimic the weapons of ancient combat. Punching combinations, similar to modern-day boxing, turn the fists into spears that jab relentlessly at an opponent. The roundhouse kick—delivered to the thigh, ribs, or head—turns the shinbone into a devastating striking surface. Elbow strikes to the face and strong knees to the abdomen mimic the motion of a battle-ax. Finally, strong front kicks, using the ball of the foot to jab at the abdomen, thigh, or face, mimic an array of weapons.

Rules: Professional bouts have five three-minute rounds, with a two-minute rest period in between each round. Fights are judged using a points system, with judges awarding rounds to each fighter, but not all rounds are given equal weight—the later rounds are more important as judges view fights as "marathons," with the winner being the fighter who's fared best throughout the entire match. The winner is determined by majority decision. Of course, a fight can also end decisively with a knockout or a technical knockout (wherein a fighter is conscious, but too injured to continue).

Rituals: The "dance" you see before each match is called the *ram muay* or *wai kru* (these terms are often used interchangeably, though the wai kru really refers to the homage paid to the *kru* or trainer). The ram muay serves to honor the fighter's supporters and his god, as well as to help him warm up, relax, and focus. Both fighters walk around the ring with one arm on the top rope to seal out bad spirits, pausing at each corner to say a short prayer. They then kneel in the center of the ring facing the direction of their birthplace and go through a set of specific movements, often incorporating aspects of the *Ramakien*. Fighters wear several good-luck charms, including armbands (*kruang rang*) and a headpiece (*mongkron*). The music you hear during each bout is live. Though it may sound like the tune doesn't change, the musicians actually pay close attention to the fight and the will speed up to match its pace—or to encourage the fighters to match theirs.

Thai Boxing

The national sport of Thailand draws enthusiastic crowds in Bangkok. Unlike some shows you can see in the resort areas down south, the city has the real thing. Daily matches alternate between the two main stadiums. The older **Lumphini Stadium** (⊠Rama IV Rd., Lumphini Park ☎02/251–4303 Ⓜ Subway: Lumphini) has matches on Friday and Saturday at 6 PM. The newer and larger **Ratchadamnoen Stadium** (⊠ Ratchadamnoen Nok Rd., Banglamphu ☎ 02/281–4205) has bouts on Monday, Wednesday, Thursday, and Sunday from 6:30 PM to 10 PM. Tickets may be purchased at the gate.

Beware the hawkers outside the stadiums who will try to sell you pricey ringside seats—you'll be able to see all the action very well and get food-and-drink service at the mid-price seats in the bleachers. The only thing you're getting with the pricier tickets is a little more comfort (a folding chair versus bleacher seating or standing room). In both stadiums there are sections that seem solely reserved for the most manic of Thai gamblers; if you find yourself accidentally sitting in one of these sections, you'll be politely redirected to the farang section.

BANGKOK ESSENTIALS

Transportation

BY AIR

About 100 airlines fly into Bangkok each day. Thai Airways, the national airline, is the only carrier to serve Thailand directly from the East Coast of the United States, with nonstop service to New York. Thai also has direct flights between Bangkok and Los Angeles, and Bangkok and London. It also flies from Hong Kong, Singapore, Taiwan, Japan, and elsewhere in Asia.

The U.S. carrier with the most frequent flights to Bangkok is Northwest Airlines. It has direct service between Bangkok and San Francisco, and serves New York, Detroit, Seattle, Dallas, Los Angeles, and other U.S. cities through Tokyo. British Airways flies nonstop to Bangkok from London. Singapore Airlines flies to Bangkok through Singapore. Japan Airlines serves Bangkok with a connection in Tokyo, and Korean Air connects Bangkok with New York and Los Angeles through Seoul, though the flight leaves at 1 AM.

Two Taiwanese airlines, China Airlines (which has a spotty safety record) and Eva Air (which doesn't), both fly frequently through Bangkok to many points in Asia, as does Hong Kong–based Cathay Pacific. Both Cathay and Eva connect to the United States through those hubs. When booking travel from the United States to Bangkok, avoid the European carriers, which offer connecting service through Europe—that routing will add many hours to your trip.

🛫 Carriers **British Airways** ☎ 02/636–1747 ⊕ www.britishairways.com. **Cathay Pacific** ☎ 02/263–0606 ⊕ www.cathay.com. **China Airlines** ☎ 02/250–9880 ⊕ www.china-airlines.com. **Eva Air** ☎ 02/269–6300 ⊕ www.evaair.com. **Japan Airlines** ☎ 02/

1

692–5185 ⊕ www.jal.com. **Korean Air Lines** ☎ 02/267–0985 ⊕ www.koreanair.com.
Northwest ☎ 02/254–0789 ⊕ www.nwa.com. **Singapore Airlines** ☎ 02/236–0440
⊕ www.singaporeair.com. **Thai Airways** ☎ 02/356–1111, 02/132–0040 at the airport
⊕ www.thaiair.com. **United Air Lines** ☎ 02/535–2232 ⊕ www.united.com.

AIRPORTS &
TRANSFERS

On September 28, 2006, the BKK code was taken over by Bangkok's
brand-new Suvarnabhumi airport (pronounced "Su-wan-na-poom"). The
$4.2 billion airport, developed for an eventual 100 million passengers
per year, is a wonder to behold, with a spectacular, flowing architectural design featuring the world's tallest control tower and the second-
largest single building in the world, along with an impressive array of
new shops and services. Suvarnabhumi is 30 km (18 mi) southeast of
the city, in the direction of Pattaya.

Bangkok's old international airport, Don Muang (now dubbed DMK),
which is 25 km (16 mi) north of the city, offers domestic flights on Nok
and One-Two-Go, as well as Thai Airlines domestic flights to major destinations like Chiang Mai, Chinag Rai, Krabi, and Phuket.

A 10-lane highway connects Suvarnabhumi to the city's outer-ring road
and is linked to the Bang Na-Chonburi Expressway, which leads to the
Eastern Gulf. Taxis, available 24 hours, are by far the most convenient
way to get to Downtown Bangkok from the airport or vice versa, and
they're cheap. You'll pay the metered fare plus a B50 airport surcharge
and tolls. The total for all of the above should be around B350–B400.
Get your taxi by taking the free airport shuttle to the airport's Public
Transportation Center, then heading to one of the taxi counters on
Level 1, near Entrances 3, 4, 7, and 8. State your destination to the dispatcher at the counter. The dispatcher will write it down for the driver,
who will lead you to the taxi. Allow 30 minutes to 1½ hours for the
trip to or from your hotel, depending on traffic. ■ TIP➔ **Don't forget to
get Thai baht at the airport, as you'll need it to pay for your taxi.**

At this writing, a city rail link between the airport and Phayathai-
Makkasan was not due to open until 2008, but the Airport Bus Express
is fully operational, and it's a good alternative to taxi service, costing
about 40% less. The bus runs from 5 AM to midnight. Head to the Airport Bus Counter on Level 1, near Entrance 8 of the Public Transportation Center. The service, which costs B150, operates four routes. You
can ask at the bus terminal which route to take to reach your hotel. Route
AE1 serves the Silom neighborhood. Route AE2 serves Khao San Road
and the Old City. Route AE3 serves Sukhumvit, and Route AE4 serves
Hua Lumphong (the city's main railway station).

Another option is prearranging a limo transfer through your Bangkok
hotel, but we don't recommend it. A hotel-arranged transfer will cost
you US$60–$75, a huge increase over the standard taxi fare, and is only
marginally more convenient than a taxi. In fact, it's not uncommon to
have a hard time finding your driver because of some flight delay or mis-
communication, in which case you'll be faced with a frantic search and/
or moral dilemma of whether to write off the transfer and take a cab—
hardly the way you want to start your vacation.

Note that when you leave the airport on an international flight, you'll be required to pay a Passenger Service Charge (PSC) of B700.

Note: The airport has more than its share of hustlers, many wearing uniforms and name tags that make them look official. Many try to get you to change your hotel to one that pays them a large commission, often claiming your hotel is overbooked. They will also hustle you into overpriced taxis or limousines. Do not get taken. Instead, follow the signs in the Public Transportation Center that point to the public taxi stand. Line up in front of a booth where an English-speaker will fill out a destination form for you. All of these taxis will use a meter.

🏛 **Suvarnabhumi Airport** ☎ 02/132-1888 general, 02/132-0000 flight information
🌐 www.airportthai.co.th.

BY BOAT & FERRY

Ferries (sometimes called "river buses") ply the Chao Phraya River. The fare for these express boats is based on the distance you travel; the price ranges from B2 to B25. At certain piers you must add a B1 jetty fee. The pier adjacent to the Oriental Hotel is convenient to many of the city's hotels. You can get to the Grand Palace in about 10 minutes, or to the other side of Krungthon Bridge in about 15 minutes. Local line boats run from 6 AM to 6 PM. If you are on Sukhumvit, Phetchaburi Road is a good place to catch them. These boats stop at every pier and will take you all the way to Nonthaburi, where you'll find a little island with vendors selling pottery. A trip up the river makes for a fun afternoon on days when it's too hot to trudge around the city. Under the Saphan Taksin Skytrain stop, there is a ferry stop where passengers can cross the river to Thonburi for B3.

Longtail boats (so called for the extra-long propeller shaft that extends behind the stern) operate as taxis that you can hire. The standard rate is B600 for two hours, though better deals can often be struck. It's a great way to see the canals, and most boats stop for quick visits at Wat Arun. Boatmen will take you anywhere you want to go, for B200–B300 per hour. The best place to hire these boats is at the Central Pier on Sathorn Bridge. Longtails for hire often quit running at 6 PM.

For a blast into Bangkok's transportation past, traditional wooden canal boats are a fun (though not entirely practical) way to get around town. Klong Saen Saep, just north of Ploenchit Road, is the main boat route. The fare is a maximum B15, and during rush hour, boats pull up to piers in one-minute intervals. Klong boats provide easy access to Jim Thompson's House and are a handy alternative way to get to Khao San Road during rush hour.

BY BUS

Bangkok has three major terminals for buses headed to other parts of the country. The **Northern Bus Terminal,** called Mo Chit, serves Chiang Mai and points north. The **Southern Bus Terminal,** in Thonburi, is for buses bound for Hua Hin, Koh Samui, Phuket, and points south. The **Eastern Bus Terminal,** called Ekkamai, is for buses headed to Pattaya, Rayong, and Trat provinces.

Most bus companies do not take reservations, and tickets are sold on a first-come, first-served basis. This is seldom a problem, however, because the service is so regular that the next bus is sure to depart before long. For example, VIP buses from Bangkok to Kanchanaburi depart every 15 minutes.

The air-conditioned orange-color 999 buses are the most comfortable. They have larger seats that recline. A hostess serves drinks and snacks and a movie is usually shown on longer trips. If no 999 bus is available on your route, stick with the air-conditioned blue VIP buses. They aren't as luxurious, but are still comfortable.

🚌 Bus Stations **Eastern Bus Terminal** ⊠ Sukhumvit Soi 40, Sukhumvit ☎ 02/391-2504 Ⓜ Subway: Sukhumvit; Skytrain: Ekkamai. **Northern Bus Terminal** ⊠ Phaholyothin Rd. behind Chatuchak Park, Northern Bangkok ☎02/936−2852 up to 66 Ⓜ Subway: Chatuchak Park; Skytrain: Mo Chit. **Southern Bus Terminal** ⊠ Pinklao-Nakomchaisri Rd., Talingchan, Thonburi ☎ 02/435−1200.

GETTING AROUND Although city buses can be very crowded, they are convenient and inexpensive. For a fare of B4 to B6 on the non-air-conditioned buses and B10 to B35 on the air-conditioned ones, you can travel virtually anywhere in the city. Air-conditioned microbuses, in which you are guaranteed a seat, charge B25. Most buses operate from 5 AM to around 11 PM, but a few routes operate around the clock.

The bus routes are confusing, but someone at the bus stop should know the number of the bus you need. You can pick up a route map at most bookstalls for B35. Buses can be very crowded, so be alert for pickpockets.

BY CAR

Thailand's highway system is good (and getting better), so driving around the country is becoming a more popular option. There are plenty of sights around Bangkok that are within easy driving distance. For longer-distance trips, driving is possible, although you may want to hire a private car with English-speaking driver, given the affordability of such a service in Thailand.

As for driving in Bangkok—don't bother. The maze of streets is difficult enough for taxi drivers to negotiate. Throw in bumper-to-bumper traffic and you'll wish that you were on a water taxi on the river or on the Skytrain soaring above the streets.

Most rental agencies in the capital let you drop off the car in a different city. Of the international chains, Avis, Hertz, and Budget have offices at the airport and in Downtown Bangkok.

BY SKYTRAIN

The Skytrain transformed the city when it opened on the king's birthday in 1999. It now has 25 stations on two lines that intersect at Siam Square. Although it covers just a fraction of the capital (it bypasses the Old City and Dusit, for example), it is surprisingly convenient for visitors. The routes above Sukhumvit, Silom, and Phaholyothin roads make traveling in those areas a breeze. If you are traveling between two points along the route, the Skytrain is by far the best way to go. The fare is B10 to B40, determined by the distance you travel. It runs from 5 AM to midnight. Although the Skytrain and subway are separate entities and use different fare and ticketing systems, the two connect at three points: Sala Daeng Station and Silom Station, Asok Station and Sukhumvit Station, and Mo Chit Station and Chatuchak Station.

🚇 Bangkok Transit System ☎ 02/617-7300 ⊕ www.bts.co.th.

BY SUBWAY

The subway stretches from Hua Lamphong Train Station to Bang Sue Train Station, stopping at 16 stations along the way. Although it only covers a small section of the city, the subway does make getting from city center out to the train stations a breeze. (What was once an hour-long affair is now a short 20-minute ride underground.) There are also convenient stops at Chatuchak, Queen Sirikit Convention Center, Thailand Cultural Center, Silom Road, and Sukhumvit Road.

The subway runs daily from 6 AM until midnight and passes every 5 minutes during rush hour and every 10 minutes during regular hours. Adult fares are B15 to B50. Fares for children and those older than 65 are 50% off the regular rates. Children whose height is less than 3 feet ride free of charge. If you plan on multiple journeys, there is also a Stored Value Card, which can be bought at ticket booths for a minimum of B100, plus a B50 deposit.

BY TAXI & TUK-TUK

Taxis can be an economical way to get around, provided you don't hit gridlock. A typical journey of 5 km (3 mi) runs about B60. Most taxis have meters, so avoid those that lack one or claim that it is broken. The rate for the first 2 km (1 mi) is B35, with an additional baht for every 55 yards after that. If the speed drops to below 6 kph (4 mph), a surcharge of one baht per minute is added. Taxi drivers may take a fare without a clue as to where they are going, so having a concierge write the name of your destination and its cross streets in Thai is always a good idea, especially if you are visiting a place that is not a well-known landmark or buried in a labyrinthine neighborhood like Chinatown.

Though colorful three-wheeled tuk-tuks are somewhat of a symbol of Bangkok, they're really only a good option when traffic is light—otherwise you can end up sitting in traffic, sweating, and sucking in car fumes. Oh, and did we mention that they're unmetered and prone to overturning? The drivers are tough negotiators, and unless you are good at bargaining you may well end up paying more for a tuk-tuk than for a metered taxi. Unscrupulous tuk-tuk drivers—all too common, especially around touristy areas—offer tours at a bargain rate, then take you directly to jewelry shops and tailors who, of course, give the drivers a commission. Don't fall for it. In many ways a tuk-tuk is not ideal, but if a trip to Bangkok does not seem complete without a spin around town in one, pay half of what the driver suggests, insist on being taken to your destination, and hold on for dear life.

At many sois you will find groups of motorcycle taxis. These "soi boys" can travel anywhere in Bangkok. Fares are negotiable, usually about the same as or perhaps a little less than taxis. A trip to go the length of a street is B10. Motorbikes can be dangerous, and helmets, when available, are often nothing more than a thin piece of plastic without a chin strap, but most locals take these taxis as part of the daily commute. Motorcycle drivers seem to know their way around the city much better than taxi drivers—they also know good side-street shortcuts. The risk and discomfort limit their desirability, but motorcycles are one of the best ways to get around Bangkok, especially if you're in a hurry.

BY TRAIN

Hua Lamphong Railway Station, the city's main station, is where you'll find most long-distance trains. Bangkok Noi Railway Station, on the Thonburi side of the Chao Phraya River, is used by local trains to Hua Hin and other nearby destinations.

🚉 Train Stations **Bangkok Noi** ✉ Arun Amarin Rd., Thonburi ☎ 02/411-3102. **Hua Lamphong** ✉ Rama IV Rd., Chinatown ☎ 02/223-0341 Ⓜ Subway: Hua Lamphong.

Contacts & Resources

BANKS & EXCHANGING SERVICES

All major banks exchange foreign currency, and most have easily accessible ATMs that accept foreign bank cards. ATMs are everywhere in tourist areas.

EMERGENCIES

In case of emergency, it's a good idea to contact the Tourist Police. The force has mobile units in major tourist areas.

For medical attention, Bunrungrad Hospital, on Sukhumvit Soi 1, and Bangkok Nursing Hospital, near Silom Road, are considered the best by most expatriates. Other good facilities include Bangkok Adventist Hospital, Bangkok Christian Hospital, and Chulalongkorn Hospital.

Bangkok has a number of reputable dental clinics, among them 11 Dental Clinic and Thaniya Dental Centre. If you want a private dentist, the aptly named Dr. Smile is conveniently located at the foot of Sala Daeng Skytrain stop.

There are many pharmacies in Bangkok, including Foodland Supermarket Pharmacy. Compared to the United States, fewer drugs require prescriptions. If you need one, the prescription must be written in Thai. Over-the-counter drugs do not necessarily have the same ingredients as those found elsewhere, so read the label carefully. If you cannot find a pharmacy, the ubiquitous 7-Eleven, AM/PM, and other convenience stores carry nonprescription medications.

🏥 Doctors & Dentists **11 Dental Clinic** ✉ 155 Sukhumvit Soi 11/1, Sukhumvit ☎ 02/255-2279 Ⓜ Subway: Sukhumvit; Skytrain: Nana. **Dr. Smile** ✉ Silom Soi 1, Silom ☎ 02/661-1156 Ⓜ Subway: Silom; Skytrain: Sala Daeng. **Thaniya Dental Centre** ✉ 52 Silom Rd., Silom ☎ 02/231-2100 Ⓜ Subway: Silom; Skytrain: Sala Daeng.

🏥 Emergency Services **Ambulance** ☎ 1669. **Fire** ☎ 199. **Police** ☎ 191. **Tourist Police** ✉ 4 Ratchadamnoen Rd., Sukhumvit ☎ 1155 Ⓜ Subway: Phetchaburi; Skytrain: Asok.

 Hospitals **Bangkok Adventist Hospital** ⊠ 430 Phitsanulok Rd., Dusit ☎ 02/282-1100. **Bangkok Christian Hospital** ⊠ 124 Silom Rd., Silom ☎ 02/235-1000 up to 07, 02/233-6981 Ⓜ Subway: Silom; Skytrain: Sala Daeng. **Bangkok Nursing Hospital** ⊠ 9 Convent Rd., Silom ☎ 02/686-2700 Ⓜ Subway: Silom; Skytrain: Sala Daeng. **Bumrungrad Hospital** ⊠ 33 Sukhumvit Soi 3, Sukhumvit ☎ 02/667-2525 Ⓜ Subway: Sukhumvit; Skytrain: Ploenchit. **Chulalongkorn Hospital** ⊠ Rama IV Rd., Pathumwan ☎ 02/252-8181.

 24-Hour Pharmacies **Foodland Supermarket Pharmacy** ⊠ 9 Patpong 2 Rd., Silom ☎ 02/233-2101 Ⓜ Subway: Silom; Skytrain: Sala Daeng ⊠ 1413 Sukhumvit Soi 5, Sukhumvit ☎ 02/254-2247 Ⓜ Subway: Sukhumvit; Skytrain: Nana.

MAIL & SHIPPING

All neighborhoods have at least one post office, and the staff at your hotel can tell you where to find the nearest one. The city's main post office is on Charoen Krung (New Road) south of Chinatown. It is more efficient than smaller ones, which can have dreadfully slow service.

The major international courier services, Federal Express, DHL, and UPS, have offices in Bangkok.

 Courier Services **DHL Worldwide** ⊠ 22nd fl., Grand Amarin Tower, New Phetchaburi Rd., Sukhumvit ☎ 02/207-0600 Ⓜ Subway: Phetchaburi; Skytrain: Asok. **Federal Express** ⊠ 8th fl., Green Tower, Rama IV Rd. ☎ 02/229-8800. **UPS** ⊠ Sukhumvit Soi 44/1, Sukhumvit ☎ 02/712-3300 Ⓜ Subway: Sukhumvit; Skytrain: Ekkamai.

TOUR OPTIONS

Virtually every major hotel has a travel desk that books tours in and around Bangkok. With only slight variations, companies usually offer half-day tours of Wat Po, Wat Benjamabophit, and Wat Traimit; half-day tours of the Grand Palace and Wat Phra Keo; and dinners featuring traditional dance. Several established agencies are good bets. Try Diethelm, East West Siam, or World Travel Service.

 Agencies **Diethelm** ⊠ Kian Gwan Bldg. 11, 140/1 Wittayu [Wireless Rd.], Sukhumvit ☎ 02/255-9150 up to 70 Ⓜ Subway: Sukhumvit; Skytrain: Ploenchit. **East West Siam** ⊠ 15th fl., Regent House, 183 Ratchadamri Rd., Lumphini ☎ 02/651-9101 Ⓜ Subway: Sukhumvit; Skytrain: Ploenchit. **World Travel Service** ⊠ 1053 Charoen Krung (New Rd.), Chinatown ☎ 02/233-5900 up to 09 Ⓜ Subway: Hua Lamphong.

Around Bangkok

TRIPS TO DAMNOEN SADUAK FLOATING MARKET,
PHETCHABURI, KANCHANABURI, AND
SANGKLABURI

The floating market in Damnoen Saduak is the only market of its kind left in the region.

WORD OF MOUTH

"The floating market is a tourist trap well worth experiencing."
—jmf314159

"Kanchanaburi is very inexpensive compared with much of Thailand. Spend $50 and you will have a pool and other luxuries. People are very friendly in town. I had many interesting conversations with locals. There weren't a lot of other tourists around."
—eurotraveller

WELCOME TO
AROUND BANGKOK

TOP REASONS TO GO

★ **Heading into the Wild**
There's a huge expanse of untouched jungle around Kanchanaburi, which is the kickoff point for trekking, elephant-riding, and river-rafting adventures.

★ **The Last Floating Market**
Most tourists know of Damnoen Saduak's floating market before they even set foot in Thailand. It's the only daily floating market left in the region.

★ **Seeing Old Siam** History awaits outside Bangkok at a Neolithic site, the remains of a Khmer temple, and in Nakhon Pathom, Thailand's oldest seat of Buddhist learning.

★ **The Bridge on the River Kwai** For a glimpse of more recent history, visit what remains of the "Death Railway," and walk across the bridge made famous by the movie of the same name.

★ **Converging Cultures** The area around Sangklaburi on the Thai-Myanmar (Burma) border is a mix of Thai, Burmese, and hill tribe communities like the Mon and Karen.

1 Day Trips from Bangkok. When most people head south, it's to make for Thailand's famous beaches, but along the way are the floating market at Damnoen Saduak and Muang Boran, a huge park with replicas of the country's landmarks. To the west of Bangkok is Nakhon Pathom, keeper of Thailand's biggest stupa.

Damnoen Saduak's floating market

2 Phetchaburi. Phetchaburi has many interesting temples and a few royal summer palaces. Located three hours south of Bangkok, it makes for a long day trip, so either hire a car and driver to make the trip easier or visit as part of a one- or two-day trip to Hua Hin.

Kanchanaburi War Cemetery

River Kwai, Kanchanaburi

Sangklaburi **4**

Khao Laem National Park

Khao Laem Reservoir

Thong Pha Phum

Si Nakharin Reservoir

Sai Yok National Park 323

BURMA (MYANMAR)

3 Kanchanaburi & Environs. Kanchanaburi, two hours west of Bangkok, is best known as the site of the famous Bridge on the River Kwai. If you're not in a hurry to get back to Bangkok, you can continue your exploration of stunning Kanchanaburi Province, with day trips to 13th-century Khmer ruins and two national parks containing waterfalls.

4 Sangklaburi. Kanchanaburi Province's farthest attraction is the city of Sangklaburi, which is on Myanmar's doorstep. Here Thai, Mon, Karen, and Bangladeshi communities mix and boats take you to see a village submerged in a reservoir.

An offering of alms at dawn on the King s Birthday.

2

GETTING ORIENTED

If you need respite from the heat, noise, and pollution of Bangkok, the surrounding countryside offers many possibilities. There are several sights directly outside the city, easily reached in a few hours by bus, train, or taxi. Kanchanaburi Province can become a mini-vacation all on its own, with Kanchanaburi city being the gateway to a first glimpse of Thailand's wilderness.

Nong Phru

Bo Phloi

U-Thong

324

Bridge of the River Kwai

Sai Yok

321

340

Pathum Thani

3 Kanchanaburi

323

Kamphaeng Saen

Kwai River

1

9

Nakhon Pathom

4

BANGKOK

7

Suan Phung

4

Damnoen Saduak

3

34

Ratchaburi

35

Samut Sakhon

Muang Boran

Samut Songkram

Ban Laem

Phetchaburi **2**

Keeng Krachan National Park

4

Gulf of Thailand

Cha'Am

0   25 mi

0   25 km

Hua Hin

Pran Buri

AROUND BANGKOK PLANNER

Tour Options

It's easy to get around on your own, but both **Asian Trails** (☎ 02/626-2000 in Bangkok ⊕ www.asiantrails. net) and **Diethelm Travel** (☎ 02/255-9150 in Bangkok ⊕ www. diethelmtravel.com) organize trips to the floating markets, trekking trips, home stays, and bicycle tours.

Regional Cuisine Highlights

The areas around Bangkok allow you to sample both regional and non-Thai ethnic foods. Kanchanaburi and Sangklaburi have Mon, Karen, Bangladeshi, and Burmese communities, each serving its own specialties. A must-try is *laphae to*, a Burmese salad of nuts and fermented tea leaves. In Nakhon Pathom try the excellent rice-based dessert *khao laam*. Phetchaburi is famous for its desserts, as well as *khao chae*, a chilled rice dish soaked in herb-infused water.

Safety

The region is generally very safe. Still, take normal precautions when dealing with strangers, and keep valuables on your person at all times when traveling by bus or train. Beware of deals—particularly involving gems—that sound ridiculously cheap. They will *always* be a rip-off.

On a more amusing note, beware the monkeys of Phetchaburi. They're cute but cunning, and may relieve you of your possessions, especially food items.

Day Trip or Overnight Stay?

An overnight stay is essential in Sangklaburi and highly recommended in Kanchanaburi and Phetchaburi. Stay in Damnoen Saduak the night before you visit the floating market to avoid a very early-morning bus ride.

Note that luxury accommodation is in short supply in most provincial towns, so be prepared to stay at a resort on the outskirts, or lower your expectations. It's best to book ahead on weekends and national holidays in Kanchanaburi. On weekends and national holidays (particularly the water festival Songkran in mid-April), Kanchanaburi and the seafood restaurants at Samut Songkram will be packed with Thais. From November to March (the high season) the floating market has more tourists than vendors.

The waterfalls of Kanchanaburi Province are at their best during or just after the rainy season (June to November).

WHAT IT COSTS In Baht

	$$$$	$$$	$$	$	¢
RESTAURANTS	Over B400	B301–B400	B201–B300	B100–B200	under B100
HOTELS	over B6,000	B4,001–B6,000	B2,001–B4,000	B1,000–B2,000	under B1,000

DAY TRIPS FROM BANGKOK

Muang Boran

❶ *20 km (12 mi) southeast of Bangkok; 2 hrs by bus.*

Updated by
Mick Elmore

Muang Boran (Ancient City) is a park with more than 100 replicas and reconstructions of the country's most important architectural sites, monuments, and palaces. The park is shaped like Thailand, and the attractions are placed roughly in their correct geographical position. A "traditional Thai village" within the grounds sells crafts, but the experience is surprisingly untouristy. The park stretches over 320 acres, and takes about four hours to cover by car. Or you rent a bicycle at the entrance for B50. Small outdoor cafés throughout the grounds serve decent Thai food. They started a dual price system in 2005 charging foreigners more than Thais, which upsets some tourists.

To get here by car, take the Samrong–Samut Prakan expressway and turn left at the Samut Prakan intersection onto Old Sukhumvit Road. You can also take an air-conditioned bus (number 511) from Bangkok's Southern Bus Terminal to the end of the line at Pak Nam, then transfer to a minibus (number 36). Muang Boran is well sign-posted on the left at Km 33. ✉ *Km 33, Old Sukhumvit Rd., Samut Prakan* ☎ *02/226–1936* 🎫 *Foreigners B300, Thais B100* ☉ *Daily 8–5.*

Damnoen Saduak

❷ *109 km (65 mi) southwest of Bangkok; 2–3 hrs by bus.*

The town's colorful floating market is a true icon of Thai tourism. The image is so evocative that it's become an ad agency favorite. Today the market, which sells mostly produce and other foods, has taken on a bit of the Disneyland effect as it is often infested with tourists and it bears only passing resemblance to the authentic commercial life of this canal-strewn corner of Thailand.

On the other hand, even though it feels a bit like a theater production, this may be your only opportunity to witness a fading Thai tradition. Twenty years ago many communities had floating markets, but with new roads replacing the need for canal commerce, this is one of the few left. ■ TIP→ **Get here before 9 AM before most tourists arrive.** Buy your breakfast from women in straw hats paddling boats laden with fruit or steaming stir-fry pans. The best way to enjoy the market is to hire a boat (holding up to six people) for around B400 per hour; after seeing the market, you can also arrange to tour the wider countryside, taking in local temples and gardens, or even travel back to Bangkok (around three hours). A second market, around a canal turn, sells strictly tourist souvenirs. Similar trips can be arranged for B500 from Kanchanaburi, which is two hours north of the market.

Where to Stay & Eat

■ TIP→ **There are morning buses from Bangkok, but the best way to get an early start is to stay overnight.** A few places are available on the main road from Samut Songkram.

¢ ✕▥ **Baan Sukchoke Country Resort.** The small wooden bungalows, are a bit rickety, but clean and comfortable nonetheless. The bungalows surround a pond connected to the canal. The water is beautifully floodlighted at night, and an outdoor restaurant serves a Thai menu (¢–$). The property is 3 km (2 mi) from the floating market; you can have the staff call a tuk-tuk or a boat (B400, up to 10 people) to take you there. ⊠ *103 Moo 5, Damnoen Saduak* ☎ *032/254301* ♺ *In-room: no a/c (some). In-hotel: restaurant* ▭ *No credit cards.*

¢ ▥ **Little Bird Hotel.** The large, basic rooms are set back from the main road, so it's quiet. The plain, municipal-looking building may be unattractive, but it's a 10-minute walk to the boats for the market and close to banks, convenience stores, and cafés. ⊠ *Moo 1/8, Damnoen Saduak* ☎ *032/254382* ♺ *In-room: no a/c (some)* ▭ *No credit cards.*

Nakhon Pathom

❸ *56 km (34 mi) west of Bangkok; 1 hr by bus.*

Reputed to be Thailand's oldest city (it's thought to date from 150 BC), Nakhon Pathom was once the center of the Dvaravati kingdom, a 6th- to 11th-century affiliation of Mon city-states. It marks the region's first center of Buddhist learning, established about a millennium ago. Today, there would be little reason to visit if it weren't for **Phra Pathom Chedi,** the tallest Buddhist monument in the world. At 417 feet, it stands just higher—but is less ornate—than the chedi at Shwe Dagon in Myanmar.

Erected in the 6th century, the site's first chedi was destroyed in a Burmese attack in 1057. Surrounding the chedi is one of Thailand's most important temples, which contains the ashes of King Rama VI.

The terraces around the temple complex are full of fascinating statuary, including Chinese figures, a large reclining Buddha, and an unusual Buddha seated in a chair. By walking around the inner circle surrounding the chedi, you can see novice monks in their classrooms through arched stone doorways. Traditional dances are sometimes performed in front of the temple, and during Loi Krathong (a festival in November that celebrates the end of the rainy season) a fair is set up in the adjacent park. ✛ *½ km (¼ mi) south of train station* ▨ *B20* ◷ *Daily 6–6.*

Next to Phra Pathom Chedi is the **Phra Pathom Chedi National Museum,** which contains Dvaravati artifacts such as images of the Buddha, stone carvings, and stuccos from the 6th to the 11th century. ⊠ *Khwa Phra Rd.* ▨ *B30* ◷ *Wed.–Sun. 9–4.*

Sanam Chan Palace was built during King Rama IV's reign. The palace is closed to the public, but the surrounding park is a lovely place to relax in the shade. ⊠ *Petchkasem Rd. west of chedi.*

On the Bangkok Road out of Nakhon Pathom (toward Bangkok) is the ⛅ **Rose Garden,** which is actually a park complex where herbs, bananas, and various flowers, including orchids and roses, flourish. Within the complex are traditional houses and a performance stage, where shows include dancing, Thai boxing, sword fighting, and even wedding ceremonies (daily at 2:45 PM). ■ TIP➜ **The park is popular with Thai families**

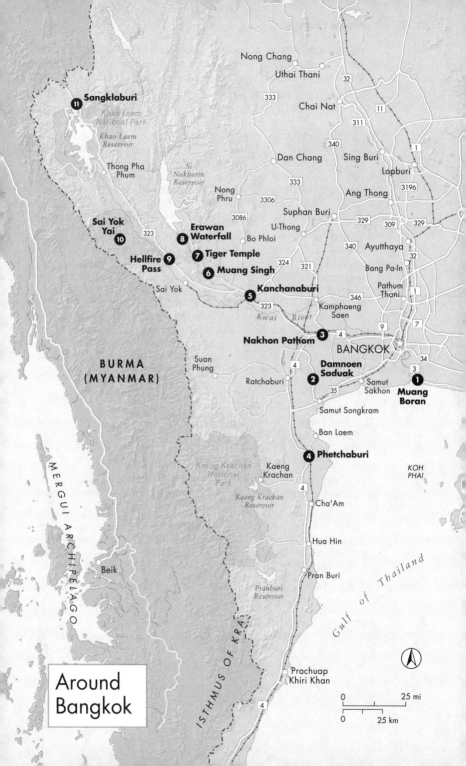

Around Bangkok

and has restaurants and a nice hotel with rooms starting at B2,500. ☒ *Km 32, Petchkasem Rd.* ☎ *034/322588* ⊕ *www.rose-garden.com* 🖃 *B20, B480 with lunch and show* ☉ *Daily 8–6.*

Next door to the Rose Garden is the **Samphran Elephant Ground & Zoo.** You can take elephant rides, and watch a 40-minute performance during which they display their historical roles in Thai warfare and industry. During the show elephants haul logs, play soccer, and even reenact the Yutha Harti, a 16th-century elephant-back battle between a Thai king and an invading Burmese prince. There are other attractions at the zoo, including an orchid nursery, but ⚠ **avoid the degrading "crocodile wrestling" show, in which practically comatose animals are tormented and dragged around by their tails.** ☒ *Km 30, Petchkasem Rd.* ☎ *02/429–0361* ⊕ *www.elephantshow.com* 🖃 *B500* ☉ *Daily 9–5.*

Where to Eat

The road from Nakhon Pathom train station has several cafés, and a market where food stalls sell one-plate Thai meals. Similar dining options are at the entrance of the chedi. Keep an eye out for Nakhon Pathom specialties such as *khao lam* (sticky rice, palm sugar, and black beans grilled in hollowed-out bamboo sections) and sweet, pink-flesh pomelo (a large citrus fruit). The Rose Garden has several places to eat, including a Japanese restaurant, and ■ TIP➜ **Samphran Elephant Ground has an open-air food court that's cheaper than the restaurant at the gate.**

Day Trips from Bangkok Essentials

Transportation

BY BUS

All buses leave from Bangkok's Southern Bus Terminal. Buses to Damnoen Saduak (two hours, B65) leave every 20 minutes starting at 5 AM; from the station, walk or take a songthaew (open-back truck) along the canal for 1½ km (¾ mi) to the floating market.

Buses depart for Nakhon Pathom (1 hour, B34) every hour from 5:30 AM to 4 PM; for Samut Songkram (1½ hours, B45) every hour 3 AM–6:30 PM.

For buses to Muang Boran (two hours, B30), take the 511, which leaves every half hour from Bangkok's Southern Bus Terminal, to the end of the line at Pak Nam. Transfer to minibus number 36 (B5), which goes to the entrance of Muang Boran. Buses also run between Nakhon Pathom and Damnoen Saduak.

Tickets are sold on a first-come, first-served basis, but services are so frequent that it's seldom a problem finding an empty seat.

BY CAR

Route 35, the main road south to Samut Songkram (one hour) is mainly a two-lane highway that can be slow going if there's heavy traffic. Add an extra half hour to all trip times for possible delays.

Driving to Muang Boran means a trip through heavy and unpredictable Bangkok traffic. It should take 1½ to 2 hours. West from Bangkok, allow 1 hour to Nakhon Pathom on Route 4.

In case of breakdowns or other road troubles it's best to call information (☎ 1133) and ask for the number of the local *tam rouat tong tiaow* (tourist police).

BY TAXI & SONGTHAEW

Bangkok's air-conditioned taxis are an often-neglected way of accessing sights outside the city. Estimate around B500 per hour of travel, depending on your bargaining skills.

Outside Bangkok, songthaews (open-back trucks) are the closest thing to taxis in most areas.

BY TRAIN

Ten trains a day run at regular intervals to Nakhon Pathom (1½ hours, B14–B20) from 7:45 AM to 10:50 PM. Some of the Nakhon Pathom trains continue on to Phetchaburi (4 hours, B94–B114) and points farther south. The trains to Kanchanaburi also stop in Nakhon Pathom. No trains go to Damnoen Saduak, Muang Boran, or Samut Songkram.

Contacts & Resources

BANKS & EXCHANGING SERVICES

ATMs and exchange facilities are common in all towns. In Damnoen Saduak, you can find them on the main road from Samut Songkram.

EMERGENCIES

🏥 Hospitals **Sanam Chan Hospital** ✉ 1194 Petchkasem Rd., Nakhon Pathom ☎ 034/219600.

VISITOR INFORMATION

The TAT (tourist information) office in Kanchanaburi covers Nakhon Pathom and Samut Songkram.

🏢 **TAT** ✉ 325 Saengchuto Rd., Kanchanaburi ☎ 034/623691.

PHETCHABURI

❹ *132 km (84 mi) south of Bangkok; 3 hrs by bus.*

This small seaport town once linked the old Thai capitals of Sukhothai and Ayutthaya with trade routes on the South China Sea and Indian Ocean. Its many wats are within, or easily accessible on foot from, the town center, particularly along Matayawong, Pongsuriya, and Phrasong roads.

Phetchaburi is famous for *khao chae*, a chilled rice dish with sweetmeats once favored by royals that has become a summer tradition in posh Bangkok hotels. You can find it around the day market on Phanit Charoen Road (look for people eating at stalls from small silver bowls), along with *khanom jeen thotman* (noodles with curried fish cake). The city was also a royal retreat during the reigns of Rama IV and Rama V (1851–1910) and has two palaces open to the public.

⚠ Watch out for the gangs of monkeys that roam the streets of the town, particularly around Khao Wang; although some of them are cute and friendly, they are clever and cunning and often steal items from vendors and passersby.

The 800-year-old Khmer-influenced **Wat Mahathat Worawihan**, on the eastern side of the Phetchaburi River, is a royal temple. Besides the magnificent architecture and main Buddha statue, an interesting feature of this wat is a subtle political joke. Look around the base of the Buddha statue outside the main temple. A ring of monkeylike Atlases supports the large Buddha image, but one of the monkeys is not like the others. See if you can find him!

Wat Yai Suwannaram, built during the Ayutthaya period by skilled craftsman, has a 300-year-old painting in its main hall, a library on stilts above a fishpond (to deter termites), and an axe mark above one of the temple doors, said to have been left by a Burmese invader.

The wood-paneled exterior of **Wat Ko Kaeo Suttharam** is considered Thailand's finest. It depicts the constellations and the 10 lives of the Lord Buddha.

Wat Kam Paeng Laeng is the largest and oldest temple in Phetchaburi. It was built during the height of the Khmer empire, known as the Bayon era. Surrounded by a laterite wall, the compound includes four Khmer-style pagodas.

Phra Nakhon Khiri Historical Park (aka Khao Wang) is a forested hillside area on the edge of Phetchaburi with one of King Rama IV's palaces and a series of temples and shrines. Many of these are set high on the hilltop and have good views. Monkeys are a major shoplifting hazard around the gift shops at the foot of the hill. There's a cable car (B30) for those who don't fancy the strenuous walk. ⊠ *Khao Wang, entrance off Phetkasem Rd.* ▦ *B40* ☉ *Daily 9–4.*

Built in 1910 as a rainy season retreat by King Rama V, **Phra Ram Ratchaniwet** was modeled on a palace of Germany's Kaiser Wilhelm, and consequently has grand European architecture with art nouveau flourishes. The dining room has impressively ornate ceramic tiles. ⊠ *Thai Military Base, Ratchadamnoen Rd.* ▦ *B50* ☉ *Daily 8:30–4.*

Where to Stay

¢ ▦ **Khao Wang Hotel.** This Chinese guesthouse hotel opposite a 24-hour Internet shop has simple rooms. You may or may not enjoy the added spectacle of monkeys climbing all over your room's window grates. ⊠ *Ratchawithi Rd.* ☎ *032/425167* ▭ *No credit cards.*

¢ ▦ **Rabieng Rooms.** A cluster of small dark-wood plank buildings hold a few basic rooms big enough for beds and not much else. The restaurant serves Thai and Western food. ■ TIP→ The hotel organizes treks of varying length into nearby Kaeng Krachan National Park. ⊠ *1 Shesrain Rd.* ☎ *032/425707* ↝ *6 rooms* ⌂ *In-room: no a/c, no TV. In-hotel: restaurant* ▭ *No credit cards.*

¢ 🖼 **Royal Diamond Hotel.** It's a long way from town, but the Royal Diamond is Phetchaburi's only choice for those seeking a hotel instead of a guesthouse. However, it's close to Khao Wang and there are a few decent cafés nearby (try Puong Petch for sizzling seafood with hot Kariang chilies or Kway Tiao Pla VIP for a variety of fish noodle dishes). ⊠ *555 Moo 1, Phetkasem Rd., Tambon Rai-Som* ☎ *032/411061 up to 70* ⤴ *58 rooms* ⚹ *In-hotel: restaurant, bar* ▭ *MC, V* ❦❖ *BP.*

Phetchaburi Essentials

Transportation

BY BUS

Buses depart Bangkok's Southern Bus Terminal for Phetchaburi (three hours, B90) every 30 minutes from 5 AM to 9 PM.

BY CAR

Route 35, the main road south to Phetchaburi (1½ hours) is mainly a two-lane highway that can be slow going if there's heavy traffic. On the way back to Bangkok from Phetchaburi, there are two possible routes. Follow signs to Samut Songkram for the shorter distance (Route 35). From Samut Songkram to Damnoen Saduak is a pleasant half-hour drive along Route 325, particularly if you go via Ampawa, which is well marked with signs.

BY TRAIN

All the numerous trains to the south of Thailand stop at Phetchaburi (four hours, B94–B114).

Contacts & Resources

BANKS & EXCHANGING SERVICES

There are ATMs that accept international cards outside several bank branches in town.

EMERGENCIES

🔳 Hospital **Meung Phet Thonburi Hospital** ⊠ Phetkasem Rd., Phetchaburi ☎ 032/415191.

VISITOR INFORMATION

The office in nearby Cha'am handles Phetchaburi's tourism.

🔳 **TAT** ⊠ 500/51 Phetkasem Rd., Cha'am ☎ 032/471005.

KANCHANABURI & ENVIRONS

Kanchanaburi

❺ *140 km (87 mi) west of Bangkok; 2 hrs by bus.*

Within and around Kanchanaburi are cave temples, museums, tribal villages, waterfalls, hikes, elephant riding, and rafting; it's also the main

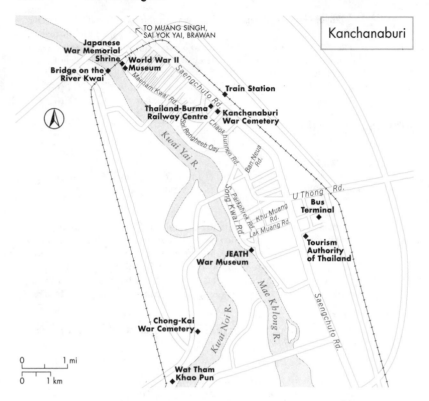

Kanchanaburi

TO MUANG SINGH, SAI YOK YAI, BRAWAN

Japanese War Memorial Shrine

Bridge on the River Kwai

World War II Museum

Saengchuto Rd.

Maenam Kwai Rd.

Train Station

Thailand-Burma Railway Centre

Kanchanaburi War Cemetery

Chaok kunnen Rd.

Soi Rongheeb Oay

Kwai Yai R.

Ban Neua Rd.

U Thong Rd.

Song Kwai Rd.

Parkphrek Rd.

Khu Muang Rd.

Lak Muang Rd.

Bus Terminal

Tourism Authority of Thailand

JEATH War Museum

Mae Khlong R.

Saengchuto Rd.

Chong-Kai War Cemetery

Kwai Noi R.

Wat Tham Khao Pun

0   1 mi

0   1 km

access point to the large national parks of western Thailand. But the city is most famous as the location of the **Bridge on the River Kwai**—a piece of the World War II Japanese "Death Railway" and subject of the 1957 film of the same name starring Alec Guinness and Richard Holden (though the film was shot in Sri Lanka).

During World War II, the Japanese, with whom Thailand sided, forced about 16,000 prisoners of war and 50,000 to 100,000 civilian slave laborers from neighboring countries to construct the "Death Railway," a supply route through the jungles of Thailand and Myanmar. It's estimated that one person died for every railway tie that was laid. Sure-footed visitors can walk across the Bridge on the River Kwai, of which the arched portions are original. In December Kanchanaburi holds a big fair and puts on a sound-and-light show depicting the Allied bombing of the bridge. Next to the bridge is a plaza with restaurants and souvenir shops.

The **Kanchanaburi War Cemetery,** next to noisy Saengchuto Road just south of the train station, has row upon row of neatly laid-out graves: 6,982 Australian, British, and Dutch prisoners of war were laid to rest here. (The remains of the American POWs were returned to the United States during the Eisenhower administration.) A remembrance ceremony is held every April 25, ANZAC (Australia and New Zealand Army Corps) Day.

2

The **Chong-Kai War Cemetery,** on the grounds of a former hospital for prisoners of war, is serene site simple, neatly organized grave markers of the soldiers forced to work on the railway. It's a little out of the way, and therefore rarely visited. To get there, hire a tuk-tuk or moto-taxi for about B40.

The **Thailand-Burma Railway Centre,** next to the Kanchanaburi War Cemetery, is certainly the best museum in town. It's small, well-designed and packed with informative displays. A walk through the chronologically arranged nine galleries gives a good overview of the railway's history. At the end of the exhibits is a coffee shop on the second floor that has a view of the cemetery. ⊠ *73 Jaokunnen Rd.* ☎ *09/549–2752* ⊕ *www.tbrconline.com* ✑ *B80 adults* ⊘ *Daily 9–6.*

A bit more than 2 km (1 mi) downriver from the bridge is the **JEATH War Museum** (JEATH is an acronym for Japan, England, America, Australia, Thailand, and Holland). The museum was founded in 1977 by a monk from the adjoining Wat Chaichumpol; it's in a replica of the bamboo huts that were used to hold prisoners of war. Among the items displayed at the museum are railway spikes, clothing, aerial photographs, newspaper clippings, and original sketches by ex-prisoners depicting their living conditions. ⊠ *Wat Chaichumpol, Bantai* ☎ *034/515203* ✑ *B30* ⊘ *Daily 8–6.*

Less than 1 km (½ mi) southwest of the Chong-Kai War Cemetery you'll find **Wat Tham Khao Pun,** one of the best cave temples in the area. A guide at the small shrine outside the cave will direct you on where to go. Inside the cave, between the stalagmites and stalactites, are Buddhist and Hindu statues and figurines. The cave complex was used as a series of storerooms by the Japanese in WWII.

Where to Stay & Eat

Kanchanaburi is laid out along the Mae Khlong and Kwai Yai rivers. The main road commercial district has a few mid-range hotels; the south end of the river, has a popular Thai weekend retreat with raft house accommodations, floating restaurants, and loud disco boats; and the northern riverbank is geared more toward backpackers, with guesthouses, bars, and Internet cafés. ■ TIP→ **The city is busy on long weekends and holidays, so book ahead for hotels and resorts.**

$ ✕ **River Kwai Floating Restaurant.** This crowded open-air restaurant is in the shadow of the railway bridge. Fish dishes (fried with pungent spices or lightly grilled), soups, and curries dominate the menu. The local specialty is *yeesok,* a fish caught fresh from the Kwai Yai and Kwai Noi rivers. Another tasty choice is the *tom yum gong,* hot-and-sour shrimp soup. ■ TIP→ **The food is toned down for foreigners, so if you want it Thai-type spicy tell them so.** ⊠ *River Kwai Bridge* ☎ *034/512595* ▤ *No credit cards.*

¢–$ ✕ **Apple & Noi's Guesthouse.** The massaman curry at this quiet garden restaurant is very popular with backpackers; it's made with heaps of palm sugar, and is a good balm for stomachs struggling with chili overdose. More authentic (hotter) dishes are available on request. ■ TIP→ **Own-**

ers Apple and Noi also teach a one-day Thai cooking course (B950, which includes six of Noi's curry pastes to take away), which starts off with a market visit by bicycle and ends with six prepared dishes. Apple runs two-day treks (minimum four people; B2,550 per person) that include a stay in a Karen village. ⊠ *52 Soi Rongheeb Oay, Chaokhunnen Rd.* 🕾 *034/512017* ☐ *MC, V.*

★ ¢-$ ✕ **Keereetara.** A new restaurant from the owners of The Resort (⇨ *below*), this classy restaurant is farther upriver and has a great views of the bridge from its terraces. It caters mostly to Thais, so the food can be quite spicy—ask them to tone the heat down ("mai phet") if you can't handle it. They serve many Thai dishes, but the fish soups and curries are the best choices. Relax with a drink and watch the river. ⊠ *43/1 River Kwai Rd.* 🕾 *01/847–9227* ☐ *MC, V.*

¢-$ ✕ **Maenam.** This is the busiest of the floating restaurants—built on a network of moored rafts—at the south end of the River Kwai Yai, where it merges with the Kwai Noi and forms the Mae Khlong. Maenam serves Thai seafood standards, such as red curry with "serpent head fish" (a freshwater relative of the catfish) and char-grilled prawns. The restaurant's riverfront serenity is disrupted periodically by the loud music of the disco and karaoke boats that meander up and down the river. The restaurant also has a singer each night. There is a separate coffee shop. ⊠ *5/7 Song Kwai Rd.* 🕾 *034/514318* ☐ *MC, V.*

¢-$ ✕ **The Resort.** This bar-restaurant occupies a white Thai-style house and draws a mostly Thai clientele. Red clay-tile floors and a low-lighted covered courtyard lend a casual elegance; the garden is particularly lovely, with tables shaded by white canvas umbrellas and palm trees. The menu is standard Thai, except for the deer and fried pig's appendix with garlic. ⊠ *318/2 River Kwai Rd.* 🕾 *01/847–9227* ☐ *MC, V.*

¢ ✕▦ **Jolly Frog Guesthouse.** These bungalow rooms are small and spartan, but some are riverfront, and all are surrounded by gardens. The cheaper rooms have fans and some have shared bathrooms. The more expensive rooms have four beds each. Because it's close to bars, Internet access, and convenience stores, the Jolly Frog is popular with backpackers and it's a good place to meet people. The restaurant (¢) has fish, burgers, pizzas, and a good selection of Thai vegetarian dishes. ⊠ *28 Soi China, River Kwai Rd., 71000* 🕾 *034/514579* 🖘 *55 rooms* ⌂ *In-room: no a/c (some). In-hotel: restaurant* ☐ *MC, V.*

★ ¢ ✕▦ **Little Creek.** The tribal-chic bungalows have peach-color walls, thatched roofs, and open-air showers. The chalets and the more expensive bungalows have air-conditioning and hot water; cheaper rooms have fans and cold water. All accommodations have verandas with bench seating. The lakeside restaurant (¢–$) has a

---

CHEAP EATS

For cheap eats, visit the **night market** on Saengchuto Road (next to the train station) that sets up early each evening. On offer is a variety of Thai stables like soups, rice dishes, and satays. The blended frozen fruit drinks are particularly good. After you grab a bite, you can peruse the market's goods—mostly clothes, CDs, and some electronic goods.

wood-fire pizza oven and charcoal grill and serves Western and Thai food while ambient world music plays in the background. Little Creek is a 10-minute drive from town; the resort provides free taxi rides or you can rent motorcycles or bicycles. ✉ *155 Moo 6, Parkphrek Rd., 71000* ☎ *034/513222* ⊕ *www.littlecreekhideawayvalley.com* ⇗ *50 bungalows* ⚬ *In-room: no a/c (some). In-hotel: restaurant, bar, pool, public Internet* ▤ *MC, V.*

$$–$$$ 🏨 **Felix River Kwai Resort.** Kanchanaburi's first luxury hotel is a bit faded now, but it's still a good value. Polished wood floors and wicker headboards decorate the cool, airy rooms. The large pool set amid tropical gardens is a great place to relax. The hotel is within walking distance of Kanchanaburi; the River Kwai bridge is 300 meters from the hotel. Rates include a buffet breakfast. ✉ *9/1 Moo 3, Tambon Thamakham, 71000* ☎ *034/551000, 02/634–4111 in Bangkok* ⊕ *www. felixriverkwai.co.th* ⇗ *255 rooms* ⚬ *In-room: safe. In-hotel: 2 restaurants, 2 tennis courts, pool, gym, spa* ▤ *AE, DC, MC, V.*

$$ 🏨 **River Kwai Village.** In the jungles of the River Kwai Valley, this resort organizes elephant riding and rafting trips, as well as the usual city excursions. Most of the simple rooms are in five single-story log cabins. You have to be slightly more adventurous to stay in one of the "raftels" (rooms set on rafts floating in the river), but they have similar amenities to the rooms on dry land. The cafeteria-style restaurant offers a combination of Thai and Western dishes, but it's more fun to eat at the casual restaurant on one of the rafts. The resort provides transportation to and from Bangkok. ✉ *72/12 Moo 4, Tambon Thasao, Amphoe Sai Yok, 71150* ☎ *034/634454, 02/251–7828 in Bangkok* ⊕ *www. riverkwaivillage.com* ⇗ *165 rooms, 26 raft houses* ⚬ *In-room: refrigerator. In-hotel: 2 restaurants, room service, pool, laundry service* ▤ *AE, DC, MC, V* ⍾ *BP.*

$ 🏨 **Kasem Island Resort.** Perched on an island in the middle of the river, this resort has one of the area's most enviable locations. Choose between bungalows with private, hot-water bathrooms and air-conditioning, or cheaper bamboo huts on rafts, with fans and private cold-water bathrooms. All have balconies and river views. Limited parking available on the mainland and the ferry is free for guests. ✉ *44–48 Chaichumpol Rd., 71000* ☎ *034/513359, 02/255–3603 in Bangkok* ⇗ *36 rooms bungalows and raft houses* ⚬ *In-room: no a/c (some), no phone, no TV (some). In-hotel: restaurant, pool* ▤ *MC, V.*

$ 🏨 **Pavilion Rim Kwai Thani Resort.** This resort near the Erawan Waterfall caters to wealthy Bangkok residents who want to retreat into the country without giving up their creature comforts. Tropical flora surrounds the complex, and the River Kwai flows serenely past. The minimally furnished rooms have polished wood floors and balcony views. The large dining room serves Thai and Western dishes. ✉ *79/2 Moo 4, Km 9, Ladya-Erawan Rd., Tambon Wangdong, 71190* ☎ *034/515772* ⇗ *200 rooms* ⚬ *In-hotel: restaurant, tennis courts, pool, gym, spa* ▤ *AE, MC, V* ⍾ *BP.*

¢ 🏨 **Sam's House.** This property is a popular launching pad for treks, which the staff here can arrange. The air-conditioned floating rooms are nice but a bit cramped and more expensive than those set away from the river.

Motorbikes (B150 per day) and cars (B1,200 per day) are available for rent. ⊠ *14/2 River Kwai Rd., 71000* ☎ *034/515956* ⊕ *www. samsguesthouse.com* ➳ *36 rooms* ↺ *In-room: no a/c (some), no TV. In-hotel: restaurant* ⊟ *No credit cards.*

Sports & the Outdoors

RAFTING Rafting trips on the Kwai Yai or Mae Khlong rivers, which take at least a full day, let you venture far into the jungle. The mammoth rafts, which resemble houseboats, are often divided into separate sections for eating, sleeping, and sunbathing. ⚠ **Be careful when taking a dip—the currents can sometimes suck a swimmer down.** The cost of a one-day trip starts at about B300. Longer trips are also available. The tour companies listed below or your hotel can help you arrange rafting trips. The Tourism Authority of Thailand office on Saengchuto Road can also be of assistance.

TREKKING Jungle treks of one to four days are possible all over the region. They typically include bamboo rafting, elephant riding, visits to Karen villages, and sampling local food (sometimes a cultural performance is also included). To ensure safety and reliability, stick to tour companies with TAT (Tourism Authority of Thailand) licenses, which will be prominently displayed on the premises.

Good Times Travel's (⊠ 63/1 River Kwai Rd. ☎ 034/624441 ⊕ www.good times_travel.com) trips take in all the usual highlights, including national parks, rafting, caves, Karen village stays, and the Tiger Temple.

RSP Jumbo Travel (⊠ 3/13 Chao Kun Nen Rd. ☎ 034/514906 ⊕ www. jumboriverkwai.com) offers everything from day trips to weeklong itineraries that include rafting, elephant riding, and off-road adventures. They also organize theme party nights; one of the most popular includes dinner and a Thai classical music concert at the Muang Singh Historical Park. Some tours are combined with stays at upmarket hotels for those who like more comfort with their adventure.

Shopping

Blue sapphires from the Bo Phloi mines, 45 km (28 mi) north of Kanchanaburi town, are for sale at many shops and stalls in the plaza near the bridge. The price is determined by the size and color of the stone, and, as usual, your bargaining skills. You'll do the best when there are few tourists around and business is slow. Stick to stalls with licenses displayed, and never buy from touts promising outrageously cheap prices.

Around Kanchanaburi Province

Muang Singh Historical Park

❻ *45 km (28 mi) northwest of Kanchanaburi; 1 hr by train.*

King Chulalongkorn reportedly discovered this 13th- to 14th-century Khmer settlement while traveling along the Kwai Noi River. The restored remains of the city range from mere foundations to a largely intact, well-preserved monument and building complex. There are also examples of Khmer statues and pottery and a prehistoric burial site. You can drive or cycle around the large grounds of Muang Singh Historical Park with the aid of taped commentary in English, Thai, or French, available at the park's entrance. Bicycle rentals cost around B20 per hour. If you don't want to make the 45-minute drive, take the train from Kanchanaburi to Tha Kilen station (B10, one hour); the park is a 1-km (½-mi) walk (turn right when leaving the station) away. There's a small café and lodgings on the grounds. ⊠ *Tha Kilen* ☒ *B40* ⊙ *Daily 8:30–5.*

Ban Khao Museum, a small two-room exhibition of 4,000-year-old Neolithic remains, is a short drive away. It may be possible to hitch a lift here. ⊠ *Ban Khao* ☒ *B30* ⊙ *Wed.–Sun. 9–4.*

Tiger Temple

❼ *25 km (15 mi) northwest of Kanchanaburi; 40 mins by bus.*

Tiger Temple (or Wat Pa Luanta Bua Yannasampanno) is a forest monastery that houses several kinds of animals on its grounds, most notably 10 tigers that have been cared for since 1999. Three cubs were born in 2003. The tigers are let out of their cages at 3 PM daily, when visitors arrive and line up to touch them. It's a unique attraction, but the monastery has caused quite a bit of controversy. Locals' concerns range from lack of safety to the possibility of the tigers being drugged to the presence of commercialism unbefitting a temple (entry fees have steadily increased, which the temple says is necessary to fund the creation of a larger environment for the tigers). In fact, many tour operators claim they'd rather not promote the sight, but have no choice because they can't afford to lose customers. The Tourism Authority of Thailand reports that there have been no cases of injury to visitors, but the risks are obvious, and you should think carefully before paying a visit. If you still insist on going, look for the sign posted on the right of the road to Sai Yok National Park. ⊠ *Km 21, Rte. 323* ☎ *034/531557 or 034/531558* ☒ *B300* ⊙ *Daily 9–4.*

Erawan National Park

★ ❽ *65 km (40 mi) northwest of Kanchanaburi; 1½ hrs by bus.*

Some of the most spectacular scenery of Kanchanaburi Province can be found in Erawan National Park. The main attraction is **Erawan Waterfall,** which has seven tiers; the topmost supposedly resembles the mythical three-headed elephant (Erawan) belonging to the Hindu god Indra. You'll need to make a rather steep 2-km (1-mi) hike to get to the top (it should take about two hours). ⚠ **Comfortable footwear is essential and don't forget to bring water!** You can swim at each level of the waterfall (levels two through five are the most popular). The first tier has a small café, and there are several others near the visitor center. There are also accommodations (bungalows for B800 sleeping up to eight, or tents sleeping up to six) in two locations—the ones nearest the waterfall are quieter.

The park is massive; the waterfall is near the main entrance—so too are the visitor center and accommodations. Other highlights of the park include five caves. One of them, **Ta Duang,** has wall paintings, and another, **Ruea,** has prehistoric coffins. The caves are much farther away, and accessed via a different road. About 2 km (1 mi) from the park is Erawan Village; songthaews leave from its market and travel to the park entrance and the caves (B500–B600). The bus to Erawan leaves Kanchanaburi's second bus station every 50 minutes; the trip takes 90 minutes. It stops at the Erawan Village market in the morning and at the park in the afternoon. If you arrive in the morning, take a songthaew from the market to the park. ⊠ *Km 44, Rte. 3199* ☎ *034/574222* ⊕ *www.dnp.go.th* ▣ *B400* ⊗ *Daily 8–4:30.*

Hellfire Pass

❾ *70 km (45 mi) northwest of Kanchanaburi; 2 hrs by bus.*

The museum at Hellfire Pass is a moving memorial to the Allied prisoners of war who built the River Kwai railway, 12,399 of whom died in the process. Along with a film and exhibits, there's a 4½-km (3-mi) walk along a section of the railway, including the notorious Hellfire Pass, one of the most grueling sections built. The pass got its name from the fire lanterns that flickered on the mountain walls as the men worked through the night. ■ TIP→ **Many people do the walk in the early morning before the museum opens, and before it gets too hot.** Allow 2½ hours round-trip for the walk. Take plenty of water and a snack; there's a small shack near the museum that sells drinks, but not much food. The pass can be busy at weekends (when an average of 500 people a day visit), and on ANZAC Day (April 25). The trail is open all hours, and admission to the museum is free. ⊠ *Km 66, Rte. 323* ☎ *01/754–2098* ⊗ *Museum daily 9–4.*

Sai Yok National Park

❿ *97 km (62 mi) northwest of Kanchanaburi; 2 hrs by bus.*

The main attraction in Sai Yok National Park is **Sai Yok Yai waterfall,** which flows into the Kwai Noi River. The waterfall, an easy walk from the visitor center, is single tier and not nearly as spectacular as Erawan. More unique are the **bat caves** (2-km [1 mi] past the waterfall) that house the thumb-size Kitti's Hog-nosed bat, the world's smallest mammal, found only in these caves. You can rent flashlights at the visitor center.

There are park-run accommodations at Sai Yok Yai in tents (from B85 per person) and guesthouses (from B800 for up to four people). The private raft houses on the Kwai Noi River (B500) are more scenic options. There's no electricity at these guesthouses; light is provided by oil lamp. Sai Yok View Raft guesthouse (01/857–2284) has more isolated raft houses (B500–B700) upstream. The raft houses near the waterfall have cheap restaurants that are more pleasant than the food stalls near the visitor center.

Buses to Sai Yok Yai leave Kanchanaburi every 30 minutes from 6 AM to 6:30 PM. The two-hour trip costs B38.

Also within the national park's boundaries—though not accessible from the Sai Yok visitor center—are **Sai Yok Noi Waterfall** and other notable caves. Despite being higher than Sai Yok Yai, Sai Yok Noi has less water, but there's enough to swim in from June to November, and the area is often packed with Thai families on weekends. It's 2 km (1 mi) from Nam Tok Station, the terminus of the Death Railway. Trains leave

Kanchanaburi each day at 5:52 AM and 10:[...]
agricultural areas then into thick jungles and p[...]
as they cling to the mountainside; the journey [...]
natively, buses run to and from Kanchanabu[...]
6 AM to 5 PM (B25) in half the time it takes or [...]
ing, take Route 323; Sai Yok Noi is at Km 6 [...]
the park are Lawa Cave, 1 km (½ mi) before S[...]
ung Cave (turn left off Route 323 after the [...]
terfall). ⊠ *Sai Yok Yai, Km 97, Rte. 323* ☎ 034/[...]
⊕ *www.dnp.go.th* ☒ *B400* ⊙ *Daily 8–6.*

Kanchanaburi & Environs Essentials

Transportation

BY BUS

Air-conditioned buses leave from Bangkok's Southern Bus Terminal for
Kanchanaburi (two hours, B79) every 20 minutes from 5 AM to 10:30
PM. Tickets are sold on a first-come, first-served basis, but services are
so frequent that it's seldom a problem finding an empty seat.

🚏 **Southern Bus Terminal** ⊠ Pinklao-Nakomchaisri Rd., Talingchan, Bangkok ☎ 02/
435–5012.

BY CAR

Allow two hours to Kanchanaburi along Route 4. The first half is on a
busy truck route that continues to southern Thailand, but the second
half more pleasant, through agricultural land. The road to Kanchanaburi
passes through Nakhon Pathomp.

BY TAXI & SONGTHAEW

In Kanchanaburi town options for getting around include pedicabs and
motorcycles with sidecars. Songthaews are better for longer forays. You
can just flag them down, and often they stop to ask if you want a ride.
A few tuk-tuks and taxis are in town, but they are harder to find.

BY TRAIN

Trains to Kanchanaburi leave from Bangkok Noi Railway Station, on
the Thonburi side of the Chao Phraya River.

Two daily trains leave Bangkok Noi at 7:45 AM and 1:50 PM (three hours,
B100 one way). On weekends and holidays, a special excursion train
(B75) leaves Hua Lamphong Station at 6:30 AM and returns at 7:30 PM,
stopping at Nakhon Pathom and Kanchanaburi.

Contacts & Resources

BANKS & EXCHANGING SERVICES

ATMs and exchange facilities are common in Kanchanaburi.

EMERGENCIES

🏥 Hospital **Thanakan Hospital** ⊠ Saengchuto Rd., Kanchanaburi ☎ 034/622360.

There is a TAT (tourist information) office in Kanchanaburi.

🔲 **TAT** ✉ 325 Saengchuto Rd., Kanchanaburi ☎ 034/623691.

NGKLABURI

⓫ *203 km (127 mi) northwest of Kanchanaburi; 3 hrs by bus.*

Sangklaburi is a sleepy town on a large lake created by the Khao Laem Dam. There was once a Mon village here, but when the dam was built in 1983, it was almost completely covered by water. (Some parts, including a temple, are still visible beneath the surface.) The Mon were relocated to a village on the lakeshore opposite Sangklaburi. The village has a temple with Indian and Burmese influences and a bronze-color pyramid chedi that's illuminated beautifully at night. Also in the village is a dry-goods market selling Chinese and Burmese clothes and trinkets, with Mon dishes available at nearby food stalls. You can reach the village by car or boat or you can walk from Sangklaburi across the country's longest wooden bridge.

The Mon arrived here 50 years ago from Myanmar, seeking religious sanctuary, and they are not allowed to travel to other areas without permission. Due to its closeness to Myanmar's border, Sangklaburi is also home to Karen and Bangladeshi communities, and its small **night market** (from 4 PM to 7 PM) attracts itinerant ethnic stalls selling food, clothing, and trinkets. Jungle trekking and visits to Karen villages are popular activities for visitors; trips can be arranged through the guesthouses listed below. You can also cross into Myanmar at Three Pagodas Pass with a passport photo and $10 (U.S. currency only—there's an exchange facility at the border), but you cannot renew Thai visas at this checkpoint, so you won't be allowed to go any farther than the Myanmar border town, Phayathonzu.

Where to Stay & Eat

Six or seven guesthouses are on the lakeside road, all with views of the wooden bridge and the Mon village. Temple's lights shimmer on the water at night. From the bus station take a motorcycle taxi (B10) or songthaew (B60). They all have restaurants, and most offer Burmese and Mon food such as *haeng leh curry* (a country dish made of whatever ingredients are on hand, but often including pork) and the coconut-and-noodle dish *kao sawy,* usually made with chicken. Nightlife consists of a shophouse karaoke bar on the same road as the guesthouses, and a single rice soup stall at the market that sells beer and local whiskey until 2 AM.

¢ ✕🔲 **Burmese Inn.** These homey bungalows, run by an Austrian and his Thai wife, are on a garden hillside above the lake. The rooms are filled with pictures and knickknacks and some are directly over the water. The room TVs only have Thai-language stations. The terrace restaurant (¢–$) has fish dishes and other Thai and Burmese options, including laphae to, a salad of nuts, beans, and fermented tea leaves. It also serves Western breakfasts, salads, and sandwiches. ✉ 52/3 Moo 3, Tambon Nongloo ☎ 034/595146 🖂 burmeseinn@yahoo.com ➷ 19 rooms ⌂ In-room: no a/c (some). In-hotel: restaurant ▭ No credit cards.

¢–$ 🏠 **Pornphailin Riverside.** The bungalows are on the water's edge, but the guesthouse is a long walk from town. All rooms have balconies and panoramic views of the lake; yet some have more windows than others. Larger rooms are less expensive on weekdays. The huge terrace restaurant serves Thai food. ✉ *60/3 Moo 1, Soi Tonpeung* ☎ *034/595322* ➥ *21 bungalows* ⚭ *In-hotel: restaurant* ⊟ *No credit cards.*

¢ 🏠 **P Guest House.** Stone bungalows with narrow log ceilings are in a stepped garden that leads down to the lakeside. Rooms are mainly fan-cooled with shared bathrooms, but three have air-conditioning and private bathrooms and cost more. The latter are on the lakeside (look at all of them to get the best view). You can rent kayaks (B100 per hour) and motorcycles (B200 per day), and the owners organize treks that include a longtail boat ride on the lake to see the submerged temple, elephant riding, and rafting (packages start at B900 per person, and include one night's stay at the guesthouse). The large terrace restaurant has an inexpensive Thai menu with a few Burmese dishes, as well as pastas, sandwiches, and Western breakfasts. ✉ *81/2 Moo 1, Tambon Nongloo* ☎ *034/595061* ⊕ *www.pguesthouse.com* ➥ *20 rooms* ⚭ *In-room: no a/c (some), no TV. In-hotel: restaurant* ⊟ *No credit cards.*

Sangklaburi Essentials

Transportation

BY BUS

There are no direct buses from Bangkok to Sangklaburi; you'll have to change buses in Kanchanaburi. Buses to Sangklaburi (two hours, B79) leave Kanchanaburi every 20 minutes from 5 AM–4 PM.

BY CAR

To Sangklaburi it's a very rewarding 2½- to 3-hour drive from Kanchanaburi on Route 323, along good roads beside fields of pomelo, corn, and banana palms, with Myanmar's mist-shrouded mountains in the distance. The journey then winds through the mountains.

BY TAXI

Motorcycle taxis are the favored way to get around this sprawling provincial town. They are so common and so easy to find, that besides walking, they're the main mode of travel for locals. In the rainy season, you get a bit wet, but that goes with the territory. For longer trips, or if you aren't comfortable on the motorcycle taxis, you can ask your hotel or guesthouse to arrange transport in a car.

Contacts & Resources

EMERGENCIES

🏥 Hospital **Sangklaburi Hospital** ✉ Sukhaphiban 2, Sangklaburi ☎ 034/595058.

VISITOR INFORMATION

The TAT (tourist information) office in Kanchanaburi covers Sangklaburi. 🏥 **Kanchanaburi** ✉ 325 Saengchuto Rd. ☎ 034/577200 or 034/623691.

The Central Plains

AYUTTHAYA, SUKHOTHAI, AND TAK PROVINCE

Wat Phra Si Sanphet was once the home of 33 kings.

WORD OF MOUTH

"If you do one of the tours of Ayutthaya, you go out on a bus and return to Bangkok on a boat. I felt very sorry for those who showed up on the boat for their hot afternoon tours of the ruins as we were leaving. The boat trip back on the Chao Phraya was a highlight in itself, with great photo ops along the way."

—Craig

"Seeing Sukhothai on bicycle is the best way to experience it."
—Vagabond

WELCOME TO
THE CENTRAL PLAINS

TOP REASONS
TO GO

★ **Sukhothai's Monuments**
It is easy to spend days of
speechless soul-searching
after encountering the mystical monuments of Thai-
land's 13th-century capital.

★ **River Views in Ayut-
thaya** This city, which can
be visited as a day trip
from Bangkok, combines
great river views—most of
its hotels offer them—with
an island full of fascinating
wats.

★ **Loi Krathong** The Central Plains, Sukhothai in
particular, is one of the
best areas to experience
this festival. Thais set elaborate candle-bearing floats
out into the river, creating
a memorable light display.

★ **Myanmar for a Day**
Myanmar (Burma), a coun-
try ruled by a military
junta with a bad human
rights record, is a mystery
to most people. A day trip
across the border from
Mae Sot may not provide
a deep understanding of
the country's situation, but
it's a start.

1 Ayutthaya & Environs.
Within easy reach of Bangkok,
Ayutthaya is a historically significant ruin, and once one of the
country's most important.
Nearby Bang Pa-In, with its famous Royal Palace, and Lopburi, with its monkey-infested
temples, are a bit farther off
the beaten track.

2 Sukhothai & Environs. To
history buffs, the soul of the
country is to be found in the
cities of Sukhothai and Si
Satchanalai. These strongholds
of architecture and culture
evoke Thailand's ancient civilizations, while Sukhothai's
well-developed tourist industry
make it the modern-day hub for
exploring the region.

Wat Sri Sawai Sukhothai

3 Tak Province. Journeying farther north, by combinations of
minibus, bus, and songthaews,
will take you from historic to geographic majesty. Within the
cooler climes of the north are
Mae Sot, a frontierlike city bordering Myanmar, and
Umphang, with its mountainous, forested isolation, natural
grandeur, hill tribe villages, and
ecotourism opportunities.

Tha
Song Yang   *Bhumiphol
Reservoir*   Mae Ping
Nat'l Park

105   Ban Tak   1

                          Tak
105

Mae Sot

1090

BURMA
(MYANMAR)   Mae Wong
National

Khlong Lan

Umphang

0   30 mi

0   30 km

Buddha image at Wat Yai Chaya Mongkol Ayutthaya Historical Park

GETTING ORIENTED

The Central Plains is one of the most overlooked regions of Thailand. Some people take a side trip from Bangkok to the ancient capital of Ayutthaya, but fewer venture farther north to the even older cities at Sukhothai and Si Satchanalai to some of the most breathtaking ruins in the country. Although some sights are decidedly off the beaten track, it isn't difficult to reach the Central Plains. If you have more than a passing interest in Thailand's history, you should make this part of your itinerary.

Si Satchanalai
101
102

Swankhalok

Sukhothai
12   New Sukhothai

Ramkhamhaeng Nat'l Park
101
Phitsanulok

115

Kamphaeng Phet
Phichit
113   11

117

1084

1

Mae Nam Nan

Nong Bua   225

Nakhon Sawan

Sawang Arom
32

Nong Chang
11

Tak Fa

21   Chai Badan

333   Chai Nat

1

Chao Phraya

340   32

Sing Buri

Dan Chang

Sam Chuk
311

21

Lopburi

1

Nong Phru

Suphan Buri

U-Thong
340

333   Ang Thong

Saraburi
329

Ayutthaya

347

1

321   Bang Pa-In

Kamphaeng Saen   Pathum Thani   1

When to Go

The driest months, between November and February, are the coolest and the busiest, with refreshing temperatures enticing travelers. From March to June, this central area, like much of Thailand, becomes almost unbearably hot; it's only slightly cooled by the rains that fall between June and early October.

November's amazing Loi Krathong festival sees both Ayutthaya and Sukhothai's historical parks explode with orchestrated light-and-sound shows. Tourists fill the towns' guesthouses and hotels, so make sure to book as soon as possible.

Safety

The cities are pretty safe, with common sense being the only precaution needed. However, do beware the monkeys in Lopburi. They are a cheeky bunch and have been known to steal anything that you can't hold onto, from your coffee cup to your camera.

Rubies, brought in from Burmese mines, are a big draw at Mae Sot, but unless you know what you're looking at, you might find yourself with substandard or fake gems, as scams on unsuspecting visitors are common.

Outdoor Adventures & Trekking

Eco-trekking options are abundant in Mae Sot and Umphang. Most center around Umphang's Thee Lor Su waterfall and range from two-day to seven-day tours (B5,500–B19,000). You can raft, trek, and ride elephants, taking in Karen villages, caves, mountains, and waterfalls. One-day or half-day tours around Mae Sot are also available and typically cost B1,500 for a full day or B350 for a half day.

Mae Sot's brightest and best-organized tour operator is **Max One Tour** (✉ 269/2 Intarakeeree Rd., Mae Sot ☎ 055/542941 or 055/542942 ⊕ www.maxonetour. com). They provide a number of tours, including a standard itinerary to Thee Lor Su waterfall and the newer Mae Sot–to–Kee District white-water rafting route. All of their tour options can be found, along with prices and previous travelers' comments, on their Web site.

No. 4 Guesthouse (✉ 736 Intarakeeree Rd., Mae Sot ☎ 055/544976 or 01/785–2095 ⊕ www.geocities. com/no4guesthouse/) is another reliable option in Mae Sot. Mr. Oom is a true adventurer and he can put together customized tours if none of his standard tours meet your needs. Note that you should seek other accommodations.

The other big tour company in the area is **Thee Lor Su Riverside Resort** (✉ Hwy. 1090, Umphang ☎ 055/561010, 038/312050, or 01/862–0533), based in the resort of the same name in Umphang. They have a unique tour of Thee Lor Su waterfall involving an initial flight over the falls and its surrounding area in a Cessna. After the first night's stay, you leave early and the rafting begins. A three-day/two-night program costs B5,500, but there has to be a minimum of five people for the trip to happen. Book well in advance. The one disadvantage is that, unlike its competitors, the resort can't guarantee English-speaking guides.

The Ultimate Tour Guide

Expert birder and excellent tour guide **Anavaj Chai-mongkol** (✉ 14/2836 Bua Thong Thani Village, Kanchanaphisek Rd., Bang Buaq Thong District, Nonthaburi ☎ 02/922–7934, 08/1792–1130 mobile), who goes by "Wat," takes individuals or groups in his SUV anywhere in the region, based on your preferences. This wise, English-speaking guide will show you around the monuments in Sukhothai and Ayutthaya; orchestrate esoteric eating expeditions; lead you on a cross-border excursion from Mae Sot to Myanmar, another country he knows well; take you on a longer journey combining the Central Plains and Isan regions; and, of course, take you bird-watching. Wat's story is extraordinary: after his first wife died, he lived in the forest for 11 years before becoming a bird-watching guide and even an erstwhile part of the guerrilla forces across the border in Myanmar, helping to fight that country's totalitarian leadership. A documentary film about Wat's life is currently touring the festival circuit in Germany. Prices run US$50–$110 per day, plus gas and other expenses, and it's money well spent.

Regional Cuisine Highlights

Although the region is not known for its cuisine, the Central Plains will feed you well if you avoid the tourist traps and stick to the local places. The staples of the region include curries made from local fowl such as water hens and partridge; a lot of fresh local fish, such as snakehead and cottonfish grilled over charcoal (*pla chon pao glua*); and a number of milder Chinese-inspired dishes, such as *gaeng jeut woon sen* (noodle consommé) and the ever-present *kuaytiew nahm* (noodle soup). More unusual is curried rat, which you'll find at stalls along the highway and at very local markets. Peruse local markets, which have cheap fast food and *khao lad gaeng* (canteen-style) restaurants that are reliable and full of variety.

Hotel Know-How

Because relatively few tourists visit the Central Plains, most hotels and guesthouses cater chiefly to a business clientele. There are some top-class hotels, but most accommodations are much more modest than in Bangkok or Chiang Mai. As elsewhere in Thailand, standards of cleanliness are high and even the most basic room will invariably have fresh linen and towels.

A new phenomenon is the appearance of lodgings run by hospitable and knowledgeable local people anxious to help visitors get to know this seemingly remote region. They open up their homes to paying guests and show them around for a modest fee. Listed in this chapter are a few of the most reputable.

For budget-conscious travelers, rooms in the Central Plains are truly a bargain—even the most expensive hotels charge less than US$60 a night. Don't expect the full range of facilities, however. Such refinements as room phones and TVs can be rare outside the cities.

WHAT IT COSTS In Baht

	$$$$	$$$	$$	$	¢
RESTAURANTS	Over B400	B301–B400	B201–B300	B100–B200	under B100
HOTELS	over B6,000	B4,001–B6,000	B2,001–B4,000	B1,000–B2,000	under B1,000

AYUTTHAYA & ENVIRONS

Updated by
Robin
Goldstein

With 92% of its land used for agriculture, it isn't surprising that Ayutthaya is known as Asia's rice field. To its west is the Suphan Buri and its continuing rice paddies, while to the northeast the region borders with Lopburi, approaching the northeastern plateau with rising forested hills. The bountiful plain has been home to Thailand's most influential and ancient Kingdoms: Lopburi and Ayutthaya.

Ayutthaya and its environs represent an important historical journey that traces Thailand's cultural developments from Buddhist art and architecture to modern government and language. ■ TIP➔ **Ayutthaya gets the most attention, drawing day-trippers from Bangkok, but a visit to Lopburi, with its Khmer temples and French-influenced Royal Palace, lends even more historical context to the museums and ransacked ruins found at Ayutthaya's historical park and the 18th-century Royal Palace in nearby Bang Pa-In.**

Ayutthaya

★ *72 km (45 mi) north of Bangkok.*

Ayutthaya was named by King Ramatibodi after a mythical kingdom of the gods portrayed in the pages of the Ramayana. The city was completed in 1350 and was a powerhouse of Southeast Asia. The city was originally chosen as a capital for its eminently defendable position: it lies in a bend of the Chao Phraya River, where it meets the Pa Sak and Lopburi rivers—to completely surround their capital with water, early residents dug a curving canal along the northern perimeter, linking the Chao Phraya to the Lopburi. However, Ayutthaya quickly changed from being essentially a military base to an important center for the arts, medicine, and technology. Trade routes opened up Siam's first treaty with a Western nation (Portugal, in 1516) and soon after, the Dutch, English, Japanese and, most influentially, the French, accelerated Ayutthaya's role in international relations under King Narai the Great. After Narai's death in 1688 the kingdom plunged into internal conflict.

Today Ayutthaya is a carefully preserved World Heritage Site and a visit provides a fascinating snapshot of ancient Siam. Scattered ruins lay testament to the kingdom's brutal demise at the hands of the Burmese in 1767. Although the modern town is on the eastern bank of the Pa Sak, most of the ancient temples are on the island. An exception is Wat Yai Chai Mongkol, a short tuk-tuk ride away.

■ TIP➔ **Ayutthaya is best appreciated in historical context, and a visit to the Historical Study Center can improve the experience for a first time visitor.** Certain sites are guaranteed to take your breath away, with Wat Phra Si Sanphet, Wat Yai Chai Mongkol, Wat Phra Mahathat, and Wat Ratchaburana being the best. Aside from the temples, Ayutthaya's friendly guesthouses, welcoming people, and floating restaurants make for a refreshing change from Bangkok. However, because Ayutthaya is in such easy reach of Bangkok, hordes of day-trippers roam the city during daylight hours, making Ayutthaya feel somewhat more touristy than the rest of the region—at least until the sun sets.

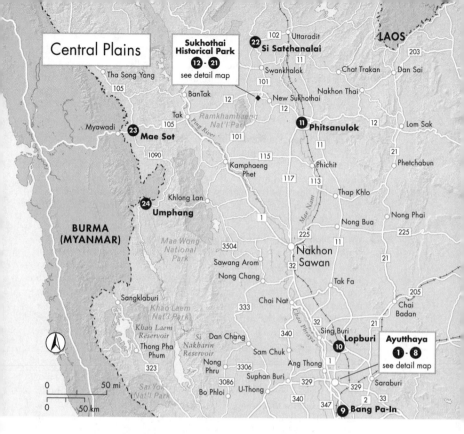

Most people find that a morning or afternoon is sufficient to see Ayutthaya. For a three-hour tour of the sites, tuk-tuks can be hired for about B700; a three-wheel samlor (small bicycle cab) costs about B500.

What to See

❶ Ayutthaya Historical. This educational center, financed by the Japanese government, houses fascinating audiovisual displays about Ayutthaya. Models of the city as a rural village, as a port city, as an administrative center, and as a royal capital reveal the site's history. ⊠ *Rotchana Rd. between Si San Phet and Chikun Rds.* ☎ *035/245124* ✎ *B100* ⊙ *Weekdays 9–4:30, weekends 9–5.*

❷ Chao Sam Phraya National Museum. This dated museum on spacious grounds is ostensibly a showcase of Buddhist sculpture, including Dvaravati (Lamphun), Lopburi, Ayutthayan, and U-Thong styles. In truth, the artifacts are poorly presented, and the best attraction is an upstairs vault in the first building, which has relics (such as a jewel-covered sword) of two of Wat Ratchaburana's original princes. ⊠ *Rotchana Rd. at Si San Phet Rd.* ☎ *035/241587* ✎ *B30* ⊙ *Wed.–Sun. 9–4.*

Elephant Kraal. Thailand's only intact royal kraal was built to hold and train elephants for martial service; it was last used during King Chulalongkorn's reign in 1903. The restored teak stockade acts as little other than a gateway to the Royal Elephant Kraal Village behind it, which cares for about 100 elephants. Though it looks like a working village, it's primarily a business—rehabilitating and parenting elephants for work on tours around Ayutthaya and also for TV and film productions (most recently Oliver Stone's *Alexander*). ✛ *5 km (3 mi) north of Ayutthaya, on Hwy. 3060 to Panead* ☎ *035/321982* ☉ *Daily 8–5.*

⑥ Viharn Phra Mongkol Bopitr. This is one of the modern structures in the Old City. The site's original temple was built in 1610. When the roof collapsed in 1767, one of Thailand's biggest and most revered bronze Buddha images was revealed. It lay here uncovered for almost 200 years before the huge modern viharn was built in 1951. Historians have dated the image back to 1538. ✉ *Off Naresuan Rd.* ☜ *Free* ☉ *Weekdays 8–4:30, weekends 8–5:30.*

★ **⑦ Wat Phanan Choeng.** This bustling merit-making temple complex on the banks of the Lopburi River is an interesting diversion from the dormant ruins that dominate Ayutthaya. A short B3 ferry ride across the river sets the scene for its dramatic origins. The temple was built in 1324 (26 years before Ayutthaya's rise to power) by a U-Thong king in atonement for the death of his fiancée. Instead of bringing his bride, a Chinese princess, into the city himself, the king arranged an escort for her. Distraught at what she interpreted to be a lackluster welcome, the princess threw herself into the river (at the site of the current temple) and drowned. ✉ *East of the Old City* ☜ *Free* ☉ *Daily 8–5.*

③ Wat Phra Mahathat. Building began on this royal monastery in 1374 and was completed during the reign of King Ramesuan (1388–95). Today, tree-shaded grounds contain what's left of its 140-foot brick prang. The prang collapsed twice between 1610 to 1628, and again in the early 20th century, and today barely reflects its former glory. The stunted ruins and beheaded Buddhas that remain in Wat Phra Mahathat are a result of the Burmese sacking this once revered temple in 1767. ✉ *Naresuan Rd. at Chee Kun Rd.* ☜ *B30* ☉ *Daily 8–6:30.*

⑤ Wat Phra Si Sanphet. This wat was the largest temple in Ayutthaya, and where the royal family worshipped. The 14th-century structure lost its 50-foot Buddha in 1767, when the invading Burmese melted it down for its 374 pounds of gold. The trio of chedis survived and are the best existing examples of Ayutthaya architecture; enshrining the ashes of several kings, they stand as eternal memories of a golden age. If the design looks familiar, it's because Wat Phra Si Sanphet was the model for Wat Phra Keo at the Grand Palace in Bangkok. Beyond the monuments you can find a grassy field where the Royal Palace once stood. The foundation is all that remains of the palace that was home to 33 kings. ✉ *Naresuan Rd.* ☜ *B30* ☉ *Daily 7–6:30.*

④ Wat Ratchaburana. Directly north across the road from Wat Phra Mahathat is Wat Ratchaburana, its Khmer-style prang dominating the skyline. King Borommaracha II (Chao Sam Phraya) built this temple in 1424 to commemorate the death of his two older brothers, whose duel for the throne ironically left their younger brother as king. Their relics were buried in a crypt directly under the base of the prang, which was

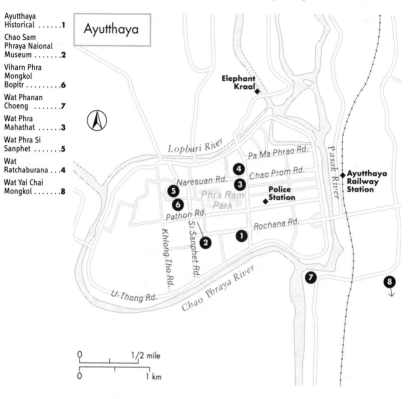

Ayutthaya

Elephant
Kraal

Lopburi River

Pa Ma Phrao Rd.

Naresuan Rd.   Chao Prom Rd.

Pasak River

Ayutthaya
Railway
Station

Phra Ram
Park

Police
Station

Ayutthaya
Railway
Station

Pathon Rd.

Si Sanphet Rd.

Khlong Tho Rd.

Rochana Rd.

U-Thong Rd.

Chao Phraya River

0 ___ 1/2 mile
0 ___ 1 km

looted in 1957. Arrests were made, however, and the retrieved treasures can now be seen in the Chao Sam Phraya National Museum.
✉ *Naresuan Rd. and Chee Kun Rd.* 🖼 *B30* ⊙ *Daily 8:30–4:30.*

8 **Wat Yai Chai Mongkol.** The enormous chedi at Wat Yai Chai Mongkol,
the largest in Ayutthaya, was constructed by King Naresuan after he defeated the Burmese crown prince during a battle atop elephants in 1593.
(A recent painting of the battle is one of the highlights of the temple.)
The chedi is now leaning quite a bit, as later enlargements are weighing down on the foundation. The complex, dating from 1357, was totally restored in 1982. Linger a while to pay your respects to the huge
reclining Buddha or climb to the top for a spectacular view. ■ TIP➔ **The
site closes at 5 PM, but you can enter after that if the gates are left open, as
they often are. The view at sunset is beautiful, and you'll completely escape
the crowds.** ⊕ *About 5 km (3 mi) southeast of the Old City on the Ayutthaya to Bang Pa-In Rd.* 🖼 *B20, free after 5 PM* ⊙ *Daily 8–5.*

Where to Stay & Eat

If you're a romantic, a stay in Ayutthaya allows you to wander among
the ruins at night. Since most tourists leave Ayutthaya by 4 PM, those
who stay are treated to genuine Thai hospitality. Don't expect luxury,
however; Ayutthaya has only modest hotels and simple restaurants.

★ **$$–$$$$**   ✕ **Pasak River Queen.** Enjoy a leisurely two-hour ride along the Pa Sak River while filling your belly with grilled seafood and some fantastic Thai dishes. The 350-passenger boat departs nightly at 6:30 PM. There's a B79 cover charge and dishes are ordered à la carte. The dock's a bit outside town; it's worth booking transportation to and from the dock ahead of time. During the summer rains, boats sometimes do not run in high-water conditions. ✉ *116 Moo 2, Borpong* ☎ *035/724520, 035/ 724504, or 035/724519* ▤ *AE, DC, MC, V.*

¢–$$ ✕ **Pae Krung Kao.** If you can't resist dining outdoors beside the Pa Sak River, this good option is near the Pridi Damrong Bridge. You can also drop by for a beer. ✉ *4 U-Thong Rd.* ☎ *035/241555* ▤ *MC, V.*

¢–$ ✕ **Tevaraj.** For good, spicy food, head for this unpretentious restaurant behind Ayutthaya's railway station. The *tom kha gai* (chicken soup with coconut) is excellent, as are the always-fresh fish dishes. ✉ *74 Wat Pa Kho Rd.* ☎ *No phone* ▤ *No credit cards.*

★ **$–$$**   🏨 **River View Place Hotel.** There may be no other hotel in Thailand that offers so much space for such a small price: the Majesty Suites, with kitchenettes and about 1,000 square feet of space, go for B2,000. An even better value at this hotel on the Pa Sak River are the more-than-adequate 700-square-foot Senior Suites. Riverview suites, meanwhile, have enormous balconies. Rooms are so spacious and sparsely furnished that they can feel somewhat empty, but facilities are brand new. The hotel operates a dinner cruise as well. All in all, it's the best lodging choice in Ayutthaya. ✉ *K. 35/5 Horatanachai, U-Thong Rd., Ayutthaya 13000* ☎ *035/241444* ✐ *riverview05@hotmail.com* ⇥ *71 suites* ☐ *In-room: safe, refrigerator, Wi-Fi. In-hotel: 2 restaurants, room service, bar, pool, gym, laundry service, public Wi-Fi* ▤ *MC, V.*

$ 🏨 **Krungsri River Hotel.** This hotel near the train station has a refreshingly cool and spacious marble-floor lobby. The rooms, although not distinguished, are clean and filled with modern furnishings. For the best views, choose a room overlooking the river. Because Ayutthaya has few overnight visitors, try to negotiate a discounted rate. Rates include a buffet breakfast. The hotel also operates river cruises. ✉ *27/2 Moo 11 Rojana Rd., Ayutthaya 13000* ☎ *035/244333* ⊕ *www.krungsririver.com* ⇥ *200 rooms* ☐ *In-room: refrigerator. In-hotel: 2 restaurants, 2 bars, pool, gym* ▤ *AE, DC, MC, V.*

$ 🏨 **U-Thong Inn.** If the gilded lobby is grandiose bordering on gaudy, the clean, tasteful rooms with firm beds and modern bathrooms make up for it. The Tower Wing has much better rooms, so make sure you ask for one there. Suites, which cost about B800 more, are really just higher-end versions of the double rooms in the tower. The hotel is not far from Wat Yai Chai Mongkol. ✉ *210 Rojana Rd., Ayutthaya 13000* ☎ *035/212531* ⊕ *www.uthonginn.com* ⇥ *77 rooms, 132 suites* ☐ *In-room: refrigerator. In-hotel: 2 restaurants, 3 bars, pool, gym, spa* ▤ *AE, MC, V.*

Bang Pa-In

🔟 *20 km (12 mi) south of Ayutthaya.*

Near Ayutthaya, in the village Bang Pa-In, is the extravagant **Royal Palace,** set in well-tended gardens. The original structure, built by King Prusat on the banks of the Pa Sak River, was used by the Ayutthaya kings until the Burmese invasion. After being neglected for 80 years, it was rebuilt during the reign of Rama IV and became the favored summer palace of King Rama V until tragedy struck. When the king was delayed in Bangkok, he sent his wife ahead on a boat that capsized. Although she could easily have been rescued, people stood by helplessly because a royal could not be touched by a commoner on pain of death. The king built a pavilion in her memory; be sure to read the touching inscription engraved on the memorial. ⊠ *B100* ⊙ *Tues.–Thurs. and weekends 8–3.*

King Rama V was interested in the architecture of Europe, and many Western influences are evident here. The most beautiful building, however, is the **Aisawan Thippaya,** a Thai pavilion that seems to float on a small lake. A series of staggered roofs lead to a central spire. The structure is sometimes dismantled and taken to represent the country at worldwide expositions.

Phra Thinang Warophat Phiman, nicknamed the Peking Palace, is a replica of a Chinese imperial court palace. It was built from materials custommade in China—a gift from Chinese Thais eager to win the king's favor. It contains a collection of exquisite jade and Ming-period porcelain.

Take the cable car across the river to **Wat Nivet Thamaprawat,** built in Gothic style. Complete with a belfry and stained-glass windows, it looks like a Christian church masquerading as a Buddhist temple.

Shopping

The **Bang Sai Folk Arts and Craft Centre** was set up by Queen Sirikit in 1982 to train farming families to make traditional crafts for extra income. Workers at the center regularly demonstrate their techniques and a small souvenir shop offers a chance to buy their crafts. ⊹ *24 km (14½ mi) south of Bang Pa-In* ☎ *035/366090 or 035/366666* ⊠ *B100* ⊙ *Weekdays 9–5, weekends 9–6.*

Lopburi

⑩ *75 km (47 mi) north of Ayutthaya, 150 km (94 mi) north of Bangkok.*

One of Thailand's oldest cities, Lopburi has been inhabited since the 4th century. After the 6th century, its influence grew under the Dvaravati rulers, who dominated Northern Thailand until the Khmers swept in from the east. From the beginning of the 10th century until the middle of the 13th, when the new Thai kingdom drove them out, the Khmers used Lopburi as their provincial capital. During the Sukhothai and early Ayutthaya periods, the city's importance declined until, in 1664, King Narai made it his second capital to escape the heat and humidity of Ayutthaya. He employed French architects to build his palace; consequently, Lopburi is a strange mixture of Khmer, Thai, and Western architecture.

Lopburi is relatively off the beaten track for tourists, who are generally outnumbered by the city's famous monkey population. Some foreigners show up on their way to or from Ayutthaya, but few stay overnight. The rarity of foreigners may explain why locals are so friendly and eager to show you their town—and to practice their English. Samlors are available, but most of Lopburi's attractions are within easy walking distance. As for the monkeys, they cluster around the monuments, particularly Phra Prang Sam Yot; most notable is the monkey banquet organized by the Lopburi Inn each November, in which a grand buffet is laid out for the monkeys and much of the town's population comes out to watch them feast.

Wat Phra Si Rattana Mahathat, built by the Khmers, is near the railway station. It underwent so many restorations during the Sukhothai and Ayutthaya periods that it's difficult to discern the three original Khmer prangs—only the central one is intact. Several Sukhothai- and Ayutthaya-style chedis are within the compound. ⊠ *Na Phra Karn Rd.* ▣ *B30* ⊙ *Daily 6–6.*

Past Wat Phra Si Rattana Mahathat is **Phra Narai Ratchaniwet.** The palace's well-preserved buildings, completed between 1665 and 1677, have been converted into museums. Surrounding the buildings are castellated walls and triumphal archways grand enough to admit an entourage mounted on elephants. The most elaborate structure is the Dusit Mahaprasat Hall, built by King Narai to receive foreign ambassadors. The roof is gone, but you can spot the mixture of architectural styles: the square doors are Thai and the domed arches are Western. North of Phra Narai Ratchaniwet is the restored Wat Sao Thong Thong. ⊠ *Ratchadamneon Rd.* ▣ *B30* ⊙ *Daily 8:30–4:30.*

North of Wat Sao Thong Thong is **Vichayen House,** built for French King Louis XIV's personal representative, De Chaumont. The house was later occupied by King Narai's infamous Greek minister, Constantine Phaulkon, whose political schemes eventually caused the ouster of all Westerners from Thailand. When King Narai was dying in 1668, his army commander, Phra Phetracha, seized power and beheaded Phaulkon. ⊠ *Vichayen Rd.* ⊙ *Wed.–Sun. 9–noon and 1–4.*

East on Vichayen Road is a Khmer shrine called **Phra Prang Sam Yot,** Lopburi's most famous landmark. The three prangs symbolize the sacred triad of Brahma, Vishnu, and Shiva. King Narai converted the shrine into a Buddhist temple, and a stucco image of the Buddha sits serenely before the central prang. The most memorable aspect of the monument is its hundreds of resident monkeys, including mothers and nursing babies, wizened old males, and aggressive youngsters. ⚠ **Hold tight to your possessions, as the monkeys love to steal anything that looks vulnerable, from a map of the city to your digital camera.** But most tourists wind up having a blast with the monkeys. Approach them and stand still for a minute, and you'll soon have monkeys all over your head, shoulders, and just about everywhere else—a perfect photo-op. ⊠ *Vichayen Rd.*

Where to Stay & Eat

★ ¢–$$ ✕ **Bualuang Restaurant.** This is the sort of local restaurant that you shouldn't miss on your travels, a place for trying true regional specialties, including bird curry (from rails to partridge to water hen), charcoal-grilled or steamed blue crabs, mussels in a hot pot, and charcoal-grilled cottonfish and snakehead fish. There are also multicourse Chinese-style set meals for six or more people. ⊠ *46/1 Moo 3, T. Tasala, A. Muang* ☎ *036/614227 up to 30* ▤ *No credit cards.*

¢–$$ ✕ **White House.** A popular haunt for travelers, the White House offers a standard range of Thai and seafood dishes, including a good duck curry, with an easy-to-use English-language menu. The location is prime, right next to the night market, and the second-floor terrace is both lively and romantic, as is the tree-shaded garden below. The owner, Mr. Piak, is a good source of information on the area. Make sure to flip through his guest book. ⊠ *18 Phraya Kumjud Rd.* ☎ *036/413085* ⊟ *AE, MC, V.*

$ ▦ **Lopburi Inn Resort.** This monkey-theme retreat is the best value in Lopburi, with stylish rooms decorated in a modern Thai style, a good range of facilities including a pleasant pool, and a generous buffet breakfast. The only drawback is its distance from the Old City and main sights— 10 km (6 mi)—but samlors to the sights are easy enough to arrange. Note that the hotel, like many properties, charges foreigners B250 (about $7) more per night than Thais. ⊠ *17/1–2 Ratchadamnoen Rd., 15000* ☎ *036/614790, 036/420777, or 036/421453* ⊕ *www. lopburiinnresort.com* ⬃ *100 rooms* ⌂ *In-hotel: restaurant, room service, 2 bars, pool, gym* ⊟ *AE, MC, V.*

¢ ▦ **Lopburi Inn Hotel.** This hotel has achieved a certain amount of fame by hosting the annual banquet for the town's resident monkeys each November. It is, however, awkwardly located between the old and new cities and dated rooms and cluttered corridors mean that it's not necessarily worth it. The dining room serves Thai and Chinese food; a buffet breakfast is included in the rates. ⊠ *28/9 Narai Maharat Rd.* ☎ *036/412300* ⊕ *www.lopburiinnhotel.com* ⬃ *130 rooms* ⌂ *In-hotel: restaurant, room service, bar, laundry service, public Internet* AE, MC, V.

Ayutthaya & Environs Essentials

Transportation

BY BUS

Buses to Ayutthaya (1½ hours) and Lopburi (3 hours) leave Bangkok's Mo Chit Northern Bus Terminal about every 20 minutes between 6 AM and 7 PM. Tickets are cheap. From Ayutthaya, Lopburi is another 1½ hours on the green 607 bus from Ayutthaya's bus terminal.

🚍 Bus Stations **Ayutthaya** ⊠ Buses to Bangkok, Naresuan Rd. ⊠ Main Bus Terminal, Soi Grand, Rojchana Rd. ☎ 035/335304. **Northern Bus Terminal** ⊠ Khamphaeng Phet 2 Rd., Bangkok ☎ 02/937-0055 or 02/936-0667.

BY CAR

Driving to Ayutthaya from Bangkok is an easy day trip once you're out of the congestion of the big city. Kanchanaphisek Road, Bangkok's outer ring road, is the best route to take, costing around B120 in tolls. Following this road will drop you into Bang Pa-In—a good opportunity to visit the Royal Palace before continuing to Ayutthaya.

BY TAXI & TUK-TUK

All forms of local transport are available from samlors to a few songthaews, but the brightly colored tuk-tuks are more frequently used. Tuk-tuks can be hired for an hour for around B200 or the day for around B600 to B700 and make easier work of Ayutthaya's historical sites.

BY TRAIN
The Northeastern Line, which heads all the way up to Isan, has frequent service from Bangkok to Ayutthaya and Lopburi. Beginning at 4:30 AM, trains depart frequently (roughly every 40 minutes) from Bangkok's Hua Lamphong Station, arriving in Ayutthaya 80 minutes later.

Trains from Bangkok's Hua Lamphong Station regularly make the hour-long trip to Bang Pa-In Station, where you can catch a minibus to the palace. Three morning and two afternoon trains depart for the three-hour trip to Lopburi. Trains back to Bangkok run in the early and late afternoon. Since Lopburi is such a short distance from Bangkok, advance tickets aren't necessary.

Contacts & Resources

BANKS & EXCHANGING SERVICES
ATMs and exchange services are abundant in Ayutthaya, on Naresuan Road, and in Lopburi on Ratchadamnoen Road.

EMERGENCIES
🔳 Emergency Number **Ayutthaya Tourist Police** ☎ 035/241446.
🔳 Hospital **Ratcha Thani Hospital** ✉ 111 Moo 3, Rotchana Rd., Ayutthaya ☎ 035/335555.

TOUR OPTIONS
The Chao Phraya Express Boat Company runs a Sunday excursion from Bangkok to Bang Pa-In Summer Palace. It departs at 8 AM and arrives in time for lunch. On the return trip, the boat stops at the Bang Sai Folk Arts and Craft Centre before arriving in Bangkok at 5:30 PM. The trip costs B350. Another option is the Manohra Song cruise; for a day and a half or longer, you can relax in suites decorated with rich woods like mahogany and teak and yards of flowing silks, and you are pampered by a private chef.
🔳 Tour Companies **Chao Phraya Express Boat Company** ✉ Maharat Pier, 2/58 Aroon-Amarin Rd., Bangkok ☎ 02/222-5330. **Manohra Song** ✉ Marriott Royal Garden Riverside Hotel, 257/1-3 Charoen Nakorn Rd., Bangkok ☎ 02/476-0021 or 02/276-0022 ⊕ www.manohracruises.com.

VISITOR INFORMATION
The Tourist Authority of Thailand has an office in Ayutthaya with helpful maps and brochures. It's open daily 8:30–4:30.
🔳 **Tourist Authority of Thailand** ✉ Si Sanphet Rd. ☎ 035/246076.

SUKHOTHAI & ENVIRONS

In the valley of the Yom River, protected by a rugged mountain range in the north and rich forest mountains in the south, lies Sukhothai. Here, laterite (red porous soil that hardens when exposed to air) ruins signify the birthplace of the Thai nation and its emergence as a center for Theravada Buddhism.

North of Sukhothai is its sister city of Si Satchanalai, which is quieter and more laid-back, but no less interesting—its historical park has the remains of more than 200 temples and monuments.

■ TIP→ **But before you reach Sukhothai and Si Satchanalai, you'll come across Phitsanulok, which in many ways makes the best base for exploring the area.** Despite its historical relevance as Sukhothai's capital for 25 years, the birthplace of King Narai the Great, and residence of the Ayutthayan Crown Princes, Phitsanulok has grown away from its roots. This onetime military stronghold has stamped over its past, with only a few reminders, like Wat Phra Si Rattana Mahathat

> ### SHOPPING
>
> Because a relatively small number of travelers venture this way, fewer crafts are for sale here than elsewhere in the country. One notable exception is around Sukhothai and Si Satchanalai, where you can find reproductions of the pottery made here when this was the capital of the country.

and the revered Phra Buddha Chinnarat image. Phitsanulok now serves as a center for commerce, transportation, and communication. In addition, its blend of entertainment and access to outward-bound excursions make it an enjoyable diversion.

Phitsanulok

⑪ *377 km (234 mi) north of Bangkok, 60 km (37 mi) southeast of Sukhothai.*

For a brief span in the 14th century, after the decline of Sukhothai and before the rise of Ayutthaya, Phitsanulok was the kingdom's capital. Farther back in history, Phitsanulok was a Khmer outpost called Song Kwae—today only an ancient monastery remains of that incarnation. The new city, which had to relocate 5 km (3 mi) from the old site, is a modern provincial administrative seat with few architectural blessings. There are outstanding attractions, however, such as the Phra Buddha Chinnarat inside Wat Phra Si Rattana Mahathat. And make sure to walk along the Nan River, lined with tempting food stalls in the evening. On the far side are many houseboats, which are popular among Thais.

With modern conveniences, Phitsanulok is an ideal base for exploring the region. Most of the sights in Phitsanulok are within walking distance, but samlors are easily available. Bargain hard—most trips should be about B20. Taxis are available for longer trips; you can find a few loitering around the train station.

Naresuan Road runs from the railway station to the Nan River. North of this street you can find **Wat Phra Si Rattana Mahathat**, a temple commonly known as Wat Yai. Built in the mid-14th century, Wat Yai has developed into a large monastery with typical ornamentation. Particularly noteworthy are the viharn's wooden doors, inlaid with mother-of-pearl in 1756 at the behest of King Boromkot. Behind the viharn is a 100-foot prang with a vault containing Buddha relics. The many religious souvenir stands make it hard to gain a good view of the complex, but the bot is a fine example of the traditional three-tier roof with low sweeping eaves, designed to diminish the size of the walls, accentuate the nave, and emphasize the image of the Buddha.

Within the viharn is what many consider the world's most beautiful image of the Buddha, Phra Buddha Chinnarat. It was probably cast in the 14th century, during the late Sukhothai period. Its mesmerizing beauty and the mystical powers ascribed to it draw streams of pilgrims—among the most notable of them was the Sukhothai's King Eka Thossarot, who journeyed here in 1631. According to folklore, the king applied with his own hands the gold leaf that covers the Buddha. Many copies of the image have been made, with the best known residing in Bangkok's Marble Temple. ⊠ *Off Ekethosarot Rd.* ☉ *Daily 8–6.*

★ Phitsanulok also has a little-known museum, **Pim Buranaket Folkcraft Museum,** that alone would justify a visit to the city. In the early 1980s, Sergeant-Major Khun Thawee traveled to small villages, collecting traditional tools, cooking utensils, animal traps, and handicrafts that were rapidly disappearing, and crammed them into a traditional house and barn. For a decade nothing was properly documented; visitors stumbled around tiger traps and cooking pots, with little to help them decipher what they were looking at. But Khun Thawee's daughter came to the rescue and now the marvelous artifacts are systematically laid out. You can now understand the use of everything on display, from the simple wood pipes hunters played to lure their prey, to elaborately complex rat guillotines. The museum is a 15-minute walk south of the railway station, on the east side of the tracks. ⊠ *Wisut Kasat Rd.* 📧 *B50* ☉ *Tues.–Sun. 8:30–4:30.*

Where to Stay & Eat

Phitsanulok has a good range of dining options, from its popular pontoon and riverside restaurants to some great little daytime canteen-style restaurants near the central clock tower on Phayalithai Road. The Muslim restaurants on Pra Ong Dam Road, opposite the town's mosque, are great for curry and roti breakfasts. The night bazaar promenade banking the Nan River contains some basic early-evening places to enjoy the sunset, including the infamous "flying vegetable restaurant," where you can have the province's famed *pak bung fire dang* (stir-fried morning glory). And the veggies do fly here—when the cooks fling the morning glory to waiters, who deftly catch the food on their plates. Akathodsarod Road near Topland Hotel is a good bet for late-night noodles.

$$-$$$$ ✕ **Boo Bpen Seafood.** Although not on the river, this upbeat seafood restaurant has the edge on the competition because of its spacious bench seating and garden atmosphere. Live bands play on a small central stage. House specialties include *gai khua kem* (roasted chicken with salt) and *boo nim tort gratium* (crab fried in garlic) and are worth a nibble, but for something more substantial, the barbecue prawns are a must, sampled with the chili, lime, and fish sauce dip. ⊠ *Sanambin Rd.* ▭ *No credit cards.*

¢-$$ ✕ **Phraefahthai.** This floating teak Thai-style house on the Nan River is the more popular of the two pontoon eateries in Phitsanulok; it draws the majority of tourists, as well as local businessmen and their families. It's strikingly lighted up at night, impossible to miss from anywhere on the river. An extensive menu in English makes it the most comfortable riverside experience. The emphasis is on fresh seafood—the *pla taptim*

(St. Peter's fish, a delicious freshwater fish) is particularly recommended, served steamed with a spicy lemon and lime sauce. ✉ *60 Wangjan Rd.* ☎ *055/242743* 🖃 *AE, DC, MC, V.*

$ 🖳 **Grand Riverside Hotel.** The new kid on the block is a fine-looking hotel. The foyer is grand, with a spiral staircase leading to well-appointed rooms. It's a great base for Phitsanulok and is within walking distance of restaurants, bars, and the city's main temple. ✉ *59 Praroung Rd., 65000* ☎ *055/248333* ↩ *81 rooms* ⚲ *In-room: safe, refrigerator, ethernet. In-hotel: restaurant, room service, bar, laundry service, public Internet* 🖃 *MC, V.*

$ 🖳 **Pailyn Hotel.** The rooms at this white high-rise are quite large, with picture windows adding plenty of light—rooms on the higher floors have the best view of the river. The large lobby and coffee shop are busy in the morning as tour groups gather, and in the evening when the disco attracts the local teenagers. It's in downtown Phitsanulok, within walking distance of most city attractions. ✉ *38 Boromatrailokart Rd., 65000* ☎ *055/252411, 02/215–7110 in Bangkok* ↩ *125 rooms* ⚲ *In-room: refrigerator. In-hotel: 2 restaurants, bar, spa* 🖃 *MC, V.*

¢–$ 🖳 **La Paloma.** This vast complex is Phitsanulok's best value high-end option. Rooms are clean and comfortable, with soft floral upholstering against classic dark-wood stain. A good selection of English-language TV channels help make it a comfy retreat. The location, however, isn't the best, with the center of the city a brisk 20-minute walk away and few independent dining or drinking options nearby. ✉ *103 Srithumtripdork Rd.* ☎ *055/217930* ↩ *239 rooms, 10 suites* ⚲ *In-room: refrigerator. In-hotel: restaurant, pool, laundry service, public Internet* 🖃 *MC, V.*

¢ 🖳 **Phitsanulok Thani Hotel.** This fresh-faced hotel has a friendly staff and a nicely designed foyer based around a small fountain leads to less attractive, though comfortable, rooms. Although away from the town center, the area around the hotel has plenty of good restaurants and pubs to choose from. Local transport to other areas of the city is easy to find. ✉ *39 Sanambin Rd., 65000* ☎ *055/211065 up to 69, 055/212631 up to 34* ⊕ *www.phitsanulokthani.com* ↩ *110 rooms* ⚲ *In-room: refrigerator. In-hotel: restaurant, bar, spa, laundry service* 🖃 *AE, DC, MC, V.*

Sukhothai

★ *56 km (35 mi) northwest of Phitsanulok, 427 km (265 mi) north of Bangkok; 1 hr by bus from Phitsanulok.*

Sukhothai, which means "the dawn of happiness," holds a unique place in Thailand's history. Until the 13th century most of Thailand consisted of many small vassal states under the thumb of the Khmer Empire based in Angkor Wat. But the Khmers had overextended their reach, allowing the princes of two Thai states to combine forces. In 1238 one of the two princes, Phor Khun Bang Klang Thao, marched on Sukhothai, defeating the Khmer garrison commander in an elephant duel. Installed as the new king of the region, he took the name Sri Indraditya and founded a dynasty that ruled Sukhothai for nearly 150 years. His youngest son became the third king of Sukhothai, Ramkhamhaeng, who ruled from 1279 to 1299. Through military and diplomatic victories he expanded

Sukhothai
Historical Park

the kingdom to include most of present-day Thailand and the Malay Peninsula.

By the mid-14th century Sukhothai's power and influence had waned, and Ayutthaya, once its vassal state, became the capital of the Thai kingdom. Sukhothai was gradually abandoned to the jungle, and a new town grew up about 14 km (9 mi) away. In 1978 a 10-year restoration project costing more than $10 million created the Sukhothai Historical Park. The vast park (70 square km [27 square mi]) has 193 historic monuments. Sukhothai is the busiest during the Loi Krathong festival, which is celebrated in the historical park each year on the full moon in November. Its well-orchestrated, three-day light-and-sound show is the highlight. At this time the town's hotels and guesthouses are booked weeks in advance.

New Sukhothai, where all intercity buses arrive, is a quiet town where most inhabitants are in bed by 11 PM. Its many guesthouses are a magnet for tourists coming to see the ruins, and as such, you'll see quite a few *farang* (foreigners), especially young British, German, and American couples, wandering around amid the locals, drinking at the bars or browsing the sidewalk food stalls. New Sukhothai's night market is sleepy by the standards of the region, and in short, you can't expect much of an urban cultural experience here.

Because the sights are so spread out, the best way to explore the park is by bicycle; you can rent one along the main street. You can also book a tour with a guide. Either way, bring a bottle of water with you—the day will get hotter than you think.

Depending on your means of transportation, this tour could take a few hours or the better part of a day. It's best to come in the late afternoon to avoid the midday sun and enjoy the late evening's pink-and-orange hues. Crowds generally aren't a problem.

What to See

⑫ Ramkhamhaeng National Museum. Most of the significant artifacts from Sukhothai are in Bangkok's National Museum, but this open, airy museum has more than enough fine pieces to demonstrate the gentle beauty of this period. You can learn how refinements in the use of bronze let artisans create the graceful walking Buddhas. ⊠ *Jarodvithithong Rd., just before entrance to historical park* 🎫 *B30* ⊙ *Daily 9–4.*

> **THE TRACES OF A NATION**
>
> The optimism that accompanied the birth of the nation at Sukhothai is reflected in the art and architecture of the period. Strongly influenced by Sri Lankan Buddhism, the monuments left behind by the architects, artisans, and craftsmen of those innovative times had a light, often playful touch. Statues of the Buddha show him as smiling, serene, and confidently walking toward a better future. Note the impossibly graceful elephants portrayed in supporting pillars.

⑭ Royal Palace. Thais imagine Sukhothai's government as a monarchy that served the people, stressing social needs and justice. Slavery was abolished, and people were free to believe in their local religions, Hinduism and Buddhism (often simultaneously), and to pursue their trade without hindrance. In the 19th century a famous stone inscription of King Ramkhamhaeng was found among the ruins of the palace across from Wat Mahathat. Sometimes referred to as Thailand's Declaration of Independence, the inscription's best-known quote reads: "This city Sukhothai is good. In the water there are fish, in the field there is rice. The ruler does not levy tax on the people who travel along the road together, leading their oxen on the way to trade and riding their horses on the way to sell. Whoever wants to trade in elephants, so trades. Whoever wants to trade in horses, so trades." ⊠ *In the Old City* 🎫 *B40 for all sights inside the Old City walls* ⊙ *Daily 8–4:30.*

⑱ Wat Chang Lom. South of the park off Chotwithithong Road is one of Sukhothai's oldest monasteries. Its bell-shaped pagoda, thought to have been built in the latter part of the 14th century, is of Sri Lankan influence and is perched on a three-tiered square base atop damaged elephant buttresses. In front of the chedi are a viharn and solitary pillars; the remains of nine other chedis have been found within this complex. ⊠ *Chotwithithong Rd., about 4 km (2½ mi) before entrance to historical park, reached by turning north down a small lane over a smaller bridge.*

⑬ Wat Mahathat. Sitting amid a tranquil lotus pond, Wat Mahathat is the largest and most beautiful monastery in Sukhothai. Enclosed in the compound are some 200 tightly packed chedis, each containing the funeral ashes of a nobleman. Towering above them is a large central chedi, notable for its bulbous, lotus-bud prang. Wrapping around the chedi is a frieze of 111 monks, their hands raised in adoration. Probably built by Sukhothai's first king, Wat Mahathat owes its present form to King Lö Thai, who in 1345 erected the lotus-bud chedi to house two important relics brought back from Sri Lanka by the monk Sisatta. This Sri Lankan–style chedi became the symbol of Sukhothai and classical Sukhothai style. Copies of it were made in the principal cities of its vassal states, signifying a magic circle emanating from Sukhothai, the spiritual and temporal center of the empire. ⊠ *In the Old City* 🖼 *B40 for all sights inside the Old City walls* ⊙ *Daily 8:30–4:30.*

㉑ Wat Saphan Hin. This pretty wat is reached by following a slate pathway and climbing a 656-foot hill. It's famous for its standing Buddha, an imposing sculpture whose hand is about as tall as you. ⊠ *North of Old City walls* 🖼 *Free.*

⑲ Wat Phra Phai Luang. This former Khmer structure, once a Hindu shrine, was converted to a Buddhist temple. Surrounded by a moat, the sanctuary is encircled by three laterite prangs, similar to those at Wat Sri Sawai—the only one that remains intact is decorated with stucco figures. In front of the prangs are the remains of the viharn and a crumbling chedi with a seated Buddha on its pedestal. Facing these structures is the *mondop,* a square structure with a stepped pyramid roof, built to house religious relics. ⊠ *North of Old City walls on Donko Rd., opposite Tourist Information Center* 🖼 *B30* ⊙ *Daily 8:30–4:30.*

⑯ Wat Sra Sri. This peaceful temple sits on two connected islands within a lotus-filled lake. The lake, called Traphong Trakuan Pond, supplied the monks with water and served as a boundary for the sacred area. A Sri Lankan–style chedi dominates six smaller chedis, and a large, stucco, seated Buddha looks down a row of columns, past the chedis, and over the lake to the horizon.

Especially wondrous is the walking Buddha beside the Sri Lankan–style chedi. The walking Buddha is a Sukhothai innovation and the most ethereal of Thailand's artistic styles. The depiction of the Buddha is often a reflection of political authority and is modeled after the ruler. Under the Khmers, authority was hierarchical, but the kings of Sukhothai represented the ideals of serenity, happiness, and justice. The walking Buddha is the epitome of Sukhothai's art; he appears to be floating on air, neither rooted on Earth nor placed on a pedestal above the reach of the common people. ⊠ *In the Old City* 🖼 *B40 for all sights inside the Old City walls* ⊙ *Daily 8:30–4:30.*

⑳ Wat Sri Chum. Like many other sanctuaries, Wat Si Chum was originally surrounded by a moat. The main structure is dominated by a breathtaking statue of the Buddha in a seated position. The huge but elegant stucco image is one of the largest in Thailand, measuring 37 feet from knee to knee. Enter the mondop through the passage inside the left inner wall. Keep your eyes on the ceiling: more than 50 engraved slabs illustrate scenes from the *Jataka,* which are stories about the previous lives of Lord Bud-

Loi Krathong

ON THE FULL MOON OF THE 12TH LUNAR MONTH, when the tides are at their highest and the moon at its brightest, the Thais head to the country's waterways to celebrate Loi Krathong, one of Thailand's most anticipated and enchanting festivals.

Loi Krathong was influenced by Diwali, the Indian lantern festival that paid tribute to three Brahman gods. Thai farmers adapted the ceremony to offer tribute to Mae Khlong Kha, the goddess of the water, to thank her for blessing the land with water.

Ancient Sukhothai is where the festival's popular history began, with a story written by King Rama IV in 1863. The story concerns Naang Noppamart, the daughter of a Brahman priest who served in the court of King Li-Thai, grandson of King Ramkhamhaeng the Great. She was a woman of exceptional charm and beauty who soon became his queen. She secretly fashioned a krathong (a small float used as an offering), setting it alight by candle in accordance with her Brahmanist rites. The king, upon seeing this curious, glimmering offering embraced its beauty, adapting it for Theravada Buddhism and thus creating the festival of Loi Krathong.

Krathong were traditionally formed by simply cupping banana leaves and offerings such as dried rice and betel nut were placed at the center along with three incense sticks representing the Brahman gods. Today krathong are more commonly constructed by pinning folded banana leaves to a buoyant base made of a banana tree stem; they're decorated with scented flowers, orange candles (said to be representative of the Buddhist monkhood), and three incense sticks, whose meaning was changed under Li-Thai to represent the three forms of Buddhist existence.

Today, young Thai couples, "loi" their "krathong" to bind their love in an act almost like that of a marriage proposal, while others use the ceremony more as a way to purge any bad luck or resentments they may be harboring. Loi Krathong also commonly represents the pursuit of material gain, with silent wishes placed for a winning lottery number or two. The festival remains Thailand's most romantic vision of tradition, with millions of Thais sending their hopes floating down the nearest waterway.

Although it's celebrated nationwide, with events centered around cities such as Bangkok, Ayutthaya, Chiang Mai, and Tak, the festival's birthplace of Sukhothai remains the focal point. The historical park serves as a kind of Hollywood back lot, with hundreds of costumed students and light, sound, and pyrotechnic engineers, preparing for the fanfare of the annual show, which generally happens twice during the evening. With the historical park lighted and Wat Mahathat as its stage, the show reenacts the story of Sukhothai and the legend of Loi Krathong; then, governors, dignitaries, and other celebrity visitors (which recently included a former Miss USA who is idolized in Thailand) take part in a spectacular finale that includes sending off the krathong representing the king and queen, and fireworks.

–Warwick Dixon

dha. The monument is open all the time, but you'll have to pay B30 if you visit before 4 PM. ⊠ *East of Old City walls* ⊞ *B30, free after 4 PM.*

⑮ Wat Sri Sawai. Sukhothai's oldest structure may be this Khmer-style one, which has three prangs—similar to those found in Lopburi—surrounded by a laterite wall. The many stucco Hindu images and scenes suggest that Sri Sawai was probably first a Hindu temple, later converted to a Buddhist monastery. ⊠ *In the Old City* ⊞ *B40 for all sights inside the Old City walls* ⊘ *Daily 8:30–4:30.*

⑰ Wat Traphang Thong Lang. The square mondop of Wat Traphang Thong Lang is the main sanctuary, the outer walls of which boast beautiful stucco figures in niches—some of Sukhothai's finest art. The north side depicts the Buddha returning to preach to his wife. On the west side he preaches to his father and relatives. Note the figures on the south wall, where the story of the Buddha is accompanied by an angel descending from Heaven. ⊠ *Just north of Old City walls* ⊞ *B30* ⊘ *Daily 8:30–4:30.*

Where to Stay & Eat

Some of the best food in town can be found at the local food stalls that line the main street before and after the bridge. If you're in the mood for something sweet, look for the stand selling delicious Thai crepes filled with condensed milk, right at the bridge on the city-center side. But it's hard to go wrong almost anywhere in or near the night market or along that street.

$ ✕ **Dream Café.** While waiting for your meal, feast your eyes on the extraordinary collection of antiques that fill this charming restaurant, which is in its third decade of existence. The rustic tile floor, the glowing teak tables and chairs, and the nooks and crannies packed with fascinating odds and ends—everything from old lamps to fine ceramics—combine in a perfect harmony to endow the Dream Café with a superlative atmosphere. The modified Thai food is not quite up to snuff, however; be sure to tell your waiter you want things spicy, not farang-style, and even then, don't expect much. Behind the restaurant are four rustic but romantic rooms, aptly named Cocoon House, set in a fairy-tale garden. ⊠ *86/1 Singhawat Rd.* ☎ *055/612081* ⌑ *4 rooms* ♨ *In-room: no a/c (some). In-hotel: restaurant* ⊟ *MC, V.*

¢–$ ✕ **Khun Tanode Restaurant.** The menu doesn't get much more exciting than the fish curry, but you'll enjoy yourself at this dimly lighted haunt nonetheless. It has a great central location right next to the main bridge and an unmatched atmosphere, simple but infinitely romantic, especially at sunset or at night. Some tables and chairs are arranged amid hanging flowers on platforms that overhang the river. Aside from the curry, try the minced pork omelet or the crispy fried chicken. ⊠ *Kuhasawan Rd.* ☎ *No phone* ⊟ *No credit cards.*

$$–$$$ ✕⊡ **Ananda Museum Gallery Hotel.** The Ananda has redefined the concept of luxury lodging in Sukhothai. As you might expect from a hotel that is also an art gallery, room design is informed by a deep sense of minimalism along with a healthy dose of feng shui. The open-air Celadon restaurant ($$), set in a lovely garden, is a relaxing place to dine, away from touristy Sukhothai. The hotel is 1 km (½ mi) from the city center and 15 minutes from the historical park. ⊠ *Jarodvithithong Rd., 64210*

Fodor'sChoice
★

☎ 055/622428 *up to 31* ⊕ *www.anandasukhothai.com* ➔ *32 rooms, 2 suites* ⚭ *In-room: safe, refrigerator. In-hotel: restaurant, room service, bar, gym, spa, public Internet* ▤ *AE, MC, V.*

$ ▥ **Pailyn Hotel.** The staff is proud to point out that King Bhumibol Adulyadej has spent the night here. It's a vast building with a subtle contemporary Thai look, including a typical stepped roof. Rooms are large, comfortable, and reasonably decorated, though the highly varnished rattan bed frames and chairs look kind of tacky. The airy central atrium and the pool are a welcome sight after a day exploring the dusty ruins. It's halfway between New Sukhothai and the Old City, so transport can be a problem. ✉ *Jarodvithithong Rd., 64210* ☎ *055/633336 up to 39, 02/215–5640 in Bangkok* ➔ *234 rooms* ⚭ *In-room: refrigerator. In-hotel: 3 restaurants, pool, gym* ▤ *MC, V.*

¢–$ ▥ **Lotus Village.** The lotus-flower ponds that dot the lush gardens of this attractive Thai-style lodging give the place its name. It's run by a charming French-Thai couple who are happy to help organize tours of Sukhothai and the surrounding area. The teak bungalows—some with fans, others with air-conditioning—are comfortably furnished and have private verandas. The inn is tucked away near the Yom River. It's best reached via Rajuthit Road, which runs along the river from the center of town. There's a breakfast room but no restaurant. ✉ *170 Ratchathani Rd., 64000* ☎ *055/621484* ⊕ *www.lotus-village.com* ➔ *10 rooms* ⚭ *In-hotel: laundry service, public Internet* ▤ *No credit cards.*

¢ ▥ **Rajthanee Hotel.** The traditional Thai entrance of this well-run hotel leads into a modern building. There's a terrace where you can also enjoy a Thai whiskey and a stylish restaurant that serves good Asian cuisine. Comfortable rooms (standards and slightly larger deluxe rooms) are clean and practically furnished with a few trimmings such as woven headboards, which help soothe the eyes from the ever-present glare of lacquer. The swimming pool is proving a welcome addition to this hotel as is its karaoke bar that lights up like a lava lamp at night. ✉ *229 Jarodvithithong Rd., 64000* ☎ *055/611031 or 055/611308* ➔ *83 rooms* ⚭ *In-room: refrigerator. In-hotel: 2 restaurants, pool* ▤ *AE, MC, V.*

Nightlife

Of the many bars and pubs that cater to tourists in Sukhothai, **Chopper Bar** (✉ 96/1 Pawee Nakhon ☎ 055/611190) is one of the best. It's on the main street, with open-air tables laid out amid twinkling lights; there's a fun garden in the back and a terrace in the front with rustic tables, shrines, greenery, flowing water, and live music. Skip the Western food.

Si Satchanalai

㉒ *80 km (50 mi) north of Sukhothai.*

With its expanse of neatly mowed lawns, Sukhothai is sometimes criticized for being too well groomed. But Si Satchanalai, spread out on 228 acres on the banks of the Mae Yom River, remains a quiet place with a more ancient, undisturbed atmosphere. It isn't difficult to find the ruins of a temple where you won't be disturbed for hours.

Most visitors to Si Satchanalai reach it as part of a tour from Sukhothai (most hotels can set you up with a guide). If you want to go on your own, hop on a bus bound for the town of Sawankhalok. Take a taxi to the historical park, asking the driver to wait while you visit the various temples. You can also tour the site by bicycle or on top of an elephant, if that's your choice of transportation. Accommodations near the park are only relatively expensive bungalows, so most visitors stay in Sukhothai.

Si Satchanalai, a sister city to Sukhothai, was governed by a son of Sukhothai's reigning monarch. Despite its secondary position, the city grew to impressive proportions, and no less than 200 of its temples and monuments survive, most of them in a ruined state but many well worth seeing. Near the entrance, **Wat Chang Lom** shows strong Sri Lankan influences. The 39 elephant buttresses are in much better condition than at the similarly named temple in Sukhothai. The main chedi was completed by 1291. As you climb the stairs that run up the side, you can find seated images of the Buddha. The second important monument, **Wat Chedi Jet Thaew,** is to the south of Wat Chang Lom. The complex has seven rows of ruined chedis, some with lotus-bud tops that are reminiscent of the larger ones at Sukhothai. The chedis contain the ashes of members of Si Satchanalai's ruling family. **Wat Nang Phya,** to the southeast of Wat Chedi Jet Thaew, has well-preserved floral reliefs on its balustrade and stucco reliefs on the viharn wall. As you leave the park, stop at **Wat Suam Utayan** to see a Si Satchanalai image of Lord Buddha, one of the few still remaining.

Sukhothai grew wealthy on the fine ceramics it produced from the rich earth around the neighboring town of Sawankhalok. The ceramics were so prized that they were offered as gifts from Sukhothai rulers to the imperial courts of China, and they found their way as far as Japan. Fine examples of 1,000-year-old Sawankhalok wares are on display at the **Sawankhalok Museum,** about 1 km (½ mi) from the town. ⊠ *Phitsanulok Rd., Sawankhalok* 🖅 *B40* ⊙ *Weekdays 10–6, weekends 10–8.*

Where to Eat

Si Satchanalai's historical park has plenty of basic eating options. Kaeng Sak restaurant at the entrance will offer a bit more variety, with some good Chinese and European dishes.

¢–$$ ✕ **Wang Yong Resort.** For a more leisurely meal, walk just east of the historical park to the pleasant riverside Wang Yong Resort, an expensive resort with attractive grounds. The restaurant is in an open-side antique wooden pavilion on the riverbank; it serves up some delectable Thai dishes such as *neua tord krapao grob* (crispy fried beef and holy basil) and *yam gai tua pu* (chicken and bean salad). ⊠ *78/2 Suwanthanas Rd.* 🖅 *055/631380* ▤ *MC, V.*

Sukhothai & Environs Essentials

Transportation

BY AIR

All air traffic to the Central Plains radiates from Bangkok, with the exception of daily flights from Chiang Mai to Sukhothai and flights between Chiang Mai and Phitsanulok, all on Thai Airways. There are several Thai Airways flights daily from Bangkok to Sukhothai and Phitsanulok. Sukhothai is roughly equidistant between its own airport (a beautiful open-air terminal built by Bangkok Airways but also used by Thai Airways) and the one in Phitsanulok, which is less than an hour away by taxi or bus. In the region, Bangkok Airways only serves Sukhothai.

📶 **Bangkok Airways** ✉ 10 Moo 1, Jarodvithithong Rd., Sukhothai ☎ 055/633266 ⊕ www.bangkokair.com. **Thai Airways** ✉ Singhawat Rd., Sukhothai ☎ 055/613075 or 055/610578 ⊕ www.thaiairways.com.

📶 Airports **Phitsanulok Airport** ☎ 055/301002. **Sukhothai Airport** ☎ 055/647220 up to 25.

BY BUS

Buses to Sukhothai depart from Bangkok's Northern Bus Terminal (Mo Chit) daily from 7 AM to 11 PM, leaving roughly every 20 minutes. There are five main companies to choose from but all charge about the same, most with prices under B300. The journey takes about seven hours. Buses from Sukhothai's new bus terminal on the bypass road depart at the same times and for the same prices.

Phitsanulok's main bus terminal, on Highway 12, is the stop before Sukhothai, shaving 1½ hours off the journey and around B40 off the ticket price. The terminal also has buses for travel to Chiang Mai via Lampang or via Phrae and Phayao and to Khon Kaen via Lomsak.

Between Phitsanulok and Sukhothai there are regular, non-air-conditioned buses for pennies, which depart roughly every hour; the trip takes about 1½ hours. To get to Si Satchanalai from Sukhothai takes 1½ hours and costs B36.

📶 Bus Stations **Phitsanulok** ✉ Mittaparp Rd. ☎ 055/242430 or 055/242030. **Sukhothai** ✉ Bypass Rd. ☎ 055/614529.

BY CAR

A car is a good way to get between the three towns. Highway 12 from Phitsanulok leads to Sukhothai and is a long, straight, and reasonably comfortable 59-km (37-mi), one-hour drive.

To get to the region from Bangkok, take the four-lane Highway 117; the drive takes about four hours.

Agencies with drop-off services, such as Avis or Budget, will be your best option around this area—they both have desks at the airport in Phitsanulok. Costs for renting economy cars up to SUVs range from B1,500 to B3,500 per day without drivers. For chauffeur-driven services, figure on an additional B1,000. Make sure to ask for an English-speaking driver. Bigger hotels in Phitsanulok offer chauffeur services at similar prices, but are more tour-oriented and generally offer no more than one day trip.

📶 Agencies **Avis** ✉ Phitsanulok Airport ☎ 055/242060. **Budget** ✉ Phitsanulok Airport ☎ 055/258556.

BY TAXI, SAMLOR & SONGTHAEW

There's a cheap, cramped, tin-can bus service in Phitsanulok, but unless ovens are your thing, you're best off using the motorized samlors or the more eco-friendly pedal-powered ones. Sukhothai is without public bus routes, and most of the population gets around in souped-up samlors or songthaews.

Contacts & Resources

BANKS & EXCHANGING SERVICES

There are plenty of ATM machines or exchange kiosks in Phitsanulok and Sukhothai. Sukhothai's banks are mainly on Sriintharathid Road, while Naresuan Road has most of Phitsanulok's banks.

EMERGENCIES

⏷ In Phitsanulok **Phitsanuwej Hospital** ✉ Khun Piren Rd. ☎ 055/21994. **Police** ☎ 055/258777.

⏷ In Sukhothai **Police** ☎ 055/613611. **Sukhothai Hospital** ✉ Jarodvithithong Rd. ☎ 055/611782.

TOUR OPTIONS

In Sukhothai, Dhanasith Kampempool's one-man agency is *the* place to go for a tour of the area. Dhanasith (or Tom, as he prefers to be called) studied and worked for more than 20 years in the United States. His English is perfect. His office is next to the Vitoon Guesthouse in Old Sukhothai: just tell Tom what you want to see and where you want to go and he'll arrange it.

⏷ Tour Company **Dhanasith Kampempool** ✉ 49 Moo 3, Jarodvithithong Rd., Old Sukhothai ☎ 055/697045 or 055/633397.

VISITOR INFORMATION

The Tourist Authority of Thailand's office in Phitsanulok has maps and brochures, and is open daily between 8:30 AM and 4:30 PM.

⏷ Tourist Information **Phitsanulok** ✉ 209/7–8 Boromtrailokanat Rd. ☎ 055/231063.

TAK PROVINCE: MAE SOT & ENVIRONS

Often overlooked, Tak Province is finally finding its feet as a destination, mainly because of the wonderful trekking opportunities on offer in the region, and the opportunity to cross the border into Myanmar.

Famed for its teak forests, the province is home to an incredible number of plants and animals, including Thailand's last remaining wild cattle and the last 50 wild water buffalo. Umphang National Park and Thung Yai Naresuan Wildlife Sanctuary are two definite highlights in this, Thailand's largest forest region.

Although the provincial hub city of Tak has little of interest for travelers, it's an inevitable transit point coming from other provinces in the Central Plains. From here, you can head off to Mae Sot and Umphang, where you have the opportunity to sample some of the country's more diverse cultural mixes, and outstanding natural beauty.

Mae Sot borders Myanmar and is a cultural melting pot, with Karen and Burmese peoples creating a vibrant mix rarely seen elsewhere in Thailand. It's also the best place to base yourself, with a range of guesthouses and tour companies preparing you for further exploration of Umphang's natural riches.

Umphang is the key to this area's spectacular tourist attractions; the small, peaceful town is your launching pad for white-water rafting tours that takes you through national parks and along gorges and ravines, passing hill tribe communities on your way to the Thee Lor Su waterfall.

Mae Sot

23 *83 km (51 mi) west of Tak city, 506 km (312 mi) north of Bangkok.*

At Mae Sot, which borders Myanmar to its west, you can find an interesting mix of local Thais, a dominant Burmese workforce, and the Karen refugees who live an ambiguous life in their 10,000-strong community, stuck between two worlds. It's definitely a frontier town, complete with black-market gems and timber smuggling, but it also provides the gateway for the natural sights of Tak Province.

Wattanaram Monastery, a Tai Yai temple dating back to 1867, was built in Myanmar by a merchant from Tongchai. A typically Burmese wat, it's notable chiefly for its ornate gold-plate bronze Buddha image (Phra Phutta Maha Muni), which measures 6½ feet by 6½ feet and is encrusted with small precious stones, adding to its prestige. There's also a long 90-foot white concrete reclining Buddha behind the ordination hall. For men, there's an herbal sauna service available daily from 8–7. The temple is 3 km (2 mi) west of Mae Sot on Route 1085.

Aside from its miniature Mon-style pagoda—precariously mounted on a boulder and overhanging a 984-foot cliff—the forest temple of **Wat Phra That Hin Kew** is not really much to look at. There is, however, a fantastic view out over the Moei River and Myanmar's forested bank, which you'll feel you've earned after a good 20-minute hike up the complex's 413 stairs. It's about 11 km (7 mi) north of town; take the 1085 road heading north and follow the signs.

FodorśChoice
★

The second Thai-Myanmar Friendship Bridge, built in 1996, is 6 km (4 mi) east of town. Crossings into the eastern frontier town of **Myawady** give a brief taste of Myanmar, but with no safe access routes incountry, return to Thailand is unavoidable. The border is open daily 8–6. No visa is required, but you will be required to pay a B500 fee upon arrival in Myanmar, and you'll have to leave your passport with the border officials for the entire duration of your stay. Myawady is quite a change from Thailand, noticeable as soon as you cross: men wearing sarongs, women and children with their faces colored in sun-screening chalk, and unpaved streets will welcome you to this less developed land. Warm welcomes in English greet you, too, along with motorbikes with homemade sidecars. Guided tours of the nominal attractions here, which can be arranged either at one of the tourist agencies that cluster on the Thai side of the border or through one of the taxi drivers on the other side, are fairly cheap at around B500. They'll take you to the Shwe Muay Wan, the city's most prominent temple; to a hilltop monastery where, if you time it right, you might be invited to lunch with the monks; and to the uniquely shaped crocodile temple, the Myikyaungon. The town occasionally erupts into a political flash point as the KNU slug it out with the Yangon-based government, sometimes resulting in the temporary closure of the bridge, but this hasn't happened in a while. The crossing is absolutely worthwhile, and not to be missed if you're in Mae Sot.

Tens of thousands of Karen have been driven into **refugee camps** in Northern Thailand by the Burmese government-backed military attacks on their Burmese villages. Karen villagers live in terror of these attacks, as they're generally being presented with two simple options: stay and work in labor camps on the government's oil pipelines or flee into the forest, where they'll be branded as enemies of the state and consequently hunted and killed. Some stand up and fight as guerrillas for the KNU, but the majority try to cross the border into Thailand, where they are recognized as political refugees. The largest Karen camp, **Bargor**, is about 40 km (25 mi) north of Mae Sot on the 1085 road to Mae Rammat. It's an arresting sight, with thousands of traditional split-bamboo huts staggered (some on stilts) over a hill range that stretches for 4 km (2½ mi). There are small checkpoints at each end, but villagers are allowed to leave during the day to farm the fields and travel into Mae Sot. You won't be able to visit this town without a guide.

Where to Stay & Eat

Mae Sot is often used as a one- or two-night stopover for trips into Umphang and therefore has a good range of cheap, friendly guesthouses, as well as some not-so-special mid-range hotels. In addition to a few good restaurants, Mae Sot is famous for its street food, centered around Intarakeeree and Prasartwithee roads. Don't miss Tui Khaosoi (65 Prasartwithee Road), a famous hole-in-the-wall Muslim noodle joint that serves up one delicious dish, *khao soi*, a bowl full of noodles that are half crispy and half wet, with chicken or beef and a broth that's thick with coconut milk. It's garnished with cilantro, red onions, pickled cabbage, lime, and chili.

Another notable noodle stand is at 115/1 Prasartwithee Road. Don't miss the *kuay tiew tai yai* (Burmese-style glass noodles with dried shrimp, fish sauce, onions, pork rinds, chili, and bean sprouts, to name a few ingredients). Also try *maing kum,* a sort of Thai wrap, with *wai* (betel leaf) wrapped around lemongrass, dried salted shrimp, peanuts, and red onions, and seasoned with lime, ginger, garlic, and chili. All this should set you back only B20 or so.

★ ¢–$ ╳ **Ruen Phae.** On the edge of a spectacular rice paddy, this restaurant consists of a set of little bungalows on stilts with low-slung tables. You'll sit on mats and dig into a variety of local fish specialties while gazing upon a lily pad–filled pond. This is a taste of the most rural cuisine and experience that the Central Plains has to offer. ⊠ *Mae Sot-Umphang Rd., Km 1* ☎ *073/082011* ▭ *No credit cards.*

¢–$ ╳ **TK Restaurant.** Don't be put off by the bright lighting, the linoleum floors, or the vaguely communist feel—this restaurant is justly popular for its hot-pot specialties such as sukiyaki (there are hot pots at the tables) and for its Chinese-influenced Thai food, which might include fresh fish from the tank in back. About half the menu is translated into English, but that half only covers the Westernized dishes, which are not recommended. ⊠ *68 Prasartwithee Rd.* ☎ *073/082011* ⊟ *No credit cards.*

¢ ✕ **Cook Phaan Torung.** At this local restaurant in the night market, you pick out what you want from a glass case and it's served up at one of the sidewalk tables. The food could hardly be any more inexpensive, rustic, or satisfying. Try the wild pig curry or the spicy whole fish—or, if you dare, *phad phed tuhn* (bamboo rat in dry curry). There's also the classic Central Plains vegetable dish, *pak boong fai dang* (morning glory with oyster sauce), and an English-language menu to boot. ⊠ *68 Prasartwithee Rd.* ☎ *073/082011* ⊟ *No credit cards.*

$$ 🏨 **Central Mae Sot Hill Hotel.** The biggest and brightest hotel in Mae Sot has spacious rooms done in a contemporary Thai design, with nice wood furnishings and marble-trim bathrooms. The courtyard surrounding the large pool is a pleasant place to get a massage or to just relax with a cocktail in hand. ⊠ *100 Asia Rd., 63110* ☎ *055/532601 up to 08* ⊕ *www.centralhotelsresorts.com* ⇨ *113 rooms* ♢ *In-room: refrigerator. In-hotel: 2 restaurants, room service, bar, 2 tennis courts, pool, gym, public Internet, airport shuttle* ⊟ *AE, DC, MC, V.*

¢ 🏨 **Ban Thai Guesthouse.** Follow the signpost down a small lane past the Fortune guesthouse and you can find this converted white wooden Thai house. Rooms are very clean and surprisingly cool, with dark varnished floors and furniture. It's popular with expats and long-term tourists, and it's a good spot to pick up some info on the area. ⊠ *740/1 Intarakeeree Rd., 63110* ☎ *055/531590, 02/9418878 in Bangkok* ⇨ *12 rooms* ♢ *In-hotel: laundry service* ⊟ *No credit cards.*

Umphang

㉔ *164 km (100 mi) south of Mae Sot, 249 km (150 mi) southeast of Tak city*

Umphang is Tak Province's largest district. It's landlocked in the Tano Thongchai mountain range, with the high mountains making up 97% of the area; there's only one access road to it from Mae Sot. Dense rain forest rich with bamboo and teak abuts the Thung Yai Naresuan and Huai Kha Kaeng wildlife sanctuaries, as part of the Western Forest range (the largest in Southeast Asia), which due to its importance as a conservation area was classified as a World Heritage Site.

The district's distinct geography and culture is ever present. The town is a center for ecotreks to hill tribe villages and some of the oldest remaining rain forest left in the country, as well as rafting expeditions along the Mekong River to Thailand's largest and most spectacular waterfall, Thee Lor Su.

"Umphang," adapted from the Karen word "umpha," refers to the border pass that the Burmese were required to have to trade with this Thai village. The document was folded, sealed, and placed inside a bamboo cane to prevent wear; its story has become an important part of Umphang's heritage. Today, rubber boats and canoes have replaced the bamboo rafts once used on the rivers and local Karen guides are employed counteracting logging activities.

Umphang town itself is a sleepy and seasonal one with 3,000 residents of mainly Karen, Mon, and Thai. The small cluster of streets is a sight for sore eyes after a twisting four-hour songthaew ride from Mae Sot.

At almost 6 km (4 mi), **Tham Takobi** (meaning "Flat Mangoes" in Karen dialect) is Thailand's fourth-longest cave complex. The cave has three levels; the lowest and narrowest is for the more adventurous (it gets very dark and narrow in parts) and follows an active stream through the system's entire length. The main tourist cave, on the other hand, is 82 feet above the streamline; it's a big, comfortable space to explore, plastered with stalagmites and stalactites, which are lighted up. There's also another cave 98 feet above the main one. There are a total of 15 entrances poking out of the caves but the well-marked tourist entrance is the recommended choice.

Takobi is an easy 2-km (1-mi) walk from Umphang town, making it an accessible and enjoyable half-day excursion. If you intend to walk the full lower level, make sure to give yourself an early start as it will take most of the day. Also take into account that the stream is seasonal: the chambers are flooded from June through December, rendering the lower cave inaccessible. Good shoes, plenty of bottles of water, and a flashlight are essential. 🖭 *Free* ⊙ *Daily 8:30–5.*

Considered one of Southeast Asia's most spectacular falls and Thailand's
Fodor'sChoice largest, **Thee Lor Su Waterfall** is in the Umphang Wildlife Conservation ★ Area. The valley's river, tracking its way from Huai Klotho, cascades down a 984-foot limestone cliff into a green translucent pool; the clearing is surrounded by virgin mountain forest. The waterfall is a 30-minute walk from the conservation area's headquarters. Note that though the conservation area is open year-round, the best time to go rafting is during the rainy season from July through October. Rafting tours are the most rewarding means of seeing Thee Lor Su and its surrounding area, with programs readily available from agents in Umphang, as well as in Mae Sot. ⊠ *27 km (17 mi) from Umphang* 🖭 *B300* ⊙ *Daily 8:30–6:30.*

Where to Stay & Eat

Umphang's about as basic as it gets when it comes to eating options. Noodle soup and basic rice dishes are the staples, and the market adjacent to the main road can supply you with some good Umphang home cooking.

¢–$$ 🏨 **Thee Lor Su Riverside.** This resort 3 km (2 mi) uphill from town is set in spacious, beautifully tended gardens, and is a great way to start your Umphang experience. There are 10 log bungalows of varying sizes for groups as small as 2 or as large as 10. Rooms are cozy, with glowing varnished wood and plenty of blankets and cushions on long communal mattresses. Gas-powered hot-water heaters in the tiled bathrooms mean you're guaranteed a hot shower on a cool morning. The larger

Lagato house, where evening barbecues take place, is the center of activities—here you can arrange one of their popular rafting tours (one includes a flight over Thee Lor Su in a Cessna before your rafting begins). ⊠ *Hwy. 1090, 63170* ☎ *038/312050, 01/278–9292, or 01/862–0533* ⊕ *www.theelorsuriverside.com* ⇄ *15 bungalows* ⌂ *In-room: no a/c, no TV (some)* ⊟ *No credit cards.*

¢–$ ⊡ **Tukasu Cottage.** Even from the stylish green sign, you can tell that something special awaits. Flowering plants and lush foliage lead you along the grounds to contemporary hill tribe–inspired bungalows. A combination of split-bamboo and dried-grass roofs cover cozy brick-and-wood rooms. The proximity to town and smart accommodations make it a good choice. ⊠ *40 Moo 6, 63170* ☎ *055/561295, 01/819–0304, or 01/825–8238* ⇄ *12 bungalows* ⌂ *In-hotel: restaurant* ⊟ *No credit cards.*

Tak Province Essentials

Transportation

There is no commercial air service to Tak Province.

BY BIKE & MOTORBIKE

This is a good way to see Mae Sot. Bai Fern Guesthouse rents bicycles for B50 a day and 100cc motorbikes for B100 a day. A passport will be required as a deposit for motorbikes.

BY BUS

Mae Sot only has bus service to and from Bangkok. Cherd Chai Travel has first-class air-conditioned buses that leave from the new bus station at the rotary at the terminus of Asia Road, just outside town, for the eight-hour journey to Bangkok (B350); the bus also stops outside the Siam Hotel in town. It also has smaller second-class air-conditioned buses departing at 5:40 PM (6 PM outside Siam Hotel) for B241. Tanjit Tour provides a luxury 32-seat VIP bus for B350 that leaves from Intarakeeree Road, 50 feet from the police station. Service to Umphang leaves from Chitlom Road and Siri Wiang Road.

Minibuses are the main link between Tak city and Mae Sot. For B44 they take you from the Tak bus terminal to the old bus station on Chidwana Road. Going both ways, minibuses depart every 30 minutes 6:30–6; the journey takes 1½ hours.

▥ Bus Stations **Cherd Chai Travel** ☎ 055/546856 or 09/7089448. **Tanjit Tour** ⊠ Intarakeeree Rd., 50 feet from the police station ☎ 055/531835.

BY CAR

Bai Fern Guesthouse in Mae Sot rents pickup trucks for B1,200 per day.
▥ **Bai Fern** ⊠ 660 Intarakeeree Rd. ☎ 055/533343 or 09/858–4186.

BY SONGTHAEW

This is the main form of travel in Mae Sot. Songthaews to Umphang are blue and can be found on Ratchaganratchadamri 2 Road, about ½ km (⅓ mi) from the Telecommunications Building. The long four-hour ride is around B100; songthaews leave every hour from 7:30 AM to 5:30 PM.

Orange songthaews from the old bus station on Chidwana Road go to Mae Sariang, making stops in Mae Hong Son and Chiang Mai, but it's an arduous six-hour trip (though it is very cheap). They run from 6:30 AM to 5:30 PM.

If you're looking simply to get to the Thai/Myanmar border, however, jump on a songthaew at Prahsartwithee Road, 60 feet from the Siam Hotel. Hop on as they come along and expect to pay B30. For around B100 you can charter one privately.

Contacts & Resources

BANKS & EXCHANGING SERVICES
The majority of banks with ATMs and exchange services are on Intarakeeree Road, but make sure to take enough cash with you for a trip down to Umphang, because it has no exchange counters or ATMs.

EMERGENCIES
⊞ **Police** ⊠ Mae Sot ☏ 055/563937. **Mae Sot Hospital** ⊠ 175/16 Seepharnit Rd., Mae Sot ☏ 055/531229 or 055/531224.

VISITOR INFORMATION
There's no official tourist information center in Mae Sot, so your best option is contacting the No. 4 Guesthouse or Max One Tour—both have a wealth of local information, maps, and advice on what to do.

The Southern Beaches

Long tail boats, pictured here at Railay Beach, are a common form of transportation.

WORD OF MOUTH

"Krabi is still my favorite beach destination and I am from Florida. It really has a wonderful sense of calm."   —Wmccawley

"Close to Bangkok, Hua Hin has beaches, temples, elephants, etc., and is less than 30 minutes from the Sam Roi Yot National Park. You can cycle around the national park or take the trips all the resorts offer. The area is undiscovered but not remote, lots of people visit but you are also in a natural part of Thailand along the coast.
                                                                —JamesA

www.fodors.com/forums

WELCOME TO THE SOUTHERN BEACHES

TOP REASONS TO GO

★ **Sunsets at Railay Beach**
The sunsets here are unbeatable however you choose to view them: floating in a kayak, strolling along the sand, or lounging in a beachfront bungalow.

★ **Boating Around Koh Tao** Don't miss snorkeling at Shark Island, stopping for lunch at Mango Bay, and climbing to the lookout on Koh Nang Yuan.

★ **Kayaking Phang Nga Bay** Phang Nga Bay's maze of islands is ideal for gliding alongside towering cliffs.

★ **Camping at Koh Similan**
This gorgeous national park has a handful of tents for rent. Hire a longtail boat to do some snorkeling while you're here.

★ **Exploring Koh Phi Phi**
The jewel of Phang Nga Bay cannot be truly appreciated from one beach. Make day trips aboard a longtail boat: Maya Bay is a must-see and quieter Loh Samah Bay is magical.

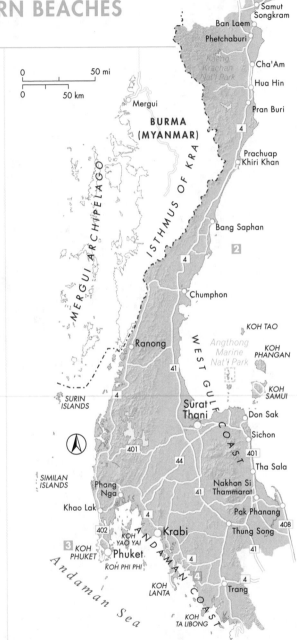

BANGKOK
Chachoengsae
Muang Boran
Phanat Nikhom
Chonburi
Sri Racha
Bang Lamung
KOH PHAI
Pattaya
Klaeng
Sattahip
Rayong
KOH SAMET
Chantaburi
CAMBODIA
EAST GULF COAST
Trat
Gulf of Thailand
KOH CHANG
Mu Koh Chang Marine Nat'l Park
Khlong Yai
KOH KUT
Kaoh Kong
KAOH KONG

1 The Eastern Gulf. Several spots are close enough to Bangkok to be easy weekend trips. Gaudy Pattaya is a wild and crazy place, but it also has a few resorts that are secluded from the insanity. Farther south are some great islands, including longtime escape-from-Bangkok favorite, Koh Samet. Koh Chang has also seen considerable growth in the past few years.

2 The Western Gulf. Cha-am and Hua Hin fill up with Bangkok escapees on weekends and holidays. The beaches only get better as you continue south along the narrow peninsula; they're all reachable from Surat Thani. Koh Samui is very developed, but perennially popular; daily flights from Bangkok make it very easy to reach.

Longtail boats line the beach.

Krabi, Koh Mor Island

3 Koh Phuket. Phuket is the hub of the western coast, with daily flights from Bangkok landing in its airport and ferries to Koh Phi Phi, Krabi, and the Similan and Surin islands departing from its docks. Though it's got its share of overdevelopment issues, Phuket has many beautiful beaches.

4 The Andaman Coast. Krabi has beautiful limestone cliffs shooting straight up out of the water that have become popular with rock climbers. Koh Phi Phi suffered severe damage from the 2004 tsunami, but it has quickly resumed its status as a prime destination for snorkeling and diving.

GETTING ORIENTED

In the miles of sandy beaches in Southern Thailand, there is pretty much something for everyone, from secluded spots in the marine National Parks to loud and gaudy resort towns, where the bar scene is a bigger draw than the beach. Thailand has two shores: the eastern shore faces the Gulf of Thailand and includes the well-known destinations of Pattaya, Koh Chang, and Koh Samui, among others; the western shore fronts the Andaman Sea, where you'll find the islands of Phuket, Koh Phi Phi, Koh Lanta, and various marine parks.

SOUTHERN BEACHES PLANNER

Safety

Driving on Phuket is dangerous. Every year hundreds of foreigners are injured in motorcycle accidents. Remember, a small wreck is much worse if you're only wearing shorts and flip-flops.

Be very careful when swimming during the monsoon season, as strong undertows often develop, especially along the west coast. Pay attention to posted warnings and listen if locals tell you not to swim in a certain place. Watch out for jellyfish.

In 2004, nearly two dozen tourists were killed in two separate ferry accidents. In both cases, the boats were ill equipped and overloaded (60 people in a boat made for 22, for example). Don't take the chance of getting on overcrowded boats; you can often hire speedboats to travel ferry routes. If you do take a ferry, travel during the day, when rescue operations are easier.

Regional Cuisine Highlights

Around the beach resorts seafood is king, usually lightly sautéed in oil and garlic or spiced up with chilies. A dish like *her thalee kanom khrok*, seafood cooked in coconut milk with spices and lemongrass, is one of the joys of visiting the south. Crabs are a real treat on Phuket. Around Surat Thani, oysters are famous; they are farmed on bamboo poles in river estuaries. Another east-coast specialty is salted eggs, coated in a mixture of salt and earth from anthills and rolled in the ashes of rice husks.

In the Gulf of Thailand, squid and shrimp are common, often lightly grilled with garlic, or in *tom yam* (hot and sour) soups with other seafood. Many of the beach-area restaurants have chefs from the northeastern province of Isan, so they cook in that style, which often means spicy. The southeast provinces Rayong, Chanthaburi, and Trat are considered fruit baskets of Thailand and during May and June there are tropical fruits in overabundance. In August, head to Surat Thani to sample rambutan, a local fruit.

In the far south, the food can get very spicy. Most of the time, Thais are very good about toning down the heat for Westerners, but you might want to ask. The magic words are *mai phet* (pronounced "my pet"), meaning "not spicy."

If prices are not listed, it's wise to ask or you might get an unpleasant surprise when they hand you the bill. Such experiences are the exception, but they happen. Note that many restaurants are seasonal—if you're traveling off-season and find a lot of closed doors, your best bet is to ask the locals for a recommendation.

WHAT IT COSTS In Baht

	$$$$	$$$	$$	$	¢
RESTAURANTS	Over B400	B301–B400	B201–B300	B100–B200	under B100
HOTELS	over B6,000	B4,001–B6,000	B2,001–B4,000	B1,000–B2,000	under B1,000

How Much Can You Do?

It's unlikely that any traveler, however intrepid, would wander down the peninsula exploring the towns along the coast. Visitors usually settle in at one resort for as many days as they have set aside. Should you wish to cover both coasts, there is a six-hour land/boat service between Phuket and Koh Samui, and both Thai Airways and Bangkok Airways have daily direct flights between the islands. You can travel from Bangkok to the beaches along the northern part of the Gulf of Thailand in a few hours. Getting to the southernmost resorts takes time. By land, count on a good 12 to 14 hours (usually through the night), or by air (including airport transfers), half a day.

If you only have two days, your best bet is to either drive south of Bangkok to Hua Hin or fly to Koh Samui—the first and last flights of the day are the cheapest fares and allow you to enjoy two full days on the island.

When to Go

In the Eastern Gulf, December to March is the best time to visit, when the seas are mostly calm and the skies mostly clear. Pattaya and Koh Samet are year-round destinations. Many places on Koh Chang and the other islands in the archipelago close down during the rainy season because the seas are rough, making boat travel difficult, and the rainy weather keeps visitors to a minimum. The big car ferries, however, continue to run on a limited schedule, and the larger resorts and many medium-range hotels stay open, offering cheaper rates.

Cha-Am and Hua Hin are year-round locations, particularly Hua Hin, which is a developed historical city that has more to offer than just the beach.

As you head farther south, the peak season depends on which side of Thailand you visit. On the Western Gulf side (including Koh Samui, Koh Phangan, and Koh Tao) the monsoon season runs from late October through December; at this time—with the exception of the week from Christmas to New Year's—prices can be halved. Peak season in the Western Gulf runs from January through early July. But even during the off-season flying to Koh Samui is still convenient, making it a year-round location. The peak season on the west coast along the Andaman Sea is November through April. The monsoon season is May through October, during which high seas can make beaches unsafe for swimming, though hotel prices are considerably lower.

Health

Health authorities have done a great job controlling mosquitoes around the southern resorts, but you'll still need a good supply of repellent. Malaria is very rare, but not unheard of in Thailand's southeast. Most accommodations either have screens on all windows and doors or at least mosquito netting over the beds. Regardless, be vigilant at dusk and dawn, and make sure there are no mosquitoes inside your net before you fall asleep! When exploring in the wilderness, use mosquito repellent with deet.

Be careful at the beach, as the sun can be stronger than you think. Wear a hat and bring along plenty of sunscreen.

Protective clothing while diving or snorkeling is a good idea, as accidentally brushing against or stepping on coral can be painful.

Keep an eye out for dangerous creatures, especially jellyfish and sea urchins. If you are stung, seek medical attention immediately.

Although Thailand has had great success stanching the spread of AIDS, those who claim that the Pattaya sex scene is safe from the epidemic are kidding themselves.

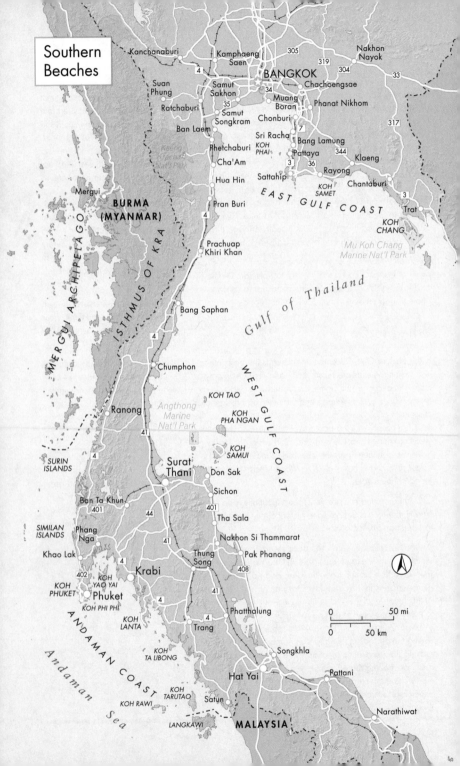

Southern Beaches

Kanchanaburi

Kamphaeng Saen

305

319

Nakhon Nayok

304

33

BANGKOK

Chachoengsae

Suan Phung

34

Muang Boran

Phanat Nikhom

Ratchaburi

Samut Sakhon

35

Samut Songkram

Chonburi

7

317

Ban Laem

Sri Racha

Bang Lamung

Rhetchaburi

KOH PHAI

Pattaya

344

Klaeng

Cha'Am

3

36

Rayong

Chantaburi

Hua Hin

Sattahip

KOH SAMET

3

Pran Buri

EAST GULF COAST

Trat

BURMA (MYANMAR)

Mergui

KOH CHANG

Prachuap Khiri Khan

Mu Koh Chang Marine Nat'l Park

MERGUI ARCHIPELAGO

Gulf of Thailand

ISTHMUS OF KRA

Bang Saphan

4

Chumphon

WEST GULF COAST

KOH TAO

Ranong

Angthong Marine Nat'l Park

KOH PHA NGAN

41

SURIN ISLANDS

4

KOH SAMUI

Surat Thani

Don Sak

SIMILAN ISLANDS

Ban Ta Khun

401

Sichon

Phang Nga

44

401

Tha Sala

Khao Lak

41

Nakhon Si Thammarat

Pak Phanang

402

KOH YAO YAI

Krabi

Thung Song

408

KOH PHUKET

4

Phuket

41

KOH PHI PHI

KOH LANTA

Phatthalung

ANDAMAN COAST

4

Trang

Andaman Sea

KOH TA LIBONG

Songkhla

KOH TARUTAO

Hat Yai

Pattani

KOH RAWI

Satun

LANGKAWI

MALAYSIA

Narathiwat

0   50 mi

0   50 km

THE EASTERN GULF

Updated by
Robin
Goldstein and
Trevor Ranges

The Eastern Gulf has long been a favorite escape from the heat and humidity of Bangkok. Its proximity to the capital means that weekend trips are possible, which in turn means that the area is overrun with sunseekers during long or holiday weekends. As the capital becomes more and more congested and its residents more affluent with disposable income, the region is growing rapidly. Some of the closer beaches have become so crowded that people now continue down the coast to quieter shores.

Many people go no farther than the coastal city of Pattaya, less than two hours south of Bangkok, which is both a notorious commercial sex hub and a popular weekend beach retreat for Bangkok residents. Pattaya is the most highly developed area in the Eastern Gulf—too much so, it seems, as two consecutive prime ministers have criticized the area as a good example of the evils of unchecked development. For years now the city has been cleaning up its beaches and its act, but it remains an eyesore to many people. But if you're looking for raucous entertainment, this is the spot, and the new world-class Sheraton resort just outside the city provides some isolation from the seedier, more frenetic side of Pattaya.

Head farther south and east for more tranquil environs. Koh Chang, Thailand's second-largest island after Phuket, has started to experience the tourism onslaught and although the pressures to overbuild are strong, at this writing it remains a charming and beautiful island.

Pattaya

 147 km (88 mi) southeast of Bangkok.

Pattaya proponents like to boast that their city has finally shed its long-standing image as the hub of Thailand's prostitution industry and emerged as a legitimate upscale beach destination. This is partly true: recent years have seen the opening of chic new restaurants and the world-class Sheraton resort. Still, Pattaya remains a city as divided as ever between sand and sex—and the emphasis still falls clearly on the latter. ⚠ **If you can't handle being surrounded at every turn by a stunning proliferation of live sex shows, hourly motels, and smut shops, then stay away from Pattaya—unless you plan on spending your entire stay within the confines of a luxury resort.** Understand, however, that commercial sex is not just a reality here: it is the lifeblood of the city.

That said, Pattaya was not always like this. Until the end of the 1950s, it was a fishing village sitting on an unspoiled natural harbor. Even after it was discovered by affluent Bangkok residents, it remained rather small and tranquil. Then came the Vietnam War, with thousands of American soldiers stationed at nearby air and naval bases. They piled into Pattaya, and the resort grew with the unrestrained fervor of any boomtown. But the boom eventually went bust. Pattaya was nearly abandoned, but its proximity to Bangkok and the beauty of the natural harbor ensured that it didn't crumble completely. In the late 1990s, after much talk and government planning, Pattaya started regaining popularity. Two

expressways were finished, making the trip from Bangkok even easier. Now that Bangkok's new international airport is open on the southeast side of the capital, it is even more convenient to visit Pattaya.

The curving bay, along which runs Beach Road, with palm trees on the beach side and modern resort hotels on the other, is the central part of the city. By the old pier are pedestrian streets where bars, clubs, and open-air cafés proliferate. South of this area is Jomtien, a beach that is somewhat overdeveloped but still pleasant enough. The northern part of the bay, over steep hills, is the quietest, most easygoing section of Pattaya. Lately, water quality in the bay is improving with the introduction of modern water- and sewage-treatment plants. Pattaya has a big water-sports industry, with a beach full of Jet Skis, paragliders, and even water-skiers.

Beaches

Some resorts, like the Royal Cliff Beach Hotel and the Sheraton, have their own beaches—rocky outcroppings around the resorts make them more secluded and more private. In addition to those smaller beaches, Pattaya has two big ones: **Pattaya Beach** on Pattaya Bay is the more active beach with Jet Skis, paragliders, and other water sports on offer all day. The bay is usually crowded with small boats. There's a nice landscaped walkway between the beach and Pattaya Beach Road. The other beach, of a bit south of the city proper, is **Jomtien Beach.** It's a long, narrow beach with grainy sand, and is quieter than Pattaya.

A third and better option is **Koh Lan,** an island 45 minutes by ferry or 15 minutes by speedboat from Pattaya Bay. The beaches here have nice white sand and the water is cleaner. There are many water sports here, too, which means that this is not where you can find that quiet place to sun and read a book. Ferries leave South Pattaya Pier daily from 10 AM to 6:30 PM and cost B20. Speedboats on Pattaya Beach are available for B1,800 round-trip, which isn't a bad deal if you have a few people to split the cost.

What to See

The **Bottle Museum** is certainly unique. Dutchman Pieter Beg de Leif created more than 300 miniatures—tiny replicas of famous buildings and ships—in bottles. ✉ *79/15 Moo 9, Sukhumvit Rd.* ☎ *038/422957* 💶 *B100* 🕑 *Daily 8:30–8.*

Though it's more famous for its nightlife, Pattaya also has quite a few activities designed for families. Children love the **Elephant Kraal,** where a few dozen pachyderms display their skills in a two-hour show. There are demonstrations of everything from their part in ceremonial rites to their usefulness in construction. Everything is staged, but it's always fun to see elephants at work and at play. Although it's a bit unsettling to see these gentle giants languishing in the city, the Elephant Kraal has a good reputation as one of the few places that doesn't mistreat the animals. One-hour elephant rides are available for an extra B700 between 8 and 5. For tickets, go to the Tropicana Hotel on Pattaya 2 Road. ✛ *5 km (3 mi) from Pattaya* ☎ *038/249145 up to 47* ⊕ *www.elephant-village-pattaya.com* 💶 *B500* 🕑 *Daily shows at 2:30 PM.*

Also popular with kids is the **Pattaya Monkey Training Center.** The pig-tailed monkeys, who live about 40 years, are adept at harvesting coconuts, a skill they are taught over the course of a year. This training is not just for show; once schooled in coconut collecting, the monkeys are each worth several thousand dollars to resorts that want their coconut trees harvested. But at this training center they are also taught a few other entertaining tricks that bring a smile to the face of even the most jaded traveler. ✉ *Km 151, Sukhumvit Rd., Soi Chaiyapruk* ☎ *038/756367 or 038/756570* 💶 *B250* 🕑 *Daily shows at 9, 11, noon, 1, 2, and 5.*

The **Ripley's Believe It or Not** is the same one you can find in America with its collection of curiosities from all corners of the world. Many are actual items, while others are replicas. There's an extensive collection here in 250 categories ranging from peculiar lifestyles to optical illusions. ✉ *3rd fl., Royal Garden Plaza, 218 Moo 10 Beach Rd.* ☎ *038/710294 up to 98* ⊕ *www.ripleysthailand.com* 💶 *B380* 🕑 *Daily 5 AM–5 PM.*

★ The **Sanctuary of Truth** is probably the most interesting place in Pattaya. The late tycoon Lek Wiriyaphen started building this massive teak structure in 1981—it's still not finished but it's open. The aim of the building, which looks like an intricate collection of carvings, was to make a statement about the balance of different cultures, mixing modern and traditional arts. The setting right next to the water north of Pattaya is pleasant, too. ⊠ *206/2 Moo 5, Naklua 12, Naklua Rd., Banglamung* ☎ *038/225407* ⊕ *www.sanctuaryoftruth.com* ✉ *B500* ◷ *Daily 8 AM–9 PM.*

Where to Eat

Much of Pattaya feels like Little America. For example, in the Royal Garden Plaza, a little mall right on Pattaya Beach Road, there's a McDonald's, a Burger King, *and* a KFC all next to one another. But Pattaya is also near Thailand's major fruit-producing provinces, as well as many fishing grounds in the Gulf of Thailand, thus ensuring both produce and seafood are fresh; lobster is a specialty. There are plenty of fancier full-scale restaurants here—a necessity because Pattaya's noise and crowds seriously detract from the simple places on the beach.

$$$$ ✕ **The Bay.** Giuseppe Zanotti's flashy new restaurant represents well the hip, modern side of Pattaya. Here you can dine at sleek modern tables overlooking the Dusit Resort's expansive pool and (you guessed it) the bay. The menu isn't just luxe (as in a rack of venison with porcini mushrooms and juniper berries), it's also unusually authentic (as in *gnochetti sardi,* Sardinian gnocchi). ⊠ *Dusit Resort, 240/2 Pattaya Beach Rd.* ☎ *038/425611* ⊕ *www.dusit.com* ▭ *AE, MC, V.*

$$$$ ✕ **Mez.** The new Sheraton resort's flagship restaurant is a wonder to be-
Fodor'sChoice hold, beginning with the most exciting menu in Pattaya. Chef Matthew
★ Woolford fuses traditional Thai ingredients with nouvelle French techniques and Indian touches to create dazzling plates like char-grilled Wagyu beef with sour green mango and roasted peanuts; a warm salad of Phuket lobster tikka with cucumber noodles, mint, and yogurt foam; or braised duck and seared foie gras in red curry with lychee and Thai basil. The atmosphere is modern but refined, with dark woods, pillows, and floor-to-glass windows that emphasize the views of gardens, waterfalls, open sea, and Coral Island in the distance. ⊠ *Sheraton Pattaya Resort, 437 Phra Tamnak Rd.* ☎ *038/259888* ⊕ *www.sheraton.com/ pattaya* ▭ *AE, DC, MC, V* ◷ *No lunch.*

$$$–$$$$ ✕ **Bruno's.** This restaurant and wine bar has built up a good reputation among the local expat community since it opened in 1986. The lunchtime set menus for B370 are a real bargain, and the set dinner menu is popular, too. The international cuisine here leans toward Swiss recipes, but you can also find a wide range of American staples. ■ TIP→ **Though the seafood and Western specialties can be pricey at dinner, the menu also includes pasta and Thai favorites that are far cheaper.** The wine list is extensive enough to necessitate a walk-in wine cellar. ⊠ *306/63 Chateau Dale Plaza, Thappraya Rd.* ☎ *038/364600 or 038/364601* ⊕ *www.brunos-pattaya. com* ▭ *AE, DC, MC, V.*

$$–$$$$ ✕ **Mantra.** This enormous, ultramodern restaurant is probably the most talked-about place to eat in Pattaya at the moment. The menu tries to cover too much geographical territory, from sushi to Italian, but at least the many cuisines come in finely realized versions: brick-oven pizza with taleggio, Gorgonzola, ricotta, pecorino, and arugula, for instance, or Wagyu beef sizzled on a lava stone. About the only cuisine you won't find here is Thai. Mantra's Kasbah-meets-soaring-wine-bar-meets-alien-invasion atmosphere is stunning. ⊠ *Amari Orchid Resort, Pattaya*

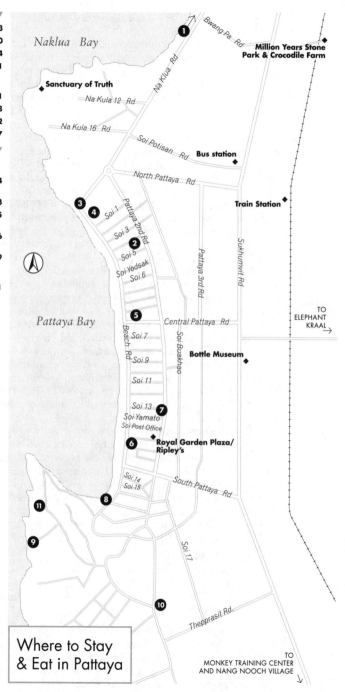

Restaurants ▼
The Bay **3**
Bruno's **10**
Mantra **4**
Mez **11**
Mum Aroi
Gourmet
Seafood **1**
Nang Nual **8**
Pic Kitchen **2**
Vientiane **7**

Hotels ▼
Amari Orchid
Resort &
Tower **4**
Dusit
Resort **3**
Montien **5**
Pattaya
Marriott **6**
Royal Cliff
Beach Hotel . . . **9**
Sheraton
Pattaya
Resort **11**

Naklua Bay

**Million Years Stone
Park & Crocodile Farm**

Bwang Pa Rd

Na Klua Rd

Sanctuary of Truth

Na Kula 12 Rd

Na Kula 16 Rd

Soi Potisan Rd

Bus station

North Pattaya Rd

Train Station

Soi 1

Pattaya 2nd Rd

Soi 3

Soi 5

Soi Yodsak

Soi 6

Pattaya Bay

Central Pattaya Rd

Pattaya 3rd Rd

Sukhumvit Rd

TO
ELEPHANT
KRAAL →

Beach Rd

Soi 7

Soi 9

Soi Buakhao

Bottle Museum

Soi 11

Soi 13

Soi Yamato

Soi Post Office

**Royal Garden Plaza/
Ripley's**

Soi 14
Soi 15

South Pattaya Rd

Soi 17

Thepprasit Rd.

TO
MONKEY TRAINING CENTER
AND NANG NOOCH VILLAGE

Where to Stay
& Eat in Pattaya

Beach Rd. ☎ *038/429591* ⊕ *www.mantra-pattaya.com* ▭ *AE, MC, V* ◷ *No lunch Mon.–Sat.*

$$ ✕ **Pic Kitchen.** This restaurant is actually a series of classic teak pavilions. You can dine inside or outside, and you can choose from table seating, floor seating, or sofas in Pic's jazz pit. The Thai dishes are consistently good, especially the deep-fried crab claws and spicy eggplant salad. All food can be made mild or spicy, but if you're really adverse to chilies, you should try the ginger-scented white snapper. ⊠ *255 Soi 5 Pattaya 2 Rd.* ☎ *038/428374* ⊕ *www.pic-kitchen.com* ▭ *AE, DC, MC, V.*

¢–$$ ✕ **Mum Aroi Gourmet Seafood.** For a very different side of Pattaya, head a bit north of the city and seek out this beautiful, romantic outdoor waterfront seafood restaurant. The almost exclusively Thai customers choose their lobsters, giant tiger prawns, crawling crabs, fresh oysters, and whole fish from a series of huge tanks and enjoy them amid shimmering pools, palm trees, and sweeping views of the bay. There is no English-language menu, so you will have to point to the seafood you want. Prices are very reasonable, especially given the upmarket feel of the place. ⊠ *83/4 Na Klua Rd., near Ananya Beachfront Condominium* ☎ *038/223252* ▭ *MC, V.*

$ ✕ **Nang Nual.** At the southern end of Pattaya Beach Road amid the bar scene is one of the city's best places for seafood. A huge array of freshly caught fish is laid out on blocks of ice at the entrance; point to what you want and explain how you'd like it cooked (most people ask for it to be grilled). A menu filled with photographs of the entrées overcomes the language barrier, and they will understand the type of cooking as long as you don't make it too complicated. For meat-lovers, the huge steaks are an expensive treat. There's a dining room upstairs, but ask for a table on the terrace overlooking the ocean. A newer branch is across from Jomtien Beach, near the Sigma Resort. ⊠ *214–10 S. Pattaya Beach Rd.* ☎ *038/428177* ⊠ *1 25/24–26 Moo 1, 2 Jomtien Beach Rd.* ☎ *038/ 231548* ▭ *AE, MC, V.*

$ ✕ **Vientiane Restaurant.** This restaurant, named after the capital of Laos, serves Laotian and Thai cuisine. The dishes from Thailand's northeastern province of Isan include arguably the best *som tam* (spicy papaya salad) in Pattaya. For something less spicy try the *gai yang* (roast chicken) with sticky rice. Laotian food is very spicy, so be sure to specify if you want those dishes mild. There's an air-conditioned dining room if it's too hot out for comfort, but if it's a pleasant evening, ask for a table outside on the terrace. The restaurant is near the Marriott Resort. ⊠ *485/18 2nd Rd.* ☎ *038/411298* ▭ *MC, V.*

Where to Stay

Pattaya is second only to Bangkok in the number of hotel rooms in Thailand. Many cater primarily to the weekend crowd, many others to the sex trade (though not the ones listed here), and still more to group tours who have Pattaya thrown into their Thailand packages.

For seclusion, you have to do some spending, but there are some excellent places to stay, like the Sheraton, the Dusit Resort, the Royal Cliff Beach Hotel, and the Pattaya Marriott Resort & Spa. Booking rooms in the better hotels is a wise idea. Be sure to ask about packages and discounts, as they'll save you a chunk of change.

$$$$ 🏨 **Dusit Resort.** Located at the northern end of Pattaya Beach, this large hotel has superb views. The beautifully kept grounds, with a lap pool and a free-form pool with a swim-up bar, are on the tip of a promontory. The rooms have comfortable sitting areas and private balconies, and the lobby is a light-soaked atrium complete with waterfalls. For a bit more you can book one of the larger "Landmark" rooms. The resort's good Cantonese and modern Italian restaurants have expansive bay views, and the new Bevarana spa is a luxurious, cutting-edge facility. This retreat is only a short songthaew ride from Pattaya attractions. ⊠ *240/2 Pattaya Beach Rd., 20150* ☎ *038/425611, 02/2636–3333 in Bangkok* ⊕ *www.dusit.com* ↵ *442 rooms, 15 suites* ⚐ *In-hotel: 3 restaurants, 3 bars, 3 tennis courts, 2 pools, water sports, public Wi-Fi* ▭ *AE, DC, MC, V.*

$$$$ 🏨 **Sheraton Pattaya Resort.** The 2005 opening of this spectacular Shera-
Fodor'sChoice ton, 1½ km (1 mi) south of town next to the Royal Cliff Beach Hotel,
★ established a new standard not just for Pattaya, but for all of the Eastern Gulf. A paradisiacal village of rooms and separate cabanas rings a series of free-form pools. The grounds are shaded by palm trees and the resort is framed by the views of the brilliant waters of the gulf. The complex includes several excellent, high-concept bars and restaurants. What further sets this resort apart are its relatively intimate size and degree of personal service—not to mention the most luxurious spa in the region. Don't miss the amazing cuisine at Mez. ⊠ *437 Phra Tamnak Rd., 20150* ☎ *038/259888, 02/2639–1734 in Bangkok* ⊕ *www.sheraton.com/pattaya* ↵ *114 rooms, 40 cabanas, 2 villas* ⚐ *In-room: safe, refrigerator, DVD. In-hotel: 4 restaurants, room service, bar, 3 pools, gym, spa, beachfront, laundry service, concierge, public Wi-Fi* ▭ *AE, DC, MC, V.*

★ **$$$–$$$$**   🏨 **Amari Orchid Resort and Tower.** Step into this open-air, modern Thai-style lobby, and you'll immediately be transported into a tropical world that's worlds away from the hectic streets of Pattaya. Classy "deluxe" rooms are comfortable and spacious, with impeccable furnishings and pleasant views of the free-form pool (or partially obstructed ocean views if you don't mind a third-floor walk-up). The gleaming new Ocean Tower wing might well vault Amari to the top of downtown Pattaya's hotel lineup. The tower will sport a new spa, executive lounge, and all rooms will have ocean-view balconies. The Orchid's buzz-worthy Mantra restaurant/bar has also fueled the resurgence of this grande dame. ⊠*Pattaya Beach Rd., 20150* ☎*038/428161* ⊕*www.orchid.amari.com* ↵ *222 rooms, 8 suites* ⚐ *In-room: safe, refrigerator, ethernet. In-hotel: 3 restaurants, 2 bars, pool, gym, spa, water sports, laundry service, concierge* ▭ *AE, MC, V.*

$$$–$$$$ 🏨 **Pattaya Marriott Resort & Spa.** This traditional-style hotel is a block from the beach. It has a large lobby that opens out onto a tropical garden and towering trees that line the path to the shimmering pool. The rooms are good size and have private balconies with ocean views. The Royal Garden Plaza is next door, so you're steps away from some of the town's best shopping, some good restaurants, and a few movie theaters. ⊠ *218 Beach Rd., Chonburi 20260* ☎ *038/412120, 02/477–0767 in Bangkok* ⊕ *www.marriotthotels.com* ↵ *300 rooms* ⚐ *In-room: safe, refrigerator, ethernet. In-hotel: 2 restaurants, bar, 4 tennis courts, pool, gym* ▭ *AE, DC, MC, V.*

$$$–$$$$ 🏨 **Royal Cliff Beach Resort.** This self-contained resort, actually a cluster of four well-kept hotels, is nothing less than an institution in Thailand. The Royal Cliff is known for its staggering size and its setting, perched high on a bluff overlooking the gulf; most rooms gaze down at the shore. But time has not been kind to the Royal Cliff: the place is starting to feel dated and impersonal, in stark contrast with the new Sheraton next door, which has easily eclipsed the Royal Cliff for best-in-Pattaya honors. On the plus side, even the standard rooms here are big and well furnished, and most have ocean-view terraces (request one ahead of time). Some lavish suites have two bedrooms, which is good for families. There are several swimming pools, each with a view. The beach is nice, but it's a bit of a hike down some stairs. The resort is about 1½ km (1 mi) south of town. ☒ *Jomtien Beach, 353 Phra Tamnak Rd., 20150* ☎ *038/250421, 02/282–1737 in Bangkok* ⊕ *www.royalcliff.com* 🛏 *966 rooms, 162 suites* ⚲ *In-room: refrigerator, Wi-Fi. In-hotel: 10 restaurants, room service, 5 bars, 2 tennis courts, 3 pools, beachfront, water sports, laundry service, concierge, public Wi-Fi* ▭ *AE, DC, MC, V.*

$$–$$$ 🏨 **Montien.** Although it couldn't be described as plush, this centrally located hotel has a laid-back atmosphere that many people prefer, and all but 17 of its rooms have terraces facing the sea. Standard rooms are aging, but "deluxe" rooms are more modern and worth the extra cost. The Montien is across from the beach, and the ocean breezes cool the hotel. The Garden Restaurant has a dance floor and stage for entertainment, which features classically kitschy Thai lounge singers each night. The hotel tends to get tour groups, but it's not overrun by them. ☒ *Pattaya 2nd Rd., Chonburi 20260* ☎ *038/428155, 02/233–7060 in Bangkok* ⊕ *www.montien.com* 🛏 *293 rooms, 7 suites* ⚲ *In-room: safe, refrigerator. In-hotel: 3 restaurants, 2 bars, 2 tennis courts, pool, public Wi-Fi* ▭ *AE, DC, MC, V.*

Nightlife

Nightlife is one of Pattaya's main draws. It goes without saying that most of that nightlife centers around the sex trade. Scattered throughout town (though mostly concentrated on Sai Song) are hundreds of beer bars, which are low-key places where hostesses merely want to keep customers buying drinks. The raunchy go-go bars are mostly found on the southern end of town. But Pattaya's, and perhaps Thailand's, most shockingly in-your-face red-light district is on Soi 6, about a block inward from the beach. The street is a sight to behold—whether that sight is interesting or sickening is your call—with hundreds of prostitutes lined up shoulder-to-shoulder, spilling out of every single bar and storefront, and catcalling to every single male passerby—morning, noon, and night. Gay bars are in the sois between Pattaya Beach Road and Pattaya 2 Road called Pattayaland.

■ TIP→ **The only bars in town that are somewhat removed from the commercial sex trade are the ones in the city's most expensive hotels.** Below we've listed a few alternatives to the red-light district scene.

In the Pattaya Marriott Resort & Spa, **Shenanigans** (☒ 218 Beach Rd. ☎ 038/710641) tries hard to conjure up an Irish pub by serving favorite brews like Guinness. A large-screen TV makes this popular with sports fans. For live music, try **Tony's** (✉ Walking Street Rd., South Pattaya ☎ 038/425795) in the heart of the nightlife district. Grab a beer and head to the outdoor terrace.

Even if you're not staying in the new Sheraton resort, it's worth the five-minute trip from town to have a drink at its bar, **Latitude** (✉ 437 Phra Tamnak Rd. ☎ 038/259888). Here you can watch the sun set over the Gulf of Siam—through plate-glass windows or alfresco—while sipping wines or well-crafted cocktails, perhaps accompanied by tapas. There's a small library adjacent to the wine bar as well. The sleek new block-buster, **Mantra** (✉ Amari Orchid Resort, Pattaya Beach Rd. ☎ 038/428–1611) is as popular for drinks as it is for food; this is the see-and-be-seen spot for businesspeople and visiting jet-setters. Don't miss the secluded table surrounded by Oriental curtains.

To get a glimpse at Pattaya's raunchier side in a way that might be more fun than strolling hostess bar–lined streets, check out one of the city's famous cabaret shows. There are memorable dance shows at **Tiffany** (✉ 6 Moo 9, Pattaya 2nd Rd. ☎ 038/421700 ⊕ www.tiffany-show.co.th), a cabaret that's famous all over Thailand. The beautiful dancers on stage are really boys, but you'd never know it. **Alcazar** (✉ 78/14 Pattaya 2nd Rd. ☎ 038/410224 up to 27 ⊕ www.alcazar-pattaya.com) provides similarly glam-boy-turned-girl entertainment and is equally famous.

Sports & the Outdoors

WATER SPORTS   Pattaya Beach is the action center for water sports. Just go to the beach and you'll easily find plenty of vendors. Jet skiing is generally B600 for 30 minutes, parasailing B500 for 15 minutes, and waterskiing starts at B1,000 for 30 minutes. All activities are available from 7 AM to 4 PM. Big inflatable bananas, yet another thing to dodge when you're in the water, hold five people and are towed behind a speedboat; riders have a screaming good time on them. They cost B1,000 or more for 30 minutes. For windsurfing, it's best to try Jomtien Beach, where you won't have to deal with all the motorized activities on Pattaya Beach.

■ TIP→ **Although Pattaya offers scuba diving, too, there are many other places in the region that are much better for diving.**

Koh Samet

❷ *30 mins by passenger ferry from Ban Phe, which is 223 km (139 mi) southeast of Bangkok.*

The 6-km-long (3-mi-long) island of Koh Samet and its beautiful beaches are accessed through the small village of Ban Phe, east of Pattaya. Two passenger ferries make the crossing, one going to Na Duan on the north shore, the other to An Vong Duan halfway down the eastern shore. You can ride a songthaew from Na Duan down the center of the narrow island, but all the island's beaches are an easy walk from either of these villages. Indeed, from the southern tip to the north is a comfortable three-hour walk.

Along with several neighboring islands, Koh Samet was made a marine national park in 1981, so there's a B200 entrance fee. The government has been unable (or unwilling) to control development on the island, and although Jet Skis are prohibited in national parks, some find their way to Samet. But there are no high-rises and just one rutted road for songthaews. Most goods are brought straight to the resorts by boat.

Koh Samet is popular with Thais and Bangkok expats, especially on weekends. Many people thought that the development of Koh Chang, a couple of hours east, would pull business away from Koh Samet, but that has yet to happen. People are not giving up on Samet just yet and it remains popular, mostly with people looking for a bit of peace and quiet and clean air. It's for the laid-back traveler who just wants to sunbathe and read on the beach.

Beaches

Koh Samet is known for its sugary beaches. The island's other name is Koh Kaeo Phitsadan (Island with Sand Like Crushed Crystal), so it isn't surprising that its fine sand is in great demand by glassmakers. The smooth water is another attraction. The beaches are a series of little bays, with more than 10 of them running along the east side of the island. The west side is mostly rocky and offers fewer accommodations.

The beaches are busier on the northern tip near Na Duan and become less so as you go south, with the exception of a congregation of bungalows near An Vong Duan, the second ferry stop.

All the beaches have licensed massage ladies walking around offering one- and two-hour Thai massages, which generally cost B50 an hour (not including tip).

Much of the north shore of the island, before the series of little bays down the east side, is rocky, but **Nanai Beach** is a nice little sandy stretch. The view is toward the mainland; the Samed Cliff Resort is just above this beach.

FodorśChoice ★ **Ao Vong Duan** is a beautiful half-moon bay, but its beach is packed with bungalows, and it's the place where you can find many Jet Skis, sailboat, and Windsurfers. It also has many restaurants. For a little more seclusion, two beaches—Ao Cho to the north and Ao Thian to the south—flank Ao Vong Duan. They're both a pleasant five-minute walk away.

Ao Kiu, near the southern end of the island, is beautiful and even more secluded. From here it's an easy walk around the southern end of the island, where you can watch the sunset. The Paradee Resort is on this beach.

Where to Stay & Eat

The island has many bungalows and cottages, with and without electricity. ⚠ **Make sure that your accommodations at least have mosquito netting: come dusk, Koh Samet's mosquitoes take a fancy to tourists.** Restaurants set up along the beach in the late afternoon; seafood is the logical choice, but there's something for everyone. While you dine, the sounds of the surf are soothing, and sometimes waves splash your feet. All three resorts below have good restaurants, but it's worth it to spend one night strolling the beaches around Ao Vong Duan and trying one of the beach restaurants. After you do, chances are you'll return.

$$$$ ▣ **Paradee Resort.** The beach here is tops—the Paradee actually spans beaches on both the east and west coasts of Samet—and is more secluded than others. Each unique bungalow has a terrace, and most have a private pool. There's also a large pool complete with a pool bar. ⚠ **The resort caters to couples; bringing small children is discouraged.** ✉ *76 Moo 4, Rayong* ☏ *02/438–9711, 02/438–9772 in Bangkok* ➘ *40 bungalows* ⚭ *In-room: safe, refrigerator, DVD, Wi-Fi. In-hotel: restaurant, room service, bar, pool, gym* ☰ *AE, MC, V.*

$–$$ ▣ **Samed Cliff Resort.** The rooms at this little cluster of bungalows are simply furnished, but they're clean and comfortable and have quite a few amenities, including hot water and air-conditioning. Out front is a small beach with white sand and calm surf. The restaurant serves Thai food, as well as a few other dishes. For dinner, venture out to one of the grills set up on the beach. This place is popular, so make reservations in advance. They offer all-inclusive packages, too. ✉ *Nanai Beach* ☏ *016/457115, 02/635–0800 in Bangkok* ⊕ *www.samedcliff.com* ➘ *30 bungalows* ⚭ *In-room: refrigerator. In-hotel: Restaurant, pool* ☰ *MC, V.*

$–$$ ▣ **Vong Deuan Resort.** This resort offers the best bungalows on Ao Vong Duan Beach and is near much of the island's activity. The best rooms are the superior ones with air-conditioning (B3,500); the other bungalows are smaller, but otherwise offer the same amenities. ✉ *Ao Vong Duan* ☏ *01/446–1944, 038/651777 in Ban Phe* ⊕ *www.vongdeuan.com* ➘ *45 bungalows* ⚭ *In-room: no a/c (some), refrigerator. In-hotel: restaurant* ☰ *MC, V.*

Chanthaburi

❸ *100 km (62 mi) east of Rayong, 180 km (108 mi) east of Pattaya.*

Buses from Rayong and Ban Phe make the 90-minute journey to the pleasant provincial town of Chanthaburi, which is on the way to Koh Chang. (You can also take a four- to five-hour bus journey from Bangkok's Eastern Bus Terminal.) Unless you're going for the gems, or the fruit in May and June, it's best to keep your visit short and continue on to Koh Chang.

The mines are mostly closed, but Chanthaburi is still renowned as a center for gems. Rubies and sapphires still rule, but stones from all corners of the world are found in the town's shops. On Gem Street, in the center of town, you can see traders sorting through gems and making deals worth hundreds of thousands of baht. The street becomes a gem market on Friday and Saturday.

Chanthaburi has played a big role in Thai history. It was here that the man who would become King Taksin gathered and prepared his troops to retake Ayutthaya from the Burmese after they sacked the capital of Siam in 1767. The King Taksin Shrine, shaped like a house-size helmet from that era, is on the north end of town and it's where locals hold a celebration in his honor from December 28 to early January.

The French occupied the city from 1893 to 1905 and some architecture from that time is still evident, particularly along the river where the city was concentrated during those years. The French influence is also evident in Thailand's largest Catholic church, the Cathedral of Immaculate Conception, which is across the river from the center of town and an easy stroll from Gem Street. A footbridge to the cathedral was washed away by a flood in 2002, but there's talk of rebuilding it. The walk to the next bridge is a bit farther now, but still an easy motorcycle taxi ride away. First built in 1711 by Christian Vietnamese who migrated to the area, the cathedral has been rebuilt four times since, and the present building was completed in the early 1900s when the city was under French control. The best time to visit is during the morning market on the grounds when local foods, fruits, and desserts are sold. But it's good for peaceful solitude anytime.

The province of Chanthaburi has few beach resorts of note, and those cater mostly to Thais. Laem Sadet, 18 km (11 mi) from Chanthaburi, is the most popular, and its accommodations range from small bungalows to low-rise hotels. Chanthaburi is once again becoming a gateway to western Cambodia as Thailand's neighbor opens its borders.

Koh Chang

★ ❹ *1 hr by ferry from Laem Ngop, which is 15 km (9 mi) southwest of Trat; Trat is 400 km (250 mi) southeast of Bangkok.*

Koh Chang, or Elephant Island, is the largest and most developed of the 52-island archipelago that was made into Mu Koh Chang National Park in 1982 (many of these islands are not much more than sandbars). Most of Koh Chang is mountainous and it has only a few small beaches. The 30-km-long (18-mi-long) island has only nine villages and 24 km (15 mi) of road linking them, with a few villages accessible only by boat. But this little paradise has been the focus of rapid development in the past few years—resorts have multiplied fourfold over the past five years.

The island is certainly in for more development. Exactly how this will all play out is unknown, but it seems like every beach has something being built or renovated, and those construction sites can certainly ruin your serenity as crews blast electric drills and saws early and late in the day. ■ TIP→ Make sure that there's no major construction project near your hotel. The places listed below are well established and, minor changes aside, they should remain pretty much the same.

To get to Koh Chang you first have to get to Trat in the east of Thailand. The easiest way is on one of Bangkok Airway's daily flights. There are also air-conditioned buses from Bangkok's Eastern and Northern bus terminals; the trip takes a little over five hours. Another option is to have a hotel or tourist office in Bangkok arrange a car or shared taxi, which is much quicker and is reasonably priced.

At the same time that the government claims it will restrict the number of cars on Koh Chang—one minister announced his intentions to make the island off-limits to vehicles from the mainland—a proliferation of new piers for car ferries have appeared along the coast south of Trat. They all accept walk-on passengers and will drop you at one of two piers on Koh Chang. Some resorts will arrange transportation from the airport; if you have to make it here on your own, take a songthaew to the pier, get the ferry to Koh Chang, and then take another songthaew to your hotel.

Songthaews are the easiest way to get around the island; just flag one down on the road. They cost between B30 and B50, or more if you venture toward the eastern part of the island.

If you plan to go many places in a day, small 100cc motorcycles are readily available for B200 a day, but drive them with care. Bicycles are harder to find for rent, but some resorts have them.

Beaches

Koh Chang's best beaches are found on the western shore. Haad Sai Khao (White Sand Beach) is the farthest north and the most developed. A few miles south is the more serene Haad Khlong Phrao, a long, curving beach of pale golden sand. Nearby Haad Kai Bae is a mix of sand and pebbles. It has a gentle drop-off, making it safe for weak swimmers. Still farther south is Haad Ta Nam (Lonely Beach), which is perhaps the most picturesque beach. But it's also the smallest one and therefore more crowded. Farther along on the southwest corner of the island is the fishing village Bang Bao, which is also experiencing development, with restaurants, dive shops, and cheap bungalows popping up.

Though the east coast is beautiful, it's mostly rugged rain forest, and beaches are in short supply.

Troops of masseurs walk the beaches—they wear uniforms and are licensed. The general price for Thai massage is B250 an hour.

Where to Stay & Eat

Despite the government's interest in turning Koh Chang into an exclusive luxury destination, mid-level and budget travelers still have plenty of options. In fact, as the tourism industry grows on the island, mid-level resorts are becoming more common than expensive upscale establishments.

Resorts are being built on some of the other islands in the marine park, including Koh Mak, which is the third-largest island in the archipelago. You can find a few bungalows for rent there, along with the Koh Mak Panorama Resort, listed below.

If the other islands interest you, the Tourism Authority of Thailand's Trat office (☎ 039/597255 and 039/597259) has information. It's near the pier at Laem Ngop, one place to catch the ferry to Koh Chang and the other islands. There's a daily ferry to Koh Mak and Koh Kharn that leaves from here as well. It's a three-hour journey to Koh Mak on the passenger ferry.

★ For seafood and skewers of chicken, pork, or beef, the neighboring Mac Resort Hotel and Koh Chang Lagoon Resort, on White Sand Beach, excel.

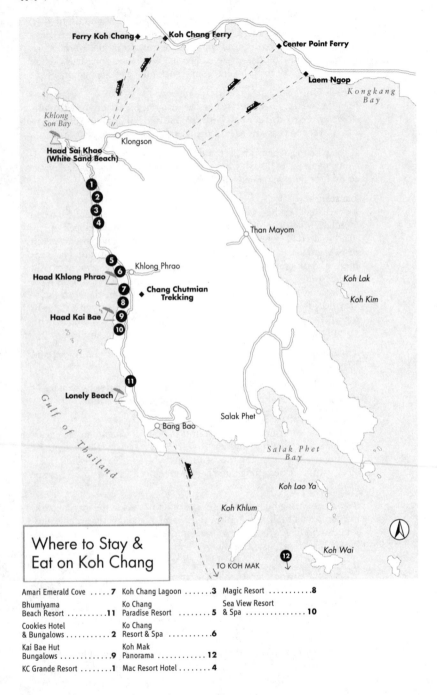

Where to Stay & Eat on Koh Chang

Both set up barbecues on the beach just before sunset. Koh Chang Lagoon Resort also offers a reasonable vegetarian selection. The only real problem is deciding which one, but you can't miss with either.

¢ ✕ **Magic Resort.** The restaurant at this resort is a rather worn wooden structure that sits over the water. A pleasant breeze usually cools the open-air dining area and there are good views of the coastline and Koh Chang's high hills. The Thai seafood is very good—try the crab if you want something spicy. There's also a reasonable Western menu. Breakfast is available all day. ⊠ *34 Moo 4, Haad Khlong Phrao Beach, Koh Chang 23170* ☎ *039/557074* ▭ *MC, V.*

$ ✕▭ **Cookies Hotel & Bungalows.** The best part of Cookies is its beachfront restaurant. The Thai food is consistently good and inexpensive and the Western backpacker fare is okay, too. The *tom yum talay* (hot-and-sour seafood soup) is a bit hot but definitely a standout; the banana shakes and the banana pancakes alone are worth a visit. As for the concrete bungalows, they're somewhat worn and basic, but they're close to the beach and prices are reasonable, even during high season. The adjacent three-story hotel is more comfortable, but although all the rooms have ocean views, the building is across the street from the beach and restaurant, so you're more likely to hear the traffic than the surf. ⊠ *7/2 Moo 4, Band Haad Sai Khao, White Sand Beach, Koh Chang 23120* ☎ *039/ 551107* ⤴ *26 bungalows, 33 rooms* ⚹ *In-hotel: restaurant, pool* ▭ *MC, V.*

★ $$$ ▭ **Amari Emerald Cove Resort.** This is currently the island's top hotel, and it lives up to its five-star standards with spacious and tastefully decorated rooms. The well-kept grounds include a 50-meter lap pool and numerous fountains, plants, and trees. With a 200-plus staff, service is exemplary, too. However, the beach is rather small and can get crowded. ⊠ *88/8 Moo 4, Haad Khlong Phrao, Koh Chang 23170* ☎ *039/552000, 02/255–3960 in Bangkok* ⊕ *www.amari.com* ⤴ *158 rooms, 7 suites* ⚹ *In-room: safe, refrigerator, DVD (some), Wi-Fi. In-hotel: 3 restaurants, 2 bars, 2 pools, gym, spa, laundry service* ▭ *AE, MC, V.*

$$$ ▭ **Ko Chang Paradise Resort.** The bungalows here are spacious and include porches and all the amenities expected in a big city hotel. They're simply furnished with a few wood accents that offset the white walls and fabrics. The pool is beachside, and some trees along the beach have swings attached to them—at high tide, you can swing out over the surf. The resort is close to Ko Chang Plaza, which has an ever-growing number of stores. ⊠ *39/4 Moo 4, Haad Khlong Phrao, Koh Chang 23120* ☎ *039/551100 or 039/551101* ⊕ *www.kohchangparadise.com* ⤴ *69 bungalows* ⚹ *In-hotel: restaurant, pool* ▭ *MC, V.*

★ $$ ▭ **KC Grande Resort.** The bungalows here vary greatly, from spacious multiroom air-conditioned ones with all the amenities, to small one-room, fan-cooled huts (though these also have a minibar and TV). This is the first property you see on the west side of the island as you drive in from the piers, and its location between a nice beach and a steep jungle-covered hill is certainly a plus. You can get a bungalow right on the beach or a row or two back. ⊠ *1/1 Moo 4, Band Haad Sai Khao, White Sand Beach, Koh Chang 23120* ☎ *039/551199, 02/539–5424 in Bangkok* ⊕ *www.kcresortkohchang.com* ⤴ *61 bungalows* ⚹ *In-room: no a/c*

4

(some), refrigerator. In-hotel: restaurant, pool, diving, laundry services ▤ *No credit cards.*

$$ ▦ **Ko Chang Resort & Spa.** This self-contained complex on the edge of the bay has a long history—it was one of the first major lodgings built on Koh Chang in the late 1980s. Rustic bungalows line the beach and the hillside, and a newer hotel building sits between the bungalows and Koh Chang's one road. The bungalows closest to the beach are nice, but they're more expensive and get more foot traffic than the hillside ones as other guests pass by to get to the beach. There's a spa offering treatments from traditional Thai massage (B300 an hour) to two-hour packages with sauna and body scrubs (B2,000). ■ TIP→ **The spa is open to nonguests—there are free transfers from any Koh Chang resort.** ✉ *Klong Prao Beach, Koh Chang 23170* ☎ *039/551082, 02/692–0094 in Bangkok* ⊕ *www.kohchangresortandspa.com* ⟲ *145 rooms* ⟐ *In-room: refrigerator. In-hotel: 2 restaurants, pool, spa* ▤ *AE, MC, V.*

★ **$–$$** ▦ **Bhumiyama Beach Resort.** The two-story bungalows here are modern and classy, with white walls and a lot of polished wood. The resort has two pools, one spilling into the other below, and landscaped grounds with several fountains and sculpture. It's next to Lonely Beach, which is beautiful, but rather small and often crowded. ✉ *Haad Tah Nam, Koh Chang 23170* ☎ *039/558067 up to 69, 02/266–4388 in Bangkok* ⊕ *www.bhumiyama.com* ⟲ *43 rooms* ⟐ *In-room: safe, refrigerator. In-hotel: restaurant, bar, 2 pools* ▤ *MC, V.*

$–$$ ▦ **Sea View Resort & Spa Koh Chang.** This resort is at the far end of Kai Bae Beach, which means it's quieter than most. Choose between bungalows just beyond the sands of Kai Bae Beach or rooms in the hotel section back and above the beach. The grounds include a big beachside pool and an attractive terrace restaurant. A spa offers everything from haircuts to three-day B14,600 packages. ✉ *10/2 Moo 4, Kai Bae Beach, Koh Chang 23170* ☎ *039/529022* ⊕ *www.seaviewkohchang.com* ⟲ *74 rooms, 2 suites* ⟐ *In-room: refrigerator. In-hotel: 2 restaurants, bar, pool, gym, spa, laundry service* ▤ *MC, V.*

$–$$ ▦ **Mac Resort Hotel.** A deluxe room with Jacuzzi and a balcony overlooking the beach or one of the bungalows clustered around the big, beachfront pool is the way to go at the Mac. It's a friendly place, with a nightly barbecue on the beach. ✉ *7/3 Moo 4, Haad Sai Khao, White Sand Beach, Koh Chang 23120* ☎ *039/551124 or 01/864–6463* ⟲ *25 rooms* ⟐ *In-hotel: restaurant, pool, public Wi-Fi* ▤ *AE, MC, V.*

★ **$** ▦ **Koh Mak Panorama Resort.** If the bungalows here look more like something you'd find on safari in Africa, it's thanks to owner Khun Luang, a Chanthaburi gem dealer who spent many years on the continent searching for rough stones. Most of the bungalows are clustered in a coconut grove above a slope that leads down to a man-made river. Bungalows have many amenities—cable TV, phone, hot water—but no air-conditioning. A few two-room bungalows on stilts right on the shoreline are a better option, but pricey at B12,000. Most of the coastline is rocky, but there's a small sandy beach near the bungalows. The sprawling open-air restaurant serves wonderful Thai food (a good thing since there's no other place to eat in the immediate vicinity). The resort can arrange transportation to Koh Mak, a small island south of Koh Chang, via speedboat from the pier at Laem Ngop. ✉ *44 Moo 1, Koh Mak 23000* ☎ *02/630–5768* *up to 69 in Bangkok, 01/858–8468 mobile* ⤙ *108 bungalows* ⟠ *In-room: no a/c. In-hotel: restaurant, bar, public Internet* ▭ *MC, V.*

¢–$ ⊡ **Kai Bae Hut Bungalows.** There are many sets of bungalows on Kai Bae Beach, which has been backpacker central on Koh Chang for awhile, but this property is the most established and reliable. One-room bungalows have fans or air-conditioning. There are a few air-conditioned hotel rooms in an adjacent building, but the bungalows are closer to the beach. With so many other resorts around, you can easily wander over to nearby restaurants for a meal. ⊠ *10/3 Moo 4, Kai Bae Beach, Koh Chang 23120* ☎ *09/936–1149 or 01/862–8426* ⤙ *38 bungalows, 20 hotel rooms* ⟠ *In-room: no a/c (some). In-hotel: restaurant, diving* ▭ *No credit cards.*

Sports & the Outdoors

ELEPHANT TREKS **Ban Kwan Chang** (☎ 01/919–3995 or 09/815–9566) in Klongson Village on the north end of the island offers a trekking program supported by the Asian Elephant Foundation. Half-day tours (from 8:30 AM until around noon) include a bathing and feeding session and a 90-minute trek into the jungle. The cost is B900 per person, which includes transportation from your hotel. There are shorter treks, as well. Most hotels can arrange trips for you, if you don't want to call yourself.

Chang Chutiman Trekking (☎ 09/939–6676 or 07/135–7424), just off Haad Khlong Phrao, offers one-hour treks for B500 and two-hour treks for B900.

HIKING Hiking trips, particularly to some of the island's waterfalls, are gaining popularity. It's a good idea to hire a guide if you plan to venture farther than one of the well-traveled routes, as good maps of the mostly jungle terrain are unheard of. At this writing, guided trips were starting to spring up. **Jungle Way** (☎ 09/223–4795) is based in the northern village of Klongson.

SCUBA DIVING & Scuba diving, including PADI courses, is readily available. Divers say
SNORKELING that the fish are smaller—there are no sharks for one thing—than in other parts of Thailand, but the coral is better and most of the dives are less than 54 feet. Prices generally run from B3,200 for a two-day PADI introductory course to more than B20,000 for dive-master certification.

Ploy Scuba Diving (☎ 01/451–1387 ⊕ www.ployscuba.com) offers a full range of dives and internationally recognized PADI courses, from beginner to dive master. Their main office is on Bang Bao Pier on the south of the island. There are offices on many of the beaches around the island, too.

OK Diving (☎ 09/936–7080), which has offices on White Sand Beach and Haad Khlong Phrao, and **Water World Diving** (⊠ Koh Chang Plaza, Khlong Phrao Beach ☎ 09/224–1031 ⊕ www.waterworldkohchang.com) both offer day dives and PADI courses, as well as snorkeling excursions.

Snorkeling off a boat costs as little as B500 a day. Snorkelers usually just tag along on dive boats, but boat excursions that feature snorkeling are available. **Thai Fon** (☎ 06/141–7498) leaves White Sand Beach each morning for a 10-hour, 15-island tour of the marine park. The trip includes stops at two or more islands (skirting the shores of the others), a buffet lunch, and two snorkeling stops. The cost is around B800. It's a good way to see some of the archipelago, including uninhabited islands, but it's a long day.

Koh Si Chang

 40 mins by ferry from Sri Racha, which is 100 km (62 mi) southeast of Bangkok.

Koh Si Chang is not known for its beaches—most of the coast is rocky—but it's off the main tourist routes, so it has an easygoing pace that makes it a real escape. It's still relatively close to Bangkok, so Thais flood the island on weekends. During the week, however, it's peaceful. Foreign visitors have increased (they're now counted by the day, not by the week), but the development mania that has taken hold of Koh Chang has not found its way here yet. This is a great island for people who want to fill their days with nothing more than a long stroll. All the sights on the island are within pleasant walks of each other, and there aren't many cars around to pose a danger to pedestrians.

For centuries Koh Si Chang was considered a gateway to Thailand—for nearly 200 years it was the spot where large ships stopped and loaded their goods onto smaller barges that then carried the goods the rest of the way to Bangkok and Ayutthaya. This practice still occurs, and ships and barges are anchored between the island the mainland. Most locals are fishermen and business folk who support fishing. Rubbish from the shipping and fishing industries lining the coast is a bit of a blight, but it's a clean island otherwise.

Koh Si Chang has been a popular retreat for three generations of royalty. In the 1800s King Rama IV noted that people on this island lived longer than most Thais (to 70 and 80 years). He concluded that this phenomenon had something to do with the island's climate and he started to spend time here. His son, King Rama V, went one step further and built a summer palace on the island, and King Rama VI would spend up to eight or nine months a year here.

To get to Koh Si Chang, you need to get on a ferry at Sri Racha, which can be reached by bus from Bangkok; ferries depart from the pier at the end of Soi 14 and run every hour from 9 AM to 6 PM. It's B40 each way. Transportation around the island is limited to motorcycle taxis, which will take you to most places for B20, and the island's unique "stretch tuk-tuks," which cost about B50 to most spots. Bicycles are not widely available.

What to See

Most people visit Koh Si Chang to relax in a friendly, nontourist-oriented community, but there are a few places worth visiting, too.

After his father King Mongkut (Rama IV) first noted people on the island lived longer here than anywhere else in Thailand, King Chulalongkorn (Rama V) built **Chudhadhuj Palace** (named after Prince Chudhadhuj who was born on the island on July 5, 1893). The palace was abandoned in 1894 when France blockaded the Gulf of Thailand during a political crisis. Few buildings remain today, but the palace gardens are great for strolling around in, and the grounds are only about 2 km (1 mi) south of town. Vimanmek Mansion was originally started here before being moved to Bangkok in 1901, and its beachside foundation remains. Nearby, an old wooden pier has been restored to its former glory.

On the north side of town is **Khao Yai Temple,** which attracts hordes of weekend visitors from Bangkok. The temple is actually a real hodge-podge of shrines and stupas that line a 400-step walkway up a steep hillside. It's an arduous climb to the main temple building, but the view of the northern half of the island, the mainland, and the rows of barges and ships is worth the effort. (You can see from the top that Koh Si Chang has no natural water sources, and the reservoir just below the temple can't seem to hold water even with a plastic lining. Nearly every roof on the island has a big water collection jar underneath.)

Wat Yai Prik, just west of town, can't be missed as you near the island by boat—it's on the top of a hill and has eight 40-foot reservoirs, as well as many smaller ones. Much of the land around the wat is covered in concrete so the rain runoff can be collected. It seems that everywhere you turn you see pipes linking the roof collection funnels to the concrete reservoirs. The wat often donates drinking water to villagers when they need it. But Yai Prik is equally dedicated to the spiritual as it is to the practical. For 26 years this was a meditation center, until its status changed in 1999—to a wat that includes meditation. Meditation courses are available; signs throughout the grounds explain Buddhist principles. It's worth a look for folks interested in the many conservation practices the residents (22 monks, one novice, and 22 nuns) employ, as well as to see a wat where simplicity rules—though donations are accepted, they don't collect wealth to build ornate temples.

Where to Stay & Eat
The island caters to mostly Thai weekend visitors, and therefore has a limited selection of guesthouses and hotels. You need to book ahead for a weekend stay, but getting a room during the week is no problem.

¢–$$ ✕ **Pan & David.** Pan and David are a Thai-American couple, and not surprisingly, their eatery offers a good mix of both Thai and Western food, as well as some inventive combinations of the two. The spaghetti with a spicy seafood sauce is tops. The open-air dining area is cooled by ocean breezes. ⊠ *167 Moo 3, Mekhaamthaew Rd.* ☎ *038/216629* ▭ *No credit cards.*

¢ ✕ **Lek Noi.** Lek Noi doesn't look like much—it's little more than a shack with plastic chairs and simple wooden tables—but many locals cite this as the best place for seafood on the island. It's a little more than a kilometer (½ mi) out of town on the way to Chudhadhuj Palace. ⊠ *Mekhaamthaew Rd.* ☎ *No phone* ▭ *No credit cards.*

$ ▦ **Rim Talay Resort.** For something a little different, stay in one of three boats that have been converted into bungalows. They're air-conditioned and sit on the beach, overlooking the rocky coast. The resort also has a hotel building, but it's rather bare-bones, and rooms aren't as comfortable as those in the converted boats. Pan & David is next door. ⊠ *130 Moo 3, Mekhaamthaew Rd.* ☎ *038/216084 up to 85* ⬦ *3 bungalows* ▤ *No credit cards.*

$ ▦ **Sichang Palace Hotel.** This is the island's biggest hotel. There's nothing particularly special about it, but it's comfortable enough and centrally located. It's often full on weekends, but nearly empty during the week. The pool is great for an afternoon dip after walking around the island. ⊠ *81 Atsadang Rd.* ☎ *038/216276 up to 78* ⬦ *56 rooms* ⚲ *In-hotel: restaurant, pool* ▤ *No credit cards.*

Eastern Gulf Essentials

Transportation

BY AIR

Because this region is so close to Bangkok, it's unlikely that you'll need to fly to get here. However, Bangkok Air does have daily flights from Bangkok to Trat.

🛦 Airport **Trat Airport** ⊠ 99 Mu 3 Tasom, Trat 23150 ☎ 039/525777 ⊕ www.bangkokair. com.

BY BUS

The bus is probably the best way to travel to the Eastern Gulf. Buses to Pattaya, Ban Phe (where you catch boats bound for Koh Samet), Chanthaburi, Trat (where ferries depart to Koh Chang), and Sri Racha (where ferries depart to Koh Si Chang) leave from Bangkok's Eastern Bus Terminal at least every hour daily.

The same buses stop in the major towns, so you can also travel between towns easily.

BY CAR

The resorts along the Eastern Gulf are fairly close to Bangkok, making a car trip here more reasonable. The drive to Pattaya takes between two and three hours. To Ban Phe it's another 90 minutes. Chanthaburi is less than four hours from Bangkok on good roads. Often the most difficult part of a drive to the region is getting out of Bangkok, which is no mean feat.

BY TRAIN

One train per day makes the round-trip journey down the eastern coast. Unfortunately, it's a third-class train with hard seats that is excruciatingly slow, and the view on the way down is an uninspiring mix of flat agricultural land and industrial estates. But if you like trains or have a good book to finish, it's a cheap option at B31. It departs from Bangkok's central Hua Lamphong Station at 6:55 AM and arrives in Sri Racha (where you disembark if you're going to Koh Si Chang) at 9:55 AM and Pattaya at 10:35 AM. The return train departs Pattaya at 2:21 PM, and Sri Racha at 3:13 PM, arriving in Bangkok at 6:25 PM. Note that this schedule is subject to change; updates are available from the 24-hour information hotline ☎ 02/220–4334. (It's also best to call this Bangkok number from Pattaya or Sri Racha.)

Contacts & Resources

BANKS & EXCHANGING SERVICES

Banks with ATMs are easy to locate in Pattaya, Chanthaburi, Trat, Koh Chang, and Sri Racha. Though hotels and resorts can also exchange currency, remember that the more remote the hotel, the less you'll get for your dollar.

EMERGENCIES

It's best to try the Tourist Police first in an emergency. Their general number is ☎ 1155.

🔳 Hospitals **Chanthaburi** ⊠ Taksin Chanthaburi Hospital, 25/14 Taluang Rd., Chanthaburi ☎ 039/351467. **Koh Chang** ⊠ Ko Chang International Clinic, 9/14 Moo 4 White Sand Beach, Koh Chang ☎ 039/551151, 01/863-3609 24 hrs ⊕ www.kohchanginterclinic. com. **Koh Si Chang (Sri Racha)** ⊠ Samitivej Hospital, 8 Soi Laemket, Choemchompon Rd., Sri Racha ☎ 038/324100. **Pattaya** ⊠ Bangkok Pattaya Hospital, 301 Moo 6, Sukhumvit Rd. Km 143, Banglamung, Chonburi ☎ 038/259911 emergency, 66/3825-9999.

VISITOR INFORMATION

🔳 Tourist Information **Tourism Authority of Thailand (Pattaya Office)** ⊠ 382/1 Moo 10, Chaihat Rd. ☎ 038/427667 or 038/428750. **Tourism Authority of Thailand (Trat office)** ⊠ 100 Moo 1, Trat-Laem Ngop Rd. ☎ 039/597259 or 039/597260.

THE WESTERN GULF

South of Bangkok lies the Western Gulf coast, hundreds of miles of shoreline where resort towns are the exception rather than the rule. Most towns along the gulf are either sleepy fishing villages or culturally and historically significant towns, such as Surat Thani. Some touristy areas have grown up out of the smaller villages, but they are considerably less developed than some of their counterparts in the other coastal areas. Thus, the allure of the Western Gulf is its charming towns, spectacular beaches, and developed—but not overgrown—tourist destinations.

About three hours south of Bangkok are the laid-back beaches of Cha-am and Hua Hin. Popular with families and weekend warriors escaping from the bustling capital, these nearby towns offer visitors quiet beaches and lots of great seafood restaurants. Bangkokians have traveled to Hua Hin since the 1920s, when King Rama VII built a palace here. Where royalty goes, high society inevitably follows, but despite the attention the city received, Hua Hin was spared the pitfalls of rapid development thanks to Pattaya's explosion onto the tourism scene. The Eastern Gulf city received most of the development dollars, as well as most of the woes of overdevelopment, while Hua Hin retained its tranquil beauty.

Another 483 km (300 mi) south is Surat Thani, the former capital of an ancient Siamese kingdom. As the center of its own civilization, Surat Thani developed its own artistic and architectural style. In modern times it has remained an important commercial and historic Thai city,

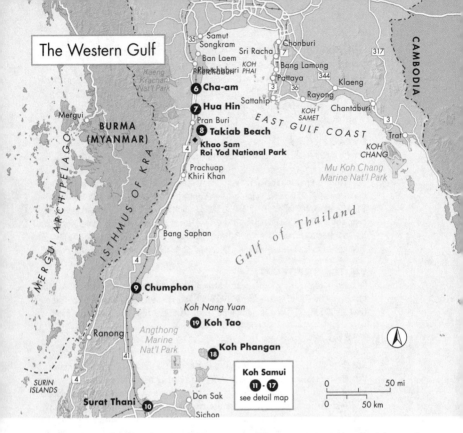

The Western Gulf

and the province is home to one of the most pristine tropical forests in Thailand, Khao Sok National Park. However, most travelers know Surat Thani only as a departure point for the islands off its coast, primarily Koh Samui.

Koh Samui is the most popular tourist destination on the Western Gulf coast, which isn't surprising, considering Samui's gorgeous beaches, perfect weather, and sparkling blue water. Samui has been developed quite rapidly since the mid 1990s, but there's still a good variety of experiences to choose from. Here, you can find beaches in all stages of development. If you can't find what you want on Samui, there are boats departing regularly to Koh Phangan, a more natural island that draws backpackers, new-age types, and hippies, and to Koh Tao, a hot spot for scuba divers.

Cha-am

6 *163 km (101 mi) south of Bangkok, 40 km (25 mi) from Petchaburi town.*

It may not be the cleanest or most picturesque seaside town, but Cha-am does offer an authentic Thai-style beach experience. The small, quiet town is centered around the main pier; its main street, full of restaurants, bars, guesthouses, and hotels, lies along a tree-lined strip of beach. You can often see Bangkok families here—gathered at large, umbrella-covered tables for all-day meals, stocking up on fresh seafood and beer from wandering vendors.

Around the pier there are beach chairs, Jet Skis, Windsurfers, and banana-boat rides for hire, but the beach here has fairly dirty sand. Most visitors head to one of the many all-inclusive resorts farther from the town beach, where the sand is generally nicer and the water is better for swimming. Other than during occasional festivals, such as the seafood festival in September, there isn't a whole lot going on in Cha-am town.

Where to Stay & Eat

Fresh seafood is available at small cafés along Ruamchit (Beach) Road, where there are also stalls selling trays of deep-fried squid, shrimp, and tiny crab (for around B25). A steadily improving mix of small hotels and guesthouses for all budgets lines this road, while a string of luxury hotels and resorts runs along the main highway south of town to Hua Hin.

$–$$$ ✕ **Poom Restaurant.** The seafood here is perhaps the best in town, evidenced by a steady stream of locals. Try the charcoal-barbecue whole fish, large prawns, crab, and squid—all fresh and accompanied by delicious chili sauce dip. The decor is nothing special—of the metal-table-and-plastic-chair variety—but there's some outside seating under the trees. The restaurant next door (owned by the same people) has an air-conditioned dining area, if you really can't take the heat. ⊠ *274/1 Ruamchit Rd., Cha-am* ☎ *032/471036* ▤ *No credit cards.*

$$$–$$$$ ▥ **Regent Cha-am.** Taking a swim couldn't be easier than at the Regent Cha-am, which has a quartet of pools spread among the dozens of bungalows that face the beach. The Lom Fang restaurant, overlooking a lake, grills up excellent fish accompanied by a spiced curry-and-lime sauce. The more formal restaurant, the Tapien Thong Grill Room, serves seafood and steak. In the evening live musicians sing your favorite pop songs in Thai. The hotel has its own car service from Bangkok. ⊠ *849/21 Cha-am Beach, Cha-am 76120* ☎ *032/451240 up to 49, 02/2510305 in Bangkok* ⊕ *www.regent-chaam.com* ◗ *630 rooms, 30 suites* ⚬ *In-room: safe, refrigerator. In-hotel: 7 restaurants, room service, tennis court, 3 pools, gym, spa, water sports* ▤ *AE, DC, MC, V.*

★ $$ ▥ **Sabaya Jungle Resort.** Whether you're relaxing in your room or chilling out in the common area, you can feel at home at this cute, personable resort. Rooms are either "Tropical," wooden bungalows with comfortable mattresses on the floor and stylish bathrooms with bamboo walls, or "Madagascar," with regular beds and TVs and housed within a concrete structure alongside the pool. The common area has comfortable chairs to relax in and have coffee or tea. Sabaya also has a competent spa staff to ensure that you know you're on holiday. The resort is not on the beach, but it's only about a block away. The water there is swimmable and water sports can be found a short walk down the beach toward town. Driving to Sabaya, turn left at the 208-km mark along Highway 4 south. ⊠ *304/7 Nong Chaeng Rd., Cha-am 76120* ☎ *032/470716 or 032/470717* ⊕ *www.sabaya.co.th* ◗ *7 bungalows* ⚬ *In-room:*

refrigerator, no TV (some). In-hotel: restaurant, spa, laundry service ▭ No credit cards.

$ ▣ **Kaenchan Beach Hotel.** Chinese box lanterns and Thai teak benches with silk cushions fill this boutique hotel's modern entrance hall and open-fronted bar and lounge. Some rooms have ocean views, and garden bungalows are also available. The price drops by 25% during the week. The Thai and international restaurant specializes in seafood. ✉ *241/4 Ruamchit Rd., Cha-am* ☎ *032/470777* ⊕ *www.kaenchanbeach. com* ⇗ *73 rooms* ⚲ *In-hotel: restaurant, bar, pool* ▭ *MC, V.*

Hua Hin

❼ *66 km (41 mi) from Cha-am, 189 km (118 mi) south of Bangkok.*

Before the introduction of low-cost air carriers in 2003, Bangkokians had few choices for weekend getaways. One of the preferred destinations has been the golden sand near the small seaside city of Hua Hin, and Bangkok's rich and famous are frequent visitors here. The most renowned visitors are the King and Queen of Thailand who now use the Klai Kangwol Palace north of Hua Hin town as their primary residence. The palace was completed in 1928 by King Rama VII, who gave it the name Klai Kangwol, which means "Far From Worries."

Hua Hin's beach is the nicest of those along this part of the coast, but it's also the most popular. The sand is soft enough for sunbathing, though wandering hawkers will frequently disrupt your solace with silk cloth and fresh fruit for sale. You can get away from them figuratively by booking a relaxing beach massage or literally by taking a horseback ride to less populated parts of the beach. Jet Skis, kayaks, Windsurfers, and all other water sports can be arranged at various areas along the beach or through any tour agent.

Hua Hin town, which has many hotels and guesthouses, is also a great place to try fresh Thai seafood dishes. Many of these restaurants are on wooden piers, allowing you to dine above the sea.

The town also has a vibrant night market where souvenirs and local foods are available in abundance. The **Chatchai Street Market** is fun to explore. In the morning vendors sell meats and vegetables. From 5 PM to 11 PM daily, stalls are erected along Dechanuchit Street. You can practice your haggling skills over goods as diverse as jewelry, clothes, vases, lamps, toys, and art. You can also sample a variety of Thai delicacies, exotic fruits, desserts, pancakes, barbecue chicken, and just about anything that can be skewered on a stick, including the local favorite, squid.

When the upper classes from the capital followed the royal family to Hua Hin, they needed somewhere to stay. The Royal Hua Hin Railway Hotel was constructed to give these weary travelers somewhere to rest their heads. Near the intersection of Damnernkasem and Naresdamri roads you can still see the hotel, now called the **Sofitel Central Hua Hin Resort.** The magnificent Victorian-style colonial building was a stand-in for the hotel in Phnom Penh in the film *The Killing Fields.* Be sure to wander through its well-tended gardens and along the lovely verandas.

OFF THE
BEATEN
PATH

KHAO SAM ROI YOD NATIONAL PARK – You'll pass rice fields, sugar palms, pineapple plantations, and crab farms as you make your way to this park, about 63 km (39 mi) south of Hua Hin. The park has two main trails and is a great place to spot wildlife, especially monitor lizards and barking deer. With a little luck you can see the dusky langur, a type of monkey also known as the spectacled langur because of the white circles around its eyes. About a kilometer (½ mi) from the park's headquarters is Khao Daeng Hill, which is worth a hike up to the viewpoint, especially at sunrise. Another 16 km (10 mi) from the headquarters is Haad Laem Sala, a nice white-sand beach—you can pitch a tent here or stay in a guesthouse. Near the beach is Phraya Nakhon Cave, once visited by King Rama V. The cave has an opening in its roof where sunlight shines through for a beautiful effect. If you don't have a car (or haven't hired one), you'll have to take a bus to the Pranburi District in Prachuab Kiri Khan Province. From here, you'll be able to get a songthaew to take you to the park. ☎ *066/3261–9078* ⊕ *www.dnp.go.th.*

Where to Stay & Eat

$–$$$ ✕ **Monsoon Restaurant & Bar.** Monsoon serves tasty tapas, afternoon tea (3 PM–7 PM), and a full menu of Thai and Vietnamese cuisine, including vegetarian entrées and a daily set menu. To wash down dishes such as *luc lac* (sautéed beef) and *tom yam goong* (spicy shrimp soup), Monsoon serves up creative cocktails like the Tonkin Wave (Midori, Creme de Banana, and pineapple juice). The restaurant is in a two-story colonial-style building, which has an elegant open-air dining room and garden terrace. ⊠ *62 Naresdamri Rd., Hua Hin* ☎ *032/531062* ⌂ *Reservations essential* ▤ *MC, V.*

¢–$$ ✕ **Hua Hin Restaurant (KOTI).** A longtime local favorite for Thai-style seafood, Koti has a no-nonsense decor and typically full tables that attest to its primary focus: good food. A large menu (in English) includes fried fish with garlic and pepper, and *hor mok talay* (steamed seafood curry). ⊠ *61/1 Petchkasem Rd., Hua Hin* ☎ *032/511252* ▤ *No credit cards.*

¢–$$ ✕ **Sang Thai.** Ignore the ramshackle surroundings and floating debris in the water—for interesting seafood dishes from grilled prawns with bean noodles to fried grouper with chili and tamarind juice, this open-air restaurant down by the wharf can't be beat. It's popular with Thais, which is always a good sign. Don't miss the *kang* (mantis prawns). ⊠ *Naresdamri Rd.* ☎ *032/512144* ▤ *AE, DC, MC, V.*

$$$$ ▦ **Chiva-Som.** Even with the proliferation of spas in Hua Hin, Chiva-Som has not been toppled from its lofty position as one of the region's, if not the world's, best destination health resort and spa. The resort focuses on holistic healing and a wholesome diet, but the setting on the beach will do you a world of good, too. Personalized programs begin with a questionnaire upon arrival, addressing diet, detoxification needs, or any other physical or mental health concerns. For the remainder of your stay obsequiously courteous staff (six per guest room) will help you heal, through educational talks in the library, Watsu treatments (shiatsu massage while floating in a body-temperature pool), and individually tailored diets. The tasteful and comfortable rooms have lots of natural

Fodor'sChoice
★

woods and private terraces that overlook the ocean. ⊠ *73/4 Petchkasem Rd., Hua Hin 77110* ☎ *032/536536* ⊕ *www.chivasom.com* ⌁ *57 rooms* ᗌ *In-room: DVD. In-hotel: restaurant, pool, spa* ▤ *AE, DC, MC, V.*

$$$$ 🏨 **Evason Hideaway and Evason Hua Hin Resort.** These neighboring properties are both located on a quiet beach in Pranburi, approximately 20 minutes south of Hua Hin. The newer Hideaway resort has villas and suites, all of which have private plunge pools and outdoor tubs, along with lounging areas with comfy daybeds shaded by umbrellas. The older Evason Resort has a few pool suites as well as more standard hotel rooms. The resorts share facilities, so there are two spas to choose from, both soft and hard tennis courts, several restaurants, and a gorgeous beachside swimming pool. Daily activities include morning tai chi and afternoon Tibetan Healing Breathing Technique classes, as well as sports as diverse as archery and windsurfing. ⊠ *9/22 Moo 5 Paknampran, Pranburi, Prachuap Kiri Khan, 77220* ☎ *032/618200 Hideaway, 032/ 632111 Resort* ⊕ *www.sixsenses.com* ⌁ *Hideaway: 38 villas, 17 suites; Resort: 145 rooms, 40 villas* ᗌ *In-room: safe, refrigerator, DVD (some), Wi-Fi. In-hotel: 3 restaurants, room service, bar, 8 tennis courts, pool, gym, 2 spas, water sports* ▤ *AE, MC, DC, V.*

★ $$$$ 🏨 **Sofitel Central Hua Hin Resort.** Even if you don't stay at this local landmark, its old-world charm makes it worth a visit. Originally built in 1923 for visitors to King Rama VII's summer palace, the hotel has wide verandas open onto splendid gardens that lead down to the beach. More than two dozen gardeners take their work very seriously, caring for the topiaries that look like shadows at night. The lounges on either side of the reception area are open to let in sea breezes. The best rooms are those on the second floor—they have unforgettable views of the ocean. ▦ TIP→ **Stay here during the low season, when rates are almost half of what they are the rest of the year.** On-site activities include badminton and two putting greens. ⊠ *1 Damnernkasem Rd., Hua Hin 77110* ☎ *032/ 512021 up to 38, 02/541–1125 in Bangkok* ⊕ *www.sofitel.com* ⌁ *207 rooms, 30 suites* ᗌ *In-room: safe, refrigerator, Wi-Fi. In-hotel: 3 restaurants, bar 2 tennis courts, 3 pools, gym, spa, water sports* ▤ *AE, DC, MC, V.*

★ $$$–$$$$ 🏨 **Anantara.** The whole resort is surrounded by a 10-foot-tall terra-cotta wall, and you will feel as if you are entering an ancient Thai village, rather than a beach resort. The lobby, like much of the resort, features numerous works of Thai art, furniture, and flowers. All rooms are within two-story brown-and-burnt-orange structures that are surrounded by five distinct gardens and a lagoon; the color scheme is so complementary and the grounds are so beautiful you could spend a whole day photographing yourself at any number of Anantara's picturesque resting spots. When you need actual rest, you can always head back to your room and collapse on the huge, comfy sofa on your balcony. At night, tiki torches light up the walkways that connect the rooms with the restaurants. Activities include Thai cooking classes, croquet, and elephant-riding classes in the resort's elephant camp. For large groups, there are even elephant polo lessons! ⊠ *43/1 Phetkasem Beach Rd., Hua Hin 77110* ☎ *032/520250* ⊕ *www.anantara.com* ⌁ *187 rooms* ᗌ *In-room: safe,* *refrigerator, ethernet. In-hotel: 4 restaurants, 3 bars, 2 tennis courts, 2 pools, gym, spa, water sports, bicycles, laundry service* ☰ *AE, MC, V.*

$ ▨ **Jed Pee Nong.** This complex of bungalows and a small high-rise building is on one of the main streets leading down to the public entrance to the beach. The bungalows are clustered around a swimming pool, but most rooms are in the hotel building. Rooms have huge beds and not much else, but the price couldn't be better. The terrace restaurant facing the street stays open late. ⊠ *17 Damnernkasem Rd., Hua Hin 77110* ☏ *032/512381* ✐ *baanjedpeenong@thaimail.com* ➥ *40 rooms* ♿ *In-room: safe. In-hotel: 2 restaurants, pool* ☰ *MC, V.*

★ **¢–$** ▨ **Fulay Guesthouse.** This unique guesthouse is built on a pier that juts out over the gulf. The Cape Cod–blue planks of the pier match the color of the trim around the whitewashed walls; rooms have kitschy effects like seashell-framed mirrors and sand-encrusted lamps. Two large, private houses claim prime real estate toward the end of the pier, with private wooden decks ideal for sipping afternoon drinks or watching early-morning sunrises. If you prefer not to sleep to the sound of the sea beneath your bed, opt for the more modern but reasonably priced Fulay Hotel across the street. ⊠ *110/1 Naresdamri Rd., Hua Hin 77110* ☏ *032/513145 or 032/513670* ⊕ *www.fulay-huahin.com* ♿ *In-room: no a/c (some), no TV (some). In-hotel: restaurant, bar, laundry service, public Internet* ☰ *MC, V.*

¢ ▨ **Pattana Guesthouse.** Two beautiful teakwood houses are hidden down a small alley in the heart of Hua Hin. The main house used to be a fisherman's residence and now holds a variety of clean, simple rooms facing a small garden bar and café. Rooms with fans have either private or shared bathrooms. ⊠ *52 Naresdamri Rd., Hua Hin 77110* ☏ *032/513393* ➥ *13 rooms* ♿ *In-room: no a/c. In-hotel: restaurant, bar, laundry service* ☰ *No credit cards.*

Takiab Beach

8 *4 km (2½ mi) south of Hua Hin.*

Khao Takiab, the beach directly to the south of Hua Hin, is a good alternative for people who wish to avoid Hua Hin's busier scene; tourists who stay in Takiab are mostly well-off Thais who prefer Takiab's exclusivity to Hua Hin's touristy atmosphere, and you can find many upscale condos and small luxury hotels here. The beach itself is wide and long, though the water is quite murky and shallow, and not very suitable for swimming. Sunbathing is the ideal activity here, especially during the low tide when the golden, sandy beach is flat and dry. To get to Takiab, flag down a songthaew (B10) on Petchkasem Road in Hua Hin. Alternatively, you can take a horseback ride from the beach in Hua Hin and trot along the coast to Takiab (horses are also available from Takiab). The usual water activities like jet skiing and banana-boating are available here, and are more enjoyable than in Hua Hin as the beach and water are less crowded. The southern part of the beach ends at a big cliff, which has a tall, standing image of the Buddha. You can hike to the top of the hill, where you find a small Buddhist monastery and several restaurants with excellent views.

Where to Stay & Eat

$–$$$ ✕ **Supatra-by-the-Sea.** The outdoor seating at this restaurant on the southern end of the beach allows you to dine beneath the tranquil gaze of the standing Buddha on the adjacent hillside. The dining room is exquisitely designed in Lanna-style and has water-lily ponds beside several tables. Entrées are mainly seafood-based, such as prawn sour soup with deep-fried green omelet, although other Thai dishes and vegetarian dishes are included on the extensive menu. The full bar serves inventive cocktails, which may be enjoyed beside the beach. ⊠ *122/63 Takiab Beach* ☎ *032/536561* ▤ *AE, MC, V.*

$$$–$$$$ ☐ **Smor Spa Village & Resort.** Smor's accommodations are nearly identical in design to neighboring Kaban Tamor Resort—spacious, single-story, mushroomlike bungalows—but the rooms at Smor have private, outdoor Jacuzzis. The spa has several treatment rooms, saunas, and steam rooms. Sun beds are available on the lawn adjacent to the beach, which is convenient when all of the sand is submerged at high tide. ⊠ *122/64 Takiab Beach, 77110* ☎ *032/536800* ⊕ *www.smorspahuahin.com* ⇨ *6 rooms* � *In-room: refrigerator. In-hotel: restaurant, spa, laundry service* ▤ *MC, V.*

$$$ ☐ **Kaban Tamor Resort.** Rooms at this stylish resort are inside two-story structures that were designed after seashells, but look more like mushrooms. The spacious, round rooms have white walls and pale wooden floors and are filled with plenty of natural light. A small pool and soft grass are alongside the beach. The open-air restaurant serves tasty Thai food. Guests at Kaban Tamor get a 20% discount at Smor Spa next to the resort. ⊠ *122/43–57 Takiab Beach, 77110* ☎ *032/521011 up to 13* ⊕ *www.kabantamor.com* ⇨ *23 rooms* � *In-room: refrigerator. In-hotel: restaurant, room service, bar, pool, laundry service* ▤ *AE, MC, V.*

Chumphon

❾ *400 km (240 mi) south of Bangkok, 211 km (131 mi) south of Hua Hin.*

Chumphon is regarded as the gateway to the south, because trains and buses connect it to Bangkok in the north, to Surat Thani and Phuket to the south, and to Ranong to the southwest. Ferries to Koh Tao dock at Pak Nam at the mouth of the Chumphon River, 11 km (7 mi) southeast of town. Most of the city's boat services run a free shuttle to the docks.

If you're overnighting here or have a couple of hours to spare before catching a bus, visit the night market. If you have more time, just north of Chumphon there's an excellent beach, **Ao Thong Wua Laen.** You can catch a songthaew on the street across from the bus station. The curving beach is 3 km (2 mi) of white-yellow sand with a horizon dotted by small islands that make up one of the world's strangest bird sanctuaries. Vast flocks of swifts breed here, and their nests are harvested for the bird's nest soup served up in the best Chinese restaurants of Southeast Asia. It's such a lucrative business that the concessionaires patrol their properties with armed guards.

Where to Stay

$ ☒ **Chumphon Cabana Beach Resort.** This friendly resort at the south end of Chumphon's Thong Wua Beach is a great place to stay if you want to make brief visits to Koh Samui and other nearby islands. The hotel wins top marks for its eco-friendly program, designed to save water and power and keep the beach free of the litter that too often disfigures Thai resorts. Accommodations are in bamboo-wall bungalows hidden in the lush foliage and rooms with private balconies in several low-rise buildings. Furnishings are simple but tasteful. ☒ *69 Thung Wua Laen Beach, 86230* ☎ *077/560245 up to 49* ⊕ *www.cabana.co.th* ☜ *73 rooms* ⌂ *In-room: refrigerator. In-hotel: restaurant, bar, diving, laundry service* ☱ *MC, V.*

¢ ☒ **Marokot Hotel.** This is not the most luxurious hotel in Chumphon, but the rooms are comfortable and the baths have plenty of hot water. The hotel is a short walk from the night market. Best of all, the rates are among the lowest in town. ☒ *102/112 Taweesinka Rd., 86000* ☎ *077/503628 up to 32* ☜ *60 rooms* ☱ *No credit cards.*

Surat Thani

⑩ *193 km (120 mi) south of Chumphon, 685 km (425 mi) south of Bangkok.*

Surat Thani is the main embarkation point for boats bound for Koh Samui. Although it's not a particularly attractive city, don't despair if you have to stay overnight while waiting for your ferry. There are some good restaurants and a handsome hotel. In addition, every night sleepy downtown Surat Thani turns into an electrifying street fair centered around the **San Chao Night Market,** which is illuminated by the lights of numerous food stalls and shop carts. The market is quite popular with Surat locals, as well as with the few tourists in town. If there are too many choices, pad thai seafood is the best solution—it's safe and consistently good. Looking for a tasty dessert? Across the street from the market, you can find Tavorn Roti, which serves delicious traditional roti.

☺ There's also the possibility of an entertaining excursion to one of Thailand's most unusual educational establishments, the **Monkey Training College** (☒ Km 91, Hwy. 401 ☎ 077/273378). Here, under almost scholastic conditions, monkeys are trained to climb high palms and collect the coconuts that are still an important part of the local economy. And for those who can't get enough of Thailand's cultural sites, the 1,000-year-old **Wat Phra Barommathat** in the ancient city of Chaiya is the most intriguing one in the area. The simian school and Chaiya are only a short songthaew ride from Surat Thani.

Where to Stay & Eat

$–$$ ✕☒ **Wang Tai Hotel.** If you find yourself searching for a place to stay in Surat Thani, this modern high-rise offers everything to prepare you for the onward journey. Rooms here overlook the Tapi River. The local tourist office is a few blocks away. The hotel's restaurant is among the best in Surat Thani, with a predominantly Thai and Chinese menu. The dim sum is excellent. ☒ *1 Talad Mai Rd., 84000* ☎ *077/283020, 02/253–*

7947 in Bangkok ✆ *230 rooms* ⬥ *In-room: refrigerator. In-hotel: 2 restaurants, room service, bar, pool, gym, laundry service* ▭ *AE, MC, V.*

Koh Samui

20 km (12 mi) by boat east of Don Sak.

Koh Samui is half the size of Phuket, so you could easily drive around it in a day. But Samui is best appreciated by those who take a slower, more casual approach. Most people come for the sun and sea, so they head straight to their hotel and rarely venture beyond the beach where they are staying. However, every beach has its own unique character and with a little exploration, you may find the one most suitable for you.

On the east coast of Samui lies **Chawaeng Beach**, the island's primary destination. Chawaeng has the best beach; the greatest variety and number of hotels, restaurants, and bars; and consequently, the largest crowds. During the day, the beaches are packed with tourists; the ocean buzzes with Jet Skis, parasailers, and banana boats. At night, the streets come alive as shops, bars, and restaurants vie for your vacation allowance.

Lamai Beach, to the south of Chawaeng, is just as long as Chawaeng Beach and nearly as nice. The water is deeper, so it's less suitable for young children, but water sports are readily available and the beach itself is much less congested. The accommodations here range from a few swanky resorts, far from the center of town, to a large selection of budget guesthouses and bungalows. Lamai's nightlife might be slightly more subdued than Chawaeng's but it's also a bit more sordid, with many beer bars blasting Thai pop music and employing numerous young Thai hostesses.

On the northern coast are the less developed beaches of **Mae Nam** and **Bophut.** Mae Nam town is a relatively busy, local business district along the road from Chawaeng to Nathorn. Mae Nam Beach, on the other hand, is one of the least developed and most natural beaches on the island. There's little nightlife and few distractions there. Bophut Beach has both high- and low-end accommodations and a small romantic fishermen's village with several nice seaside restaurants, bars, and boutique shops.

Nathorn Town, on the west coast of Samui, is the primary port on the island, where ferries and transport ships arrive from and depart to the mainland. Nathorn has the island's governmental offices, including the Tourism Authority of Thailand (TAT). There are also banks, foreign exchange booths, shops, travel agents, restaurants, and cafés by the ferry pier. There are even a few places to rent rooms, although there would be little reason to stay in Nathorn—nicer accommodations can be found a short songthaew ride away.

The high-class resorts of **Choengmon Beach,** on the northeastern cape, provide luxury accommodations and service on small, often private, beaches. Several other high-end resorts and alternative health retreats are on various beaches around the rest of the island. These include many international chains, designer-boutique resorts, and top-tier spas.

CLOSE UP

Diving & Snorkeling Responsibly

DECADES OF VISITORS SCUBA-DIVING IN THAILAND'S ISLANDS and reefs has had far greater negative effects on marine life than the 2004 tsunami. Considering that the number of visitors is quickly returning to pre-tsunami levels, every diver needs to be aware of, and consequently minimize, his or her impact.

As fascinating as something you see may be, **do not touch anything** if possible, and **never stand on anything other than sand.** Coral is extremely fragile, urchins are as painful as they look, and sharks may be no threat to divers, but you can appreciate the foolishness of grabbing one's tail. Other dangers to both you and the environment are less obvious: eels live within holes in rocks and reef; turtles are mammals that require air to breathe and even some dive instructors are guilty of "hitching a ride" on them, causing the turtles to expend precious air. Let instructors know you find this behavior unacceptable. Furthermore, **don't feed fish human food**—feeding the fish bread, peas, or even M&Ms may be entertaining, but it rewards more aggressive fish to the detriment of species diversity.

Divers should also **make sure equipment is securely fastened or stored,** so that no items are lost or scrape against coral. Divers should also **maintain level buoyancy** to prevent inadvertent brushes with coral, as well as to save air. Snorkelers who need to remove their masks should pull them down around their necks rather than up on their foreheads. Masks can fall off and quickly sink, and a mask on the forehead is considered a symbol of distress. When snorkeling, you can **minimize underwater pollution by checking your pockets** before jumping into the water. Conscientious divers can clip a stuffsack to their BCDs to pocket random trash they encounter. Lastly, it seems like a no-brainer, but apparently many people need to be reminded: **don't flick your cigarette butts into the water.**

Sunscreen is a must anytime you are exposed to Thailand's tropical sun. Snorkeling unprotected is a guaranteed skin disaster (and painful obstacle to the rest of your holiday); however, sunblock, when dissolving into the water from hundreds of visitors each day, is bound to take its toll on the marine environment. You can limit the amount of sunscreen you must slather on by covering your back with a Lycra Rashguard or a short- or long-sleeve shirt while snorkeling.

Follow the credo: "Leave only footprints, take only memories (or photographs)." Try to minimize your impact on this ecosystem in which you are only a visitor.

4

OFF THE BEATEN PATH

MU KOH ANGTHONG NATIONAL MARINE PARK – Although some visitors prefer to enjoy sunbathing on the white sand and swimming in the blue sea of Samui Island, many choose a trip to Angthong National Marine Park. Angthong is an archipelago of 42 islands, which cover some 250 square km (90 square mi) and lie 35 km (22 mi) northwest of Samui. The seven main islands are Wua Ta Lap Island, which houses the national park's headquarters; Phaluai Island; Mae Koh Island; Sam Sao Island;

Hin Dap Island; Nai Phut Island; and Phai Luak Island. The islands feature limestone mountains, strangely shaped caves, and emerald-green water. Most tourists do a one-day trip, which can be arranged by most travel agents on Samui. Prices vary from agent to agent since they all offer different tours (i.e., some offer kayaking around several islands, while others take you out on small speedboats to do snorkeling or more comprehensive tours of the numerous caves and white-sand beaches). If you're interested in more than a one-day tour, you can hire a taxi-boat to take you out to the national park's headquarters on Wua Talap Island where there are five huts for rent and a campsite. If you stay overnight you should also have time to hike up to the viewpoint at the top of Wua Talap. The park is open year-round, although the seas can be rough and the waters less clear during the monsoon season (October through December). ☎ *077/286025 or 077/420225* ⊕ *www.dnp.go.th.*

Sports & the Outdoors

Although many people come to Samui to chill out on the beach, there are dozens of activities, certainly more than one vacation's worth. In addition to the activities listed below, you can arrange paintball, go-karting, shooting, and bungee jumping through most hotels and tour agents on the island.

You can go up into the mountains and explore the jungle and some of the waterfalls by car. If you're more adventurous, you can get a different view of the jungle by sailing through the air on a zipline. **Canopy Adventures** (☎ 077/414150) will have you zipping among six tree houses on 330 yards of wire strung across the tree canopies. If you prefer to stay on the ground, you can arrange a ride at the **Sundowner Horseranch** (☎ 077/424719) in Ban Thale. Elephant treks are available through **Samui Namuang Travel & Tour** (☎ 077/418680). The interior of the island can also be explored on mountain bikes from **Red Bicycle** (☎ 077/232136).

Finally someone has figured out how to fit an actual golf course on the island; Santiburi Dusit Resort has build a driving range and an 18-hole course, at the **Santiburi Samui Country Club** (☎ 077/421710 up to 14 in Samui, 02/6644270 up to 74 in Bangkok), using the natural terrain of the Samui mountains to create a challenging multilevel golfing experience. Also, one enterprising company, **Extra Golf Club** (☎ 077/422255), has built a 3-hole course. Alternatively, you can shoot a round of Frisbee golf (same idea as regular golf, but Frisbees are tossed from the putting area to the "holes," which are actually baskets). Head to **Frisbee Golf** (☎ 091/894–2105), near Bophut, laugh your way through a round of "golf," and grab an ice-cold beer at the end.

Mae Nam

❶ *10 km (6 mi) northeast of Na Thon.*

Mae Nam lies on the northern coast of Samui. Its long and narrow curving beach has coarse golden sand shaded by tall coconut trees. It's a very quiet beach, both day and night, with little nightlife and few restaurants. The gentle waters are great for swimming, but water sports are limited to what your hotel can provide. Several inexpensive guesthouses and a few luxurious resorts share the 5-km (3-mi) stretch of sand. Mae Nam

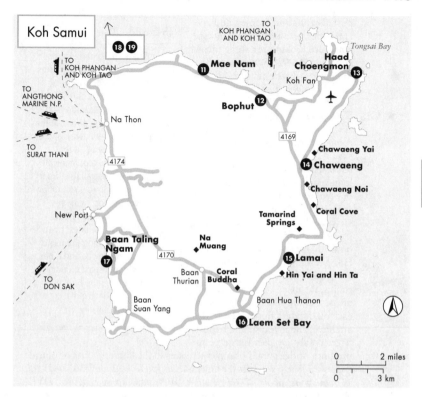

is certainly the most "un-Samui" of Samui's beaches; a place for those who want simple relaxation on an otherwise highly developed island.

Mae Nam is also the departure point for speedboats and Lomprayah Catamaran leaving Samui for Phangan and Koh Tao. Transport on these boats can be arranged from anywhere on the island.

WHERE TO
STAY & EAT

$–$$$

✕ **Kohseng.** This two-story seafood restaurant has been feeding Mae Nam locals for decades. Although the interior is quite simple, the big sign in front of the restaurant shows off the stars it has earned, along with a few suggested dishes from Khun Muek Daeng, Thailand's renowned food critic. Once inside, don't be intimidated by the local crowd—menus are in both Thai and English and the staff speaks English. The most famous dish, stir-fried crab with black pepper, is highly recommended. ⊠ *95 Soi Kohseng, Mae Nam Beach* ☎ *077/425365* ⌨ *Reservations essential* ▭ *No credit cards.*

¢–$$

✕ **Angela's Bakery & Café.** Angela's, on the main road running through Mae Nam, serves salads and sandwiches, both traditional and inventive. The "Hot Bandana" is a tasty vegetarian sandwich baked inside a bread bowl and wrapped in a bandana. Entrées represent Samui's British influence: bangers and mash, fish-and-chips, and the like. In addition, Angela's sells 20 types of bread, more than 40 desserts, a variety of imported meats and cheeses, and several types of muffins, just in case you were looking for some picnic goodies. ✉ *64/29 Samui Ring Rd., Mae Nam Beach* ☎ *077/427396* ⊕ *www.angelasbakery.com* ⊟ *No credit cards.*

★ **$$$$** ⌕ **Napasai.** The name means "clear sky" and if you book a beachfront room, you can enjoy the view of the sky *and* the sea from your outdoor terrace, from inside the room as you lounge on L-shaped floor cushions, or even from your bathtub. Garden spa rooms make up for their lack of views with large living rooms and spacious showers and bathrooms, both adjacent to an outdoor waterfall. Multilevel private pool villas are the epitome of luxury: the bedrooms, the living room and kitchen areas, and the swimming pools are each on different floors. The staff is attentive, and if you should happen to get a rainy day, they'll arrange impromptu bridge games or other activities in the library or bar or outside the resort to help you pass the time. ✉ *Ban Tai, Koh Samui* ☎ *077/429200* ⊕ *www.pansea.com* ⇆ *69 rooms* ♨ *In-room: safe, refrigerator, DVD, Wi-Fi. In-hotel: 2 restaurants, room service, 2 bars, 2 tennis courts, pool, gym, spa, laundry service, public Wi-Fi* ⊟ *AE, DC, MC, V.*

> **THE SPA LIFE**
>
> The ultimate spa experience on the island is at **Tamarind Springs** (✉ 205/7 Thong Takian, Lamai Beach ☎ 077/230571 or 077/424436 ⊕ www.tamarindretreat.com). Leave your cell phone at the door, put the camera away, and, oh yeah, forget about all that stress and tension, too. Many different options are available, from Thai massage to herbal relaxation to the "Over the Top" massage package, which lasts 2½ hours. The spa employs the latest treatment trends, including the use of Tibetan singing bowls, and it has added additional spas, dipping pools, and a tearoom, built harmoniously into Tamarind's boulder-strewn hillside.

★ **$$$$** ⌕ **Santiburi Resort and Spa.** The villas on this beachfront estate make you feel as if you're staying at a billionaire's holiday hideaway; accordingly, this is one of the most expensive lodgings on the island. The carefully chosen furnishings in the teak-floor rooms are casual, yet elegant. The "less is more" philosophy extends to the huge bathrooms, which have shiny black tiles. Floor-to-ceiling French windows flood the living rooms with light. The main building, a classic Thai pavilion overlooking the oval swimming pool, has European and Thai restaurants. The private beach is ideal for water sports and has a jetty for the hotel's own cruise ship, a 60-year-old junk. ✉ *12/12 Samui Ring Rd., Mae Nam Beach, 84330* ☎ *077/425031 up to 38, 02/636–3333 in Bangkok, 800/223–5652 in U.S.* ⊕ *www.santiburi.com* ⇆ *71 villas and suites* ♨ *In-room: safe, refrigerator, DVD, Wi-Fi. In-hotel: 3 restaurants, room service, 2 bars, golf course, 2 tennis courts, pool, gym, spa, beachfront, diving, water sports, laundry service, public Internet* ⊟ *AE, DC, MC, V.*

$$$–$$$$ ⌕ **Amarin Victoria Hotel.** For those who want more urbane lodging, Amarin Victoria is a "city hotel" near the sea. The decor is hip and trendy; polished concrete walls lead to comfortable yet stylish rooms. Black and white are the predominant colors here, and most rooms have multiple, pivoting doors that allow the various sections to open to each other. The rooftop pool and lounge area compensate for the hotel's short distance from the beach. ✉ *12/71 Samui Ring Rd., Mae Nam Beach, Koh Samui, 84330* ☎ *077/425611 up to 15* ⊕ *www.amarinsamuiresort.com* ➽ *46 rooms, 14 suites* ⚘ *In-room: safe, refrigerator, DVD, Wi-Fi. In-hotel: restaurant, room service, bar, pool, spa, laundry service, public Wi-Fi* ⊟ *AE, DC, MC, V.*

$–$$ 🏠 **The Florist.** This guesthouse is quite small and you're likely to feel that you are sharing rooms in someone's home. Most rooms have balconies with partial sea views, but the huge seafront room has a full-view of Phangan from its large deck, outdoor tub, and huge sun bed. Although the rooms in the old wing have aging furniture and a slightly musty smell, they are private enough that you can keep doors open at night to allow the breeze to blow through. Rooms in the new wing have a boutiquey decor, with wooden furniture and Thai art on the walls. ✉ *190 Mae Nam Beach, 84330* ☎ *077/425671 up to 72* ➽ *15 rooms, 1 suite* ⚘ *In-room: safe, refrigerator, no TV (some). In-hotel: restaurant, pool, laundry service* ⊟ *AE, DC, MC, V.*

Bophut

⑫ *11 km (7 mi) east of Na Thon.*

A small headland separates Mae Nam from the north shore's other low-key community, Bophut. The beach here is quite narrow, but more than wide enough for sunbathing. During the rainy season the runoff waters make the sea slightly muddy. Otherwise, the water is like glass, good for swimming (though it's deep enough to be unsuitable for young children). Lodgings here range from backpacker hangouts to upscale resorts. Unlike ultraquiet Mae Nam, Bophut has a bit more nightlife—Central Bophut, referred to as the fishermen's village, has a beachside strip of old two-story Chinese shophouses that have been converted into restaurants, bars, and boutiques. Although the scene is small, there's ample variety, including Italian and French cuisine, English and Australian pubs, and even a few clubs with DJs. Bophut, quaint and romantic, has a devoted following of return visitors who enjoy its compact and quiet environment.

WHERE TO STAY & EAT
¢–$$$

✕ **Happy Elephant.** Owner Khun Sasothon displays the day's freshest seafood on ice in front of his restaurant. Choose your favorite and specify how you'd like it cooked. After a drink at the bar, sit outside on the deck perched above the beach and dine under the stars. You can spot the twinkling lights of Koh Phangan across the ocean. Other dishes are also delicious—the *tom yam pla nam sai* (spicy soup with fish) is strongly recommended. On the Beach, the adjoining restaurant has a larger menu and a canopied, outdoor patio that is cooled by large fans. Wi-Fi is available for restaurant patrons in both establishments. ✉ *79/1 Moo 1* ☎ *077/245347* ⊟ *AE, MC, V.*

$ ✕ **Starfish and Coffee.** You won't find any starfish on the menu, but there's a great deal more on offer here than just coffee. Fresh seafood is prepared in a variety of ways; fish, crab, squid, prawns, and mussels are cooked with garlic and pepper, chili and basil, and a number of other primarily Thai styles. The interior is a funky fusion of Thai and Chinese styles. Seating is outdoors by the sea or indoors on rattan chairs or floor pillows. A decent selection of international wines is on the menu, but interestingly, only a scant few choices of coffee. ✉ *51/7 Moo 1, Bo Phut Village* ☎ *077/427201* ▤ *MC, V.*

★ $$$$ ✕▣ **Anantara Resort Koh Samui.** Anantara captures the essence of Samui: coconut trees dot the grounds, monkey statues and sculptures decorate the entire resort, and, of course, there is a beautiful beach. All rooms have ocean views from their large patios and are designed in a modern Lanna style. Each room also has a tank with several colorful Thai fighting fish. You'll feel like a rock star performing on stage when dining at the Full Moon Italian Restaurant—the dining room is a large open platform beside the swimming pool. The High-Tide Thai restaurant allows you to interact with your chef, who is working near your table and will alter any dish to your exact specifications. Booking a treatment at the stylish spa is a must. ✉ *101/3 Samui Ring Rd., Bophut Beach, 84320* ☎ *077/428300* ⊕ *www.anantara.com* ⬤ *82 room, 24 suites* ♻ *In-room: safe, refrigerator, DVD, Wi-Fi. In-hotel: 2 restaurants, room service, bar, pool, tennis court, gym, spa, water sports, bicycles, laundry service, public Wi-Fi* ▤ *AE, DC, MC, V.*

$$$$ ▣ **Bandara Resort and Spa.** Bandara gets high marks immediately for convenience: it's on the nicest stretch of Bophut Beach, and although the resort's facilities will be able to meet nearly all of your needs, the restaurants, bars, and shops in the fisherman's village are a short walk away. The deluxe rooms in the large, multistory complex aren't particularly special, but they all have decks with daybeds. Private villas have gardens complete with outside tubs and showers and shady daybeds perfect for massages. Five spa treatment rooms provide a variety of facials and massages. The seaside restaurant serves seafood and Thai dishes. ✉ *178/2 Moo 1, Bophut, Koh Samui, 84320* ☎ *077/245795, 02/2368260 in Bangkok* ⊕ *www.bandararesort.com* ⬤ *151 rooms* ♻ *In-room: refrigerator, DVD, Wi-Fi. In-hotel: 2 restaurants, 2 bars, 3 pools, gym, spa, diving, water sports* ▤ *MC, V.*

$$–$$$$ ▣ **Peace Resort.** Formerly the budget accommodation Peace Bungalow, Peace Resort was renovated in 2006 and is now a vibrant mid-range resort, although it maintains the same friendly spirit and attitude. Clusters of cottages have bright yellow rooms, with green-and-blue trim and lots of natural lighting. Superior rooms have big beds and tile floors; deluxe rooms also have separate living rooms. Bathrooms in both have mini indoor gardens. The staff is very friendly and helpful. ✉ *178 Samui Ring Rd., Bophut Beach, 84320* ☎ *077/425357 or 077/427063* ⊕ *www.peaceresort.com* ⬤ *102 rooms* ♻ *In-room: safe, refrigerator, ethernet. In-hotel: restaurant, room service, bar, pool, spa, laundry service* ▤ *MC, V.*

$ ▣ **The Lodge.** The Lodge is small, elegant two-story building, a renovated Chinese shophouse in the center of the fishermen's village. The building has one terrace facing the street, perfect for people-watching, and the other terrace overlooks the ocean and distant Koh Phangan. The rooms have warm and romantic lighting and the location, on the beach in central Bophut, can't be beat. ✉ *91/1 Fisherman's Village, Bophut Beach, 84320* ☎ *077/425337* ⊕ *www.lodgesamui.com* ⬤ *7 rooms, 2 penthouses* ♻ *In-room: safe, refrigerator. In-hotel: bar, laundry service* ▤ *MC, V.*

$ 🏠 **Red House.** This is no misnomer: The Red House has red walls, red furniture, and red bedding—almost too much red, though considering it's a converted Chinese shophouse, the red lanterns seem particularly appropriate. There is a small seaside patio for snacks and coffee and a rooftop garden with the best view in Bophut. A small boutique in the front sells mostly cool women's shoes and a few Chinese-style women's tops. ⊠ *Fisherman's Village, Bophut, Koh Samui* 📞 *077/245647* 🌐 *www.design-visio.com* 🛏 *4 rooms* 🛁 *In-room: refrigerator, Wi-Fi. In-hotel: restaurant, room service, bar, laundry service* ▭ *MC, V.*

¢–$ 🏠 **Cactus Bungalows.** Colorful, funky huts are set in an unmanicured, natural environment. Instead of clunky bedsteads, mattresses rest on rounded platforms, giving rooms an organic feel. The bar and restaurant by the beach is pretty basic, but it does have a pool table. As you can imagine, Cactus Bungalows is a pretty laid-back place. ⊠ *175/7 Moo 1, Bophut Beach, 84320* 📞 *077/245565* 🌐 *www.sawadee.com/hotel/samui/cactus* 🛏 *13 bungalows, 1 suite* 🛁 *In-room: no a/c (some). In-hotel: restaurant, bar, laundry service* ▭ *MC, V.*

Haad Choengmon

⓭ *20 km (12½ mi) east of Na Thon.*

On the northeast coast of Samui lies Haad Choengmon. Choengmon is one of several small beaches that line the northeastern cape. A few guesthouses, a handful of resorts, and some restaurants are scattered along the shore of this laid-back beach. The sand is firm and strewn with pebbles and shells, but adequate for sunbathing. For a little adventure, walk east to the bend in the beach and wade through the water to **Koh Fan Noi,** the small island 30 yards offshore. The water all along the beach is swimmable, with a shallow shelf, and there are all varieties of water sports to choose from, including catamarans, Sunfish, Windsurfers, and kayaks.

Off the western shore of the northeastern tip of Koh Samui is **Koh Fan** (not to be confused with Koh Fan Noi), a little island with a huge seated Buddha image covered in moss. Try to visit at sunset, when the light off the water shows the statue at its best.

WHERE TO STAY

★ $$$$ 🏠 **SALA Samui.** Bright, nearly all-white rooms have both retractable and open doorways that lead to private courtyards on one side, and curtain enclosed bathrooms on the other. Only some rooms have small private pools in their courtyards, but all have large oval bathtubs, which are nearly as nice and certainly as romantic. The two-bedroom Presidential Pool Villa has a larger pool and more space to fill with equally lavish accoutrements. SALA restaurant, beside the pool and overlooking the beach, has a wonderful evening atmosphere. ⊠ *10/9 Moo 5 Baan Plai Laem, Koh Samui, 84320* 📞 *077/245889* 🌐 *www.salasamui.com* 🛏 *69 rooms* 🛁 *In-hotel: restaurant, room service, bar, 2 pools, spa, beachfront, public Wi-Fi* ▭ *AE, DC, MC, V.*

$$$$

Fodor'sChoice

★ 🏠 **Sila Evason Hideaway & Spa.** From the moment you're greeted by the management and introduced to your private butler, you'll realize that this is not just another high-end resort—you're about to embark on an amazing experience. Your butler will escort you via electric car to your private villa. The rooms have plush bedding, tubs arranged near shutters that open to give you flawless ocean views, separate outdoor showers, and a variety of lighting options. The 30-meter pool on the cliff matches the color of the ocean and the infinity edge is level with the horizon, making you feel like you could swim off into the sea. Dining on the Hill serves an exquisite and comprehensive breakfast buffet, and Dining on the Rocks has a romantic private terrace perfect for indulging in innovative and exotic cuisine. The resort even employs its own consultants to make sure it is environmentally friendly. ⊠ *9/10 Bay View Bay, 84320* ☎ *077/245678* ⊕ *www.sixsenses.com* 🛏 *66 villas* ⚏ *In-room: safe, refrigerator, DVD, Wi-Fi. In-hotel: 2 restaurants, room service, 2 bars, pool, gym, spa, beachfront, laundry service, concierge, public Wi-Fi* ⊟ *AE, DC, MC, V* ⎟⚏⎥ *BP.*

★ **$$$$** ⊞ **Tongsai Bay.** The owners of this splendid all-suites resort managed to build it without sacrificing even one of the tropical trees that give the place a refreshing and natural sense of utter seclusion. The suites, contained in luxurious wooden bungalows, have large private terraces. They also have outdoor bathtubs or private pools and some have beds outside the rooms, protected by mosquito nets. Furnishings are nothing short of stunning, with individual touches such as fresh flowers. The resort is perfect for honeymooners, as the entire resort exudes a "love at first sight" vibe. It's on a private beach just to the north of Choengmon that is suitable for sunbathing. The water is okay for cooling off in, but better for water sports, like windsurfing, which are available from the resort. ⊠ *84 Tong Sai Bay, 84320* ☎ *077/245480 or 077/245544* ⊕ *www.tongsaibay.co.th* 🛏 *83 suites* ⚏ *In-room: safe, refrigerator, DVD. In-hotel: 3 restaurants, room service, bar, 2 tennis courts, 2 pools, gym, spa, beachfront, laundry service, public Internet* ⊟ *AE, DC, MC, V* ⎟⚏⎥ *BP.*

$$$–$$$$ ⊞ **White House Beach Resort and Spa.** Step back in time as you pass under the Khmer-style stone facade and enter the classic lobby, which is filled with giant Chinese vases, Persian carpets, and classic Lanna art. Beyond the lobby, lush gardens with tall palms, fragrant flowers, and vines provide the surroundings for a row of two-story concrete buildings with nearly 9-foot-tall wooden doors and Ayutthaya-style roofs. The decoration in the rooms contributes to the old-world feeling of opulent style, with silk comforters and throw pillows covering the beds and separate sitting rooms in ground-floor rooms. The pool is surrounded by Thai sandstone art. ⊠ *59/3 Choeng Mon Beach, 84320* ☎ *077/247921 up to 23* ⊕ *www.hotelthewhitehouse.com* 🛏 *32 rooms, 8 junior suites, 3 Thai suites* ⚏ *In-room: safe, refrigerator, DVD. In-hotel: restaurant, pool, spa, public Wi-Fi* ⊟ *AE, DC, MC, V.*

$$–$$$ ⊞ **Samui Honey Cottages.** The cottages at this small, cozy resort on one of Samui's quieter beaches have glass sliding doors and peaked ceilings. Bathrooms have showers with glass ceilings. Dine alfresco under hanging gardens, or walk down the beach and have fresh seafood at the beachside restaurant across the channel from Koh Fan Lek. ⊠ *24/34 Choeng Mon Beach, 84320* ☎ *077/245032 or 077/279093* ⊕ *www.samuihoney. com* 🛏 *19 bungalows, 1 suite* ⚏ *In-room: safe, refrigerator. In-hotel: restaurant, laundry service* ⊟ *MC, V.*

$ ⊞ **Island View II.** The small bungalows here each have room for a bed, a small desk, and little else. But there are few reasons to stay indoors, and the bungalows do have their own decks with tables and chairs. A small beach bar and restaurant sits just 10 yards from the water and beachside massage is available next door. ⊠ *Choeng Mon Beach, 84320* ☎ *077/245360* ✉ *islandview_02@hotmail.com* ⇥ *9 rooms* ⚑ *In-room: refrigerator. In-hotel: restaurant, bar, laundry service* ▤ *No credit cards.*

Chawaeng

⓮ *20 km (12½ mi) east of Na Thon.*

Koh Samui's most popular beach is Chawaeng, a fine stretch of glistening white sand, divided into two main sections—Chawaeng Yai (yai means "big") and Chawaeng Noi (noi means "little"). Travelers in search of sun and fun flock here, especially during the high season. But despite the crowds, Chawaeng is no Pattaya or Patong—the mood is very laid-back.

Chawaeng Yai is divided by a coral reef into two sections: the secluded northern half is popular with backpackers, while the noisy southern half is packed with tourists who flock to the big resorts. Many of the women, young and old, wear little to the beach at Chawaeng Yai (note that locals find this display of skin offensive, although they usually say nothing). Chawaeng Noi is not as developed. The salt air has yet to be permanently tainted by the odor of suntan oil, but there are already hotels here, and more are on the way.

South of Chawaeng is **Coral Cove,** popular with scuba divers. It's not as idyllic as it once was, because unthinking travelers have trampled the beautiful coral while wading through the water (and worse, many have broken off pieces to take home as souvenirs). To see the lovely formations that still exist a little farther from shore, get a snorkel and swim over the reef—just be careful not to inflict further damage by stepping on it.

WHERE TO STAY & EAT

$$–$$$$ ✕ **Betelnut.** Owner and internationally experienced chef Jeffrey Lord oversees both the dining room and the kitchen, greeting guests and explaining the menu before rushing back to the kitchen to assist with his concoctions. The style is Californian-Asian fusion cuisine. Try "The Buddha jumped over the wall" as a starter, or blackened tuna with Samui salsa for an entrée. Also excellent is the summer roll with prawns and scallops, covered with sesame sauce. For dessert, try one of the interesting ice cream flavors, like red chili, a great mix of sweet and tingly. ⊠ *Soi ColiburiSouth Chawaeng Beach* ☎ *077/413370 or 077/414042* ⊕ *www.betelnutsamui.com* ▤ *MC, V.*

★ **$$–$$$$**   ✕ **Eat Sense.** If you wandered onto Eat Sense's manicured grounds from the street or approached it from the beach, you might assume that it's simply another boutique beach resort. Although there certainly is room for a resort on the grounds, Eat Sense focuses solely on serving up great Thai food. The dining area has several small fountains and towering palms from which hang giant paper lanterns. Dine on the patio beside the beach or on couches beneath white umbrellas, sip creative cocktails (like the Sabai Sabai Samui, winner of a Samui bartending competition) served in coconut shells, and nosh on exotic seafood creations, such as Phuket lobster with eggplant and Kaffir leaves in a green curry paste. Reservations are recommended, particularly during the high season. ✉ *Near Central Samui Resort* ☎ *077/414242* ▭ *MC, V.*

¢–$ ✕ **Ninja.** This no-frills dining room is authentic Thai and therefore very popular with locals and foreigners alike. The Thai curries like *massaman* (peanut-based) or *panaeng* (chili paste and coconut milk) are solid choices, but you really can't go wrong here. Save room for classic Thai desserts, such as *khao niew mamuang* (mango and sticky rice). Ninja's expansive menu includes large color photographs of every dish on the menu, along with phonetic Thai and English captions. ✉ *Samui Ring Rd., Chawaeng Beach* ☎ *No phone* ▭ *No credit cards.*

$$$–$$$$ ✕▦ **Muang Kulaypan Hotel.** This hotel puts a little more emphasis on design than some of its neighbors. Instead of the teak, antiques, and flowing fabrics you'll find at most resorts going for a "classic Thai" look, here you'll get simple lines, minimal furnishings, and sharp contrasts. There's a sort of subtle Javanese-Thai theme throughout, reflected in the artwork selected for the rooms. The VIP Inao suite allows you to sleep in a bed once used by King Rama IV. Bussaba Thai restaurant serves uncommon but authentic Thai food. Note that rooms on the wings, farther from the main road, are considerably quieter. Standard rooms are the only rooms that don't have ocean views. ✉ *100 Samui Ring Rd., North Chawaeng Beach, 84320* ☎ *077/230849 or 077/230850* ⊕ *www.kulaypan.com* ⤶ *41 rooms, 1 suite* ⚲ *In-room: safe, refrigerator. In-hotel: restaurant, room service, bar, pool, gym, laundry service, public Wi-Fi* ▭ *AE, DC, MC, V* ❙◎❙ *BP.*

$$$$ ▦ **The Briza.** Rather than try another iteration of Thai design, The Briza chose what can best be described as a fusion of Indian and Chinese styles for its variety of villas. Duplex villas are more minimalist, with concrete floors, daybeds on the ground floor, and spacious baths and bedrooms on the second floor. Outside the rooms, the deck chairs beside the pool convert into massage beds. Pool villas have open-air living rooms and large, canopied beds facing small terraces with Jacuzzis. Beachfront pool villas look out over the quieter northern end of Chawaeng Beach, which is ideal for guests who want seclusion from the chaos of the main drag. ✉ *173/22 Moo 2, Chawaeng Beach, Koh Samui, 84320* ☎ *077/ 231997, 02/2513118 up to 21 in Bangkok* ⊕ *www.thebriza.com* ⤶ *57 villas* ⚲ *In-room: safe, refrigerator, DVD, Wi-Fi. In-hotel: restaurant, pool, spa* ▭ *AE, MC, V* ❙◎❙ *BP.*

$$$$ ▦ **Central Samui Beach Resort.** This spacious resort has larger grounds and more amenities than any other resort on Chawaeng Beach. The main building, which has the rooms, is set back behind a large field separating it from the beach. Badminton, basketball (hung from a coconut tree), and Ping-Pong cover one side of the field; a sunbathing area, which runs from the grass to the pool, occupies the other. Multiple happy hours run at different hours at the indoor, pool, and beach bars. Dining possibilities include an excellent Japanese restaurant, as well as two others serving Thai and Chinese dishes. The beach has a large cordoned-off swimming area to protect swimmers from Jet Skis. Rooms have hardwood floors and bathtubs with doors that open into the main body of the room. ✉ *38/2 Samui Ring Rd., South Chawaeng Beach, 84320* ☎ *077/ 230500* ⊕ *www.centralhotelsresorts.com* ⤶ *199 rooms, 9 suites* ⚲ *In-room: safe, refrigerator, Wi-Fi. In-hotel: 4 restaurants, room service, 3*

bars, tennis courts, 3 pools, gym, diving, water sports, laundry service, public Wi-Fi ⊟ *AE, DC, MC, V.*

★ $$$$ 🔲 **Muang Samui Spa Resort.** Arrive at your room via a meandering garden path with small bridges and stepping stops that crosses a flowing, fish-filled stream. Brick walls instead of standard concrete provide an atmosphere reminiscent of ancient Ayutthaya. The Royal Suite has two Jacuzzis, one indoor, one outdoor. Other guests must "settle" for lavishly decorated Junior Suites with teak floors and elaborate carved-wood headboards. Even the swimming pool blends perfectly into its surroundings, with a waterfall and grassy, palm tree islands within its waters. The resort offers Thai cooking classes. ⊠ *13/1 Moo 2, Chawaeng Beach, Koh Samui, 84320* ☎ *077/429700 up to 09, 02/553–1008 up to 09 in Bangkok* ⊕ *www.muangsamui.com* ⟿ *53 suites* ⚹ *In-room: safe, refrigerator, DVD, Wi-Fi. In-hotel: 2 restaurants, room service, bar, pool, gym, spa beachfront, water sports, laundry service* ⊟ *AE, MC, DC, V.*

★ $$$$ 🔲 **Poppies.** More than 80 competent and friendly employees are on hand to attend to the guests at this romantic beachfront resort on the quieter southern end of Chawaeng. A large number of them are employed by the restaurant, which is as popular (and remarkable) as the resort itself and serves Thai and seafood under the stars or in the dining room. Cottages have living rooms with sofa beds, making them suitable for families or larger groups. The floors and trim are of handsome teak, and silk upholstery gives the place a decadent feel. Baths have sunken tubs and showers made of marble. Because of the friendly staff, southern location, and first-rate restaurant, the majority of guests are repeat visitors or word-of-mouth referrals. In addition, a 2006 renovation gave the resort a "face-lift," which included new bathrooms, a new reception area, a new spa, and an upgraded pool. ⊠ *Samui Ring Rd., South Chawaeng Beach, 84320* ☎ *077/422419* ⊕ *www.poppiessamui.net* ⟿ *24 rooms* ⚹ *In-room: safe, refrigerator, DVD, Wi-Fi. In-hotel: restaurant, room service, pool, spa, laundry service, public Wi-Fi* ⊟ *AE, DC, MC, V.*

★ $$$–$$$$ 🔲 **Iyara Beach Hotel and Plaza.** The Iyara is a getaway for young, European urbanites who don't want to give up the luxuries of home. The complex includes a maze of boutiques, including Lacoste and Bossini. Bronzed bodies lounge around the beachside pool and book spa treatments at the nearby Four Seasons–operated spa. Iyara studio rooms have peaked ceilings, wooden floors, and large bathtubs with sea views. Superior rooms have mattress on the floor, Japanese style, and lack sea views. Cabanas, including deluxe pool rooms, are closest to the beach, and have teak furniture and outdoor daybeds. ▪ TIP→ **Particularly in low season, this is one of the most reasonably priced beachfront hotels on Chawaeng.** ⊠ *90/13–16 Chawaeng Beach, Koh Samui, 84320* ☎ *077/231629 up to 41* ⊕ *www. iyarabeachhotelandplaza.com* ⟿ *69 rooms* ⚹ *In-room: safe, refrigerator. In-hotel: restaurant, pool, spa, beachfront, concierge* ⊟ *MC, V.*

$$–$$$ 🔲 **Al's Resort.** The newer deluxe villas at the resort are fashionably Thai, with wooden bed frames, trims, and desks; Thai art on walls; and outdoor showers. Older deluxe beach-view rooms are refurbished concrete rooms with boutique touches like loose-stone floors outside the baths, canopies over the beds, and stylish lighting, but look somewhat

contrived. Suites around the pool are similar to the villas, but have more amenities like DVD players and wet bars in the sitting rooms. The beachside swimming pool thumps with hip-hop beats to please a young, fun clientele. The large, semicircular restaurant and bar has glassed-in walls for full views of the beach and the sea. ⊠ *200 Moo 2, Chawaeng Beach, Koh Samui, 84320* ☎ *077/422154* ⊕ *www.alsresort.com* ⇗ *26 rooms, 17 villas* ♿ *In-room: DVD (some). In-hotel: restaurant, room service, 2 bars, pool, spa, laundry service* ▭ *MC, V* � *BP.*

$$ 🏨 **Montien House.** Two rows of charming bungalows line the path leading to the beach at this comfortable little resort. Each modest bungalow has a private patio surrounded by tropical foliage. Rooms are furnished in a spare style, which is nonetheless quite cozy. Penthouses in an adjacent building provide more-luxurious accommodation, with separate living and dining rooms. The management is attentive and helpful. ⊠ *5 Moo 2, Central Chawaeng Beach, 84320* ☎ *077/422169* ⊕ *www.montienhouse.com* ⇗ *57 rooms, 3 suites* ♿ *In-room: refrigerator. In-hotel: restaurant, bar, pool, laundry service, public Internet* ▭ *MC, V.*

★ $–$$ 🏨 **AKWA guesthouse.** Rooms at Australian proprietor Timothy Schwan's guesthouse have giant pop-art paintings on the walls, chairs in the shape of giant hands, and kitschy lamps. Smaller details, like a collection of books, including Thai language manuals and beach novels; a stack of DVDs atop the TV; colorful beach towels; and even the odd stuffed animal, really make it feel like you're crashing in a friend's well-designed bedroom. A penthouse room has a huge terrace with two teak sun beds, an outdoor dining area, and a lazy banana bed with a sweeping 180-degree view; indoors, a private bathtub overlooks the terrace towards Chawaeng Beach. ■ TIP→ **Breakfasts are arguably the best on the island,** although other meals are quite decent as well, and the vibe in the lobby's bar-restaurant is friendly and easygoing. ⊠ *28/12 Moo 3, Chawaeng Beach Rd., Chawaeng Beach* ☎ *04/660–0551* ⊕ *www.akwaguesthouse. com* ⇗ *5 rooms* ♿ *In-room: refrigerator, DVD, Wi-Fi. In-hotel: restaurant, room service, bar* ▭ *No credit cards.*

$ 🏨 **Al's Hut.** A row of white huts follows a path beneath towering tamarind trees from the entrance of the resort, straight down to the beach. The trees provide a shady, beautiful setting and the huts are set far enough apart to make the resort feel less crowded than many of its neighbors. Doors to the huts have multicolor glass, but the rooms are otherwise simple and cozy. Al's is centrally located, on the nicest section of beach, and close to all the action. It's a great value. ⊠ *159/86 Moo 2, Chawaeng Beach, 84320* ☎ *077/231650* ⊕ *www.alshutsamui.com* ⇗ *32 rooms* ♿ *In-room: refrigerator. In-hotel: restaurant* ▭ *MC, V.*

NIGHTLIFE   There are plenty of places to go in the evening in Chawaeng. Soi Green Mango is a looping street chockablock with beer bars and nightclubs large and small, including the enormous **Green Mango,** and trendy DJ club **Mint Bar.** At the corner of Beach Road and Soi Green Mango is the multilevel, open-air, chill-out bar called **The Deck.**

Ark Bar (☎ 077/422047 ⊕ www.ark-bar.com) is one of Samui's original nightlife venues on the beach. They throw a party with free barbecue every Wednesday, starting at 2 PM. Farther south, across from

Central Samui Beach Resort down Soi Coliburi (which looks like an unnamed street) there are several clubs, the most popular and stylish of which is **POD** (☎ 018/914–042).

The popular **Reggae Pub** (☎ 077/422331), on the far side of the lagoon opposite Chawaeng's main strip, is a longtime favorite. It has several bars and dance floors. **Coco Blues Company** (☎ 077/414354 ⊕ www.cocobluescompany.com), on the northern side of town, has live blues music nightly from their house band and visiting blues artists. The **Islander Pub & Restaurant** (✉ Central Chawaeng, near Soi Green Mango ☎ 077/230836) has 11 televisions channeling Thai, Australian, and Malaysian satellites and holds in-house pool competitions and a quiz night.

The newest edition to the Samui scene is **Q Bar Samui** (☎ 081/956–2742), an upscale nightclub from the owners of the Q Bar in Bangkok. Sexy bartenders pour premium spirits while international DJ's spin. It's high up on the hillside to the north of Chawaeng Lake—the drive home could be disastrous for motorbike riders, so plan on a safer form of transportation like a taxi.

Lamai

⓯ *18 km (11 mi) southeast of Na Thon.*

A rocky headland separates Chawaeng from Koh Samui's second-most-popular beach, Lamai. It lacks the glistening white sand of Chawaeng, but its clear water and long stretch of sand made it the first area to be developed on the island. Lamai does have more of a steeply shelving shoreline than Chawaeng, which makes the swimming a bit better. It's not as congested as Chawaeng, though there are plenty of restaurants and bars, many of which are geared to a younger, party-oriented crowd and those (to put it gently) who are looking for Thai companions. Chawaeng Beach Road's rampant commercialization is quite a bit more family-friendly than Lamai's semisordid strip. However, if you are young and looking for fun, there are more budget accommodations available here than in Chawaeng, and there are quite a few happening clubs. And the farther from central Lamai you wander, the more likely you are to discover a nice resort with a beautiful beach and a quieter scene than you will find in Chawaeng.

Every visitor to Koh Samui makes a pilgrimage to Lamai for yet another reason: at the point marking the end of Lamai Beach stand two rocks, named **Hin Yai** (Grandmother Rock) and **Hin Ta** (Grandfather Rock). Erosion has shaped the rocks to resemble weathered and wrinkled private parts. It's nature at its most whimsical.

About 4 km (2½ mi) from Lamai, at the small Chinese fishing village of Baan Hua Thanon, the road that forks inland toward Na Thon leads to the **Coral Buddha,** a natural formation carved by years of erosion. Beyond the Coral Buddha, toward Na Thon, lies the village of Baan Thurian (famous for its durian trees), where a track to the right climbs up into jungle-clad hills to the island's best waterfall, **Na Muang.** The 105-foot falls are spectacular—especially just after the rainy season—as they tumble from a limestone cliff into a small pool. You are cooled by the spray and warmed by the sun. For a thrill, swim through the curtain of falling water; you can sit on a ledge at the back to catch your breath.

WHERE TO
STAY & EAT
$$-$$$$

✕ **The Cliff.** Halfway along the road from Chawaeng to Lamai is the Cliff, which is actually perched on a big boulder overlooking the sea. You can have lunch or dinner either inside the spartan dining room or out on the scenic deck. The lunch menu includes sandwiches and hamburgers; dinner features steaks and Mediterranean grill. The prices are a bit high for the small servings, and the service isn't great, but the Cliff is a nice place to stop to have a drink and check out the view. In the evening, cooler-than-thou staff serve cocktails in the enclosed, air-conditioned club. ⊠ *124/2 Samui Ring Rd., Lamai Beach* ☎ *077/414266* ⊕ *www.thecliffsamui.com* ⌒ *Reservations essential* ▭ *AE, MC, V.*

¢–$ ✕ **Mr. Pown Seafood Restaurant.** This place is nothing fancy, but it serves up reliable Thai dishes and seafood, as well as some German and English fare. Try the red curry in young coconut (a moderately spicy, not quite "red" curry with cauliflower and string beans served inside a coconut) or the catch of the day. The staff is courteous. ⊠ *Central Lamai Beach* ▭ *No credit cards.*

$$$$ ▦ **Pavilion.** Just far enough from central Lamai, the Pavilion offers a little respite from the downtown hustle and bustle. Rooms in the main building are more modern and more expensive than the stand-alone thatched bungalows, but are not necessarily better. Although Junior Suites have large outdoor daybeds and Jacuzzis, rooms 201 to 208 are the best of the rest. Superior spa rooms have outdoor Jacuzzis and huge wooden-canopy beds. Note that construction of junior pool villas, scheduled for completion in 2008, could be a distraction for those seeking tranquillity. The stylish restaurant serves tasty Thai and Italian, as well as fresh seafood. ⊠ *124/24 Lamai Beach, 84320* ☎ *077/424030* ⊕ *www.pavilionsamui.com* ⌒ *52 rooms, 8 suites* ⌂ *In-room: safe, refrigerator, DVD, Wi-Fi. In-hotel: restaurant, room service, 2 bars, pool, spa, laundry service, public Wi-Fi* ▭ *AE, MC, V.*

$$$$ ▦ **Renaissance Koh Samui Resort & Spa.** At the far northern end of Lamai, the Renaissance is technically on its own secluded, private beach (two small beaches to be exact). Most rooms are in multistory buildings connected by elevated walkways that pass through tropical gardens. All have outdoor Jacuzzis on terraces with ocean views, opulent decoration, and floor-to-ceiling glass doors leading from the bedroom to the deck. Separate villas have jumbo Jacuzzis, daybeds, fishponds, gardens, and even miniature waterfalls within their private, gated compounds. Shuttle service is available to Chawaeng Beach, where guests are free to use the facilities at the Princess Resort. ⊠ *208/1 North Lamai Beach, 84320* ☎ *077/429300* ⊕ *www.renaissancehotels.com/usmbr* ⌒ *45 rooms, 33 suites* ⌂ *In-room: safe, refrigerator, DVD (some). In-hotel: 2 restaurants, room service, bar, 2 pools, gym, spa, beachfront, water sports, bicycles, laundry service, public Wi-Fi* ▭ *AE, DC, MC, V.*

$$ ▦ **Aloha Resort.** Ask for a room with a view of the ocean at this beachfront resort—many overlook the parking lot. However, all rooms have private terraces or balconies that do face in the general direction of the beach. The rooms are divided between those in the main building and

those in attractive, refurbished bungalows, which lack a view but are closer to the beach and pool. The rooms have carpets, furniture, and bedding that appear to have not been replaced since the resort first opened 20 years ago, but Aloha is one of the few family-style accommodations you'll find in Lamai. The popular restaurant, Mai Thai, serves Thai, Chinese, and European food, while the more casual Captain's Kitchen has a nightly barbecue. ⊠ *128 Moo 3, 84130* ☎ *077/424014* ⊕ *www. alohasamui.com* ↩ *74 rooms* ⛄ *In-room: refrigerator. In-hotel: 2 restaurants, room service, bar, pool, beachfront, laundry service, public Wi-Fi, airport shuttle* ▭ *AE, MC, V.*

★ **$–$$** ▦ **Lamai-Wanta.** Incredibly spartan rooms are kept immaculately clean, which is not surprising considering the owners-managers are a nurse and doctor couple. The two beachfront villas are their private residences, the other 10 bungalows and 40 attached rooms are for guests. Rooms have king-size beds and many tall, thin windows with interior shutters. Another highlight is an infinity-edge swimming pool directly on the beach surrounded by beach chairs, a beach bar, and restaurant. If you have come to Lamai to relax and enjoy the beach, Lamai-Wanta has all that you need, plus a small on-site clinic (in case you crash your motorbike). ⊠ *Central Lamai Beach, 84320* ☎ *077/424550* ⊕ *www.lamaiwanta. com* ↩ *40 rooms, 10 bungalows* ⛄ *In-room: safe, refrigerator, Wi-Fi. In-hotel: restaurant, bar, pool* ▭ *AE, MC, V* ▯⦿▯ *BP.*

NIGHTLIFE Central Lamai is where all the action is. The one-stop, sprawling party spot **Bauhaus** has foam parties on Monday and Friday nights. In the dead center of town there's a muay thai boxing ring that features women boxers on weekends and *muay thai* (Thai kickboxing) exhibitions staged regularly during the high season. The boxing ring is surrounded by beer bars with highly skilled Connect Four players, and across the street, is the heart of Lamai's club scene: **Fusion,** a dark, chilled-out open-air club spinning hip-hop and progressive house; **SUB,** a huge indoor dance club that also has an outdoor party area with enormous projection TV screen; and **Club Mix,** another megasize club featuring international and local DJs.

Laem Set Bay
16 *17½ km (11 mi) south of Na Thon.*

This small rocky cape on the southeastern tip of the island is far from the crowds. It's a good 3 km (2 mi) off the main road, so it's hard to reach without your own transport. You may want to visit the nearby **Samui Butterfly Garden,** 2 acres of meandering walks enclosed by nets that take you through kaleidoscopic clouds of butterflies. It's open daily 10 to 4.

Baan Taling Ngam
17 *3 km (2 mi) south of Na Thon.*

The southern and western coasts are less developed, and with good reason—their beaches are not as golden, the water isn't as clear, and the breezes aren't as fresh. But there's one very good reason to come here: a luxury hotel on a pretty stretch of shore with magnificent views of nearby islands and even the mountainous mainland.

✕⊡ **Le Royal Meridien Baan Taling Ngam.** Its name means "home on a beautiful bank," but that doesn't come close to summing up the stunning location of this luxurious hotel. Most of the rooms are built into the 200-foot cliff, but the beachside villas are even better. The swimming pool is a magnificent trompe l'oeil, looking as if it's part of the ocean far below. There's a second pool by the beach where you can find an activities center. The beach is extremely narrow, so sunbathing is not feasible at high tide, but you can swim here. The southeast corner of the island is also closest to Angthong National Marine Park, making it the best resort from which to explore that island chain. You can dine on Thai and European fare at the Lom Talay; seafood is served at the more casual Promenade. ✉ 295 Taling Ngam Beach, 84140 ☎ 077/429100, 02/6532201 up to 07 in Bangkok ⊕ www.lemeridien.com ➷ 40 rooms, 30 villas ⚷ In-room: safe, refrigerator, DVD, ethernet. In-hotel: 2 restaurants, room service, bar, tennis court, 7 pools, gym, spa, water sports, bicycles, laundry service, concierge, public Internet ▤ AE, DC, MC, V.

Koh Phangan

⑱ 12 km (7 mi) by boat north of Koh Samui.

As Koh Samui developed into an international tourist hot spot, travelers looking for a cheaper and/or more laid-back scene headed for Koh Phangan. Decades ago, the few wanderers who arrived here stayed in fishermen's houses or slung hammocks on the beach. Gradually, simple bungalow colonies sprang up on even the most remote beaches, and investors bought up beach property with plans for sprawling resorts. Although some large commercial development did occur, a funny thing happened on the way to Samui-like development: the allure of Koh Tao's crystalline waters starting drawing away a lot of the attention. While Haad Rin boomed as a result of its world-famous Full Moon Party, most of Koh Phangan's smaller beaches continued to develop, but at a much less rapid pace. For now, most of Phangan remains a destination for backpackers looking for beautiful beaches with budget accommodation and hippies (old-school and nouveau) searching for chilled-out beaches and alternative retreats.

Since the island's unpaved roads twist and turn, it's easier to beach-hop via boat, although most beaches are now accessible via songthaew pickup trucks (it's *not* advisable to attempt most of Koh Phangan's roads on motorbike). If you want to find the beach that most appeals to you, take a longtail boat around the island—the trip takes a full day and stops in many places along the way. Boats from Koh Tao and the mainland alight at Thong Sala, an uninteresting town, where taxis can shuttle you around the island, including to the larger beaches of Chalok Lam, in the north, and Haad Rin, at the southeast tip of the island, which is divided by a long promontory into **Haad Rin West** and **Haad Rin East.**

★ Most backpackers and tourists without a game plan, head straight to the sprawling concrete village between the two beaches of Haad Rin. Unless you are here for the Full Moon Party, or have banking or postal needs, take a songthaew or a boat up the east coast to **Haad Thong Nai**

Pan, a horseshoe bay divided by a small promontory. The most beautiful, and most remote beach, accessible almost exclusively by boat, is **Haad Kuat (Bottle Beach),** which has gorgeous white sand and only five simple accommodations. **Haad Yao** and **Haad Salad** on the northwest coast are similarly remote beaches for those looking for relaxation. **Haad Sarikantang** (Leela Beach), **Haad Yuan,** and **Haad Thien** are close to Haad Rin and are good choices for those interested in going to the Full Moon Party, but who want to stay in a nicer, more relaxing beach environment.

Haad Rin East & West

Haad Rin Town has many good restaurants, shops, and bars. It's densely built up, and not very quiet, but full of fun. The town is sandwiched between Haad Rin West and Haad Rin East. The west side is where the main pier of the island is located and where literally boatloads of visitors disembark, most of whom stay in Haad Rin town or along the beach on Haad Rin East.

Haad Rin West has swimmable water, but you needn't settle for this beach when Haad Rin East is only a short walk away. Haad Rin East is a beautiful beach lined with bungalows and bars, although the water isn't nearly as pristine as the more remote beaches. Once a month, Haad Rin East gets seriously crowded when throngs of young people gather on the beach for an all-night Full Moon Party. Check your calendar before heading to Phangan as the island starts to fill up at least a week prior to the big event. Boats from Thong Sala, the major town, take about 40 minutes to reach Haad Rin East, but most people travel on songthaews, which take only 15 minutes. Nearby is the smaller but quieter beach of Haad Sarikantang (Leela Beach) if you want to stay away from the crowds but still want to be close to the party.

WHERE TO
STAY & EAT

¢–$$ ✕ **Lucky Crab Restaurant.** The extensive menu includes entrées from all around the world, which is appropriate on a beach that hosts visitors from virtually everywhere. Despite the hundreds of selections on the menu, the specialty at the Lucky Crab is barbecue seafood, served with 12 different sauces. Select your fish, select your sauce, then enjoy the breeze from the ceiling fans while you await your tasty food at this fun and friendly eatery. Also worth trying is the sizzling seafood in a hot pan. ✉ *94/18 Haad Rin W, Koh Phangan* ☎ *077/375125 or 077/375498* ▭ *No credit cards.*

¢–$ ✕ **Nira's Bakery and Restaurant.** As you walk into the restaurant, you'll be bombarded by the mouthwatering smell of fresh-baked goods. The owner picked up his baking skills while living and working in Germany, and then opened this funky bakery in the mid-1980s, before the island even had electricity. Traditional homemade lasagna, fresh fruit juices, and gourmet sandwiches are a few of the specialties available at the juice bar, sandwich bar, and air-conditioned bakery. ✉ *130 Central Haad Rin, Koh Phangan* ▭ *No credit cards.*

$$–$$$ ▦ **Phangan Buri Resort and Health Spa.** This is the latest multimillion-baht, modern hotel development in Haad Rin. What you get is an international-standards hotel room, complete with modern amenities, but lacking the Thai island vibe. Still, rooms have touches of Thai style, including Thai art on the walls. A computer in every room helps e-mail-

addicted travelers stay in touch with their less fortunate friends and family back home. Deluxe beachfront rooms have sea views and are next to the seaside swimming pool and spa, where a variety of treatments are available. ⊠ *120/1 Moo 6, Haad Rin Nai Beach 84280* ☏*077/375481* ⊕ *www.phanganburiresort.net* ⇲ *106 rooms* ⚑ *In-room: safe, refrigerator, ethernet. In-hotel: restaurant, 2 bars, 2 pools, spa* ▭ *AE, MC, V* ⦿| *BP.*

★ ¢–$$ 🖼 **Coco Hut Resort.** Coco Hut Resort is on Leela Beach, a five-minute walk from Haad Rin West. Although Leela Beach is not as beautiful as Haad Rin, it's quieter and much more relaxing. Rooms range from backpacker rooms with shared bath in a large wood-and-concrete building to cute clapboard huts on the beachfront and hill. Rooms on the beach are either air-conditioned or fan-cooled, so that even budget travelers can afford the nicest huts. Rooms away from the beach are connected by a boardwalk and have ladders leading up to tiny lofts; newer bungalows on the hill have high ceilings and lots of windows with impressive ocean views. The resort provides a slew of services and amenities, including beach volleyball, rafts, and kayaks to keep you busy during the low tide, when the water is too shallow for swimming. ⊠ *130/20 Leela Beach, Koh Phangan 84280* ☏ *077/375368* ⊕ *www.cocohut.com* ⇲ *76 bungalows, 24 rooms* ⚑ *In-room: no a/c (some), refrigerator. In-hotel: restaurant, bar, pool, water sports, public Wi-Fi* ▭ *MC, V.*

★ ¢–$$ 🖼 **Sarikantang.** This small resort, with both wooden and concrete bungalows on Leela Beach, is a short walk from Haad Rin. All the concrete rooms have outdoor showers and baths, hot water, air-conditioning, and hammocks, while some of the wooden bungalows have only cold water and fans and none of the other standard amenities like TVs or minibars. The rooms are behind the pool, and although none of them are beachfront, almost all have ocean views. The two suites have large stone bathtubs that look over cozy living rooms, across the decks, and out to the sea. The spa, which is right on the beach, provides excellent massages while you listen to the waves lap the shore. This is a family-run resort that genuinely tries to help you enjoy your stay, much unlike some of the larger resorts nearby. ⊠ *129/3 Leela Beach, Koh Phangan 84280* ☏ *077/375055 or 077/375056* ⊕ *www.sarikantang.com* ⇲ *47 rooms* ⚑ *In-room: no a/c (some), safe (some), refrigerator (some), DVD (some), no TV (some). In-hotel: restaurant, pool, spa, laundry service, public Wi-Fi* ▭ *MC, V.*

¢–$ 🖼 **Sea View Haad Rin Resort.** The simple, wooden, fan-cooled huts directly on the beach at the "quieter" northern end of Haad Rin are the best deal in the area—for the best location. In fact, the beachfront rooms with fans and hammocks on their porches are arguably better than air-conditioned huts in the second row. ⊠ *134 Haad Rin Nok Beach, 84280* ☏ *077/375160* ⇲ *40 rooms* ⚑ *In-room: no a/c (some), no phone, no TV. In-hotel: restaurant* ▭ *No credit cards.*

NIGHTLIFE Haad Rin East is lined with bars and clubs—music pumps and drinks pour from dusk until dawn, seven days a week, 365 days a year. All this culminates in a huge beach party with tens of thousands of revelers every full moon (or the night after, if the full moon lands on a major Buddhist holiday). Check out ⊕ www.fullmoonparty.com for details. If you're only here for a night, check out **Cactus** and **Drop In Club,** two of the most popular nightspots, both right on the beach.

Haad Thong Nai Pan

If Haad Rin is too crowded, take a boat up the east coast to Haad Thong Nai Pan, a horseshoe bay divided by a small promontory. On the beach of the southern half are several guesthouses and restaurants, as well as the area's sole ATM. The northern part of the bay is called Tong Nai Pan Noi, where a glistening crescent of sand curves around the turquoise waters. The best time to visit this long stretch of white-sand beach is from December to August, as the area can be hard to reach by boat during the monsoon months (September–November). However, a bumpy road can be your alternative during those months.

WHERE TO
STAY & EAT

★ **$$$–$$$$**

Panviman Resort. The big attraction at this friendly resort is its two restaurants, one of which is a circular Thai-style dining area that is open to the ocean breezes; the other is seaside. Superior rooms have hardwood floors, spacious decks with ocean views, and convenient access to the gorgeous, multitiered swimming pool. Superior cottages are more like small wooden houses than bungalows and sit on the hill above the small private beach. Family cottages are enormous, with tall glass windows for walls on both stories. The resort provides shuttle service to Bangkok. ✉ 22/1 Thong Nai Pan Noi Bay, 84280 ☎ 077/445101 up to 09, 077/445220 up to 24 ⊕ www.panviman.com ☞ 72 rooms, 14 cottages, 18 deluxe cottages ☼ In-room: no a/c (some), safe, refrigerator. In-hotel: 2 restaurants, bar, pool, beachfront, laundry service ☐ MC, V.

¢–$ **Star Hut Resort.** A friendly and chilled-out resort on Tong Nai Pan Noi, Star Hut has simple wooden huts with rattan walls, thatch roofs, and wraparound decks ideal for enjoying this beautiful and peaceful remote beach. Rooms 1, 110, 210, and 310 are beachfront. The open-air restaurant provides service with a smile (an unfortunate rarity at many of the other tourist-jaded resorts in the area). ✉ Tong Nai Pan Noi ☎ 077/445085 ✉ star_hut@hotmail.com ☞ 26 rooms ☼ In-room: no a/c (some). In-hotel: restaurant, public Wi-Fi ☐ MC, V.

¢ **Dolphin.** Dolphin's small, clean, basic bungalows are situated in a veritable Garden of Eden on the southern end of Tong Nai Pan Yai. The rooms are Thai-style huts the way beach bungalows should be designed: built entirely of wood with shuttered windows, fans, mosquito nets, and hammocks slung on the decks. Sadly, they are not beachfront, but sit behind an ultracool beach bar, which has a variety of shady lounge areas for people to relax and play cards, sip cocktails, or just laze away the days. ✉ Tong Nai Pan Yai ☎ 077/445135 ✉ kimgiet@hotmail.com ☞ 20 rooms ☼ In-room: no a/c, no phone, no TV. In-hotel: bar ☐ No credit cards.

Haad Yuan

Haad Yuan is a small, beautiful beach between Haad Rin and Haad Thien. Despite its proximity to Haad Rin (a 10-minute boat ride), Haad Yuan is worlds away: the beach is not built up (there are just a few resorts) and it's extremely quiet most of the month. However, because of its location, the rooms at the resorts fill up quickly about a week prior to the

Full Moon Party; in high season arrive a week before the event to secure a room or book in advance.

WHERE TO STAY
¢ **Barcelona Resort.** For very few baht you get a private cottage with doors on two walls that fold open to reveal a wraparound deck. Every cottage, large and small, is on the hill overlooking the powdery beach. Rooms are simple, with fans with mosquito nets, but slightly larger and breezier than your average beach bungalow. ⊠ *Haad Yuan* 🕿 *No phone* 🛏 *25 rooms* ⚹ *In-room: no a/c, no TV. In-hotel: restaurant, laundry service* ▭ *No credit cards.*

Haad Kuat (Bottle Beach)

Haad Kuat is one of the most remote beaches on Koh Phangan. The only ways to get there are by boat from Chalok Lam, on a 20-minute songthaew ride from Thong Sala Pier, or on a longtail boat from nearby Thong Nai Pan. It might be more difficult to get to than any other beach, but it's definitely worth the hassle. The beach itself is about a quarter-mile-long stretch of fine, white sand. The water is a beautiful sparkling blue, perfect for swimming, especially on the western end of the beach. There are only five resorts on Haad Kuat, so the beach isn't too crowded in the morning or late in the afternoon (though it does receive many daytrippers from the rest of the island midday). The scene is young and fun: each guesthouse blares the latest Western hits in the common areas for travelers chilling out on triangular pillows. If you prefer peace and quiet, stick to the beach or string a hammock up in front of your hut. If you get tired of lounging around, follow the steep trail up to the viewpoint above the western end of the beach.

WHERE TO STAY & EAT
¢ ✕🖾 **Smile Bungalows.** There are only five guesthouses on Haad Kuat, and Smile Bungalow, on the far western end of the beach, is the best of the bunch. The restaurant has the most comfortable seating area, with both standard wooden tables, and foot-high tables surrounded by triangular pillows. The huts are built on the hillside overlooking the beach, and have large wooden decks and bright bathrooms decorated with shells. The bungalows higher up on the hill are duplexes and have great ocean views. The staff at Smile Bungalows is friendly and fun, and frequently hang out with the guests in the evening when the music gets turned up, the lights turned down, and playing cards and beer bottles cover all the tables. The beach in front of Smile Bungalows is also the best spot for swimming. The one small drawback is that the bungalows only have electricity from 6 PM to 6 AM. ⊠ *Haad Kuat* 🕿 *091/780–2881* 🛏 *25 rooms* ⚹ *In-room: no a/c, no TV. In-hotel: restaurant, laundry service* ▭ *No credit cards.*

Koh Tao

⑲ *47 km (29 mi) by boat north of Koh Phangan.*

Less than a decade ago, the tiny island of Koh Tao could be compared to the one inhabited by Robinson Crusoe: no electricity, no running water, no modern amenities of any kind. Today it's built up with air-conditioned huts with cable TV, tattoo parlors, discos, and a few 7-11s. Dozens of small bungalow colonies offer every level of accommodation, from ultrabasic to modern luxury. The peace and quiet has disappeared from the main beaches, but the primary reason to come here is still the underwater world. ■ TIP➜ **Koh Tao is an excellent place to get your scuba certification, as many operators don't have pools, so the initial dives must be done in the shallow, crystal-clear ocean water.** Advanced divers will appreciate the great visibility, decent amount of coral, and exotic and plentiful marine life.

Sairee, the island's longest, most popular beach, is a crescent-shape beach with palm trees arching over the pellucid, aquamarine water as if they are yearning to drink from the sea. Along the thin sliver of golden sand sit rustic, traditional wooden beach huts with bohemian youths lounging in hammocks; novice divers practicing in seaside pools; and European students on holiday, sipping cocktails at basic beach bars. On the far northern end of the beach a few "upscale" resorts provide urban amenities amid manicured landscapes that manage to blend in with their surroundings enough to create idyllic beach environments rather than artificial resort settings. Sairee Beach is west-facing and therefore great for watching the sun set and for kayaking to Koh Nang Yuan. Chalok Baan Kao Beach, on the southern shore, is another nice beach, which is popular with travelers of all stripes. Travelers looking for real peace and quiet head to the smaller, more isolated beaches and bays, which generally have only a few guesthouses each, a more laid-back scene, and nice snorkeling conditions directly off the beach.

Getting to Koh Tao is easy—it's on the scheduled ferry routes out of Koh Phangan and Koh Samui, and several boats a day make the trip from Chumphon on the mainland. Catamarans take 1½ hours, high-speed Seatran vessels take 2 hours, and regular ferry service takes 6 hours. If you want to check out Koh Tao, but want to stay in the extravagant hotels only available on Koh Samui, **Lomprayah Catamaran** (⊕ www.lomprayah.com) has 1¾-hour trips twice daily at 8 AM and noon. Lomprayah Catamaran stops at Koh Phangan on their way from Koh Samui (at 8:30 and 12:30), if you wish to jump on or off there. Lomprayah even has boat-and-bus packages available to get you from Bangkok or Hua Hin to Koh Tao. In addition, speedboats leave at 8:30 AM from Bophut Pier, taking snorkelers on day trips to the island and its neighbor, Koh Nang Yuan.

Where to Stay & Eat

★ ¢–$$ ✗ **Papa's Tapas.** Low, warm lighting and relaxing music contribute to the upscale feel of Papa's—the elegance of this restaurant is indicative of Koh Tao's growing popularity and prosperity. Each of the five courses on the set menu is served with a luscious beverage, such as a Japanese plum martini, that complements the food. You can also sample delectable seafood, meat, and vegetarian tapas (like lemon and tandoori black tiger prawns or coffee-flavor duck breast with a vanilla foam) à la carte. There is also a small hooka lounge where hip patrons lounge on beanbags while puffing on flavored tobaccos or Cuban cigars and sip on glasses of absinthe. Reservations are recommended during the high season. ⊠ *Next to the 7-11 on the northern end of Sairee Beach* ☎ *077/457020* ▭ *No credit cards.*

$$–$$$$ 🖼 **Charmchuree Villa.** Whether you opt to stay in one of the uniquely
Fodor'sChoice   designed tropical villas or the superior or deluxe rooms, you'll enjoy a
   ★   tiny corner of heaven on the private beach at Jansom Bay. Rooms and
thatch-roof villas are built into the landscape, constructed on or around
massive boulders and trees, and situated to maximize exposure to the
magnificent views of Nang Yuan, Jansom Bay, and Sairee Beach. Indoor-
outdoor baths and semidetached living rooms are great features, as is
lots of deck space for chairs, hammocks, and triangular pillows. The
spa, Elvis Bar, and spectacular snorkeling (free equipment rental for guests)
are both found at the beach, which is just a three-minute walk from the
farthest rooms. ■ TIP➜ **Nonguests can use the beach (not as exotic as Nang
Yuan, but quieter and just as satisfying) for B100.** ✉ *30/1 Moo 2, Jansom
Bay, Koh Tao, 84280* ☎ *077/456393 or 077/456394* ⊕ *www.
charmchureevilla.com* ⤵ *40 rooms* ⚭ *In-room: safe, refrigerator. In-
hotel: 3 restaurants, room service, bar, spa, water sports, laundry serv-
ice, public Wi-Fi* ▤ *MC, V.*

$$–$$$$ 🖼 **Koh Tao Coral Grand Resort.** Coral Grand, on the quieter, northern end
of Sairee, is a great place to get your scuba certification. Rooms here are
colorfully painted, traditional wooden Thai beach huts built to 21st-cen-
tury hotel standards, including clean, spacious, sunken bathrooms with
stone floors. Air-conditioned standard rooms are the same as deluxe rooms,
but are simply smaller and lack some amenities (like phones and minibars), a minor detail considering how little time you'll actually spend in
your room. Those interested in the nicest Deluxe Beach and Captain Suites
should be aware that rooms 304 and 403 are adjacent to the sometimes
noisy restaurant and beach bar. Much cheaper and more basic fan rooms
are available for those strictly visiting the resort for its scuba courses.
Guests at neighboring resorts, including Koh Tao Cabana, are welcome
to take scuba courses here as well. ✉ *15/4 Moo 1, Sairee Beach, Koh
Tao, 84280* ☎ *077/456431 up to 33* ⊕ *www.kohtaocoral.com* ⤵ *42
rooms* ⚭ *In-room: no phone (some), safe, refrigerator (some). In-hotel:
restaurant, room service, bar, pool, beachfront, diving, water sports,
laundry service, public Internet* ▤ *MC, V.*

★ **$$–$$$**   🖼 **Koh Tao Cabana.** Koh Tao Cabana, on the far northern end of Sairee
Beach, is one of the few boutique resorts on the island. Choose between
the circular, thatch-roof White Sand Villas or the more traditional cottages. The Mediterranean-style villas have tile and wood floors, four-
poster beds, chill-out nooks, and panoramic windows. The wooden
cottages, which are farther up the hill away from the beach, have bam-
boo-frame beds, native art, and decks that face south towards Sairee
Beach. Rooms on the hill have stairs leading down to a snorkeling spot.
■ TIP➜ **The stylish restaurant, just above the water, is open to the public** and
serves up tasty Western, Thai, and seafood specialties; it's open for dinner only. ✉ *16 Moo 1, Baan Hadd Sai Ree, Koh Tao, 84280* ☎ *077/
456250 or 077/456504* ⊕ *www.kohtaocabana.com* ⤵ *33 villas and cottages* ⚭ *In-room: safe, refrigerator. In-hotel: restaurant, laundry service, public Internet* ▤ *AE, MC, V* ⱺ *BP.*

$–$$ 🖼 **Mango Bay Grand Resort.** Mango Bay may not have a beach, but the
spectacular view from the enormous deck, spacious restaurant, and
cliff-side rooms easily makes up for the lack of a sandy shore. All rooms

have balconies overlooking the crystalline waters of Mango Bay, a favorite of dive boats and day-trip snorkelers. Air-conditioned rooms are in wooden huts with comfortable beds, mosquito nets, and deck chairs for staring at the amazing hues of the water and reef below. Fan-cooled rooms are simply smaller and have no amenities but are cozy and have decks with the same amazing view. Room A9, at the top, is a hike, but the view is the best of the best. ⊠ *Mango Bay* ☎ *077/456949* ⊕ *www. kohtaomangobay.com* ↬ *14 rooms* ⌂ *In-room: no a/c (some), refrigerator, DVD. In-hotel: restaurant, room service, bar, laundry service, public Internet* ⊟ *No credit cards* ⊗ *Closed Sept.–Dec. 20.*

¢–$$ ▨ **Black Tip Dive Resort and Watersport Center.** Black Tip Dive Resort is on Tanote Bay, on the "remote" eastern shore of Koh Tao. Although the sand here is course, the bay is great for snorkeling, full of colorful coral, large fish (the water drops off steeply around the large boulders in the center of the bay), and even small black-tip reef sharks that cruise the northern side of the bay around sunset. Naturally, this is a great location to do your scuba certification. Rooms, located on the hill above the bay, are set in a nicely landscaped garden and are a stylish blend of natural wood and painted, curvaceous concrete walls. Note that some rooms do not have hot water; the deluxe bungalows are the only ones that have minibars and TVs. Some economy rooms share a bathroom with one other room. A pickup truck taxi makes the run to Mae Haad five times daily, and a taxi-boat for trips around the island is available from the Mt. Reef Resort at the south end of the bay. Room discounts are available if you sign up for a dive course. ⊠ *40/6 Tanote Bay, 84280* ☎ *077/456867* ⊕ *www.blacktipdiving.com* ↬ *25 bungalows* ⌂ *In-room: no a/c (some), refrigerator (some), no TV (some). In-hotel: restaurant, bar, pool, diving, water sports* ⊟ *MC, V.*

¢ ▨ **SB Cabana.** Certainly not a place for those unaccustomed to roughing it, SB Cabana has old-school wooden beach huts. At high tide the ocean laps at the stilts of these simple, wooden structures, which have no amenities—just fans and cold-water showers. They may be best for backpackers, but if you're willing to be a little adventurous, you'll find great accommodations here: clean, comfortable, and centrally located. Only rooms A9–A16 are beachside; A9 is the newest, largest, and nicest of the pack. ⊠ *Sairee Beach* ☎ *077/456005* ↬ *60 huts* ⌂ *In-room: no a/c, no phone, no TV. In-hotel: restaurant, bicycles* ⊟ *No credit cards.*

Western Gulf Essentials

Transportation

BY AIR

Thai Airways, One-Two-Go, and budget carrier Thai Air Asia fly to Surat Thani daily. Bangkok Airways, the sole airline with direct service to Koh Samui, offers up to 25 flights a day from Bangkok. Direct flights from Phuket, Pattaya, and Chiang Mai to Samui are also available from Bangkok Airways, with routes from Krabi and Trat (Koh Chang) planned for the near future.

Compared to other flights around Thailand, flights to Koh Samui are quite expensive. Following the introduction of low-cost airlines in 2003, flights to neighboring countries are often cheaper than flights to Koh Samui. Some discount fares are available from the Bangkok Airways Web site—the first and last flights of the day are less than half the cost of the other flights. Also, most flights are on propeller planes, which take about 30 minutes longer, so when booking, check for flights on the few 717s, which are less frequent but more spacious and a bit faster. Reservations are essential during holiday seasons. Thai Air Asia, if booked a few days in advance, has incredibly low fares to Surat Thani that arrive early enough to catch a midday ferry to the islands.

AIRPORTS & TRANSFERS There are two airports in the Western Gulf, at Surat Thani and Samui (there used to be airports at Chumphon and Hua Hin, but they are no longer in service for commercial flights). Samui Airport, privately owned by Bangkok Airways, levies a B400 airport tax from every passenger for each domestic departure.

For those who would like to go straight from Surat Thani Airport to Koh Samui or Koh Phangan, Seatran Ferry provides free daily transfers to Donsak Pier that leave the airport at noon. Samui Airport has a minivan shuttle service to anywhere on the island for B100 to B200, depending on your destination.

🛫 Carriers **Bangkok Airways** ☎ 17711 ⊕ www.bangkokairways.com. **One-Two-Go** ☎ 1126 ⊕ www.onetwo-go.com. **Thai Air Asia** ☎ 02/515-9999 ⊕ www.airasia.com. **Thai Airways** ☎ 02/6282000 ⊕ www.thaiairways.com.

🛫 Airport Information **Koh Samui** ☎ 077/425011 up to 12. **Surat Thani** ☎ 077/441230 up to 32.

BY BOAT & FERRY

Boats depart from the mainland to the trio of islands from Chumporn and Suratthani. There are a number of ferry services, including high-speed catamarans, slower passenger ferries, and "speed boats," as well as large "slow boats," which are car ferries. The main boat operators are Lomprayah, SeaTran, Songserm, and Raja.

Boats from Chumporn service Koh Tao; those from Surratthani service Koh Samui. Traveling to Koh Phangan, you must first go to either of the other two islands. Some ferry lines require that you disembark, wait for some time, and then board a second ship to Koh Phangan. To make things more complicated, schedules and routes are subject to change and do so frequently.

To Koh Samui: Several times a day Seatran, Songserm, and Raja ferries make the 1½- to 3-hour journey between Surat Thani's Donsak Pier and Koh Samui's Na Thon Pier. Seatran departs hourly from 6 AM to 7 PM and provides the quickest trip. The cost on Seatran is B150, which includes free shuttle service to and from Surat Thani's airport, train station, or bus terminal. Specific time tables for all ferries are available at the airport and from any tour operator on either end of the route.

To Koh Phangan: Seatran Discovery (a partner of Seatran ferry) connects Surat Thani with Phangan via Koh Samui. Boats depart hourly from

Suratthani's Donsak Pier to Na Thon Pier in Koh Samui; the price includes the hour bus ride from the airport to Donsak Pier. The first leg of the voyage takes about 2½ hours total. Passengers must then disembark and catch a second boat to Koh Phangan's Thong Sala Pier. Be aware that only two Seatran boats depart Samui for Phangan, at 8 AM and 1:30 PM. This leg of the journey takes about 30 minutes. Return travel from Phangan to Samui is at 10:30 AM and 4:30 PM and then continues on to Samui. Traveling on another ferry provider, Songserm, has the advantage of not having to switch boats on Samui; however, Songserm makes the Surat Thani-Samui-Phangan run only once a day, leaving Suratthani at 8 AM and returning from Phangnan at 12:30 PM. There are a number of ways to travel between Phangan and either Samui or Koh Tao—Lomphrayah and SeaTran boats are the best options. Boats to and from Koh Tao take 2 to 2½ hours.

To Koh Tao and Koh Nang Yuan: For visitors who wish to go straight from Bangkok or Hua Hin to Koh Tao and Koh Nang Yuan, Lomprayah Travel makes it easy and affordable. They offer joint tickets that include a VIP bus ride (leaving from Bangkok's famous Khaosan Road) to Chumphon's Catamaran Pier and ferry service aboard a massive, high-speed catamaran. The catamaran takes passengers to Koh Tao's Mae Haad pier in an hour and a half; it departs twice a day and costs B650 from Hua Hin, B850 from Khaosan Road, and B550 from Chumphon. The same boat continues its journey to Koh Phangan and Koh Samui, respectively. From Suratthani, Seatran Discovery services Koh Tao with stops at both Samui and Phangan. Between Koh Phangan and Koh Samui, Seatran and Lomphrayah are again the best options.

Getting to Koh Nang Yuan from Koh Tao can be done easily by hiring a longtail boat from Sairee Beach. The journey takes about 15 minutes and costs B50 per person.

Interisland Trips: From Koh Samui to Koh Phangan, most ferry companies will drop you off at Phangan's Thong Sala Pier. However, if you wish to go straight to Haad Rin, the Full Moon Party beach, the Haad Rin Queen ferry line takes you directly from Samui's Big Buddha Pier (Bangrak) to Haad Rin West five times daily for B100.

Lomprayah Travel also provides service from Koh Samui's Mae Nam Pier, twice daily. It reaches Koh Phangan in 30 minutes and then continues its journey to Koh Tao (two hours).

🚢 Boat & Ferry Lines **Lomprayah** ☎ 02/629-2569 or 02/629-2570 in Bangkok, 077/427765 in Samui, 077/456176 on Koh Tao ⊕ www.lomprayah.com. **Raja Ferry** ☎ 077/471151 up to 53 Donsak Pier, 077/377452 up to 53 Koh Phangan. **Seatran Ferry & Express** ☎ 077/275060 Surat Thani, 077/471174 Donsak Pier, 077/426000 up to 02 Koh Samui, 077/238679 Koh Phangan ⊕ www.seatranferry.com. **Songserm** ☎ 077/377704 Tha Thong Pier in Surat Thani, 077/420157 Koh Samui.

BY BUS

Buses to Cha-am, Hua Hin, Chumphon, and Surat Thani (the latter two are departure points for Koh Samui and other islands) leave from Bangkok's Southern Bus Terminal. Buses to Cha-am (2½ hours, B113) leave every 30 minutes from 6:30 AM to 7 PM; buses to Hua Hin (3 hours, B130) leave hourly. Expect a long bus ride to Chumphon and Surat Thani;

the outbound journey could take 6 to 9 hours. Buses usually leave at night and arrive at your destination in the morning. Costs are around B300–B590. Minivans to Hua Hin from Khao San Road charge B150 per person and are generally faster than buses.

Buses can also transport you between destinations within the south. A daily bus travels from Phuket to Surat Thani, arriving in time for the ferry to Koh Samui. Check with the bus station a day prior to departure for exact times and to reserve a seat.

🚌 Bus Stations **Bangkok** ✉ Southern Bus Terminal, Baromratchchonnani Rd. ☎ 02/435-5605. **Cha-am** ✉ Cha-am Beach ☎ 032/471654 or 032/433288. **Chumphon** ✉ Tha Tapao Rd. **Hua Hin** ✉ Dechanuchit St. **Surat Thani** ✉ Taladmai Rd.

BY CAR

Driving to Cha-am and Hua Hin is rather easy because the journey is short. But to Chumphon and Surat Thani, it's a long drive from Bangkok, one that can be tiresome and boring. There's only one highway (Petchkasem Road) as far south as Chumphon, where it divides into one road following the Andaman Sea coast to Phuket and another snaking along the Gulf of Thailand to Surat Thani, where the ferries cross to Koh Samui. The highway narrows to a one-lane road once you leave the greater Bangkok sprawl. The road is heavily trafficked by long-haul transport trucks, and driving this road if you're not familiar with Thai driving habits can be unsettling, especially at night.

Budget and Hertz have counters at the Koh Samui airport, and National has its counter in Samui town. TA Car Rental is a local reputable company based on Samui. Otherwise, car rentals can be arranged from your hotel or any tour operator, as there are numerous authorized Budget agents as well as many smaller rental companies, which offer cheaper rates than the major car-rental agencies with perhaps less professional assistance in the event you have an accident. Remember that although Thais are legally required to drive on the left side of the road, they frequently drive on the wrong side, too. In addition, roads on Samui are very narrow, and traffic laws are not strictly enforced. Also, although Thai people are generally very friendly and helpful, in the event of an accident, there's often an automatic assumption that it's your fault simply because you're a visitor (and have more money). Remember to remain calm, and realize that what is the just solution may not always be the ultimate outcome.

Motorbikes can also be rented on Koh Samui. They're cheap and convenient and therefore especially popular modes of transportation for many visitors. Remember that helmets are required by law and covered shoes recommended by common sense. Although there are several decent hospitals on the islands, they are frequently filled with Western tourists sometimes seriously injured from motorbike crashes. Drive carefully.

In many tourist areas there's often car service available for hire. This can be a better option than renting a car. Many of the major car-rental agencies charge fares comparable to or greater than fares in Western cities. In comparison, it may be cheaper and more convenient to hire a car with a driver who knows his way around and is liable for accidents. Hiring a car for a day is usually much cheaper than taxis as well, and multiple days are usually cheaper per day than several single day trips.

🖪 Local Agency **TA Car Rental** ✉ Choengmon Beach, Koh Samui ☎ 077/245129.

BY TAXI, TUK-TUK & SONGTHAEW

Most areas of the south have a variety of different motorized taxi services from samlors to tuk-tuks to songthaews. Traveling around Cha-am is easiest by motorbike taxi, which can be found on any street corner or flagged down. Don't forget to wear your helmet. Hua Hin has more transportation options, including motorbike taxis, samlors, and tuk-tuks at negotiable prices. Surat Thani, a bigger town, has songthaews and regular bus services throughout the day. Samui has many songthaews that circle Samui Ring Road and cost B20–B50 during the day. At night these songthaews become chartered taxis for negotiable prices. "Metered" taxis can be found in the larger towns and on Samui. They don't actually run their meters, however, and are unscrupulous bargainers. Taxis do not normally meet incoming flights at the airport in Koh Samui. If you're likely to be needing a taxi throughout your stay on Samui, ask your driver for his card and you can negotiate lower, multiday rates.

BY TRAIN

The *Southern Line* train from Bangkok's Hualamphong Station leaves throughout the day, beginning at 8:05 AM and running until 10:50 PM. Trains going south along the Western Gulf stop at Kanchanaburi, Hua Hin, Chumphon, and Surat Thani, continuing all the way to Sungaikolok. The 12 daily trips from Bangkok to Hua Hin take three to four hours. The journey to Chumphon takes seven to eight hours. The best option to Chumphon is the first train at 8:05 AM or the 7:30 PM train. On the first one, you arrive fairly early so that you can still enjoy your day, and the latter is the last overnight sleeper train.

Many express trains from Bangkok's Hua Lamphong railway station stop at Surat Thani on their way south. The journey takes just less than 12 hours, and the best trains are the overnighters that leave Bangkok at 6:20 PM and 7:30 PM, arriving in Surat Thani a little after 6 AM. First-class sleeping cabins are available only on the 7:30 PM train. There are later trains departing from Bangkok, but there are no sleeping beds available on them.

Surat Thani is the closest train station to Phuket. A bus service links the two cities. The State Railway of Thailand, in conjunction with Songserm Travel, issues a combined train and bus ticket to Phuket for B670. The bus ride takes about five hours. There's a similar deal for passengers headed to Koh Samui.

🖪 **State Railway of Thailand** ☎ 1690 ⊕ www.railway.co.th.

Contacts & Resources

BANKS & EXCHANGING SERVICES

Banks are easy to locate in all mainland towns and on Koh Samui (in Chawaeng, Lamai, and Mae Nam). All banks will exchange foreign currency and most have ATMs. ATMs are increasingly easier to find in previously remote areas, such as Sairee Beach on Koh Tao and Haad Thong Nai Pan Yai on Koh Phangan. Bank of Ayudhya provides Western Union money transfer in a number of locations (central Sairee near AC Resort and Haad Rin, Phangan near Chicken Corner, and in the Central Samui Beach Resort); look for the yellow Bank of Ayudhya and matching yellow Western Union signs. Remember that hotel exchange rates differ significantly (and for the worse) from those at banks or currency exchange houses. Remote islands like Koh Phangan and Koh Tao do not widely accept credit cards, but have many eager currency exchangers. Some places will add a small service charge, typically 3%, when you pay with a credit card.

EMERGENCIES

If you're on the mainland, Surat Thani Hospital has a good reputation. The Bangkok-Samui Hospital near Chawaeng is your best bet on the islands. There are many emergency clinics on both Koh Tao and Phangan (perhaps in proportion to the number of places renting motorbikes). On Koh Tao, Maehad Clinic, across from the post office in Mae Haad, provides 24-hour on-call service. Haad Rin Inter Clinic on Phangan has an English-speaking doctor on call 24-hours and accepts all major credit cards. For any emergencies, call tourist police at ☎ 1699, a 24-hour service.

🚩 Hospitals **Haad Rin Inter Clinic** ✉ 116/20 Haad Rin, Haad Rin, Koh Phangan ☎ 077/375342 or 01/318–5085. **Mae Haad Clinic** ✉ Mae Haad Blvd., across from Post Office, Mae Haad, Koh Tao ☎ 077/456640 or 091/081–7797. **Samui International Hospital** ✉ Chawaeng Beach, Koh Samui ☎ 077/421230. **Surat Thani Hospital** ✉ Surat-Phun Phin Rd., Surat Thani ☎ 077/272231.

TOUR OPTIONS

Dive Deep runs trips from Koh Samui to Angthong National Marine Park and other destinations.

🚩 Tour Operator **Dive Deep** ✉ Chawaeng Beach Resort, Koh Samui ☎ 077/230155.

VISITOR INFORMATION

The Tourism Authority of Thailand has offices in several resorts in Southern Thailand. You can drop by for maps and brochures, as well as information about local excursions.

🚩 Tourist Information **TAT Central Region Office 2** ✉ Petchkasem Rd., Cha-am, Petchaburi ☎ 032/471005 or 032/471502 🌐 www.tourismthailand.org. **Hua Hin** ✉ Petchkasem Rd. ☎ 032/511367. **Koh Samui** ✉ Na Thon ☎ 077/421281. **Petchaburi Town** ✉ Radvitee Rd. ☎ 032/402220. **Surat Thani** ✉ 5 Talat Mai Rd. ☎ 077/281828.

KOH PHUKET

Phuket was one of the region's economic powerhouses—millions of tourists visited the island every year and many beaches were exhibiting the rampant overbuilding that turned Pattaya from peaceful getaway to eyesore. The 2004 tsunami, however, changed all that. Although only a few of the island's many beaches were directly affected (the worst damage actually occurred north of the island along the Andaman Coast), the beaches that were hit were hit really hard, and the island suffered its share of destruction and casualties. But it's important to note that most of the island wasn't hit at all, and the affected areas have, at this writing, completely recovered. In fact, if you've never been to Phuket, you will likely love it; returning visitors will find a new island that eagerly greets its next wave of tourism.

Koh Phuket is linked to the mainland by a causeway, and the rest of the world by an international airport. Its indented coastline and hilly interior make the island seem larger than its 48-km (30-mi) length and 21-km (13-mi) breadth. Before tourism, Koh Phuket was already making fortunes out of tin mining and rubber plantations. Then backpackers discovered Koh Phuket in the early 1970s. Word quickly spread about its white, sandy beaches and cliff-sheltered coves, its plunging waterfalls and impressive mountains, its cloudless days and fiery sunsets.

This love of Phuket has brought serious problems. Entrepreneurs built massive resorts, first at Patong, then spreading out around the island. Before the tsunami, there was no easy way to navigate the island, which was plagued by horrendous traffic and overdevelopment. Some would say Phuket was being loved to death. Now, many hope the tsunami's silver lining will be a bit of thought and reflection as the rebuilding continues.

Even though it may seem like every other business here is a tour operator or dive shop or tailor or jeep rental or pub, there's still a lot to love about the island. The beaches are beautiful and this is a top destination for snorkeling and diving (with more than 180 registered dive shops). The island offers some of the most exclusive resorts and spas in the world yet the food, drink, and accommodations are cheap compared to most visitors' home countries (though Phuket is quite expensive by Thai standards). And direct flights to the island make this a very convenient getaway.

⚠ **When planning your trip, keep in mind that the monsoon season runs from May to October, and swimming on the west side of the coast is not advisable during this time as the current can be dangerous.**

This section starts with Phuket Town, the hub of the island, and is organized counterclockwise from there. It's best to pick one or two choice spots and stick with them. The frazzling travel between destinations can very well undo any relaxation you enjoyed the previous day.

Numbers in the text correspond to numbers in the margin and on the Koh Phuket map.

Phuket Town

 862 km (539 mi) south of Bangkok.

Though very few tourists linger here, Phuket Town, the provincial capital, is one of the more interesting places on the island. About one-third of the island's population lives here, and the town is an intriguing mix of old Sino-Portuguese architecture and the influences of the Chinese, Muslims, and Thais that inhabit it. The old Chinese quarter along Talang Street is especially good for a stroll, as its history has not yet been replaced by modern concrete and tile. And this same area also has a variety of antiques shops, art studios, and cafés.

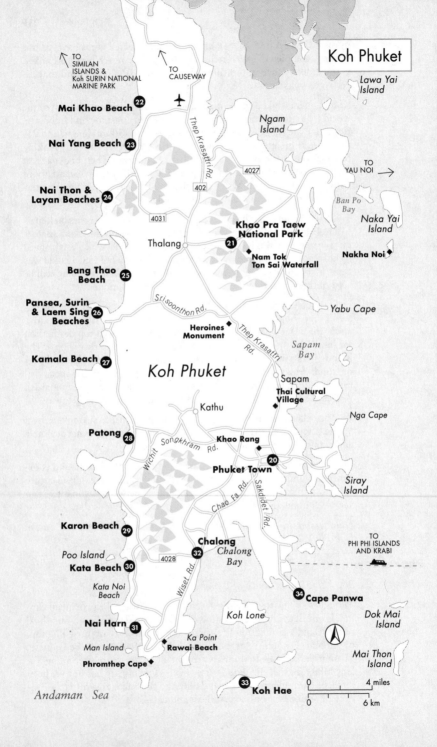

The other major thoroughfares in town are Ratsada, Phuket, and Ranong roads. Ratsada connects Phuket Road, where you can find the Tourism Authority of Thailand office, to Ranong Road, where there's an aromatic local market filled with fruits, vegetables, spices, and meats. Ranong Road also has a songthaew terminal, where minibuses depart for the most popular beaches every half hour. The fare is B15–B30.

If you want to get your bearings, there's a fine view of Phuket Town and the island's interior from the top of **Khao Rang,** a hill northwest of town. It can be a tricky drive—you'll need to watch carefully for street signs, as many aren't marked or are covered by foliage. From the town's center, take either Ranong or Thalang Road west and turn north on Kho Sim Bi Road. Follow the winding, forested road up to the top.

4

The **National Museum,** opposite the Heroines Monument, has an interesting exhibition of the island's culture and history, including its encounter with the Burmese and their defeat by the island's two heroines. ⌧ *12 km (7 mi) north of Phuket Town* ☎ *076/311426* ⌨ *B30* ⊙ *Daily 9–4.*

Where to Eat

$–$$ ✕ **Khanasutra, A Taste of India.** This restaurant's name is not making false promises—the Sikh owner and Indian chef turn out flavorful, authentic Indian cuisine. The fish tikka is recommended. Part of the unique decor is a bedouin-style tent, where you can have a few cocktails after dinner. ⌧ *18–20 Takua Pa Rd., Phuket Town* ☎ *091/894–0794* ⊟ *No credit cards* ⊙ *No lunch Sun.*

¢–$ ✕ **Kopi de Phuket.** For a good cup of coffee, try this artistically designed shop, which also serves snacks, sandwiches, breads, and shakes. It's across from the Honda Shop/Nai Yao Restaurant. It opens daily at 9:30 AM. ⌧ *Phuket Rd.* ☎ *No phone* ⊟ *No credit cards.*

¢ ✕ **Wilai.** Thai fast food is served from big vats at this little shop in the heart of the old Sino-Portuguese district. The owner makes different dishes every day to keep her regular customers interested. She focuses on curries, vegetables, fish, and soups, and she'll warn hapless foreigners away from the spicy ones. Try a traditional cup of coffee, made with a cloth bag. Ask the owner about the temple in her backyard. The restaurant closes at 4 PM. ⌧ *14 Talang Rd.* ☎ *076/222875* ⊟ *No credit cards* ⊙ *No dinner.*

Where to Stay

$$–$$$$ ▦ **Royal Phuket City Hotel.** This is arguably Phuket Town's best address. Rooms are spacious and contemporary, but don't have great views. The large Club Asia health club is popular with locals. The top-floor Thai Thai Room has outdoor seating and great views; the Cappuccino 154 deli on the ground floor caters its baked goods to other coffee shops around town. ⌧ *154 Phang Nga Rd., Phuket, 83000* ☎ *076/233333* ⊕ *www.royalphuketcity.com* ⇆ *251 rooms* ⌂ *In-room: safe, refrigerator. In-hotel: 3 restaurants, bar, pool, gym, spa, laundry service, public Internet* ⊟ *AE, DC, MC, V.*

$$ ▦ **Metropole.** The grand old Metropole—the town's first luxury hotel—has a shuttle service to the closest beaches, so you can stay in town and commute to the sea. The advantages are not only cheaper accommodation, but the opportunity to visit more than just one beach. Rooms are bright, with picture windows that let in a lot of sun. A spacious lounge is a cool retreat during the day, and the karaoke bar is fun at night. The hotel's handsome Chinese restaurant serves great dim sum; for Western food, try the Metropole Café. ✉ *1 Montri Rd., 83000* ☎ *076/215050 or 076/214020* ⊕ *www.metropolephuket.com* ☞ *248 rooms, 20 suites* ♿ *In-room: refrigerator. In-hotel: 2 restaurants, pool, gym, laundry service, public Internet, airport shuttle* ▭ *AE, DC, MC, V* �‖⦾ *EP.*

$–$$ ▦ **The Taste.** For a slightly more expensive, but still budget, option try this small guesthouse, formerly called XVI (The 16). A pair of old shophouses were gutted and renovated by local Thai architect Khun Malida in a chic style that wouldn't be out of place in London or New York. The 12 uniquely decorated rooms feature spartan but stylish open layouts finished in wood, steel, and glass. The downstairs bar features house music until the wee hours. ✉ *16 Ratsada Rd., 83000* ☎ *076/222812* ⊕ *www.thetastephuket.com* ☞ *12 rooms* ♿ *In-room: DVD (some). In-hotel: bar* ▭ *MC, V.*

¢ ▦ **Talang Guesthouse.** This inexpensive hotel is becoming ever more popular with backpackers, offering basic fan-cooled and some air-conditioned rooms in an old building. Two rooms on the roof are spacious and, naturally, have the best sunset views. Rooms toward the front overlook the street, so they're not as quiet. ✉ *37 Talangs Rd., 83000* ☎ *076/214225* ☞ *13 rooms* ♿ *In-room: no a/c (some), no TV* ▭ *No credit cards.*

Khao Pra Taew National Park

㉑ *19 km (12 mi) north of Phuket Town.*

Thailand's islands have several national parks, and this one is home to Phuket's last remaining virgin forest and populations of endangered animals. The park boasts two easily accessible waterfalls. From Highway 4027, watch the signs and turn west toward Bang Pae Waterfall and the Gibbon Rehabilitation Center. You'll have to pay the standard foreigner's fee to the park: B200 (Thais pay B20). The park advertises the good deeds of the Gibbon Center, and indeed it's a worthy cause. (What they don't tell you is that the center, which sits near the parking lot at Bang Pae, receives none of your entrance fee.) After visiting the center, follow the paved trail along the waterfall. It's a relatively easy hike, quite lush in the rainy season.

To access **Tonsai Waterfall** on the other side of the park, follow the signs and turn east off Highway 402. Here, you can find two trails (600 meters and 2 km [1 mi]), through rich tropical evergreen forest. Expect buckets of rain in the monsoon season. Gibbons, civets, macaques, mouse deer, wild boar, lemurs, and loris live in the park, but spotting one would be a rare and impressive feat.

Both park entrances have bathrooms, parking lots, and food stalls. If you plan to visit both waterfalls, make sure you get entrance tickets at your first stop—they're good for both sites.

Mai Khao Beach

㉒ *37 km (23 mi) northwest of Phuket Town.*

This is Phuket's northernmost beach, still a haven for leatherback turtles that lay their eggs here between November and February. It's an increasingly rare event, but one new nest was found less than two weeks after the tsunami hit.

The Marriott Resort and next-door Sirinath Marine National Park (established to protect the turtles) are the only things to occupy this beach, which connects with Nai Yang Beach, to form Phuket's longest stretch of sand. It's great for running, sunbathing, and swimming (in the hot season, although dangerous during the monsoons).

Where to Stay & Eat

$$$$ ✕▨ **J. W. Marriott Resort & Spa.** Wow. This secluded resort offers the
Fodor'sChoice longest stretch of sand on the island. It has luxurious rooms with im-
★ peccable classic Thai design and an unbeatable spa with amenities that meet or exceed those in the guest rooms. The Marriott is the only thing on this beach, but it has everything you need and then some, including the flagship spa of Marriott Asia and a cooking school. ⊠ *231 Moo 3, Mai Khao, 83110* ☎ *076/338000* ⊕ *www.marriott.com/HKTJW* ⇋ *265 rooms* ⅋ *In-room: safe, refrigerator, DVD, ethernet. In-hotel: 6 restaurants, room service, 4 bars, 2 tennis courts, 3 pools, gym, spa, concierge, laundry service* ▭ *AE, MC, V* ⍿⚆⍿ *EP.*

Nai Yang Beach

㉓ *34 km (20 mi) northwest of Phuket Town.*

Nai Yang Beach is really a continuation south of Mai Khao, making a long stretch of sand good for running or swimming in the dry season. Casuarina trees line the gently curving shore. It's a far quieter beach than most, with a strip of trees and a small string of beachside restaurants and bars, tour guides, tailors, and shops. Fishing boats anchor nearby, making for picture-perfect sunrises and sunsets. Nai Yang did suffer some damage from the tsunami, but its businesses were fully operational by that spring.

Where to Stay & Eat

At this writing, the Pearl Village Resort was being turned into a new resort, the Indigo Pearl (⊕ www.phuket.com/indigo-pearl). Though we were unable to confirm details before publication, it's worth looking into this resort as an option for the area, as it will easily be the swankiest property on the beach with the most daring design.

¢–$ ✕ **Bank Restaurant.** Nai Yang Beach has a number of seafood restaurants with tables in the sand, but this is definitely one to try. It's run by a woman whose husband goes out fishing each night and returns by morning with the day's catch. Red tablecloths and lights hanging from the trees give this beachside spot a romantic air. ⊠ *Nai Yang Beach* ☎ *091/978–5728* ▭ *No credit cards.*

$-$$$ ⊡ **Nai Yang Beach Resort.** These basic bungalows are a short walk from the beach. They surround a small fishpond and come with a variety of amenities—choose between fans or air-conditioning, and with or without TVs and minibars. The higher the price, the better the view, although none of the rooms overlook the sea. ⊠ *65/23–24 Nai Yang Beach Rd., Moo 5, T. Sakhu, Thalang, Phuket, 83140* ☎ *076/328300* ⊕ *www.naiyangbeachresort.com* ➳ *36 rooms* ⌂ *In-room: no a/c (some), refrigerator (some), no TV (some). In-hotel: restaurant* ⊟ *MC, V* ⦿❘ *EP.*

Nai Thon & Layan Beaches

㉔ *30 km (18½ mi) northwest of Phuket Town.*

Just a few miles north of Bang Thao Bay, follow a smaller highway off the main routes (4030 and 4031) along a scenic coastline reminiscent of California's Pacific Coast Highway. These beaches are good for swimming in the dry season. There's more development on the way, but for now they're two of the island's quiet gems.

Where to Stay

$$$$ ⊡ **Bundarika Villa.** On a quiet, isolated beach, Bundarika has the ideal environment for relaxation; accordingly, the resort has a special focus on wellness for both body and mind. You can begin each day with a tai chi or yoga class. If you need a change of scenery during the day, you can take a stroll across the sandbar at low tide to a small offshore island. In the evening, dine on cuisine designed with your health in mind. All accommodations are private villas with peaked roofs, dark stained wood, and artfully placed flowers, statues, and silk pillows. Within the walls of your private compound, covered sala tables and chairs are set up so you can enjoy afternoon tea or coffee beside your small private pool. ⊠ *89 Moo 6, Layan Beach, 83110* ☎ *076/317200* ⊕ *www.bundarika.com* ➳ *20 villas* ⌂ *In-room: safe, refrigerator, DVD. In-hotel: restaurant, bicycles, laundry service, concierge, public Wi-Fi* ⊟ *AE, MC, V.*

$$$$ ⊡ **Pavilions.** Many resorts claim that they're set up so that you never have to leave your villa, but Pavilions really means it. Each private villa here has a pool and a small kitchen. All meals are delivered to your room, as are massages and spa treatments. Rooms have enormous tubs, covered outdoor beds with fans, and ocean views from either the bed or the pool. It's the ideal honeymoon retreat. ■ TIP→ **If you feel the need to mingle with other guests, at the peak of the hill there is a bar with panoramic views; nonguests often drop in here, too, for tapas and spectacular sunsets.** Note that all rooms are nonsmoking and the resort does not allow children. The beach is a bit far away, but there is shuttle service available on demand. ⊠ *31/1 Moo 6, Cherngtalay, Thalang, 83110* ☎ *076/317600, 091/621–4841 in Bangkok* ⊕ *www.pavilions-resorts.com* ➳ *30 villas* ⌂ *In-room: safe, refrigerator, DVD, Wi-Fi. In-hotel: room service, bar, spa, concierge* ⊟ *AE, DC, MC, V.*

$$$$ ⊡ **Trisara.** Opulence is the standard at the Trisara resort; rooms feature a variety of Thai wooden art pieces, silk throw pillows on the divans, and 32-inch plasma TVs hidden in the walls. The spacious library contains an abundance of literature, magazines, music, and games for the occasional rainy day. The restaurant serves meals on an enormous wooden deck built over a giant pool, beneath swaying palms and beside the resort's small, private beach. Guests enjoy golf at a 36-hole course just 15 minutes away. If you simply love Trisara (which translates roughly to "inner peace"), then you can purchase one of the villa homes. ⊠ *60/ 1 Moo 6, Srisoonthorn Rd., Cherngtalay, 83110* ☎ *076/310100 or 076/ 310355* ⊕ *www.trisara.com* ⇨ *42 rooms* ♻ *In-room: safe, refrigerator, DVD, Wi-Fi. In-hotel: restaurant, room service, bar, 2 tennis courts, pool, gym, spa, beachfront, diving, water sports* ⊟ *AE, MC, DC, V.*

★ **$$$–$$$$** 🖼 **Layan Beach Resort & Spa Village.** The spa is the focus of this resort, which is tucked away on a hillside overlooking the sea, a small beach, and nearby island. In fact, the spa looks like it's own exclusive set of villas. You won't find much else around here, for now. The standard rooms aren't terribly exciting, but they're spacious and bright. ⊠ *62 Moo 6, Layan Village, 83110* ☎ *076/313412 up to 14* ⊕ *www. layanphuket.com* ⇨ *52 rooms and villas* ♻ *In-hotel: 2 restaurants, 2 pools, gym, spa, bicycles* ⊟ *AE, MC, V* 🍴 *EP.*

Bang Thao Beach

㉕ *22 km (14 mi) northwest of Phuket Town.*

Once the site of a tin mine, Bang Thao Beach (a resort area collectively called Laguna Phuket) now glistens with the more precious metals worn by its affluent visitors. Due to the ingenuity of Ho Kwon Ping and his family, this area was built nearly 20 years ago in a spot so damaged from mining, most thought it beyond repair. Now it's recovered enough to support an array of accommodations, eateries, and golf courses set around the lagoons. The beach itself is a long stretch of white sand with vendors offering a variety of sports equipment rental, inexpensive seafood, beach massages, and cocktails. The beach is good for swimming in the hot season; the lagoon for kayaking anytime.

The once-quiet bay was one of the island's major destinations, though it's been quieter since the 2004 tsunami. A free shuttle service transports visitors among the five resorts that line the shore. Of the Laguna quintet, the odd man out is the Dusit, which doesn't match up to the other four. None are cheap. As anywhere on the island, some of the older resorts are showing signs of age and tropical weather damage, despite frequent renovations.

Where to Stay & Eat

¢ ✕ **Seafood.** The friendly women at this popular street-side shanty serve made-to-order seafood, noodles, and stir-fry. Every meal comes with a bowl of aromatic cardamom soup. It's safe for foreign bellies, but if you're wary of street food or spicy food, you probably won't be comfortable here. ⊹ *About 5 km (3 mi) from the resorts, heading east. Look for a small sign on the left side of the road that says* SEAFOOD. *If you reach the mosque, you've gone too far* ☎ No phone ⊟ No credit cards.

$$$$ 🖼 **Allamanda Laguna Phuket.** Unlike the other four resorts in the area, this all-suites property sits on the lagoon instead of the beach and therefore, offers lower rates. You definitely get more bang for your buck here than at the other four resorts. Suites come in various configurations (one or two bedrooms), but all have kitchenettes. Shuttle boats between the resort and the beach run every 30 minutes 8–5. The scenic trip across the lagoon takes approximately 10 minutes. ⊠ *29 Moo 4 Srisoonthorn Rd., Cherngtalay, 83110* ☎ *076/324359* ⊕ *www.allamanda.com* ⤳ *235 suites* ⚴ *In-room: kitchen. In-hotel: 2 restaurants, 3 pools, spa, water sports, children's programs (ages 4–14), laundry service* ▭ *AE, MC, V* ⓐ *EP.*

$$$$ 🖾 **Banyan Tree Phuket.** Of the quintet of resorts on Laguna Beach, this is the most exclusive—and expensive. Your secluded villa has a bathroom as big as the bedroom; an outdoor shower for rinsing off after a swim is a nice addition. Teak floors and locally woven fabrics remind you that you are in Thailand. The king-size bed is on a raised platform so that you can gaze out onto your garden. The most expensive villas have their own private pools. Rejuvenating treatments in the spa include herbal massages. ⊠ *33 Moo 4 Srisoonthorn Rd., Cherngtalay, Amphur Talang, 83110* ☎ *076/324374* ⊕ *www.banyantree.com* ⤳ *132 villas* ⚴ *In-room: safe, refrigerator, DVD, Wi-Fi. In-hotel: 3 restaurants, 2 bars, 18-hole golf course, 5 tennis courts, pool, gym, spa, beachfront, water sports, bicycles, children's programs (ages 3–12), laundry service, concierge, airport shuttle* ▭ *AE, MC, V* ⓐ *EP.*

$$$–$$$$ 🖾 **Bang Thao Beach Resort & Spa.** On the southern edge of Bang Thao Beach—and not part of the Laguna complex—this Best Western facility offers cheaper accommodation that's right on the beach. You can get very nice sea views and the basic, decent rooms you expect of Best Western, for one-half to two-thirds the price of the other resorts, especially in low season, when rates drop dramatically. The place can be a little difficult to find, though, as it's on a small, twisty road connecting Bang Thao and Surin Beach. ⊠ *124/29 Moo 3, Tumbon Cheung Thalay, 83110* ☎ *076/ 270680 up to 85* ⊕ *www.bangtaobeach.com* ⤳ *243 rooms* ⚴ *In-room: safe, refrigerator. In-hotel: 2 restaurants, bar, 3 pools, gym, spa, beachfront, laundry service, public Internet* ▭ *AE, MC, V* ⓐ *EP.*

$$$–$$$$ 🖾 **Laguna Beach Resort.** Laguna Beach is in the same league as the Sheraton, but less expensive. The resort has traditional Thai and Angkor details, including a vast, meandering pool with replica Angkor Wat wall carvings. In addition, this resort has less of an amusement park feel than its neighbor, but still has plenty of kids' activities. ⊠ *Bang Thao Bay, Phuket, 83110* ☎ *076/324352* ⊕ *www.lagunabeach-resort.com* ⤳ *252 rooms* ⚴ *In-room: safe, refrigerator. In-hotel: 5 restaurants, room service, golf course, 4 tennis courts, pools, diving, water sports, bicycles, children's programs (ages 4–12), laundry service, public Internet* ▭ *AE, MC, V* ⓐ *EP.*

Pansea, Surin & Laem Sing Beaches

26 *21 km (12 mi) northwest of Phuket Town.*

South of Bang Thao is a jagged shoreline with little inlets. Once secluded, these areas are developing quickly with villas, restaurants, high-end resorts, cheap backpacker hotels, and what is becoming the usual Phuket beach slurb. Surin Beach is about 550 yards of sand where you can get a beer and pretty much anything else that you want. There's a public parking lot above the beach, which is literally a garbage dump in the off-season. Dozens of sites are under construction between here and Laem Sing. So many little restaurants, with Thai and Western food for a few dollars, have popped up, it's nearly impossible to recommend one over another.

Head north a bit and things change. On the spit of land separating these beaches from Bang Thao sit two of the island's most luxurious resorts, though you may never find them without careful sleuthing. An overgrown sign points the way up a small road to the Chedi; no sign marks the Amanpuri beyond that.

Where to Stay

★ $$$$ **Amanpuri Resort.** You'd be hard-pressed to find a more elegant hotel in Thailand—nor one quite as expensive (the nightly rate for the largest of the villas is more than $7,000!). The reception area, with beautifully polished teak floors, is completely open in the dry season so that you can enjoy the ocean breezes. Here you can find two palm-shaded restaurants overlooking the blue-tiled swimming pool. Choose between rooms in secluded hillside pavilions or immense villas with private swimming pools. Pavilion prices differ according to the view offered; villas have between two and six bedrooms. The split-level bar has stunning sunset views. ⊠ *Pansea Beach, Phuket, 83000* ☎ *076/324333* ⊕ *www.amanpuri.com* ⥲ *40 pavilions, 31 villas* △ *In-room: safe, refrigerator, no TV, Wi-Fi. In-hotel: 2 restaurants, bar, 4 tennis courts, 3 pools, gym, spa, beachfront, water sports, laundry service* ⊟ *AE, D, MC, V* ⏐○⏐ *EP.*

★ $$$$ **Chedi.** Almost completely hidden by a grove of coconut palms, this resort has more than 100 thatch-roof cottages overlooking a quiet beach. You know this place is special when you walk into the lobby, which has a sweeping view of the Andaman Sea. The decor is sleek and geometric. An octagonal pool is set amid the tropical flora. Each of the cottages has its own sundeck. The interiors, done in wood and stone, with high, pointed ceilings, are simple but elegant. ⊠ *118 Moo 3, Cherngtalay, Phuket, 83110* ☎ *076/324017* ⊕ *www.phuket.com/chedi* ⥲ *108 chalets* △ *In-room: safe, refrigerator, Wi-Fi. In-hotel: 3 restaurants, bar, 4 tennis courts, pool, spa, beachfront, water sports, laundry service, concierge* ⊟ *AE, MC, V* ⏐○⏐ *EP.*

$–$$ **Surin Bay Inn.** For cheaper accommodations near Surin Beach (only a few minutes' walk away), try this small hotel. Some rooms have balconies overlooking the street along the beach. This is one of the cleanest, nicest budget options in the area. ⊠ *106/11 Surin Beach, 83110* ☎ *076/271601* ⊕ *www.surinbayinn.com* ⥲ *12 rooms* △ *In-room: safe, refrigerator, ethernet. In-hotel: restaurant, bar, laundry service, public Internet, airport shuttle* ⊟ *MC, V* ⏐○⏐ *BP.*

Kamala Beach

㉗ *18 km (11 mi) west of Phuket Town.*

South of Bang Thao is Kamala Beach, a curving strip of coral sand backed by coconut palms. Before the tsunami, Kamala town was quickly turning into a beach strip of shops and restaurants, like so many others. But unlike the more upscale enclaves to the north, Kamala Beach had some reasonably priced accommodations, set apart from the development. Kamala Beach suffered some of the worst destruction on Phuket during the tsunami, but it has fully recovered.

Lodging

$$ ☐ **Baan Chaba.** If you're looking for a bungalow or hotel on the beach, you'll find several options at the north end of Kamala (none of which have views of the beach, some of which are absurdly priced). This one has newly designed concrete, tile, and wood rooms with nicer trimmings than the others, and wood furniture. Each bungalow has a porch. Post-tsunami renovated rooms now feature air-conditioning and hot water. There is no restaurant at the resort, but you'll find plenty of beachside options just a few feet away. ☒ *95/3 Moo 3, Kamala Beach, Kathu, Phuket, 83120* ☎ *076/279158* ⊕ *www.baanchaba.com* ☎ *8 bungalows* ♨ *In-room: refrigerator. In-hotel: laundry service, public Internet* ▭ *No credit cards* ¶⊙¶ *EP.*

Patong

28 *13 km (8 mi) west of Phuket Town.*

You'd hardly believe it today, but Patong was once the island's most remote beach, completely cut off by the surrounding mountains and only accessible by boat. In 1959 a highway linked Patong with Phuket Town, and the tranquil beachfront was bought up by developers who knew the beautiful beach wouldn't stay a secret for long. Today, the cat is definitely out of the bag: Patong is a thriving beach resort community frequented by both Bangkokians, down for a weekend of fun in the sun, and international visitors. ■ TIP→ Patong is a great place for new visitors to Thailand who are looking for a nice beach with characteristic Thai experiences, like muay thai, street shopping, and authentic Thai food, as well as familiar facilities, like Starbuck's, sushi bars, and chain hotels.

The beach was hit hard by the 2004 tsunami, and anything close to the water was destroyed. The area has fully recovered, however, and as a result of post-tsunami redevelopment, Patong's beach road has undergone a beautification that includes a mosaic inlaid sidewalk. You can now stroll along several miles of boutique shops, Western restaurants and bars, ice cream parlors, and upscale nightlife venues, interspersed with traditional Thai market stalls selling food, cheap T-shirts, and knockoff goods. Patong has something for travelers of any age or demeanor.

The beach itself, which used to be cluttered with beach umbrellas, now has ample room for both sun-

PATONG'S SULLIED REPUTATION

Patong has, on occasion, been portrayed as a sleazy environment crawling with prostitutes, but this is a gross exaggeration. It is a far cry from Pattaya or Patpong in Bangkok, and most visitors are oblivious to anything untoward, spending the majority of their days playing on the beach and their evenings at the tasteful bars and tasty restaurants along Thaweewong Road. The sex trade does exist here, but Patong is a suitable destination for families and couples, as well as singles.

bathing and playing soccer or Frisbee on the beach. Every conceivable beach activity from wakeboarding to jet skiing to parasailing is available. Like Chawaeng on Koh Samui, Patong became so popular because it was the nicest beach on the island, and now its popularity has caused some degradation of the environment, particularly noticeable when the monsoon rains wash the grime off the street and onto the beach. That said, it's still a nice stretch of sand for walking, swimming, or sunbathing.

Where to Stay & Eat

$$$$ ✕ **Otowa.** This Japanese-French fusion restaurant sits between its two other cliff-top neighbors, offering the same spectacular views. The chef has cooked in Tokyo and Monaco before settling in Thailand. Menu items include foie-gras sushi, goose liver, and Kobe beef, and abalone cooked in burgundy butter. ⊠ *223 Prabaramee Rd., Kalim Beach, Patong* ☎ *076/344254* ⌚ *Reservations essential* 🖃 *AE, MC, V.*

$$–$$$$ ✕ **Baan Rim Pa.** If you suffer from vertigo, take a pass on this restaurant.
FodorsChoice You dine on a terrace that clings to a cliff at the north end of Patong Beach.
★ There are tables set back from the edge, but you'll then miss the gorgeous ocean views. The food is among the best Phuket has to offer. Well-thought-out set menus make ordering simpler for those unfamiliar with Thai food. They've turned down the heat on many favorites, so you may be disappointed if you like spicier fare. The restaurant has a piano bar open Tuesday through Sunday. ⊠ *Prabaramee Rd., Kalim Beach, Patong, Phuket* ☎ *076/340789* ⌚ *Reservations essential* 🖃 *AE, MC, V.*

★ ⊙ **$$$$** 🏨 **Holiday Inn.** This is no ordinary Holiday Inn: this stylish, modern hotel exudes the kind of sophistication that most people would never imagine possible from a Holiday Inn or from Patong in general. The hotel has two wings. In the main wing, the superior rooms above the terrace are nicer. A colorful hallway leads to the Kids' Suites, which have bunk beds and Playstations in the children's room; Family Suites are larger—a king-size parents' room is connected to a pirate-theme kids' room that has two separate beds. The hotel has two activities centers for kids (featuring Thai culture, arts, and crafts classes), as well as a children's pool with a waterfall. The Busakorn wing has a separate reception area; Thai-style, peaked-roof rooms; and an adults-only swimming pool surrounded by Singha and elephant sculptures and fountains. The main swimming pool, like the rest of the resort, is across the road from the beach but is buffered from the street by an Italian café/restaurant which is a great place to watch the sun set. ⊠ *52 Thaweewong Rd., Patong Beach, 83150* ☎ *076/340–0608* ⊕ *www.phuket.com/holidayinn* ↘ *405 rooms* ⌂ *In-room: safe (some), refrigerator, DVD (some). In-hotel: 4 restaurants, room service, 3 bars, 6 pools, gym, spa, children's programs (ages 5–12), concierge, laundry service* 🖃 *AE, MC, V.*

★ **$$–$$$** 🏨 **Impiana Phuket Cabana.** This hotel's chief attraction is its unbeatable location, right in the middle of the city facing the beach. Furthermore, the post-tsunami renovations have made the Impiana the nicest resort in Patong. Towering flower displays stand in the lobby, where Buddhist Thai art adorns the walls, and large sliding glass doors exit to the beachside bar and adjacent pool. Among the hotel's other highlights are good travel services, a reputable dive shop, an outstanding restaurant, and a festive cigar/tapas bar, La Salsa, with pictures of Che smoking stogies and Fidel hamming it up with Hemingway. The beachside spa has glass doors and windows so that you can enjoy the view while having your treatments or massages. ⊠ *41 Taweewong Rd., 83150* ☎ *076/340138* ⊕ *www.impiana.com* ⤴ *70 rooms* ⬥ *In-room: safe, refrigerator. In-hotel: 3 restaurants, room service, 2 bars, pool, spa, diving, laundry service, public Wi-Fi, airport shuttle* ⊟ *AE, MC, V* ⦿| *EP.*

$$ ⊞ **QVC Patong Beach Resort.** This small beach hotel is at the southern end of Patong Beach, away from the noise, but close enough to the action. The beach, just across a relatively quiet road, is narrow at high tide, but lacks the clutter of boats and Jet Skis found along the main stretch of Patong. Rooms have either sea views or no views; sea-view rooms have balconies. All guest rooms have Thai-style wooden bed frames and silk throw pillows, which are a nice touch. There is no pool on-site, but guests can use the pool at the hotel next door. The restaurant serves breakfast only, which is included in the price of the room. ⊠ *22–26 Thaweewong Rd., Kathu-Patong, 83150* ☎ *076/342197 or 076/342198* ⊕ *www.qualityvacationclub.com* ⤴ *18 rooms* ⬥ *In-room: safe, refrigerator, Wi-Fi. In-hotel: restaurant, public Internet* ⊟ *MC, V* ⦿| *BP.*

Nightlife

The vast majority of tourists only venture as far as Bang La Road, a walking street that is more of a carnival atmosphere than something disturbingly sleazy; children pose for photos with flamboyant and friendly transvestites, honeymooning couples people-watch from numerous beer bars along the traffic-free promenade, and everyone else simply strolls the strip, some stopping to dance or play Connect Four, Jenga, or a curiously popular nail-hammering game with friendly Thai hostesses.

Patong has a reputation for its happening nightlife, and the seedy side of it is easily avoidable. Some of the more tasteful nightlife venues are on Thaweewong Road, including **Saxophone** (⊠ 188/2 Andaman Bazaar, Thaweewong Rd. ☎ 076/346167), a branch of the legendary Bangkok jazz and blues bar, and the neighboring **Rock City,** both of which provide live music nightly, and a number of pubs and bars, some of which have live music and other shows.

With the varied nightlife in Patong, it's no surprise to find a sensational drag show here. The famous **Simon Cabaret** (⊠ 8 Sirirach Rd. ☎ 076/342011) treats you to a beautifully costumed and choreographed show. There are two shows daily, at 7:30 and 9:30.

There are also regularly scheduled muay thai fights at the arena on the corner of Bang La and Rat-U-Thit Songroipee roads.

Karon Beach

㉙ *20 km (12 mi) southwest of Phuket Town.*

Just south of Patong lie Karon Beach and its smaller northern counterpart, Karon Noi. Bunches of hotels, restaurants, tailors, dive operators, and gift shops have sprung up along the main Karon Beach to accommodate the tourists tempted by this long stretch of white sand and good dry-season swimming (it's good for running year-round). A sprawling Meridien resort is wedged into Karon Noi. If none of the following options tickle your fancy, there are literally dozens upon dozens of others. It's best to call hotels individually, as some were still under repair as of this writing. Most businesses, however, are back to normal.

☮ The Flintstones-style buildings along the road in central Karon village belong to **Dino Park Mini Golf** (✉ Karon Beach ☎ 076/330625 ⊕ www. dinopark.com ☞ B240 adult ☉ Daily 10 AM–midnight). Street side are a dinosaur-theme bar and restaurant, but the real fun is inside: 18 holes of miniature golf, featuring a swamp, a lava cave, and a real live Tyrannasaurus Rex (well, the kids will think so!).

Where to Stay & Eat

$$–$$$$ ✗ **On the Rock.** Built, you guessed it, on a rock overlooking Karon Beach, this restaurant has great views of the water. Seafood is the specialty, but Italian and traditional Thai dishes are on the menu, too. This restaurant is part of the Marina Cottage hotel. ✉ *South end of Karon Beach* ☎ *076/330625* ▤ *AE, MC, V.*

$$$–$$$$ ▦ **Le Meridien.** Between Patong and Karon Beach sits this sprawling resort. There are more bars, cafés, and restaurants in this hotel than in many small towns. Its range of outdoor diversions—everything from tennis to waterskiing—means you never have to leave the property. There are hundreds of guests at any given time, yet the resort never feels too crowded, thanks to its thoughtful design. Two huge wings are where you'll find the sumptuous rooms, which are furnished in teak and rattan. Most have sea views, others overlook the pair of pools. ✉ *8/5 Moo 1, Karon, Muang, Phuket, 83100* ☎ *076/340480* ⊕ *www.lemeridien-phuket.com* ☞ *470 rooms* ☝ *In-room: safe, refrigerator, ethernet. In-hotel: 7 restaurants, room service, 2 tennis courts, 2 pools, gym, spa, beachfront, diving, water sports, children's programs (ages 3–12), laundry service, concierge, public Internet* ▤ *AE, DC, MC, V* ❖ *EP.*

★ $$$–$$$$ ▦ **Marina Cottage.** This surprisingly quiet option has its cottages spread out over a lush hillside separating Karon from Kata Beach. Those cottages higher on the hill are the quietest. A wonderful pool and second restaurant (the other is On the Rock, listed above) are surrounded by more trees and plants. Best of all, Marina Cottage has its own beach access, keeping the hordes at bay. The post-tsunami renovations upgraded half of the jungle rooms around the pool to have all the latest high-tech amenities, including minicomputers and DVD players; note that some older rooms don't have certain amenities, like TVs. ✉ *47 Karon Rd., 83100* ☎ *076/ 330493 or 076/330625* ⊕ *www.marinaphuket.com* ☞ *89 rooms* ☝ *In-room: refrigerator, DVD (some), no TV (some), ethernet (some). In-hotel: 3 restaurants, pool, diving, public Internet* ▤ *MC, V* ❖ *EP.*

★ $$$–$$$$ ▦ **Moevenpick Resort and Spa.** Live Thai music greets you as you enter an expansive lobby lavishly decorated with Thai art. Six types of rooms include two-bedroom family villas, one-bedroom plunge pool villas, and rooftop villas that have penthouse salas with deck chairs and outdoor Jacuzzis. Wander across the beautifully landscaped grounds, past the jungle gym and volleyball and badminton courts, follow the scent of incense to the spa, or continue toward the sea, where sand has been transported across the road to create an authentic "beach" bar. The main pool has a domed, thatch-roof platform within the water. ✉ *509 Patak Rd., Karon Beach, 83100* ☎ *076/396139* ⊕ *www.moevenpick-phuket. com* ⤳ *339 rooms* ⚭ *In-room: safe, refrigerator, ethernet. In-hotel: 2 restaurants, room service, 3 bars, 3 tennis courts, 3 pools, gym, spa, diving* ⊟ *AE, DC, MC, V.*

$$–$$$ ⊡ **In On the Beach.** This new place way at the north end of Karon is truly on the beach. Many of the rooms have good sea views. It's a quick walk from here to the rest of the sprawl of Karon Beach. ✉ *Moo 1, Patak Rd., Karon Beach, Phuket, 83100* ☎ *076/398220* ⊕ *www.karon-inonthebeach.com* ⤳ *30 rooms* ⚭ *In-hotel: restaurant, laundry service, public Internet* ⊟ *MC, V* ⑩ *CP.*

$$ ⊡ **Phuket Orchid Resort.** This resort is slightly inland, but the beach is just a short walk away. The lack of a beachfront brings the rates down considerably, but the lower rates make it very popular. A hodgepodge of Thai, Khmer, and Chinese architectural and design flourishes are everywhere, even in the sprawling pool and surrounding patios. And yes, lots of orchids are sprinkled about the main lobby. Some rooms have direct pool access. If you want a no-smoking room, be sure to demand it when booking. ✉ *34 Luang Pohchuan Rd., Karon Muang, Phuket, 83100* ☎ *076/396519* ⊕ *www.katagroup.com* ⤳ *525 rooms* ⚭ *In-room: safe, refrigerator. In-hotel: 3 restaurants, room service, bar, 2 pools, spa, laundry service, public Internet* ⊟ *AE, MC, V* ⑩ *EP.*

Kata Beach

➌ *22 km (13 mi) southwest of Phuket Town.*

Of the three most popular beaches on the west coast of Phuket, this is the calmest of the lot. A shady sidewalk runs the length of the beach. Club Med dominates a large hunk of the beachfront, keeping the development frenzy to the southern end. There's also a committed group of regulars here who surf the small local breaks. To the south, Kata Noi is almost exclusively taken up with the very long and expensive Kata Thani Phuket Beach Resort. This is a public beach (as all beaches in Thailand are), so be sure to exercise your beach rights and soak up some sun on delightfully quiet Kata Noi if you're in the area.

Where to Stay

$$$$ ⊡ **Kata Thani Phuket Beach Resort.** This long, sprawling lodge fronts most of the Kata Noi beach. This seems to intimidate day-trippers, whose general absence keeps nearly 1 km (½ mi) of smooth sand delightfully calm. Glass-walled suites in the Thani wing have some of the best ocean views on the island. You can shower and watch the sun set at the same time through huge bathroom windows. Regular rooms (if you can call them that) in the Buri wing are very tastefully furnished, with all the bells and whistles you'd expect in this price range (some have pool views, others ocean views). ✉ *14 Kata Noi Rd., Karon, Muang, Phuket, 83100* ☎ *076/330124* ⊕ *www.katathani.com* ⤳ *479 rooms* ⚭ *In-room: safe, refrigerator, Wi-Fi. In-hotel: 6 restaurants, 2 tennis courts,*

CLOSE UP

A Festival for Health and Purity

PHUKET'S MOST IMPORTANT FESTIVAL is its annual Vegetarian Festival, held in late September or early October. Though no one knows the precise details of the event's origins, the most common story is that it started in 1825, when a traveling Chinese opera group fell ill. The Taoist group feared that their illnesses were the result of their failure to pay proper respects to the nine Emperor Gods. After sticking to a strict vegetarian diet to honor these gods, they quickly recovered. This made quite an impression on the local villagers, and the island has celebrated a nine-day festival for good health ever since. Devotees, who wear white, abstain from eating meat, drinking alcohol, and having sex. Along with detoxing the body, the festival is meant to renew the soul—not killing animals for food is supposed to calm and purify the spirit.

The festival involves numerous temple ceremonies, parades, and fireworks.

But what most fascinates visitors are the grisly body-piercing rituals. Some devotees become mediums for warrior spirits, going into trances and mutilating their bodies to ward off demons and bring the whole community good luck. These mediums pierce their bodies (tongues and cheeks are popular choices) with all sorts of things from spears to sharpened branches to florescent lightbulbs. Supposedly, the presence of the spirits within them keeps them from feeling any pain.

The events are centered around the island's five Chinese temples. Processions are held daily from morning until mid-afternoon. The Tourism Authority of Thailand office in Phuket Town can provide a list of all activities and their locations. Note that you might want to invest in earplugs—it's believed that the louder the fireworks, the more evil spirits they'll scare away.

5 pools, gym, spa, children's programs (ages 4–12), laundry service, public Wi-Fi ▭ AE, MC, V ⍾⊙⍾ EP.

¢–$ ▦ **Da Bungalows.** Across the street from Mama Tri's Boathouse sits a set of snug, white bungalows high on the hill with views of the beach and ocean. Some of the rooms are surprisingly spacious; all come with pleasant balconies. The friendly owner Da also runs the local surf shop, which doubles as the hotel office. The place is small and popular with the international surfer crowd (they rent boards in the lobby and on the beach by Mom Tri's), so it's best to call in advance about rooms. ⊠ 235/1 Kohktanode Rd., A. Muang, Phuket, 83100 ☎076/333055 ➴8 rooms ⌂ In-room: no a/c (some). In-hotel: laundry service ▭ No credit cards.

¢–$ ▦ **Kata Noi Bay Inn.** If you want to enjoy the serenity of Kata Noi without draining your wallet, here's the spot. All but a few of the simple, clean rooms have air-conditioning and all have small balconies. Most rooms overlook the Kata Thani across the road, but some manage to squeeze in a small view of the beach. ⊠ 4/16 Moo 2, Patak Rd., Kata Noi Beach, Phuket, 83100 ☎ 076/333308 up to 09 ➴ 22 rooms ⌂ In-room: no a/c (some), refrigerator, no TV. In-hotel: restaurant ▭ MC, V ⍾⊙⍾ EP.

Nai Harn

㉛ *18 km (11 mi) southwest of Phuket Town.*

South of Kata Beach the road cuts inland across the hills before it drops into yet another beautiful bay, Nai Harn. On the north side of the bay is the gleaming white Royal Meridien Phuket Yacht Club. On the south side is a nice little beach, removed for now from the tailors and cheap restaurants that have sprung up at the entrance to the Royal Meridien.

From the top of the cliff at **Phromthep Cape,** the southernmost point on Koh Phuket, you're treated to a fantastic, panoramic view of Nai Harn Bay, the coastline, and a few outlying islands. At sunset, you can share the view with swarms of others who pour forth from tour buses to view the same sight. If you're driving, arrive early if you want a parking spot. There's a lighthouse atop the point.

Where to Stay & Eat

$–$$$ ✕ **Phromthep Cape Restaurant.** Although it doesn't look like much from the Phromthep Cape parking lot, views from the tables out back are hard to beat. Just slightly down the hill from the lighthouse, you get unobstructed sights of the cape and coastline. Plus, you get lower prices and better views than most places on the island that boast of their panoramas. The restaurant serves Thai food and some Western fare. ✉ *94/6 Moo 6, Rawai Beach, 83130* ☎ *076/288656* ⊕ *www.phuketdir.com/ phromthepcaperest* ⊟ *AE, MC, V.*

$$$$ ✕▦ **Royal Meridien Phuket Yacht Club.** This place used to be home to the annual King's Cup Regatta—now the only yachts here are decorative carvings on the walls. But the place is still every inch a luxury destination, and it was recently renovated. Beautifully appointed rooms in a modern Thai style all have balconies overlooking the sea with views of Promthep Cape in the distance. The building's layout has balconies staggered up the hillside. Some would say this is to afford each room a perfect view of the sea. Others would say it allows you to look down and see your sun-tanning neighbors. ✉ *Nai Harn Beach, Phuket, 83130* ☎ *076/380200* ⊕ *www. lemeridien.com* ⋈ *110 rooms and suites* ⚫ *In-room: safe, refrigerator. In-hotel: 3 restaurants, room service, 2 tennis courts, pool, gym, spa, beachfront, water sports, laundry service* ⊟ *AE, DC, MC, V* ❲◎❳ *EP.*

Chalong

㉜ *11 km (7 mi) south of Phuket Town.*

The waters in horseshoe-shape Chalong Bay are usually calm, as the entrance is guarded by Koh Lone and Koh Hae. It's not a scenic stop in itself—it's more of a working port than a beach. From the jetty you can charter boats or book one-day or half-day trips to Koh Hae, Koh Lone, and other nearby islands for snorkeling, diving, parasailing, and other activities (B650–B1,200). Waterfront businesses survived the tsunami just fine.

Not far from Chalong Bay you can find **Wat Chalong,** the largest and most famous of Phuket's Buddhist temples. It enshrines gilt statues of two revered monks who helped quell an 1876 Chinese rebellion. They're wrapped in brilliant saffron robes. Wats are generally open during daylight hours, and you can show up at 5 PM to see the resident monks pray.

Where to Eat

★ $ ✕ **Kan Eang.** Grab a palm-shaded table next to the seawall and order some delicious grilled fish. Be sure that your waiter understands whether you want yours served *phet* (spicy hot) or *mai phet* (not spicy). Succulent and sweet crabs should be a part of any meal here. It's right on the waterfront to the south of the pier. ⊠ *44/1 Viset Rd.* ☎ *076/381212* ▭ *AE, MC, V.*

Koh Hae (Coral Island)

33 *10 km (6 mi) from Chalong Bay.*

Although this was once a quiet island, it's now a playground for (primarily) Asian tour groups. Before the tsunami slowed tourism down, as many as 1,000 day-trippers would race to the island each morning in an armada of speedboats that dropped them on shore. But after lunch the crowds leave and a quiet island remains. That's the time to be at Koh Hae. After a few repairs, the Coral Island Resort has returned to normal operations.

Where to Stay & Eat

$$ ✕🏨 **Coral Island Resort.** This nice set of beachfront cottages works hard to keep a stiff upper lip in the face of the daily hordes that descend upon the rest of the beach. It's the only place to stay on the island. Signs keep most of the nonguests at bay, leaving a quieter oasis around the resort. All the boat traffic stirs up the water, but also chases the fish to this end of the beach, making for decent snorkeling right in front of the hotel. Plus, the very friendly staff spend most of their mornings cleaning up the day-tripper's garbage, making this the cleanest stretch of beach. Several magnificent hornbills chatter at the guests here in the evenings, and you can sleep with your windows open and drift off to the sound of waves lapping at the beach. ⊠ *48/11 Chaofa Rd., Chalong Bay, Phuket, 83130* ☎ *076/281060* ⊕ *www.coralislandresort.com* 🛏 *64 rooms* ⟁ *In-hotel: restaurant, bar, pool, diving, water sports* ▭ *AE, MC, V* ⦿ *EP.*

Cape Panwa

34 *10 km (6 mi) south of Phuket Town.*

Heading south out of Phuket Town (or northeast from Chalong Bay), follow the signs for Makham Bay, but don't stop there. This route will take you past the PTT petroleum dump, Phuket's deep-sea port, and a Thai Navy base. At the end of the road is the Phuket Aquarium. Just a little farther on is Cape Panwa, where you can find several public spots to pull over and gaze over the ocean and outlying islands.

Where to Stay & Eat

★ $$–$$$ ✕🏨 **Cape Panwa Hotel.** It could be argued that Sheraton made a mistake when it pulled out of this lovely place for its massive joint on Laguna Beach. Set in a hillside coconut grove with a secluded beach, this resort is the only thing here. And what a wonderful thing it is. Basic rooms are basic yet tastefully appointed and have wonderful sea views. The several villas on the property are very nice and come with every convenience. The Panwa House Restaurant is in an antique-filled plantation house right off the beach. And the beach, though small, is perfectly secluded, accessible only from the resort or by boat. You can snorkel right in the bay. The resort also features its own boat jetty and a tram to take you from the beach up the hill to your room. ⊠ *27 Moo 8, Sakdidej Rd., Cape Panwa, Phuket, 83000* ☎ *076/391123 up to 25* ⊕ *www. capepanwa.com* ⚓ *246 rooms, 6 villas* ⚄ *In-room: safe, refrigerator, DVD, ethernet. In-hotel: 6 restaurants, 3 bars, tennis courts, 2 pools, gym, beachfront, water sports* ▭ *AE, D, MC, V* ¶⊘ *EP.*

Koh Phuket Essentials

Transportation

BY AIR

Although flights to Phuket used to be quite expensive, the emergence of discount airlines has dropped prices dramatically. A flight now costs around B1,000–B1,500, little more than taking the train and a bus from Bangkok—but the trip takes just over an hour, rather than a full day.

Thai Airways flies between Bangkok and Koh Phuket 10 times daily. Bangkok Airways has four flights daily between Phuket and Bangkok and Phuket Air offers one flight a day between Bangkok and Phuket.

New, low-cost airlines include Air Asia, Nok Air, and Orient Thai, all of which offer two to three flights per day. With Air Asia, book and buy your tickets all online for the best fares. If you are flexible with your dates or itineraries, then you can find some ridiculously cheap fares on Air Asia. With Orient Thai, you can book online for an added fee or just go to the airport to buy a ticket for the best price. Keep in mind that planes fill up fast during the high season, and the lowest fares are mostly available if booked weeks or months in advance.

AIRPORTS & TRANSFERS — Phuket's airport is at the northern end of the island. All hotels are to the south. Be sure to check whether yours offers a free shuttle. Taxis meet all incoming flights. Fares are higher than in Bangkok; expect to pay B700 to Patong, Kata, or Karon, or B400 to Phuket Town. On your way back to the airport, you have to book a taxi for a minimum of B400. Many hotels charge B350–B400 per person.

There are also frequent minibus and van services to Phuket Town, Patong, Kata, and Karon that costs between B80 and B120. However, it might be worth springing for a cab as not all van drivers are reputable and might try to take you on an extended detour to a friend's shop or restaurant.

🛪 **Air Asia** ☎ 02/515-9999 in Bangkok ⊕ www.airasia.com. **Bangkok Airways** ☎ 076/351235 ⊕ www.bangkokair.com. **Nok Air** ☎ 02/900-9955 in Bangkok ⊕ www.nokair.com. **Orient Thai** ☎ 076/328620 ⊕ www.orient-thai.com. **Phuket Air** ☎ 076/351337 ⊕ www.phuketairlines.com. **Thai Airways** ☎ 076/211195 ⊕ www.thaiairways.com.

BY BUS

Numerous buses in various classes leave from Bangkok's Southern Bus Terminal, generally in the late afternoon and evening. The trip takes from 12 to 14 hours, depending on the bus and road conditions. You need to go to either a travel agent or to the bus station to check exact times and purchase tickets in advance, especially for VIP buses. Costs run from B278 for a non-air-conditioned bus to B970 for an air-conditioned VIP bus. VIP buses with ample legroom, padded footrests, and comfortable seats are well worth the added price. Be sure to have a long-sleeve shirt or sweater handy to combat the powerful air-conditioning. There will be stops along the way for food, drinks, and bathroom breaks.

Most long-haul VIP buses travel overnight, but you can leave Phuket on the 7 AM bus and arrive in Bangkok that evening. Day trips are recommended as Thailand's highways grow even more dangerous at night.

There are buses from Phuket to pretty much every major destination in Southern Thailand. This includes, but is not limited to: Surat Thani, Krabi, Trang, Hat Yai, Satun, Phang Nga, and the ferry crossing to Koh Samui. You can check departure times at your hotel or the centrally located bus station just east of Montri Road, two blocks north of Phang Nga Road in Phuket Town.

BY CAR

Here's a neat trick for the long-distance drivers in the crowd. You can take Highway 4 from Thonburi in Bangkok all the way to the Causeway at the north end of Phuket Island, where it turns into Highway 402. It's a long drive, but once you're out of the capital all you have to do is follow the compass due south. Follow Highway 4 to Chumphon, where it jogs west and south and follows the Andaman Sea coast to Phuket island. Phuket Town is 862 km (517 mi) from Bangkok; bus companies make the trip in 13–15 hours. Your results may vary.

Phuket isn't an island on which to take a leisurely Sunday drive. If you are driving, make sure you pick up at least two or three tourist maps (available at the airport, travel agencies, and most any tourism-related office), as they differ in details. Streets are poorly marked, and you'll need all the help you can get.

Residents of Phuket readily admit that their traffic is insane. Roads are badly congested and badly marked. That said, Phuket is the only island where you might want a car to get around. (Though it should be noted that even the Tourism Authority of Thailand recommends tourists avoid motorbikes here, either as taxis or rentals.) All hotels can arrange for car rentals, and many have booking offices on the premises. Look for Avis, Budget, and Hertz at the airport. In town you can find rental cars at various private shops near the Pearl and Metropole hotels, as well as shops along all the major beaches. Prices will be a little lower than those at the airport, but not a lot.

You can rent a Suzuki Caribian (called a jeep) for as little as B700 per day in the off-season. It's clunky but reliable transportation, though they tend to leak in heavy rains. Add another B500 for a Thai driver to deal with the nutty traffic. Small Toyota sedans start at B1,500 in the low season and can double in the high. The above prices do not include fuel, but do include a basic insurance plan.

BY TAXI, TUK-TUK & SONGTHAEW

You'll never have a problem finding transportation in Phuket. There are no fleets of taxis here—what you'll find are the ubiquitous little red trucks known as tuk-tuks. And if you don't find one, don't worry; they'll find you. And they will be happy to take you to your destination for an absurd price. Be ready to bargain hard or simply walk away. Fares within any one town shouldn't be much more than B20 per trip, but they will often demand a flat B100. Keep in mind you can catch a minivan from the airport to Phuket Town for B100, a distance of 30 km (19 mi).

There's supposedly a bus service in Phuket Town, but good luck finding one or a route map. The best and cheapest way of getting between beaches on the island is by the ubiquitous songthaews. You catch them in front of the market on Ranong Road or at the bus stops in the beach towns. These are marked on most maps and locals can help you find them. Prices run from B15 to B30 per trip depending on the beach you're visiting. They run every half hour from 7 AM to 5 PM. If you miss that last songthaew, you may well spend B400 on a tuk-tuk for a ride that costs you only B15 earlier in the day. Hint: if you just missed that last songthaew, you can sometimes arrange a cut-rate ride on the sly with a hotel taxi driver who wants to go home or to a different beach town for dinner. If he drives alone, he makes no money. If he takes you for, say, half the normal hotel fare, he gets to keep that, which will probably pay for his dinner.

BY TRAIN

Surat Thani is the closest train station to Phuket. A bus service links the two cities. Express trains from Bangkok's Hua Lamphong railway station stop at Surat Thani on their way south. The journey takes 12 hours or so. Note that if you leave Bangkok at 3 PM, you'll arrive to a dark train station in Surat Thani at around 3 AM. Sleepers are not available on all trains, so check first at a train station or with a travel agent. Prices vary depending on type of seat and speed of train. You can travel for as little as B400 in a hard, hot seat. These days, it's cheaper to fly a budget airline than to take a first-class sleeper that only gets you to Surat Thani. Regardless, if you want to save a night's lodging by spending it on a train, connecting buses to Phuket leave Surat Thani around 7 AM, coinciding with the arrival of the last sleeper train from Bangkok. Bus tickets are available on the second floor of Hua Lamphong train station in Bangkok.

Contacts & Resources

BANKS & EXCHANGING SERVICES

Banks are easy to locate in Phuket Town, Patong, Karon Beach, and Kata Beach. All banks will exchange foreign currency and most have ATMs. Remember that hotel exchange rates are never as good as those at banks or currency exchange houses. The more remote the hotel, the less you'll get for your dollar.

EMERGENCIES

🔲 Emergency Numbers **Fire** ☎199. **Marine Police** ☎076/211883. **Police** ☎191. **Tourist Police** ☎1155, 076/219878 in Phuket.

🔲 Hospitals **Bangkok Phuket Hospital** ✉2/1 Hongyok Rd., Phuket Town ☎076/254429 or076/254430. **Phuket International Hospital** ☎076/249400.

TOUR OPTIONS

As the saying goes, you can't throw a stone at a dog in Phuket without hitting a tour operator. Nearly all of them are selling the same package tours and renting the same cars and motorcycles, so feel free to comparison shop and haggle over prices. Common half-day sightseeing tours include visits to Wat Chalong, Rawai Beach, Phromthep Cape, and Khao Rang. Other half-day tours take in the Thai cultural village and the cultured-pearl farm on Nakha Noi island.

It's not unreasonable to pay the extra money to book a trip or rental through your hotel: it's more convenient, you may be less likely to get ripped off, and it will give you an extra venue to complain to should something go wrong. In general, be wary of what tour operators tell you; they are in business to sell you a trip to the beach, not to tell you how to get there on your own. If you feel you have been ripped off or cheated, note the offender's name and other info and be sure to report him to the local Tourism Authority of Thailand office. Also let the manager at your hotel know, so he or she can steer other tourists clear.

Try Santana for diving and canoeing. They were Patong's first operator for such things and are still in business. Also, they will pick you up so you don't have to travel into Patong.

Dive Asia, in Kata Beach, is a certified PADI instructor and operator, in business since 1988.

John Gray's Sea Canoe is known internationally for ecotourism trips, including canoe trips through Phang Nga Bay. You can pick up a descriptive flyer at one of the ubiquitous travel shops, then book a tour directly from the company.

🔲 **Dive Asia** ☎076/330598 ⊕ www.diveasia.com. **John Gray's Sea Canoe** ☎076/254505 ⊕www.johngray-seacanoe.com. **Santana** ☎076/294220 ⊕www.santanaphuket.com.

VISITOR INFORMATION

The Tourism Authority of Thailand has offices in several resorts in Southern Thailand. You can drop by for maps and brochures, as well as information about local excursions.

🔲 **Tourism Authority of Thailand** ✉73–75 Phuket Rd. ☎076/212213 ⊕ www.phukettourism.org.

THE ANDAMAN COAST

The Andaman Coast stretches from Ranong Province, bordering Myanmar (Burma) to the north, to Satun Province, flanking Malaysia to the south. Along this shore are hundreds of islands and thousands of beaches. Because of their proximity to Phuket, Phang Nga and Krabi provinces are the two most popular destinations on the Andaman Coast.

The effects from the 2004 tsunami varied greatly around the region. Generally speaking, west-facing coasts were hardest hit, followed by south- and north-facing shores. East-facing beaches and areas shielded to the west by other bodies of land were less harmed.

Cleanup was undertaken almost immediately, and considering the popularity of this region and the inherent economic value of these beautiful beaches and islands, reconstruction proceeded rapidly. In some instances, Khao Lak for example, many resorts built in the year preceding the tsunami were to be rebuilt exactly as they had been the year before, with reopenings occurring regularly. The impact on the beaches and underwater marine life was harmful in some regard and beneficial in others. However, most beaches were not adversely affected by the waves; many areas were actually cleansed by the deep ocean water and are more beautiful than they have been in many years.

Phang Nga Bay National Park is Phang Nga's most heralded attraction, drawing thousands of day-trippers from Phuket. There are dozens of little islands to explore, as well as offshore caves and startling karst formations rising out of the sea. Most visitors make an obligatory stop at Phing Kan Island, made famous by the James Bond movie *The Man with the Golden Gun*.

The Similan and Surin Islands National Parks are well known to scuba divers for their crystalline waters and abundant marine life. You can camp or stay in a national park bungalow on either of the islands; no commercial lodging is available in either park. Many divers opt to stay on live-aboard ships departing from Phuket or Khao Lak.

Prior to the tsunami, Khao Lak, the departure point for boats to the Similans, was an up-and-coming beach "town" in its own right. Khao Lak Lamru National Park attracted nature lovers, while the beaches along this coast drew beachgoers who wanted a vibe more tranquil than Phuket has to offer. Although most resorts were destroyed, the "town" was spared and Khao Lak was nearly back to business as usual by 2006. Travelers looking for even greater seclusion head to the Koh Yao Islands, which have cultural tours and homestays that provide insight on southern Thai lifestyles.

Krabi Province lies to the east of Phuket. Its capital, Krabi Town, sits on the northeastern shore of Phuket Bay. Once a favorite harbor for smugglers bringing in alcohol and tobacco from Malaysia, the town has been transformed into a gateway to the nearby islands. Ao Nang, a short distance from Krabi Town, has evolved into a quaint beach town. Ao Nang, and nearby Noppharat Thara, exist simply to cater to tourists, and restaurants and shopping abound. With its coast lined with longtail boats, Ao Nang is a more convenient base of operations than Krabi Town for exploring nearby islands and beaches. Longtail boats and ferries depart Ao Nang to Koh Phi Phi, Koh Lanta, Nang Cape, and the multitude of smaller islands in eastern Phang Nga Bay.

Andaman Coast

The islands of Koh Phi Phi were once idyllic retreats, with secret silver-sand coves, unspoiled stretches of shoreline, and limestone cliffs dropping precipitously into the sea. But then the islands were portrayed in *The Beach* (2000). By the time the film had been released on DVD, Phi Phi was a hot property. Sadly, Koh Phi Phi was also hit hard by the tsunami, which destroyed many resorts, restaurants, bars, and shops along all but the east-facing beaches. The untouched beaches are certainly still beautiful and the affected areas were quickly cleaned up. By fall 2006, many restaurants, bars, and smaller guesthouses had sprung up to fill the demand for lodging on this ultrapopular tourist destination, and major resorts are scheduled to reopen by spring 2008.

Farther south, more-adventurous travelers are discovering the relative serenity of Krabi's "hidden" gem, Koh Lanta. Koh Lanta, one of the largest islands in Thailand, has many beautiful beaches, accommodations to please both budget and spendthrift travelers, and a few activities such as elephant trekking in the jungle.

Numbers in the text correspond to numbers in the margin and on the Andaman Coast map.

Phang Nga Bay National Marine Park

㉟ *100 km (62 mi) north of Phuket, 93 km (56 mi) northwest of Krabi.*

Fodor'sChoice
★

The best way—actually, the only way—to visit Phang Nga Bay is by boat. Talk with one of the travel agencies on Phuket that offer half-day tours of the area or hire your own boat and spend as long as you want. There are two inlets, just before you reach the town of Phang Nga, where you can arrange for longtail boats. Most tour buses go to the western inlet, where you can rent a boat for about B1,300 for two hours. The second inlet sees fewer foreign tourists, so the prices are better—about B800 for three hours. The bay can be explored via tour boat, speedboat, or sea canoe. Most tourists don't arrive from Phuket until 11 AM, so if you get into the bay earlier, you can explore it in solitude. To get an early start, you may want to stay overnight in the area. Be sure to take time to appreciate the sunsets, which are particularly beautiful on the island of **Koh Mak.**

There are several key sights around Phang Nga Bay. The island of **Koh Panyi** has a Muslim fishing village consisting of houses built on stilts. Restaurants are no bargain, tripling their prices for tourists. Beautiful **Koh Phing Kan,** now known locally as James Bond Island, is well worth a visit. The island of **Koh Tapu** resembles a nail driven into the sea. **Kao Kien** has overhanging cliffs covered with primitive paintings of elephants, fish, and crabs. Many are thought to be at least 3,500 years old. **Tham Lot** is a stalactite-studded cave that has an opening large enough for boats to pass through.

Where to Stay

$$$$
Fodor'sChoice
★

Aleenta Resort and Spa Phan-Nga. Stylish design, a romantic atmosphere, and a beautiful beach contribute to the Aleenta experience. Two-story lofts have glass walls overlooking the sea; you can watch the sunset from the bed, the sofa, or from your small poolside deck. Pool suites have outdoor tubs and showers and glass walls that retract so that the rooms are open air. Pool villas don't have sea views, but their retractable glass doors open onto a wooden deck that connects separate bedroom and living room areas to each other and to private pools and large outdoor tubs. Breakfast is served by the beach, as are sunset cocktails. The library has movie nights complete with popcorn. Located just over the Sarasin bridge north of Phuket, Aleenta is on a quiet Phang Nga beach a brief drive to Phuket, Phang Nga Bay, or Khao Lak. ⊠ *33 Moo 5, Khokkloy, Phang Nga, 82140* ☎ *076/580333* ⊕ *www.aleenta.com* ⊅ *15 suites and villas* ⌂ *In-room: refrigerator, Wi-Fi. In-hotel: restaurant, room service, 2 bars, pool, spa, beachfront, concierge, public Wi-Fi* ⊟ *AE, DC, MC, V.*

$-$$
Phang Nga Bay Resort Hotel. Each of the comfortable rooms at this modern resort has a private terrace overlooking a jungle-ringed estuary. The four levels are set back to ensure picture-perfect views from everywhere. The nearest beaches are more than 1 km (½ mi) away, but the hotel operates a boat to bring you there. Rooms are conventionally but comfortably furnished, with all modern amenities. The restaurant, which has a terrace overlooking the water, serves Thai, Chinese, and

Western dishes. ✉ *20 Thaddan Panyee, 820* *rooms △ In-room: refrigerator. In-hotel: 2 resta* *pool ⊟ AE, MC, V.*

¢–$ 🏠 **Ao Phang Nga National Park.** In addition to tl you can rent tents), the park has a few well-l grounds. The bungalows have one to three be ple, fan-cooled affairs or plusher, with air-cor bars. Near the bungalows and visitor center boats to explore the park. Rates vary based (uals in your party. ✉ *80 Ban Tha Dan Koᵤ ᵣanyi, 82000* 🕾 *076/ 522236, 02/562–0760 for reservations* ⊕ *www.dnp.go.th* ➦ *15 bungalows △ In-room: no a/c (some), refrigerator, no TV (some). In-hotel: restaurant* ⊟ *No credit cards.*

Koh Yao (Yao Island)

36 *45 mins by boat from Bangrong Pier, Phuket or 45 mins by boat from Chaofa Pier, Krabi.*

Koh Yao Yai and Koh Yao Noi are the two large islands in the center of Phang Nga Bay. Both are quiet, peaceful places, fringed with sandy beaches and clear water. Most inhabitants still make their living through traditional means such as fishing, rubber tapping, and batik-painting. Considering their size and proximity to Phuket and Krabi, it's surprising how little development these islands have seen. During the 1990s many tourists began to discover the islands and the impact was, unsurprisingly, negative. So, to reduce the impact on the land and their culture the villagers residing on Koh Yao organized the "Koh Yao Noi Ecotourism Club" to regulate growth on the islands. They've certainly been successful—they even picked up a 2003 award for tourism development sponsored by Conservation International and *National Geographic Traveler.*

A visit to Koh Yao will allow you to experience the local culture and customs while exploring the beauty of the islands (kayak and mountain bike are popular transportation options). The Ecotourism Club provides homestays if you really want the full experience of the islands; otherwise, most resorts provide day tours or information for self-guided exploration.

Where to Stay & Eat

$$$$ ✕🏠 **Koyao Island Resort.** Koyao Island Resort has arguably the best view
FodorsChoice of any beach resort in Thailand. From east-facing Haad Pa Sai you have
★ a panoramic vista of a string of magnificent islands. The bungalows are almost entirely open-air, so you not only admire the surroundings, you're part of them—you can even throw open the doors and watch the sunrise from your bed! An ideal romantic hideaway, Koyao Island Resort even arranges private beach barbecues. Although the beach is not great for swimming or sunbathing, there are beach chairs on the grass beside the sea, and kayaks and mountain bikes are available for use around the island. Boats can be hired to visit nearby islands for diving or snorkeling, and day trips, including cultural tours to batik-dying and fish-

villages, can be arranged. The restaurant serves great fresh seafood; you select your meal from the saltwater pond. ✉ *24/2 Koh Yao Noi, Phang Nga, 82160* ☎ *076/597474 up to 76* ⊕ *www.koyao.com* ⊅ *15 villas* ♿ *In-room: safe, refrigerator, DVD, ethernet. In-hotel: restaurant, spa* ▭ *AE, MC, V.*

¢ ▣ **Koh Yao Homestay.** Koh Yao Homestay is organized by a community of Koh Yao residents who welcome tourists to share their way of life. The community provides visitors with lodging in their own homes, meals (consisting primarily of fish caught by village fishermen), and knowledge about their local customs. Visitors learn about rubber-tapping, batik-dying, fishing, rice-farming, coconut-harvesting, and other traditional trades from the people who have practiced them for centuries. More environmentally friendly and less invasive on the island's indigenous people than resort development, the homestay program is a unique way to learn about local people while helping to preserve their way of life. ✉ *Baan Laem Sai, Koh Yao Noi, Phang Nga, 82160* ☎ *076/597428* ⊕ *www. kohyaohomestay.com* ▭ *No credit cards.*

Khao Lak

㊲ *80 km (50 mi) north of Phuket.*

The coastal area collectively known as Khao Lak was one of Thailand's hottest new resort destinations prior to the 2004 tsunami. Originally just a launching point for boat trips to the idyllic Similan Islands, Khao Lak quickly blossomed into a tourist destination in its own right. Unfortunately, Khao Lak bore the full brunt of the tsunami and it devastated most of the resorts along the coast, killing thousands of Thais and international tourists. Very few resorts were not completely destroyed. And though the area's shops, restaurants, and bars are on the road that runs along a hill (far beyond the high-water mark), the destruction of the resorts and the devastating death toll halted all tourist arrivals, causing undamaged businesses to shut down. But the extent of the destruction also makes Khao Lak the region's greatest success story—only two years after the catastrophe, Khao Lak is amazingly back on its feet.

Khao Lak Lamru National Marine Park's rolling green hills and abundant wildlife is a primary attraction. The park grounds cover more than 325 square km (125 square mi) from the sea to the mountains, including a secluded sandy beach and several waterfalls. The park preserves some pristine tropical evergreen forest that is often supplanted in the south by fruit and rubber trees. Wildlife includes wild pigs, barking deer, macaques, and reticulated pythons. Walking trails lead to waterfalls with swimmable pools. Three rudimentary cabins are available for overnight stays, as are tent rentals for visitors who do not have their own. The park headquarters, on the road from Khao Lak Beach to Khao Lak town, provides information about exploring or staying in the park. ☎ *076/ 720023, 02/579–0529 National Park Division in Bangkok* ⊕ *www.dnp. go.th.*

Khao Lak Beach proper lies to the south of the national park, while most resorts and dive operators purporting to hail from "Khao Lak" actually line the coasts of Nang Thong, Bang Niang, Khuk Khak, and Bang

Sak beaches to the north. As a result of Khao Lak's (once again) boom-ing popularity, many properties are beginning to stay open more dur-ing the low season; however, Khao Lak is best visited near or during the high season (November to May) when you can be sure that all businesses are in full operation.

Where to Stay & Eat

¢–$$ ✕ **Jai Restaurant.** This simple restaurant in central "Khao Lak town" pleases locals and visitors alike; the presence of locals in a restaurant is always a good sign in a tourist town. Choose your own fish or jumbo prawns from the display boat and select a cooking style. The deep-fried snapper with chili sauce (not spicy) and the spicy vegetable salad with cashew nuts are both highly recommended. ✉ *5/1 Moo 7, Khao Lak* ☎ *076/485390* ▱ *No credit cards.*

$$$$ ▢ **Mukdara Beach Resort.** This expansive resort was hit hard by the tsunami but has been rebuilt to look almost identical to how it looked before: gorgeous. Accommodations are in large, Thai-style, peaked-roof villas in landscaped tropical gardens landscaping or in rooms in a three-story building farther from the beach (only the top floor has an ocean view). Deluxe rooms are luxurious, with hardwood floors, glass-enclosed baths that see through to the living room, and sundecks. Villas have canopy beds, triangular floor pillows, lounge areas, and outdoor rain showers. ✉ *26/14 Moo 7, Thanon Khuk Khak, Takuapa, Phang Nga, 82190* ☎ *076/429999* ⊕ *www.mukdarabeach.com* ⇥ *70 rooms, 64 villas, 7 suites* ⚙ *In-room: safe, refrigerator, ethernet. In-hotel: 6 restaurants, 2 bars, tennis court, gym, spa, laundry service, public Internet* ▱ *AE, D, MC, V.*

★ $$$$ ▢ **The Sarojin.** This exquisite boutique resort to the north of Khao Lak makes you feel not only like you're on holiday, but that you are *some-one* on holiday. The Sarojin's smaller size makes it more intimate and exclusive than nearby megaresorts. There are three types of rooms and they all have something special: garden rooms have large oval tubs in pebble-strewn indoor gardens; suites have outdoor tubs; and pool res-idences have private plunge pools and salas with lounge chairs. At the Ficus restaurant you can have breakfast beneath an ancient ficus tree growing beside a large pond with lily pads. The resort provides a vari-ety of activities, including cooking classes, river rafting, elephant trekking, and day trips to the Similan Islands aboard a private speedboat. ✉ *60 Moo 2, Kukkak, Takuapa, Phang Nga, 82190* ☎ *076/427900 up to 04* ⊕ *www.sarojin.com* ⇥ *56 rooms* ⚙ *In-room: safe, refrigerator, DVD, Wi-Fi. In-hotel: 2 restaurants, room service, pool, gym, spa, water sports, bicycles, concierge* ▱ *AE, DC, MC, V.*

$$$–$$$$ ▢ **Baan Krating.** Baan Krating was one of the few properties that didn't have to rebuild—it has a fortunate (and wonderful) location on a cliff above a rocky beach. The beautiful view and a path to the beach that travels within Khao Lak Lamru National Park give the resort a quiet, natural atmosphere. Rooms are in wooden cottages that are "rustic" in the sense that they do not have the usual explosion of silk fittings and Thai art that most resorts of this class have, but you'll hardly have to sacrifice any comfort here. Each room has a few deck chairs out front for gazing at the sea. ✉ *28 Khao Lak, Takuapa, Phang Nga, 82190*

☏ 076/423088 ⊕ *www.baankrating.com* ⇆ *24 cottages* ⚴ *In-room: safe, refrigerator. In-hotel: restaurant, pool, laundry service, public Internet* ⊟ *MC, V.*

$$$–$$$$ ⊞ **Khao Lak Seaview Resort and Spa.** Seaview Resort's stunning tiered swimming pool epitomizes the luxury available to its guests. Octagonal villas have high ceilings, four-poster beds, and whirlpool tubs. The resort's small private stretch of sand is nice, but the beach and the ocean are slightly better at beaches farther north. Regardless, the water is swimmable and, as Seaview is situated on the south end of Nang Thong Road, the resort is ideally located for romantic beach walks. That is, if you can tear yourself away from the stunning tiered swimming pool long enough to explore the beach. ✉ *18/1 Moo 7 Petchkasem Rd., Khuk Khak, 82190* ☏ *076/420625* ⊕ *www.khaolak-seaviewresort.com* ⇆ *156 rooms, 41 villas* ⚴ *In-room: safe, refrigerator. In-hotel: 2 restaurants, room service, 2 bars, tennis court, 2 pools, gym, spa, beachfront, laundry service, public Internet* ⊟ *AE, DC, MC, V.*

$$$–$$$$ ⊞ **La Flora.** La Flora is a lovely boutique resort with terrific service. Rooms are fashionably decorated in modern Asian aesthetic and most have balconies or daybeds. Villas have even more features like writing desks and private outdoor rain showers. Although La Flora is more likely to appeal to urban professional couples looking for a romantic hideaway, families are well accommodated in two-bedroom villas that have Jacuzzis overlooking the beach. Bang Niang Beach is great for sunbathing and swimming, and a small reef for snorkeling is directly in front of the resort. A new wing on the neighboring beachfront property is expected for completion in December 2007, adding 70 rooms and another swimming pool. ✉ *59/1 Moo 5, Khuk Khak, Phang Nga, 82190* ☏ *076/428000 up to 28* ⊕ *www.lafloraresort.com* ⇆ *57 rooms, 13 villas* ⚴ *In-room: safe, refrigerator, DVD (some). In-hotel: restaurant, room service, bar, pool, gym, spa, beachfront, water sports, laundry service, public Wi-Fi* ⊟ *AE, D, MC, V.*

$$$–$$$$ ⊞ **Le Meridien Khao Lak Beach & Spa Resort.** Le Meridien is on an isolated 12-km (7-mi) stretch of beach to the north of Khao Lak town. Most rooms are either in the Family wing or Spa wing, the former having connecting parents' and kids' rooms and views of the pool and "kids beach," the latter positioned closer to the spa and adults-only swimming pool. Beautifully furnished villas have peaked roofs, spacious baths with tubs and outdoor showers, and comfortable sofas from which to watch the plasma TVs. Beachside villas have long, thin pools ending in Jacuzzis beside the beach. Le Spa earned the resort the 2006 World Travel Award for Asia's and Thailand's Leading Spa Resort. ✉ *9/9 Moo 1, Tambol Kuk Kak, Amphur Takua Pa, Phang Nga, 82190* ☏ *076/427500* ⊕ *www.starwoodhotels.com* ⇆ *243 rooms* ⚴ *In-room: safe, refrigerator, DVD, ethernet. In-hotel: 4 restaurants, room service, 2 bars, 3 pools, gym, spa, diving, children's programs (ages 3–12), laundry service, concierge* ⊟ *AE, D, MC, V.*

★ $–$$ ⊞ **Nang Thong Bay Resort.** The majority of rooms here are surprisingly inexpensive cottages that face the beach and are surrounded by manicured gardens. White concrete beachfront cottages have contemporary Thai interiors, outdoor garden showers, and decks with sun chairs. Beyond the pool (which has a great pool bar) and garden stands two modern, two- and three-story complexes with studios and roomy one-bedroom suites. Long walks along the beach are magical at sunset. Reasonably priced spa services are available next door at the Seaview Resort. ⊠ *Khao Lak, Takuapa, Phang Nga* ☏ *076/485088 up to 89* ✐ *nangthong1@hotmail.com* ↷ *82 rooms* ⚘ *In-room: refrigerator. In-hotel: restaurant, bar, pool, laundry service, public Internet* ▤ *MC, V.*

$ 🏨 **Green Beach Resort.** Standard clapboard bungalows exteriors have wooden floors, rattan walls, and bamboo furniture. The brick-enclosed outdoor showers in deluxe rooms have semi-incongruous wooden sinks—the only boutique-style element in otherwise generic bathrooms. Sea-view bungalows have much better locations than the standard ones, which are located beside a barren lot. All bungalows have decks and chairs. Budget rooms can have the air-conditioning shut off for discounted rates. ⊠ *13/51 Moo 7, Haad Nangtong, Khuk Khak, 82190* ☏ *076/ 420046* ✐ *greenbeach_th@yahoo.com* ↷ *40 bungalows* ⚘ *In-room: refrigerator. In-hotel: restaurant, public Internet* ▤ *MC, V* ⊗ *Closed May–Nov.*

¢ 🏨 **Khao Lak Nature Resort.** The best budget option in the area is near the Khao Lak Lamru National Park. Basic wooden huts have rattan walls and many windows that look out into the surrounding forest. A trail leads to a small sandy beach within the national park. New rooms are scheduled for completion in November 2007. ⊠ *26/10 Khao Lak, Takuapa, Phang Nga, 82190* ☏ *04/7440520* ↷ *39 huts* ⚘ *In-room: no a/c (some), no phone, no TV. In-hotel: restaurant* ▤ *No credit cards* ⊗ *Closed May–Nov.*

Mu Koh Similan National Marine Park

Fodor'sChoice
★

70 km (45 mi) 1½ hrs by boat from Thaplamu Pier.

The Similan Islands National Park consists of the nine Similan Islands, as well as Koh Tachai and Koh Bon, which are located farther north. The diving around the Similan Islands is world class, with visibility of up to 120 feet; abundant blue, green, and purple coral; and rare marine life, such as the whale shark, the world's largest fish. The tsunami had a considerable effect on the islands. Shallow reefs were particularly hard hit, and as of this writing islands 1, 2, and 3 were indefinitely closed to divers, snorkelers, and visitors. However, many reefs were less affected and the underwater experience on the Similan Islands is fantastic. ▰ TIP➔ **If you plan to dive, contact a dive operator in Phuket or Khao Lak; there are no dive shops on the islands, though snorkeling gear is available for rent from the ranger stations.**

In addition to sparkling, crystal-clear water, the Similan Islands also have ultrafine, powdery white-sand beaches and lush tropical forests. The national park service allows visitors to stay on the beaches of Koh Miang (Island 4) and Koh Similan (Island 8). Koh Miang, where the park headquarters is located, has bungalows with 24-hour electricity and even some with air-conditioning (B2,000 with air-conditioning, B1,000 without); some bungalows have ocean views as well. Beachside camping is also available on Koh Miang (the park rents out roomy tents, large enough to stand in, which have two camping cots, for B450). Koh Similan has no bungalows, but has the same large tents for rent (B450), as well as an area for visitors to set up their own tents for B80 per person. If you choose to visit the island to stay at the park, expect to pay B1,800–B2,000 for a round-trip boat transfer. Once on the island, you can hire a long-tail boat to explore the other islands for about B500 per day. Alternatively, tour groups, such as **Jack's Similan** (☎ 076/443205 ⊕ www.jacksimilan.com), have their own smaller tents set up in this area and rent them out for the same fee charged by the national park. There are also overnight packages, which include tours of the islands, as well as camping and food.

■ TIP→ **The park is extremely popular with Thais, so book well in advance if you're planning a visit during a Thai holiday. The islands are more enjoyable, and more explorable, if visited midweek.** The park entrance fee is B200 per visit. Note that the islands are normally closed to visitors from mid-May until early November. ☎ 076/595045 for campsite reservations, 02/562–0760 for bungalow reservations ⊕ www.dnp.go.th.

Mu Koh Surin National Marine Park

60 km (37 mi), 2 hrs by boat from Kuraburi Pier.

Koh Surin is a remote island paradise practically unknown to anyone other than adventurous scuba divers and Thais. Five islands make up Mu Koh Surin National Park, each featuring sea turtles, varieties of shark, and plentiful coral. If you get tired of sun and sea, there are several hiking trails that lead to waterfalls and a sea gypsy village.

The tsunami hit the Surin islands quite hard, damaging shallow reefs and destroying all park structures. As of this writing all dive sites had reopened and conditions were good. Coral at snorkeling sites in shallow water received considerable damage, but most dive sites were protected by their deeper water and were generally unaffected. The visibility and diversity of marine life is spectacular, and this is arguably the most unspoiled Thai island retreat, owing to its remote location and low number of visitors. Note that the park is normally closed during the rainy season (June–November).

There are 15 newly built, comfortable fan-cooled wooden huts on Koh Surin Nua (B2,000), and tent camping is allowed at a site that has decent facilities, including toilets and showers. You may bring your own tent and camp for B80, or rent one that sleeps two from the national park for B450. ☎ 02/562–0760 inquiries and bungalow reservations ⊕ www.dnp.go.th.

Krabi Town

38 *814 km (506 mi) south of Bangkok, 180 km (117 mi) southeast of Phuket, 43 km (27 mi) by boat east of Koh Phi Phi.*

Krabi Town is a pleasant place to visit, but most visitors pause just long enough to grab some cash, arrange onward travel, and catch up on the news at one of the cafés on Uttarakit Road. However, there are several decent restaurants, a Tourism Authority of Thailand office, and a night market for souvenir shopping that may keep you in town a bit longer. Krabi locals are determined to keep Phuket-style development at bay, and so far—despite the opening of an airport 12 km (7 mi) from town—they are succeeding.

Just 3 km (2 mi) from Krabi Town is **Wat Tham Sua.** Built in 1976 as a monastery and meditation retreat, Wat Tham Sua is both respected by the local population and popular with tourists. Locals come to participate in Buddhist rituals, tourists to climb the 1,277 steps to panoramic views of the cliffs, Krabi Town, Krabi River, and the Panom Benja mountain range. There's also a cave with many chambers, which can be fun to explore, though it's not terribly attractive. A really large tree grows outside the entrance. The wat is between Krabi Town and the airport. ⊠ *Tambon Muang Chum, 4 km (2½ mi) after Wachiralongkorn Dam.*

Where to Stay & Eat

¢–$ ✕ **Chao Fa Pier Street Food Stalls.** Looking for local quality food at a low price? This strip of street-side food stalls serves everything from simple fried rice to more sophisticated southern delicacies such as *kanom jeen* (rice noodles topped with whatever sauces and vegetables you want). Open from nightfall until midnight, these stalls serve as an excellent opportunity to discover some exotic and enjoyable Thai foods. ⊠ *Chao Fa Pier, Khong Kha Rd.* ▭ *No credit cards.*

¢–$ ✕ **Ruen Pae.** This massive floating restaurant aboard a large, flat barge serves Thai standards, with an emphasis on seafood dishes. It's at the Chao Fa Pier beside the night market. ⊠ *Ut-tarkit Rd.* ☎ *076/611956* ▭ *No credit cards.*

★ ¢ ✕ **Relax Coffee and Restaurant.** The menu at this street-side café includes more than 10 different breakfast platters; a number of sandwiches, such as chicken satay, served on freshly baked brown bread, baguette, or ciabatta; many Thai dishes, including 10 different barracuda dishes; and, not surprisingly, a huge variety of coffee drinks, like raspberry latte frappés. ⊠ *7/4 Chaofa Rd.* ☎ *075/611570* ▭ *No credit cards* ⊙ *Closed 2nd and 4th Fri. of each month.*

$$–$$$$ ▥ **Krabi Maritime Park and Spa Resort.** This resort extends over 25 acres, and features a mangrove forest, a sprawling lagoon, a large swimming pool, and views of Krabi's signature limestone cliffs. The spa has a Jacuzzi that sits upon small tented piers above the lagoon. The large rooms look out over water, forest, and stunning cliffs. ⊠ *1 Tungfa Rd., 81000* ☎ *075/620028 up to 46* ⊕ *www.maritimeparkandspa.com* ⇲ *221 rooms* ♻ *In-room: refrigerator. In-hotel: restaurant, room service, bar, pool, gym, spa, laundry service* ▭ *AE, MC, V.*

¢–$ ▥ **City Hotel.** Rooms in the old wing of this hotel are simple but very clean and come with air-conditioning or fans; rooms in the new wing are standard, modern hotel rooms with carpeting and air-conditioning. Both buildings are near the night market and the river. ⊠ *15/2–4 Sukon Rd., 81000* ☎ *075/611961 or 075/621280* ⇲ *124 rooms* ♻ *In-room: no a/c (some). In-hotel: laundry service* ▭ *No credit cards.*

¢–$ ▥ **Krabi City Seaview Hotel.** This resort could have also added "riverside" to its name, as only a walking path separates it from the Krabi River. However, not all rooms have either river or sea views. Top-floor rooms have carpeted floors and small balconies, but the two second-floor rooms have large picture windows with the best views. The cheapest, ground-floor rooms have tile floors and no views. The resort is a five-minute walk from Chao Fa Pier, a quiet and beautiful location. Another five minutes along the walking path to the south leads to Thara Nature Park. ✉ *77/1 Kohngka Rd., 81000* ☎ *075/622885 up to 88* ⊕ *www.krabicityseaviewhotel.com* ↩ *30 rooms* ⚅ *In-room: refrigerator. In-hotel: bar, public Internet* ⊟ *MC, V.*

Ao Nang

★ ❸❾ *20 km (12 mi) from Krabi Town.*

Although Ao Nang Beach is not much of an attraction, the strip facing it underwent a face-lift in 2002 that transformed it into a pleasant promenade of hotels, shops, and restaurants. During the day, longtail boats depart Ao Nang for the more spectacular beaches and waters of Hong, Poda, Gai, Lanta, and the Phi Phi Islands, as well as nearby Railay Beach. Less adventurous types can find nicer sand and better water for swimming on the far eastern end of the beach or at Noppharat Thara Beach National Park to the west. In the evening, storefronts light up the sidewalk and open-air restaurants provide excellent venues to kick back with a beer and watch the crowd go by. For a more romantic atmosphere, head to the half dozen seafood restaurants atop a pier extending from the bend in Liab Chai Haad Road in between Ao Nang and Noppharat Thara beaches.

Noppharat Thara Beach, a 15-minute walk from central Ao Nang is quiet and relaxing. The renovated walking path was extended here from Ao Nang in 2004, but as of this writing, the development had not yet followed it. The national park at the western end has shady casuarina trees and a clean, quiet beach.

A narrow river pier delineates the western edge of Noppharat Thara National Park. Here you can catch boats departing from the pier to Railay, Phi Phi, and Lanta, or simply cross to the other side and enjoy the unspoiled natural beauty of **Laem Son Beach.** Farther north are the beaches of **Klong Muang** and **Tubkaak,** beautiful stretches of sand with amazing views that are occupied by upmarket resorts.

Where to Stay & Eat

$–$$$ ✕**Ao Nang Cuisine.** Believe the hype! The sign outside the restaurant brags that its chef, Mrs. Phaichat, is world famous, having worked at several well-known Thai eateries, including Chao Phraya Restaurant in Hollywood, California. The melt-in-your-mouth chicken satay (curry chicken skewers), an otherwise ordinary dish, is prepared superbly here, with a side of spicy peanut sauce. More elaborate Thai dishes are available for tourists who are tired of street-side barbecue seafood. ✉ *245/4 Liab Chai Haad Rd.* ☎ *075/695399* ⊟ *MC, V.*

$$$$ ⊡ **The Cliff.** You can get a good view of the cliff that inspired the hotel's name as soon as you enter the lobby. But then your attention will quickly shift to burned bricks, charred wooden tiles, and natural wooden beams that create an atmosphere reminiscent of ancient Srivijaya Period

of Siam. The Cliff's villas are set around a nonchlorinated, ozone-treated swimming pool. The rooms, each with outdoor shower, feature glass bay doors on two sides. The suite is on stilts above a small private fishpond and is particularly popular with honeymooners. ⊠ *85/2 Liab Chai Haad Rd., Ao Nang, 81000* ☎ *075/638117 up to 18* ⊕ *www.k-bi.com* ⟿ *20 rooms, 1 suite* ⚐ *In-room: refrigerator. In-hotel: restaurant, room service, pool* ⊟ *AE, DC, MC, V.*

★ **$$$$** 🖼 **The Tubkaak.** The elegant wooden buildings here each resemble a *kor lae*, a traditional Southern Thai fishing boat. Tubkaak Beach is calm and lovely, and the rooms have spectacular views of the Hong Islands. All superior and deluxe rooms are a few steps from the free-form swimming pool, while sea-view villas are only steps from the beach. A cozy library and bar has books and games for rainy days and relaxing evenings. The small size of the Tubkaak makes you feel at home and friendly staff make everyone feel like family. ⊠ *123 Taab Kaak Beach, Nongtalay, 81000* ☎ *075/628400* ⊕ *www.tubkaakresort.com* ⟿ *44 rooms, 2 suites* ⚐ *In-room: safe, refrigerator. In-hotel: restaurant, pool, spa, water sports, laundry service* ⊟ *AE, MC, V.*

$$$–$$$$ 🖼 **Sheraton Krabi Beach Resort.** The Sheraton Krabi is built around an expansive mangrove forest, and there's a wide, sandy beach on the premises. All of the contemporary and colorful standard rooms overlook the forest, while the six suites have views of the sea. There are many activities to keep guests occupied, including aerobics, sailing, and tennis on lit courts. The pool, restaurants, and bar are down by the beach, where various water sports are available, and the sunbathing and swimming are great. ⊠ *155 Klong Muang Beach, Nongtalay, 81000* ☎ *075/628000* ⊕ *www.sheraton.com* ⟿ *246 rooms, 6 suites* ⚐ *In-room: safe, refrigerator. In-hotel: 2 restaurants, room service, 2 bars, tennis court, pool, gym, diving, water sports, bicycles, laundry service, concierge, public Internet* ⊟ *AE, DC, MC, V.*

★ **$$–$$$** 🖼 **Alis Hotel and Spa.** Whitewashed walls and red, ceramic tile floors contribute to the Morrocan design at Alis Hotel. The top-floor club rooms and honeymoon suite have blue wooden doors facing a two-story atrium hallway. Inside, wood-frame beds and small tables and chairs are nice, but the real treat lies up a flight of stairs that leads to a private sunbathing deck with a large, round wooden tub. The honeymoon suite has mosaic-style tile floors, bead curtains, and an atmosphere worthy of the extra baht. The minitheater beside the lobby is ideal for rainy days. ⊠ *125 Moo 3, Ao Nang, 81000* ☎ *075/638000, 02/801–0760 in Bangkok* ⊕ *www.alisthailand.com* ⟿ *34 rooms* ⚐ *In-room: refrigerator. In-hotel: restaurant, 2 bars, pool, spa, laundry service, public Wi-Fi* ⊟ *MC, V* |○| *BP.*

★ **$$–$$$** 🖼 **Phra Nang Inn.** When selecting a room at this inn on the shore of Ao Phra Nang Beach, you can choose between the coconut wing and the betel-nut wing. The difference? Well, the rooms in the former are constructed from coconut palms, while those in the latter . . . well, you get the picture. The resort has a wonderfully kooky vibe—you might find headboards decorated with bright paintings of seashells and fish in the coconut wing and a few pieces of furniture might look like they're made from tree branches in the betel-nut wing. Even the bar, called the 75 Million Year Pub, is a little odd. The central location is also a big plus. ✉ *119 Liab Chai Haad Rd., Ao Nang, 81000* ☎ *075/637130* ⊕ *www. phrananginn.com* ⤶ *74 rooms* ⌂ *In-room: safe, refrigerator. In-hotel: 2 restaurants, bar, 2 pools, spa, laundry service, public Internet, airport shuttle* ▤ *AE, DC, MC, V.*

$$ 🏨 **Best Western Anyavee Ao Nang Resort & Spa.** The resort is a cluster of four-story buildings in Thai design, including northern-style peaked roofs. The large swimming pool has a waterfall you can swim through to have a drink at the pool bar. Rooms are contemporary Thai, austere but tastefully trimmed with hardwood. The resort is on a small rise a bit far from the sea, but that means it overlooks the hills and water around (and below) it. ✉ *31/3 Liab Chai Haad Rd., Ao Nang, 81000* ☎ *075/ 695051 up to 54* ⊕ *www.anyavee.com* ⤶ *71 rooms* ⌂ *In-room: safe, refrigerator. In-hotel: restaurant, pool, spa, laundry service, public Wi-Fi, airport shuttle* ▤ *AE, DC, MC, V.*

★ **¢–$** 🏨 **Emerald Bungalow.** On isolated Laem Son Beach, Emerald Bungalow is a family-run resort that provides genuine Thai hospitality. Tall pines, arching coconut trees, flowers, and ferns abound, and many birds, including a few chickens, inhabit the grounds. Budget-conscious travelers can enjoy proximity to the beach from basic wooden huts. Larger, newer air-conditioned villas have individually designed layouts and interior design, but all include some Thai art. The resort is across the river from Noppharat Thara National Park. ✉ *Noppharat Thara Beach, 81000* ☎ *091/892–1072 or 091/956–2566* ⌂ *In-room: no a/c (some). In-hotel: restaurant, laundry service* ▤ *No credit cards.*

¢ 🏨 **J Mansion.** Top-floor rooms peek out over surrounding buildings for a nice view of the sea. The primary reason to stay here is to save money for day trips and nightlife—the view is a nice bonus. Large, bright rooms have tile floors, and all rooms are available without the air-conditioning turned on for an extra discount. The hotel is very close to the action in town, as well as to the minibus and longtail boat junction. ✉ *23/3 Moo 2, Ao Nang Beach, 81000* ☎ *075/637878* ⤶ *21 rooms* ⌂ *In-room: refrigerator. In-hotel: restaurant, public Internet* ▤ *AE, DC, MC, V.*

Nightlife

Funky tunes and an extremely inviting atmosphere courtesy of proprietors Oil (a native Southerner) and Jeff (her Canadian husband) make most people become repeat customers at the aptly named **Bad Habit Bar** (✉ Noppharat Thara Beach, Liab Chai Haad Rd., Ao Nang ☎ 075/ 637882 or 06/279–2712). Drink prices are reasonable (beer for B50 and cocktails for B100). It's one of the nicest pubs in the area and good times are pretty much guaranteed. The bar is midway down Noppharat Thara Beach directly across from the beach and next to the Andaman Spa. Upstairs at **The Loft** restaurant enjoy the view of the beach and dine on the small specials menu, changed weekly, featuring fusion Thai-Western food like pasta and Thai green curry sauce.

Encore Café (✉245/23 Liab Chai Haad Rd., Nang Beach, Ao Nang ☎075/ 637107) has live music five to seven nights a week from prominent local and expat musicians who play rock, reggae, blues, jazz, funk, folk, and fusion Western-Thai tunes. Hidden back behind the main road in Central Ao Nang, Encore Café is one of the few places to hear quality music while knocking back some beers and eating Thai and Western pub grub.

Nang Cape/Railay Beach

★ ❹ *15 mins by longtail boat east of Ao Nang.*

Don't strain your neck admiring the sky-scraping cliffs as your longtail boat delivers you to Nang Cape, four interconnected beaches collectively referred to as Railay Beach; the isolated beaches of Tonsai, Phra Nang, East Railay, and West Railay, only accessible by boat, are sandy oases surrounded by vertical sandstone cliffs. The four beaches are connected by walking paths and each have their own attractions. Tonsai Beach, with a pebble-strewn shore and shallow, rocky water, caters to budget travelers and rock climbers. West Railay has powdery white sand, shallow but swimmable water, gorgeous sunset views, and many kayaks for hire. East Railay, a mangrove-lined shore unsuitable for beach or water activities, draws rock-climbing enthusiasts, as well as younger travelers looking for late-night drinks and loud music. Phra Nang Beach, one of the nicest beaches in all Krabi, is ideal for swimming, sunbathing, and rock climbing.

Where to Stay & Eat

★ $$$$ ✕⛨ **Rayavadee Premier Resort.** Scattered across 26 landscaped acres, this magnificent resort is set in coconut groves with white-sand beaches on three sides. The lobby faces East Railay, the pool looks out over West Railay Bay, and the beach bar and restaurant are the only structures on Phra Nang Beach—Rayavadee has the only direct access to this beautiful stretch of sand. Circular pavilions built in traditional Thai style have spacious living rooms with curving staircases that lead up to opulent bedrooms and baths with huge, round tubs. Some of the best rooms have secluded gardens with private hot tubs. Four restaurants assure variety—the beachfront Krua Pranang, set in a breezy pavilion, serves outstanding Thai food. ✉ *214 Railay Beach, Ao Nang, 81000* ☎ *075/620740* ⊕ *www.rayavadee.com* ⇨ *98 rooms 5 suites* ⚐ *In-room: safe, refrigerator, DVD. In-hotel: 4 restaurants, room service, bar, pool, tennis court, gym, spa, beachfront, water sports, laundry service, public Internet, airport shuttle* ▤ *AE, DC, MC, V.*

$$–$$$$ ✕⛨ **Railay Bay Resort and Spa.** Great Thai food and a beachside patio and bar from which you can watch the sunset are a few good reasons to visit Railay Bay Resort and Spa. Basic cottages and rooms in a row of modern two-story buildings are suitable reasons to lodge here, also. Get a massage in a room overlooking the beach and pool and you may never want to leave. This resort in the center of West Railay appeals to people who like a natural environment—one that comes with plenty of amenities, such as a minimart, Internet, and air-conditioning. A walking path connects West and East Railay for easy access to Phra Nang Beach. ✉ *145 Moo 2, Railay West Beach, Krabi, 81000* ☎ *075/622570 up to 72* ⊕ *www.krabi-railaybay.com* ⇨ *141 rooms, 10 suites* ⚐ *In-room: safe, refrigerator. In-hotel: restaurant, pool, spa, public Internet* ▤ *MC, V.*

$$–$$$$ 🏠 **Railei Beach Club.** Each of the 24 privately owned homes here is in-
Fodor'sChoice   dividually designed (and named), giving each its own unique charac-
★   ter. Solly's house, a two-story glass house on the beach, is particularly
popular. The houses sleep between two and eight persons and most have
large decks and kitchens. Powdery white sand is a short walk away and
kayaks are available. Feeling lazy? The staff can go into town and shop
for you. Really lazy? A cook can be arranged. Two small rooms are
available in the clubhouse, next to the common area and reception; they
have no kitchens, so you must have your meals down the beach at other
resorts, but they are the best deal on all of Nang Cape. Booking ahead
is a must. Note that there's no electricity from 6 AM to 6 PM. 🏠 *Box
8, Krabi, 81000* ☎ *075/622582* ⊕ *www.raileibeachclub.com* � *24
houses* ⚲ *In-rooms: no a/c, safe, kitchen. In-hotel: airport shuttle*
🍽 *No credit cards.*

$$$ 🏠 **Koh Jum Lodge.** Located on the island of Koh Jum, in Phang Nga Bay
between Krabi, Phi Phi, and Koh Lanta, Koh Jum Lodge has rooms in
16 wooden cottages designed in traditional Thai architectural style.
Bungalows are on the grounds of a coconut palm plantation in a tropical garden setting. All cottages are near the beach, facing Phi Phi Island to the west, each benefiting from sunset and sea views. Although
the resort is open all year, public boats do not service it year-round. During the high season (November to mid-May), boats from Krabi to Koh
Lanta stop offshore, where longtail boats ferry you to the island. The
remainder of the year you must contact the resort to hire a B2,500 longtail for the 40-minute ride out to the island from Krabi. ✉ *286 Moo 3,
Koh Siboya, Kua Klong, Krabi, 81130* ☎ *075/618275* ⊕ *www.
kohjumlodge.com* ➥ *16 bungalows* ⚲ *In-room: no a/c, no phone, no
TV. In-hotel: restaurant, pool, public Internet* 🍽 *MC, V.*

$$–$$$ 🏠 **Railay Princess Resort and Spa.** Thai-style lamps and silk throw pil-
lows on the beds and sofas are nice touches at this quiet retreat located
midway between East and West Railay beaches. All rooms have balconies
that look out over the pool and the lotus- and fishpond to the surrounding cliffs. A teak walkway connects the restaurant to the swimming pool.
✉ *145/1 Moo 2, Railay Beach, Ao Nang, 81000* ☎ *075/622605 or 075/
624356* ⊕ *www.railayprincessresortandspa.com* ➥ *59 rooms* ⚲ *In-room:
refrigerator. In-hotel: restaurant, pool, spa, water sports, laundry service* 🍽 *MC, V.*

¢–$$ 🏠 **YaYa Resort.** This large complex of three- and four-story wooden build-
ings looks like a small village—something like the castaways on Gilli-
gan's Island would have developed after three or four generations. In
fact, it's one of the oldest resorts on the cape and has undergone sev-
eral renovations over the years. Well . . . some of the rooms have. Newer
rooms have tile floors, air-conditioning, and standard amenities. Older
ones have moldy wood and dodgy bedding. Nonetheless, the resort has
a funky, tropical vibe, and is centrally located on East Railay Beach: not
immediately near anything, but a short walk from everything including
beaches, climbing, and nightlife. ✉ *1 Moo 2, Railay Beach, Ao Nang,
81000* ☎ *075/622593* ⊕ *www.yayaresort.com* ➥ *86 rooms* ⚲ *In-
room: no a/c (some), refrigerator (some), no TV (some). In-hotel: restau-
rant, laundry service, public Internet* 🍽 *No credit cards.*

¢ ⊡ **Railay Highland Resort.** While admiring the sweeping view of the towering limestone cliffs, take a closer look and you may see teeny people scaling the rock face. Awake early and you can witness the sunrise over the distant bay. The restaurant and bar have amazing views, the rooms are set back in the hillside, spread out among the trees. Basic huts with rattan walls and thatched roofs have mattresses on the floor with mosquito nets. There's no hot water, but electricity runs 24 hours. This is a great spot for rock climbers or people who want to chill out and don't mind roughing it a bit. ⊠ *Moo 1, Railay East Beach, Krabi, 81000* ☎ *075/621731* ⇨ *20 bungalows* ⚅ *In-room: no a/c, no TV. In-hotel: restaurant, bar, diving, laundry service* ⊟ *No credit cards.*

Sports & the Outdoors

ROCK-CLIMBING Climbers discovered the cliffs around Nang Cape in the late 1980s. The mostly vertical cliffs rising up out of the sea were, and certainly are, a dream comes true for hard-core climbers. Today, anyone daring enough can learn to scale the face of a rock in one of the most beautiful climbing destinations in the world. There are 500 to 600 established routes. Notable climbs include the Tonsai Beach overhang and Thaiwand Wall, where climbers must use lanterns to pass through a cave and then rappel down from the top. Beginners can learn some skills through half-day or full-day courses for fixed rates of B800 or B1,500, respectively. Most climbing organizations are found on East Railay. **Cliffs Man** (☎ 075/621768 ⊕ www.thaiclimb.com), **Tex** (☎ 075/631509 ⊕ www.texrockclimbing.com), and **King Climbers** (☎ 075/637125 ⊕ www.railay.com) are a few of the originals. King Climbers provides rescue services, though hopefully you won't need them.

Slightly less adventurous, or more spendthrift, types can try the free climb to "the lagoon." The lagoon isn't all that impressive, but the view from the top is spectacular. The trailhead for the fairly arduous climb up the occasionally near-vertical mud, rock, vine, and fixed-rope ascent is along the path to Phra Nang Beach, immediately across from the gazebo. Watch out for monkeys!

Koh Phi Phi

➍ *48 km (30 mi) or 90 mins by boat southeast of Phuket Town; 42 km (26 mi) or 2 hrs by boat southwest of Krabi.*

The Phi Phi Islands consist of six islands. **Phi Phi Don,** the largest of the islands, is shaped like a butterfly: The "wings," covered by limestone mountains, are connected by a flat 2-km (1-mi) narrow body featuring two opposing sandy beaches. Phi Phi Don is the only inhabited island.

The tsunami drastically changed the face of the islands, Phi Phi Don in particular. It devastated Loh Dalam Bay and a great deal of Tonsai Bay, too, where much of the "town" was, as well as the docks where tourists would pour off ferries every day. Practically all of the resorts along the narrow body between the two beaches were destroyed. Newer, better constructed shops, bars, and restaurants at Tonsai were strong enough to survive the waves. But only resorts and businesses on Long Beach and the more remote, east-facing beaches were spared heavy damage.

The Tsunami's Effect on Thailand's Underwater World

THE WAVES FROM THE 2004 TSUNAMI WERE CATACLYSMIC, but to a far greater extent on land than underwater. Shallow reefs were upturned and countless fish were left stranded far ashore, but the underwater impact was relatively mild. Official reports found 13% of coral reefs sustained severe damage, while 40% had no noticeable impact at all. Almost immediately after the event, more than 200 experts had examined over 300 dive sites to asses the damage. Their reports indicate that within 5 to 10 years, depending on the level of impingement by divers and fishermen, damaged reefs will have naturally regrown.

Shallow dive sites, such as Similan Island's Snapper Alley, were most affected by the waves. The waves primarily upturned table coral and buried shallow reefs with a blanket of sand, causing greater harm to crustaceans than to fish. As many dive sites, particular those around Koh Surin and Richileu Rock, are in deeper water, they were generally unaffected. That said, Similan and Surin islands accounted for half of the severely damaged sites. The popular dive site China Wall off Koh Miang, damaged severely by the tsunami, has since been reopened to the public.

Damage off Phi Phi Island was a combination of ocean surge and debris from the island. At Lanah Bay, up to 90% of the coral was destroyed. Most damaged reefs, with the exception of Bamboo Island, were not in popular snorkeling areas. Hard coral around the islands was particularly hard hit, but numerous volunteers contributed to cleaning up tons of debris and turning table coral over to its original upright position. Phi Phi dive sites are more renowned for the variety of marine life, such as leopard sharks, and this is still the case, although turtles and other marine life that feed off coral may see reduced numbers.

Phi Phi Dive Camp ⊕ www. phiphidivecamp.com has established a floating coral nursery and deployed cement blocks near Viking Cave by Phi Phi Ley. The cement blocks have been positioned into formations that will be seeded by coral fragments from the nursery to develop artificial reefs. The dive camp provides a four-day reef-monitoring course that is educational to the diver, promotes responsibility regarding reef treatment, and collects useful for data for its ongoing reef-monitoring program.

More than two years on, it's difficult to say that the diving, on the whole, is worse as a result of the tsunami. One dive operator suggested that the huge decline in divers in the year and a half following the tsunami had a great restorative effect on most marine life— it may have outweighed the destruction caused by the waves. Reports cite a greater diversity of fish around the Similan Islands after the event. Experts from the Global Coral Reef Monitoring Network postulate that much-needed coastal management implemented as a result of the tsunami may have a long-term benefit on the ecosystem. Prior to the tsunami, nearly 50% of Thailand's reefs were considered deteriorated and less than 20% were in good or excellent shape.

With the exception of those around Similan Islands 1, 2, and 3 (closed prior to the tsunami), all dive sites in Thailand are open to divers, some indisputably beautiful. Especially around the Similan and Surin islands, there are many dive spots that remain world class.

The Post-Tsunami Recovery

Both of Thailand's coasts had been experiencing a tourism boom for years—with many places facing the consequences of overdevelopment—when the tsunami hit the Andaman Coast on December 26, 2004. Several beaches on Phuket, the beach area of Khao Lak, and much of Koh Phi Phi were devastated by the waves, and although many areas on the Andaman Coast were unaffected by the tsunami, tourism on that shore came to a near standstill in the months following the disaster.

More than two years after the catastrophe, things are considerably different. Phuket beaches affected by the waves have been completely redeveloped, including much improved beachfront sidewalks, street lighting, restaurants, bars, and cafés on par with Western beach destinations. Phi Phi Island has rebuilt a bit more slowly. Most development along Tonsai and Loh Dalam has focused on upgrading salvageable budget accommodation to nicer, mid-range standards to fill the void left as the largest resorts plan their reconstruction (many scheduled for completion in early 2008). Bars and restaurants catering to the hordes of visitors returning to Phi Phi are plentiful. Khao Lak has seen most of its resorts rebuilt, with construction on pace to offer more 2007

accommodation, dining, and activities than it did prior to 2004. All along this lengthy, beautiful coast, accommodation from budget to boutique to five-star has been, and continues to be, built. In fact, simply looking at the tsunami-affected areas as they stand now, one would be hard-pressed to image that such destruction had occurred.

As the building continues, the issue of overdevelopment remains in the spotlight. Once adventurous travelers find a new, secluded, undeveloped beach and start talking about it, rapid development follows at a frightening pace. In many spots this development hasn't been regulated or monitored properly and the country is now pulling in the tourist dollar at the expense of the environment. It's a cycle that's hard to stop. Redevelopment in the tsunami areas began quite slowly, while developers and local businesses awaited government regulations. In some instances, the planning paid off (Phi Phi now has much-needed waste-water treatment facilities), but as most areas waited for regulations that never arrived, no-holds-barred development quickly followed. Where these areas will be two years from now is anyone's guess.

Tsunami Memorials

ON THE EASTERN END OF LOH DALAM BEACH is the Phi Phi Tsunami Memorial Park, a tiny garden with a small plaque listing some of the names of those who lost their lives in the 2004 tsunami. Several benches have been dedicated to the memory of others lost in the disaster. The memorial is a little sad, partly because it is only moderately well maintained, but also because it seems so small in relation to the devastation that claimed 5,395 lives. Regardless, it is a nice little park, and looking out across the beach and sea, one cannot help but be moved.

Another memorial, this one underwater, is located 66 feet deep, off the coast of Monkey Beach. The granite memorial consists of three pyramid-shape plaques arranged in the shape of an equilateral triangle; the plaques are the exact number of centimeters apart as the number of victims taken by the sea. The bases of the pyramids contain philosophical quotations, and the three markers symbolize the elements of land, water, and air, in which humans must learn to live in balance. In the center of the triangle rests a single granite stand that describes the tsunami's occurrence. In addition, 2,874 (the number of missing persons) centimeters from the memorial is a traditional Thai sala made from tsunami debris. It is the first underwater memorial monument on Earth.

But Phi Phi is one of Thailand's premier tourist destinations, so developers have scrambled to meet the renewed tourist demand. If you were unaware that such a catastrophe had taken place, you would think it was a beautiful island under a lot of development, rather than one that was recently destroyed and is being rebuilt. The rapid return of backpackers and divers forced initial redevelopment to focus on budget accommodations, including many cute beach bungalows. Resorts less affected by the tsunami consequently renovated their facilities to cater to more well-to-do travelers. Several of the finest hotels on the island, Phi Phi Cabana, Charlies, and Phi Phi Princess, all of which were devastated by the tsunami, were more patient to rebuild and are scheduled to open in Feburary 2008.

As a result of the original destruction, farther-flung beaches are now getting the attention that they deserve. Visitors forced to look elsewhere for lodging have discovered the magic of sandy and swimmable Laem Tong Beach and peaceful and beautiful Long Beach, which had lived in the shadow of busier Tonsai Beach.

The popularity of the Phi Phi Islands stems from the outstanding scuba diving; leopard sharks, turtles, and sea horses are some species still frequenting popular reefs. The tsunami actually had surprisingly little effect on the dive sites here, with 75% of coral reefs sustaining low to no impact. The best dive sites were relatively unaffected and those hardest hit were not good snorkeling sites to begin with.

A popular day trip from Phi Phi Don is a visit to nearby **Phi Phi Lae** via longtail or speedboat. The first stop is Viking Cave, a vast cavern of limestone pillars covered with crude drawings. Most boats continue on for an afternoon in Maya Bay, aka "The Beach." If you don't mind huge crowds (the snorkelers practically outnumber the fish), Maya Bay is a spectacular site. If you get a really early jump on everyone, cruise into a secluded bay, and leave first tracks along the powdery sand beach, you've done it right; otherwise, secluded Loh Samah Bay, on the opposite side of the island, is smaller but just as special.

Alternatively, you can take a 45-minute trip by longtail boat to circular **Bamboo Island,** with a superb beach around it. The underwater colors of the fish and the coral are brilliant. The island is uninhabited, but you can spend a night under the stars if you're adventuresome. You can also hike up to a series of viewpoints toward the 1,030-foot peak on the east side of the island. The trail-head is near Tonsai Bay; ask your hotel for directions.

Where to Stay & Eat

¢–$$$　✕ **Chao Koh Restaurant.** As you stroll Tonsai's walking path, you'll surely notice the catches of the day on display in front of Chao Koh Restaurant. Kingfish, swordfish, and barracuda, grilled with garlic and butter, white wine, or marsala sauce, and served with rice or a baked potato, is a mere B200. Clams, crabs, shrimp, Phuket lobster, and live rock lobsters are available by weight. Chao Koh also serves a variety of Thai salads, appetizers, noodles, and curry dishes, but the seafood is obviously their specialty. ⊠ *Tongsai Bay* ☎ *075/620800* ▭ *No credit cards.*

¢–$$　✕ **Thai Cuisine.** Fresh seafood is not hard to come by on Phi Phi, but even so, Thai Cuisine's selection of white shark, barracuda, swordfish, lobster, and crab have people lining up outside to get a table. In addition to finely cooked fish, Thai Cuisine makes great fried rice. Look for the restaurant with all rattan walls and ceiling across from Phi Phi Bakery in the middle of Tonsai's beach road, near the pier. ⊠ *Central Tonsai Beach, Koh Phi Phi* ☎ *091/979–2525* ▭ *No credit cards.*

¢–$　✕ **Pearl Restaurant.** Nothing fancy here, just genuine Thai food prepared and served by genuinely friendly Thai people. They also serve breakfast and a few Western dishes, including pizza. ⊠ *Next to Cosmic Restaurant, Tonsai Village* ☎ *07/164–5716* ▭ *No credit cards.*

¢　✕ **Phi Phi Bakery.** Craving fresh baked donuts, Danish, croissants, or real coffee rather than Nescafé? Check out Phi Phi Bakery, which serves American, Continental, and Thai breakfast specials and freshly baked pastries. They also serve Thai and Western standards for lunch and dinner. ⊠ *97 Moo 7, Tonsai Village* ☎ *091/894–0374* ▭ *No credit cards.*

$$$$　✕▯ **Holiday Inn Resort.** The Holiday Inn couldn't have a better location— Fodor'sChoice it's on more than 50 acres of tropical gardens along a private beach, which ★ has gorgeous blue water with a sandy sea floor, where you can swim and snorkel year-round. Most bungalows have identical design with parquet floors, comfortable indoor daybeds, and decks with lounge chairs. However, a few rooms are family-style duplexes; those numbered 100–118 are also beachfront. A late 2007 expansion of the resort will add more beachfront rooms, hillside rooms with spectacular beach views, and an

additional pool, bar, and restaurant. The Terrace Restaurant, serving Thai and international cuisines, has splendid views of the sea, and the cliff-side satay bar has one of the few sunset viewpoints on the entire island. Classes in Thai culture, arts, cooking, and language are offered throughout the week. The resort offers boat service from Phuket. ⊠ *Cape Laemtong, 81000* ☎ *075/621334 or 075/620798* ⊕ *www.phiphi-palmbeach. com* ⊅ *130 bungalows* ⚇ *In-room: safe, refrigerator. In-hotel: 4 restaurants, room service, 4 bars, 2 tennis courts, 2 pools, gym, spa, beachfront, diving, water sports, laundry service* ⊟ *AE, MC, V.*

★ **$$$$** ▦ **Zeavola.** Zeavola takes its name from a flower, the name of which translates in Thai to "love of the sea." That certainly is fitting, as the water off the powdery white-sand Laem Tong Beach is simply stunning. From the beach, sandy garden paths meander between semisecluded teak villas with outdoor sala entryways. Though the resort and its amenities are thoroughly modern, there's a decided old-world charm to the place: baths have small mirrors and exterior iron plumbing and beds have cream-color mosquito nets. Chill out by the sea to relaxing tunes piped through all-weather Bose speakers. You can even relax on a simple mat outside your villa while fresh coffee percolates. Need privacy? Flick a switch and bamboo shades enclose your sala. ⊠ *11 Moo 8, Laem Tong, Koh Phi Phi, 81000* ☎ *075/627000* ⊕ *www.zeavola.com* ⊅ *52 villas* ⚇ *In-room: safe, refrigerator, DVD. In-hotel: 2 restaurants, spa, beachfront, diving, laundry service* ⊟ *AE, MC, V* ⧉ *BP.*

$$-$$$$ ▦ **Phi Phi Natural Resort.** Beautiful sunrise views from the deluxe seaside bungalows are this resort's biggest draw. The 20 deluxe rooms along the rocky shoreline have wooden floors and Thai arts and crafts. The resort is on a hill between the north end of Laem Tong Beach and a smaller secluded beach, which is quite private, but less than ideal for swimming. Budget rooms also have good views, as they are high up on the hill. ⊠ *Moo 8, Laem Tong Beach, 81000* ☎ *075/613000* ⊕ *www.phiphinatural.com* ⊅ *70 rooms* ⚇ *In-room: safe (some), refrigerator. In-hotel: restaurant, room service, bar, pool, public Internet* ⊟ *MC, V.*

$$-$$$$ ▦ **Phi Phi Viewpoint Resort.** On the western hillside overlooking Loh Dalam Bay, Phi Phi Viewpoint Resort was the sole survivor of the tsunami that devastated the resorts on this beautiful beach. Although the hillside huts are stacked pretty tightly next to and on top of each other, the six beachfront huts will give you a little more breathing room and privacy. The outdoor bar and the pool also have outstanding views of the beach and bay. Note that some huts don't have hot water. ⊠ *107 Loh Dalam Bay, 81000* ☎ *075/622351 or 075/618111* ⊕ *www.phiphiviewpoint. com* ⊅ *54 huts, 1 suite* ⚇ *In-room: no a/c (some), refrigerator. In-hotel: restaurant, bar, pool, diving, water sports, public Wi-Fi* ⊟ *MC, V.*

$$-$$$ ▦ **Bay View and Arayaburi Resorts.** All rooms at these two neighboring resorts are on a hill at the far eastern end of Tonsai Bay. Every bungalow has a large deck with a great view of both Phi Phi Lae and Tonsai Bay. These two resorts share everything but their names. The only difference between them is the room decor: Bay View is older and its rooms have hardwood floors, whereas Arayaburi is newer and its rooms have tile floors—the wood-floor rooms feel more traditional and natural, which suits the environment better. Arayaburi rooms are closer to the small "private" beach, which is slightly better than the water in front of the reception area, which is quite shallow and not great for swimming. The resort is on the quietest spot along Laem Hin Beach and it's only a short (although sometimes slippery) 15-minute walk along the rocks to gorgeous Long Beach. Electric cars transfer guests from distant rooms to the reception and restaurant areas. ✉ *69 Laem Hin Beach* ☎ *076/281360 up to 64* ⊕ *www.phiphibayview.com* ↪ *109 bungalows* ⚘ *In-room: safe, refrigerator. In-hotel: restaurant, room service, pool, public Internet* ▭ *AE, D, MC, V.*

$$–$$$ 🛏 **Phi Phi Erawan Palm Resort.** Erawan Palm is a small, comfortable resort in the middle on Laem Tong Beach, next to the sea gypsy village. The spacious cottages all have wooden floors and ceilings with golden curtains and comforters. The beach bar is great for lazy afternoon cocktails and there is a small museum about the sea gypsy community that you can check out when you need a break from the beach. ✉ *Moo 8, Laem Tong Beach, 81000* ☎ *075/627500* ⊕ *www.pperawanpalms.com* ↪ *18 cottages* ⚘ *In-room: refrigerator, ethernet. In-hotel: restaurant, room service, bar, pool, diving, laundry service, public Internet* ▭ *AE, MC, V.*

$–$$ 🛏 **Chao Koh Phi Phi Lodge.** Chao Koh Phi Phi Lodge is a collection of basic but comfortable bungalows near Tonsai Bay. Major renovations in spring 2005 added a swimming pool and family-style suites. Several simple fan huts survived both the tsunami and the renovation, so the place still welcomes budget travelers. Evenings, the lodge runs a popular seafood restaurant by the sea, with a nice view of the bay. ✉ *Tongsai Bay, 81000* ☎ *075/620800* ⊕ *www.chaokohphiphi.com* ↪ *44 bungalows* ⚘ *In-room: no a/c (some), safe, refrigerator (some). In-hotel: restaurant, pool, diving, public Internet* ▭ *MC, V.*

¢–$$ 🛏 **Paradise Resort.** Book ahead (it's popular) and don't settle for less than beachfront. These are the best beachfront rooms on Long Beach and the other rooms aren't all that special. All rooms have tile floors and are relatively characterless, though superior rooms are slightly better than family rooms, which are far from the beach. You probably won't spend much time in your room, though, as the beach is gorgeous and there are many trees in front of the resort that provide much-needed shade. ✉ *Long Beach* ☎ *091/968–3982 up to 89* ⊕ *www.paradiseresort.co.th* ↪ *25 rooms* ⚘ *In-room: no a/c (some). In-hotel: restaurant, water sports, laundry service* ▭ *No credit cards.*

★ ¢–$$ 🛏 **Phi Phi Villa Resort.** Large, thatch-covered huts in a natural setting give Phi Phi Villa a relaxing island feeling quite different from bustling Tonsai Bay, a short walk away. All bungalows have small patios with wooden handrails, and interiors large enough to fit desks, chairs, wardrobes, and enormous bathrooms. The resort is on a stretch of private beach where boats are prohibited from landing; the absence of longtails that clutter Tonsai's shore makes the beach here more suitable for swimming, although it's still shallow and quite rocky. It's great for travelers who want to stay close to the action without being a part of it. The cheapest rooms lack air-conditioning, hot water, and basic amenities, but they do have access to everything else, including a new yoga center, the first on Phi Phi. ⚠ **Rooms closest to the beach are only for sound sleepers or night owls, as the reverberations from Hippies Bar and Carpe Diem beach bar can be heard late into the night.** ✉ *Tonsai Bay, 81000* ☎ *075/601100* ⊕ *www.phiphivillaresort.com* ↪ *55 bungalows* ⚘ *In-room: no* *a/c (some), refrigerator (some), no TV (some). In-hotel: restaurant, room service, 2 bars, pool, diving, laundry service* ☰ *MC, V.*

¢–$ 🏠 **Maprao Resort.** Not for those unaccustomed to roughing it a bit, Maprao resort is a great place for those who don't mind a few geckos in their room (to say the least). Six styles of bungalows are available, from the two-story, beachfront Holy Tree, which has a large deck and breezy sea view, to the Roof Terrace Bungalows, which feature rooftop sun chairs. Bamboo bungalows on stilts with shared baths are available for budget travelers; newer concrete bungalows have small lofts above the baths with fans and mosquito nets for families with adventurous kids. Maprao is on a small private beach between Tonsai and Long Beach, accessible only by foot or by boat. ✉ *Between Tonsai and Long beaches* ☎ *075/622486* ⊕ *www.maprao.com* 🛏 *25 rooms* ⚤ *In-hotel: restaurant, bar, diving* ☰ *No credit cards.*

¢ 🏠 **Twin Palm Bungalow.** It doesn't get more basic than these small bamboo bungalows (nor does it need to). Were the island covered with these, it couldn't be more ideal. Thrown up in a sandy field, just off the beach, which once housed larger bungalows prior to the tsunami, they will inevitably be replaced by more permanent structures that may be "nicer" and more expensive, though not necessarily better. Check 'em out while you can. Reception is in the minimart on Loh Dalam Beach. Some rooms have shared bathrooms. ✉, *Central Loh Dalam Beach* ☎ *084/185–8296* 🛏 *24 bungalows* ⚤ *In-room: no a/c, no phone, no TV. In-hotel: restaurant* ☰ *No credit cards.*

Nightlife

Many people come to Phi Phi for two reasons only: to go to Maya Bay during the day, and to party in Tonsai Bay at night. As a result, a large number of bars were constructed, primarily out of concrete, most of which were strong enough to survive the impact from the waves. Once you head down the side streets away from the beach there are mazes of bars and clubs competing in stereo wars, filled with young travelers eager to drink and dance the night away. If you like Khao San Road in Bangkok, you will love Tonsai Bay at night. The most popular of these bars, located near the 7-11 in the center of "town," are **Tiger Bar** and **Reggae Bar.** Along the path running parallel to the sea, there are several popular bars, notably **Apache Bar,** which has an impressive "katoey" (drag cabaret) show, and farther to the east are fire shows at the popular beach bars **Hippies Bar** and **Carpe Diem.** More remote beaches around the island have more subdued nightlife, primarily centered around resort restaurants and bars. One of the best of these is **Sunflower Bar,** which is on the eastern end of Loh Dalam Beach, next to the Tsunami Memorial Park. Constructed almost entirely of driftwood or old wooden bungalows, this laid-back beach bar often has local reggae bands jamming beneath the stars.

Koh Lanta

42 *70 km (42 mi) south of Krabi Town; 2–3 hrs from Ao Nang.*

Long, uncrowded beaches, crystal-clear water, and a laid-back natural environment are Koh Lanta's main attractions. Although "discovered" by international travelers in early 2000, Koh Lanta remains fairly quiet. Early development resulted in the construction of hundreds of budget bungalows and several swanky resorts along the west coast of Lanta Yai (Lanta Noi's coast is less suitable for development), however, as one of the largest islands in Thailand, Lanta was able to absorb the "boom" and therefore remains relatively uncluttered. In addition, Lanta is approximately 70 km (44 mi) south of Krabi Town, far enough outside established tourist circuits that visitor arrivals have increased more slowly than at other Krabi and Phang Nga beaches and islands. Most smaller resorts are closed during the low season (May though October). However, some do open in late October and remain open until mid-May—during these (slightly) off times, the weather is still generally good, and you can find that the rates are much lower and the beaches much less crowded.

The tsunami was a mixed blessing for Koh Lanta. It had a small effect on the buildings along the coast, and most damage was repaired within months of the disaster. However, it had a beneficial effect on the environment, cleansing the beaches and replenishing the shore with clear deep-ocean water. Before the tsunami it was hard to imagine how Koh Lanta could be any more beautiful, but afterwards the water was bluer and more sparkling, the sand whiter and softer. Though the huge decrease in visitor arrivals to the island initially caused its share of economic hardship, it wasn't long before word of Koh Lanta's renewal spread and lucky travelers again found their way to its shores.

Sports & the Outdoors

Diving, snorkeling, hiking, and elephant trekking are a few activities available on Koh Lanta and the nearby islands. Diving and snorkeling around Koh Lanta can be arranged through dive and tour operators, though most people choose to book through their own resort. Popular nearby dive sites are **Koh Ha** and **Koh Rok** off Koh Lanta. If you would like to enjoy Koh Lanta from another viewpoint, elephant trekking is available near Phra Ae (Long) Beach. A boat trip to the famous **Emerald Cave** on **Koh Muk** is a worthwhile experience; it's easiest to inquire at your resort about day trip options.

Klong Dao Beach

Klong Dao Beach is a 2-km-long (1-mi-long) beach on the northern coast of Lanta Yai. Most resorts along Klong Dao are larger facilities catering to families and couples looking for a quiet environment. The water is shallow but swimmable, and at low tide the firm, exposed sand is ideal for long jogs on the beach.

WHERE TO STAY & ✕⬚ **Time for Lime.** Time for Lime is a large, open-air kitchen right off
EAT the beach where you can learn to cook Thai food (with Chinese,
$ Malaysian, and Indian twists), using fresh seafood and vegetables. Instruction is provided in selecting the best ingredients and then cooking and presenting your own visual feast. It's fun, easy, and taught in a great environment. Spartan but cozy accommodation is available for those who wish to take multiple classes or just enjoy the smell of Thai cooking. Each night, the restaurant serves a different three-course set menu for B600, and reclining chairs are placed on the recessed sandbar while music plays and cocktails are served. Note that you should reserve

workshops at least two days in advance. ⊠ *72/2 Klong Dao Beach, Lanta Yai, 81150* ☏ *075/684590 or 089/967–5017* ⊕ *www.timeforlime.net* ➟ *9 rooms* ⚒ *In-room: no a/c, no phone, refrigerator, no TV, Wi-Fi. In-hotel: restaurant, bar* ☰ *No credit cards.*

¢–$ ✕⌂ **Chaba Guesthouse and Picasso Restaurant.** Once you spot the giant mushrooms, you'll know you've found Picasso Restaurant and Chaba Guesthouse. Thai people believe that southerners make the best food, and Picasso Restaurant lives up to this southern reputation. Proprietor and artist Khun Toi creates pastel-color oil paintings incorporating shells and driftwood from Klong Dao Beach. Finished products adorn the walls of the restaurant, which itself is a Monet-inspired swirl of impressionist pastels and sculpture. Toi's style of art has even been granted a patent by the Thai government. The guesthouse part of the operation offers colorful, comfortable bungalows. ⊠ *Klong Dao Beach, Lanta Yai, 81150* ☏ *075/684118 or 099/738–7710* ⊕ *www.krabidir.com/ chababungalows* ➟ *20 bungalows* ⚒ *In-room: safe, refrigerator. In-hotel: restaurant, bar, laundry service, public Internet* ☰ *No credit cards.*

★ $$$$ ⌂ **Costa Lanta.** The coolest thing about Costa Lanta is the room design; each room at this trendy boutique resort is a convertible box, so if you're too hot you can open up the "walls" and allow the breeze to blow through your room. The resort keeps the design elements minimal, so as to place an emphasis on nature. The result?: "camping" for people who don't want to camp without air-conditioning and a nice bathroom. Even the water in the swimming pool appears greenish and pondlike. The resort is at the northern end of Klong Dao Beach—the quiet end of an already quiet beach. Isolation is a blessing here, as the resort has almost everything you might need, including a pool table and a spa. The water here is swimmable, and snorkeling around Kaw Kwang Cape, while not exceptional, is pleasant and there are fish to be seen. ⊠ *212 Klong Dao Beach, Lanta Yai, 81150* ☏ *075/618092* ⊕ *www.costalanta.com* ➟ *22 rooms* ⚒ *In-room: safe, refrigerator. In-hotel: restaurant, bar, pool, spa* ☰ *AE, DC, MC, V.*

★ $$$$ ⌂ **Twin Lotus Resort and Spa.** Twin Lotus is as much an architectural and interior-design exhibition as it is a sophisticated and tranquil retreat. At times the resort seems traditionally tropical (Thai massage is offered on thatched sala islands set amid a lily pond), but at other times, it's creatively modern (the swimming pool is fringed with waterfalls). Occasionally, the two styles meld: deluxe superior rooms have colorful tile floors, but incredibly romantic outdoor baths. The resort's main dining area is a feast for the eyes as well as the palate, and the two bars make up for the fairly isolated location on the quiet northern end of Klong Dao Beach. ⊠ *199 Moo 1, Klong Dao Beach, Koh Lanta Yai, 81150* ☏ *075/607000, 02/361–1946 up to 49 in Bangkok* ⊕ *www. twinlotusresort.com* ➟ *78 rooms* ⚒ *In-room: safe, refrigerator, DVD. In-hotel: 2 restaurants, room service, 2 pools, spa, diving, water sports, public Internet* ☰ *AE, MC, V.*

☾ $–$$$ ⌂ **Southern Lanta.** With a fun-slide plunging into a big pool and several two-bedroom villas each with large multibed rooms, Southern Lanta is quite popular with families. Standard rooms are bungalows built closely to each other with slightly run-down exteriors, but comfortable interiors. Seaside rooms are newer and have sofas indoors and deck chairs outdoors for maximum lounging. ⊠ *105 Klong Dao Beach, Lanta Yai, 81150* ☎ *075/684175 up to 77* ⊕ *www.southernlanta.com* ⤵ *80 rooms, 10 suites* ♿ *In-room: refrigerator. In-hotel: 2 restaurants, bar, 2 pools, gym, spa, public Internet* ⊟ *MC, V.*

Phra Ae Beach (Long Beach)

Long and wide, Phra Ae Beach (aka Long Beach) is Lanta Yai's main tourist destination. The sand is soft and fine, perfect for both sunbathing and long walks. The water is less shallow than at other Lanta beaches, and therefore more suitable for diving in and having a swim. However, kayaks, catamarans, and other water activities, while available, are not as ubiquitous as on other islands. Although most lodging consists of simple budget bungalows, the beachfront does have several three- and four-star resorts. Along the beach and on the main road are many restaurants, bars, Internet cafés, and dive operators.

WHERE TO
STAY & EAT
¢–$

✕▣ **Funky Fish Bar and Bungalows–Mr. Wee Pizzeria.** Feeling funky? Dine while you recline on a triangular Thai pillow atop one of dozens of elevated wooden platforms. Mr. Wee serves thin-crust pizzas that should satisfy both American and Italian palates. We enjoyed pizza Raul: mozzarella, tomato, mushroom, and shrimp. They also serve Thai and Italian food as well as ice cream and other desserts. Funky Fish is also a happening bar at night, and they rent super simple wood and rattan bungalows with thatched roofs and tile baths. ⊠ *241 Moo 3 Phra Ae Beach, Lanta Yai* ☎ *07/274–0750* ♿ *In-room: no a/c, no phone, no TV. In-hotel: restaurant, bar* ⊟ *No credit cards* ⊗ *Closed June–Sept.*

$$$$

▣ **Layana Resort and Spa.** The majority of rooms are in two-story garden pavilions set around a football field–size grass clearing that opens to the sea. The ocean and beach suites are the finest rooms here, the former featuring rooftop, open-air salas with large desks and mosquito-net enclosed daybeds ideal for afternoon lounging or romantic evenings. Beach suites have beds in the center of the rooms looking directly out to sea. The suites also have outdoor rainfall showers and glass-enclosed garden bathtubs. ⊠ *272 Moo 3, Saladan, Phra Ae Beach, Koh Lanta, 81150* ☎ *075/607100, 02/713–2313 in Bangkok* ⊕ *www.layanaresort. com* ⤵ *50 rooms* ♿ *In-room: safe, refrigerator, DVD, Wi-Fi. In-hotel: restaurant, bar, pool, spa, beachfront, diving, water sports* ⊟ *AE, DC, MC, V.*

$$

▣ **Lanta Nakara.** If you're staying in a resort on a beautiful, white-sand beach with crystal-clear, blue water you should treat yourself to a room with a view. Fortunately, if you stay at Lanta Nakara (formerly Lanta Resortel), you will have such a view, even if you get stuck in a room at the back—most wooden bungalows are positioned so that you can look down a sandy walkway to the beach. So whether lying in bed and looking through the picture window, or lounging on one of two daybeds on the deck, you'll appreciate the tranquillity of the Andaman Sea. Ask for one of the rooms away from the restaurant and pool to ensure quiet. When it gets too hot, retreat to the air-conditioned bliss of your cottage, which has wooden floors and rattan walls—a perfect blend of island design and modern amenities. ⊠ *172 Moo, Phra Ae Beach* ☎ *075/*

684178 ⊕ *www.lantalongbeach.com/nakara.html* 🛏 *44 cottages* ⚿ *In-room: refrigerator. In-hotel: restaurant, bar, pool, laundry service, public Wi-Fi* ▤ *MC, V.*

$–$$ ▦ **Lanta Long Beach Resort.** The exteriors of the thatched roof wooden huts appear weathered and worn and the restaurant is now a short walk away at the neighboring, co-owned Nakara, but the resort's simplicity is its charm. The rooms are rustic—floors and walls are made of wood the way Thai huts should be, natural, but airtight, to keep the mosquitoes out. Some huts, however, have a few amenities like air-conditioning, large windows, and decks with roll-down wind-rain screens. Years of expansion have resulted in a variety of rooms for the thriftiest backpacker as well as the spendthrifty hippie. Construction of the "nicer" Nakara resort benefits L.L.B Resort guests, who may now use the swimming pool next door. ⊠ *172 Moo 3, Phra Ae Beach, Lanta Yai, 81150* ☎ *075/684178* ⊕ *www.lantalongbeach.com* 🛏 *95 rooms* ⚿ *In-room: no a/c (some), refrigerator (some), no TV (some). In-hotel: restaurant, bar, pool, laundry service, public Wi-Fi* ▤ *MC, V.*

¢–$ ▦ **Best House.** The entry to Best House is an inviting high-ceiling room with many comfortable chairs, white tile floors, and wooden beams, trim, and hand railings. The rooms are spacious and comfortable, the closest thing to "normal" Western hotel rooms on an island of bungalows and upscale spa-resorts. The place isn't on the beach, but it's very close to it. All rooms are equally nice, but air-conditioned rooms have the added luxury of hot water, which is unavailable in cheaper, fan rooms. ⊠ *5/1 Moo 3, Phra Ae Beach, Lanta Yai, 81150* ☎ *091/174–0241* ⊕ *www.krabidir.com/besthouse* 🛏 *40 rooms* ⚿ *In-room: no a/c (some). In-hotel: laundry service* ▤ *No credit cards* ☉ *Closed June–Sept.*

¢ ▦ **Somewhere Else.** If you like your huts to be innovative, check out Somewhere Else. The six octagonal rooms in the front of the clearing are particularly cool. They have fold-down windows, wooden floors, and loose-pebble bathroom floors. This resort is nothing fancy (expect cold water and fans) but it has a great vibe, and you'll enjoy playing Ping-Pong with friendly staff in the common room or just watching the sunset on the chill-out pillows strewn on various wooden platforms. Note that there's no hot water. ⊠ *253 Moo 3, Phra Ae Beach, Lanta Yai, 81150* ☎ *091/536–0858 or 089/731–1312* 🛏 *16 rooms* ⚿ *In-room: no a/c. In-hotel: restaurant, laundry service* ▤ *No credit cards* ☉ *Closed June–Sept.*

Klong Nin Beach

Klong Nin Beach, approximately 30 minutes south of Long Beach by car or boat, is one of the larger, nicer beaches toward the southern end of Lanta Yai. Klong Nin is less developed and more tranquil than Long Beach. A typical day on Klong Nin could consist of a long walk on the silky soft sand interrupted by occasional dips in the sea, a spectacular sunset, a seaside massage, and a candlelit barbecue beneath a canopy of stars. Central Klong Nin, near Otto bar, is the best for swimming, as rocks punctuate the rest of the shoreline. Kayaks are available from some resorts and longtail boat taxis are for hire along the sea. Most resorts here rent motorbikes as well, as the road to the south is much smoother than the road from Long Beach.

WHERE TO
STAY & EAT
¢–$
Fodor'sChoice
★

✕ **Cook Kai.** From the outside, the restaurant appears to be a standard, wooden Thai beach restaurant. Once inside, fairy lights along the ceiling light up your eyes and the food does likewise to your taste buds. Sizzling "hotpan" dishes of seafood in coconut cream and sweet-and-sour shrimp are succulent. Specials, such as duck curry served in a hollowed-out pineapple, change daily. Everything on their extensive menu tastes amazing. They even share their recipes, offering cooking classes upon request. ☒ *Moo 6, Klong Nin Beach* ☎ *091/606–3015* ▤ *No credit cards.*

$$$$ ⌂ **Rawi Warin Resort and Spa.** This enormous resort encompasses an entire hillside along the road from Klong Khong Beach to Klong Nin and makes great use of the land to create a comprehensive vacation retreat. In addition to its luxuriously outfitted rooms, the resort features, among many other things, a 24-seat minitheater, a music room, a video game room, a dive shop, and a beautiful private beach. Landscaping marvels include wooden walkway bridges that cross a lagoon to several gazebos. Hotel and room decor is Thai style with an emphasis on the sea; the restaurant-bar area attempts to resemble a fishing village. ☒ *139 Moo 8, Lanta Yai Island, Krabi, 81150* ☎ *075/607400 up to 48, 02/ 434–5526 in Bangkok* ⊕ *www.rawiwarin.com* ⇆ *186 rooms* ⌂ *In-room: safe, refrigerator. In-hotel: 3 restaurants, 3 bars, room service, tennis court, 5 pools, gym, spa, diving, bicycles, children's programs (ages 5–10), laundry service, public Wi-Fi, airport shuttle* ▤ *AE, DC, MC, V.*

$$–$$$ ⌂ **Srilanta.** One of the first upscale resorts in the area to market the "less is more" philosophy, Srilanta remains a cool yet classy island getaway for trendy urbanites. Breezy rooms are primitive but have comfortable lounging areas and are tastefully decorated with flowers. Unfortunately, most rooms have no view, and the beach is a short walk down the hill. Suites, in addition to having larger rooms, also feature cable TV and in-room DVD players. The beachside pool, sunbathing lawn, spa, and common areas follow stylish Hindu and Balinese themes. The spa has massage tables on a platform above a large fishpond. Srilanta is reasonably priced for what you get (one of the nicest resorts on one of the nicest beaches), but the service is quite ordinary for such an extraordinary resort. ☒ *111 Moo 6, Klong Nin Beach, Lanta Yai, 81150* ☎ *075/697288, 02/712– 8858 in Bangkok* ⊕ *www.srilanta.com* ⇆ *49 rooms, 3 suites* ⌂ *In-room: refrigerator, no TV (some). In-hotel: 2 restaurants, bar, pool, spa, beachfront, laundry service, public Internet* ▤ *AE, DC, MC, V.*

¢–$ ⌂ **Lanta Miami Bungalows.** The Lanta Miami is on the beach, it's affordable, and the staff is incredibly friendly—you truly need little more. The rooms are spacious, and have big beds and tile floors, though you can probably spend your days on the beach or under a shady palm. Note there's no hot water or air-conditioning in some rooms. ☒ *13 Moo 6, Klong Nin Beach, Lanta Yai, 81150* ☎ *075/662559* ⊕ *www.lantamiami. com* ⇆ *22 rooms* ⌂ *In-room: no a/c (some), refrigerators. In-hotel: restaurant, laundry service* ▤ *No credit cards* ☉ *Closed June–Sept.*

¢–$ ⌂ **Lanta Paradise Resort.** It's only a short walk along the beach to the best swimming spot, but the sand gets so hot you'll be glad to have the pool outside your room. Bungalows come in all permutations from fan-cooled and cold-water-only to air-conditioned, with hot water and all the standard amenities. The beachfront rooms are the best of the lot and have the most amenities (even TVs). Shady twin massage beds and southern Thai–style elevated dining tables with chill-out pillows and peaked roofs (both by the beach) help you keep your cool. There's even a hip little hippie beach bar that sells shell necklaces. ✉ *67 Moo 6, Klong Nin Beach, Lanta Yai, 81150* ☎ *089/473–3279* ⊕ *www. lantaparadiseresort.com* 🛏 *35 rooms* ♿ *In-room: no a/c (some), refrigerator (some), no TV (some). In-hotel: restaurant, bar, pool, laundry service, public Internet, airport shuttle* ▤ *No credit cards* ⊙ *Closed June–Sept.*

Southern Lanta Beaches

Southern Lanta beaches consist of several widely dispersed small coves and beaches ending at Klong Chak National Park. Immediately south of Klong Nin the road suddenly becomes well paved (much smoother than the road from Long Beach to Klong Nin), making the southern beaches accessible by road as well as by taxi boat. The nicest of the southern beaches is Bakantiang Beach, a beautiful one to visit on the way to the national park.

WHERE TO STAY & EAT ✕ **Same Same But Different.** This restaurant is tucked away in a shady grove near the southern end of Bakantiang Beach. The "dining room"

★ ¢–$ is very Robinson Crusoe, enclosed by a rudimentary roof with a dozen tables on the sand and wood bar. Have your longtail boat drop you off here and pick you up on the northern end of the beach an hour or so later, so you have time for a swim before you eat, and a nice walk on the beach when you're done. Same Same serves some southern Thai dishes, typically spicy. We recommend the fried prawns with tamarind sauce topped with fried shallot and chili. Smoothies and ice-cold beer are perfect for combating the afternoon heat. ✉ *85 M. 5 Bakantiang Beach, Lanta Yai* ☎ *091/787–8670* ▤ *No credit cards.*

$$$$ ⊡ **Pimalai Resort and Spa.** Pimalai Resort and Spa is a premier resort encompassing hundreds of acres of beachfront and hillside along southern Bakantiang Beach. Standard rooms are luxurious enough, but exclusive villas have full kitchens, private pools, and drivers to shuttle you to the spa, beach, or other facilities around the sprawling resort. The spa was carefully landscaped with tall palms and sloping trails. The soothing sounds of streams and waterfalls around the spa and classical Thai music in the lobby are just as tranquilizing as the treatments. Thai royalty and celebrities have been guests here. Booking ahead is essential. ✉ *99 M. 5 Bakantiang Beach, Lanta Yai, 81150* ☎ *075/607999* ⊕ *www. pimalai.com* 🛏 *79 rooms, including 7 suites, 40 private houses* ♿ *In-room: safe, refrigerator, DVD. In-hotel: 3 restaurants, room service, 3 bars, pool, gym, spa, beachfront, diving, public Internet, airport shuttle* ▤ *AE, DC, MC, V.*

★ **$–$$** ⊡ **Narima Resort.** The owners staggered the bungalows when they were built so that almost all could enjoy the awesome view of Koh Ha. If that were not enough, they strung hammocks on each deck and threw in a couple of palm-straw rocking chairs. The rooms have cloth canopy ceilings and rattan walls. It almost doesn't matter that the shore here is rocky rather than sandy. The guests do not seem to mind; many take courses with the in-house dive shop, practicing in the pool or the crystal-clear sea. Others snorkel or just soak up the view from the large Jacuzzi. Owner-manager Dr. Jotiban is a doting, pleasant host. ⊠ *98 M. 5 Klong Nin Beach, Lanta Yai, 81150* ☎ *075/662668 or 075/662670* ⊕ *www.narima-lanta.com* ⇨ *32 rooms* ⌂ *In-room: refrigerator. In-hotel: restaurant, pool, laundry service, public Internet* ⊟ *MC, V.*

Andaman Coast Essentials

Transportation

BY AIR

Six domestic airlines, ranging from pricey boutique to no-frills budget, travel to Phuket and Krabi international airports daily. Thai Airways, Bangkok Airways, and Phuket Air are among the more sophisticated ones—food and full service are offered on board. Budget airlines, like Nok Air, Air Asia, and One-Two-Go by Orient Thai Air, provide similar service, but food and beverages must be purchased on board for a reasonable price. Each day, more than 20 domestic flights fly from Bangkok to Phuket, whereas only 10 flights go to Krabi. One-way prices from Bangkok to either destination range from B500 to B2,500; flight duration averages about one hour to either destination.

AIRPORTS & TRANSFERS Most travelers head to Phuket International Airport as flights generally cost less and arrive with greater frequency. Phuket International Airport lies on the northern end of the island. A ride to Phuket Town (where you get the ferry to Phi Phi and Krabi) takes about 45 minutes; and to Khao Lak it's about 1½ hours. Krabi International Airport is very close to Krabi Town, only a 20-minute taxi ride away. It's a 45-minute trip to Ao Nang from Krabi's airport, and 2 hours by taxi or minibus to Koh Lanta.

Both Krabi and Phuket international airports have taxis waiting outside, but they also have cheaper minivan service to most tourist destinations. Minivans won't leave until they're full, which can happen either very quickly or after a considerable time. Using the toilet prior to visiting the taxi stand may result in missing the only minivan available until the next flight arrives. Other times, you may have to wait 30 minutes before they are certain that they will have to drive off with empty seats. You're better off checking in with the minivans first to make sure you get a seat and if it looks like its not going to be full—or if you're headed to somewhere off the beaten path—opt for a taxi. Minibuses from Krabi Airport to Krabi Town cost B100, to Ao Nang, B200. Taxis are B350 and B600, respectively. Taxis from the airport to Koh Lanta cost B2,300, whereas minibuses (which depart from Krabi Town/Ao Nang rather than the airport) cost only B300–B400.

🔲 Info **Air Asia** ☎ 02/515-9999 in Bangkok, 075/623554 in Krabi ⊕ www.airasia.com. **Bangkok Airways** ☎ 1771 or 02/655-5555 ⊕ www.bangkokair.com. **Nok Air** ☎ 1318 ⊕ www.nokair.com. **Orient Thai Air** ☎ 1126, 02/267-3210 in Bangkok ⊕ www.fly12go.com. **Phuket Air** ☎ 02/679-8999 ⊕ www.phuketairlines.com. **Thai Airways** ☎ 02/628-2000 in Bangkok, 075/636541 in Krabi ⊕ www.thaiairways.com.

BY BOAT & FERRY

Ferry travel is the easiest way for travelers to island-hop. The most popular routes start in Phuket, stopover on Koh Phi Phi, and then continue on to Ao Nang and Koh Lanta or vice versa. However, ferry routes are seasonal, so always double-check schedules.

Boats running the Phuket–Koh Phi Phi routes operate year-round. Seatran and Royal Fern Ferry depart from Ratsada Pier on Phuket at about 8 AM and 1:30 PM for the two-hour journey to Phi Phi Don. PP Cruiser also takes about two hours to reach Phi Phi Don, but departs from Makham Pier. One-way prices on any carrier range from B250 to B350 per person.

PP Family and Ao Nang Travel & Tour also offer other inter-beach and interisland connections. Routes connect Phuket, Koh Phi Phi, Krabi Town, Ao Nang, Nang Cape (Railay Beach), and Koh Lanta in a multitude of ways. Ao Nang Travel departs from Ao Nang, whereas PP Family connects at Krabi. Most boats traveling between Krabi/Ao Nang and Phuket stop at Nang Cape (Railay Beach) and Koh Phi Phi. PP Family boats between Krabi and Koh Lanta stop briefly at Koh Jum. These routes are usually more convenient than land transfer, however, boats servicing Koh Lanta are in daily operation only from mid-October to May. Fares from Krabi/Ao Nang to Lanta or Phi Phi both cost around B350.

Speedboats to the Similan and Surin islands from Phuket or Khao Lak operate only when the national parks are open to the public (November–May). Speedboats to Surin National Park depart from Kuraburi Pier in Takuapa District in early morning once a day. Speedboats to Similan National Park leave from Thaplamu Pier in Tai Muang District at 8:30 AM.

Fisherman boats from Phuket's Bang Rong Pier take you to Koh Yao Yai and Noi five times daily starting from 8:30 AM for a mere B50 per person. The journey takes 45 minutes to one hour.

Longtail boats from Krabi Town and Ao Nang to Nang Cape serve tourists all year round. Travel via longtail from Ao Nang takes 15 minutes and costs B60 per person. Longtails from Chao Fa Pier in Krabi Town cost B120 per person but will not leave until boats are full.

📡 Boat & Ferry Lines **Ao Nang Travel & Tour Co.** ✉ 183/87 Phang Nga Rd., Muang, Phuket, 83000 ☎ 076/232040 or 076/232041 ⊕ www.krabi-tourism.com/aonangtravel. **PP Family Co.** ✉ Kohngka Rd. (Kohngka Pier), Krabi 81000 ☎ 075/612463 ⊕ www. ppfamily.com. **Royal Fern Co.** ✉ 148/11 Suthat Rd., Talad Yai, Muang, Phuket, 83000 ☎ 076/232240, 076/232317, or 076/232975 ⊕ www.phuketdir.com/royalfernco/. **Seatran Travel** ✉ 64/423 Anupas-Phuket-Karn Rd, Ratsada, Muang, Phuket, 83000 ☎ 076/355410 up to 12, 076/219391 ⊕ www.seatran.co.th.

BY BUS

Buses from Bangkok to Krabi, Phang Nga, and Khao Lak leave from Bangkok's Southern Bus Terminal. VIP and first-class buses leave once every evening around 6 or 7 PM. Public buses leave Krabi for Bangkok at 8 AM and 4 and 5:30 PM. Reservations are recommended for VIP and first-class, especially during Thai holidays. Trips to and from the Andaman Coast take at least 12 hours. If you are pressed for time, flying is a much quicker option, and costs only a little more if booked in advance or if travel is done on off-peak days.

Bus and boat combination tickets are available from Krabi to Koh Samui and Koh Phangan, departing on the seven-hour journey at 9 AM, 11 AM, or 4 PM.

There's also bus service from Phuket to Krabi, Phang Nga, and Khao Lak. First-class buses (B117) leave Phuket every hour for the three-hour journey to Krabi. There is no direct bus from Phuket to Khao Lak, but you can take a local bus that is bound for Ranong, Surat Thani, or Kuraburi and ask to get dropped off in Khao Lak.

Songthaews are the most cost effective way to travel between Krabi Town and Ao Nang. Fares should be no more than B50 between the two towns. In Krabi Town they can be hired from the corner of Maharat Soi 4 and Pruksa Uthit Road. In Ao Nang, they cruise the main road looking for passengers and have Krabi–Ao Nang signs displayed.

BY CAR

If you are driving from Bangkok, Phang Nga is 788 km (400 mi) and Krabi is 814 km (505 mi) south, as the crow flies. The main road that leads south is Petchkasem Road or Highway 4, which narrows to a one-lane road once you leave the greater Bangkok sprawl. The road is heavily trafficked by long-haul transport trucks and driving without familiarity of Thai driving habits can be unsettling, especially at night.

Krabi Airport has Avis, National, and Budget rental counters. Budget also has an office in Ao Nang. Prices start from B1,200/day. There is a B300 extra charge to have the car picked up elsewhere in Krabi if you are planning on departing via boat, rather than heading off from the airport. Call ahead and ask about frequent specials, including a pick-up in Krabi and drop-off in Phuket combo. Numerous other local agencies rent simple four-wheel-drive jeeps for around B1,200, which are ideal for exploring many of the islands that have muddy, rugged road conditions.

BY TAXI

Taxis are the most expensive way to travel by land in Southern Thailand, usually only worth the cost if you're traveling with a group that can split the cost. A taxi ride from Krabi Airport to Ao Nang costs B600. In many touristy destinations, un-registered taxi drivers are in every corner touting for customers. Make sure you negotiate a price that you are happy with prior to accepting a ride. A good negotiator can often procure a taxi and driver for an entire day for little more than the price of a rental car.

BY TRAIN

There is no train service to Phuket, Phang Nga, or Krabi. The nearest train station for travel to Phang Nga is to the east in Surat Thani and the nearest to Krabi and Phuket is to the south in Trang. However, bus tickets can be purchased at Bangkok's Hua Lamphong train station for buses departing Surat Thani after the overnight train has arrived there.

The bus should take five to six hours to either destination and cost around B500.

Contacts & Resources

BANKS & EXCHANGING SERVICES

Banks and ATMs are easy to locate in big towns like Krabi Town and Ao Nang. All banks will exchange foreign currency. Remember that hotel exchange rates differ significantly from those at banks or currency exchange houses. The more remote the hotel, the less you'll get for your dollar. Most major credit cards are accepted by medium to large tour operators and accommodations. Some will charge a service fee for accepting your card.

Western Union is available in Krabi Town at Kongka Pier, at Siam City Bank.

EMERGENCIES

Tourist police are on call 24/7; call 1699 or 1155 in the Andaman Coast area if you need assistance. Hospitals in Krabi and Phuket should be able to deal competently with most medical emergencies; if you have more serious problems, you should try to get back to Bangkok.

It's a good practice to alert your hotel's staff if you are taking day trips to more remote islands.

🛂 Emergency Numbers **Marine Police** ☎ 076/211883. **Tourist Police** ☎ 1155, 1699, 076/219878 in Phuket, 075/637028 in Ao Nang.

🛂 Hospitals **Bangkok Phuket Hospital** ✉ 2/1 Hongyok Rd., Phuket Town ☎ 076/254425. **Koh Lanta Hospital** ✉ Lanta Old Town ☎ 075/697068. **Krabi Hospital** ✉ 325 Uttarakit Rd., Krabi Town ☎ 075/631768, 075/631769, or 075/611210. **Phang Nga Hospital** ✉ 436 Petchkasem Rd., Phang Nga Town ☎ 076/412034.

VISITOR INFORMATION

The Tourism Authority of Thailand (TAT) has a central office covering Phang Nga, Krabi, and Phuket at the visitor information center in Phuket Town. Krabi and Phang Nga towns have their own small TAT offices, where you can pick up maps and brochures, as well as information about local excursions. Tour operators and your hotel's tour desk are also good sources of information.

🛂 **Krabi** ✉ Uttarakit Rd. ☎ 075/622163. **Phuket** ✉ Phuket Rd. ☎ 076/211036, 076/212213, or 076/217138.

Northern Thailand

Wat Phra That Doi Sutnep in Chiang Mai province.

WORD OF MOUTH

"You could easily spend two or three days in Chiang Mai and then hire a driver explore the other wonderful areas of Northern Thailand. Those who spend a few days in Chiang Mai shopping and then simply go to a luxury resort miss out."

—glorialf

"Pai is really the place to trek from. We hiked to within a couple of kilometers of the Myanmar border, and it was beautiful."

—blackmarble

WELCOME TO NORTHERN THAILAND

TOP REASONS TO GO

★ **Natural Wonders** You don't have to venture far from Chiang Mai to see the region's natural beauty. You can hike to spectacular waterfalls and be back in the city in time for dinner.

★ **Shopping** The region is world famous for its silks, and the night markets of Chiang Mai and Chiang Rai have an astonishing range of handicrafts, many of them from hill tribe villages.

★ **Eating** The region's cuisine is said to be the country's tastiest. Chiang Mai has excellent restaurants, but even the simplest food stall can dish up delicious surprises.

★ **Temples** The golden spires of thousands of temples dot the region. Even the simplest one will tell you volumes about Buddhist faith and culture.

★ **Sports** The country's most beautiful golf courses are here, and nongolfers have an almost unlimited variety of sports to choose from—rock climbing, white-water rafting, and paragliding are just a few.

Elephants in Chiang Mai.

1 Chiang Mai & Environs. Northern Thailand's principal city is a vibrant regional hub, modern and expanding rapidly outside its historic, moat-ringed, and partially walled center. Its famous Night Bazaar attracts shoppers from around the world, who are catered to with world-class hotels and restaurants.

2 Nan & Environs. Northern Thailand's most remote provincial capital is a fascinating destination. Nan is reached by a long but worthwhile drive from Chiang Mai along empty highways lined by fruit orchards, paddy fields, and jungle-clad uplands. The city's Pumin temple and its unique frescoes are reason enough to tackle the journey.

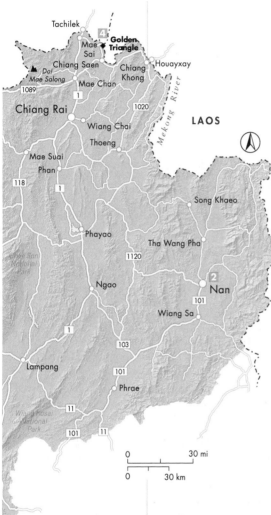

GETTING ORIENTED

A journey through Northern Thailand feels like venturing into a different country from the one ruled by far-off Bangkok: the landscape, the language, the architecture, the food, and even the people of this region are quite distinct. Chiang Mai is the natural capital of the north. The city is not a smaller version of Bangkok, but a bustling metropolis in its own right. Just beyond the city rises the mountain range that forms the eastern buttress of the Himalayas, and the region overall has some of the country's most dramatic scenery. The northernmost part of the region borders both Myanmar (Burma) and Laos, and improved land crossings into Laos from here have made forays into that country popular side trips.

3 The Mae Hong Son Loop. Set two or three days aside for traveling Thailand's famous tourist trail, which begins and ends in Chiang Mai, winding through spectacular mountain scenery for much of the way. Although the route is named after its principal town, Mae Hong Son, the quiet village of Pai has become a major destination.

4 The Golden Triangle. The northernmost region of Thailand is mostly known for its former role as the center of the opium trade; it has a museum devoted to the subject that's a worthy side trip. Beyond its fascinating past, the area has much to recommend it: mountain scenery, boat trips on the Mekong River, and a few luxurious resorts.

Workers in a rice field

NORTHERN THAILAND PLANNER

How Much Can You Do?

To really get a feel for Northern Thailand, plan on spending at least a week here.

If You Have 2 Days Spend your first day exploring the streets of Chiang Mai. On the second day rise early and drive up to Wat Phra That Doi Suthep. In the afternoon, visit the Elephant Training Center at Mae Sa.

If You Have 5 Days On your first two days, cover the major sights in and around Chiang Mai. On the third day, fly to Mae Hong Son and take a tour of a nearby Karen village. Set out the next day (by hired car or bus) for Chiang Rai. You might want to consider overnighting in Tha Ton or Chiang Dao. On the fifth day make a circular tour to Chiang Saen to see its excavated ruins and meet the Mekong River, then to Ban Sop Ruak to visit the magnificent new Hall of Opium. Finally, head to Mae Sai for a look at Burmese crafts in the busy local markets.

If You Have 7 Days If you're lucky enough to have a week or more in Northern Thailand, you'll have plenty of time to stay for a few nights with a hill tribe family. Treks to these mountain villages, most often done on elephants, can be arranged from Chiang Mai, Chiang Rai, Mae Hong Son, and other communities.

Getting Around

Northern Thailand appears to be a very remote area of Asia, far from the country's capital, Bangkok, or other major centers. In fact, this region, bounded on the north, east, and west by Myanmar and Laos, is easily accessible, and its main cities and towns are linked to Bangkok by frequent and reliable air services and connected regionally by a network of highways. An excellent regional bus service also links every town and most villages, however remote.

Chiang Mai is Northern Thailand's self-described "hub," although the country's main north–south artery, Highway 1, bypasses the city and actually connects Bangkok with Chiang Rai and the Golden Triangle. An arm of the motorway, Highway 11, branches off for Chiang Mai at Lampang, itself a major transport hub with a long-distance bus terminal, railroad station, and airport. There are several flights a day from Bangkok to Chiang Mai and Chiang Rai, and regular flights from the capital to Lampang, Mae Hong Son, and Nan.

From Chiang Mai you can reach the entire region on well-paved roads, with travel times not exceeding eight hours or so. The journey on serpentine mountain roads to Mae Hong Son, however, can be very tiring, requiring a stopover in either the popular resort town of Pai or quieter, more sedate Mae Sariang. Similarly, Chiang Rai offers a convenient stopover on the road north to the Golden Triangle.

Lampang is less than two hours' drive south from Chiang Mai, and is also a convenient and comfortable center from which to explore the nearby national parks and lakes. Nan, whose temples rival those of Chiang Mai and Lampang, sits in a remote valley with few routes in and out—if you're traveling there from Bangkok, it's advisable to do one leg of the journey by air.

When to Go

Northern Thailand has three seasons. The region is hottest and driest from March to May. The rainy season runs from June to October, with the wettest weather in September. Unpaved roads are often impassable at this time of year. The best season to visit is winter from November to March, when days are warm, sunny, and generally cloudless and nights pleasantly cool. (At higher altitudes, it can be quite cold in the evening.)

It's advisable to book hotel accommodation a month or two ahead of the Christmas and New Year holiday periods and the Songkran festival, which falls in mid-April.

Health

Malaria and other mosquito-borne diseases are virtually unknown in the urban centers in the north, but if you're traveling in the jungle during the rainy season (June to October), you might consider taking antimalarials. If you're trekking in the mountains or staying at hill tribe villages pack mosquito repellent. It's advisable to spray your room about a half hour before turning in, even if windows have mosquito screens and beds have mosquito nets. Some treks are particularly arduous, so find room in your backpack for lotions to soothe aching muscles. A small first-aid kit is also advisable.

Safety

Chiang Mai and other communities in Northern Thailand are generally safe. However, it's a good idea to leave your passport, expensive jewelry, and large amounts of cash in your hotel's safe when you go out. Keep a copy of your passport's relevant pages with you at all times, as police can demand proof of identification and levy a fine if you can't produce it. Always walk holding bags on the side of you that faces away from the street, as Chiang Mai has its share of motorcycle thieves who snatch your bag as they drive by.

Regional Cuisine Highlights

The cuisine in the northern part of the country differs significantly from the rest of Thailand, although most restaurants serve both types. Locals prefer the glutinous *khao niao* (sticky rice), using handfuls of it to scoop up sauces and curries, but you'll have no problem finding plain *khao suay* (steamed rice) or fragrant jasmine rice. A truly northern and very popular Muslim specialty is *khao soy*, a delicious pork or chicken curry with crispy and soft noodles, served with pickled cabbage and onions. Lively debates take place on the best khao soy restaurants and at least one establishment—Just Khao Soy in Chiang Mai—serves only this dish.

Another specialty is *hang led*, a pork curry spiced with ginger. Chiang Mai's sausages are nationally famous—try *sai ua* (crispy pork sausage) and *mu yo* (spicy sausage). Noodles of nearly every variety can be bought for a few baht from food stalls, and some fried-noodle dishes, particularly pad thai, have found their way onto many menus. Also try *nam pik ong* (pork, chilies, and tomatoes), *gaeng ke gai* (chicken curry with chili leaves and baby eggplant), and *kap moo* (crispy pork served with *nam pik num*, a mashed chili dip). Western food is served at all larger hotels, although the local version of an "American" or "English" breakfast can be a shock.

WHAT IT COSTS In Baht

	$$$$	$$$	$$	$	¢
RESTAURANTS	Over B400	B301–B400	B201–B300	B100–B200	under B100
HOTELS	over B6,000	B4,001–B6,000	B2,001–B4,000	B1,000–B2,000	under B1,000

CHIANG MAI & ENVIRONS

Updated by
Robert Tilley

Chiang Mai, known as the "Rose of the North," has ambitious plans: it wants to expand beyond its role as a provincial capital to become a gateway to Myanmar, Laos, and western China. New luxury hotels are shooting up, attracting more business and leisure travelers. The airport is being expanded to accommodate more and larger airplanes, and already there has been an increase in the number of direct flights from Europe and Asia. And although the country's main highway, Highway 1, bypasses Chiang Mai as it runs between Bangkok and Chiang Rai, officials have made sure the city is at the center of a spider's web of highways reaching out in all four directions of the compass, with no major city or town more than a day's drive away.

It's a long way between Bangkok and Chiang Mai—nearly 700 km (420 mi)—but there are several very comfortable options for making the journey. Because of the distance, most visitors decide to fly from Bangkok to Northern Thailand. The 70-minute flight to Chiang Mai and the 90-minute flight to Chiang Rai are relatively inexpensive. (If you have the time to shop around, you can arrange return flights with most travel agents for as low as US$40.) The airports of both Chiang Mai and Chiang Rai are a 10- to 15-minute taxi ride from city centers. Express trains and long-distance buses take either an entire day or night to cover the distance. Trains are among the most comfortable in Southeast Asia, and even second-class sleeper accommodations compare favorably with American and European standards. Long-distance buses—the most comfortable are termed VIP—have fully reclinable seats, hostesses serving snacks and drinks, and TV (although they usually show absurd Thai comedies). The bus fare (B500–B670) includes lunch or supper at a stop along the way.

Regional buses connect Chiang Mai to nearby towns such as Lamphun and Lampang, which make them easy excursions. The Golden Triangle and the mountains near the Myanmar border, home of many hill tribes, are farther afield, but are readily accessible by air or by bus.

Chiang Mai

696 km (430 mi) north of Bangkok.

Chiang Mai's rich history stretches back 700 years to the time when several small tribes, under King Mengrai, banded together to form a new nation called Anachak Lanna Thai. Their first capital was Chiang Rai, but after three decades they moved it to the fertile plains near the Mae Ping River to a place they called Napphaburi Sri Nakornping Chiang Mai.

The Lanna Thai eventually lost their independence to Ayutthaya and, later, to Myanmar. Not until 1774—when the Burmese were finally driven out—did the region revert to the Thai kingdom. After that, the region developed independently of Southern Thailand. Even the language is different, marked by a more relaxed tempo. In the last 50 years the city has grown beyond its original borders; the provincial capital has exploded beyond its moated city walls, expanding far into the neighboring countryside.

First impressions of modern Chiang Mai can be disappointing. The immaculately maintained railroad station and the chaotic bus terminal are in shabby districts, and the drive into the city center is far from spectacular. First-time visitors ask why they can't see the mountains that figure so prominently in the travel brochures. Once you cross the Ping River, Chiang Mai begins to take shape. The Old City is roughly 2½ square km (1 square mi), bounded by a moat where fountains splash and locals stroll along a flower-bordered promenade. Much of the wall that once encircled the city has been restored, and the most important of its five original gates, called Pratou Tha Phae, fronts a broad square where markets and festivals are constantly in full swing. Chiang Mai's brooding mountain, Doi Suthep, is now in view, rising in steps over the Old City.

> ## TEMPLE KNOW-HOW
>
> Most temple complexes open about 6 AM and don't close until 6 or 8 PM, although the hours can be irregular and the doors may be locked for no reason. If that's the case, approach any monk and explain you'd like to visit. He'll normally open up the temple. There's no admission charge, but leave some change in one of the collection boxes found throughout the compound. (By making a donation you're also "making merit" and easing your journey to the hereafter.) In some temples, caged birds are for sale—you're expected to set them free, another means of making merit.

Enter the Old City and you're in another world. Buildings more than three stories high have been banned, and guesthouses and restaurants vie with each other for the most florid decoration. Many of the streets and *sois* (alleys) have been paved with flat, red cobblestones. Strolling these narrow lanes, lingering in the quiet cloisters of a temple, sipping hill tribe coffee at a wayside stall, and fingering local fabrics in one of the many boutiques are among the chief pleasures of a visit to Chiang Mai. Whenever you visit, there's bound to be a festival in progress.

Getting Around Chiang Mai

Under a multimillion dollar program to improve the sometimes chaotic transport system, Chiang Mai's songthaews are gradually being phased out, to be replaced by metered taxis. It will take a few years before taxis are a familiar sight on Chiang Mai roads, but you can have your hotel arrange one for you. The basic charge is B30, plus a B20 booking fee. If you hire a taxi for a day (B1,000–B1,400, depending on mileage), negotiate the price in advance or, better yet, arrange it the evening before and have the driver collect you from your hotel in the morning. Do not pay the driver until you have completed the trip.

Motorcycles are a cheap and popular option. Rental agencies are numerous, and most small hotels have their own agency. A car and driver is the most convenient way to visit the temples outside the city. If you're planning on driving yourself you'll need an international license—and strong nerves. Try to avoid driving in the city during rush hours, which

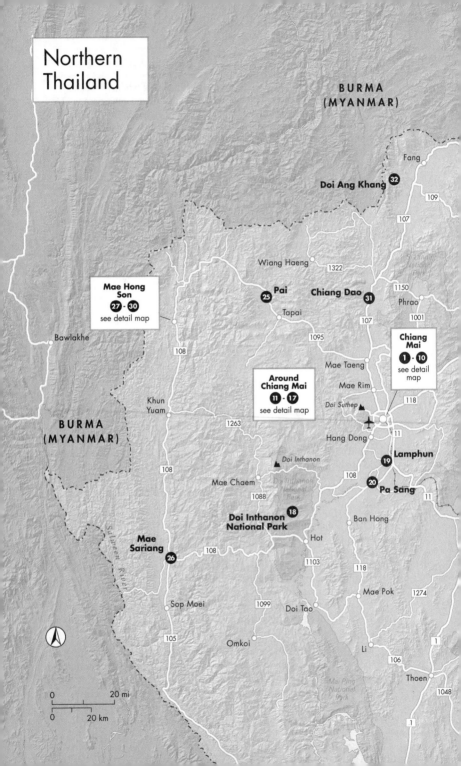

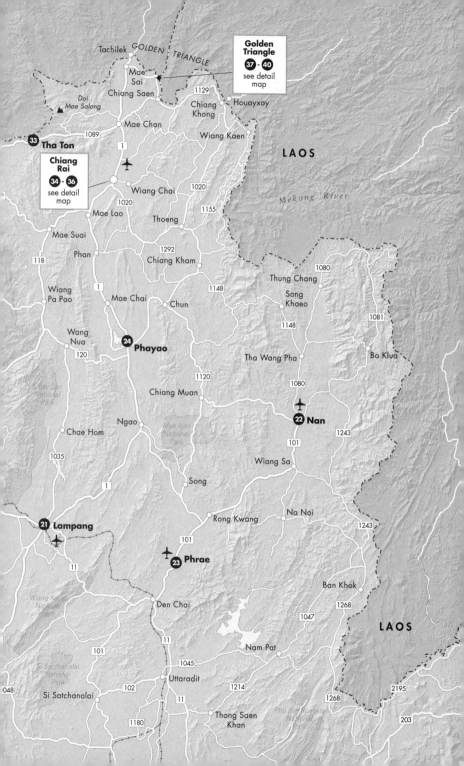

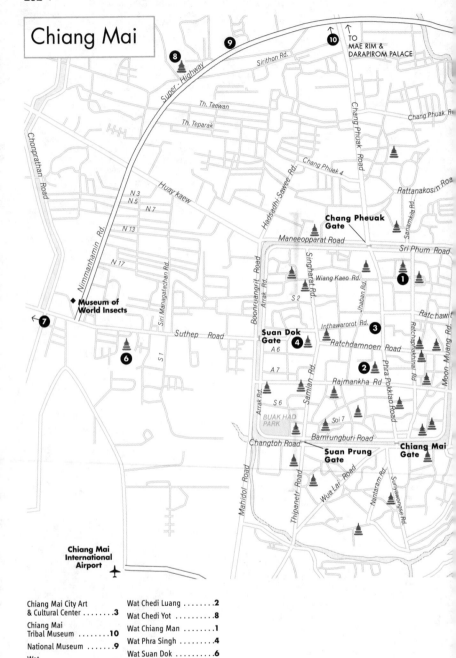

Chiang Mai

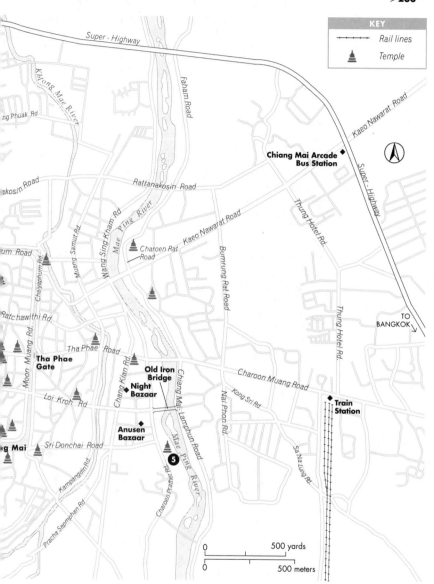

KEY

+—+—+ Rail lines

🛕 Temple

Super - Highway

Faham Road

Khlong Mae River

ng Phuak Rd

Kaeo Nawarat Road

Chiang Mai Arcade ◆
Bus Station

Super - Highway

akosin Road

Rattanakosin Road

Thung Hotel Rd

um Road

Muang Sing Kham Rd.

Muang Samut Rd.

Mae Ping River

Charoen Rat
Road

Kaeo Nawarat Road

Burnrung Rat Road

Chaiyapum Rd.

Ratchawithi Rd.

Thung Hotel Rd.

TO
BANGKOK

Moon Muang Rd.

Tha Phae Road

**Tha Phae
Gate**

Chang Klan Rd.

**Old Iron
Bridge**

Charoen Muang Road

Loi Kroh Rd

**Night
Bazaar**

Chiang Mai-Lamphun Road

Nai Phon Rd.

Kong Sri Rd

◆ **Train
Station**

**Anusen
Bazaar**

g Mai

Sri Donchai Road

❺

Mae Ping River

Sa Na Lung Rd.

Kampangdin Rd.

Charoen Prathet Rd.

Pracha Sampphan Rd.

0 ———— 500 yards

0 ———— 500 meters

starts as early 7 in the morning and 3 in the afternoon, and pay special attention to no-parking restrictions (usually 9 AM–noon and 3 PM–6 PM). Parking is prohibited on many streets on alternate days, but the explanatory signs are in Thai. Your best bet is to note on which side of the street vehicles are parking. Chiang Mai's traffic police are merciless and clamp and tow away vehicles parked illegally. Parking lots are numerous and charge as little as B20 for all-day parking.

Chiang Mai Proper

Covering roughly 2½ square km (1 square mi), the patchwork of winding lanes that make up Chiang Mai's Old City is bounded by remains of the original city wall and a wide, water-filled moat. Connected by about half a dozen major thoroughfares, this system of one-way streets can be confusing for a newcomer. The plan, however, keeps traffic moving quite effectively around the moat, which is crossed by bridges at regular intervals. The compact Old City can be explored easily on foot or by bicycle. Tuk-tuks and songthaews cruise the Old City and can easily be flagged down if you tire or want to take a trip outside the ancient walls. Count on paying B50 for a tuk-tuk ride to the Night Market area or B15 if a songthaew is going that way.

Start any tour of the Old City at the Tha Pae Gate, which leads through the ancient city walls into the oldest part of Chiang Mai. Heading west on Ratchadamnoen Road and turning north on Ratchaphakhinai Road will bring you to the first of the area's major sights, Wat Chiang Man, the oldest temple in Chiang Mai. Backtracking down Ratchaphakhinai Road and heading west on Ratchadamnoen Road will bring you to Wat Chedi Luang and Wat Phra Singh. Several other worthwhile temples are outside the city walls. To the east is the serene Wat Chaimongkol. It's an easy walk from the Tha Pae Gate if the sun isn't too strong. You'll want to take a tuk-tuk to Wat Suan Dok, one of the largest temples in the region. A bit farther away are the verdant grounds of Wat Umong.

WHAT TO SEE **Chiang Mai City Art & Cultural Center.** The handsome city museum is housed
❸ in a colonnaded palace that was the official administrative headquarters of the last local ruler, Chao (Prince) Inthawichayanon. Around its quiet central courtyard are 15 rooms with exhibits documenting the history of Chiang Mai. ■ TIP→ **In another small, shady courtyard is a delightful café.** The palace was built in 1924 in the exact center of the city, site of the ancient city pillar that now stands in the compound of nearby Wat Chedi Luang. In front of the museum sits a statue of the three kings who founded Chiang Mai. ⊠ *Phrapokklao Rd.* ☎ *053/217793 or 053/*
❿ *219833* ▭ *B90* ⊘ *Tues.–Sun. 8:30–5.* **Chiang Mai Tribal Museum.** This museum has more than 1,000 pieces of traditional crafts from the hill tribes living in the region. The varied collection—farming implements, hunting traps, weapons, colorful embroidery, and musical instruments—is one of the finest in the country. It's in Ratchangkla Park, off the road to Mae Rim, about 1 km (½ mi) from the National Museum. ⊠ *Ratchangkla Park, Chotana Rd.* ☎ *053/210872* ▭ *Free* ⊘ *Daily 9–4.*

♻ **Museum of World Insects & Natural Wonders.** Save a visit to this offbeat museum for a rainy day. Children love its oddball display of creepy-crawlies, which include enormous centipedes, beetles, moths, gaudy butterflies, and the world's largest collection of individual mosquito species. ✉ *72 Soi 13, Nimman-hemin Rd.* ☎ *053/211891* 🏷 *B200* ⊙ *Daily 8:30–4:30.*

❾ National Museum. This Northern Thai–style building contains many statues of Lord Buddha, including a bust that measures 10 feet high. There's also a huge Buddha foot-print of wood with mother-of-pearl inlay. The exhibits have been skill-fully arranged into topics such as the early history of the Lanna region, the founding of Chiang Mai, and the development of city's distinctive

> **TOURIST POLICE**
>
> Chiang Mai has a Tourist Police, which can be helpful in dealing with minor emergencies, thefts, or shady antiques dealers. Expatriate volunteers now assist the Tourist Police—they wear black uniforms and a "Tourist Police" badge. The volunteers' powers are limited, but they are equipped to handle most situations or at least direct you to someone who can assist you further.

art forms. The centerpiece of one display is a regal bed covered with mosquito netting that was used by an early prince of Chiang Mai. ✉ *Super Hwy., Chiang Mai–Lampang Rd.* ☎ *053/221308* 🏷 *B30* ⊙ *Daily 9–4.*

★ **❺ Wat Chaimongkol.** Although rarely visited, this small temple is well worth the journey. Its little chedi contains holy relics, but its real beauty lies in the serenity of the grounds. Located outside the Old City near the Mae Ping River, it has only 18 monks in residence. ✉ *Charoen Prathet Rd.*

❷ Wat Chedi Luang. In 1411 King Saen Muang Ma ordered his workers to build a chedi "as high as a dove could fly." He died before the struc-ture was finished, as did the next king. During the reign of the follow-ing king, an earthquake knocked down about a third of the 282-foot spire, and it's now a superb ruin. The parklike grounds contain a vari-ety of assembly halls, chapels, a 30-foot-long reclining Buddha, and the ancient city pillar. ✉ *Phrapokklao Rd. between Ratchamankha and Ratchadamnoen Rds.*

Fodor's Choice
★

❽ Wat Chedi Yot. Wat Photharam Maha Viharn is more commonly known as Wat Chedi Yot, or Seven-Spired Pagoda. Built in 1455, it's a copy of the Mahabodhi temple in Bodh Gaya, India, where the Buddha is said to have achieved enlightenment. The seven intricately carved spires rep-resent the seven weeks that he subsequently spent there. The sides of the chedi have striking bas-relief sculptures of celestial figures, most of them in poor repair but one bearing a face of hauntingly contemporary beauty. The temple is just off the highway that circles Chiang Mai, but its green lawns and shady corners are strangely still and peaceful. ✉ *Super Hwy. between Huay Kaew Rd. and Chang Puak Rd.*

❶ Wat Chiang Man. Chiang Mai's oldest monastery, dating from 1296, is typ-ical of Northern Thai architecture. It has massive teak pillars inside the bot (chapel), and two important images of the Buddha sit in the small build-ing to the right of the main viharn. ■ TIP→ **The Buddha images are suppos-edly on view only on Sunday, but sometimes the door is unlocked.**

★ **❹** ✉ *Ratchaphakhinat Rd.* **Wat Phra Singh.** In the western section of the Old

Massages & Spa Treatments

CHIANG MAI has no shortage of massage parlors (the respectable kind) where the aches of a day's strenuous sightseeing can be kneaded away with a traditional massage. Your hotel can usually organize either an in-house massage or recommend one of the city's numerous centers. Good massages with or without accompanying herbal treatments are given at **Suan Samoon Prai** (✉ 105 Wansingkham Rd. ☎ 053/252716). A two-hour full-body massage costs B200. If you want to do a good deed for Thai society as well as enjoy a great massage, stop by Chiang Mai's **women's prison** (✉ 115 Ratvithee Rd.). Female inmates trained in Thai massage are allowed to practice their trade in a room adjoining the prison's shop (where handicrafts from the prison workshops are sold). A two-hour Thai massage costs B150—money well spent in assuring these (remarkably cheerful) women a solid foundation for life outside the prison walls.

Chiang Mai also has dozens of spas specializing in Thai massage and various treatments involving traditional herbs and oils. The original **Oasis Spa** (✉ 102 Sirimungklajan Rd. ☎ 053/227494 ⊕ www. chiangmaioasis.com) has grown into a chain of three establishments in Chiang Mai. All offer a full range of different types of massage from Swedish to traditional Thai and a slew of mouthwatering body scrubs like Thai coffee, honey and yogurt, or orange, almond, and honey. The other two branches are at Samlan Road and in the Amora Hotel on Charyaphum Road. The number above will connect you to all three.

At the **Ban Sabai Spa Village** (✉ 17/7 Charoen Prathet Rd. ☎ 053/285204) you can get your massage in a wooden Thai-style house or in a riverside sala. Treatments of note include a steamed herb massage, wherein a bundle of soothing herbs is placed on the body, and various fruit-based body masques like honey-tamarind or pineapple.

City stands Chiang Mai's principal monastery, Wat Phra Singh, which was extensively renovated in 2006. The beautifully decorated wat contains the Phra Singh Buddha, with a serene and benevolent expression that is enhanced by the light filtering in through the tall windows. Note the temple's facades of splendidly carved wood, the elegant teak beams and posts, and the masonry. Don't be surprised if a student monk approaches you to practice his English. ✉ *Phra Singh Rd. and Singharat Rd.*

6 **Wat Suan Dok.** To the west of the Old City is one of the largest of Chiang Mai's temples, Wat Suan Dok. It's said to have been built on the site where bones of Lord Buddha were found. Some of these relics are believed to be inside the chedi; others were transported to Wat Phra That Doi Suthep. At the back of the viharn is the bot housing Phra Chao Kao, a superb bronze Buddha figure cast in 1504. Chiang Mai aristocrats are buried in stupas in the graveyard. ✉ *Suthep Rd.*

7 **Wat Umong.** The most unusual temple in Chiang Mai is Wat Umong, dating from 1296. According to local lore, a monk named Jam liked to

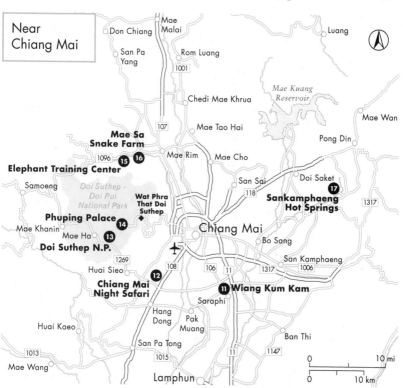

go wandering in the forest. This irritated King Ku Na, who often wanted to consult with the sage. So he could seek advice at any time, the king built this wat for the monk in 1380. Along with the temple, tunnels were constructed and decorated with paintings, fragments of which may still be seen. Beyond the chedi is a pond filled with hungry carp. Throughout the grounds the trees are hung with snippets of wisdom such as "Time unused is the longest time." ⊠ *Off Suthep Rd., past Wat Suan Dok.*

Near Chiang Mai

Beyond the highway that surrounds Chiang Mai you will find plenty to hold your attention. The most famous sight is Wat Phra That Doi Suthep, the mountaintop temple that overlooks the city. The mountain road that skirts Doi Suthep, winding through the thickly forested Mae Sa Valley, is lined with tourist attractions for much of its way, from bungee-jumping towers to orchid farms.

WHAT TO SEE **Chiang Mai Night Safari.** Modeled on Singapore's famous game park, the Chiang Mai Night Safari realized a long-held dream of Thaksin Shin-nawatra, the country's former prime minister (he was deposed in a military coup in September 2006). The 100-acre reserve on the edge of the Doi Suthep-Pui National Park, 10 km (6 mi) from downtown Chiang Mai, has more than 100 species of wild animals, including tigers, leop-

Monk Chat

IF YOU'RE LIKE MOST PEOPLE, a visit to Chiang Mai's numerous temples is likely to leave you full of unanswered questions. Head to Wat Suan Dok or Wat Chedi Luang, where help is at hand. The monks and novice monks who reside in the two temples eagerly welcome foreign visitors for chats about the history of their temples, the Buddhist faith, and Thai history and culture. Their enthusiasm isn't totally altruistic—they're keen to practice their English.

The talkative monks at Wat Suan Dok are all students of a religious university attached to the temple. Their "monk chat" takes place 5:30–7:30 PM on Monday, Wednesday, and Friday. Their counterparts at Wat Chedi Luang can be approached Monday to Saturday noon–6:30 PM as they relax under the trees of their parklike compound. They urge foreign visitors to converse with them about Lanna culture, life in a monastery, or, as one monk put it, "anything at all."

ards, jaguars, and elephants. The park is open afternoons and all day on weekends, as well as until midnight daily, but for a real thrill board one of the special trams and tour the grounds after dark. ⊠ *Km 10, Chiang Mai–Hod Rd.* ⊠ *B100 daytime, B500 nighttime* ⊗ *Weekdays 1 PM–4 PM and 6 PM–midnight, weekends 10–4 and 6 PM–midnight.*

Chiang Mai Zoo. On the lower slopes of Doi Suthep, this zoo's cages and enclosures are spaced out along paths that wind leisurely through shady woodlands. If the walk seems too strenuous, you can hop on an electric trolley that stops at all the sights. The most popular animals are two giant pandas, Lin Hui and Chuang Chuang—the only ones in captivity in Southeast Asia. ⊠ *100 Huay Kaew Rd.* ☎ *053/221179* ⊠ *B30, B200 to view the pandas* ⊗ *Daily 9–5.*

Darapirom Palace. This Lanna-style mansion was the last home of Jao Dararasamee, daughter of a late-19th-century ruler of Chiang Mai and the favorite wife of King Chulalongkorn. The low-eaved and galleried building has been restored and furnished with many of the princess's antiques, including clothes she designed herself. It's a living museum of 19th-century Lanna culture and design, well worth the 12 km (8 mi) journey from Chiang Mai. ⊠ *Chiang Mai–Mae Rim Rd.* ⊠ *B20* ⊗ *Tues.–Sun. 9–5.*

⑬ Doi Suthep National Park. You don't have to head to the distant mountains to go trekking during your stay in Chiang Mai. Doi Suthep, the 3,542-foot peak that broods over the city, has its own national park with plenty of hiking trails to explore. One of these paths, taken by pilgrims over the centuries preceding the construction of a road, leads up to a gold-spired wat. ■ TIP→ **It's a half-day hike from the edge of the city to the temple compound. Set off early to avoid the heat of the midday sun.** If it's not a public holiday, you'll probably be alone on the mountain.

An easy hike lasting about 45 minutes brings you to one of Chiang Mai's least known but most charming temples, **Wat Pha Lat.** This modest ensemble of buildings is virtually lost in the forest. Make sure to explore the compound, which has a weathered chedi and a grotto filled with images of the Buddha. After you leave Wat Pha Lat, the path becomes steeper. After another 45 minutes you emerge onto the mountain road, where you can flag down a songthaew if you can't take another step. Otherwise follow the road for about 200 yards and pick up the path in a break in the forest. The trail leads inexorably upward, emerging just below the *naga*-flanked (nagas are mythical snakes believed to control the irrigation waters in rice fields) staircase that leads to Wat Pra That. A funicular can carry you to the top, but the true pilgrim's way is up the majestic steps. Your reward is a breathtaking view.

> ### THE MAE SA VALLEY
>
> This very beautiful upland valley winds behind Chiang Mai's Doi Suthep and Doi Pui mountain range. A well-paved 100-km (60-mi) circular route begins and ends in Chiang Mai, and is lined by resorts, country restaurants, tribal villages, two bungee-jumping installations, an elephant center, a snake farm, a monkey colony, orchid hothouses, and the Queen Sirikit Botanical Gardens. The route follows Highway 1001 north from Chiang Mai, turning left at Mae Rim onto Highways 1096 and then 1269, returning to Chiang Mai from the south on Highway 108. **Nakornlanna C. Ltds** a taxi service (☎ 053/279291 or 053/271242).

The trail begins at the entrance of the national park, reached by a 5-minute ride in one of the songthaews FodorsChoice ★ that wait for passengers at the end of Huay Kaew Road, near the entrance to Chiang Mai Zoo. **Wat Phra That Doi Suthep** is perched on the top of 3,542-foot Doi Suthep. You can find songthaews to take you on the 30-minute drive at Chuang Puak Gate, the Central Department Store on Huay Kaew Road and outside the entrance to Wat Phra Singh. When you arrive, you are faced with an arduous but exhilarating climb up the broad, 304-step staircase flanked by 16th-century tiled balustrades taking the customary form of *nagas* (mythical snakes believed to control the irrigation waters in rice fields). ■ TIP➔ **If you find the ascent too daunting, there's a funicular railway that provides a much easier way to the top.**

As in so many chapters of Thai history, an elephant is closely involved in the legend surrounding the foundation of Wat Phra That, Northern Thailand's most revered temple and one of only a few enjoying royal patronage. The elephant was dispatched from Chiang Mai carrying religious relics from Wat Suan Dok. Instead of ambling off into the open countryside, it stubbornly climbed up Doi Suthep. When it finally came to rest, and after turning in a pattern of circles given symbolic significance by the party accompanying it, the solemn decision was made to establish a temple on the site that would contain the relics. Over the centuries the temple compound grew into the glittering assembly of chedis, bots, viharns, and frescoed cloisters you see today. The vast terrace, usually smothered with flowers, commands a breathtaking view of Chiang Mai, spread out like an apron on the plain below. Constructing the temple was quite a feat—until 1935 there was no paved road to the temple. Workers and pilgrims alike had to slog through thick jungle. The

Northern Thailand Then and Now

AS LATE AS 1939 Northern Thailand was a semiautonomous region of Siam, with a history rich in tales of kings, queens, and princes locked in dynastic struggles and wars. The diversity of cultures you'll find here today is hardly surprising, since the ancestors of today's Northern Thai people came from China, and the point where they first crossed the mighty Mekong River, Chiang Saen, became a citadel-kingdom of its own as early as 773. Nearly half a millennium passed before the arrival of a king who was able to unite the citizens of the new realm of Lanna ("a thousand rice fields").

The fabled ruler King Mengrai (1259–1317) also established a dynasty that lasted two centuries. Mengrai's first capital was Chiang Rai, but at the end of the 13th century he moved his court south and in 1296 founded a new dynastic city, Chiang Mai. Two friendly rulers, King Ngarm Muang of Phayao and King Rama Kampeng of Sukhothai, helped him in the huge enterprise, and the trio sealed their alliance in blood, drinking from a chalice filled from their slit wrists. A monument outside the city museum in the center of Chiang Mai's Old City commemorates the event. Nearby, another monument marks the spot where King Mengrai died, in 1317, after being struck by lightning in one of the fierce storms that regularly roll down from the nearby mountains.

Lanna power was weakened by waves of attacks by Burmese and Lao invaders, and for two centuries—from 1556 to the late 1700s—Lanna was virtually a vassal Burmese state. The capital was moved south to Lampang, where Burmese power was finally broken and a new Lanna dynasty, the Chakri, was established under King Rama I.

Chiang Mai, nearby Lamphun (also at the center of Lanna-Burmese struggles), and Lampang are full of reminders of this rich history. Lampang's fortified Wat Lampang Luang commemorates with an ancient bullet hole the spot where the commander of besieging Burmese forces was killed.

To the north is Chiang Rai, a regal capital 30 years before Chiang Mai was built. This quieter, less-developed town is slowly becoming a base for exploring the country's northernmost reaches. In the far north, the Chiang Saen, site of the region's first true kingdom, is being excavated, its 1,000-year-old walls slowly taking shape again. Chiang Saen is on the edge of the fabled Golden Triangle. This mountainous region, bordered by Myanmar to the west and Laos to the east, was once ruled by the opium warlord Khun Sa, whose hometown, Ban Sop Ruak, has a magnificent museum, the Hall of Opium, tracing the story of the spread of narcotics.

Chiang Mai and Chiang Rai are ideal bases for exploring the hill tribe villages, where people live as they have for centuries. The communities closest to the two cities have been overrun by tourists, but if you strike out on your own with a good map you may still find some that haven't become theme parks. Most of the villages are bustling crafts centers where the colorful fabrics you see displayed in Bangkok shop windows take shape before your eyes. The elaborately costumed villagers descend into Chiang Mai and Chiang Rai every evening to sell their wares in the night markets that transform thoroughfares into tented bazaars.

road was the result of a vast community project—individual villages throughout the Chiang Mai region contributed the labor, each laying 1,300-foot sections. ⊠ *Huay Kaew Rd.* 🚠 *B70 (includes funicular railway fare); entry to the National Park B400* ☉ *Daily 6–6.*

☺ **⑮ Elephant Training Center.** Animal shows aren't everybody's idea of fun, but the Elephant Training Center in the Mae Sa Valley, is actually quite entertaining. The big fellows are treated well and seem to enjoy showing off their skills. They certainly like the dip they take in the river before demonstrating log-rolling routines and giving rides. ⊠ *Between Mae Rim and Samoeng* 🚠 *B500* ☉ *Daily 8:30–noon.*

⑯ Mae Sa Snake Farm. If you're fascinated by slithering creatures, you'll find them not only at Chiang Mai Zoo but at this snake farm on the Mae Sa Valley road. There are cobra shows at 11:30 AM, 2:15 PM, and 3:30 PM, during which the snakes are "milked" for their venom. ⊠ *Mae Rim–Samoeng Rd.* ☏ *053/860719.*

NEED A BREAK?

If you're visiting the Elephant Training Center or the Mae Sa Snake Farm, stop for lunch at **Mae Sa Valley Resort** (⊠ Mae Rim–Samoeng Rd. ☏ 053/291051). It's a pretty place, with thatched cottages in beautifully tended gardens. The owner's honey-cooked chicken with chili is particularly good.

⑭ Phuping Palace. The summer residence of the royal family is a serene mansion that shares an exquisitely landscaped park with the more modest mountain retreats of the crown prince and princess. The palace itself cannot be visited, although the gardens are open daily 9–5, unless any of the royal family is in residence (usually in January). Flower enthusiasts will swoon at the sight of the roses—among the lovely blooms is a variety created by the king himself. A rough, unpaved road left of the palace brings you after 4 km (2½ mi) to a village called Doi Pui Meo, where most of the Hmong women seem busy creating finely worked textiles (the songthaew return fare there is B300). On the mountainside above the village are two tiny museums documenting hill tribe life and the opium trade. ⊠ *Off Huay Kaew Rd., 6 km (4 mi) past Wat Phra That Doi Suthep.*

⑰ Sankamphaeng Hot Springs. Among the most spectacular in Northern Thailand, these hot springs include two geysers that shoot water about 32 yards into the air. The spa complex, set among beautiful flowers, includes an open-air pool and several bathhouses of various sizes. There's a rustic restaurant with a view over the gardens, and small chalets with hot tubs are rented either by the hour (B200) or for the night (B800). Tents and sleeping bags can also be rented for B80. The spa is 56 km (35 mi) north of Chiang Mai, beyond the village of San Kamphaeng. Songthaews bound for the spa leave from the riverside flower market in Chiang Mai. ⊠ *Moo 7, Tambon Ban Sahakorn Mae-On* ☏ *053/929077 or 053/929099* 🚠 *B20* ☉ *Daily 8–6.*

⑪ Wiang Kum Kam. When King Mengrai decided to build his capital on the Ping River, he chose a site a few miles south of present-day Chiang Mai. He selected a low-lying stretch of land, but soon realized the folly of his choice when the river flooded during the rainy seasons. Eight years after establishing Wiang Kum Kam, he moved to higher ground and

Back to School

IF SPENDING TIME IN monasteries makes you wonder about the lives of the monks, or if you find yourself so enthralled by delicious dishes that you want to learn how to prepare them, you're in luck. Chiang Mai has hundreds of schools offering classes in anything from aromatherapy to Zen Buddhism. Alternative medicine, cooking, and massage are the most popular courses, but by no means the most exotic. In three weeks at the Thailand's Elephant Conservation Center near Lampang you can train to become a fully qualified mahout.

Cooking: Chiang Mai has dozens of classes—some in the kitchens of guesthouses, others fully accredited schools—teaching the basics of Thai cuisine. Courses cost B800–B1,000 a day. Among the best cooking classes is the **Baan Thai Home Cooking Course** (⊠ 11 Ratchadamnoen Rd. ☎ 053/357339). **Chiang Mai Cookery School** (⊠ 42/7 Moon Muang Rd. ☎ 053/206388 ⊕ www. thaicookeryschool.com) is attached to one of the city's best Thai restaurants, The Wok. One of the city's most popular budget lodgings, **Gap's House** (⊠ 4 Ratchadamnoen Rd., Soi 3 ☎ 053/278140), also runs an excellent cooking school. A trek through the mountains usually involves eating simple meals cooked over an open fire. One Chiang Mai cooking course teaches how to prepare these simple, flavorful meals. The so-called "jungle course" is organized by **Smile House** (⊠ 5 Rachamankha Rd., Soi 2 ☎ 053/208661) and costs about B800.

Dancing: Surprise your friends by learning the ancient art of Thai dancing at the **Thai Dance Institute**

(⊠ 53 Kaokrang Rd., Nuanghoy ☎ 053/801375). A two-hour course teaching you a few of the graceful movements costs B800.

Jewelry: One- to five-day courses in jewelry making are offered at **Nova Artlab** (⊠ 201 Tha Pae Rd. ☎ 053/ 273058 ⊕ www.nova-collection.com). You can also study sculpture, leatherwork, painting, and photography–all for B1,100 a day.

Language: The **American University Alumni** (⊠ 73 Ratchadamnoen Rd. ☎ 053/278407) has been around for more than 20 years. Charges vary according to the duration of the course and the number of pupils. **Corner Stone International** (⊠ 178/ 233 Moo 7, Nhongkwai, Hang Dong ☎ 053/430450) has both group and individual instruction.

Massage: Held at the Chiang Mai University Art Museum, the **Thai Massage School** (⊠ Nimmanhemin Rd. ☎ 053/907193 ⊕ www.tmcschool. com) is authorized by the Thai Ministry of Education. Courses lasting two to five days cost B2,560 to B4,800. The **Chetawan Thai Traditional Massage School** (⊠ Opposite Rajabhat University, on Pracha Uthit Rd. ☎ 053/410360 ⊕ www. watpomassage.com) is affiliated to Bangkok's famous Wat Po massage school. Courses cost B800 a day.

Yoga: The **Yogasala** (⊠ 48/1 Rachamankha Rd. ☎ 05/208452 ⊕ www.cmyogasala.com) has a five-day yoga course that costs B1,500. The **Yoga Center** (⊠ 65/1 Arak Rd. ☎ 061/ 927375) has five-day workshops costing B1,800. The 90-minute "open classes" on Tuesday, Thursday, and weekends cost B200.

began work on Chiang Mai. Wiang Kum Kam is now being excavated, and archaeologists have been amazed to uncover a cluster of buildings almost as large as Chiang Mai's Old City. **Chiangmai Cattleya Tour & Travel Services** (⊠ 141/24 Moo 2, San Kamphaeng Rd. ☎ 053/ 248829) offers morning and afternoon tours for B700. ⊠ *4 km (2½ mi) south of Chiang Mai on the old Chiang Mai–Lamphun Rd. ☎ No phone* ⌦ *Free.*

Where to Eat

All of the city's top hotels serve reasonably good food, but for the best Thai cuisine go to the restaurants in town. Several good restaurants serving Northern Thai cuisine are across from the Amari Rincome Hotel on Nimmanhemin Road, about 1½ km (1 mi) northwest of downtown. Also try the food at the Anusan Market, found near the Night Bazaar. Chiang Mai also has Northern Thailand's best restaurants serving European food, and some of its French, Italian, and Spanish restaurants rival those of Bangkok.

$$$–$$$$ ✕ **The House.** A white stucco city mansion is home to central Chiang Mai's most elegant restaurant and bar. Reserve a table either inside the teak-floored, chandelier-lighted dining room, where a guitarist plays nightly, or in the neighboring tapas bar, a sybaritic den of plump cushions and oriental carpets. The plate of mixed tapas is a meal in itself, and the accompanying Spanish wines are superb (but expensive). You can also peruse a more comprehensive menu in the restaurant. ⊠ *199 Moon Muang Rd.* ☎ *053/419011 up to 14* △ *Reservations essential* ⊟ *AE, MC, V.*

$$–$$$ ✕ **Chez Daniel.** Although Chiang Mai has fancier French restaurants, none can match the value offered by Daniel at his charming restaurant on the airport road. A typical three-course lunch menu of salad, home-cured charcuterie, and crepes in Daniel's own alcohol-laced orange sauce costs less than B200, while the B350 menu often features free-range chicken from royal project farms. The dining room is classic French, with Gallic attention to table settings and tableware. ⊠ *251/18 Mahidol Rd.* ☎ *053/204800* ⊟ *MC, V.*

$$–$$$ ✕ **Mi Casa.** The Basque chef and his charming Singaporean wife offer an eclectic international menu with a distinctly Spanish emphasis at their very appealing restaurant, which is in a converted Thai house tucked away near the Chiang Mai University campus. The mixed tapas (at B280) are an Iberian dream and would serve as a meal for two. A B250 lunchtime set menu features prime beef, pork, and fish, all prepared in a highly imaginative fashion. Reservations are advised. ⊠ *60 Moo 6 Suthep Rd.* ☎ *053/810088* ⊟ *MC, V* ☉ *Closed Mon.*

★ $–$$ ✕ **The Gallery.** Awards have been heaped on this very attractive riverside restaurant, both for its architecture (a combination of Chinese and Lanna styles) and its cuisine, which embraces dishes from three continents. Guests enter through a gallery (the "Elephant Collection"), cross a secluded courtyard with an open-air barbecue, and proceed into a teak-floored dining area with tables set with eggplant-color linen. A Northern Thai string ensemble plays in the evening, while a subtly integrated bar-café offers some of Chiang Mai's best jazz and blues. ⊠ *25–29 Charoen Rat Rd.* ☎ *053/248601* ⊟ *AE, DC, MC, V.*

Where to Stay & Eat in Chiang Mai

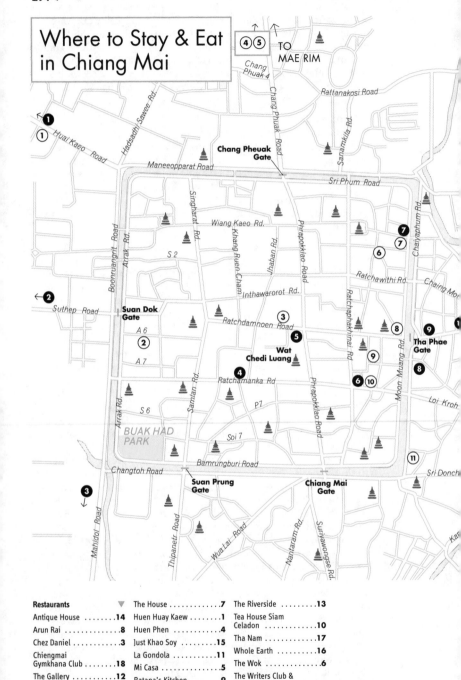

TO MAE RIM

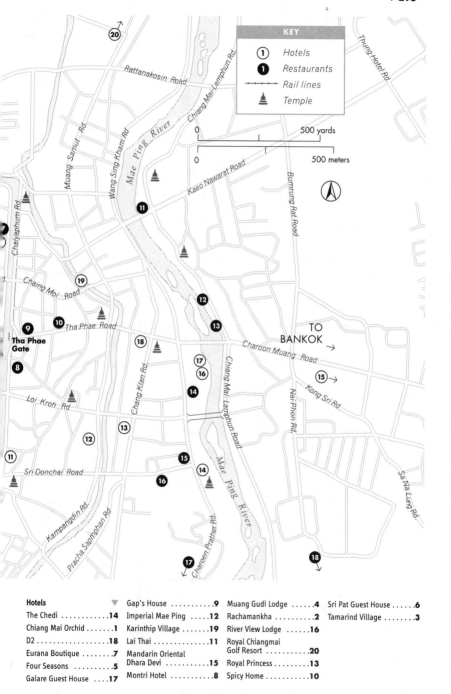

Hotels		
The Chedi	**14**	
Chiang Mai Orchid	**1**	
D2	**18**	
Eurana Boutique	**7**	
Four Seasons	**5**	
Galare Guest House	**17**	
Gap's House	**9**	
Imperial Mae Ping	**12**	
Karinthip Village	**19**	
Lai Thai	**11**	
Mandarin Oriental Dhara Devi	**15**	
Montri Hotel	**8**	
Muang Gudi Lodge	**4**	
Rachamankha	**2**	
River View Lodge	**16**	
Royal Chiangmai Golf Resort	**20**	
Royal Princess	**13**	
Spicy Home	**10**	
Sri Pat Guest House	**6**	
Tamarind Village	**3**	

★ **$** ✕ **Antique House.** Built in 1870, this teak-beamed home is one of Chiang Mai's true treasures. It's furnished with antiques from Chiang Mai's finest shops. If you like the chair you're sitting on or the table in front of you, it's possible to add to your (surprisingly modest) bill an order for a replica from a local workshop. The menu, of course, is authentic northern cuisine. A big surprise is the wine list—small but very interesting. ✉ *71 Charoen Prathet Rd.* ☎ *053/276810* ▭ *MC, V.*

$ ✕ **Chiengmai Gymkhana Club.** The son of the author of *Anna and the King of Siam* was among the founders of Chiang Mai's delightfully eccentric Chiengmai Gymkhana Club. Harking back to when it was founded, the club insists on keeping the spelling of the city used back in 1898. Polo isn't played as often now, but a very horsey crowd gathers regularly at the restaurant for lunch and dinner. Visitors are more than welcome. The food is remarkably good, with a variety of local and foreign dishes. Sporty types can enjoy a round of golf on the 9-hole course or a set or two of tennis. ✉ *349 Chiang Mai–Lamphun Rd.* ☎ *053/ 241035 or 053/247352* ▭ *MC, V.*

$ ✕ **Just Khao Soy.** Northern Thailand's favorite dish, khao soy, has been turned into a work of art at Shane Beary's stylish, brick-floored restaurant one block from the river. The eponymous dish—a bowl of meat soup topped up with crispy fried noodles—is served on an artist's palette, with the various condiments taking the place of the paint pots. Diners are issued aprons—eating khao soy can be messier than tackling lobster. ✉ *108/2 Charoen Prathet Rd.* ☎ *053/818641* ▭ *DC, MC, V.*

$ ✕ **La Gondola.** Chiang Mai has more than a dozen Italian restaurants, but La Gondola is regarded as one of the best. A glassed-in dining room is bordered on two sides by a terrace overlooking the river. There's something festive about the white-and-gold decor, matched by crisp table linens and sparkling table settings. The pasta certainly has no match elsewhere in Chiang Mai, and it would be hard to find a more comprehensive wine list. Reservations are advised on weekends. ✉ *Rimping Condominium, 201/6 Charoen Rat Rd.* ☎ *053/306483* ▭ *AE, DC, MC, V.*

$ ✕ **The Riverside.** Housed in a century-old teak house on the banks of the Mae Ping River, this casual restaurant serves Western favorites given some extra zing by the Thai chef. The conversation-laden atmosphere attracts young Thais as well as Westerners, and with lots of beer flowing the food gets only partial attention. Choice tables are on the deck, where you're treated to views of Wat Phra That, the golden-spired temple that sits on the summit of distant Doi Suthep. ✉ *9–11 Charoen Rat Rd.* ☎ *053/ 243239* ⌕ *Reservations not accepted* ▭ *MC, V.*

$ ✕ **Whole Earth.** On the second floor of an attractive old house, this longtime favorite serves delicious and healthy foods. It's mostly vegetarian fare, but there are a few meat dishes for the carnivorous, such as *gai tahkhrai* (fried chicken with lemon and garlic). Many of the favorites here, including the tasty eggplant masala, are Indian dishes. The dining room is air-conditioned, and the garden terrace that surrounds it takes full advantage of any breezes. The service is sometimes slow. ✉ *88 Sri Donchai Rd.* ☎ *053/282463* ⌕ *Reservations not accepted* ▭ *MC, V.*

★ **¢–$** ✕ **Huen Huay Kaew.** Thai families escape the heat of the city by dining at this rustic restaurant built of bamboo and ancient teak and perched by the edge of a waterfall at the base of Doi Suthep mountain. Some of the tables in the multitiered dining area are so close to the cascade that diners are cooled by the spray. The Thai food is outstanding—the *gaeng som* fish curry is cooked in a delicious tamarind reduction, and the deep-fried pork ribs come with a sauce that blends several flavors of the Thai kitchen. ⊠ *31/2 Moo 2, Huay Kaew Rd.* ☏ *053/892698* ⊟ *No credit cards.*

¢–$ ✕ **Ratana's Kitchen 1 & 2.** The original Ratana's Kitchen, especially popular with budget-minded tourists, became too small for its expanding clientele, so the owners opened an offshoot around the corner. The menus of both offer a vast choice of more than 50 low-priced dishes, ranging from basic Thai fare to Western favorites. ■ TIP➡ **If you arrive in Chiang Mai early in the morning, make straight for Ratana's Kitchen 2 for a hearty breakfast, served starting at 5 AM.** ⊠ *320–322 Tha Pae Rd.* ⊠ *82 Charyaphum Rd.* ☏ *053/874173* ⊟ *No credit cards.*

★ ¢–$ ✕ **Tea House Siam Celadon.** Escape the hustle and bustle of busy Tha Pae Road by stepping into the cool interior of this exquisitely restored century-old Chinese merchant's house. You enter through a showroom of fine celadon pottery and an adjoining courtyard flanked by tiny boutiques selling Lanna fabrics. The fan-cooled tearoom is a teak-floored salon furnished with wrought iron and glass. The menu is limited, mostly sandwiches and salads, but the pastries are among Chiang Mai's best. ⊠ *158 Tha Pae Rd.* ☏ *053/234518* ⊟ *AE, MC, V* ⊗ *No dinner.*

¢–$ ✕ **Tha Nam.** The Ping River meanders past the outdoor terrace of this rambling old Thai house. The upper floor, where a classical trio plays for evening diners, is so old and creaking that it tilts like the main deck of a schooner in a storm. The lower terrace is a lush tropical garden, shaded by enormous trees older than the house itself. The extensive menu is packed with Thai specialties—try the *hang led* (pork curry with ginger) or the chicken wrapped in pandanus leaves. ⊠ *43/3 Moo 2, Chang Klan Rd.* ☏ *053/275125* ⊟ *AE, MC, V.*

¢–$ ✕ **The Wok.** One of Chiang Mai's best cooking schools is fronted by this excellent restaurant. If the ancient teak house at the heart of the establishment is crowded, grab a table in the shrub-festooned garden. The menu is packed with local specialties like *nam prik ong* (minced pork dip), and the puddings are a delight—particularly the black rice and the pumpkin in coconut milk. ⊠ *44 Rachamankha Rd.* ☏ *053/208287* ⊟ *AE, MC, V* ⊗ *No lunch Mon.*

¢–$ ✕ **Writers Club & Wine Bar.** You don't have to be a journalist to dine at Chiang Mai's unofficial press club—the regulars include not only media types but anyone from hard-up artists and eccentric local characters to successful entrepreneurs. Local venison, wild boar, and rainbow trout frequently appear on the ever-changing menu, and the house wines are that rare vintage—good and sensibly priced. Reservations are recommended on Friday and Sunday. ⊠ *141/3 Ratchadamnoen Rd.* ☏ *053/ 814187* ⊟ *No credit cards* ⊗ *Closed Sat.*

¢ ✕ **Arun Rai.** This simple, open-sided restaurant has prepared such traditional northern dishes as frogs' legs fried with ginger for more than 30 years, adding to the menu at about the same rate as they increase the size of the airy dining room. Try the *tabong* (boiled bamboo shoots fried in batter) and *sai ua* (pork sausage with herbs). There's also a take-out service for customers in a hurry. ⊠ *45 Kotchasarn Rd.* ☎ *053/276947* ⚒ *Reservations not accepted* ⊟ *No credit cards.*

★ ¢ ✕ **Huen Phen.** The small rooms in this restaurant, once a private home, are full of handicrafts that are typical of the region. Select a table in any of the dining rooms or out among the plants of the garden. The house and garden are open only in the evening; lunch is served in a street-front extension packed daily with hungry Thais. The *kaeng hang led* (northern pork curry) with *kao nio* (sticky rice) is a specialty. The *larb nua* (spicy ground beef fried with herbs) and deep-fried pork ribs are two more dishes you won't want to miss. ⊠ *112 Rachamankha Rd.* ☎ *053/ 277103* ⊟ *MC, V.*

Where to Stay

Hopes of a big increase in tourist arrivals have fueled a hotel building boom in Chiang Mai, with several grand openings planned for 2007. The most luxurious of the new hotels rival those in Bangkok and one, the Mandarin Oriental Dhara Devi, justly claims to be among Asia's finest. Prices, however, are about half what you'd expect to pay in the capital (although in January and February surcharges tend to close the gap). The west side of Chiang Mai, toward Wat Phra That Doi Suthep, is where you'll find several of the most expensive hotels; it's a quieter part of the city, but also far from many points of interest. Unlike in Bangkok, the luxury hotels do not enjoy a monopoly on river frontage, and some charming and modestly priced guesthouses are right on the water. There are also small hotels and guesthouses within the walls of the Old City that are cheap and ideally located for sightseeing.

$$$$ ▦ **The Chedi.** The city's newest waterfront hotel sits in isolated splendor between the Mae Ping River and one of the city's busiest streets. Rooms and suites have their own private courtyard entrances and terraces overlooking either the river or the mountains. ⊠ *123 Charoen Prathet Rd., 50200* ☎ *053/253333* ⊕ *www.ghmhotels.com* ⇌ *84 rooms* ♿ *In-room: safe, refrigerator, Wi-Fi. In-hotel: restaurant, room service, pool, gym, spa, laundry service, concierge* ⊟ *AE, DC, MC, V* ⦿❘ *BP.*

$$$$ ▦ **Four Seasons.** Formerly the Regent, the magnificent Four Seasons stands

Fodor'sChoice on a hilltop above the lush Mae Rim Valley. It commands a view of ver-

★ dant mountains, tropical gardens, and its own manicured rice paddies. The accommodations are in clusters of Lanna-style buildings. Each suite has an outdoor *sala* (gazebo) ideal for breakfast or cocktails. Rooms of polished teak are furnished with richly colored fabrics and traditional art. ▮ TIP➔ **The restaurant, which serves beautifully presented Thai dishes, overlooks the valley.** ⊠ *Mae Rim–Samoeng Old Rd., 50180* ☎ *053/298181, 800/545–4000 in U.S* ⊕ *www.fourseasons.com/ chiangmai* ⇌ *67 suites* ♿ *In-room: safe, refrigerator, DVD, ethernet. In-hotel: 2 restaurants, room service, bar, 2 tennis courts, pool, gym, spa, laundry service* ⊟ *AE, DC, MC, V.*

★ $$$$ ▦ **Mandarin Oriental Dhara Devi.** This extraordinary resort is one of the most lavish in Southeast Asia. Regal in scale and style, it's a huge contrast to the shabby neighborhood that guests must navigate to reach it. Even the most modest of its accommodations is palatial. The "residences"—really freestanding villas, many with private pools—are grouped around landscaped rice fields worked by buffaloes. Concerts are given in the cultural center (with a library of 5,000 volumes) or in the outdoor amphitheater. A temple and weathered chedi were built to add historical character. ■ TIP→ **Even if you're not staying the night, book a table for dinner and visit the pavilion-like King's Room—so named because the king dined here.** ☒ *51/4 Chiang Mai–San Kampaeng Rd., Moo 1, Tambon Tasala, 50000* ☎ *053/888888* ⊕ *www.mandarinoriental.com/chiangmai* ⇱ *101 suites, 34 residences* ⚲ *In-room: safe, kitchen, DVD, Wi-Fi. In-hotel: 3 restaurants, room service, 2 bars, 2 tennis courts, pools, gym, spa, laundry service, concierge, airport shuttle* ▭ *AE, DC, MC, V.*

★ **$$$$** ▣ **Rachamankha.** On a quiet lane near Wat Pra Singh, the Rachamankha is one of the newest of the city's luxury resorts. Visually an extension of the temple compound, the hotel is a series of hushed brick courtyards enclosed by triple-eaved Lanna-style buildings. Most of the rooms, all furnished with Lanna or Chinese antiques, are set along green lawns planted with tall palms and fragrant frangipani. Collections of rare 19th-century Lanna scripture boxes and Burmese manuscript chests stand guard outside the rooms. The courtyard swimming pool is a blue haven of peace. ☒ *Rachamanka Rd., Soi 9, 50200* ☎ *053/904111* ⊕ *www.rachamankha.com* ⇱ *21 rooms, 1 suite* ⚲ *In-room: safe, refrigerator. In-hotel: restaurant, room service, bar, pool, laundry service, airport shuttle* ▭ *AE, DC, MC, V* ⦿ *CP.*

$$$–$$$$ ▣ **D2 Hotel.** The sturdy old Chiang Inn has been demolished to make
FodorsChoice way for Chiang Mai's most daringly modern hotel, a complete break
★ from the traditional Lanna style that's been so in vogue. Clean lines, brushed steel and glass surfaces, and cubist upholstery dictate the interiors, from the vast, airy, and light lobby to the beautifully lighted rooms, where a wealth of cushions compensate for the slightly minimalist look. The hotel abuts Chiang Mai's famed Night Bazaar and is surrounded by bars and restaurants. ☒ *100 Chang Klan Rd., T. Chang Klan, A. Muang, 50100* ☎ *053/999999* ⊕ *www.d2hotels.com* ⇱ *131 rooms* ⚲ *In-room: safe, refrigerator, DVD, ethernet. In-hotel: restaurant, room service, bar, pool, gym, spa, public Internet, laundry service, concierge, parking (no fee)* ▭ *AE, MC, V.*

$$$–$$$$ ▣ **Tamarind Village.** A canopy of towering, interlaced bamboo leads to the main entrance of this stylish, village-style hotel in the center of the Old City. Beyond the entrance is a blue pool, embraced by whitewashed corridors that lend a feeling of contemplative peace. Rooms, furnished in tones of cream and teak, surround a garden dominated by a venerable 200-year-old tamarind tree. ☒ *50/1 Ratchadamnoen Rd., 50200* ☎ *053/418898* ⊕ *www.tamarindvillage.com* ⇱ *40 rooms* ⚲ *In-room: safe, refrigerator. In-hotel: restaurant, room service, pool, spa, laundry service, concierge* ▭ *AE, MC, V.*

$$$ ▣ **Imperial Mae Ping.** The elegant curved facade of the Imperial Mae Ping resembles the side of a luxury cruise ship tethered to the center of Chiang Mai. Everything about the hotel is vast, from the extensive gardens to the marble, mirrored, pillared lobby. Rooms are furnished in shades of softly lighted ocher. Two of the floors have butlers assigned to each room. Four restaurants serve Thai, Chinese, Japanese, and Western food, and a beer garden provides a great place to end a hot day of sightseeing. ⊠ *153 Sri Donchai Rd., 50100* ☎ *053/283900, 02/261–9460 in Bangkok* ⊕ *www.imperialmaeping.com* ⇆ *336 rooms, 35 suites* ♨ *In-room: refrigerator. In-hotel: 4 restaurants, room service, 2 bars, pool, spa, laundry service* ⊟ *AE, DC, MC, V.*

$$$ Royal Chiangmai Golf Resort. Although this luxurious resort in the hills about 25 km (18 mi) outside Chiang Mai is geared for golfers (green fees are included in the room rate), visitors who value tea over tee are also pampered—and receive a B1,000 rebate if they renounce the pleasure of playing the resort's fine 18-hole course. The luxuriously appointed rooms, in gleaming white wings that embrace a large swimming pool, overlook either the golf course or the surrounding rolling countryside. ⊠ *169 Moo 5, Prao Rd., 5000* ☎ *053/849301, 02/233–7950 in Bangkok* ⊕ *www.royalchiangmai.co.th* ⇆ *60 rooms* ♨ *In-room: refrigerator. In-hotel: restaurant, golf course, pool, gym, spa, airport shuttle* ⊟ *AE, MC, V.*

$$ ▦ Chiang Mai Orchid. With teak pillars lining the lobby, the Chiang Mai Orchid is a grand hotel in the old style. The rooms are tastefully furnished and trimmed with hardwoods. The lavish honeymoon suite is often used by the crown prince. You can dine at either the formal Le Pavillon, which serves French fare, or at Phuping, where you can enjoy Chinese favorites. The more informal Mae Rim Café features a buffet. Stop for a cocktail in the lobby bar where a pianist plays nightly, or the cozy Opium Den. The hotel is a 10-minute taxi ride from the center of Chiang Mai. ⊠ *23 Huay Kaew Rd., 50200* ☎ *053/222099, 02/714–2521 in Bangkok* ⊕ *www.chiangmaiorchid.com* ⇆ *266 rooms* ♨ *In-room: safe (some), refrigerator. In-hotel: 2 restaurants, room service, 2 bars, pool, gym, spa, laundry service, public Internet* ⊟ *AE, DC, MC, V.*

$$ ▦ Muang Gudi Lodge. Lanna-style boutique resorts are springing up throughout Chiang Mai and beyond, so it's a delight to find a mountain retreat designed in the more graceful Sukhothai fashion. Two finely tapering Sukhothai chedis guide the way to this exquisitely conceived and furnished hotel in the hills north of Chiang Mai. The Sukhothai style is maintained throughout the breathtakingly beautiful ensemble, from the arabesque arches of the interior galleries to the airy, luxuriously appointed bedrooms. Even the courtyard swimming pool is a small replica of the pools that cooled Sukhothai more than eight centuries ago. ⊠ *815 Mae Rim-Samoeng Rd., Tambon Rim Tai, 50180* ☎ *053/299900* ⊕ *www.muanggudilodge.com* ⇆ *25 rooms* ♨ *In-room: refrigerator. In-hotel: restaurant, room service, pool, gym, spa, bicycles, laundry service, public Internet* ⊟ *AE, MC, V.*

Fodor'sChoice
★

$ ▦ Eurana Boutique Hotel. The former S.P. Hotel has blossomed into one of Chiang Mai's most attractive boutique hotels, a haven of peace and understated luxury on a quiet lane near busy Sompet market. You step through an archway, walk along a winding path lined with tropical shrubs and into a courtyard atrium ringed by rooms furnished in homey Lanna style. ■ TIP➔ **The Violet restaurant is among the best in this corner of the Old City.** ⊠ *Soi 7, Moon Muang Rd., 50200* ☎ *063/214522* ⊕ *www. euranaboutiquehotel.com* ⇆ *72 rooms* ♨ *In-room: refrigerator. In-hotel: restaurant, pool, spa* ⊟ *MC, V.*

$ ⊞ **Karinthip Village.** A statue of a mythical winged elephant welcomes you at the entrance of the Karinthip, one of many traditional Lanna touches that distinguish the hotel from others in this otherwise rather shabby corner of town. Chinese influences are also present, particularly in the furnishings of many of the rooms. For an extra B1,000 or so you can sleep in a Lanna-style four-poster, while B6,000 suites have whirlpool bath tubs and crimson-and-pink bedrooms complete with Chinese-style lounge chairs. ⊠ *50/2 Changmoikao Rd., 50300* ☎ *053/235414 or 053/ 874302* ⊕ *www.karinthipvillage.com* ➘ *62 rooms, 5 suites* ⌂ *In-hotel: restaurant, bar, pool, laundry service* ⊟ *AE, DC, MC, V.*

★ **$** ⊞ **River View Lodge.** Facing a grassy lawn that runs down to the Mae Ping River, this lodge lets you forget the noise of the city. The restful rooms have terra-cotta floors and wood furniture; some have private balconies overlooking the river. The terrace and gazebo overlooking the secluded riverside pool are pleasant retreats for an afternoon coffee or tea or an evening cocktail. It's an easy 10-minute walk to the Night Bazaar. ⊠ *25 Charoen Prathet Rd., Soi 4, 50100* ☎ *053/271109* ⊕ *www. riverviewlodgch.com* ➘ *33 rooms* ⌂ *In-room: no a/c (some), safe. In-hotel: restaurant, pool, laundry service, public Internet* ⊟ *MC, V.*

$ ⊞ **Royal Princess.** This centrally located hotel is ideal if you'd like to step out of the lobby and right into the tumult of downtown Chiang Mai. The bustling Night Market is right at the front door and the famous Night Bazaar is barely a block away. Rooms have been upgraded and reflect the light, airy atmosphere of the lobby, where a pianist or a Thai trio play nightly. The swimming pool and its tropical garden terrace and bar are a welcome retreat after a day's sightseeing or shopping. ⊠ *112 Chang Klan Rd., 50100* ☎ *053/281033* ⊕ *http://chiangmai.royalprincess. com* ➘ *182 rooms, 16 suites* ⌂ *In-room: safe, refrigerator, ethernet. In-hotel: 4 restaurants, room service, 2 bars, pool, gym, laundry service, airport shuttle* ⊟ *AE, DC, MC, V.*

★ **¢** ⊞ **Galare Guest House.** The location is the envy of many of the city's top hotels—its gardens lead right down to the Mae Ping River. Even better, it's a short walk to the Night Bazaar. The teak-paneled rooms are simply but adequately furnished and overlook a tidy garden. The terrace restaurant faces the river. The staff is happy to assist with all travel requirements, from bus, train, and plane tickets to visas to Myanmar and Laos. ⊠ *7 Charoen Prathet Rd., Soi 2, 50100* ☎ *053/818887* ⊕ *www.galare.com* ➘ *35 rooms* ⌂ *In-room: refrigerator, ethernet (some). In-hotel: restaurant, room service, laundry service, public Internet* ⊟ *MC, V.*

¢ ⊞ **Gap's Guesthouses.** The very popular Gap's House has spawned a second guesthouse, Gap's House 2, on the western edge of the city moat. It lacks some of the rustic charm of the original, but the service is friendlier and more efficient and bicycle rentals are included in the very low room rate. Both guesthouses are well placed for exploring the Old City, but the original Gap's House is the quieter of the two, sunk dreamily in a backstreet tropical oasis. Both guesthouses offer reliable tours, and the original Gap's House still ranks as one of Chiang Mai's leading cooking schools. ⊠ *Gap's House: 3 Ratchadamnoen Rd., Soi 4, 50100* ☎ *053/278140* ⊕ *www.gaps-house.com* ➘ *18 rooms* ⌂ *In-hotel: bar, restaurant* ⊠ *Gap's House 2: 43 Arak Rd.* ☎ *053/274277* ⊕ *www.gaps-*

house2.com ⮌ *11 rooms* ☖ *In-room: no a/c (some). In-hotel: bicycles, laundry service, public Internet* ☰ *MC, V.*

★ ¢ ▦ **Lai Thai.** This rambling guesthouse on a busy thoroughfare just outside the moat is a budget traveler's favorite, so book far ahead. Rooms, some of them cooled with lazily turning fans, are huddled around a courtyard with a small swimming pool. ■ TIP➡ **The adjacent open-air restaurant is also always buzzing with activity—this is the place to pick up helpful hints from seasoned travelers.** The staff is happy to arrange excursions in the area, but the prices are a bit higher than you'll find at nearby travel agencies. ⊠ *111/4–5 Kotchasarn Rd., 50100* ☎ *053/271725* ⊕ *www.laithai. com* ⮌ *110 rooms* ☖ *In-room: refrigerator. In-hotel: restaurant, pool, laundry facilities* ☰ *AE, DC, MC, V.*

¢ ▦ **Montri Hotel.** Next to the Tha Pae Gate, this hotel's central location, bordering the moat and Pratou Tha Phae, makes up what it lacks in creature comforts. It's adjacent to the bars and restaurants on Tha Pae Road and Loi Khroh Road and is an easy walk to the Night Bazaar. Most of the rooms lack a view of the moat, but they are quiet. ⊠ *2–6 Ratchadamnoen Rd., 50200* ☎ *053/211069 or 053/418480* ⊕ *www. hotelthailand.com/chiangmai/montri* ⮌ *75 rooms* ☖ *In-room: safe, refrigerator. In-hotel: restaurant, laundry service, public Internet, airport shuttle* ☰ *MC, V.*

¢ ▦ **Spicy Home.** The incredibly low rates at this very friendly little timber-built guesthouse include an evening meal, making this an incredible deal. Kun Mim, who runs the place, is an excellent cook and has a small business on the side teaching Thai cooking. The evening meals around her dining table attract not only paying guests but friends as well, so they are a great way of breaking the ice on a first visit to Chiang Mai. There are only five rooms (basic but functional and clean, sharing two bathrooms), so it's essential to book ahead. ⊠ *42/1 Rachamankha Rd., 50200* ☎ *09/5566727* ⮌ *5 rooms without bath* ☰ *No credit cards.*

¢ ▦ **Sri Pat Guest House.** This family-run establishment is one of the best deals in the Old City. The spotlessly clean and stylishly furnished little hotel sits on a cobbled lane a short walk from the moat. The light and airy rooms have twin beds with crisp linens and tiled baths. Som Pet market, with its jumble of stalls selling every kind of fresh produce, is just around the corner. ⊠ *16 Moon Muang Rd., Soi 7, 50200* ☎ *053/ 218716* ✉ *sri-pat@sri-patguesthouse.com* ⮌ *18 rooms* ☖ *In-hotel: restaurant* ☰ *No credit cards.*

Nightlife

This being Thailand, Chiang Mai has its share of Bangkok-style hostess bars. If you don't want to be hassled, there are also dozens of places where you can grab a beer and listen to live music. Many restaurants, such as the Riverside, double as bars later in the evening.

BARS The western end of Loi Khroh Road, the southern end of Moon Muang Road, and the vast **Bar Beer Center** next to the Top North Hotel on Moon Muang Road have bars where the "working girls" usually outnumber the customers, but pool tables and dartboards are valid rival attractions.

Step through the gnarled door of **The Pub** (⊠ 189 Huay Kaew Rd. ☎ 053/211550) and you could be anywhere in rural England. The bar area is hung with the usual pub paraphernalia and there's a large hearth where a log fire burns on cold evenings. The clientele is drawn mostly from Chiang Mai's large expat community. Foreign residents also favor the rather shabby **Red Lion** (⊠ 123 Loi Kroh Rd. ☎ 053/818847).

O'Malley's Irish Pub (⊠ Anusarn Market, Chang Klan Rd. ☎ 053/271921) serves draught Guinness. Regulars say it's Chiang Mai's most authentic Irish bar. **U.N. Irish Pub & Restaurant** (⊠ 24 Ratvithee Rd. ☎ 053/214554) has a nightly entertainment program, varying from live music to movies, from quiz games to live sports. The upstairs bar, with French doors onto the street, and a small side garden are cool places to while away a warm evening.

Most bars serve wine, but two have made it their specialty: **Darling** (⊠ 49/21 Huay Kaew Rd. ☎ 053/227427) is a chic place on a busy main road, compared by many to a smart New York bar but run by a British couple. The **Writers Club & Wine Bar** (⊠ 141/3 Ratchadamnoen Rd. ☎ 053/814187) is Chiang Mai's unofficial press club but open to anyone who enjoys networking in good company. The decor is "eclectic colonial."

DANCE CLUBS   Local tuppies (Thai yuppies) crowd the discotheques and music bars of the Nimmanhemin Road area, fast becoming Chiang Mai's major night scene. Visiting ravers under 40 won't feel out of place in haunts like **Warm Up** (⊠ 251 Nimmanhemin Rd.) or the **Monkey Club** (⊠ Soi 9, Nimmanhemin Rd.). If you prefer to remain anonymously unobtrusive on the disco floor, then **Bubbles** (⊠ Charoen Prathet Rd. ☎ 053/270099) is the place, where the spotlights pierce the gloom only at 2 AM closing time. It adjoins the Pornping Tower Hotel. The **Horizon Club** (⊠ Loy Kroh Rd. ☎ 053/905000), in the basement of the Central Duang Tawan Hotel, is a popular addition to the local night scene.

In the Chiang Mai Orchid Hotel, **Club 66** (⊠ 100–102 Huay Kaew Rd. ☎ 053/222099) caters to a stylish, sophisticated crowd. For sophisticated dining and dancing, try the Empress Hotel's **Crystal Cave Supper Club** (⊠ 199/42 Chang Klan Rd. ☎ 053/270240).

CABARET   In the Las Vegas–style cabaret show staged nightly at the **Simon Chiang ★   Mai** (⊠ 177 G Bldg., Chang Phuak Rd. ☎ 053/410321) the girls are actually boys. The costumes and sets are so spectacular, and the dance routines so decorous, that people take the whole family. The theater isn't easy to find, tucked behind the Novotel Hotel in the Chang Phuak district. Performances are at 7:30 PM and 9:30 PM.

KHANTOKE   Khantoke (or kantoke) originally described a revolving wooden tray on which food is served, but it has now come to mean an evening's entertainment combining a seemingly endless menu of northern cuisine and presentations of traditional music and dancing. With sticky rice, which you mold into balls with your fingers, you sample delicacies like *kap moo* (spiced pork skin), *nam prik naw* (a spicy dip made with onions, cucumber, and chili), and *kang kai* (a chicken and vegetable curry).

Among the best of places offering khantoke is the sumptuously temple-like **Khum Khantoke** (⊠ Chiang Mai Business Park, 139 Moo 4, Nong Pakrung ☎ 053/304121). Another popular place for khantoke is **Kan-**

toke Palace (✉ 288/19 Chang Klan Rd. ☎ 053/272757). The **Vista Hotel** (✉ 252 Phrapokklao Rd. ☎ 053/210663) has a nightly khantoke show and dinner in its **Khum Kaew Palace,** costing B160 for hotel guests and B260 for other visitors. The **Old Chiang Mai Cultural Center** (✉ 185/3 Wualai Rd. ☎ 053/275097), a fine ensemble of traditional teak-built houses, accompanies a multicourse dinner with traditional music and dancing. The B320 charge includes transport to and from your hotel.

MUSIC A rough, unnamed alleyway off Ratchaphakinai Road has become the in-place for local night owls, who nightly pack the dozen or so open-air or open-sided music bars. The best of them are **Babylon (formerly the Rasta Café)** and **Heaven Beach.** Thai rock is the specialty of the vast beer hall called **Sai Lom Joi** (✉ 125 Chang Klan Rd. ☎ 053/247531). **Tha Nam** (✉ 43/3 Moo 2, Chang Klan Rd. ☎ 053/275125) has nightly performances of Thai classical music.

The east bank of the Ping River between Nawarat Bridge and Nakorn Ping Bridge resounds nightly with live music. Most of the decibels come from the **Riverside** (✉ 9–11 Charoen Rat Rd. ☎ 053/243239). Next door, the **Good View** (✉ 13 Charoen Rat Rd. ☎ 053/241866) has a variety of bands that play nightly. Farther along the riverbank, the **Gallery** (✉ 25–29 Charoen Rat Rd. ☎ 053/248601) has a café-bar adjacent to its restaurant where some of the city's best jazz can be heard nightly. A few doors down, crowds pack in late every night to hear one of Chiang Mai's finest guitarists, Lek, at the **Brasserie** (✉ 31 Charoen Rat Rd. ☎ 053/241665).

Sports & the Outdoors

BOATING **Two-hour cruises** along Chiang Mai's Ping River depart daily between 8:30 AM and 5 PM from the **River Cruise Seafood Restaurant** (✉ Charoen Prathet Rd. ☎ 053/274822) landing at Wat Chai Mongkol, Charoen Prathet Road. A dinner cruise sets off nightly at 7:30 PM.

For a taste of how the locals used to travel along the Ping River, take a ride in a scorpion-tail boat. Two companies operate services from the east bank of the river, between Nawarat Bridge and Rattanakosin Bridge. The large rudder at the stern of this sturdy Siamese craft gives it its name. **Scorpion-tail boat tours** (✉ Charoen Rat Rd. ☎ 01/885–0663 or 01/884–4621) has several trips daily between 10 AM and 5:30 PM, and there are dinner cruises departing at 7 PM.

GOLF Chiang Mai is ringed by championship golf courses that will challenge players of all levels. The **Chiengmai Gymkhana Club** (☎ 053/241035) has a 9-hole course just 1 mi from the city center; green fees are B400 per day. Farther out, on the road north to San Khamphaeng, is the city's principal championship course, the **Chiang Mai-Lamphun Golf Club** (☎ 053/880880 ⊕ chiangmaigolf.com). **Northern Express Tour** (✉ Chiang Mai–Lamphun Rd., Soi 9, Nong Hoi ☎ 09/850–7344) has a "tee off service" that delivers golfers to any one of four courses near Chiang Mai. The service costs B800. Between the airport and the city center, near the junction of Hangdong and Mahidol roads, there's a two-tier driving range, with a good restaurant and coffee shop.

HORSEBACK RIDING
North of Chiang Mai, **J & T Happy Riding** (✉ Mae Rim–Samoeng Rd. ☎ 05/036–1227) sponsors trail rides through the beautiful Mae Sa Valley. Beginners are welcome. The stables are opposite the Mae Sa Orchid Farm.

ROCK CLIMBING
You can go rock climbing right in the center of Chiang Mai at The Peak, a three-story-tall artificial rock face. **The Peak Rock Climbing School** (✉ 282 Chang Klan Rd. ☎ 053/820777 ⊕ www.thepeakadventure. com) offers climbs for first-timers costing B300 and three-day courses for more advanced climbers costing B5,800. A four-day tour that includes climbs up rock faces in the Pai and Mae Hong Son areas costs B7,100. The facility is on Chang Klan Road behind the Night Bazaar.

THAI BOXING
Professional muay thai (Thai boxing) contestants square off every Thursday night at the **Tha Pae Boxing Stadium** (✉ The Beer Bar Center, Moon Muang Rd., behind True Blue Pub). The program starts at 9 PM; admission is B400.

Shopping

Day-to-day life in Chiang Mai seems to revolve around shopping. The delightful surprise is that you don't have to part with much of your hard-earned money—even the most elaborately crafted silver costs a fraction of what you'd expect to pay at home. Fine jewelry, weighed and priced at just above the current market value, pewter, leather, and silk are all on display all around the city.

Fodor'sChoice
★
The justifiably famous **Night Bazaar,** on Chang Klan Road, is a kind of open-air department store filled with stalls selling everything from inexpensive souvenirs to pricey antiques. In the afternoon and evening traders set up tented stalls, confusingly known as the Night Market, along Chang Klan Road and the adjoining streets. You're expected to bargain, so don't be shy. Do, however, remain polite. ■ TIP➔ **Many vendors believe the first and last customers of the day bring good luck, so if you're after a real bargain (up to 50% off) start your shopping early in the day.**

Another permanent bazaar, the **Kalare Night Bazaar,** is in a big entertainment complex on the eastern side of the Night Market on Chang Klan Road; it's clearly marked. It's packed with boutiques, stalls, cheap restaurants, and a beer garden featuring nightly performances of traditional Thai dances. If you're in Chiang Mai on a Sunday, make for the so-called **Walking Street Market** on Ratchadamnoen Road. It's cheaper and far more authentic than the market on Chang Klan Road.

SHOPPING GUIDES

Before setting off on a shopping expedition in Chiang Mai, buy a copy of *Shopping Secrets of Chiang Mai,* a comprehensive 280-page visitors' guide containing in-depth information on virtually everything the city has to offer. It's available in most bookstores. Or page through the local English-language monthlies *Guidelines* or *Art & Culture Lanna*. Both are packed with advertisements and information featuring an astonishing variety of local crafts by trustworthy dealers. The magazines are available free of charge in most hotels.

5

ANTIQUES   If you follow certain common-sense rules—examine each item very carefully for signs of counterfeiting (new paint or varnish, tooled damage marks) and ask for certificates of provenance and written guarantees that the goods can be returned if proved counterfeit—shopping for antiques should present few problems. ■ TIP→ **Reputable stores will *always* provide certificates of provenance,** aware that penalties for dishonest trading are severe (if you're ever in doubt about a deal contact the Tourist Police).

The Night Bazaar in Chiang Mai has two floors packed with antiques, many of which were manufactured yesterday (and hence come with no guarantee of authenticity). Some stalls have the genuine article, among them **Lanna Antiques** (⊠ Chang Klan Rd.). It's the second booth on the second floor.

The road south to Hang Dong (take the signposted turn before the airport) is lined with antiques shops. Just outside Hang Dong you'll reach the craft village of Ban Tawai. You could spend an entire morning or afternoon rummaging through its antiques shops and storerooms.

ART   Chiang Mai has a vibrant artists' scene, and several small galleries dot the city. **La Luna** (⊠ Charoen Rat Rd. ☎ 053/306678 ⊕ www.lalunagallery. com) has regular exhibitions by top local and regional artists. The **Writers Club and Wine Bar** (⊠ 141/3 Ratchadamnoen Rd.) has a permanent, rotating exhibit of work by Myanmar artists, many of whom are political dissidents and unable to show in their native country. A number of other restaurants feature displays of Thai art. The best of them is **The Gallery** (⊠ 25–29 Charoen Rat Rd. ☎ 053/248601).

HANDICRAFTS   For local handicrafts, head to two of Chiang Mai's main shopping streets, Tha Pae Road and Loi Kroh Road. On Tha Pae Road **Living Space** (⊠ 276–278 Tha Pae Rd. ☎ 053/ 874156 ⊕ www.livingspacedesigns. com) is worth seeking out for its very original and aesthetic collection of home decor items. Across the Nawarat Bridge, Charoen Rat Road is home to a row of refurbished old teak houses with a handful of boutiques selling interesting crafts such as incense candles and carved curios. Farther afield, along Nimmanhemin Road near the Amari Rincome Hotel, a whole neighborhood of crafts shops has developed. The first lane on the left, Soi 1, has some of the most rewarding.

The money you pay for a woven mat or carved mask goes directly to the local communities at the **Hilltribe Products Promotion Center** (⊠ 21/17 Suthep Rd. ☎ 053/277743). Here

---

OTOP

To encourage each *tambon* (community) to make the best use of its special skills, the government set up a program called **OTOP** (⊠ 29/ 19 Singharat Rd. ☎ 053/221174 or 053/223164 ⊕ www.depthai.go.th). The program, which stands for "One Tambon, One Product," has been a great success. It's center has a two-story showroom with a collection that rivals many of the city's galleries and museums. The ground floor has an exquisite display of furniture and decorative items. Upstairs are smaller items—baskets, carvings, ceramics, and textiles.

you can discover a wide range of handicrafts by Akha, Hmong, Karen, Lahu, Lisu, and Yao people in their native villages. On the other side of town, **Thai Tribal Crafts** (⊠ 208 Bumrungrat Rd. ☎ 053/241043 ⊕ www.ttcrafts.co.th) has more than 25 years' experience in retailing the products of Northern Thailand's hill tribe people. Chiang Mai's largest handicrafts retail outlet is called the **Northern Village** (⊠ Hang Dong and Mahidol Rds.). The massive store takes up two floors of the Central Airport Plaza Shopping Center. The selection here is astounding: silks and other textiles, ceramics, jewelry, and carvings.

> **HAPPY KIDS**
>
> Children can't get enough of the **Red Bull** (⊠ Huay Kaew Rd.), an amusement park next to Chiang Mai's Central Department Store. The rides are exhilarating enough to keep parents amused.

For two of Chiang Mai's specialties, lacquerware and exquisite paper products, take a taxi or songthaew to any of the outlets along San Kamphaeng Road (also known as the Golden Mile). Large emporiums that line the 10-km (6-mi) stretch sell a wide variety of items. Whole communities here devote themselves to their traditional trades. One community rears silkworms, for instance, providing the raw product for the looms humming in workshops. Among the crafts you can find are hand-painted umbrellas made from lacquered paper and tree bark. Hundreds of these are displayed at the **Umbrella Making Center** (⊠ 11/2 Moo 3, Bor Sang ☎ 053/338324). The artists at the center will paint traditional designs on anything from a T-shirt to a suitcase—travelers have discovered that this is a very handy way of helping identify their luggage on an airport carousel.

Outside the city center, the highways running south and east of Chiang Mai—those leading to Hang Dong and San Kamphaeng—are lined for several miles with workshops stocked with handicrafts of every description. They're a favorite destination for tuk-tuk drivers, who receive a commission on goods bought by their passengers. ⚠ **Be very specific with tuk-tuk drivers about what you're looking for before setting out—otherwise you might find yourself ferried to an expensive silverware outlet when all you want to buy is an inexpensive souvenir.**

Near Hang Dong, 12 km (7 mi) from the city center, is the crafts village of **Ban Tawai,** whose streets are lined with antiques shops. Four kilometers (2½ mi) beyond Ban Tawai is the **Ban Tawai Tourist Village,** an entire community of shops dealing in antiques and handicrafts. At workshops you can see teak, mango, rattan, and water hyacinth being worked into an astonishing variety of attractive and unusual items. If you end up buying a heavy teak piece of furniture, the dealers here will arrange for its transport. Beyond the Hang Dong–Ban Tawai junction is a large Lanna-style crafts center called **Baan Mai Kham** (⊠ 122 Chiang Mai–Hod Rd. ☎ 04/040–5007).

JEWELRY   Chiang Mai is renowned for its gems and semiprecious stones. ⚠ **Avoid the unscrupulous dealers at the Night Market and head to any of the more reputable stores.** If gold is your passion, make for the Chinese district. All the shops that jostle for space at the eastern end of Chang Moi Road are reliable, invariably issuing certificates of authenticity. The city's silver district, Wualai Road, is lined for several hundred yards with shops where you can sometimes see silversmiths at work. **Thongyon Silverware** (✉ 1 Soi 7, Wualai Rd. ☎ 053/202796) has been in business for more than 16 years, so you're assured of reliable service.

A very attractive Chiang Mai specialty features orchid blooms or rose petals set in 24-karat gold. There's a spectacular selection at the **Royal Orchid Collection** (✉ 94–120 Charoen Muang Rd., 2nd fl. ☎ 053/ 245598). **Eaze** (✉ Central Airport Plaza, 2nd fl.) also has a good selection of these blooms in gold.

Reliable jewelry shops include **Nova** (✉ 201 Tha Pae Rd. ☎ 053/ 273058) is a reliable jewelry shop with an attached jewelry school. **Shiraz** (✉ 170 Tha Pae Rd. ☎ 053/252382) is a long-established and reliable shop. Ask for Mr. Nasser. **Sherry** (✉ 59/2 Loi Kroh Rd. ☎ 053/ 273529) is a small treasure trove of a boutique crammed in between the bars and restaurants of one of the city's busiest streets.

Claiming to be the world's largest retailer of jadeite, The **Orchid Jade Factory** (✉ 7/7 Srivichai Rd., opposite the entrance to Doi Suthep ☎ 053/ 295021 up to 23) claims to be the world's largest retailer of jadeite. The hard-sell tactics here can be slightly annoying, but the showrooms are truly a treasure trove of fabulous jade jewelry and ornaments, and visitors are invited to watch the craftspeople at work.

PAPER The groves of mulberry trees grown in Northern Thailand aren't only used to feed the silkworms—their bark, called *saa,* produces a distinctive, fibrous paper that is fashioned into every conceivable form: writing paper and envelopes, boxes, book covers, and picture frames. In Chiang Mai, **HQ PaperMaker** (✉ 3/31 Samlan Rd. ☎ 053/814717) is the biggest and best outlet. Its first floor is a secluded gallery whose works include paintings done by elephants at the Elephant Conservation Center near Lampang. **Siam Promprathan** (✉ 95/3 Moo 4, Ratchawithi Rd., San Kamphaeng ☎ 053/331768 or 053/392214) also has a wide selection of saa paper products.

TEXTILES Chiang Mai and silk are nearly synonymous, and here you can not only buy the product but also see it being manufactured. Several companies along San Kamphaeng Road open their workrooms to visitors and explain the process of making fine silk, from the silkworm to the loom. ⚠ These shops are a favorite destination of package tours, so prices tend to be higher than in other parts of town or at the Night Market.

Silk and other local textiles can be reliably bought at **Shinawatra Thai Silk** (✉ 18 Huay Kaew Rd., and at the Mandarin Oriental Dhara Devi Hotel ☎ 053/221076 or 053/888535), **Studio Naenna** (✉ Soi 8, 138 Huay Kaew Rd. ☎ 053/226042), **Vaniche** (✉ 133 Boonraksa Rd.), and **Eaze** (✉ 2nd fl., the Airport Plaza ☎ 053/262786).

Textiles woven in hill tribe villages can be found at **Nicha** (✉ 86/1 Charoen Rat Rd. ☎ 053/288–0470).

Doi Inthanon National Park

⓲ *90 km (54 mi) southwest of Chiang Mai.*

Doi Inthanon, Thailand's highest mountain (8,464 feet), rises majestically over a national park of staggering beauty. Many have compared the landscape with that of Canada—only the tropical vegetation on its lower slopes and the 30 villages that are home to 3,000 Karen and Hmong people remind you that this is indeed Asia. The reserve is of great interest to nature lovers, especially birders who come to see the 362 species that nest in its thick forests of pines, oaks, and laurels. Red-and-white rhododendron run riot here, as do other plants found nowhere else in Thailand.

A 48-km (30-mi) toll road winds to the mountain's summit, where the ashes of Chiang Mai's last ruler, King Inthawichayanon, are contained in a stupa that draws hundreds of thousands of pilgrims annually. Hiking trails penetrate deep into the park, which has some of Thailand's highest and most beautiful waterfalls. The Mae Klang Falls, just past the turnoff to the park, are the most accessible, but the most spectacular are the Mae Ya Falls, the country's highest, and the Siribhum Falls, which plunge in two parallel cataracts from a 550-yard-high cliff above the Inthanon Royal Research Station. The station's vast nurseries are a gardener's dream, filled with countless varieties of tropical and temperate plants. Rainbow trout—unknown in the warm waters of Southeast Asia—are raised here in tanks fed by cold streams plunging from the mountain's heights, then served at the station's restaurant. The national park office provides maps and guides for trekkers and bird-watchers. ■ TIP→ **Accommodations are available: B1,000 for a two-person chalet, B6,500 for a villa for up to eight people.** ✉ *Amphur Chomthong, 50160* ☎ *053/ 268550 or 053/268–5550* ⊕ *www.dnp.go.th* 🖃 *B400 per person, B30 per car* ☽ *Daily 9–6.*

Lamphun

⓳ *26 km (16 mi) south of Chiang Mai.*

Lamphun claims to be the oldest existing city in Thailand (but so does Nakhon Pathom). Originally called Nakhon Hariphunchai, it was founded in AD 660. Its first ruler was a queen, Chamthewi, who has a special place in Thailand's pantheon of powerful female leaders. There are two striking statues of her in the sleepy little town, and one of its wats bears her name. Queen Chamthewi founded the eponymous dynasty, which ruled the region until 1932.

Lamphun and the countryside surrounding it are known throughout Thailand for the *lamyai*, a sweet cherry-size fruit with a thin shell. In this region it's a big business. In the nearby village of Tongkam, the "10,000-baht lamyai tree" is said to net its owner that sum each year. A good time to visit is during the annual lamyai festival, which brings the town to a halt in the first week of August. There are parades, exhibitions, a beauty contest, and copious quantities of lamyai wine. Buy yourself a jar of lamyai-flower honey—reputed to have exceptional healing and aphrodisiacal powers. You can find it on sale throughout the town.

Minibus songthaews (B15) travel from Chiang Mai to Lamphun. It's also a pleasant day's trip to drive south on Highway 106, a very busy but beautiful and shady road lined by 100-foot rubber trees.

Lamphun's architectural treasures include two monasteries. About 2 km (1 mi) west of the town's center is **Wat Chamthewi**, often called the "top-less chedi" because the gold that once covered the spire was pillaged sometime during its history. Work began on the monastery in AD 755, and despite a modern viharn added to the side of the complex, it retains an ancient weathered look. Suwan Chang Kot, to the right of the entrance, is the most famous of the two chedis, built by King Mahantayot to hold the remains of his mother, the legendary Queen Chamthewi. The five-tier sandstone chedi is square; on each tier are Buddha images that get progressively smaller. All are in the 9th-century Dvaravati style, though many have obviously been restored. The other chedi was probably built in the 10th century, though most of what you see today is the work of 12th-century King Phaya Sapphasit. ■ TIP→ You probably want to take a *samlor* (bicycle rickshaw) down the narrow residential street to the complex. Since this is not an area where samlors generally cruise, ask the driver to wait for you. ⊠ *Lamphun–San Pa Tong Rd.* The temple complex of FodorśChoice ★**Wat Phra That Hariphunchai** is dazzling. Through the gates, guarded by ornamental lions, is a three-tier, sloping-roof viharn, a replica of the original that burned down in 1915. Inside, note the large Chiang Saen–style bronze image of the Buddha and the carved *thammas* (Buddhism's universal principals) to the left of the altar. As you leave the viharn, you pass what is reputedly the largest bronze gong in the world, cast in 1860. The 165-foot Suwana chedi, covered in copper and topped by a golden spire, dates from 847. A century later, King Athitayarat, the 32nd ruler of Hariphunchai, added a nine-tier umbrella, gilded with 14 pounds of gold. At the back of the compound—where you can find a shortcut to the center of town—there's another viharn with a standing Buddha, a sala housing four Buddha footprints, and the old museum. ⊠ *Inthayongyot Rd.* 🖅 *Free* 🕙 *Wed.–Sun. 8:30–4.*

Just outside Wat Phra That Hariphunchai, the **National Museum** has a fine selection of Dvaravati-style stuccowork. There's also an impressive collection of Lanna antiques. ⊠ *Inthayongyot Rd.* 🕾 *053/511186* 🖅 *B30* 🕙 *Wed.–Sun. 9–4.*

Where to Stay & Eat

¢–$ ✕ **Add Up Coffee Bar.** This attractive riverside haunt, next door to the visitor information center, is more than just a coffee shop. The menu has the usual Thai dishes, but its list of Western specialties is full of surprises—pork chops, for instance, served with a garlic-apple compote. The ice cream is made under American license and is delicious. ⊠ *Lob-muangnai Rd. 22* 🕾 *053/530272* 🖃 *MC, V.*

¢–$ ✕ **Lamphun Ice.** The odd name of this restaurant seems to come from its origins as an ice-cream parlor. The interior has cozy booths that give it the feel of a vintage soda fountain. The Asian food served here is the real thing—try the sensational Indian-style crab curry. ⊠ *Chaimongkon*

Rd., opposite southern gate of Wat Phra That Hariphunchai ☎ *053/ 511452* ▤ *MC, V.*

¢–$ ✕ **Ton Fai.** This restaurant, named for the colorful flame tree, occupies an ancient house and its shady backyard. Inside you can climb the stairs to a teak-floored dining room with tables set beneath the original rafters. The room is cooled by the breeze that wafts in from the nearby river through the shuttered windows. The menu is simple, but has plenty of tasty Northern Thai specialties. ⊠ *183 Chaimongkol Rd., Tambon Nai Muang* ☎ *053/530060* ▤ *No credit cards.*

¢   **Supamit.** From this hotel's fifth-floor restaurant you have fine views of Wat Chamthewi, located on the opposite side of the street. Lamphun's best hotel, the Supamit has simple but adequately furnished and clean rooms. After a day touring the city's temples the airy lobby offers a cool and soothing retreat. ⊠ *Chamthewi Rd.* ☎ *053/534865* ⏎ *50 rooms* ♨ *In-hotel: restaurant, bar* ▤ *MC, V.*

Shopping

Lamphun's silk and other fine textiles make a visit to this charming city worthwhile. It has its own version of Venice's Rialto bridge, a 100-yard-long covered wooden bridge lined on both sides with stands selling mostly silk, textiles, and local handicrafts. The bridge is opposite the main entrance to Wat Phra That Hariphunchai, Inthayongyot Road. The market is open daily 9–6. Eight kilometers (5 mi) from Lamphun on the main Lampang highway is one of the area's largest silk businesses, **Lampoon Thai Silk** (⊠ 8/2 Panangjitawong Rd., Changkong ☎ 053/510329 ⊕ www.thaisilk.th.com), where you can watch women weave at wooden looms.

Pa Sang

❷⓪ *12 km (7 mi) south of Lamphun, 38 km (19 mi) south of Chiang Mai.*

At one time every other shop in this little town offered locally designed and woven cloth in traditional Lanna designs, but now these eye-catching fabrics are harder to find. However, you can still buy fine examples of local work in the market. Even if you're not shopping for textiles, a visit to Pa Sang takes you through some beautiful countryside, much of it part of the Khun Tan National Park.

About 5 km (3 mi) south of Pa Sang is **Wat Phra Bhat Tak Pha,** commonly known as the Temple of the Buddha's Footprint. You can climb the 600 steps to the hilltop chedi, but the main attraction here is the two huge imprints representing Lord Buddha's foot, found indented in the floor inside the temple. ■ TIP➡ **As you enter, buy a piece of gold leaf to affix in the imprint.** ⊠ *Pa Sang-lee Rd.*

The highway between Chiang Mai and Lampang runs through the mountainous **Doi Khun Tan National Park,** a wild upland area of great natural beauty. Since the Bangkok–Chiang Mai railroad also crosses the area, the park is run by Thailand's Royal State Railway. It has its own railroad station, an immaculately kept structure at the northern end of the country's longest railroad tunnel. A small chedi near its entrance contains the ashes of the German engineer who led construction work on tunneling through the mountain in the early years of the 20th century. When World War I broke out in 1914, Emil Eisenhofer was repatriated, but was so taken with Thailand (or Siam as it then was) that he returned after the war and he and his German wife made their home in Bangkok. His last wish was for his remains—and those of his wife—to be buried at the site of his greatest professional accomplishment. Floral tributes are regularly placed on his chedi by passing travelers.

The park has a small resort of six bungalows, the **Khun Tan Nature Land Resort** (⊠ Tambon Si Bua Ban ☎ 053/561030). The bungalows cost B800–B3,000. There's a second small resort just off the Chiang Mai–Lampang Highway, near the entrance to the park: **Kuntan Viewpoint Resort** (☎053/80222). It has 20 chalets, grouped around a small lake, costing B500 each. The resort's restaurant has a fascinating gallery of photographs documenting the construction of Eisenhofer's tunnel.

Lampang

㉑ *65 km (40 mi) southeast of Lamphun, 91 km (59 mi) southeast of Chiang Mai.*

At the end of the 19th century, when Lampang was a thriving center of the teak trade, the well-to-do city elders gave the city a genteel look by buying a fleet of English-built carriages and a stable of nimble ponies to pull them through the streets. Until then, elephants had been a favored means of transport—a century ago the number of elephants, employed in the nearby teak forests, nearly matched the city's population. The carriages arrived on the first trains to steam into Lampang's fine railroad station, which still looks much the same as it did back then. More than a century later, the odd sight of horse-drawn carriages still greets visitors to Lampang. The brightly painted, flower-bedecked carriages, driven by hardened types in Stetson hats and cowboy boots, look very touristy, but the locals also use them to get around the city. They pay considerably less than the B150 for a short city tour visitors are charged.

Apart from some noteworthy temples, not much else remains of Lampang's prosperous heyday. An ever-dwindling number of fine teak homes can be found among the maze of concrete. Running parallel to the south bank of the Wang River is a narrow street of ancient shops that once belonged to the Chinese merchants who catered to Lampang's prosperous populace. ■ TIP→ **The riverfront promenade is a pleasant place for a stroll; a handful of cafés and restaurants with terraces overlook the water.**

Workers from Myanmar were employed in the region's rapidly expanding logging business, and these immigrants left their mark on the city's architecture. Especially well preserved is **Wat Sri Chum**, a lovely Burmese temple. Pay particular attention to the viharn, as the eaves are covered with beautiful carvings. Inside you can find gold-and-black lacquered pillars supporting a carved-wood ceiling. To the right is a bronze Buddha cast in the Burmese style. Red-and-gold panels on the walls depict temple scenes. ⊠ *Sri Chum Rd.*

Near the banks of the Wang River is **Wat Phra Kaew Don Tao,** dominated by its tall chedi, built on a rectangular base and topped with a rounded spire. More interesting, however, are the Burmese-style shrine and adjacent Thai-style sala. The 18th-century shrine has a multitier roof. The interior walls are carved and inlaid with colored stones; the ornately engraved ceiling is painted with enamel. The sala, with the traditional three-tier roof and carved-wood pediments, houses a Sukhothai-style reclining Buddha. Legend has it that the sala was once home to the Emerald Buddha, which now resides in Bangkok. In 1436, when King Sam Fang Kaem was transporting the statue from Chiang Rai to Chiang Mai, his elephant reached Lampang and refused to go farther. The Emerald Buddha is said to have remained here for the next 32 years, until the succeeding king managed to get it to Chiang Mai. ☒ *Phra Kaew Rd.* Near

FodorśChoice
★

the village of Ko Khang is **Wat Phra That Lampang Luang,** one of the most venerated temples in the north. It's also one of the most striking. Surrounded by stout laterite defense walls, the temple has the appearance of a fortress—and that's exactly what it was when the legendary Queen Chamthewi founded her capital here in the 8th century. The Burmese captured it two centuries ago, but were ejected by the forces of a Lampang prince (a bullet hole marks the spot where he killed the Burmese commander). The sandy temple compound has much to hold your interest, including a tiny chapel with a hole in the door that creates an amazing, inverted photographic image of the Wat's central, gold-covered chedi. The temple's ancient viharn has a beautifully carved wooden facade; note the painstaking workmanship of the intricate decorations around the porticoes. A museum has excellent wood carvings, but its treasure is a small emerald Buddha, which some claim was carved from the same stone as its counterpart in Bangkok. ✛ *15 km (9 mi) south of Lampang* ☒ *Free* ☉ *Tues.–Sun. 9–4.*

FodorśChoice
★

☺ On the main highway between Lampang and Chiang Mai is Thailand's internationally known **Elephant Conservation Center.** So-called training camps are scattered throughout the region, but many of them are little more than overpriced sideshows. This is the real thing: a government-supported research station. Here you can find the special stables that house the white elephants owned by the king, although only those who are taking the center's mahout training course are allowed to see them. The 36 "commoner" elephants (the most venerable are over 80 years old) get individual care from more than 40 mahouts. The younger ones evidently enjoy the routines they perform for the tourists—not only the usual log-rolling, but painting pictures (a New York auction of their work raised thousands of dollars for the center). There's even an elephant band—its trumpeter is truly a star. The elephants are bathed every day at 9:30 and 1:15, and perform at 10, 11, and 1:30. You can even take an elephant ride through the center's extensive grounds, and if you fancy becoming a mahout you can take a residential course in elephant management. ☒ *Baan Tung Kwian* ☏ *054/228034 or 054/229042* ☒ *B70* ☉ *Daily 8–4.*

Where to Stay & Eat

¢–$ ✕ **Krua Bangkok.** The management of this riverside restaurant has introduced Vietnamese dishes to its mostly Thai menu. It was a good move,

Thailand's Elephants

THE UNITED STATES HAS ITS eagle. Britain acquired the lion. Thailand's symbolic animal is the elephant, which has played an enormous role in the country's history through the ages.

It even appeared on the national flag, as it did when Thailand was Siam. It's a truly regal beast—white elephants enjoy royal patronage and several are stabled at the National Elephant Institute's conservation center near Lampang.

But the elephant is also an animal of the people, domesticated some 2,000 years ago to help with the heavy work and logging in the teak forests of Northern Thailand. Elephants were in big demand by the European trading companies, which scrambled for rich harvests of teak in the late 19th century and early 20th century. At one time there were more elephants in Lampang than people.

Early on warrior rulers recognized their usefulness in battle, and "Elephants served as the armored tanks of premodern Southeast Asian armies," according to American historian David K. Wyatt. The director of the mahout training program at the Lampang conservation center believes he is a reincarnation of one of the foot soldiers who ran beside elephants in campaigns against Burmese invaders.

While many of Thailand's elephants enjoy royal status, the gentle giant is under threat from the march of progress. Ivory poaching, a cross-border trade in live elephants, and urban encroachment have reduced Thailand's elephant population from about 100,000 a century ago to just 2,500 today. Despite conservation efforts, even these 2,500 face an uncertain future as mechanization and a 1988 government ban on private logging threw virtually all elephants and their mahouts out of work. Hundreds of mahouts took their elephants to Bangkok and other big cities to beg for money and food. The sight of an elephant begging for bananas curbside in Bangkok makes for an exotic snapshot, but the photo hides a grim reality. The elephants are kept in miserable urban conditions, usually penned in the tiny backyards of city tenements. It's been estimated that the poor living conditions, unsuitable diet, and city pollution combine to reduce their life expectancy by at least five years.

A nationwide action to rescue the urban elephants and resettle them usefully in the country—mostly in Northern Thailand—is gathering pace, though. The National Elephant Institute near Lampang is a leader in this field, thanks largely to the efforts of an American expert, Richard Lair, and two young British volunteers. The 40 or so elephants that have found refuge at the center actually pay for their keep by working at various tasks, from entertaining visitors with shows of their logging skills to providing the raw material (dung) for a papermaking plant. The center has a school of elephant artists, trained by two New York artists, and an elephant orchestra. The art they make sells for $1,000 and more on the Internet, and the orchestra has produced two CDs. Several similar enterprises are dotted around Northern Thailand. All are humanely run. The alternative—a life on the streets of Bangkok—is just too depressing to consider.

—Robert Tilley

as the Vietnamese-style egg rolls are the best this side of Hanoi. You dine either indoors beneath massive teak beams and slowly revolving fans or on the flagstone terrace overlooking the Wang River. A Thai group plays folk music every night. ⊠ *340 Tipchang Rd.* ☎ *054/310103* ⊟ *AE, MC.*

¢–$ ✕ **Riverside.** A random assortment of wooden rooms and terraces gives this place an easygoing charm. Perched above the sluggish Wang River, it's a great place for a casual meal. The moderately priced Thai and European fare is excellent, and on weekends the remarkable chef serves up the best pizza east of Italy. Most nights a live band performs, but there are so many quiet corners that you can easily escape the music. There are a handful of rooms on the lower floor if you want to stay over for the authentic American breakfast. ⊠*328 Tipchang Rd.* ☎*054/221861* ⊟ *AE, MC, V.*

$–$$ ▥ **Lampang River Lodge.** Facing the Wang River, this lodge is in a forest. The simple but comfortable rooms are in Thai-style wooden pavilions near a small lake where you can rent boats. The vast, airy restaurant is often crammed with tour groups, but you shouldn't have a problem securing a quiet corner. To get away from the crowds, totter over the swaying bridge to the riverside bar. The complex is 6 km (4 mi) south of Lampang. ⊠ *330 Moo 11, Baan Klang Rd., Tambon Champoo, 52000* ☎ *054/336640* ⊕ *www.lampangriverlodge.com* ⇆ *60 rooms* ⌂ *In-hotel: restaurant, bar, pool, laundry service* ⊟ *AE, MC, V.*

$ ▥ **Lampang Wiengthong.** One of the city's best hotels, this modern high-rise has a number of luxuriously appointed rooms and suites. Its "Drinks Palace" features live music most nights. ■ TIP→ **The Wiengthip coffee shop and Wiengpana restaurant rank among Lampang's smartest eateries.** ⊠ *138/ 109 Phaholyothin Rd., 52100* ☎ *054/225801* ⊕ *www. lampangwiengthonghotel.com* ⇆ *235 rooms* ⌂ *In-hotel: 2 restaurants, bar, pool, laundry service* ⊟ *AE, MC, V.*

¢ ▥ **Asia Lampang.** Although this hotel sits on a bustling street, most of the rooms are quiet enough to ensure a good night's sleep. Some are newly renovated, so ask to see a few before you decide. The airy terrace is just the place to relax on a warm evening. If you fancy singing along with the locals, there's a delightfully named karaoke room, the Sweety Music Room. ⊠ *229 Boonyawat Rd., 52100* ☎ *054/227844, 02/642–5497 Bangkok reservations* ⇆ *71 rooms* ⌂ *In-room: refrigerator (some). In-hotel: restaurant, bar, laundry service* ⊟ *MC, V.*

¢ ▥ **Boonma Guesthouse.** An ancient mansion was dismantled and its timbers recycled to make this charming little Lanna-style guesthouse in the heart of Lampang's Chinese quarter. Insist on one of the two upstairs rooms in the main house—they're large and denlike, with creaking teak floors and raftered ceilings. They share a country house–like lounge where antlers hang on the weathered walls. ⊠ *256 Taladkao Rd., Tambon Suandok, 52100* ☎*054/322653 or 054/218394* ⇆*8 rooms* ⌂ *In-hotel: restaurant* ⊟ *No credit cards.*

Shopping

Lampang is known for its blue, white, and orange pottery, much of it incorporating the image of a cockerel, the city's emblem. ■ TIP→ **If you're driving, you can find the best bargains at markets a few miles south of the city** on the highway to Bangkok, or north of the city on the road to Chiang Mai. The biggest outlet is 2 km (1 mi) from the city center, on the road to Phrae, at **Indra Ceramic** (⊠ 382 Vajiravudh Damnoen Rd. ☎ 054/315593). You can see the ceramics being made and also paint your own designs. The extensive showrooms feature a ceramic model city. In Lampang proper, Phaholyothin Road has several small showrooms. The best place for pottery is **Srisawat Ceramics** (⊠ 316 Phaholyothin Rd. ☎ 054/225931).

Chiang Mai & Environs Essentials

Transportation

BY AIR

In peak season, flights to Chiang Mai are heavily booked. Thai Airways has almost hourly flights from 7 AM to 9 PM from Bangkok (70 minutes, B2,370) and two direct flights daily from Phuket (110 minutes, B4,640). Bangkok Airways has one daily flight from Bangkok Wednesday through Friday and on Sunday and three daily flights on Tuesday and Saturday). Three budget airlines offer flights for as little as B1,600: Orient Thai Airlines (five flights daily), Air Asia (three flights daily), and Nokair (nine flights daily). They are easiest booked online, at travel agencies, or at airport booths.

A new, privately operated carrier, PBair operates a twice-daily flight from Bangkok to Lampang (one hour).

🛪 Carriers **Air Asia** ⊕ www.airasia.com. **Bangkok Airways** ⊠ 2nd fl., Chiang Mai International Airport, Chiang Mai ☎ 053/276176 ⊕ www.bangkokair.com. **Nokair** ☎ 1318 ⊕ www.nokair.co.th. **Orient Thai Airlines** ⊕ www.orient-thai.com. **PBair** ☎ 02/261-0220 up to 25 ⊕ www.pbair.com. **Thai Airways** ⊠ 240 Phrapokklao Rd., Chiang Mai ☎ 053/920999 ⊕ www.thaiairways.com.

AIRPORTS & TRANSFERS Chiang Mai International Airport is about 10 minutes from downtown, a B100 taxi ride. Lampang Airport is just south of downtown. Songthaews run to city centers for around B50.

🛪 **Chiang Mai International Airport** ☎ 053/270222. **Lampang Airport** ☎ 054/218199.

BY BUS

So-called VIP buses ply the route between Bangkok and Chiang Mai, stopping at Lampang on the way. The privately operated coaches depart Bangkok's Northern Bus Terminal at Mo Chit almost hourly. For around B400–B500 you get a very comfortable 10-hour ride in a modern bus with reclining seats, blankets and pillows, TV, onboard refreshments—a lunch or dinner at a motorway stop is even included in the ticket price. You can take cheaper buses, but the faster service is well worth a few extra baht.

Chiang Mai's Arcade Bus Terminal serves Bangkok, Mae Hong Son, and destinations within Chiang Rai Province. Chiang Phuak Bus Terminal serves Lamphun and destinations within Chiang Mai Province. From Lampang, air-conditioned buses leave for Lamphun, Phrae, and Nan.

Buses from Chiang Mai to Lampang (stopping at the Elephant Conservation Center) leave every half hour from near the Tourism Authority of Thailand office on the Lamphun Road. From an area diagonally opposite, songthaews leave at regular intervals for Lamphun. Both air-conditioned and non-air-conditioned buses connect Lampang to cities in the north as well as to Bangkok. Lampang's bus station is 2 km (1 mi) south of the city, just off the main highway to Bangkok.

🚍 Bus Stations Arcade Bus Terminal ⊠ Super Hwy. and Kaew Nawarath Rd., Chiang Mai ☎ 053/242664. **Chiang Phuak Bus Terminal** ⊠ Rattanakosin Rd., Chiang Mai ☎ 053/211586. **Lampang Bus Terminal** ⊠ Chantasurin Rd., Lampang ☎ 054/227410.

BY CAR

The well-paved roads around Chiang Mai, between Chiang Mai and Chiang Rai or south to Lampang are no problem for most drivers. Even the mountainous Mae Sa route north of Chiang Mai is perfectly drivable. Two major car-rental agencies in Chiang Mai are Avis and Hertz. Budget has a good range of four-wheel-drive vehicles for trips off the beaten path.

BY TAXI & TUK-TUK

Metered taxis are being introduced gradually in Chiang Mai, replacing the noisier, dirtier songthaews. If you manage to flag down one of the small fleet of taxis, the basic charge is B30—reckon on paying around B50 for a ride across the Old City. Tuk-tuks are generally cheaper, but you are expected to bargain with the driver—offer B20 or so less than the driver demands. The songthaews that trundle around the city on fixed routes are the cheapest form of transport—just B15 if your destination is on the driver's route. If he has to make a detour you'll be charged an extra B20 or so—settle on the fare before you get in. If your Thai is limited, just hold up the relevant number of fingers. If you hold up three and your gesture evokes the same response from the driver, you'll be paying B30. Drivers of taxis and songthaews are scrupulously honest, at least in Chiang Mai.

BY TRAIN

The State Railway links Chiang Mai to Bangkok and points south. As the uninteresting trip from Bangkok takes about 13 hours, overnight sleepers are the best choice. The overnight trains are invariably well maintained, with clean sheets on the rows of two-tier bunks. ■ TIP→ **Parting with a few extra baht for a first-class compartment is strongly recommended. In second class, you could be kept awake by partying passengers.**

Trains for the north depart from Bangkok's Hualamphong Railway Station and arrive in the Chiang Mai Railway Station. Overnight sleepers leave Hualamphong at 2:30 PM, 6 PM, 7:40 PM, and 9:30 PM, arriving at 5:35 AM, 6:50 AM, 8:55 AM, and 12:05 PM. Return trains leave at 6:55 AM, 4 PM, 4:45 PM, 5:50 PM, and 9:50 PM and arrive in Bangkok at 9:20 PM, 6:05 AM, 6:25 AM, 7 AM, and 12:30 PM. The second-class carriages (the fare is B441–B741) are reasonably comfortable. First-class carriages (B1,253) are recommended if you value a good night's sleep. The Nakornping Special Express leaves Bangkok at 6 PM and arrives in Chiang Mai at 6:50 AM. The return trip departs at 5:50 PM and arrives in Bangkok at 7 AM.

Most Bangkok–Chiang Mai trains stop at Lampang and at Lamphun, where a bicycle samlor can take you the 3 km (2 mi) into town for about B30. The train to Lampang from Chiang Mai takes approximately 2½ hours; from Bangkok, it takes 11 hours.

🚆 Train Station **Chiang Mai Station** ✉ Charoenmuang Rd. ☎ 053/244795 or 053/247462.

Contacts & Resources

BANKS & EXCHANGING SERVICES

Banks are swift and professional in all the region's major cities, and you can expect friendly assistance in English. ATMs are everywhere to be found and are clearly marked. Instructions for using the machines are in English.

EMERGENCIES

🚨 Emergency Numbers **Police** ☎ 191. **Tourist Police** ✉ 105/1 Chiang Mai–Lamphun Rd., Chiang Mai ☎ 1699 or 053/248130.
🏥 Hospital **Lanna Hospital** ✉ 103 Super Hwy., Chiang Mai ☎ 053/357234.

INTERNET, MAIL & SHIPPING

Internet cafés are on virtually every street corner in Chiang Mai, and you'll have no trouble locating one in the region's smaller towns. Charges vary enormously, ranging from B15 an hour to B2 a minute. Sometimes a half-hour's Internet use includes a free cup of coffee. Rates in hotel business centers are much higher than in Internet cafés. Wireless Internet access is offered by several outlets, the best of which, The Library, is run by an English university lecturer. His friendly café also serves food, delicious pastries, and Italian ice cream.

Post offices are normally open weekdays 8:30 to 4:30 and for a few hours Saturday morning. Chiang Mai's main post office is also open Sunday 9–noon.

📧 **The Library** ✉ Ratchadamnoen Rd. 141/8 ☎ 053/272012.
📧 Post Offices **Chiang Mai** ✉ 402 Charoenmuang Rd. ☎ 053/241070. **Lampang** ✉ Tipchang and Thibpawan Rds. ☎ 054/224069.

TOUR OPTIONS

Every other storefront in Chiang Mai seems to be a tour agency, and not all of them are professionally run. You'd be wise to pick up a list of agencies approved by the Tourism Authority of Thailand before choosing one. Prices vary quite a bit, so shop around, and carefully examine the offerings. Each hotel also has its own travel desk with ties to a tour operator. The prices are often higher, as the hotel adds its own surcharge.

Chiang Mai's Trekking Club is an association of 87 licensed guides with enough experience among them to manage the most demanding customer. "Tell us what you want and we can arrange it," is the club's boast. The club has its own café where you can meet the guides over a drink.

Summit Tour & Trekking and Top North also offer good tours at reasonable prices. World Travel Service is another reliable operator. Chiangmai Cattleya Tour & Travel Services has morning and afternoon tours of Wiang Kum Kam for B700. Chiangmai Tic Travel (ask for Pom or Tinar) arranges custom tours of Northern Thailand, ranging from day trips to weeklong holidays.

🛈 **Chiangmai Cattleya Tour & Travel Services** ✉ Hillside Plaza and Condotel 4, 50 Huay Kaew Rd., Chiang Mai ☎ 053/223991. **Chiangmai Tic Travel** ✉ 147/1 Ratchadamnoen Rd., Chiang Mai ☎ 053/814174. **Summit Tour & Trekking** ✉ Thai Charoen Hotel, Tapas Rd., Chiang Mai ☎ 053/233351. **Top North** ✉ 15 Soi 2, Moon Muang Rd., Chiang Mai ☎ 053/278532. **Trekking Club** ✉ 41/6 Loi Khroh Rd., Soi 6, Chiang Mai ☎ 053/818519. **World Travel Service** ✉ Rincome Hotel, Huay Kaew Rd., Chiang Mai ☎ 053/221044.

VISITOR INFORMATION

In Chiang Mai you can find an office of the Tourist Authority of Thailand on Chiang Mai–Lamphun Road. It's in a small building on the eastern bank of the Mae Ping River, opposite the New Bridge, and opens daily 8:30–4:30.

Lampang's tourist office is on Thakhraonoi Road near the clock tower. The TAT office in Lamphun, opposite the main entrance to Wat Hariphunchai, has irregular hours, but is generally open weekdays 9–5.

🛈 Tourist Information **Tourist Authority of Thailand** ✉ 105/1 Chiang Mai–Lamphun Rd., Chiang Mai ☎ 053/248604.

NAN & ENVIRONS

Visitors looking for off-the-beaten-track territory usually head north from Chiang Mai and Chiang Rai to the Golden Triangle or west to Mae Hong Son. Relatively few venture east, toward Laos, but if time permits, it's a region that's well worth exploring. The center of the region is a provincial capital and ancient royal residence, Nan, some 70 km (42 mi) from the Laotian border. The city is very remote; roads to the border end in mountain trails and there are no frontier crossings, although there are ambitious, long-term plans to run a highway through the mountains to Luang Prabang.

Two roads link Nan with the west and the cities of Chiang Mai, Chiang Rai, and Lampang—they are both modern highways that sweep through some of Thailand's most spectacular scenery, following river valleys, penetrating forests of bamboo and teak, and skirting upland terraces of rice and maize. Hill tribe villages sit on the heights of the surrounding Doi Phu Chi mountains, where dozens of waterfalls, mountain river rapids, and revered caves beckon travelers with time on their hands. Here you can find Hmong and Lahu villages untouched by commercialism, and jungle trails where you, your elephant, and mahout beat virgin paths through the thick undergrowth.

The two routes from Chiang Mai to Nan pass through a pair of ancient towns, Phayao or Phrae, both of them worth an overnight stay. Phrae is center of Thailand's richest teak-growing region and Phayao sits on a beautiful lake. The region has three wild, mountainous national parks, Doi Phak Long, 20 km (12 mi) west of Phrae on Route 1023; Doi Luang,

Trekking

IN THE 1960S A FEW INTREPID people in Northern Thailand started wandering through the countryside, finding rooms at the hill tribe villages. By 1980 tour companies were organizing guided groups and sending them off for three- to seven-day treks. The level of difficulty of a Northern Thailand trek varies: you might traverse tough, hilly terrain for several hours or travel mostly by pickup and hike just the last few miles. Days are spent walking forest trails between villages, where you can sleep overnight. Accommodations are in huts, where the bed can be a wooden platform with no mattress. Food is likely to be a bowl of sticky rice and stewed vegetables. Travel light, but be sure to wear sturdy hiking shoes and to pack a sweater. Mosquito repellent is a must.

Always use a certified guide. It's important to pick one who's familiar with local dialects and who knows which villages are not overrun with tour groups. It's also imperative that you discuss the route; that way you'll know what to expect. You can usually tell whether the guide is knowledgeable and respects the villagers, but question him thoroughly about his experience before you sign up. The best way to select a tour that is right for you is to talk to other travelers. Guides come and go, and what was true six months ago may not be today. The charge for a guided trek is around B800 per day.

Try to avoid the hot months of April and May, when trekking can be sweaty work even at high altitudes. The best time of year to make for the hills is the cool, dry season, between November and March.

Trekking is more than a popular pastime in Northern Thailand—it's big business. Some of the more accessible villages, particularly those inhabited by the long-necked women of the Karen people, have consequently come to resemble theme parks. Be clear about what you expect when booking a trek. Insist on the real thing, perhaps offering a bit more to achieve it. Better still, ask your hotel to recommend a good local guide. Gather as much information as you can from those who have just returned from a trek. Their advice will save you time, money, and frustration.

which reaches into the outskirts of Phayao; and Doi Phukku, on the slopes of the mountain range that separates Thailand and Laos, some 80 km (48 mi) northeast of Nan.

Nan

㉒ *318 km (200 mi) southeast of Chiang Mai, 270 km (167 mi) southeast of Chiang Rai, 668 km (415 mi) northeast of Bangkok.*

Near the border of Laos lies the city of Nan, a provincial capital founded in 1272. According to local legend, Lord Buddha, passing through Nan Valley, spotted an auspicious site for a temple to be built. By the late 13th century Nan was brought into Sukhothai's fold, but it maintained a fairly independent status into the 20th century. Only in the last two decades have modern roads been cut from Phayao and Phrae to bring this region into closer communication with authorities in Bangkok.

Nan is rich in teak plantations and fertile valleys that produce rice and superb oranges. The town of Nan itself is small; everything is within walking distance. Daily life centers on the morning and evening markets. ■ TIP→ **The Nan River, which flows past the eastern edge of town, draws visitors at the end of Buddhist Lent, in late October or early November, when traditional boat races are held.** The longtail boats are all carved out of a single tree trunk, and at least one capsizes every year, to the delight of the locals. A few weeks later, in mid-December, Nan honors its famous fruit crop with a special Golden Orange and Red Cross Fair—there's even a Miss Golden Orange contest. It's advisable to book hotels ahead of time for these events.

To get a sense of the region's art visit the **National Museum,** a mansion built in 1923 for the prince who ruled Nan, Chao Suriyapong Pharit-tadit. The house itself is a work of art, a synthesis of overlapping red roofs, forest green doors and shutters, and brilliant white walls. There's a fine array of wood and bronze Buddha statues, musical instruments, ceramics, and other works of Lanna art. The revered "black elephant tusk" is also an attraction. The 3-foot-long, 40-pound tusk is actually dark brown in color, but that doesn't detract at all from its special role as a local good luck charm. ⊠ *Phalong Rd.* ☎ *054/710561* ☒ *B30* ⊙ *Daily 9–5.*

Fodor'sChoice ★ Nan has one of the region's most unusual and beautiful temples, **Wat Pumin,** whose murals alone make a visit to this part of Northern Thailand worthwhile. It's an economically constructed temple, combining the main shrine hall and viharn, and qualifies as one of Northern Thailand's best examples of folk architecture. To enter, you climb a short flight of steps flanked by two superb nagas, their heads guarding the north entrance and their tails the south. The 16th-century temple was extensively renovated in 1865 and 1873, and at the end of the 19th century murals picturing everyday life were added to the inner walls. Some have a unique historical context—like the French colonial soldiers disembarking at a Mekong river port with their wives in crinolines. A fully rigged merchant ship and a primitive steamboat are portrayed as backdrops to scenes showing colonial soldiers leering at the pretty local girls corralled in a palace courtyard. Even the conventional Buddhist images have a lively originality, ranging from the traumas of hell to the joys of courtly life. The bot's central images are also quite unusual—four Sukhothai Buddhas locked in conflict with the evil Mara. ⊠ *Phalong Rd.* ☒ *Free* ⊙ *Daily 8–6.*

Nan is dotted with other wats. **Wat Hua Wiang Tai** (⊠ Sumonthewarat Rd.) is the gaudiest, with a naga running along the top of the wall and lively murals painted on the viharn's exterior. **Wat Suan Tan** (⊠ Tambon Nai Wiang) has a 15th-century bronze Buddha image. It's the scene of all-night fireworks during the annual Songkran festival. **Wat Ming Muang** (⊠ Suriyaphong Rd.) contains the city pillar. **Wat Chang Kham** (⊠ Suriyaphong Rd.) has one of only seven surviving solid-gold Buddha images from the Sukhothai period. Its large chedi is supported by elephant-shaped buttresses.

Where to Stay & Eat

¢–$ ✕ **Ruen Kaew.** Its name means Crystal House, and this riverside restaurant really is a gem. Guests step in through a profusion of bougainvillea onto a wooden deck directly overlooking the Nan River. A Thai band and singers perform from 6:30 PM every night. The Thai menu has some original touches—the chicken in a honey sauce, for instance, is a rare delight. ✉ *1/1 Sumondhevaraj Rd.* ☎ *054/710631* ▤ *V*

¢–$ ✕ **Suriya Garden.** This substantial restaurant on the banks of the Nan River is a larger version of the nearby Ruen Kaew, with a wooden deck overlooking the water. Like its neighbor, it has added some interesting specialties to its conventional Thai menu—Chinese-style white bass or pig's hooves, for instance. A band and solo vocalists perform nightly. ✉ *9 Sumondhevaraj Rd.* ☎ *054/710687* ▤ *MC, V.*

$ ▦ **City Park Hotel.** Nan's top hotel is a low-rise, ranch-style complex of buildings on the outskirts of the city, set in 12 acres of gardens. Rooms overlook either the gardens or the landscaped pool, and all have private balconies. The Chumpoo-Thip restaurant serves fresh produce from the hotel's own kitchen garden, where guests can walk and learn about the herbs and spices that season Thai cuisine. ✉ *99 Yantarak-itkosol Rd., 55000* ☎ *054/741343 up to 52* ⊕ *www.thecityparkhotel.com* ⊅ *129 rooms* ☾ *In-room: refrigerator. In-hotel: restaurant, room service, tennis court, pool, laundry service* ▤ *AE, MC, V.*

¢–$ ▦ **Dhevaraj.** Built around an attractive interior courtyard, which is romantically lighted for evening dining, the Dhevaraj has all the comforts and facilities of an top-class hotel. Rooms are cozily furnished and the bed linen is high quality. The location couldn't be better, across from the city market and within a short walk of all the sights. A welcome plate of fresh fruit in your room is a nice touch, but ▪ TIP➡ **it's advisable to shun the complimentary "American" breakfast (congealed fried eggs, warped ham, and tasteless sausage) for a cup of Thai rice soup at the market.** ✉ *466 Sumondhevaraj Rd., 55000* ☎ *054/751577* ⊕ *www.dhevarajhotel.com* ⊅ *160 rooms* ☾ *In-room: refrigerator. In-hotel: 2 restaurants, pool, laundry service* ▤ *MC, V.*

¢ ▦ **Nan Fah Hotel.** A reminder of the past, this old wooden Chinese hotel is worth a visit even if you're disinclined to stay in its rather dark rooms. The wide-plank floors are of a bygone age. A balcony overlooking the street is a great place to take in the town. Marvelous antiques are scattered around the hotel, and the delightful owner is happy to sell you some in the shop in the lobby. A live band plays in the restaurant at night, so if you're planning on turning in early, ask for a room at the back of the hotel. ✉ *436–440 Sumondhevaraj Rd., 55000* ☎ *054/710284* ⊅ *14 rooms* ☾ *In-hotel: restaurant, bar* ▤ *No credit cards.*

Sports & the Outdoors

Nan is the ideal center from which to embark on treks through the nearby mountains, as well as raft and kayak trips along the rivers that cut through them. Khun Chompupach Sirsappuris has run Nan's leading tourist agency, **Fhu Travel and Information** (✉ *453/4 Sumondhevaraj Rd.* ☎ *054/*

710636 or 01/287–7209 ⊕ www.fhutravel.com) for 20 years and knows the region like her own backyard. She speaks fluent English, and has an impressive Web site describing tours and prices.

Phrae

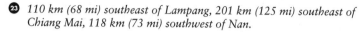 *110 km (68 mi) southeast of Lampang, 201 km (125 mi) southeast of Chiang Mai, 118 km (73 mi) southwest of Nan.*

A market town in a narrow valley, Phrae is well off the beaten path. The town's recorded history starts in the 12th century, when it was called Wiang Kosai, the Silk City. It remained an independent kingdom until the Ayutthaya period. Remains of these former times are seen in the crumbling city walls and moat, which separate the Old City from the new commercial sprawl.

On the northeastern edge of town stands **Wat Chom Sawan,** a beautiful monastery designed by a Burmese architect and built during the reign of King Rama V (1868–1910). The bot and viharn are combined to make one giant sweeping structure. Phrae's oldest building is **Wat Luang,** within the Old City walls. Although it was founded in the 12th century, renovations and expansions completely obscure so much of the original design that the only original section is a Lanna chedi with primitive elephant statues. A small museum on the grounds contains sacred Buddha images, swords, and texts.

On a hilltop in Tambon Pa Daeng, 10 km (6 mi) southeast of Phrae, stands another ancient temple, **Wat Phra That Cho Hae.** It was built in the late 12th century, and its 108-foot chedi is coated in gold. The chedi is linked to a viharn, a later construction, that contains a series of murals depicting scenes from the Buddha's life. The revered Buddha image is said to increase a woman's fertility. Cho Hae is the name given to the cloth woven by the local people, and in the fourth lunar month (June) the chedi is wrapped in this cloth during the annual fair. About 2 km (1 mi) from Wat Cho Hae is another smaller wat, **Wat Phra That Chom Chang,** whose chedi is said to contain a strand of Lord Buddha's hair.

Phrae is renowned in Northern Thailand for its fine teak houses. There are many to admire all over the city, but none to match what is claimed to be the world's largest teak structure, the **Ban Prathap Chai,** in the hamlet of Tambon Pa Maet near the southern edge of Phrae. Like many such houses, it's actually a reconstruction of several older houses—in this case, nine of them supported on 130 huge centuries-old teak posts. The result is remarkably harmonious. A tour of the rooms open to public view give a fascinating picture of bourgeois life in the region. The space between the teak poles on the ground floor of the building is taken up by stalls selling a variety of handicrafts, including much carved teak. The B30 admission charge includes a carved elephant key ring—a charming touch.

Where to Stay & Eat

For a quick bite, there's a night market at Pratuchai Gate with numerous stalls offering cheap, tasty food.

¢ ✕ **Ban Jai.** For authentic Lanna cuisine, you can't do better than this simple but superb restaurant. You're automatically served *kanom jin* (Chinese noodles) in basketwork dishes, with a spicy meat sauce, raw and pickled cabbage, and various condiments. If that's not to your taste, then order the *satay moo,* thin slices of lean pork on wooden skewers, served with a peanut sauce dip. In the evenings, every table has its own brazier for preparing the popular northern specialty, *moo kata,* a kind of pork stew. The open-sided, teak-floored dining area is shaded by ancient acacia trees, making it a cool retreat on warm evenings. ⊠ *Chatawan Rd. 3* ☎ *No phone* ⊟ *No credit cards.*

$ ▦ **Maeyom Palace Hotel.** Phrae's top hotel is scarcely palatial, but has comfortable, well-appointed rooms at a modest price. There are plenty of amenities, including a very pleasant pool and an outdoor bar. Rooms have Lanna touches, such as distinctive carvings on the walls. The two restaurants serve a comprehensive menu of Thai and European dishes; the more elegant of the two, the Maeyom, has an impressive wine list, including the best Thai vintages, and a menu that features such fine European specialties as beef rolls with mushroom filling. ⊠ *181/6 Yantarakitkosol Rd., 54000* ☎ *054/521028 up to 35* ✆ *wccphrae@hotmail. com* ⥅ *104 rooms* ⌂ *In-room: safe, refrigerator. In-hotel: 2 restaurants, room service, pool, laundry service, public Internet* ⊟ *AE, MC, V.*

¢ ▦ **Nakorn Phrae Tower.** A curious but effective combination of a conventional high-rise and a Lanna-style aesthetic distinguishes this very comfortable central Phrae hotel. Traditionally dressed staff (the women in sarongs) offer a friendly welcome, and the Lanna touches extend to decorative features of the rooms, where local woods frame the beds and work areas. Phrae has very little nightlife, so the piano-player in the lounge bar is a very popular local performer. ⊠ *3 Muanghit Rd., 54000* ☎ *054/ 521321* ⥅ *139 rooms* ⌂ *In-room: safe, refrigerator. In-hotel: restaurant, bar, laundry service* ⊟ *AE, DC, MC, V.*

Phayao

㉔ *150 km (90 mi) northeast of Chiang Mai, 160 km (96 mi) north of Lampang, 188 km (116 mi) northwest of Nan.*

Nearly as old as Chiang Mai and Chiang Rai, Phayao was for several centuries the center of a powerful kingdom, acquiring great prosperity and influence during the 13th-century reign of King Ngum Muang (who helped found Chiang Mai). A statue of the monarch stands in the municipal park that borders a natural lake called Kwan Phayao, which attracts anglers from as far as Bangkok. The hyacinth-studded lake is ringed by a breezy promenade bordered by restaurants, cafés, and bars. ■ TIP→ **If you're staying the night, make sure to see the sunset over the still, mountain-backed lake.** One of the region's most impressive monasteries, **Wat Sri Khom Kham,** stands on the shores of Kwan Phayao. It's reputed to have been founded after a visit to the site by Lord Buddha.

Where to Stay & Eat

¢–$ ✕ **Sang Chan.** Of all the restaurants bordering the lake, Sang Chan is probably the best. Fishing nets draping the exterior signal what to expect on the menu—lake fish predominate, and the freshly caught tilapia with garlic and pepper is a treat. The pillared dining room, its walls almost entirely of glass, has a pleasantly Italianate feeling. On warm evenings it's an unforgettable experience to watch the sun set over the lake from the garden terrace. ☒ *17/4 Chai Kwan Rd.* ☎ *053/431971* ▭ *MC, V.*

$ ▦ **Gateway Hotel.** The pink facade of the town's only international-class hotel is a local landmark. The hotel stands back from the lake, giving rooms on the upper floors views of the water and the distant mountains. The pastel shade of the stark exterior is matched by the subdued tones of the interior decor, though there are colorful Lanna touches such as fabrics and wall hangings. ☒ *7/36 Pratuklong 2 Rd., 56000* ☎ *053/ 411333* ✎ *info@chiangraihotel.or.th* ◁ *108 rooms* ♨ *In-hotel: restaurant, bar, pool, gym, laundry service* ▭ *AE, DC, MC, V.*

Nan & Environs Essentials

Transportation

BY AIR
A new, privately operated carrier, PBair flies from Bangkok to Nan on Monday, Tuesday, Friday, and Sunday. The flight takes 80 minutes.
▮ **PBair** ☎ 02/261-0220 up to 25 ⊕ www.pbair.com.

AIRPORTS & Songthaews meet incoming flights and charge about B50 for the 3-km TRANSFERS (2-mi) drive into central Nan.
▮ **Nan Airport** ☒ Thawangpha Rd. ☎ 054/710377.

BY BUS
Several air-conditioned buses leave Bangkok and Chiang Mai daily for Nan, stopping en route at Phrae. The journey from Bangkok to Nan takes 11 hours and costs B400 to B600; it's 8 hours from Chiang Mai to Nan and the cost is B300 to B400. From Lampang, air-conditioned buses leave for Phrae (three hours) and Nan (five hours). There's local bus service between Nan, Phrae, and Phayao.

BY TAXI & TUK-TUK
City transport in Nan, Phrae, and Phayao is provided by a combination of tuk-tuks, songthaews, and samlors. All are cheap and trips within a city should seldom exceed B30.

BY TRAIN
Nan is not on the railroad route, but a comfortable way of reaching the city from Bangkok is to take the Chiang Mai–bound train and change at Den Chai to a local bus for the remaining 146 km (87 mi) to Nan. The bus stops en route at Phrae.

Contacts & Resources

BANKS & EXCHANGING SERVICES
You'll have no problem finding banks with ATMs in this region.

EMERGENCIES

Nan Hospital on Thawangpha Road is equipped to treat most conditions, but in the case of serious illness it's advisable to make for Chiang Mai. ■ TIP→ **Take a basic medical kit on any tour into the mountains, and make sure it includes sufficient supplies of mosquito repellent.**

INTERNET

Nan, Phayao, and Phrae each have several Internet cafés, and all listed hotels have business facilities.

TOUR OPTIONS

All of the companies listed below offer the same types of trips, which range from city tours of Nan and short cycling tours of the region to jungle trekking, elephant riding, and white-water rafting.
Fhu Travel ✉ 453/4 Sumondhevaraj Rd., Nan ☎ 054/710636 ⊕ www.fhutravel.com. **Inter Tours** ✉ 10/10 Khaluang Rd., Nan ☎ 054/710195. **River Raft** ✉ 50/6 Norkam Rd., Nan ☎ 054/710940.

VISITOR INFORMATION

Tourist information about Nan Province, Nan itself, Phayao, and Phrae is handled by the Tourism Authority of Thailand's regional office in Chiang Rai.
TAT ✉ 448/16 Singhaklai Rd., Chiang Rai ☎ 053/744674 or 053/744675.

THE MAE HONG SON LOOP

If you're driving to Mae Hong Son, the best way to get there is along a mountainous stretch of road known to adventure travelers as "The Loop." The route runs from Chiang Mai to Mae Hong Son via Pai if you take the northern route, and via Mae Sariang if you take the southern one. Which route offers the best views is the subject of much heated debate. Most people hedge their bets by taking one route to get there and the other to return. The entire Loop is 615 km (369 mi) long.
■ TIP→ **Allow at least four days to cover it—longer if you want to leave the road occasionally and visit the hot springs, waterfalls, and grottos found along the way.**

Pai

❷❺ *160 km (100 mi) northwest of Chiang Mai, 110 km (66 mi) east of Mae Hong Son.*

Disastrous floods and mud slides in the surrounding mountains devastated this very popular tourist haunt in 2005, but the town rapidly recovered and now only a few high-water marks on the walls of some buildings and empty swathes of riverside land remind the visitor of the catastrophe. A building boom is again in full swing as the former market town struggles to cope with another annual flood—the thousands of visitors, mostly backpackers, who outnumber the locals in high season.

It was exhausted backpackers looking for a stopover along the serpentine road between Chiang Mai and Mae Hong Son who discovered Pai in the late 1980s. In 1991 it had seven modest guesthouses and three restaurants; now its frontier-style streets are lined with restaurants and bars of every description, cheap guesthouses and smart hotels, art galleries, and chic coffeehouses, while every class of resort, from back-to-nature to luxury, nestles in the surrounding hills. Somehow, though, Pai has managed to retain its slightly off-the-beaten-path appeal.

Although Pai lies in a flat valley, a 10-minute drive in any direction brings you to a rugged upland terrain with stands of wild teak, groves of towering bamboo, and clusters of palm and banana trees, hiding out-of-the-way resorts catering to visitors who seek peace and quiet. At night, the surrounding forest seems to enfold the town in a black embrace. As you enter Pai from the

> ## PAI: DEMURE HAMLET OR PARTY TOWN?
>
> Pai has a sizable Muslim population, which is why some of the guesthouses post notices asking foreign visitors to refrain from public displays of affection. Immodest clothing is frowned upon, so bikini tops and other revealing items are definitely out. The music bars close early, meaning that by 1 AM the town slumbers beneath the tropical sky. Nevertheless, quiet partying continues behind the shutters of the teak cabins that make up much of the tourist lodgings. This is, after all, backpacker territory.

direction of Chiang Mai, you'll cross the so-called World War II Memorial Bridge, which was stolen from Chiang Mai during the Japanese advance through Northern Thailand and rebuilt here to carry heavy armor over the Pai River. When the Japanese left, they neglected to return the bridge to Chiang Mai. Residents of that city are perfectly happy, as they eventually built a much handsomer river crossing.

Where to Stay & Eat

$–$$ ✕ **Pai Corner.** German Thomas Casper (Tom to his regulars) has been running this simple, thatch bar and restaurant for more than 13 years, and he's such a mine of information that he wrote the town's definitive guidebook. German specialties figure largely (literally) on the menu, but classic Northern Thai dishes such as *kao soi* can also be found. ⊠ *53, Moo 4, Raddamrong Rd.* ☎ *010/303195* ⊟ *No credit cards.*

¢–$ ✕ **All About Coffee.** One of Pai's historic merchant houses has been converted into a coffee shop that could grace any fashionable city street in the world. More than 20 different kinds of java are on the menu, which is also packed with delicacies from the café's own bakery. The mezzanine floor has a gallery of works by local artists. ⊠ *100, Moo 1, Chaisongkram Rd.* ☎ *053/699429* ⊟ *No credit cards.*

¢–$ ✕ **Edible Jazz.** Try the burritos at this friendly little café. The international menu matches the flavor of the music. It's one of few places in Pai where you can hear live jazz. ⊠ *Tambon Viengtai* ☎ *053/232960* ⊟ *No credit cards.*

¢–$ ✕ **House of Glass.** Glass isn't much in evidence at this open-air restaurant, but modern touches like picture windows would probably spoil its unique character. The buffet is an unbeatable value—pumpkin soup, various curries, fish-and-chips, and fresh fruit, all for B69. ⊠ *Tambon Viengtai* ☎ *No phone* ⊟ *No credit cards.*

$–$$ ✕⊡ **Belle Villa.** This appealing little resort's 24 teak chalets (traditional
Fodor'sChoice outside, pure luxury inside) are perched on stilts in a tropical garden
★ that blends seamlessly with the neighboring rice paddies and the foothills
of the nearby mountains. A thatched-roof reception area adds an additional exotic touch. The terrace restaurant, overlooking the pool and a
lotus-covered pond, is one of the region's best, serving fish from the Pai
River and lamb from New Zealand. ⊠ *113 Moo 6, Huay Poo-Wiang
Nua Rd., Tambon Wiang Tai, 58130* ☎ *053/698226, 02/693–2895 in
Bangkok* ⊕ *www.bellevillaresort.com* ⥲ *24 chalets* ⟁ *In-room: safe,
refrigerator, Wi-Fi. In-hotel: restaurant, room service, bar, pool, laundry service* ⊟ *AE, DC, MC, V.*

$–$$ ⊡ **Brook View.** The brook babbles right outside your cabin window if
you insist on a room with a view at this well-run little resort. The teak
cabins are tiny, but scrupulously clean. Those at the water's edge have
terraces where you can soak up the uninterrupted view of sugarcane fields
and the mountains beyond. ⊠ *132 Moo 1, Tambon Wiang Tai, 58130*
☎ *053/699366* ✎ *brookviewpai@yahoo.com* ⥲ *12 rooms* ⟁ *In-hotel:
spa* ⊟ *No credit cards.*

$–$$ ⊡ **Paivimann Resort.** "Vimann" means "heaven," and this fine new re-
sort, opened in 2006, certainly commands a heavenly spot on the banks
of the Pai River. Deluxe rooms in the main house, a stately building constructed almost entirely of teak, are enormous and opulently furnished
in Lanna style. Two-story villas are arranged along a path that leads down
to the river. The hotel has its own motorcycle taxi service to ferry guests
around Pai. ⊠ *Moo 3, Tetsaban Rd., 58130* ☎ *053/699403* ⊕ *www.
paivimaan.com* ⥲ *12 rooms* ⟁ *In-room: refrigerator. In-hotel: restaurant, room service, bar, parking (no fee)* ⊟ *AE, MC, V.*

¢   ⊡ **Cave Lodge.** The chatter of gibbons wakes you up at this remote mountain lodge between Pai and Mae Hong Son. The cave after which it is
named, just a short walk from the lodge, is one of the region's most spectacular caverns, with wall paintings and prehistoric coffins. The Australian owner of the lodge organizes treks and river tours in the
surrounding jungle. ⊠ *90 Moo 2, 15 Moo 1, Pang Mapa, Mae Hong
Son, 58150* ☎ *053/617203* ⊕ *www.cavelodge.com* ⥲ *10 rooms* ⟁ *In-
hotel: restaurant, bar* ⊟ *AE, MC, V.*

¢   ⊡ **Tree House.** The rooms with the best views at this riverside "hotel"
outside Pai are only for the most adventurous travelers—they're nestled
in the upper branches of an enormous rain tree. There are three of these
wooden cabins, which are simply furnished and share two bathrooms.
For those who prefer to keep their feet on the ground, there are seven
simple bungalows on the riverbank. ⊠ *90 Moo 2 Moo 3, Tambon
Machee, 58130* ☎ *01/911–3640* ⊕ *www.paitreehouse.com* ⥲ *10
rooms* ⟁ *In-hotel: restaurant, bar* ⊟ *AE, MC, V.*

Nightlife

In high season, Pai is packed with backpackers looking for a place to
party. Most of them congregate at **Bepop** (⊠ *188 Moo 8, Tambon
Viengtai* ☎ *053/698046*). Bands perform there nightly beginning at
9:30. A good place to chill out in the early evening is the aptly named
Ting Tong ("crazy") Bar (⊠ *55 Moo 4, Tambon Viengtai* ☎ *048/073781*).
On warm, rainless evenings you can lie on cushions and count the stars.

Sports & the Outdoors

While in Pai, you can join a white-water rafting trip sponsored by **Pai in the Sky Rafting** (⊠ 114 Moo 3, Tambon Viengtai ☎ 053/699090). The two-day outing on the Khong River sends you through steep-sided gorges, past spectacular waterfalls, and over 15 sets of rapids. An overnight stop is made at the "Pai in the Sky" camp, near the confluence of the Pai and Kohong rivers, before reaching the end point outside Mae Hong Son. The trips, costing B2,000, are made daily June to February, when the rivers are at their peak.

Mae Sariang

㉖ *175 km (105 mi) southwest of Chiang Mai, 140 km (85 mi) south of Mae Hong Son.*

The southern route of the Loop runs through Mae Sariang, a neat little market town that sits beside the Yuam River. With two very comfortable hotels and a handful of good restaurants, the town makes a good base for trekking in the nearby Salawin National Park or for boat trips on the Salawin River, which borders Myanmar.

Near Mae Sariang, the road winds through some of Thailand's most spectacular mountain scenery, with seemingly endless panoramas opening up through gaps in the thick teak forests that lines the route. You'll pass hill tribe villages where time seems to have stood still and Karen women go to market proudly in their traditional dress. In the village of Khun Yuam, 100 km (60 mi) north of Mae Sariang, you can find one of the region's most unusual and, for many, most poignant museums, the **World War II Memorial Museum.** The modest little building commemorates the hundreds of Japanese soldiers who died here on their chaotic retreat from the Allied armies in Myanmar. Locals took in the dejected and defeated men. A local historian later gathered the belongings they left behind: rifles, uniforms, cooking utensils, personal photographs, and documents. They provide a fascinating glimpse into a little-known chapter of World War II. Outside is a graveyard of old military vehicles, including an Allied truck presumably commandeered by the Japanese on their retreat east. ⊠ *Mae Hong Son Rd.* ⊡ *B10* ⊙ *Daily 8–4.*

Where to Stay & Eat

¢–$ ✕ **Riverside.** This restaurant, on the open-air terrace of an inexpensive guesthouse, is on a bend of the Yuam River, commanding an impressive view of rice paddies and the mountains beyond. The menu is simple, but the panoramic view is reason enough to eat here. The guesthouse, a rambling wooden building cluttered with antique bits and bobs ranging from worm-eaten farm implements to antlers, has 18 reasonably comfortable rooms (B180–B350). ⊠ *85 Langpanich Rd.* ☎ *053/681188 or 053/682592.*

¢ ⊡ **Riverhouse Hotel.** Cooling breezes from the Yuam River waft through the open-plan reception area, lounge, and dining room of this attractive hotel. Rooms are a simple but elegant synthesis of white walls, dark woods, and plain cotton drapes, with small terraces overlooking the river (Room 23 has a lamyai tree growing through its outside deck). ■ TIP→ **The**

12 rooms are quickly taken in high season, so if the hotel is full, the nearby, larger Riverhouse Resort (under the same management) is recommended. It's more expensive (B1,550–B2,700) but has more facilities. ✉ *77 Langpanich Rd., 58110* ☎ *053/621201* ⊕ *www.riverhousehotels.com* ⇨ *12 rooms* △ *In-hotel: restaurant, bar* ▭ *No credit cards.*

Mae Hong Son

245 km (147 mi) northwest of Chiang Mai via Pai, 368 km (230 mi) via Mae Sariang.

Stressed-out residents of Bangkok and other cities have transformed this remote, mountain-ringed market town into one of Northern Thailand's major resort areas. Some handsome hotels have arisen in recent years to cater to them. Overseas travelers also love the town because of its easy access to some of Thailand's most beautiful countryside.

For a small town, Mae Hong Son has some notable temples, thanks to immigrants from nearby Myanmar, where Burmese architecture and decorative arts were historically more advanced. Two of the temples, Wat Chong Kham and Wat Kham Klang, sit on the banks of a placid lake in the center of town, forming a breathtakingly beautiful ensemble of golden spires. Within a short drive are dozens of villages inhabited by the Karen, the so-called "long-neck" people. Fine handicrafts are produced in these hamlets, whose inhabitants trek daily to Mae Hong Son to sell their wares at the lively morning market and along the lakeside promenade.

Although Mae Hong Son offers a welcome cool retreat during the sometimes unbearably hot months of March and April, the mountains can be obscured during that part of the year by the fires set by farmers to clear their fields. One of the local names for Mae Hong Son translates as "City of the Three Mists." The other two are the clouds that creep through the valleys in the depths of winter and the gray monsoons of the rainy season.

Sights to See

★ ☺ **Thampla-Phasua Waterfall National Park.** About 16 km (10 mi) from Mae Hong Son, this park has one of the region's strangest sights—a grotto with a dark, cisternlike pool overflowing with fat mountain carp. The pool is fed by a mountain stream that is also full of thrashing fish fighting to get into the cave. Why? Nobody knows. It's a secret that draws thousands of Thai visitors a year. Some see a mystical meaning in the strange sight. The cave is a pleasant 10-minute stroll from the park's headquarters. ✉ *70 Moo 1, Huay Pa* ☎ *053/619036* ▭ *Free.*

> **SUNSET VIEWS**
>
> For a giddy view of Mae Hong Son and the surrounding mountains, take a deep breath and trudge up Doi Kong Mu, a hill on the western edge of town. It's well worth the effort—from here you can see the mountains on the border of Myanmar (it's particularly lovely at sunset). There's another shade of gold to admire—a flame-surrounded white-marble Buddha in a hilltop temple called Wat Phra That Doi Kong Mu.

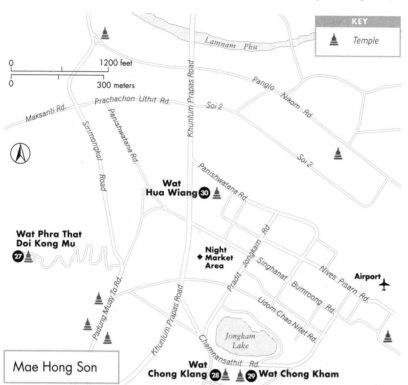

KEY

🛕 Temple

Lamnam Phu

1200 feet

300 meters

Maksanti Rd.

Prachachon Uthit Rd.

Khunlum Prapas Road

Soi 2

Panglo Nikom Rd.

Sirimongkol Road

Panishwatana Rd.

Soi 2

Panishwatana Rd.

Wat Hua Wiang 30 🛕

Wat Phra That Doi Kong Mu 27 🛕

Pradit Jongkam Rd.

Singhanat Rd.

Night ◆ Market Area

Bumroong Rd.

Nives Pisarn Rd.

Airport ✈

Padung Muay To Rd.

Khunlum Prapas Road

Udom Chao Nitet Rd.

Jongkam Lake

Chamnansathit Rd.

Mae Hong Son

Wat Chong Klang 28 🛕   🛕 29 **Wat Chong Kham**

5

---

29 **Wat Chong Kham.** A wonderfully self-satisfied Burmese-style Buddha, the cares of the world far from his arched brow, watches over the temple, which has a fine pulpit carved with incredible precision. ⊠ *Chamnansathit Rd.*

FodorsChoice
★

28 **Wat Chong Klang.** This temple is worth visiting to see a collection of figurines brought from Myanmar more than a century ago. The teakwood carvings depict an astonishing range of Burmese individuals, from peasants to nobles. ⊠ *Chamnansathit Rd.*

30 **Wat Hua Wiang.** Mae Hong Son's most celebrated Buddha image—one of the most revered in Northern Thailand—is inside this temple. Its origins are clear—note the Burmese-style long earlobes, a symbol of the Buddha's omniscience. ⊠ *Panishwatana Rd.*

27 **Wat Phra That Doi Kong Mu.** On the top of Doi Kong Mu, this temple has a remarkable view of the surrounding mountains. The temple's two chedis contain the ashes of 19th-century monks. ⊠ *West of Mae Hong Son.*

Where to Stay & Eat

¢–$ ✕ **Bai Fern.** Mae Hong Son's main thoroughfare, Khunlum Prapas Road, is lined with inexpensive restaurants serving local cuisine. Bai Fern is among the best. In the spacious dining room you eat in typical Thai style, amid solid teak columns and beneath whirling fans. Among the array of Thai dishes, pork ribs with pineapple stands out as a highly individual and tasty creation. ⊠ *87 Khunlum Prapas Rd.* ☎ *053/611374* 🖶 *MC, V.*

¢–$ ✕ **Moom Sabei.** This open-air restaurant and bar opposite Rooks Holiday Hotel & Resort has folk music during the evenings that makes it a favorite with locals. "Thai fondue"—pork stewed on open braziers—is a specialty here and it goes well with the beers on tap. Japanese sukiyaki is also on the surprisingly cosmopolitan menu. ⊠ *117/30 Khunlum Prapas Rd.* ☎ *053/613838* 🖶 *No credit cards.*

★ $$ 🏨 **Imperial Tara Mae Hong Son.** Set amid mature teak trees, this fine hotel was designed to blend in with the surroundings. Bungalows in landscaped gardens have both front and back porches, giving the teak-floored and bamboo-furnished rooms a light and airy feel. Golden Teak, which serves excellent Thai, Chinese, and European dishes, has a glassed-in section for chilly mornings and evenings. The restaurant and bar face the valley, as does the beautifully landscaped pool area. ⊠ *149 Moo 8, Tambon Pang Moo, 58000* ☎ *053/611473, 02/261–9000 in Bangkok* ⊕ *www.imperialhotels.com/taramaehongson/* ⟿ *104 rooms* ⚐ *In-room: refrigerator. In-hotel: restaurant, bar, pool, gym, laundry service* 🖶 *AE, DC, MC, V.*

$ 🏨 **Rim Nam Klang Doi.** This retreat, about 5 km (3 mi) outside Mae Hong Son, is an especially good value. Some of the cozy rooms overlook the Pai River, while others have views of the tropical grounds. A minivan shuttles you to town for B100. ⊠ *Ban Huay Dua, 58000* ☎ *053/224339* ⟿ *39 rooms* ⚐ *In-hotel: restaurant, pool* 🖶 *MC, V.*

¢ 🏨 **Panorama Hotel.** This centrally located hotel lives up to its name with upper-floor rooms that have sweeping views of the mountains surrounding the city. Twenty of the rooms are in a guesthouse annex. All rooms are simply but comfortably furnished, decorated with Northern Thai handicrafts. ⊠ *51 Khunlum Prapas Rd., 57150* ☎ *053/611757* ⟿ *463 rooms* ⚐ *In-room: refrigerator. In-hotel: restaurant, room service, bar, public Internet* 🖶 *MC, V.*

¢ 🏨 **Piya.** Eleven small bungalows, all huddled around a tree-shaded tropical garden, make up this friendly guesthouse. Sadly, none faces placid Lake Jong Kham, which is just across the road, but their secluded position at least ensures peace and quiet. ⚠ **One drawback: windows of the rooms are sealed because of the air-conditioning, so don't expect fresh air and the sound of birds singing.** Rooms are simply furnished, and the dining area is also spartan, but at least it overlooks the lake. ⊠ *1 Soi 6, Khunlum Prapas Rd., 58000* ☎ *053/611260* ⟿ *11 bungalows* ⚐ *In-hotel: restaurant* 🖶 *No credit cards.*

Sports & the Outdoors

TREKKING Many people come to Mae Hong Son to visit the villages belonging to the Karen people, whose women often extend their necks to unbelievable lengths by wrapping more and more brass bands around them starting at adolescence. Most of the Karen people still live in Myanmar. In Northern Thailand there are three villages, all near Mae Hong Son, with a total of more than 30 families, all of whom are accustomed to posing for photographs. Some visitors find there's an ethical dilemma in visiting these villages, as tourism may perpetuate what some find to be a rather barbaric custom. At the same time, tourist dollars also help to feed these people, many of whom are refugees from government oppression in Myanmar and who enjoy no civil rights in Thailand (they are not recognized as an ethnic hill tribe by the Bangkok government). With as many as 150 tourists visiting each day during the peak season, a village can make good money by having their long-necked women pose for snapshots.

The Mae Hong Son Loop Essentials

Transportation

BY AIR

A new, privately operated carrier, PBair, flies from Bangkok to Mae Hong Son on Wednesday, Friday, and Sunday. Thai Airways has a daily flight between Chiang Mai and Mae Hong Son (35 minutes, B1,270). Note that in March and April, smoke from slash-and-burn fires often prevents planes from landing at the airport in Mae Hong Son. A daily air service between Chiang Mai and Pai began in early 2007. The privately run service, operated by SGA, uses 12-seater aircraft for the 20-minute flight.
📱 **SGA** ☎ 02/641-4190 ⊕ www.sga.co.th/en-GB.

AIRPORTS & TRANSFERS The Mae Hong Son Airport is at the town's northern edge. Songthaews run to the city center for around B50.
📱 **Mae Hong Son Airport** ☎ 053/612057.

BY BUS

Chiang Mai's Arcade Bus Terminal serves Mae Hong Son. Several buses depart daily on an eight-hour journey that follows the northern section of the Loop, via Pai.
📱 Bus Station **Arcade Bus Terminal** ⊠ Super Hwy. and Kaew Nawarath Rd., Chiang Mai ☎ 053/242664.

BY CAR

If you're going to rent a car, you'll probably do it in Chiang Mai, but Avis also has an office at Mae Hong Son Airport, if needed.

▪ TIP→ **The road to Mae Hong Son from Chiang Mai has more than 1,200 curves, so make sure your rental car has power steering.** The most comfortable way to travel the route and enjoy the breathtaking mountain scenery is to let somebody else do the driving. The Loop road takes you there from either direction; the northern route through Pai (six hours) is a more attractive trip; the southern route through Mae Sariang (eight hours) is easier driving.
📱 **Avis** ⊠ Mae Hong Son ☎ 053/620457.

Contacts & Resources

BANKS & EXCHANGING SERVICES
You'll have no problem finding banks with ATMs in Mae Hong Son.

EMERGENCIES

⚡ Emergency Number **Tourist Police** ✉ Rajadrama Phithak Rd., Mae Hong Son ☎ 053/611812.

⚡ Hospital **Srisangwarn Hospital** ✉ Singhanat Bamrung Rd., Mae Hong Son ☎ 053/611259 or 053/612520.

INTERNET

Internet cafés are easy to find in Mae Hong Son.

VISITOR INFORMATION

The TAT office in Chiang Mai is responsible for Pai. For more information on the area, check out the *Pai Post* (⊕ www.paipost.com).

THE ROAD TO CHIANG RAI

Winding your way from Chiang Mai to Chiang Rai, the hub of the fabled Golden Triangle, will take you past Chiang Dao, best known for its astonishing cave complex; Tha Ton, a pretty riverside town on the Myanmar border, which has many outdoor activities; and Doi Ang Khang, a small, remote settlement—with one very fancy resort.

Chiang Dao

★ ③ *72 km (40 mi) north of Chiang Mai.*

Near the village of Chiang Dao, north of Chiang Mai, you can find Thailand's most spectacular caves. This complex of cathedral-proportioned caverns penetrates more than 2 km (1 mi) into Doi Chiang Dao, an astonishing 7,500-foot mountain that leaps up almost vertically from the valley floor. ■ TIP→ **About half the caves have electric lights, but make sure you have a flashlight in your pocket in case there's a power failure.** If you want to explore more of the mountain, hire a guide.

Where to Stay

¢ 🖾 **Rim Doi Resort.** Rim Doi means "on the edge of the mountain," so it's fitting that two extraordinary peaks loom over this peaceful little resort near Chiang Dao. After a day exploring the nearby caves or venturing into the mountains, it's just the place to relax and prepare for the journey farther north. You'll probably be tempted to stay longer than just a night. Just B200 buys you a comfortable bed in a rustic bungalow, while a more stylish room in a modern extension overlooking a placid lake is an unbeatable B500. ✉ *46 Moo 4, Muang Ghay* ☎ *053/375028* ⊕ *www.rimdoiresort.com* ➴ *40 rooms* ♿ *In-hotel: restaurant, bar* ▭ *MC, V.*

Doi Ang Khang

③ *60 km (36 mi) north of Chiang Dao.*

North of Chang Dao lies one of the most remote corners of Northern Thailand. Literally at the end of the road, the only thing beyond Doi Ang Khang is the jungle. Ang means "bowl," which aptly describes the location of this small settlement. Here you can find a large agricultural research station, an important part of a governmental project to wean villagers away from opium production. The fields, orchards, and hothouses sit in the shadow of towering peaks.

Where to Stay

$$–$$$ ☒ **Ang Khang Nature Resort.** Amari, which normally runs luxurious city hotels, manages this stylish country resort in the mountains near Doi Ang Khan. Rooms have all the comforts of Amari's downtown digs, with teak furnishings and locally woven fabrics. All rooms have private balconies, many of them with spectacular views of the mountains. ⊠ *1/1 Moo 5 Baan Koom, Tambon Mae Ngon, Amphoe Fang, Doi Ang Khang, 50320* ☎ *053/450110* ⊕ *www.amari.com/angkhang* ⤶ *76 rooms* ⌂ *In-room: refrigerator. In-hotel: restaurant, bicycles, laundry service, public Internet* ⊟ *AE, DC, MC, V.*

Tha Ton

③③ *90 km (54 mi) north of Chiang Dao.*

North of Chiang Dao lies the pretty town of Tha Ton, which sits on the River Kok right across the border from Myanmar. The local temple, Wat Tha Ton, is built on a cliff overlooking the town. From the bridge below, boats set off for trips on the River Kok, some of them headed for Chiang Rai, 130 km (78 mi) away. This small resort town is a pleasant base for touring this mountainous region. An interesting side trip from Tha Ton takes you 45 km (27 mi) northeast on Highway 1089 to **Mae Salong,** where descendants of Chinese Nationalist soldiers who fled Mao Tse Tung's forces made their home near the top of a mountain called Doi Mae Salong. The slopes of the mountain are now covered with fruit orchards and coffee plantations. ■ TIP➔ **Visit in December and January and you can find the area swathed in cherry blossoms.**

Where to Stay

♻ **$$** ☒ **Maekok River Village Resort.** Every possible activity—from hiking to canoeing, from practicing your golf swing to mastering the basics of Thai cuisine—can be arranged at this friendly, comfortable hotel. Kids love many of the more unusual offerings, such as learning how to ride an elephant. Rooms are as large as apartments, but if you need more space there are also nine family villas. ⊠ *84 Moo 3, Ban Thaton, Amphoe Mae Ai, 50280* ☎ *053/459328* ⊕ *www.maekok-river-village-resort. com* ⤶ *29 rooms* ⌂ *In-room: refrigerator, ethernet. In-hotel: 3 restaurants, room service, 2 bars, pool, gym, spa, laundry facilities, public Internet.*

CHIANG RAI & THE GOLDEN TRIANGLE

This fabled area is a beautiful stretch of rolling uplands that conceal remote hill tribe villages and drop down to the broad Mekong, which is backed on its far side by the mountains of Laos. Although some 60 km (36 mi) to the south, Chiang Rai is its natural capital and a city equipped with all the infrastructure for touring the entire region.

The region's involvement in the lucrative opium trade began in the late 19th century, when migrating hill tribes introduced poppy cultivation.

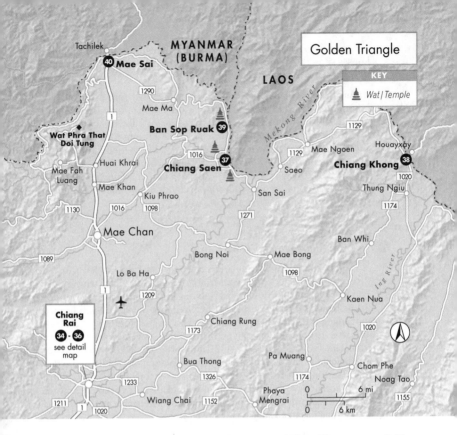

Chiang Rai
34 - 36
see detail
map

For more than 100 years the opium produced from poppy fields was the region's main source of income. Even today, despite vigorous official suppression and a royal project to wean farmers away from the opium trade, the mountains of the Golden Triangle conceal isolated poppy plantations. Scarcely a week goes by without a bloody clash between Thai police and suspected opium traders.

Despite its associations with the opium trade, the Golden Triangle is still regarded as a geographical area, varying in size and interpretation from the few square yards where the borders of Thailand, Myanmar, and Laos actually meet to a 40,000-square-km (15,440-square-mi) region where the opium-yielding poppies are still cultivated. That region includes much of Thailand's Chiang Rai Province, where strenuous and sometimes controversial police raids have severely curbed opium production and trade. The royal program to encourage farmers to plant alternative crops is also paying dividends.

Whatever the size of the actual triangle is thought to be, its apex is the riverside village of Ban Sop Ruak, once a bustling center of the region's opium trade. An archway on the Mekong riverbank at Ban Sop Ruak invites visitors to step symbolically into the Golden Triangle, and a large golden Buddha watches impassionately over the river scene. In a nearby valley where poppies once grew stands a huge museum, the Hall of Opium, which describes the history of the worldwide trade in narcotics.

Chiang Rai

180 km (112 mi) northeast of Chiang Mai, 780 km (485 mi) north of Bangkok.

Once again, an elephant played a central role in the foundation of an important Thai city. Legend has it that a royal elephant ran away from its patron, the 13th-century king Mengrai, founder of the Lanna kingdom. The beast stopped to rest on the banks of the Mae Kok River. The king regarded this as an auspicious sign and in 1256 built his capital, Chiang Rai, on the site. But little is left from those heady days: the Emerald Buddha that used to reside in Wat Phra Keo is now in Bangkok's Grand Palace, and a precious Buddha image in the 15th-century Wat Phra Singh has long since disappeared.

Chiang Rai attracts more and more visitors each year, and it's easy to see why. Six hill tribes—the Akha, Yao, Meo, Lisu, Lahu, and Karen—all live within Chiang Rai Province. Each has different dialects, customs, handicrafts, and costumes, and all still venerate animist spirits despite their increasing acquaintance with the outside world. As in Chiang Mai, they make daily journeys to the markets of Chiang Rai. The best of these is a night bazaar, just off Phaholyothin Road, which has a cluster of small restaurants and food vendors.

■ TIP→ **Climbing to the top of Doi Tong, a modest hill on the northeastern edge of Chiang Rai, is a great way to learn the lay of the land.** From the grounds of a 13th-century temple called Wat Doi Tong, you have a fine view of the Mae Kok River and the mountains beyond. Chiang Rai has very few sights of note, so a leisurely walk around town will take at most a few hours.

Sights to See

34 **Wat Doi Tong.** Near the summit of Doi Tong, this temple overlooks the Mae Kok River. The ancient pillar that stands here once symbolized the center of the universe for devout Buddhists. The sunset view is worth the trip. ⊠ *Winitchaikul Rd.*

35 **Wat Phra Keo.** The Emerald Buddha, which now sits in Thailand's holiest temple, Wat Phra Keo in Bangkok, is said to have been discovered when lightning split the chedi housing it at this similarly named temple at the foot of the Doi Tong. A Chinese millionaire financed a jade replica in 1991—al-

THE RUBBER TRIANGLE

En route to the Golden Triangle you'll pass through a small area known as the Rubber Triangle—and not because of any rubber trees. It's an offshoot of Bangkok's famous Cabbages and Condoms restaurant, which was founded by Thai politician Mechai Viravaidya, who led a successful campaign to combat AIDS. The **Cabbages and Condoms Inn and Restaurant** (⊠ Wiang Pa Pao, Chiang Rai ☎ 053/952312 ⊕ www.pda.or.th) is about halfway between Chiang Mai and Chiang Rai, and is identified by a sign, "YOU HAVE ARRIVED AT THE RUBBER TRIANGLE." Proceeds go toward funding development programs.

Chiang Rai

though it's not the real thing, the statuette is still strikingly beautiful. ✉ *Trairat Rd.*

36 **Wat Phra Singh.** This 14th-century temple is worth visiting for its viharn, distinguished by some remarkably delicate wood carving and for colorful frescoes depicting the life of Lord Buddha. A sacred Indian Bhoti tree stands in the peaceful temple grounds. ✉ *Singhaklai Rd.*

Where to Eat

¢–$ ✕ **Kasalong.** Chiang Rai's best seafood restaurant is a 15-minute tuk-tuk drive south of the city, but the journey is worth it. A large variety of seafood and lake fish is prepared according to Thai or Chinese recipes. The *tabtim* (sweet-tasting lake fish) in garlic and pepper sauce is particularly recommended. Although the restaurant sits on the busy superhighway, opposite the Big C megastore, you dine in a pleasant garden setting. ✉ *556/13 Super Hwy. Rd.* ☎ *053/754908* ▤ *MC, V.*

¢–$ ✕ **Toktong.** This teak-built, open-sided restaurant on one of Chiang Rai's busiest roads serves some of the city's best Northern Thai food in an airy, garden setting. The crispy pork and spicy dip are particularly tasty. A live folk music group performs in the evening. ✉ *45/12 Pahalyotin Rd.* ☎ *053/756369* ▤ *MC, V.*

¢–$ ✕ **Cham Cha.** Climb the stairs at this busy restaurant to avoid the lunchtime crowds and take a first-floor table overlooking the garden dominated by the handsome cham cha tree, which gives it its name. Avoid the Western dishes on the menu and go for traditional Northern Thai specialties such as *tom djuet,* a delicious soup laced with tofu and tiny pork dumplings. You can find the restaurant next to the Chiang Rai tourist office. ⊠ *447/ 17 Singhaklai Rd.* ☎ *053/744191* ▤ *No credit cards* ☉ *Closed Sun. No dinner.*

¢–$ ✕ **Hawnariga.** The name of this traditional Thai restaurant means "clock tower," and that's just where it's located, in the center of town. Orchids hang from the thatched palm-leaf roof of the large, open-sided restaurant. Two fishponds

> ### THE STORY OF THE NAME
>
> U.S. Assistant Secretary of State Marshall Green coined the term "Golden Triangle" in 1971 during a preview of the historic visit by President Richard Nixon to China. The Nixon Administration was concerned about the rise of heroin addiction in the United States and wanted to stem the flow of opium from China, Thailand, Myanmar, and Laos. The greatest source of opium was the wild territory where the Mekong and Ruak rivers formed porous borders between Thailand, Myanmar, and Laos—the "golden triangle" drawn by Green on the world map.

are connected by a brook that skirts the tables, and they provide fat tabtim for the menu. ⊠ *402/1–2 Banpapragarn Rd.* ☎ *053/711062* ▤ *V.*

Where to Stay

$$–$$$$ ▣ **The Legend.** This newer hotel could truly become something of a local legend. It's built in exclusively Lanna style on an island in the Mae Kok River, just a short walk from the city center. Rooms are furnished with exquisite Northern Thai antiques and reproductions, while public areas are a Lanna-style mixture of whitewashed walls, brickwork, and dark teak. The airy restaurant and landscaped swimming pool are on the riverbank, with views of the mountains beyond. For real seclusion, book one of the villas, which have their own private pools. ⊠ *124/15 Kohloy Rd., A. Muang, 57000* ☎ *053/910400 or 053/719649, 02/642–5497 in Bangkok* ⊕ *www.thelegend-chiangrai.com* ⇆ *79 rooms* ⚅ *In-room: safe, refrigerator, DVD, ethernet. In-hotel: 3 restaurants, bar, pool, spa, concierge, parking (no fee)* ▤ *AE, DC, MC, V.*

$$–$$$$ ▣ **Rimkok Resort.** Because it's across the Mae Kok River, and a taxi ride from town, this quiet hotel has more appeal for tour groups than for independent travelers. The main building is designed in modern Thai style with palatial dimensions—a long, wide lobby lined with boutiques leads to a spacious lounge and dining room. Rooms are in wings on either side, and most have views of the river from picture windows. ⊠ *6 Moo 4 Chiang Rai–Tathon Rd., Rimkok Muang, 57100* ☎ *053/716445, 02/279–0102 in Bangkok* ⊕ *www.rimkokresort.com* ⇆ *256 rooms* ⚅ *In-room: refrigerator. In-hotel: 4 restaurants, room service, 2 bars, pool, laundry service* ▤ *AE, DC, MC, V.*

★ $$ ▣ **Dusit Island Resort.** This gleaming white high-rise, which sits on an island in the Mae Kok River, has tons of amenities. On the premises you

CLOSE UP

The Hill Tribes: "Owners of the Mountains"

ONE OF THE MAIN ATTRACTIONS of trekking in Northern Thailand is meeting and staying with the hill tribe people who populate the more remote mountain areas. Some day trips include brief stops at villages, which are little more than Disneyland-type theme parks. But if you book a trek of three days or more you're sure to encounter authentic hill tribes living as they have for centuries.

Many hill tribe people claim they are victims of official discrimination, and it's indeed difficult for the majority to win full Thai citizenship because so many originate from beyond Thailand's borders. But the Thais themselves normally treat this exotic minority in their midst with respect and some measure of sympathy—it's significant that in the Thai language they are not described as "tribes" but as Chao Khao ("owners of the mountains").

For all the rigors of their hard existence, they're good-humored and friendly people who warmly welcome visitors. Whenever Westerners call to stay they usually organize a spontaneous party at which home-brewed whiskey flows copiously. "There was a birthday party in every one of the three villages we stayed at," mused one trekker, back in Chiang Mai, "that's some coincidence, isn't it?" If you stay overnight in a hill tribe village you'll be invited to share the community's simple food and sleep on the floor in one of their basic huts.

Before you leave on your trek, ask the tour operator to identify the hill tribes you'll be visiting and to describe their culture and traditions. It'll add greatly to the pleasure of your visit. There are nine hill tribes living in the mountains of Northern Thailand. They number about half a million, a mere 1% of Thailand's population. Most of them are descendants of migratory peoples from ancient Myanmar and China—one tribe, the Mien (called Yao by the Thais), write in Chinese script and follow Chinese Taoist religious rites.

Half of Thailand's hill tribe population are **Karen,** who mostly inhabit the mountainous northern and northwestern regions bordering Myanmar. They're not only the most numerous hill tribe people but also the most interesting, many of them sharing a common aim of the Karen people of eastern Myanmar: the establishment of an autonomous state. Hopes of eventual independence, fueled by empty British colonial promises, pushed many Karen onto the Allied side during Japan's World War II invasion of Southeast Asia. There are old soldiers in the West who remember Karen courage with gratitude.

Western missionaries brought Christianity to the Karen in colonial Burma, and today the Christian faith is followed in many communities over the border in Thailand. Traditionally, though, the Karen hold animist beliefs, usually mingled now with Buddhist practices.

The Karen are the most settled of the hill tribes, living in permanent villages of well-constructed houses and farming plots of land that leave as much of the forest as possible undisturbed. (The slash-and-burn farming methods of some other hill tribes bring them constantly into conflict with the authorities.) Though the long-neck Karen women receive the most attention, all Karen women are skilled weavers. Styles of dress vary throughout all the distinct groups, but unmarried women generally wear loose, white blouses, while married women wear bold colors (a lot of blue and red).

The next most populous hill tribe is the **Hmong.** You'll recognize the women of this group at work in the night markets of Chiang Mai and Chiang Rai by their colorful costumes and heavy silver jewelry. There are two divisions of Hmong, White and Blue; White Hmong women wear baggy black pants and blue sashes, while Blue Hmong women wear knee-length pleated skirts. There are 80,000 Hmong in Thailand, although numbers will drop as many are being resettled in the United States, mainly in California, near Fresno—the reward for Hmong assistance to American forces in neighboring Laos during the Vietnam War.

The Hmong of Thailand have been progressively weaned away from cultivating their traditional crop, the opium-producing poppy, and today most Hmong communities farm profitable alternatives such as coffee and tea.

The poor cousins of the Hmong, the 33,000-strong **Akha,** also thrived on opium-production, shielded from outside interference and control by the relative inaccessibility of the remote mountaintop sites they chose for their settlements. They're of Tibetan origin and a gentle, hospitable people, whose women wear elaborate headdresses decorated with silver, beads, and feathers. Every Akha village is defined by a set of wooden gates, which are often decorated with charms meant to ward off evil spirits.

The tribe you're most likely to meet on day trips out of Chiang Mai and Chiang Rai are the businesslike **Lisu.** More than any other hill tribe, this 25,000-strong community has recognized the earning power of tourism, and as tourist buses draw up, Lisu women scramble to don their multicolor costumes and line up for photographs.

No matter which tribe you visit, remember that the people of these villages tend to be more conservative, so be respectful and follow a few simple guidelines. Dress modestly. Keep a respectful distance from religious ceremonies or symbols—don't touch any talismans unless given permission to do so. Avoid loud or aggressive behavior and public displays of affection. And although charging tourists for snapshots is a big business for some of the villages, always ask permission before taking a person's picture.

—Robert Tilley

can find the largest outdoor pool in Northern Thailand. The complex's three wings all have rooms overlooking the shore. The spacious rooms, filled with modern renditions of traditional Thai furnishings, have unexpected extras like large marble baths. The Peak grills up delicious steaks, while Chinatown stir-fries Cantonese fare. The casual Island Café, where a buffet breakfast is served, serves Thai food all day. All three dining rooms have impressive views. ⊠ *1129 Kraisorasit Rd., 57000* ☎ *053/715777, 02/238–4790 in Bangkok* ⊕ *http://chiangrai.dusit.com* ⤢ *176 rooms* ♨ *In-room: safe, refrigerator, ethernet. In-hotel: 3 restaurants, room service, 4 bars, 2 tennis courts, pool, gym, laundry service, airport shuttle* ▤ *AE, DC, MC, V.*

$$ ▦ **Wiang Inn.** In the heart of downtown, this low-slung hotel is among the best in central Chiang Rai. Spacious rooms are decked out in dark woods and fine fabrics. Outside is a small outdoor pool surrounded by exotic greenery. The Golden Teak restaurant serves Thai, Chinese, and other fare. ⊠ *893 Phaholyothin Rd., 57000* ☎ *053/711533 up to 35* ⊕ *www.wianginn.com* ⤢ *260 rooms* ♨ *In-room: refrigerator. In-hotel: 2 restaurants, pool, gym, public Internet* ▤ *AE, DC, V.*

¢ ▦ **Ben's Guest House.** This family-run inn has repeatedly won accolades for its comfortable and extremely reasonable accommodations. The steep-eaved Lanna-style home and an annex are at the end of a quiet lane on the western edge of town. Transportation into Chiang Rai is easy to arrange. ⊠ *35/10, San Khon Noi Rd., Soi 4, 57000* ☎ *053/716775* ⤢ *28 rooms* ▤ *No credit cards.*

¢ ▦ **Chiang Rai Inn.** All the accommodations at this Lanna-style hotel, near the bus station, look out over a cool, palm-shaded courtyard. Some of the comfortable rooms have sitting areas. The casual restaurant, furnished in cane and bamboo, serves an excellent choice of Northern Thai dishes. ⊠ *661 Uttarakit Rd., 57000* ☎ *053/71700 up to 03* ⤢ *77 rooms* ♨ *In-room: refrigerator. In-hotel: restaurant, laundry facilities* ▤ *MC, V.*

¢ ▦ **Golden Triangle Inn.** Don't confuse this cozy guesthouse with the backpackers' hangout at Ban Sop Ruak. ■ TIP➔ **This comfortable little place is all too popular—advance reservations are necessary—because of its ideal location in the center of town.** Wood-ceiling rooms are cooled by slowly turning fans. The café serves Thai and Western fare, while the terrace bar has a wide range of fruity drinks. Next door is a travel agency that arranges treks into Laos. ⊠ *590–2 Phaholyothin Rd., 57000* ☎ *053/711339* ⤢ *39 rooms* ♨ *In-room: no a/c (some). In-hotel: restaurant, bar* ▤ *No credit cards.*

★ ¢ ▦ **White House.** The charming Indian-Thai couple who run this attractive inn are justifiably proud of what they regard as their own home. Rooms are huddled around a courtyard. Nearby is a small pool and an open-air café. The owners also run an efficient travel service and a modest business center. ⊠ *789 Phaholyothin Rd., 57000* ☎ *053/713427 or 053/744051* ⤢ *36 rooms* ♨ *In-room: no a/c (some), no TV (some), refrigerator. In-hotel: 2 restaurants, pool, laundry services, public Internet* ▤ *MC.*

Shopping

Chiang Rai has a **night market**, on Robviang Nongbua Road, and although it's much smaller than Chiang Mai's, there's a large variety of handicrafts and textiles on offer. **T.S. Jewelry & Antiques** (✉ 877–879 Pha-holyothin Rd. ☎ 053/711050) has a very large selection of jewelry and antiques from Northern Thailand and neighboring Myanmar and Laos.

Sports & the Outdoors

Chiang Rai is an excellent base from which to set out on tours trekking through the nearby mountains or canoeing and rafting on the region's rivers. Tour operators charge about B800 a day (including overnight stops in hill tribe villages).

Some 90 km (54 mi) due east of Chiang Rai is perhaps the region's most beautiful national park, **Phu Sang,** which has one of Thailand's rarest natural wonders, cascades of hot water. The temperature of the water that tumbles over the 85-foot-high falls never drops below 33°C (91°F), and a nearby pool is even warmer. The park has some spectacular caves and is crisscrossed by nature trails teeming with birdlife. One hour's drive north lies the mountainous border with Laos, straddled by 5,730-foot-high Phu Chee Fah, a favorite destination for trekkers and climbers. You reach the Phu Sang National Park via Thoeng, 70 km (42 mi) east of Chiang Rai on Route 1020. The park rents lodges for B800 to B1,000 a night. Entrance to the park costs B400, and B30 for a vehicle. Call 054/401099 for reservations.

BOATING Both **Inbound-Outbound Tour Service** (✉ 199/38 Phaholyothin Rd. ☎ 053/715690) and **Four Lens Tour** (✉ 131/6 Moo 13, Mae Korn Intersection ☎ 053/700617 up to 20 ⊕ www.4lens.com) offer longtail boat trips on the Kok River, but if you want something more adventurous, catch a bus to the border town of Tha Thon and board a longtail boat there and ride the rapids to Chiang Rai. The 130-km (78-mi) trip takes four hours by high-powered longtail boat, or two days by raft. The trip takes you through one of the region's most remote areas, through gorges and thick jungle and past hill tribe villages. Inbound-Outbound can help you book the trip.

GOLF Chiang Rai has one of Northern Thailand's finest golf courses, the **San-tiburi Country Club** (✉ 12 Moo 3, Huadoi-Sobpao Rd. ☎ 053/662821 up to 26 🖨 053/717377), laid out by the celebrated Robert Trent Jones Jr. The par-72, 18-hole course is set among rolling hills 10 km (6 mi) outside Chiang Rai. The ranch-style clubhouse has an excellent restaurant and coffee shop and the facilities also include a sauna. Visitors are welcome and clubs, carts, and shoes can be rented. Reservations are requested.

Chiang Saen

🕗 *59 km (37 mi) north of Chiang Rai, 239 km (148 mi) northeast of Chiang Mai, 935 km (581 mi) north of Bangkok.*

On the banks of the Mekong River sits Chiang Saen, a one-road town that in the 12th century was home to the future king Mengrai. Only fragments of the ancient ramparts survived the incursion by the Burmese in 1588, and the rest of the citadel was ravaged by fire when the last of the Burmese were ousted in 1786. The government-financed excavation project now under way is well worth visiting. Chiang Saen is now being developed as a major Mekong river port, and it's the embarkation point for river trips to Myanmar, Laos, and China.

Only two ancient chedis remain standing to remind the visitor of Chiang Saen's ancient glory. Just outside the city walls is the oldest chedi, **Wat Pa Sak,** whose name refers to the 300 teak trees that were planted in the surrounding area. The stepped temple, which narrows to a spire, is said to enshrine holy relics brought here when the city was founded. Inside the city walls stands the imposing octagonal **Wat Phra That Luang.** Scholars say it dates from the 14th century.

Next door to Wat Phra That Luang is the **National Museum,** which houses artifacts from the Lanna period, as well as some Neolithic discoveries. The museum also has a good collection of carvings and traditional handicrafts from the hill tribes.

☎ *053/777102* ✉ *B30* ☉ *Wed.–Sun. 9–4.*

Where to Stay

$ 🏨 **Chiang Saen River Hill Hotel.** Part of the Old City wall guides the way to this stylish, quietly located hotel, a short walk from the local boat jetty. Rooms are attractively decorated with Lanna arts and crafts, including the odd old cart wheel or two. The nightly buffet supper is "spiced down" to suit the tastes of the tour groups who favor this hotel, but it's a hearty, diverse meal. ✉ *714 Moo 3, Tambon Wiang, 57150* ☎ *053/ 650826 or 053/777396* ✍ *chiangsaen@hotmail.com* ⇥ *60 rooms* ♨ *In-hotel: restaurant, bar, parking (no fee)* ⊟ *No credit cards.*

★ ¢ 🏨 **Gin's Guest House.** A local lawyer, Kun Gin ("as in the drink"), and his wife run this charming guesthouse, which is a true home away from home. Rooms are just as you'd expect to find in your favorite aunt's country retreat. Some have large hearths for chilly nights. Kun Gin's a mine of local information and can organize everything from a trip across the nearby Mekong to a two-night cruise to China. If the house is full in high season you'll be lodged in bivouac-style wooden chalets in the extensive, tree-shaded garden, so early booking is recommended. ✉ *Ban Sop Ruak Rd., 57150* ☎ *053/650847* ⇥ *9 rooms* ⊟ *No credit cards.*

Chiang Khong

㊳ *53 km (33 mi) northeast of Chiang Rai.*

The recently paved road east out of Chiang Saen parallels the Mekong River en route to Chiang Khong, a town with magnificent views across the river to Laos. Songthaews ply the route, but you can also hire a speedboat to go down the river, a thrilling three hours of slipping between the rocks and rapids. Not too many tourists make the journey, especially to villages inhabited by the local Hmong and Yao tribes. ■ TIP→ **The rugged scenery along the Mekong River is actually more dramatic than that of the Golden Triangle.**

Across the river from Chiang Khong is the Laotian town of **Houay Say,** where you can find beautiful antique Laotian textiles. Thais are permitted to cross the river, but foreigners require visas. Numerous guesthouses in Chiang Khong accommodate overnight visitors. A 15-day visa can be acquired in Chiang Khong from **Ann Tour** (✉ 6/1 Moo 8, Saiklang Rd. ☎ 053/655198).

Ban Sop Ruak

39 *8 km (5 mi) north of Chiang Saen.*

Ban Sop Ruak, a village in the heart of the Golden Triangle, was once the domain of the opium warlord Khun Sa. More than a decade ago, government troops forced him back to Burmese territory, but his reputation still draws those eager to see evidence of the man who once held the region under his thumb.

Opium is so linked to the history of Ban Sop Ruak that the small town now has two museums devoted to the subject. The smaller one, **Opium Museum,** is in the center of town. A commentary in English details the growing, harvesting, and smoking of opium. Many of the exhibits, such as carved teak opium boxes and jade and silver pipes, are fascinating. ✉ B30 ☉ *Daily 7–6.*

Fodor'sChoice ★ Opened in 2004, the magnificent **Hall of Opium** is a dazzling white stucco, glass, marble, and aluminum building nestling in a valley above the Mekong. The site of the museum is so close to former poppy fields that a plan is still being considered to extend the complex to encompass an "open-air" exhibit of a functioning opium plantation. The museum traces the history of the entire drug trade (including a look at how mild stimulants like coffee and tea took hold in the West). It even attempts to give visitors a taste of the "opium experience" by leading them through a 500-foot-long tunnel where synthetic aroma traces of the drug and atmospheric music waft between walls bearing phantasmagoric bas-relief scenes.

The entrance tunnel emerges into a gallery of blinding light, where the nature of the opium-producing poppy is vividly described on an information panel erected in front of an imitation field of the insidiously beautiful flower. It's an arresting introduction to an imaginatively designed and assembled exhibition, which reaches back into the murky history of the opium trade and takes a long, monitory look into a potentially even darker future. ■ TIP→ **The Hall of Opium is so large in scope and scale that two days are hardly enough to take it all in. A visit is ideally combined with an overnight stay,** either at the Hall's own Greater Mekong Lodge (double rooms from B1,800 including breakfast) or, for a sheer splurge, at the luxurious Anantara, just across the road. ☎ 053/784444 ⊕ *www. maefahluang.org* ✉ B300 ☉ *Tues.–Sun. 10–3:30.*

Even if you don't stay overnight, pay a visit to the sumptuous **Imperial Golden Triangle Resort,** which has the best views over the confluence of the Mae Sai, Ruak, and Mekong rivers.

Where to Stay

$$$$ ▦ **Four Seasons Tented Camp.** Modeled on an African safari camp, this collection of canvas-roof bungalows sits in thick jungle in Northern Thailand's famed Golden Triangle. It's "designed for the active adult,"

meaning it combines a touch of soft adventure with all the comforts of a luxury hotel. The "tents" are floored with polished teak and furnished with Thai silks; handhammered copper bathtubs with room for two dominate the bedrooms. Activities include elephant riding, boat trips on the nearby Mekong River, jungle treks, and Thai cooking classes. Evenings are spent African-safari style, over sundowners and opulent dinners. ⌂ *Box 18, Chiang Saen Post Office, Chiang Saen, 57150* ☎ *053/784477* ⊕ *www.fourseasons.com/goldentriangle* ⊲ *15 tents* △ *In-room: safe, refrigerator, Wi-Fi. In-hotel: restaurant, bar, spa, laundry service, concierge* ▤ *AE, DC, MC, V.*

SHORT BORDER EXCURSIONS

Longtail excursion boats captained by experienced river men tie up at the Ban Sop Ruak jetty, and the B500 fee covers a 90-minute cruise into the waters of Myanmar and Laos and a stop at a Laotian market. You can take a short trip into Myanmar by visiting the Golden Triangle Paradise Resort, which sits in isolated splendor on the Burmese bank of the Mekong, about 1 km (½ mi) upstream from the Golden Triangle. The Thai immigration office at the Ban Sop Ruak jetty makes a photocopy of your passport for the Burmese authorities for B200.

$$ ▦ **Anantara Golden Triangle.** The
Fodor'sChoice Anantara is one of the Golden Tri-
★ angle's top addresses. Mythical figures line your way to a palatial entrance, which leads into a vast, open-plan, two-floor area encompassing an excellent restaurant, opulently furnished lounge, and reputedly the longest bar in Northern Thailand. Rooms are luxuriously furnished in indigenous woods and draped with handmade Thai fabrics. Louvered glass doors lead to bathrooms with terra-cotta tubs big enough for a pool party. Picture windows opening onto private balconies command spectacular views of the confluence of the Mekong and Ruak rivers. ■ TIP➡ **The former Opium Den Bar has become the best Italian restaurant north of Chiang Mai.** ⊠ *Chiang Saen, 57150* ☎ *053/784084, 02/476–0022 in Bangkok* ⊕ *www.anantara.com* ⊲ *106 rooms, 4 suites* △ *In-room: safe, refrigerator. In-hotel: 2 restaurants, room service, 2 bars, 2 tennis courts, pool, gym, spa, laundry service, concierge, airport shuttle* ▤ *AE, DC, MC, V.*

$–$$ ▦ **Imperial Golden Triangle Resort.** From the superior rooms in this higheaved, Lanna-style hotel you are treated to magnificent views of three rivers rushing together. The smart restaurant, the Border View, lives up to its name, but the best way to enjoy the panorama is to soak it up with a glass of Mekong whiskey on the terrace. Classical Thai dance is performed in the evening during high season. ⊠ *222 Ban Sop Ruak* ☎ *053/784001, 02/261–9000 Bangkok reservations* ⊕ *www.imperialhotels.com* ⊲ *74 rooms* △ *In-room: refrigerator. In-hotel: 2 restaurants, pool, laundry service* ▤ *AE, DC, MC, V.*

$ ▦ **Café De River.** Rooms at this oddly named but perfectly conventional hotel, halfway between Chiang Saen and Ban Sop Ruak, directly overlook the Mekong, and the bright little café itself sit above its swirling waters. The hotel is comfortable and scrupulously clean, and run by a very friendly local family. ⊠ *455 Moo 1 Chiang Saen, 57150* ☎ *053/784477* ⊲ *20 rooms* △ *In-hotel: restaurant, bar* ▤ *MC, V.*

Spirited Thailand

CLOSE UP

THE ANIMIST BELIEFS of many of the region's hill tribe people have mingled with traditional Buddhism.

If you're touring rural areas of the north, you might be lucky enough to witness one of the many festivals in which invisible spirits play major roles. The most impressive of these is Wat Pa, or "Tree Ordination," during which threatened trees, such as teak, are ritually dressed in saffron robes, making them holy and theoretically immune from destruction by illegal loggers. The ritual is led by monks, who hand out the robes to villagers, who then select a tree and "dress" it.

Spirits are widely believed to live in the forests, and whenever a tree is felled a ceremony of contrition has to take place. When a house is built, offerings to the spirits who once owned the timber are placed in all four corners. The garden will usually have a "spirit house," an elaborate

dollhouse to act as home for the spirits of the land on which a new house is built. If the house is extended then the spirit house is enlarged, too. You'll find spirit houses everywhere, from gardens to gas stations. On the Lampang–Chiang Mai highway there's a veritable city of them at a point in the mountains believed to be thickly populated by spirits.

Spirits are invoked at most family ceremonies from homecomings to weddings to funerals. Their influence is particularly valued in time of illness—villagers firmly believe that most maladies arise when a body "loses" one of the spirits assigned to protect it. A medicine man is commonly called upon to conduct a ceremony in which thread is wound around the patient's wrist, in the belief that the absent spirit is then reattached to the suffering body.

¢ ⊞ **Golden Home.** The Mekong River is just across the road from this small resortlike guesthouse. There are just seven wooden cabins, each with a tiny terrace overlooking a flower-smothered yard. The night market that borders the river is a short walk away. ⊠ *41 Moo 1, Wiang, Chiang Saen, 57150* ☎ *053/784205* ⇥ *7 cabins* ⚴ *In-room: refrigerator. In-hotel: parking (no fee)* ⊟ *No credit cards.*

Mae Sai

④⓪ *25 km (15 mi) west of Ban Sop Ruak, 60 km (36 mi) north of Chiang Rai.*

From Ban Sop Ruak you can travel west on a dusty road to Mae Sai, a town that straddles the Mae Sai River. At this market town the merchants trade goods with the Burmese. For the best view across the river into Myanmar, climb up to **Wat Phra That Doi Wao**—the 207-step staircase starts from behind the Top North Hotel.

Foreigners may cross the river to visit **Thachilek** on a one-day visa, obtainable at the bridge for $10. It's a smaller version of Mae Sai, but with no less than three casinos, packed with Thai gamblers. For $30 you can get a three-night visa that lets you travel 63 km (39 mi) north to **Keng-tung,** a quaint town with colonial-era structures built by the British alongside old Buddhist temples.

Where to Stay & Eat

¢ ✕ **Rabiang Kaew.** Set back from the main road by a wooden bridge, this restaurant built in the northern style has an unmistakable charm. Antiques adorning the dining room add to its rustic style. The Thai fare is tasty and expertly prepared. ⊠ *356/1 Phaholyothin Rd.* ☏ *053/731172* ⊟ *MC, V.*

¢ ▣ **Mae Sai Guest House.** Backpackers rank this riverside guesthouse, about 2 km (1 mi) west of the bridge, as the best in Mae Sai. It's certainly among the cheapest, with a single bed in a dormitory room without air-conditioning costing just B100. A small garden area, running down to the river, surrounds the main building. ⊠ *688 Wiengpangkam, 57130* ☏ *053/732021* ⬐ *20 bungalows* ⊟ *No credit cards.*

¢ ▣ **Piyaporn Place.** Mae Sai's top hotel is a long walk from the center of town and the markets, but the friendly staff arranges transport to both. The large rooms are furnished and decorated in teak and local fabrics. Many of them have fine views of the town and neighboring Myanmar. ⊠ *77/1 Moo 1, Weianghum, 57130* ☏ *053/734511* ⬐ *60 rooms* ⚷ *In-hotel: restaurant, bar, pool* ⊟ *MC, V.*

¢ ▣ **Wang Thong.** This riverside hotel was originally intended to cater to business executives trading across the nearby Thai-Burmese border, but now the guests are mostly travelers. Choose a room high up on the river side so you can spend an idle hour or two watching the flowing waters and the flowing pedestrian traffic across the bridge. Its rooms are modern and functional. ⊠ *299 Phaholyothin Rd., 57130* ☏ *053/733388* ⬐ *150 rooms* ⚷ *In-room: refrigerator. In-hotel: 2 restaurants, 2 bars, pool, laundry service* ⊟ *MC, V.*

Shopping

Thais take household goods and consumer products across the river, where the Burmese trade them for sandalwood, jade, and rubies. Though you may want to see Myanmar, the prices and quality of the goods will not be better than in Mae Sai. Near the bridge, **Mengrai Antique** (⊠ Phaholyothin Rd. ☏ 053/731423) has a matchless reputation.

▬ TIP➔ Rubies aren't the only red gems here. Mae Sai is also justifiably proud of its sweet strawberries, which ripen in December or January.

The Golden Triangle Essentials

Transportation

BY AIR

Thai Airways has three daily flights from Bangkok to Chiang Rai.

Chiang Rai International Airport is 6 km (4 mi) northeast of the city. Incoming flights are met by songthaews and tuk-tuks, which charge about B50 for the journey to central Chiang Rai.

▣ Carrier **Thai Airways** ⊠ 240 Phrapokklao Rd., Chiang Mai ☏ 053/920999 ⊕ www.thaiair.com.

▣ Airport Information **Chiang Rai International Airport** ☏ 053/793048.

BY BOAT & FERRY

At Tha Thon, a pretty little riverside border town, longtail boats and rafts set off daily for the 130-km (78-mi) trip downstream to Chiang Rai. High-powered longtail boats leave from a pier near the town bridge at 12:30 PM and take about five hours to negotiate the bends and rapids of the river, which passes through thick jungle and past remote hill tribe villages. The fare is B160. For a more leisurely ride to Chiang Rai, board a raft, which takes two days and nights to reach Chiang Rai, overnighting in hill tribe villages. Fares are around B1,000. ■ TIP→ **Take bottled water, an inflatable cushion, and (most important) a hat or umbrella to shade you from the sun.** The best time to make the trip is during October and November, when the water is still high but the rainy season is past.

BY BUS

Destinations in Chiang Rai and the Golden Triangle are serviced by buses that leave regularly from Chiang Mai's two terminals. Buses to Chiang Rai leave regularly between 8 AM and 7:15 PM from Bangkok's Northern bus terminal and between 6:15 AM and 5 PM from Chiang Mai's Arcade terminal. The VIP bus trip from Bangkok costs B700, the air-conditioned A1 service costs B452; from Chiang Mai the fare is B139. It's an exhausting journey of at least 12 hours from Bangkok. The journey from Chiang Mai takes between 3 and 4 hours.

🚩 Bus Station **Chiang Rai Bus Terminal** ✉ Prasopsook Rd., Chiang Rai 📞 053/711369.

BY CAR

Roads are well paved throughout the Golden Triangle, presenting no problem for drivers. The area is bisected by the main north–south road, Highway 110, and crisscrossed by good country roads. In Chiang Rai, the most prominent companies are Avis, National, and Budget. Budget has a good range of four-wheel-drive vehicles for trips off the beaten path.

BY TAXI & TUK-TUK

Tuk-tuks are the common way of getting around Chiang Rai, and a trip across town costs B40–B50. Songthaews can also be hailed on the street and hired for trips to outlying areas. The fare inside the city is B10—farther afield is a matter of negotiation.

Contacts & Resources

BANKS & EXCHANGING SERVICES

Banks are swift and professional in all the region's major cities and in tourist destinations such as the Golden Triangle, and you can expect friendly assistance in English. ATMs are everywhere to be found and are clearly marked.

EMERGENCIES

🚩 **Overbrooke Hospital** ✉ Singhaklai Rd., Chiang Rai 📞 053/711366. **Police** 📞 053/711444 in Chiang Rai.

INTERNET, MAIL & SHIPPING

Internet cafés are on virtually every street corner in Chiang Rai, and you'll have no trouble locating one in the region's smaller towns. Charges vary enormously, ranging from B15 an hour to B2 a minute. Sometimes a half hour's Internet use includes a free cup of coffee. Rates in hotel business centers are much higher than in Internet cafés. Post offices are normally open weekdays 8:30 to 4:30 and for a few hours on Saturday morning.

📋 Post Office **Chiang Rai** ✉ 21 Uttarakit Rd. ☎ 053/711444.

TOUR OPTIONS

The major hotels in Chiang Rai and the Golden Triangle Resort in Chiang Saen organize minibus tours of the region. Their travel desks will also arrange treks to the hill tribe villages. Should you prefer to deal directly with a tour agency, try Golden Triangle Tours or Track of the Tiger, a pioneer of "soft adventure tourism" in Northern Thailand. Its very comprehensive program, concentrated in the Chiang Rai region, covers mountain biking, canoeing, rafting, rock climbing, river barge cruises, trekking, botany trails, golf, and cooking courses.

Dapa Tours is a nonprofit company run by Akha people to raise money for their villages.

📋 **Dapa Tours** ✉ 115 Moo 2, Rimkok Rd., Chiang Rai ☎ 053/711354. **Golden Triangle Tours** ✉ 590 Phaholyothin Rd., Chiang Rai ☎ 053/711339. **Track of the Tiger** ✉ Maekok River Village Resort, Box 3, Mae Ai, Chiang Rai ☎ 053/459355 ⊕ www.maekok-river-village-resort.com.

VISITOR INFORMATION

For information in Chiang Rai try the Tourist Information Center on Singhaklai Road.

📋 Tourist Information **Tourist Information Center** ✉ Singhaklai Rd., Chiang Rai ☎ 053/744674.

Isan

There are many statues on the grounds of Wat Khaek in Nong Khai.

6

WORD OF MOUTH

"We spent three days in Khao Yai National Park. What a gem for outdoors lovers! One evening, we climbed a rocky hill to see bats swarm out of their caves. The next day we took a moderate hike through the forest and saw gibbons and great hornbills. What a treat—climbing along elephant trails, seeing wild orchids and beautiful tropical birds."

—Kay

WELCOME TO ISAN

Songthaew

TOP REASONS TO GO

★ **Roads Less Traveled**
Tour buses are rare on the roads of the sprawling northeast plateau, and you'll probably only run into a few other *farang*.

★ **Khmer ruins** Thailand's finest Khmer temples are living histories, too, with Hindu shrines sometimes supplanted by Buddhist monuments.

★ **Nature Preserves** Two of the country's most popular national parks are here, including Phu Kra Dueng, where you can find a profusion of wildflowers in spring.

★ **Drifting down the Mekong** The Mekong's murky waters are a fixture in the eastern landscape. Take a boat trip, dine in a floating restaurant, or just take in the views from a waterfront hotel.

★ **Som Tam** This spicy-and-sour green-papaya salad is a staple of the entire country, but its birthplace is Isan, and that's where it's still the best.

Thai Laos style temple.

1 Korat & Environs. The capital of Isan, Korat, is Thailand's second city, and it's justifiably famous for its fresh food, friendliness, and impressive parkland. But the real gems of this region, known as Lower Isan, are its ancient Khmer temples, which often share Hindu and Buddhist histories.

2 Along the Mekong. The legendary Mekong River forms Thailand's border with Laos to the east and north, and its banks are home to some of the country's most beautiful and off-the-beaten-path towns. In some places, you might not see another foreigner for weeks. In others, you'll find the occasional five-star resort with river views.

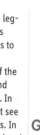

GETTING ORIENTED

The vast swath of Thailand known as Isan has often been characterized, if not stigmatized, by the existence of the Korat plateau, which makes up a good portion of the region. If much of Isan's landscape is flat and featureless, this is hardly true of the region's culture. Travelers to Isan have the option of visiting the mountains around Korat and Loei, experiencing the traditional life of the provinces along the length of the Mekong River from Nong Khai, or visiting the wealth of Khmer architecture found in the southern stretch of the region bordering Cambodia. The best way to approach the region is from one of the major cities, Korat or Udon Thani.

6

LAOS

CAMBODIA

Phimai, Issan.

3 Udon Thani & Environs. This fast-growing region includes the boomtown of Khon Kaen, along with Surin, famous for its elephants. Get into the rural parts of the region, and you'll see miles upon miles of picturesque rice paddies and expansive, pink sunsets above low-lying marshland—for many people the iconic image of Southeast Asia.

ISAN PLANNER

When to Go

The ideal time to visit Isan is during the cooler winter months between late October and February, when the rains stop, the temperatures are more agreeable, and the flora more abundant. But this major rice bowl of Thailand looks its best when the vast plains are filled with the calming sight of rice fields in full production, which happens August through December.

The region is not affected by the traditional high season, either in terms of costs or volume of visitors, but you should be prepared for crowds and steep accommodation price rises during major public festivals. It's also worth bearing in mind that discounts are prevalent during the off-season, particularly the rainy season, June through October.

Safety

Theft isn't particularly common in the region, but it's not unheard of, so it's advisable to take the normal precautions like ensuring rental cars are locked and possessions are out of sight. Motorbikes are more prone to theft than cars.

The Mekong towns pose little trouble for travelers, with the strong currents of the river itself being their only real danger. Swimming, diving, or kayaking are not recommended.

How Much Can You Do?

In the best of all possible worlds, you'd take two weeks in order to visit the whole region on a circular route. The good news is that even on a short trip you can get a sense of the region. If you are short on time, you may want to base yourself in Korat, a four-hour journey by train from Bangkok. The town can serve as a base for trips to the nearby Khmer ruins at Phimai. Surin, Buri Ram, and Si Saket, a little farther away, are also good bases from which to visit more ruins.

Getting Around

All the region's cities are accessible by bus from the major centers of Korat, Udon Thani, and Ubon Ratchathani, all of which are easily reached from Bangkok. There are two train routes from Bangkok, both running through Korat, where the line splits—one way to Udon Thani via Khon Kaen, the other heading to Ubon Ratchathani via Buri Ram, Surin, and Si Saket.

Tour companies are not common in the area, but it's possible to rent a car or hire a driver in the larger cities. Hiring a private driver for your whole trip is a more expensive, but quite appealing, option, especially if you're able to hire an English-speaking driver, as English is not commonly spoken in Isan. Songthaews are found all over, but for short trips locals tend to prefer motorbike taxis and pedal-powered samlors over tuk-tuks. Most of Bangkok's taxi drivers come from Isan, but you rarely find a car taxi here.

Regional Cuisine Highlights

The cuisine of the country's easternmost region is nationally famous for its fiery, chili-based salads and soups, most notably *som tam*, a deliciously spicy, sour green-papaya salad. In som tam, garlic, chilies, pickled crabs, dried shrimp, peanuts, and string beans are ground with a mortar and pestle; fish sauce, sugar, and lime juice are added, and the mixture is tossed with light, crunchy green papaya to make an intensely flavorful and healthy dish. Som tam is a national obsession, and in Isan, its birthplace, it is eaten by locals daily.

The one Isan dish that you may have encountered in Thai restaurants at home is *laab*, a spicy salad of boiled minced meat with chili, lime, fish sauce, sugar, lime juice, roasted rice powder, red onions, and mint leaves. Best is *laab moo*, the pork version. Laab is usually accompanied with cucumber and the ubiquitous *khao niao* (glutinous sticky rice), which is preferred to the more refined *khao suay* (steamed rice). The Isan way to do things is to take a small ball of sticky rice in your fingers and dip it into the laab juice.

An Isan cook is generous with spices, and herbs like basil and mint are liberally added to meat dishes. An especially tasty dish is *nua namtok*, which is sliced beef lightly grilled and garnished with shallots, dried chilies, lemon juice, and fresh mint leaves. Pork is popular, eaten in a style called *moo pan* (a fatty slab beaten flat and roasted over charcoal) and another called *moo yor* (an appetizer of sweet ground pork wrapped in a banana leaf). River fish is another specialty of the region; *pla nin pao*, for instance, is a whole fish stuffed with lemongrass, caked over with salt, and grilled over an open fire.

Each province claims to have the best *gai yang* (roast chicken), but Si Saket and Udon Thani brag the loudest. Especially popular in Korat is *sai krog Isan*, a sausage filled with minced pork, garlic, and rice. It's usually cooked and eaten with sliced ginger, dry peanuts, and grilled chilies. But be warned—it's *very* spicy. Korat noodles, on the other hand, are sweet. Here, as elsewhere, the locals douse just about everything with *balah*, fermented fish sauce.

Crossing into Laos

Foreigners can cross into Laos at Nong Khai, Nakhon Phanom, and Mukdahan. You'll need a Laotian visa costing US$30, which can be obtained from the Laotian Embassy in Bangkok, the consulate in Khon Kaen, or directly at the border crossings. Some hotels and guesthouses in Nong Khai can also obtain visas for an added fee.

Hotel Tips

Because relatively few tourists visit Isan, most hotels and guesthouses cater chiefly to a business clientele. There are some top-class hotels in larger towns like Korat, Khon Kaen, and Udon Thani, but most accommodations are much more modest. As elsewhere in Thailand, standards of cleanliness are high and even the most basic room will invariably have fresh linen and towels.

Isan is a bargain—with the exception of Khon Kaen's Sofitel, it is difficult to spend more than US$50 a night even at the top-end hotels. Remember that such refinements as room telephones, TVs, and even hot water can be rare outside the cities.

6

WHAT IT COSTS In Baht

	$$$$	$$$	$$	$	¢
RESTAURANTS	Over B400	B301–B400	B201–B300	B100–B200	under B100
HOTELS	over B6,000	B4,001–B6,000	B2,001–B4,000	B1,000–B2,000	under B1,000

KORAT & ENVIRONS

Updated by
Robin
Goldstein

The provinces stretching from Korat through Buri Ram, Surin, Si Saket, and on to Ubon Ratchathani are known as Lower Isan. The area is particularly renowned for its Khmer architecture; its delicious cuisine centering around pungent spices, vegetables, and river fish; and the continued influence of Khmer culture, particularly with regard to minority dialects and a musical style called *kantrum* (traditional music with singing in the Khmer language), which can be found east of Korat.

A trip to this part of the country would not be complete without visiting the famous Khmer prasats in Phimai, Buri Ram, Surin, and Si Saket. Here ruins have intricate engravings cut from sandstone and towering structures fashioned in laterite, which are somewhat more imposing than the soft touches of limestone stucco and red brick found in equivalent historical sites in the Central Plains.

The national park of Korat and the rivers of Ubon Ratchathani offer some variety to your trip, and while on your travels you may want to take the opportunity to buy the fine silks produced here or enjoy some of the local Thai folk rock ballads, known as *pleng per chavit* (songs for life). The food will take chili lovers to paradise. If you're lucky enough to be here during the rice production period, the harmonious pace of rural life among the rice fields will provide you with an unforgettable image of traditions in practice.

Korat

❶ *259 km (160 mi) northeast of Bangkok.*

Considered the gateway to the Northeast, Korat is the largest city in Isan and the second-largest city in Thailand. Its size resulted from the need for a strong frontier city to govern the towns of the vast northeastern plateau. Korat is a modern mini-metropolis, complete with huge shopping malls, a few high-rise hotels, and a wonderful bustling night market, which serves as a good introduction to Isan's lively, friendly, local feel.

The city also has a very distinct culture from the rest of Isan (its own dialect and musical style, for example) and a strong sense of self, which grew out of its prestigious past. Indeed, many people in the city will describe themselves as Korat people as opposed to Isan people. Above all, the city reveres its beloved *Ya Mo,* short for Thao Suranaree, a local woman who led her people to victory over the invading Laotians. Her monument can be found in front of Phratu Chumpol, one of the four gates leading into the Old City, and homage is paid to her throughout the city.

Where to Eat

★ $–$$ ✕ Nai-Ruen. Nai-Ruen may be in the basement of the Sima Thani Hotel,

THE NAME GAME

It's easy to get confused by the name of the city: Korat's official name is Nakhon Ratchasima, and it's labeled as such on maps and many highway signs, but Thai people call the city Korat.

Isan

VIETNAM

LAOS

Mekong River

13 Nakhon Phanom
12 That Phanom
11 Mukdahan
10 Khong Jiam
Pakxé

9 Ubon Ratchathani
8 Si Saket
7 Prasat Khao Phra Wihan
Prasat Hin Wat Sra Kamphaeng Yai
Prasat Sikharaphum
6 Surin
Sangkah
Prasat Muang Tam
5 Phanom Rung
4 Buri Ram
3 Phimai
Prakhon Chai
Chok Chai

19 Nong Khai
VIENTIANE
18 Chiang Khan
14 Udon Thani
16 Loei
17 Phu Kra Dueng National Park
Ban Chiang
Khon Kaen

15
1 Korat (Nakhon Ratchasima)
2 Khao Yai National Park
Saraburi
Lopburi

Nakhon Phanom
Thakhèk
Sakhon Nakhon
Savannakhét
Amnat Charoen
Trakan Phutphon

Phrae
Uttaradit
Si Satchanalai
Sawankhalok
Si Samrong
Sukhothai
Phitsanulok
Phichit
Nakhon Thai
Chat Trakan
Dan Sai
Lom Sak
Phetchabun
Chum Phae
Kaeng Khlo
Chaiyaphum
Nong Phai
Chai Nat
Nakhon Sawan
Sing Buri
Ang Thong
Suphan Buri
Pak Chong

Wang Saphung
Nong Bua Lamphu
Ban Phai
Borabu
Maha Sarakham
Kalasin
Roi Et
Yasothon
Suwannaphum
Tha Tum
Prathai
Phang Khun
Wanon Niwat
Somdet
Prasat

40 mi
40 km

222
212
13
8
2
9
13
212
22
223
213
227
212
202
13
24
2172
221
2328
226
214
24
219
202
23
214
23
207
202
2
205
2
226
24
304
24
21
225
21
21
1
32
340
329
1
11
11
11
117
115
12
12
201
203
1268
2013
1143
12
228
22
101
211

but it elevates the all-you-can-eat buffet concept to a new level. Throw out all of your preconceived notions about buffets (quantity over quality, lack of freshness, and so on), because everything at this one is spot-on and impeccably fresh. It's a great opportunity to sample dozens of Isan specialties at once. The Thai food is best, but also decent are the Chinese food, the sushi, the noodle soups, and the steak. (Yep, they're all included.) The B150 lunch is easily the top value in town, especially if you're hungry. ⊠ *Sima Thani Hotel, 2112/2 Mittraphat Rd.* ☎ *044/ 213100* ▤ *MC, V.*

★ ¢–$ ✕ **Korat Buri.** On Korat's busiest nightlife street is this romantic restaurant, where you can enjoy real local food (there's no English menu) while being serenaded by live music in a garden that's decked out with lanterns and shaded by big, arching trees. Try the *pla chon samunprai* (snakehead fish deep-fried with lemongrass, ginger, crispy chilies, and spicy sauce) or the *kha mu tod krob* (pork leg with a sweet-and-spicy sauce). ⊠ *Yom-Marat Rd.* ☎ *044/269108* ▤ *MC, V* ⊗ *No lunch.*

¢–$ ✕ **Rabieng-Pa.** The name means "forest terrace," which makes sense given the amount of greenery surrounding the courtyard's fountain. Rabieng-Pa's food is Isan to the core, and you'll find some unique dishes here; for example, try the *lahp plah-chaun taut,* fried snakehead fish with ground rice and mint, and don't miss the *poo-mah daung,* fresh raw blue swimming crabs in a hot chili sauce. Prices are more than fair, and another advantage of the place is its English-language menu. However, the atmosphere here isn't as charming as at Korat Buri. ⊠ *284 Yom-Marat Rd.* ☎ *044/243137* ▤ *MC, V.*

¢ ✕ **Sumlanlap Restaurant.** Popular with locals, this restaurant serves up a selection of Isan dishes, of which *laab phet,* a spicy minced duck salad, is a particular hit. The restaurant has basic furnishings and cement floors, but the fine fare at very reasonable prices more than makes up for the lack of ambience. If you feel brave, you can try the bull penis salad (be sure to let us know what it's like). ⊠ *163 Watcharasarit Rd.* ☎ *044/243636* ▤ *No credit cards.*

Where to Stay

The city, which is home to the Thai second army and air force, hosts annual U.S. army exercises, called "Cobra Gold," in November and December. If you're traveling during this time, make your reservations in advance, as the city's hotels fill up.

$$ ▦ **Royal Princess.** Regal it's not, but this gleaming nine-story showplace does have finely furnished guest rooms complete with executive desks and comfortable chairs. The expansive lobby has eye-catching silk in its souvenir shops. A small garden and pool offer some relief from the glare of the noonday sun. ■ TIP➜ **The formal restaurant serves the best Cantonese food in town.** ⊠ *1137 Suranarai Rd., 30000* ☎ *044/256629* ⊕ *www.royalprincess.com* ⇨ *179 rooms, 10 suites* ⌂ *In-room: refrigerator. In-hotel: 2 restaurants, 2 bars, pool, gym, laundry service, public Wi-Fi* ▤ *AE, DC, MC, V.*

$–$$ ▦ **Sima Thani.** At one of Korat's most distinguished hotels, a soaring lobby features fountains with rushing water and a tastefully executed elephant theme. Go for one of the deluxe rooms, which have beautiful

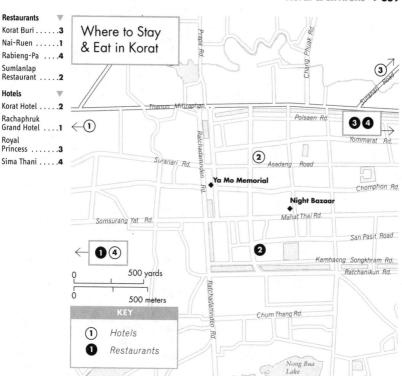

Where to Stay & Eat in Korat

beddings and Asian flair. Most high-end hotels in Isan have Chinese restaurants and this one is no exception; its eatery is decent. ✉ *2112/2 Mittraphat Rd., 30000* ☎ *044/213100, 02/253–4885 in Bangkok* ⊕ *www.simathani.com* 🛏 *245 rooms, 20 suites* ♿ *In-room: refrigerator, Wi-Fi. In-hotel: 2 restaurants, room service, 2 bars, pool, gym, laundry service, concierge* ▭ *MC, V.*

$ 🏨 **Rachaphruk Grand Hotel.** The dark, polished-granite lobby of this modern high-rise leads to a relaxing lounge. Check out the signed photos of Thai celebrity guests behind the front desk. The light and airy rooms are decorated mostly in primrose and pale woods; Japanese-style window screens can be opened to provide a commanding view of the city. The hotel is popular with visiting U.S. servicemen and women in November and December. ✉ *311 Mittraphat Rd., 30000* ☎ *044/26122* ⊕ *www.rachaphruk.com* 🛏 *159 rooms* ♿ *In-room: refrigerator. In-hotel: restaurant, room service, bar, pool, gym, laundry service* ▭ *AE, MC, V.*

¢ 🏨 **Korat Hotel.** This is one of the city's oldest hotels and probably its most famous. Upon entering the lobby, you'll be greeted by a life-size bronze of Luang Por Koon, the province's most famous monk. The lobby opens up into a 24-hour dining area with polished stone floors, chandeliers, and oil paintings. The rooms have an old-world feel. ✉ *191 Asdang Rd., 30000* ☎ *044/257057* 🛏 *103 rooms, 2 suites* ♿ *In-room:*

refrigerator. In-hotel: 2 restaurants, bar, laundry service, public Wi-Fi ▭ *MC, V.*

Nightlife

Korat has a lively nightlife, much of which is concentrated on Jomsurangyath Road, near the edge of the Old City. Another good street to try is Yom-Marat Road, within the Old City, where you can find a number of bars and restaurants. **Bule's Saloon Pub and Restaurant** (✉ 264 Yom-Marat Rd. ☎ 044/256538) is a longtime favorite for Western rock music lovers in the city. You'll feel like you're in a mountain lodge as you sit back and listen to the fine guitar licks of the owner. It's one of the few places outside Bangkok where you can hear bands play a repertoire that includes Pink Floyd, Led Zeppelin, and the Rolling Stones.

> ### PLENG KORAT
>
> At the Suranaree Monument on Ratchadamnoen Road, in front of Chumpol Gate, you can find regular performances of *Pleng Korat*, an oratory sung on request here in a style unique to the province. Performers wear traditional costumes and can be enticed into singing for about B400 for a half-hour performance. *Pleng Korat* was a favorite of the famous Suranaree and is still popular with merit-making Buddhists, as well as passing tourists. The performers usually pack up by 6 PM.

You spot the lively **Coco Beet Pub and Restaurant** (✉ Yom-Marat Rd. ☎ 044/247993) by its waterfall-effect windows. Inside you'll be wowed by the owner's unique decorating taste—a kitschy mishmash of decors—and the fine covers of Thai and Western pop songs coming from the marvelous live band. The crowd is mainly made up of the well-to-do local party set. **Huaplee** (✉ 577 Yom-Marat Rd. ☎ 044/247993), across the road from Coco Beet, serves straightforward Thai meals including six preparations of frog, but the place is even more popular for drinks. Unfortunately, it's also a hostess bar, as is the custom here.

Long Tiem (✉ 38 Suranara Rd. ☎ 044/272198) is a pub and restaurant set in a wooden Thai-style house with an enormous beer garden. It's a great choice for those who prefer the local Thai rock known as pleng per chavit (songs for life). A dreadlocked tattoo artist located to the rear of the establishment can provide you with the ultimate souvenir of your evening. **Living Bar** (✉ Rachaphruk Grand Hotel, 311 Mittraphat Rd. ☎ 044/261222 ⊕ www.rachaphruk.com) is a happening disco-bar where foreigners and locals hit the dance floor together.

Shopping

Between 6 and 9 PM head to Korat's **Night Bazaar,** on Manat Road in the center of town. A block-long street is taken over by food stands and vendor stalls and is crowded with locals. If you're looking to buy local products during the day, head to the **Suranaree Monument.** The shops facing the monument sell souvenirs at reasonable prices, including locally produced silks, pottery, and *kao tang* rice snacks.

A side trip to **Pak Thongchai Silk and Cultural Centre**, 32 km (20 mi) south of Korat, offers a chance to see how locals make silk, from the raising of silkworms to the spinning of thread and the weaving of fabric. You can buy silk at some 70 factories in the area. From Bus Station 1 buses to Pak Thongchai leave every hour (B60 one-way). They drop you at the market, from where you can explore the surrounding lanes for silk outlets and factories.

For ceramics, drive out to the village of **Ban Dan Kwian**, 15 km (10 mi) southwest of Korat. The rust-color clay here is used for reproductions of classic designs. The village can be easily reached by taking a songthaew from Kamhang Songkram Road, near the police station. Trucks leave every 20 minutes and the trip costs a nominal B30.

Khao Yai National Park

2 *130 km (80 mi) southwest of Korat.*

Khao Yai is Thailand's oldest national park (established in 1962). The reserve covers 2,168 square km (833 square mi) and spreads over four provinces. ■ TIP→ **It's a frequent destination for Thais seeking to escape Bangkok and on weekends the park can feel crowded.**

On entering the park and winding your way up into the forested hills, you'll soon find yourself confronted by hordes of pleading macaque monkeys loitering on the road in search of handouts. But these are not the only wildlife you'll likely to encounter here—of particular note are the wild elephants, tigers, leopard cats, and barking deer that can sometimes be observed at the salt licks. Elephants generally roam only at night, but occasionally one pops out during the day.

Trekking trails, bicycle paths, view points, and bird-watching towers are prolific in this huge evergreen forest, and many of the park's splendid waterfalls are easily accessible by car or bicycle. ⚠ **Leech socks, which can be purchased at the visitor center, are advised when walking on the trails to keep the minuscule but annoying leeches off your ankles.** The park is particularly easy to get around, and frequent information points and warning signs such as "Cobra Crossing" will help keep you from harm's way (though evening strolls are still not advised). Hiking trails from the park headquarters are 1 km to 8 km (½ mi to 5 mi).

From Korat take a bus from Bus Station 1 to Pak Chong for B50; buses leave hourly for the 1½-hour trip. At Pak Chong take a local songthaew to the park's entrance. Note that it's another 20 km (12 mi) from the park entrance to the visitor center, so it's best to negotiate a ride into the heart of the camp or else you'll need to hire an additional taxi at the entrance. That said, the best way in is by rental car or hired driver from Korat or Bangkok, which will also allow you to stop along the way at one of the many roadside fruit stalls (look for custard fruit) or curry puff vendors. ⊠ *Khao Yai National Park, Pakchong District* ☎ *B400 per person, plus B150 per car* ☺ *Daily 6 AM–9 PM.*

The otherwise undistinguished Jungle House resort, along the road into Khao Yai, operates **elephant rides** around the surrounding forest. ⊠ *Khao Yai National Park, Pakchong District* ☎ *B200* ☺ *Daily dawn–dusk.*

OFF THE BEATEN PATH

MUAK-LEK – About 40 km (25 mi) from Khoa Yai Park along Route 1 (Friendship Road) is the most famous place in Thailand to get curry puffs. These warm, flaky, snack-size pastry pockets are similar to empanadas or samosas, but the range of spices makes them uniquely Thai. They're stuffed with such ingredients as salted chicken, pork, sweet taro, and soybean paste. Look for the series of stalls on the left side of the road brandishing baked goods in big glass cases.

Where to Stay & Eat

The park provides a variety of cabin accommodations at reasonable rates, though many prefer to camp at one of the park's two designated sites. Tents and bedding, along with bicycles, are available for hire on-site. If you don't wish to sleep under the stars, there are several resorts and plenty of pleasant restaurants located along Thanarat Road, which leads to the park entrance. ■ TIP→ **The park's headquarters, next door to the informative visitor center, can help arrange lodgings and guided treks.**

$-$$$ ✕ **Chokchai Steakhouse.** It's not surprising that this steak house has American pretensions: it's near a cattle ranch, started by an American nicknamed the "Little Cowboy," which provides the restaurant's meat. Don't expect world-class cuts here, but Chokchai does about as well with the genre as the budget-busting spots in Bangkok that import their meat from Australia. ⊠ *170 Moo 2 Mittraphat Rd.* ☏ *044/328553 or 044/328232* ▤ *No credit cards.*

★ **$-$$** ✕ **Ya Ka Restaurant.** Most people come to this casual, open-air restaurant along the road into Khao Yai for one reason: the show-stopping grilled snakehead fish, which comes fresh out of the tanks and is then salted, skewered, and grilled over an open fire. But equally worth trying are the deep-fried, ground snakehead fish with a spicy salad and the pork leg with red gravy. Enjoy it all with sticky rice, spicy som tam, and friendly smiles from the staff. ⊠ *101/3 Khao Yai Rd.* ☏ *044/297151* ⊕ *www.yakarestaurant.com* ▤ *No credit cards.*

★ **$-$$** 🛏 **Juldis.** A luxurious resort and spa set back from an unassuming road leading to Khao Yai, the Juldis is a delightful place to spend the night if you're devoting a full day to exploring the park. The spa is relaxing, the pool is pleasant, and the gardens in back create a wonderfully isolated feeling. Skip the food at the steak house (although it does become a pub at night) and try the Thai-Chinese restaurant instead. Choose one of the "deluxe" rooms with balconies overlooking the forest—they're a better deal for only a few baht more. There are also some much pricier but lovely houses and bungalows in the garden. ⊠ *54 Moo 4, Thanarat Rd., Km 17, Thambol Moo-Sri, Pakchong, 30130* ☏ *044/297297* ⊕ *www.khaoyai.com* ⇆ *156 rooms* ♨ *In-room: refrigerator. In-hotel: 2 restaurants, room service, 3 bars, 2 tennis courts, pool, gym, spa, bicycles, laundry service, concierge* ▤ *AE, DC, MC, V.*

Phimai

❸ *60 km (37 mi) northeast of Korat.*

The town of Phimai boasts a verdant city square, an energetic market, tough muay thai boxers, and locally produced noodles, but it is most famous for its magnificent Khmer architecture at the Prasat Hin Phimai, right in the middle of it all. The town's quiet streets come to life with the arrival of tour buses ferrying tourists to the site, but it's still possible to rent a bicycle and explore the area in relative peace. Phimai is dotted with the remnants of ancient edifices, walls, and gates, and the sense of history surrounding this friendly town will not be lost on you.

> ## THE PRASAT
>
> The Khmer influence is evident in the occasional *prasat*, or tower, that dots the region. The prasat wasn't a royal residence, but rather a retreat for those traveling from the Khmer temple of Angkor in present-day Cambodia.

■ TIP➔ **The Phimai festival, held on the second weekend of November, brings the crowds to see boat races and cultural shows, so it's best to book in advance if you wish to stay overnight at this time.**

Phimai can easily be reached by bus from Bus Station 1 in Korat. Buses depart regularly (take the line headed for Phimai and Chumphuang) and cost B30.

★ **Prasat Hin Phimai,** in the center of town, is one of the great Khmer structures in Isan. Built sometime in the late 11th or early 12th century (believed to predate Angkor Wat), it has been carefully restored and frequently appears in music videos and movies. To enter the prasat is to step back eight centuries. Most fascinating, perhaps, is that the temple was first Hindu when founded by Jayavarman V, then was adapted into a Buddhist temple in the 11th century, when Jayavarman VII of Angkor Thom himself converted to Buddhism. Buddhist images replaced Hindu ones. Some Hindu iconography remains, but a giant phallus at the entrance of the temple, for one, was covered up.

By the time you pass through the external sandstone wall and the gallery, you're swept up in the creation and destruction of the Brahman gods engraved on the lintels. A quartet of *gopuras* (gate towers) guards the entrances, with the main one facing south toward Angkor. The central white sandstone prang, towering more than 60 feet, is flanked by two smaller buildings, one in laterite, the other in red sandstone. The principal prasat is surrounded by four porches whose external lintels depict Hindu gods and scenes from the Ramayana. Inside, the lintels portray the religious art of Mahayana Buddhism. ✉ *Tha Songkhran Rd.* ☎ *044/ 471568* 🎫 *B40* 🕙 *Daily 7:30–6.*

The excellent **Phimai National Museum,** adjacent to the site, contains priceless treasures from the Dvaravati and Khmer civilizations—notably great works of Khmer sculpture. The museum's masterpiece is a stone statue of King Jayavarman VII found at Prasat Hin Phimai. ✉ *Tha Songkhran Rd.* ☎ *044/471167* 🎫 *B30* 🕙 *Daily 9–4.*

From Prasat Hin Phimai, take a 2-km (1-mi) excursion to the village of **Sai Ngam,** home of the world's largest banyan tree. It's said to be more than 350 years old, which is easy to believe if you examine its mass of intertwined trunks. Walk along the raised footpaths in the shade of this vast natural phenomenon; it was once believed that the roots of the tree stretched as far as the center of town. The adjoining food stalls make it a favorite picnic spot for Thai families, and across the lake you'll see a faithful reconstruction of a traditional northeastern house.

Where to Stay & Eat

★ ¢–$ ✕ **Bahn Muong Restaurant.** In Phimai, the Thais like to eat at the seafood restaurants out by the lake, and you shouldn't pass up the chance to do so, too. At Bahn Muong, the freshwater "catch of the day" takes on new meaning: when you order a fish, they row out to a netted-in area in the lake and come back with the catch. Enjoy your simply grilled snakehead fish with a spicy dipping sauce (*pla nin tap tim pao*) in one of the thatched-roof cabanas, reached by walking across rickety wooden planks. ⊠ *Bahn Samitt Rd.* ☎ *01/997–4970* ▭ *No credit cards.*

¢–$ ✕ **Baiteiy Restaurant.** This wonderful, relaxing restaurant is only five minutes from the prasat and is within sight of the Khmer marvel. Naturally, the theme here is ancient Khmer—the walls are made of local laterite bricks, the ceiling is made of bamboo, and Khmer designs and engravings are all around. The restaurant serves traditional Thai fare with some emphasis on local dishes, such as stir-fried Phimai noodles. ▮ TIP→ **You can also rent bicycles here for a few hours or by the day.** ⊠ *276 Moo 7, Phimai Choomphuang Rd.* ☎ *044/287103* ▭ *MC, V.*

¢ ▦ **Phimai Inn Hotel.** This friendly hotel is a good value; however, its lobby is strange and impersonal, and you're well advised to choose one of the (relatively) pricier rooms in the newer building—they're in far better shape than those in the old building, which tend to be ratty and don't all have air-conditioning. The newer rooms have wooden furnishings and pale pastel hues; "VIP" rooms have carpeting and minibars. There's an enormous pool in the middle of it all. The hotel is on the bypass at the edge of town. ⊠ *33/1 Bypass Rd.* ☎ *044/287228 or 044/287229* ⇌ *80 rooms* ⌂ *In-room: no a/c (some), refrigerator (some). In-hotel: 2 restaurants, pool, laundry service* ▭ *MC, V.*

Buri Ram

➍ *90 km (56 mi) east of Korat.*

The provincial capital of Buri Ram lies between Korat and Surin and is a good gateway for those visiting the nearby Khmer prasats, some of the finest in the country. Founded in the late 18th century by the first king of the Chakri dynasty, this somewhat neglected city, which translates as "City of Pleasantness," is turning a corner, as evidenced by the $1 million conversion of an ancient moat into an attractive public park.

More peaceful than its neighboring cities, Buri Ram provides an opportunity to pick up some bargain silk products and sample the Isan lifestyle by eating local specialties such as laab (minced pork or chicken salad with lime juice, fish sauce, cilantro, chilies, and ground rice powder) at the bustling Night Bazaar, or listening to local folk rock in one of the city's live country music venues.

Where to Stay & Eat

If you really want to mix it up with the locals and get a sense of how people dine out in Buri Ram, head to the Night Bazaar (4 PM to 11 PM) at the end of Romburi Road. There's plenty of cheap, ready-to-order food, along with fresh produce. It's at its best after 6 PM.

¢–$ ✕ **Bamboo Bar & Restaurant.** This simple country-style restaurant in the heart of town is only minutes from the train station and even closer to the city's nightspots. You'll find such Western dishes as ploughman's lunch and fish-and-chips; the ham-and-cheese baguettes are particularly popular. It's a good place to meet the local expat crowd, kick back in front of some cable TV, and get some tips on what to do and see in the area. ⊠ *14/13 Romburi Rd.* ☎ *044/625577* ▤ *No credit cards.*

¢–$ ✕ **Phu Tawan.** A popular evening eatery, ◼ TIP→ **Phu Tawan is a must for Thai folk rock music lovers.** A booming band plays to an excitable local crowd, who spend all evening jumping up to dance and sing along with the musicians. It's only a minute's walk from the Thepnakorn Hotel. Recommended dishes are the local spicy minced pork dish laab moo and *yum takrai,* a lemongrass-and-dried-shrimp salad. ⊠ *99 Jira Rd.* ☎ *044/ 621327 or 01/669–3660* ▤ *No credit cards* ◔ *No lunch.*

¢ ✕ **Champ Korean Grill.** Next to the Thepnakorn Hotel and across the street from Phu Tawan, this fun, outdoor local restaurant represents a fusion of Korean and Thai cuisines. You order a plate full of raw beef, pork, and squid, and then cook it all on a grill that is built into your table. The meat sizzles in pork fat that comes in slabs that you need to balance on the top of the table grill; the fat renders down the sides of the metal, cooking the meat. The atmosphere is festive, the prices are low, and the spicy sauces offer a Thai touch. ⊠ *397 Jira Rd., Muang* ☎ *No phone* ▤ *No credit cards* ◔ *No lunch.*

$–$$ ▦ **Thepnakorn Hotel.** This is as close as Buri Ram has to a top-end hotel and a serviceable place to rest up while investigating the nearby ruins. The English-speaking staff will give you a warm welcome, though the aesthetic and quite drab look of the place lends a slightly depressing tone to it all. The value is good by Western standards, but not by the standards of Buri Ram. It's a 5- to 10-minute tuk-tuk ride from the center of town. ⊠ *139 Jira Rd., 31000* ☎ *044/613400 up to 02* ⊕ *www. thepnakorn-hotel.com* ⌁ *166 rooms* ⚒ *In-room: refrigerator. In-hotel: 2 restaurants, room service, 2 bars, pool, gym, spa, laundry service* ▤ *MC, V.*

¢–$ ▦ **Vongthong Hotel.** This relatively small low-rise hotel is aging a bit, and furnishings feel dated, but it's clean, with decent facilities, and represents an excellent value in a town without a lot of compelling hotel options. It's only a few blocks from the railway station. ⊠ *512/1 Jira Rd., 31000* ☎ *044/612540* ⌁ *71 rooms* ⚒ *In-room: ethernet. In-hotel: restaurant, 2 bars, laundry service* ▤ *MC, V.*

Phanom Rung

❺ *65 km (40 mi) south of Buri Ram.*

Fodor'sChoice The restored hilltop shrine of **Prasat Hin Khao Phanom Rung,** 65 km (40 ★ mi) from the city, is a supreme example of Khmer art. The approach to the prasat sets your heart thumping—you cross an imposing bridge and climb majestic staircases to the top, where you're greeted by a magnificent reclining Vishnu lintel. This architectural treasure hit the headlines when it mysteriously disappeared in the 1960s, then reappeared at the Chicago Art Institute. After 16 years of protests it was finally returned to its rightful place. Step under the lintel and through the portal into the double-walled sanctuary. Intricate carvings in a style similar to those found in Lopburi cover the interior walls, and in the center of the prasat stands the great throne room dedicated to the Hindu Lord Shiva.

Built in the 12th century under King Suriyaworamann II, one of the great Khmer rulers, it was restored in the 1980s at a cost of $2 million. It's one of the few Khmer sanctuaries without later Thai Buddhist additions. ■ TIP→ **For insight into this and other nearby Khmer architecture it's well worth having a look in the visitor center,** which can be found beyond the souvenir stalls, along the shaded path where you catch your first glimpse of the prasat. The center has commendably clear information; the exhibits that shed light on the magnificent stone carvings found at Phanom Rung are particularly recommended. In the gardens outside the temple area, don't miss the huge bamboo tree creaking in the wind. ☎ 044/631746 ⌨ B40 ⊙ *Daily 6–6, visitor center 9–4.*

Scattered around the area are other Khmer prasats in various stages of decay, many of them overgrown by vegetation. One of these has been rescued by Thailand's Department of Fine Arts. **Prasat Muang Tam** is only a couple of miles from the base of Phanom Rung hill. It's estimated to be 100 years older than its neighbor, starting off as a 10th-century Hindu sanctuary. Its main building symbolically represents the universe, with lesser towers emanating from the center. Today four towers remain, all containing carvings of Shiva and his consort Uma, Varuna on a swan, Krishna with cows, and Indra on the elephant Erawan. The complex is flanked by ceremonial ponds, with five-headed nagas (water serpents that appear in Buddhist folklore) lying alongside it. ✛ *8 km (5 mi) southeast of Prasat Hin Khao Phanom Rung* ☎ 044/631746 ⌨ B40 ⊙ *Daily 6–6.*

Where to Eat

¢–$ ✕ **Gift and Katit.** Of the several casual open-air restaurants lined up outside the entrance to Phanom Rung, this is one of the most reliable choices. Ignore the dumbed-down English menu and go straight for the local specialty, pla nin pao, a whole river fish covered with salt, stuffed with lemongrass, and grilled over an open fire. Try the delicious *laab moo* spicy salad. If you're standing with your back to the park, Gift and Katit is to the left of the restroom complex. ⊠ *Phanom Rung Historical Park* ☎ 01/878–7148 or 09/425–3822 ▤ No credit cards ⊙ No dinner.

Surin

❻ *52 km (30 mi) east of Buri Ram, 198 km (119 mi) east of Korat.*

With its Phanom Don Rak mountain range bordering Cambodia to the south, Surin has always been heavily influenced by Cambodian culture, and a large proportion of the local population speaks a Khmer dialect. Its strategic location also made Surin an assembly point for the elephant armies during the early Rattanakosin period; to this day the city is best known for its elephants. Everywhere you look in this bustling city you'll see homage paid to these noble creatures in the form of sculptures, artwork, and even street-lamp motifs. In addition, Surin shares with its neighboring provinces a wealth of ancient Khmer structures, found outside the city in varying states of decay or restoration.

Surin is famous, above all, for its annual **Elephant Roundup,** held the third week of November. The impressive show includes elephants performing tricks while their mahouts reenact scenes of capturing them in the wild. The main show is held at the Sri Narong Stadium in town, and starts at 7:30 AM. Ticket prices start at B300, rising to B500 if you're seated in the stands with the sun at your back. If you'd like to get up close to the animals, you can take a short ride for a small fee at the end of the performance or you can hand-feed them in the paddock to the rear of the stadium. The town is packed with visitors at Roundup time, so make sure you have a hotel reservation if you plan to join them. Surin has also become something of a year-round expat center, full of farang who have married Thais—it's a good place to absorb that subculture, perhaps over a beer at Farang Connection.

On the road between Si Saket and Surin is **Prasat Sikhoraphum,** a five-prang Khmer pagoda built in the 12th century. The central structure has engraved lintels depicting Shiva, as well as carvings of Brahma, Vishnu, and Ganesha. The bus (No. 3) from Korat stops at Surin bus station, which has a regular bus service to the site's adjoining village. ✛ *36 km (24 mi) east of Surin* ▣ *B40* ☽ *Daily 6–6.*

Nestled amid thick vegetation beside the Cambodian border, 75 km (47 mi) from the far south of the city, is a series of three prasats collectively known as **Prasat Ta Muean.** All lie on an ancient road stretching from Phimai to Angkor. The first prasat you see is Prasat Ta Muean, built in the Jayavarman VII period of the late 12th century and believed to be one of 17 rest stops made for pilgrims traveling the route. The second, smaller, site, Prasat Ta Muean Tot, acted as an ancient hospital and was also constructed in the 12th century. But these are only teasers for what lies farther on, directly beside the Cambodian border: Prasat Ta Muean Thom.

Thom means big, and Prasat Ta Muean Thom is indeed the largest of the three sites. It was constructed in the 11th century, making it the oldest of the sites as well. The contrasting textures and colors of the pink sandstone towers and the rugged gray laterite of the viharns set against the backdrop of the forest are something to behold.

The prasat's survival over the ages is made particularly poignant by the existence of unexploded grenades and land mines in the vicinity, left over from more troubled times. Some have even reported the distant crack of gunfire, and the area is kept a close eye on by the Thai army, whose checkpoints you'll pass on your approach to the area. For these reasons ⚠ **it's strongly advised that visitors don't wander off into the forest and that they admire the structures at Prasat Ta Muean Thom from cleared paths only.**

Prasat Ta Muean is situated on a newly surfaced road, but it's still a bit isolated and is often a difficult place to get to via public transportation (at any rate, it can be a slow trip). Therefore it's best to drive or take a tour provided by Saren Travel.

Where to Eat

The small but busy provincial capital of Surin has plenty of standard shophouse-style eateries where you can order basic rice or noodle dishes. Sirirat Road has many late-night dining spots, but if you want to mix with the locals in the evenings, head to the Night Bazaar on Krung Sri Nai Road between 5 PM and 11 PM.

¢–$ ✕ **Larn-Chang.** This delightful, wooden house restaurant is by a pond (its name means "big pond"). You can have a relaxing Thai meal in the restaurant's garden. Try the manta ray in Isan soup. The restaurant has an English-language menu and is open until midnight. ⊠ *199 Seepatai Samon Rd.* ☏ *044/512869* ▭ *No credit cards.*

¢ ✕ **Che Took Restaurant.** With a constant stream of customers passing underneath its thatched-straw roof, Che Took is a bit frenetic. But it's popular for a reason: it's won many awards for the high quality of its food, which includes Isan- and Thai-style fish dishes. ⊠ *Lukmuang Rd.* ☏ *06/ 865–8893* ▭ *No credit cards.*

¢ ✕ **Farang Connection.** If you have a craving for some Western fare (and company), this foreigner-run restaurant is the place to go. The small restaurant acts as a meeting point for expats and provides additional services such as motorbike rental, Internet, and tour services. The upper level also has a big-screen TV (which shows Premiership matches) and a dartboard; the menu includes cottage pie, bangers-and-mash, and Cornish pasties. The beer list, which features such gems as John Smith's Smooth Bitter, is perhaps the best in Thailand. ⊠ *257/11 Jitbumroong Rd.* ☏ *044/511509* ⊕ *www.farangconnection.com* ▭ *No credit cards.*

Where to Stay

$ ▦ **Majestic.** At this top-class hotel (at least by Surin standards), the furnishings are basic and the TVs are aging, but the level of amenities and comfort is slightly higher than elsewhere in town. All rooms have terraces, most overlooking a big lagoon. ⊠ *99 Chitbamrung Rd., 320000* ☏ *044/713980* ⊕ *www.surinmajestic.net* ⤳ *69 rooms, 3 suites* ⚕ *Inroom: refrigerator. In-hotel: restaurant, bar, pool, public Wi-Fi, laundry service* ▭ *AE, MC, V.*

$ ▦ **Thong Tarin Hotel.** Ask for a corner room at Surin's most stylish hotel—they're larger and have commanding views of the city. This is a popular choice for those looking for a night on the town, as it's only minutes from local watering holes; the hotel's beer garden attracts its own crowd of locals every evening. There's also a nightclub with live music and the popular Big Bite Restaurant on premise. The rates leap during Elephant Roundup week. ⊠ *60 Sirirat Rd., 32000* ☏ *045/ 514281 up to 88* ⊕ *www.thongtharinhotel.com* ⤳ *212 rooms, 11 suites rooms* ⚕ *In-room: refrigerator. In-hotel: 2 restaurants, bar, pool, spa, laundry service, public Internet* ▭ *AE, DC, MC, V.*

¢ ▦ **Phet Kasem Grand Hotel.** This longtime favorite surrounds you with Khmer art reproductions as you enter its two-tier lobby area. Rooms are furnished with wood and colorful Thai fabrics; the bathrooms have marble floors. The pool and terrace buffet area are favorite gathering points in the evening. The staff is charming and friendly. ⊠ *104 Jitbam-roong Rd., 32000* ☎ *044/511274* ↪ *157 rooms, 5 suites* ⚄ *In-room: refrigerator. In-hotel: 2 restaurants, bar, pool, laundry service, public Wi-Fi* ⊟ *MC, V.*

Shopping

About 15 km (10 mi) north of Surin a small road leads to **Khwao Sinarin,** a village famous for its excellent silk. Silver jewelry is now made here as well, and you can find bargains for bracelets and necklaces with a minimal amount of negotiation. You can detour south to **Ban Butom,** 12 km (7 mi) from Surin, where villagers weave the straw baskets sold in Bangkok. They'll be happy to demonstrate their techniques.

Nightlife

Surin hops at night, especially on weekends; most of the activity, including the red-light activity, centers around Sirirat Road, about a block from the Thong Tharin Hotel. The best strategy is to cruise that strip, along with Sirinpukdee Road. At the **Hip Hop** (⊠ Sirirat Rd. and Surinpukdee Rd. ☎ 045/265141), a young, boisterous crowd dances to a thumping beat until the wee hours. More chilled-out is **2Be Bar** (⊠ 97/8 Surinpukdee Rd. ☎ 044/531836). The recent opening of this sleek, hip lounge represents a new era in Surin nightlife: the city now has a chic cocktail bar that's not a girlie bar. It opens at 6 PM and keeps going until midnight.

Prasat Khao Phra Wihan

❼ *94 km (59 mi) southeast of Si Saket, 101 km (63 mi) southwest of Ubon Ratchathani.*

Fodor'sChoice
★
In the 1963 resolution of a contentious territorial dispute between Thailand and Cambodia, the World Court awarded these spectacular mountaintop Khmer ruins to Cambodia. Ironically, however, even after the border was redefined, the temple, which sits on a cliff high above the rest of Cambodia, could only be accessed from a Thai road. It is no wonder that Thais are still bitter about the loss, because the World Court's decision stripped Khao PhraWihan not just from Thailand, but also from the rest of the world's tourists when Cambodia closed the ruin site to the public. The site later became a Khmer Rouge stronghold, and even after the Cambodian government opened the ruins again in the early 1990s, access to the area was only intermittent—because of fighting—until the fall of Pol Pot in 1998.

That long period of neglect now forms part of Khao Phra Wihan's unique allure. Admire the ornate 12th-century Khmer lintels in red laterite honoring Shiva and other Hindu icons, and you will revel in the fact that the temples have for the most part not been reconstructed. As you wander through the temple complex, which proudly stretches along a misty bluff for more than a kilometer, you'll step over column fragments that seem to have crumbled only days earlier.

Aside from the steep entrance fee, crossing the border into Cambodia presents no obstacles other than showing your passport at a checkpoint. They won't stamp it, as no visa is required to make this trip. You'll leave your car, taxi, or bus at the Thai side of the checkpoint, which has a basic information booth (without much material in English), bathrooms, and such, then walk across the border for about a kilometer along a paved road. The road gives way to an area of lavalike sandstone before descending into a large market area where fried bananas, drinks, and fake consumer products are sold. ⚠ **Everything offered by the hawkers is fake, from the Rolexes and Patek Philippes to the bottles of Johnnie Walker to the antique coins to the ivory. Even the cigarettes here are fake—packs and cartons are stuffed full of ratty, low-grade cigarettes and stamped with forged logos.** You might want to take the opportunity to taste a (real) can of Cambodian beer, though. Even if fighting off the pushy vendors, postcard salespeople, and wannabe tour guides is exhausting, it's still less irritating than dealing with their counterparts at Angkor Wat or the Grand Palace in Bangkok. Perhaps this is because, relatively speaking, so few tourists come through the area that farang are still a genuine curiosity, and you'll get some genuine smiles amid all the sales pitches. The ruins are spread over four levels, with the access to the first level having the steepest ascent (after this the going gets a little easier). You pass gopura gateways and naga terraces on your ascent through this compound, which was adapted to suit the landscape, utilizing the natural bedrock of the mountain to form the base of causeways and courtyards. The principal temple structure is on the steepest level, perched on a cliff that plunges into thick rain forest. It's a long climb to the top, but the effort is rewarded by a truly breathtaking view of the jungle beyond. On a clear day you can see not just Cambodia and Thailand but also Laos.

You'll also see some grim reminders of the Khmer Rouge regime that killed 1.7 million people over the course of two horrific decades in Cambodia. ⚠ **Minefields in the brush outside the temple area have been cleared through French efforts, but it's still not a good idea to wander in the unmarked areas outside the site itself and its access paths.** A cannon that was once used by Khmer Rouge guerrillas to patrol the jungle from the cliff top is still relatively intact; behind its shield, you can operate a crank that raises and lowers the barrel. And everywhere you'll see graffiti carved into the rock by Khmer Rouge operatives; their battalion numbers are often scrawled beneath their names.

If you don't have a rental car or a private driver along already, tour operators in Ubon Ratchathani and Surin offer trips to the ruins, and it's certainly worth the expense. Alternatively, you can take a local bus to Kantharalak, 80 km (50 mi) from the city, and then seek out a songthaew or local van to the border from there. The bus to Kantaralak leaves regularly from Si Saket's bus terminal and costs around B30. 🚌 *B400.*

Si Saket

❽ *312 km (187 mi) east of Korat, 61 km (36 mi) west of Ubon Ratchathani.*

With the exception of a newly constructed temple, **Phrathat Ruang Rong,** which is said to be one of the biggest in the northeastern part of the country, the provincial, unexciting town of Si Saket is best known for its pickled garlic and onions. But in early March, when the lamduan flower blooms, the town comes alive in a riot of yellows and reds. Locals celebrate with a three-day festival, the **Lamduan Ban Fair,** which centers around the beautiful Somdej Sri Nakharin Park.

Prasat Hin Wat Sra Kamphang Yai, just outside Ban Sa Kamphang, is in better condition than many of the region's other Khmer sanctuaries. It has been carefully restored, even down to the items that have been lost or stolen over the last 900 years. Particularly spectacular are the lintels of the middle stupa, which depict the Hindu god Indra riding his elephant Erawan. The main gate, inscribed with ancient Khom letters, is thought to be from the 10th century, built during the reign of King Suriyawomarann. The temple behind the prasat is a Thai addition, its walls covered with pictures illustrating Thai proverbs. ✛ *40 km (25 mi) south of Si Saket.*

Where to Stay & Eat

$–$$ ✕ **P.S. House.** This family restaurant tries a little harder to impress with its brightly colored decor and detailed menus. It's notable for its wealth of steaks (including saba fish and ostrich meat). ✉ *820/14–16 Si Saket-Ubon Rd.* ☎ *02/208–9335* ▤ *No credit cards.*

¢–$ ✕ **Somkid Restaurant.** Dishes at this Chinese-style eatery are served with a thick rice soup. The plain plastic seating and wooden tables don't do justice to the quality of the food. The restaurant receives regular customers into the wee hours—it's open until 3 AM. ✉ *332/1–3 Ratchagarn Rot Fai Rd.* ☎ *045/614195* ▤ *No credit cards.*

¢ ▦ **Kessiri Hotel.** This stylish choice gives a nod to the Thai architecture traditions—there's even a naga fountain at the entrance to the small lobby area. Local art and fabrics are in abundance here, as is rich ocher-color paneling, which dominates both the lobby and the modest-size rooms. ✉ *1102–05 Khukran Rd.* ☎ *045/614006* ⇌ *93 rooms* ⚒ *In-room: refrigerator. In-hotel: 2 restaurants, laundry service* ▤ *No credit cards.*

¢ ▦ **Phrompiman Hotel.** Near the train station, the night market, and the city's main restaurant and bar district, this hotel is probably the best positioned in the city, and it is the largest hotel in Si Saket. The superior air-conditioned rooms are very reasonably priced and are decorated with Thai mural reproductions. However, its sparse lobby area does feel kind of lonely. ✉ *849/1 Lukmuang Rd.* ☎ *045/612677* ⇌ *192 rooms* ⚒ *In-hotel: 2 restaurants, laundry service, public Wi-Fi* ▤ *MC, V.*

Ubon Ratchathani

❾ *227 km (141 mi) east of Surin, 167 km (100 mi) south of Mukdahan.*

Ubon Ratchathani, known as the "Royal City of the Lotus," is Eastern Isan's largest city, but there is a positively provincial air about the place, especially at night, when, aside from the night market, quiet pervades, interrupted only by strains of music from nightclubs or the outdoor restaurant. Although you'll find pockets of hipness and the occasional fusion restaurant, the city, which is simply known as Ubon, is nowhere near as lively as its neighbors of Surin or Korat. Nor are there a whole lot of sights to see here. Ubon is, however, considered the gateway to the so-called "Emerald Triangle," the verdant region where Thailand, Laos, and Cambodia meet. Here you can see the sun rise over Thailand, sparkling on the surface of the third-largest province's three major rivers, the Mekong, Mun, and Chi.

Ubon was established on the bank of the Mun River in the late 18th century during a time of conflict with the Laos capital, Vientiane. Today, the city enjoys good relations with its neighbors—at least on the surface. Ubon is famous for its political heritage, musical performers, and *moo yor* (processed pork wrapped in a banana leaf and steamed), but is best known for its Candle Procession in late July. Candles are traditionally offered to monks at the start of Buddhist Lent, Kao Pansa, and villages throughout the area compete to produce the finest float adorned with huge beeswax sculptures of Buddhist-inspired mythical figures and a towering candle or *tien*. The floats are paraded through the downtown area accompanied by musicians and local dancers. The festival is held over two days and is centered at Thung Sri Muang Park.

In the northern reaches of Ubon you can find the Indian-style pagoda **Wat Nong Bua**, a copy of the famous one in India where the Buddha attained enlightenment more than 2,500 years ago. The rectangular white chedi is breathtaking. Another nice temple is **Wat Maha Wanaram,** which houses a revered Buddha image named Phra Chao Yai Impang, believed to have magical powers. Check out the wax float at the rear of the chedi, used in the Candle Procession.

More wax candles, as well as comprehensive and interactive exhibits concerning the history of the province and its makeup, can be found at Rajabhat University of Ubon's **Culture and Art Centre.** This unique white building houses in its basement an interesting museum that celebrates the lives of local wax sculptors, as well as musicians and singers who perform in the famous Isan *morlam* style. Morlam is traditional Laotian music with strong rhythms and dynamic vocals. The genre has been augmented with electronic keyboards, helping to keep it alive and as popular, nationally, as ever. ⊠ *Changsanit Rd.* ▭ *Free* ☉ *Mon.–Sat. 8:30–4.*

Where to Eat

Locals love the evening food stalls along Ratchabut Road, beside Thung Sri Muang Park, but another popular spot is Haad Ku Dua, a beach along the banks of the Mun River about 7 km (4½ mi) out of town. Here you walk out over wooden gangways to thatched rafts where your food is brought to you as you recline on reed mats. Try such favorites as *pla chon* (snakehead fish, which is white with a size, texture, and flavor similar to mullet) or the ubiquitous gai yang (roast chicken). Back in town, Sappasit Road also offers a great selection of eateries both day and night.

$–$$$
FodorśChoice
★

✕ **Jumpa-Hom.** It is refreshing to find a fusion restaurant that expands upon its own regional culinary traditions, rather than jumping from one world cuisine to the next. At Jumpa-Hom, in the midst of an urban jungle full of palms, lanterns, and flowing fountains full of floating reeds, you can try such Thai-Chinese creations as "noodle envelopes" (like dim sum rice noodles) stuffed with Chinese sausage and served in a sweet soy sauce. White deep-sea tiger prawns are baked in a casserole with *woon sen* (glass noodles) and tender whole garlic cloves. Although most customers are locals, there is an English-language menu that may just be the most eloquent in all of Thailand. ✉ *49/3 Phichit Rangsan Rd.* ☎ *045/260398 or 045/265671* ▭ *MC, V* ⊘ *No lunch.*

¢ ✕ **Dee Amnuay Choke.** This bustling, friendly Chinese-style restaurant has an extensive menu and speedy service. This is arguably the most popular restaurant in town for late-evening diners (it's open until 3 AM), and you'll literally be rubbing shoulders with the locals. The place feels like a big warehouse, but the food is outstanding and great value for the money. Try the *phad poo pong garee*, a crab curry, which, like other dishes here, you can select straight from a massive bowl. Order by pointing to what looks good—it's hard to go wrong. ✉ *377–379 Sappasit Rd.* ☎ *045/241809* ▭ *No credit cards* ⊘ *No lunch.*

¢ ✕ **Indochine.** This long-established Vietnamese restaurant is showing its age, but it's still a favorite for both visitors and locals. The exquisite wooden entrance leads to a treasure trove of rooms with regional decor and antiques from around Southeast Asia. Upstairs you'll find the dinner restaurant, which is more luxurious than the ground floor and reminiscent of a piano bar. A popular dish is *nem nuong*, minced pork balls on skewers. There's an illustrated English-language menu with good explanations of the dishes. ✉ *168–170 Sappasit Rd.* ☎ *045/245584 or 045/254126* ▭ *MC, V.*

Where to Stay

★ **$–$$** ▦ **Tohsang City Hotel.** The Tohsang's elegant lobby, decorated with Thai flair in subdued shades of purple and beige, feels more refined than its surroundings. But even if this is the one cosmopolitan boutique hotel in a town full of cinder-block high-rises, its low prices are still reflect the deals you'd expect to find in Ubon. The restaurant and piano bar are equally mellow and comfortable, and many of the well-appointed, carpeted rooms overlook the quiet, leafy residential neighborhood in which the hotel sits, a few blocks away from the city center. ✉ *251 Palochai Rd., Muang District* ☎ *045/245531* ⊕ *www.tohsang.com* ➥ *74 rooms, 2 suites* ⚭ *In-room: refrigerator. In-hotel: restaurant, bar, laundry service, public Internet* ▭ *MC, V.*

$ ▦ **Laithong Hotel.** Locally made crafts and colorful textiles decorate the basic but comfortable rooms at this popular high-rise hotel. Don't expect luxury amenities or out-of-the-ordinary service here, but it's a reasonable higher-end choice near downtown. There's a lobby pub where you can relax with a beer. ✉ *50 Pichit Rangsan Rd.* ☎ *045/264271* ⊕ *www.laithonghotel.net* ➥ *124 rooms* ⚭ *In-room: refrigerator. In-hotel: restaurant, room service, 2 bars, airport shuttle* ▭ *AE, DC, MC, V.*

¢ ▦ **Sri Isan Hotel.** There are only two reasons to stay at this small hotel. The first is if you crave an extremely central location for exploring the city's markets and nightlife and don't mind the noise. The second is if you want to save about half of the US$35 or so that you would pay at the top hotels in town. The rooms here are modest in size but well maintained and tastefully decorated. The hotel's central staircase, with mosaic-tile balustrades, winding up four floors is probably the fanciest feature; the lobby is barebones. The staff is pleasant and helpful. ✉ *62 Ratchabut Rd.* ☎ *045/261011* ⊕ *www.sriisanhotel.com* ➥ *23 rooms, 10 suites* ⚭ *In-room: refrigerator. In-hotel: restaurant, laundry service, public Internet, public Wi-Fi* ▭ *MC, V.*

Shopping

Chong Mek Border Market, 87 km (54 mi) east of Ubon, is right over the Laos border and is very popular with visitors to the area. The small market, stretching across either side of the road, is interesting in itself, but most people seem to come here to buy wild orchids, which are sold at rock-bottom prices and in such abundance that you can't help but fear for the conservation of the flora of Laos. Other forest products on sale include seasonal wild mushrooms, ant eggs, and young bamboo shoots. Vendors quote prices in baht.

Take a passport just in case you're asked for it, but there are no official checkpoints before the market, no visa requirements, and only a nominal B5 admission fee. If you want to continue farther into Laos, however, you'll have to pay the full visa entry fee at the checkpoint past the market, which is around US$30. After entering Laos, you can continue on by bus or hire a private car. Note that driving is on the right side of the street in Laos, so cars coming from Thailand will suddenly be fish out of water; also, if you plan to continue in a rental car or with a private driver, you'll have to apply in advance for a car entry permit.

There is also quite an extensive market on the Thai side of the border, selling clothing, food, and other market goods sans orchids.

Under your own steam, the best way to get the market is to take an hourlong bus ride from Ubon to Phiboon; buses leave every 12 minutes and cost B20. From Phiboon take another bus or songthaew ride to the border. The market is open daily from 8 AM to at least 5 PM, sometimes later.

Nightlife

Although Ubon tends to be quieter by night than its neighbors of Korat and Surin, there is one world-class nightspot, **U-Bar** (✉ 97/8–10 Pichit Rangsan Rd. ☎ 045/265141 ⊕ www.u-bar.co.th), where the yuppie twentysomethings of Ubon gather to listen to live Thai rock music, while sipping mojitos, kamikazes, or bottles of Johnnie Walker. The throbbing ground floor, where the music happens, is done up in bold blacks and reds, whereas the upstairs lounge has a more playful Austin Powers feel, with faux-vintage furniture and a little outdoor terrace.

Korat & Environs Essentials

Transportation

BY AIR

There are Thai Airways and Phuket Airlines flights each day from Bangkok to Buri Ram and Ubon Ratchathani. Due to its distance from town, as well as its limited popularity with travelers, the airport at Korat is no longer served by Thai Airways flights from Bangkok. Ubon Ratchathani's airport is close to downtown, but Buri Ram's is 30 km (18 mi) from town.

🛈 Airline **Thai Airways** ☎ 044/255542 ⊕ www.thaiair.com.

BY BUS

Most of the towns in Isan are served by buses from Bangkok's Northern Bus Terminal. Korat is a major transport hub, with direct bus services to and from Bangkok, Pattaya, Chiang Mai, and Phitsanulok. A bus journey from Bangkok will take roughly 4 hours and cost B150; from Chiang Mai it will take roughly 11 hours, costing around B350, depending on the standard of the bus.

In general, buses are a bit cheaper than trains. Remember that many towns don't have formal bus terminals, but rather a spot along a main road where most buses stop.

Korat has two bus stations—the older terminal in the city center and the newer one north of Mittraphat Road. Buses to and from Bangkok mostly use the old terminal, while buses to other destinations in Isan depart from the newer terminal.

Buses to Ubon Ratchathani from Korat take upward of six hours and cost around B200. The best and most established company for this trip is Nakornchai Air (⊕ www.nca.co.th), which passes through all the cities in this area, starting from Ubon Ratchathani and going as far as Chiang Mai (overnight). These buses offer, among other things, a steward service, meal stops, movies, safety belts, and inflating massage seats.

Korat to Buri Ram by bus takes around two hours, to Surin around three hours, and to Si Saket five hours. Service is regular and information concerning schedules can be obtained from TAT offices and the bus stations. Tickets are best bought at the bus station. Only the bigger companies have a booking service, which it's best to use, unless you wish to risk a long bus journey standing up.

BY CAR

The region's roads are well maintained, particularly those along the east–west route connecting Phitsanulok and Ubon Ratchathani and the north–south route of Nong Khai and Korat. The two routes intersect at Khon Kaen. You should experience no difficulty finding your way around on these roads; if you plan to explore farther afield, remember that few road signs are in English.

As with the rest of the country, access to tourist destinations has improved greatly with new asphalt roads and frequent tourist attraction signs in English. If you still feel more comfortable being led, hire a car and driver from a tour operator. Costs are around B1,500 per day.

It's advisable to carry your passport, along with your driver's license, with you at all times while driving, as police checkpoints are fairly common (though typically a traffic policeman will wave a foreign tourist on).

When driving motorbikes, make sure your vehicle is visibly taxed and insured and that you wear a helmet at all times. In the past it was common for people not to bother wearing a helmet in the evenings, but government crackdowns have made it common practice to drive as safely at night as during the day.

Budget rental cars are available at the airport in Ubon Ratchathani.

In Korat, the local agency L.A. Trans Services will deliver a car to your hotel.

🖬 Agencies **Budget** ✉ Ubon Ratchathani Airport ☎ 045/240507. **L.A. Trans Services** ✉ Korat ☎ 044/267680.

BY TAXI, TUK-TUK & SONGTHAEW

Cities in this part of the country do not have taxis like in Bangkok. The most common means of getting around is by either tuk-tuk, samlor, or motorbike taxi. In all cases, the price is negotiated when you get in—no meters here. Generally speaking, fares within city limits range from B30 to B40. The pedal-power samlors (tricycles) are perhaps the more romantic option, but take the longest to reach your destination.

The cheapest means of getting around town, and often between small towns, is by songthaew, where prices can be as low as B20 for a short trip. They may not be as direct, but are certainly a good bargain; fellow passengers will typically help you determine where to get off if you tell them your destination.

BY TRAIN

The Northeastern Line runs frequent service from Bangkok to Isan (there are dozens of trains each day from Bangkok to Korat alone). All trains go via Ayutthaya to Kaeng Khoi Junction, where the line splits. One track goes to Korat, continuing east to Buri Ram, Surin, and Si Saket before terminating at Ubon Ratchathani; the other line goes north toward Nong Khai.

The train station for Ubon Ratchathani Province is not actually in the city itself, but in Warinchamrab, directly across the river. Ubon is a 10-minute songthaew ride from there. Train prices vary according to speed of the train and class of seat. The regular train, with fans and no frills, is wildly cheap. For example, a one-hour ride from Buri Ram to Surin costs B10. If you are traveling on a Friday or Sunday evening, it's advisable to book in advance.

🚆 Train Stations **Buri Ram** ⊠ Niwas Rd. **Korat** ⊠ Mukhamontri Rd. **Si Saket** ⊠ Ratchagarn Rot Fai Rd. **Surin** ⊠ Nong Toom Rd. **Ubon Ratchathani** ⊠ Sathanee Rd., Warinchamrab District.

Contacts & Resources

BANKS & EXCHANGING SERVICES

You'll have no difficulty finding banks with ATMs in larger towns. They're identifiable by a blue-on-white sign. In smaller towns and villages you might have to seek out the foreign exchange counter of a local bank, though there are a number of ATMs even in the smallest of towns and it's only in villages that you'll have problems.

EMERGENCIES

🚩 In Korat **General Emergencies** ☎ 191. **Police** ☎ 044/242010. **Maharat Hospital** ⊠ Chang Phuak Rd. ☎ 044/254990.

🚩 In Ubon Ratchathani **Police** ☎ 045/254216. **Rom Gao Hospital** ⊠ Auparat Rd. ☎ 045/254053.

TOUR OPTIONS

Tour companies in the area provide one-day tours of the major sights, as well as overnight tours that extend over two or three provinces. The companies in Ubon can also deal with visas and trips to Laos. The companies listed below are reliable, but English-speaking guides are few in number, so don't forget to specify that you require one. Otherwise, you may find yourself paying for a driver and pointer only.

🚩 Tour Companies **Greenleaf Travel** ⊠ 51/1 Moo 2, Tessaban 15 Rd., Pakchong District, Korat ☎044/280285. **Nanta Travel** ⊠334 Suranari Rd., Korat ☎044/251339. **Sakda Travel** ⊠150/1 Kantalak Rd., Ubon Ratchathani ☎045/321937 ⊕ www.sakdatravel.com. **Saren Travel** ⊠ 202/1-4 Tesaban 2 Rd., Surin ☎ 044/520174.

VISITOR INFORMATION

The Tourist Authority of Thailand has developed a network of offices to promote tourism in Lower Isan. The TAT office in Korat provides information for its own province plus Buri Ram and Surin. The TAT in Ubon Ratchathani takes care of information for Ubon and Si Saket. At both offices you can find English-speaking staff willing to answer queries and provide you with free maps, pamphlets for local guides, and other brochures. Office hours are 8:30 to 4:30 daily, though there are typically less staff on duty on a Sunday.

🚩 Tourist Information **Korat** ⊠ 2102-2104 Mittraphat Rd. ☎ 044/213666. **Ubon Ratchathani** ⊠ 264/1 Khuan Thani Rd. ☎ 045/243770.

ALONG THE MEKONG

The Mekong River, known in Thailand as *Mae Nam Khong,* is Southeast Asia's major waterway, starting in China's Qinghai Province near the border with Tibet. The Mekong crosses Yunnan Province, China, and forms the border between Myanmar and Laos as well as the majority of the border between Laos and Thailand, flowing across Cambodia and southern Vietnam into a rich delta before flowing into the South China Sea for a total distance of 4,200 km (2,610 mi).

More than 65 million people live along its banks, the river providing all of them with 80% of their daily protein intake and 20 million people with their sole source of income. Tides are turning, though, with the construction of a series of Chinese hydroelectric/irrigation dams, which are seriously affecting the Mekong's flow (in 2004 commercial river-shipping operations had to close when the river was less than 3 feet deep).

In many ways the town of Mukdahan can be seen as symbolic of Thailand's future relationship with the Mekong. Plans to build bridges linking it to Laos, and farther afield with Vietnam, will make it more than just the river-reliant oddity it is today by turning it into a major international transit hub. If you're coming from Bangkok or elsewhere in Thailand, you'll probably be approaching from Ubon; from there, you'll drive east to the Chong Mek crossing to Laos, then north along the river to Mukdahan.

The small but active riverside community of That Phanom, with its revered Phra That Phanom temple and its dizzying 171-foot pagoda, is the focal point of the region, while Laotian influences—dialect, customs, and architecture—spread out from the provincial capital, Nakhon Phanom.

Khong Jiam

⑩ *77 km (48 mi) east of Ubon Ratchathani, 29 km (18 mi) north of Chong Mek Border Market.*

If you're heading east from Ubon to the Mekong, Khong Jiam is the first town you'll hit. It's a sleepy village (technically a so-called "district" of Ubon) notable for its pretty, flag-lined boardwalk along the Mekong River, which has food stalls and other vendors, and for its spectacular luxury hotel, the Tohsang. At the boardwalk, which overlooks the bend in the Mekong famous for its two colors (the uncharitable might call them yellow and brown). This is the point where the River Mae Nam Moon, which begins in the Khao Yai forest and winds its way through much of Isan, past Ubon, Phimai, and Korat, empties into the Mekong. Here you can wander along the riverbank and take in the views or hire a local boatman to float you around for a bit; you can also enjoy a fresh fish lunch for pennies at one of the delicious open-air restaurants.

Where to Stay & Eat

¢ ✕ **Chuan Chom.** This is the northernmost, and most elaborate, of the string of food stalls and restaurants along Khong Jiam's boardwalk; it's near the District Office, right where the unpaved road for vehicles ends. Beneath a green corrugated tin roof, at simple picnic tables overlooking the Mekong, you can enjoy local river fish such as *lod pla nua orn gra thiem,* a plate of battered, deep-fried whisker snapper, which are meant to be eaten whole, head, tail, and all (you might want to remove the dorsal bone on the larger ones). Also good is *pla buek phad cha* (spicy stir-fried giant catfish with ginger and sweet basil). And it all costs only pennies. ⊠ *Khong Jiam* ☎ *042/351334* ⊟ *No credit cards.*

$$–$$$$ 🛏 **Tohsang Khongjiam.** The finest resort along the Mekong River in FodorśChoice Thailand is an all-encompassing experience in relaxation. The pool and ★ hot tub are encircled by the Tohsang's exotic garden of vegetation; meals or drinks can be taken on tables spectacularly perched above expanses of river with views of Laos beyond. In the resort's manicured jungle you can enjoy an outdoor Thai massage, mineral bath, or herbal steam treatment; lounge in front of the river amid palm fronds; or take one of the Tohsang's kayaks out along the Mekong. Private villas are posh, but the "deluxe" corner rooms have sizable terraces with better vistas, and at about US$63, they're one of the world's greatest hotel values. ⊠ *68 Mu 7, Huany-Mak-Tai* ☎ *045/351174 up to 76* ⊕ *www. tohsang.com* ↪ *44 rooms* ⚬ *In-room: refrigerator. In-hotel: 2 restaurants, 2 bars, pool, gym, spa, bicycles, public Internet* ⊟ *AE, MC, V.*

Mukdahan

⑪ *167 km (100 mi) south of Ubon Ratchathani.*

Mukdahan is Thailand's newest (73rd) province, its status being upgraded from that of district in 1982. In 2007, Mukdahan is due to be permanently linked to its mirror city, Savannakhet in Laos, by the second Laos–Thailand friendship bridge. Once the bridge is built, with increased trade via Route 9 and the Vietnamese port town of Danang, this town is expected to boom. Indeed, Mukdahan's main selling point is its international transit links with Laos's second city and the connection through to the Vietnamese border at Lao Bao.

The town itself is no oil painting, filled as it is with modern white concrete like so many standardized Thai provincial towns. Despite its redeveloped riverside promenade, it doesn't utilize its key geographical element, the Mekong. With its tiled walkway and absence of natural shading, this promising waterfront locale seems overly sanitized, offering only a dashed exposure of the majestic river.

The Indochinese market, stretching roadside from the promenade, is the focus of Mukdahan's bustle, with daily trade boats crossing to and from Savannakhet. The majority of goods are standard, cheap Vietnamese, Russian, and Chinese imports, with a profusion of items like car accessories and telescopic lenses. There's also the fabled promise of mudmee silks, but you might need one of those telescopic lenses to hunt out quality fabrics here.

With a Laos visa and B50 in hand for the boatman, you can visit **Savannakhet**, Laos's most populated province. Primarily a transit town, Savannakhet holds very little of interest for tourists, but proves a valuable link for travel farther down the Mekong, bus or plane options to Vientiane, as well as providing an opportunity (170 km [106 mi] away) to follow the Ho Chi Minh trail. For those looking for direct access into Vietnam, a cramped 250-km (155-mi), seven-hour bus trip can get you there.

Where to Stay & Eat

Mukdahan has mostly simple street-side eateries, but there are some good alternatives. Try **BJ Nong Gai Tun** (✉ Phitak Phanomkhet Rd. ☎ 042/630986) opposite the Palace Hotel for some good noodle soup, such as *nong gai tun yaa cheen* (boiled chicken leg soup with Chinese herbs).

Lang Koo Fat (✉ Phitak Phanomkhet Rd. ☎ 042/630986) is one of two Vietnamese shopfront restaurants downtown, and the best option for some Vietnamese spring rolls and the ever-popular *naem nuang* (processed pork served with transparent rice paper, vegetables, lettuce, and chilies).

Try **Ban Rattiya Jaew Horn 2** (✉ Soi Talat Tesaban 2, Phitak Phanomkhet Rd. ☎ 042/614789) for some Isan hospitality and *laab pla* (spicy minced fish salad) with sticky rice. There's also a night market along Songnang Sanid Road, where you can feast on standard Thai fast food.

$ ▥ **Ploy Palace Hotel.** This hotel represents the latest technology in Mukdahan accommodations, which isn't saying much. Still, rooms are clean, with river views and surprisingly modern amenities; the staff is friendly; and the price is right. ✉ *40 Phitak Phanomkhet Rd.* ☎ *042/631111 up to 20 ⤺ 149 rooms, 5 suites ⚐ In-room: Wi-Fi. In-hotel: 2 restaurants, bar, pool, public Wi-Fi ▭ MC, V.*

That Phanom

⑫ *40 km (24 mi) north of Mukdahan, 50 km (31 mi) south of Nakhon Phanom.*

North of Mukdahan is the village of That Phanom, site of northeast Thailand's most revered shrine. No one knows just when **Phra That Phanom** was built, though archaeologists believe its foundations were in place by the 5th century. The temple has been rebuilt several times, most recently after it completely collapsed in 1975. Its chedi now stands 171 feet high, with a decorative tip of gold that weighs more than 20 pounds. The shape of the structure is characteristic of Lao Buddhist architecture. A small museum houses the shrine's ancient bells and relics, including the supposed collarbone of the Buddha. ■ TIP→ **Droves of devotees attend an annual festival, usually held in February. The normally sleepy town comes to life as thousands fill the narrow streets.**

Where to Stay & Eat

That Phanom has some cheap dining options along Phanom Panarak Road, but it is noted for its uniquely designed riverside restaurants. *Pla pow* (in this case, river fish grilled on an open fire) is the main dish on offer, served with chili dips and sticky rice. The street that runs along the river, a few blocks east of the shrine, is called Rimkhong Road. On the inland side of the road there are seven restaurants, of which the most reliable are **Urng Kum Pla Pow,** an extremely simple, brightly lighted shack with a friendly staff and fresh fish, or the slightly more elaborate, two-level **Ngarm Da Song Fang Khong,** which has better river views from the upper floor, plus a menu with English translations; try *pad cha pla* (fried fish in spicy sauce), with some laab pla (spicy minced fish salad) to pep it up.

The river side of the road is where things really get interesting. Kitschy would hardly be the word to describe the six or so river restaurants, most of which are reached by descending rickety wooden staircases to the riverbank below the street. Water laps a few feet from the creaky wooden floors of these restaurant-bars (a few of which are also brothels). You'll find plenty of decent grilled fish, but you'll also find groups of revelers enjoying free-flowing Thai whiskey.

Two of the more barlike places are **Nat Pop** and **Thondae Koon. Pae Choke Amnuay,** a bit farther south, seems to take the food somewhat more seriously (this is all relative, of course), as revealed by the fish logo on the sign above. It's a floating restaurant, with the entire structure moored a few feet out into the water. The karaoke stage at the front of the restaurant is flanked by bottles of Johnnie Walker and shrines to the king; twinkly Christmas lights and a fish tank with the river's fresh catch complete the scene. It's certainly an unforgettable Thai experience.

That Phanom is not as luxurious as Nakhon Phanom, but it's certainly a welcoming stay. Most of its accommodation takes the form of small concrete bungalow-style blocks placed near the Mekong River, with a couple of uninspiring Chinese hotels standing near the bus pick-up point for Bangkok. Two more-interesting options are the rather eccentric Niryana Guesthouse and the Kritsada Rimkhong Resort, which offers the only real river views.

¢ ⊡ **Kritsada Rimkhong Resort.** This expanding bungalow complex is by no means a resort, but with the addition of two air-conditioned two-room wooden bungalows on stilts, it edges ahead of the competition. Cool tile flooring and dark varnished furniture in the rooms are pleasant; there are views of the Mekong River from balconies. The ground-level concrete bungalows are spacious; some only have fans, so be sure to request air-conditioning if you need it. ⊠ *90–93 Rimkhong Rd., 48000* ☎ *042/540088* ⊕ *www.geocities.com/ksdresort* ⇥ *14 rooms* ⬙ *In-room: no a/c (some), refrigerator* ⊟ *No credit cards.*

¢ ⊡ **Niryana Guesthouse.** That Phanom's only true guesthouse, the Niryana's slightly weather-beaten look belies the value to be found within. The owner is a real character, and she will be happy to provide you with local maps and make suggestions for cycling tours to take in the surroundings. The small corridors are filled with oil and acrylic artwork done by the owner herself; rooms are replete with woven bamboo bedsteads and antique wooden furniture. During high season (November through February), breakfasts of French baguettes and Laotian coffee are on offer to set you up for the day ahead. Thai lessons are also available. ⊠ *110 Moo 14, Rimkhong Rd., 48000* ☎ *042/540088* ⇥ *6 rooms* ⬙ *In-room: no a/c* ⊟ *No credit cards.*

Nakhon Phanom

⓭ *50 km (31 mi) north of That Phanom, 252 km (156 mi) east of Udon Thani.*

Nakhon Phanom translates from Sanskrit as the "City of Mountains," and although this sleepy town boasts no actual mountain views to savor, it does represent the last chance for you to enjoy the spectacular sunrise over the Mekong from a top-story hotel room. The long, well-kept river promenade provides pleasant strolls and panoramic views, with opportunities for quick forays into local temples. In spite of Nakhon Phanom's provincial location, there is a fair bit of nighttime activity, especially on weekends, and there is a bustling night market.

The town also hosts a small but uneventful Indochinese market, opposite the immigration office, for some basic shopping (the market closes early). With a Laos visa and B30 for the ferry crossing, you can propel yourself away from the nearby harbor and into the Laotian town of **Tha Khaek.** It's not the most obvious crossing point, as you have to travel either farther down the Mekong to Savannakhet or up to the capital Vientiane (both of which have more convenient transport links with Mukdahan and Nong Khai). The town is typical of Laotian border ports, with some surviving French colonial architecture mixed up with newer facilities. To this end, Tha Khaek proves to be little more than a stepping stone.

Renu Nakhon, a small village 50 km (31 mi) south of Nakhon Phanom, represents one of the province's more interesting side trips. Based around the temple of **Wat Phra That Renu Nakhon,** this small, tourist-oriented fabric center is focused on the production and sale of predominantly mudmee silks and cottons. The shophouses at the temple's entrance make shopping easy, with dozens of local designs, fabrics, and ready-to-wear shirts and jackets on sale. Saturday is market day and village weavers from surrounding households set up shop offering homespun fabrics along with some unessential tourist treats and the chance for a good haggle.

Thailand's Partying Provinces

IN A NATION THAT LOVES TO HAVE A GOOD TIME, Isan bangs the drum the loudest and puts so much into its festivals that you soon forget this is Thailand's poorest region. Isan treats national celebrations and ceremonies with such gusto and enthusiasm that people flock from around the country to experience them. From the rice paddies to the bustling cities, the region rocks during its festivals, which are often begun as reverent affairs of Buddhist worship, but are more often than not fueled by a simple passion for living . . . and copious amounts of *sato* (rice whiskey).

Singing and dancing are always major components of any Isan festival. Brass bands often boom in processions and troops of young students in traditional costumes dance in elegant lines. Then come the good ole boys and their traditional Isan instruments: the *kahn* and *wuud* bamboo organs, the *pin* guitars and *pong larng* xylophones, followed by the *dit hai* performers, traditionally garbed young women who dance as their fingers effortlessly rise and fall to pluck notes from stringed fish pots.

There's a festival in Thailand every month of the year, often called *Heet Sib Song* (the 12 customs), and associated with various forms of Buddhist merit-making or ceremony. Of particular note are the third month's *Boon Khao Jee* in Roi Et, which features unique roasted rice-and-egg offerings; the sixth month's *Boon Bung Fai*, a rocket festival best known in Yasathon; and *Boon Khao Pansa*, the start of Buddhist Lent, marked with the incomparable Candle Procession in Ubon Ratchathani. But what also makes the region stand out are some of the more unique parties found here. These include the *Elephant Roundup* of Surin on the third weekend in November for its shows and spectacle and the *Phi Ta Korn* ghost festival of Dan Sai District in Loei, which is held at the end of June or early July. This festival includes a procession of dancers holding elongated wooden phalluses that they lightheartedly poke at the giggling onlookers. Their antics follow the awakening of the spirit of a monk, Pra Ub Pa Kud, which resides in a stream in the form of white marble. Once his spirit is led back to the local temple it's believed he'll protect the village from harm for another year.

But the pièce de résistance has to be the *Bon Fai Naak* festival in Nong Khai in late October. Here, thousands of onlookers crowd the banks of the mighty Mekong in anticipation of the supernatural conflagrations of the mythical (or not so mythical) *nagas*, water serpents that appear in so much Buddhist folklore. All eyes are focused on the waters of this famous river. Anticipation rises and then the whoops and cheers erupt as into the night sky from the very depths of the waters ascend multicolor balls of fire and light. The nagas have not disappointed and have breathed their mysterious life into another moon-drenched night. The authenticity of these annual, unearthly fireballs has been the matter of much speculation, but that fails to stop the throngs who come for the wonder and pure fun of it. This is Isan—suspend your disbelief and have a thumping good time.

–Ivan Benedict New

If it all seems a bit much, take a short walk behind the temple grounds, where you can watch households busily weaving.

Where to Stay & Eat

Along the blocks surrounding the intersection of Nakhon Phanom's main two streets, there are several bright, bustling local restaurants serving the typical Chinese-Thai soups and stews, which prominently feature innards. These places generally stay open until the wee hours.

The city is also just a couple of hundred kilometers from Vietnam, so you should keep your eyes open for the ladies that set up in storefronts, creating **Vietnamese dumplings** right before your eyes. First, the batter is ladled, crepe-style, onto a searingly hot drum that acts as a large pan; sometimes, egg is ladled onto the skin, too. Another dish to look out for is the "Vietnamese pizza," which is made with thin, crispy, pizza-size rice crackers topped with the soft rice skin—a play on two of the utterly distinct textures that rice can assume—along with minced pork and chili.

¢–$$ ✕ **Satang.** Nakhon Phanom has several restaurants that set up sidewalk
FodorsChoice   tables along the Mekong, making for quite a romantic dining experi-
★   ence at night, and Satang is the best of them. Alternatively, you can dine in a two-story, open-air space at the restaurant itself, which is across the riverfront street and also offers unobstructed river views. The food is as impressive as the setting, from the complex *ho mook pla* (fish with cabbage, green peppercorns, and chilies in a fragrant red curry with Kaffir lime leaf, steamed in tinfoil) to the showstopping *pla tap tim look tao yum ma muang*: deep-fried chunks of fresh white fish served with a separate, challengingly spicy salad of green mango, peanut, red onion, and red chili, whose juicy acidity plays beautifully off the crispy fish. ✉ *766 Soonthornvijit Rd.* ☎ *042/522658* ▭ *No credit cards.*

¢–$ ✕ **Waranya Meringue Bakery.** Here's your chance to take advantage of Nakhon Phanom's proximity to Vietnam and try Vietnamese fare in a bright, simple space that is slightly classier and more café-like than the market stalls. Aside from the quality baked goods—both Vietnamese and Western—and coffee, there is a raft of interesting and authentic Vietnamese specialties (listed only in Thai in the menu), including *nam-nuang* (grilled minced pork balls served with raw bananas, star fruit, and local vegetables) and *yum wua pao* (crispy slices of veal, blackened on the outside and rare on the inside, in a spicy salad). ✉ *32–32/1 Thumrongprasit Rd.* ☎ *042/514237* ▭ *No credit cards.*

$–$$ ▥ **Nakhonphanom River View Hotel.** This is Nakhon Phanom's only five-star hotel, with a spread of rooms from standard to presidential. The rooms are clean and airy, though the views aren't as panoramic as you might hope from this riverside location. If you're willing to spend more, you can get one of the river-view rooms, which really do have splendid vistas. There's a beautiful waterfront pool where you can pamper yourself with a massage right on the edge of the legendary river. Ask for low-season discounts; rates can dip as low as B900. ✉ *9 Nakhonphanom-Thatphanom Rd.* ☎ *042/522333 up to 40* ⊕ *www.northeast-hotel.com* ☞ *122 rooms* ♻ *In-room: refrigerator. In-hotel: restaurant, 2 bars, pool* ▭ *MC, V.*

¢–$ ▦ **Mae Nam Kong Grand View.** If you're looking for reasonably priced views over the Mekong River, then this is the place. This friendly, clean, and comfortable five-story hotel can be a rewarding stay if you snag an east-facing corner room—big windows give you a magnificent view of the Mekong. The balconies make it a really good value, even if this is one of the more expensive options in Nakhon Phanom. ⊠ *527 Soonthornvijit Rd.* ☎ *042/513564* ⤴ *114 rooms, 2 suites* ♿ *In-room: refrigerator. In-hotel: restaurant, bar* ⊟ *AE, MC, V.*

Nightlife

Nakhon Phanom has a surprisingly robust nightlife along Thumrongprasit Road and in the surrounding area. It all begins with **Bar Koo** (⊠ 39 Thumrongprasit Rd. ☎ 042/514100), an expansive outdoor space with beautiful fountains and live music from 8 PM to midnight on a big soundstage. Also extremely popular is **Ohio** (⊠ 31 Thumrongprasit Rd. ☎ 044/531836), a bar-restaurant that attracts a beautiful, young crowd.

Along the Mekong Essentials

Transportation

BY AIR

Thai Airways has one flight daily between Bangkok and Nakhon Phanom.

🔢 **Airline Thai Airways** ☎ 042/513014 ⊕ www.thaiair.com.

BY BUS

Direct service from Bangkok to Nakhon Phanom leaves from Bangkok's Northern Bus Terminal every half hour from 7 PM to 8:30 PM; the trip takes 11 hours. Buses back to Bangkok leave from Nakhon Phanom's bus station, on Highway 22, as well as from Nakorn Pranarak Road, next to the market. Buses depart every 15 minutes from 5:30 PM to 6:30 PM. Costs both ways are B635 for VIP buses and B410 for first-class air-conditioned buses.

Air-conditioned bus connections from Nakhon Phanom to Udon Thani (five hours) and Nong Khai (seven hours) leave from 5:30 AM to 3 PM, with Nong Khai buses stopping services at 11 AM. Both cost B122 one way.

Buses from Nakhon Phanom to That Phanom (one hour) and Mukdahan (three hours) take the same route starting at 6 AM and running every 40 minutes until 5 PM. Costs are B17 (fan) or B40 (air-conditioning) to That Phanom and B40 (fan) or B56 (air-conditioning) to Mukdahan. Khon Kaen (five hours) can also be reached, with buses leaving Nakhon Phanom roughly every two hours from 6:10 AM to 4 PM; the fare is B97 (fan) or B175 (first-class with air-conditioning). Buses to Ubon Ratchathani (four hours) cost B97 (fan) or B164 (first-class with air-conditioning).

That Phanom District has two private companies operating nightly buses to Bangkok found on Chaiyangun Road, while Mukdahan's bus terminal on Highway 212 has fan buses leaving every half hour to Ubon Ratchathani (3 hours; B51) between 6:30 AM and 5 PM. Buses to Bangkok

(11 hours) are also available here between 8 AM and 6 PM at a cost of B336 for first-class air-conditioned buses and B575 for 24-seat VIP buses.

🚌 Bus Stations Mukdahan ✉ Hwy. 212 ☎ 042/611421. **Nakhon Phanom** ✉ Klang Muang Rd. ☎ 042/513444. **That Phanom** ✉ Thai Sangaon Tour, Chaiyangun Rd. ☎ 042/541757 or 09/863-1243 ✉ Cherd Chai Tour, Chaiyangun Rd. ☎ 042/541375 or 01/768-3559.

BY CAR

Roads from Udon Thani (via Sakhon Nakhon) to Nakhon Phanom, That Phanom, and Mukdahan, and trailing the 212 Mekong River road down to Ubon Ratchathani, are in reasonable condition, but they're narrow, two-lane squeezes.

Nakhon Phanom and That Phanom can also be reached from Khon Kaen. Mukdahan to Khon Kaen requires some cross-country drives following the good 212 and 2136 roads to the town of Phon Thong, then the 2116 road skirting Roi Et, which becomes a minefield of potholes until Yang Talat town when it improves, taking you on to the 209 and into Khon Kaen.

Driving from Bangkok to the Mekong towns, you should use the faster Highway 2 until Khon Kaen and then backtrack the route described above.

Mukdahan is the Mekong route's only prospect for car rental; passport photocopies and an international driver's license are required.

🚌 Agencies Mekong World Holiday ✉ 2820 Thumrongprasit Rd. ☎ 042/515775. **S. P.B.R. Tour** ✉ 165/2 Thumrongprasit Rd. ☎ 042/512384 or 01/873-7495.

BY TAXI, TUK-TUK & SONGTHAEWS

Tuk-tuk and car taxis aren't really an option along the Mekong; songthaews are the most common means of public transport. Negotiate your price before getting on. Motorbike taxis and the ever-present pedal-powered samlors are available, but since these towns are so manageable in size, walking is the more enjoyable option.

BY TRAIN

There are no direct train links with Nakhon Phanom or Mukdahan; however, the Northeastern Line does make stops in Ubon Ratchathani to the east and Khon Kaen, Udonthani, and Nong Khai to the northeast. Trains bound for Ubon leave from Hualamphong station in Bangkok at 5:45 AM, 6:40 AM, 6:45 PM, 9 PM, and 11:40 PM, taking approximately 11 hours and costing from B175 for third-class seats up to B1,080 for a first-class sleeper. Khon Kaen trains leave at 8:20 AM, 8 PM, and 8:45 PM, taking around 8 hours and costing between B200 and B1,000. Udon Thani and Nong Khai trains leave at the same time as Khon Kaen's, adding an extra 2 and 3 hours and costing B175 to B1,077 and B183 to B1,117, respectively.

Contacts & Resources

BANKS & EXCHANGING SERVICES

You'll have no difficulty finding banks with ATMs in all larger towns. They're easily identifiable by a blue-on-white sign. In smaller towns and villages you might have to seek out the foreign exchange counter of a local bank.

EMERGENCIES

⚡ In Mukdahan **Police** ☎ 042/611333. **Mukdahan International Hospital** ✉ Chatu Phadung Rd. ☎ 043/236005.

⚡ In Nakhon Phanom **Police** ☎ 042/511266. **Nakhon Phanom Hospital** ✉ Apiban-buncha Rd. ☎ 042/511422.

⚡ In That Phanom **Police** ☎ 042/515554. **That Phanom Hospital** ✉ Hwy. 212. ☎ 042/541735.

TOUR OPTIONS

North by North East Tour, based in Nakhon Phanom, organizes the most comprehensive packages for seeing the Mekong stretch. This tour company has some good four-day/three-night programs for this area, including visits to ethnic Lao and traditional Isan villages, the Laotian towns of Savannakhet and Tha Khaek, Ho Chi Minh's residence, Wat Phra That Phanom, and Indochinese markets, as well as Pha Taem National Park, Mukdahan National Park, and Khao Phra Viharn's temple complex on the Cambodian border. Prices are good and online booking is available on their informative Web site.

⚡ Tour Company **North by North East Tours** ✉ 746/1 Sunthornvichit Rd., Nakhon Phanom ☎ 042/513572 or 042/513573 ⊕ www.thaitourism.com/ISAN/default.asp.

VISITOR INFORMATION

The Tourist Authority of Thailand has only one office in this area, responsible for Nakhon Phanom, That Phanom, and Mukdahan. It stocks good maps of all the towns, but lacks English information for its host province. There is, however, an essential booklet in English for Mukdahan, with all its attractions covered.

⚡ Tourist Information **Tourist Authority of Thailand** ✉ 184/1 Sunthornvichit Rd., Nakhon Phanom ☎ 042/513490.

UDON THANI & ENVIRONS

Prehistory, geography, myth, superstition, and Vietnam War–era boom towns make this area of Northern Isan one of the richest and most varied destinations in Thailand. Its geography, spreading east from the mountain ranges of Petchabun, through to the rich depths of the Mekong River, give this region one of the most varied terrains in the country.

Thailand's largest fossilized remains have been unearthed in Isan's plateau, along with proof of Southeast Asia's oldest Bronze Age civilization. Although its soils are of archaeological value, the vast waters of the Mekong have been valued even more. During the Ayutthaya period (1350–1758) these small riverside communities saw strategic garrison towns spring up, heralding territorial disputes between Laos and Siam that continued until 1907 and the Siamese-French treaties.

The French colonization of Laos from 1893 to 1953 and its gaining of all territories east of the Mekong River left a strong influence on these bordering towns in the form of architecture and a diversity in culture and surroundings that can be found in few other places in Thailand. The start of the Vietnam War, however, brought this area into the 20th-century with a bang. Thailand's major alliance with the United States during the war helped bring money into this whole region, causing its greatest economic thrust and spawning overnight boomtowns that today stabilize Thailand's poorest reaches.

Most travelers making their way into Laos find themselves spending some time in Nong Khai, the main crossing point into the country. Although Nong Khai has little to offer other than temple tours and the annual, mysterious spectacle of balls of fire rising from the Mekong during the *Bon Fai Naak* festival, it does offer a wide range of accommodation and might be your last chance to immerse yourself in Thailand before you venture into the tropics of Laos.

Udon Thani serves as the best stopover point for this region, with transit links on the way to the lower reaches of the Isan plain, as well as into Laos. ■ TIP→ **Those looking for a bit of Bangkok sophistication (without the grime) will enjoy Udon Thani, with its mix of foreign foods and tongues and the pumping bars and clubs that make for a memorable night out.**

Loei is the prime natural attraction for this region, containing the last mountainous ranges of Northern Thailand, culminating in the evergreen heights of its deservedly famous Phukradung National Park. With the Laotian-influenced festival of Phi Ta Khon and the strong French colonial styles of architecture in Chiang Khan, the region is as rich culturally as it is naturally.

Khon Kaen, aside from its Cretaceous bones and wartime legacy, is the quintessential Isan city. It holds the key to Isan's heart with its generous hospitality, wild foods, and royal fabrics. Whether on excursions out to rural Isan communities or scooting around its Bangkok-style pubs and clubs, you're guaranteed a true slice of Isan life.

Udon Thani

⓮ *564 km (350 mi) northeast of Bangkok, 401 km (250 mi) northwest of Ubon Ratchathani.*

As the site of a major U.S. Air Force base during the Vietnam War, Udon Thani quickly grew in size and importance. There are still traces of the massive U.S. presence in its hostess bars and shopping malls, but the independent Thais have managed to keep hold on the city.

The **Udon Thani Provincial Museum** opened in January 2004 and showcases most of the province's sights. The museum occupies the impressive Rachinuthit building, which was built during Rama VI's reign and was originally used as a girls' school. Divided into two floors and seven sections, the museum takes you through the history, geology, archaeology, anthropology, and urban development of the city. Sliding across the buffed golden teak floorboards from one room to the next you pass models of ethnic groups and miniatures of attractions, as well as ethnic artwork. ✉ *Phosi Rd.* 🎟 *Free* ⊙ *Daily 9–4.*

The chief attraction near Udon Thani is **Ban Chiang**, about 60 km (36 mi) east of the city. At this Bronze Age settlement, archaeologists have found evidence to suggest a civilization thrived here more than 7,000 years ago. The United Nations declared it a World Heritage Site in

1992. The peculiar pottery—red-on-cream with swirling geometric spirals—indicates that this civilization was ahead of its time in cultural development. Even more intriguing are the copper bells and glass beads found here, many of which are similar to some found in North and Central America. This poses the question: did Asians trade with Americans 7,000 years ago, or even migrate halfway around the world? You can reach Ban Chiang from Udon Thani on the local bus, or take a car and driver for about B600.

OFF THE
BEATEN
PATH

BAN PHUE One hour by bus northwest of Udon Thani is a 1,200-acre mountainside retreat near the village of Ban Phue. It's littered with rocks of all sizes, some in shapes that the faithful say resemble Buddhist and Hindu images. The 131-foot pagoda is in the style of the revered Wat That Phanom. Take the path to the right of the temple and you'll reach a cave with silhouette paintings thought to be 4,000 years old.

Where to Stay & Eat

Udon Thani is famous for its version of gai yang, or roast chicken, which you can try at stalls on virtually every street.

$ ✕ **Steve's Bar and Restaurant.** Steve, an ex-fireman from England, and his Thai wife serve up traditional pub classics at this long-standing expat haunt in the center of town. An indoor air-conditioned dining room fills up with those craving authentic steak-and-kidney pies and fish-and-chips. Portions are large and it's a good spot to catch sports on the big screen. ✉ 254/26 Prajaksilapakom Rd. ☎ 042/244523 ⊕ www.stevesbarudon.com ⊟ No credit cards.

¢–$ ✕ **Rabiang Phatchanee.** On the edge of the lake at Nong Prajak Park you find this pleasant, traditional Thai restaurant. An extensive menu features standard favorites alongside some interesting variations. Pla deuk fu phat phet (fried crispy catfish with a chili sauce) is fiery but ever so tasty, while som pla choh tot (sour soup with water mimosa and snakehead fish) is authentic Isan food, though quite sharp. Live music plays in the background. ✉ 53/1 Bannon Rd. ☎ 042/241515, 042/244015, or 042/325890 ⊟ MC, V.

$–$$ ▦ **Charoensri Grand Royal.** Just to make sure you get the message, the city's top hotel calls itself both grand *and* royal. It's certainly luxurious, with softly carpeted rooms furnished in pale woods and decorated in restful pastels. The two restaurants serve Thai, Chinese, and Western food, and there's a variety of beers on tap in the pleasant beer garden. ✉ 277/1 Prajaksilapakom Rd., 41000 ☎ 042/343555 ⬎ 260 rooms ♨ In-room: refrigerator. In-hotel: 2 restaurants, room service, 2 bars, pool, gym, concierge ⊟ AE, DC, MC, V.

$ ▦ **Ban Chiang Hotel.** Ban Chiang is a nicely furnished hotel, tastefully decorated with local paintings. The rates make it quite a bargain, and you'll be tempted to spend your savings on pampering yourself at the hotel spa. ✉ 5 Mookmontri Rd., 41000 ☎ 042/327911 ⬎ 149 rooms ♨ In-room: refrigerator. In-hotel: restaurant, pool, gym, spa, public Internet, airport shuttle ⊟ AE, DC, MC, V.

¢ ▦ **City Lodge Hotel.** The name is uninspiring, but City Lodge is actually an excellent English-owned boutique hotel. It's tastefully designed with a decidedly modern bent: heavy on pastel shades and chrome fittings,

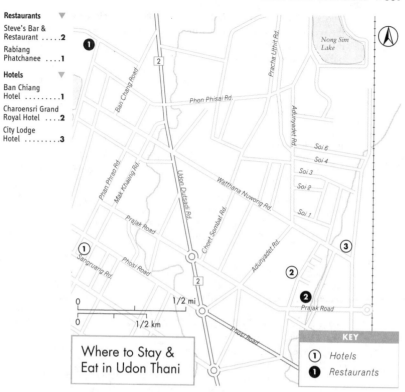

**Where to Stay &
Eat in Udon Thani**

KEY

① Hotels

❶ Restaurants

with contemporary furnishings and arresting local art. The hearty complimentary breakfast and well-stocked bar make this place particularly good value. ⊠ 83/14–15 Wottananuvong Rd., 41000 ☎ 042/224439 🛏 10 rooms ⚒ In-room: refrigerator. In-hotel: restaurant, laundry facilities ▤ No credit cards.

Khon Kaen

⓯ 190 km (118 mi) northeast of Korat, 115 km (69 mi) south of Udon Thani.

Thailand's third-largest city, Khon Kaen has seen rapid growth due to the government's efforts to bolster the economy of the northeastern region. You'll see high-rise hotels shooting up and shopping malls under construction everywhere you look. Khon Kaen has long been renowned for its mudmee silk, celebrated each December with a huge festival. The city can feel chaotic, but its pleasures include dining in seafood restaurants along Lake Bueng Kaen Nakhon and interacting with the city's rousing party scene at one of its hopping nightclubs.

At **Chonnabot**, 50 km (31 mi) to the south, you can see the silk being processed, from its cocoon stage through its spinning and dying to its weaving on hand looms.

About 80 km (50 mi) west of Khon Kaen is **Phuwiang National Park,** where the world's oldest fossils of carnivorous dinosaurs, the Siam Mityrennous Esannensil, were discovered. There are dinosaur museums at the park entrance, at Phu Pratu Teema, as well as in the nearby village of Kok Sanambin. To get there from Khon Kaen, take Highway 12 (Khon Kaen-Chumpae) west for about 50 km (31 mi), until you reach Route 2038; head north for about 40 km (25 mi) until you reach the park. ▨ B400 ⊙ Daily 6–6.

Where to Stay & Eat

It would be a crime to dine in Khon Kaen without experiencing the romance of a restaurant on Bueng Kaen Nakorn Lake (really a large pond), which is about five minutes south of the city center. On its banks, you'll find a dozen well-priced seafood restaurants. In town, however, there is also a wealth of restaurants and cheap food stalls on Klangmuang Road; options along this stretch are as varied as Vietnamese, homemade pizza, and local Isan cuisine. A good late-night food stop is the night market off Namuang Road, which is open until the wee hours.

¢–$$ ✕ **Bua Luang.** This enormous, open-plan lakeside restaurant is perched on the northern end of Lake Bueng Kaen Nakhon, extending out into the water. It's the biggest in the city, but the setting justifies the place's renown. The menu is a blend of Isan, Thai, and Chinese. One specialty worth trying is the *tom yam mapow orn* (prawns with coconut palm heart in a spicy hot-and-sour soup). ⊠ Rob Bueng Rd. ☎ 043/222504 or 043/320202 ▤ MC, V.

¢–$ ✕ **Pla Payai.** Perhaps the best place in town to try true regional Isan food, Pla Payai's open kitchen prepares complex but light dishes like *mok lab pla tong* (lightly grilled minced fish steamed in banana leaf). You also can't go wrong with the *laab ped*—a minced-duck version of the classic salad, with chilies, red onion, lime, fish sauce, rice powder, and cilantro. One of Khon Kaen's many great places to eat on the lake, Pla Payai is a supremely local joint; if you don't speak Thai, you'll have to stumble and bumble through the ordering process. ⊠ Rob Bueng Rd. ☎ 043/225411 ▤ No credit cards.

¢–$ ✕ **Sam Yan Seafood.** This big temple to fresh seafood is renowned for its first-rate preparations, such as *poop had phong garee* (fried crab in curry), *poop had prigtai dum* (fried crab with black pepper), and *salad hoi shell* (a mixed shellfish salad). You can also order a whole fresh grouper. All of this is enjoyed in classic Khon Kaen fashion—in the open air on the edge of the lake. ⊠ 120/16 Rob Bueng Rd. ☎ 043/223687 ▤ No credit cards.

$$ ▥ **Sofitel Raja Orchid.** Khon Kaen's skyline is dominated by the gleaming 25-story facade of the Sofitel Raja Orchid, easily Isan's most luxurious hotel. Everything about it is first-rate—the rooms are elegant, furnished with native woods and handwoven silks. If you're looking to splurge, there's always the 6,500-square-foot royal suite, which has its own helipad. The hotel is like a multistory shopping mall, with numerous restaurants (though none too impressive); Isan's largest karaoke bar, Studio 1; and the Funhouse, a disco that really lives up to its name. German visitors marvel at Thailand's first microbrewery, the Krönen Brauhaus, where you can even order bratwurst. ⊠ 9/9 Prachasumran Rd., 44000

Fodor'sChoice
★

☏ 043/322155, 800/221–4542 in U.S. ⊕ www.sofitel.com ⤴ 293 rooms ♿ In-room: refrigerator. In-hotel: 5 restaurants, room service, 3 bars, pool, gym, laundry service, concierge ☰ AE, DC, MC, V.

$ 🏠 **Charoen Thani Princess.** One of the many bold new additions to the Khon Kaen hotel scene that has accompanied the city's unprecedented business boom, this 19-floor hotel has a multistory lobby full of fountains, a relaxing pool, and a bustling bar, along with the requisite disco-karaoke-snooker entertainment options. Ask for an upper floor to take in great city views, even though Khon Kaen's not much to look at. ✉ 260 Sri Chan Rd., Naimuang, 40000 ☏ 043/220400 up to 14 ⊕ www.dusit.com ⤴ 287 rooms, 33 suites ♿ In-room: refrigerator. In-hotel: 2 restaurants, room service, 3 bars, pool, gym, laundry service, concierge ☰ AE, DC, MC, V.

¢–$ 🏠 **Bussarakam Hotel.** This new high-rise in the center of town is more affordable than some of its neighbors. The lobby is palatial in the slightly overdone Thai way, and rooms are done in soothing pale shades. ✉ 68 Pimpasut Rd., 40000 ☏ 043/4333–3666 ⊕ www.bussarakamhotel. com ⤴ 155 rooms ♿ In-room: refrigerator, ethernet. In-hotel: 2 restaurants, room service, laundry service, concierge ☰ MC, V.

Shopping

Khon Kaen is littered with souvenir shops. Locally made woven bamboo products can be found at **Moradok Thai** (✉ 87/89–90 Ammat Rd. ☏ 043/243827). Silver trinkets are on sale at the centrally located **Gloom Prae Phaan** (✉ 131/193 Chattaphadoong Rd. ☏ 043/337216). Most notable, however, is the province's famed mudmee silks and cottons. If you don't have time to make it to Chonnabot, Ban Muang Pha, or Phu, then pay a visit to **Rin Thai Silk** (✉ 412 Namuang Rd. ☏ 043/ 220705 or 043/221042). This small but well-stocked shop carries numerous mudmee, silks, and cottons.

Loei

16 152 km (90 mi) west of Udon Thani, 43 km (26 mi) south of Chiang Khan.

Loei, one of Thailand's most sparsely populated provinces, is a fertile basin fed by the Loei and Man rivers, tributaries of the Mekong, making it one of the country's most geographically scenic regions. Its unique topography, bordered by the Eastern and Western Phetchabun mountain ranges, and its susceptibility to China's winter winds, result in Loei bearing some of the most dramatic temperatures in the country. Summers can reach 104°F (40°C), while winter nights can drop to freezing.

Once the site of a prehistoric Bronze Age mining settlement, Loei started life in the 15th century when the kingdoms of Ayutthaya and Lan Xang, in Laos, built Phra That Si Song Rak temple in what is now the Dan Sai District. The temple's name literally translates as the "sublime love of two" and served as a sign of beneficial relations between the two kingdoms at a time when Myanmar was infringing on domains based on the Mekong. In 1853, King Rama IV bestowed Muang Loei Thai with town status and present-day Loei achieved its independent provincial status in 1933.

The province is a rare blend of culture and language between its Northern Thai neighbors, Laotian migrations, and northeastern affection. The result is a warm, traditional lifestyle and the unique Thai Loei language. Dan Sai District has its animated Phi Ta Khon festival in June, which is reminiscent of the Puyoe Yayoe festival in Muang Kaen Tao, Laos.

Despite its rich, embracing nature, the town itself is rather drab, with predictable concrete blocks and shophouses lining the streets. As a short stopover, Loei can be useful as a place to gather information, but the places worth exploring lie out of town. Phu Kra Dueng National Park is Loei's most visited station for its evergreen plateau, and Chiang Khan, with its Laotian roots and colonial architecture, is the heart of the province.

Where to Stay

$$ **Loei Palace.** The sinuous white facade of the massive Loei Palace dominates the city's skyline. Surrounded by well-tended gardens, the pool is a welcome sight after a day exploring the mountains. The excellent restaurant, serving Thai, Chinese, and other dishes, reassures you that sophisticated cuisine is still to be found in this remote region. An interesting outing offered by the hotel is to the Chateau de Loei, Thailand's top vineyard. ✉ *167/4 Charoenrath Rd., 42000* ☎ *042/815668* ⊕ *www.amari.com* ⌨ *123 rooms, 33 suites* ⌂ *In-room: refrigerator. In-hotel: 2 restaurants, bar, pool, gym, laundry service, public Wi-Fi* ▭ *AE, DC, MC, V.*

$$ **Phu Pha Nam Resort.** With the exception of the rustic tiled floors of its pavilion-style restaurant and the stone walls in the billiards room, this entire hotel seems to be constructed of richly colored teak. You sleep on carved teak beds in teak-floor rooms, all of which have sitting areas with picture windows framing views of the nearby hills. The resort is on a 52-acre estate about 70 km (42 mi) south of Loei. ✉ *252 Moo 1, Koakngam Amphur Dansai, 42120* ☎ *042/892055, 02/254–3000 in Bangkok* ⊕ *www.phuphanamresort.com* ⌨ *71 rooms* ⌂ *In-room: refrigerator. In-hotel: restaurant, pool, gym, water sports, bicycles, public Internet* ▭ *AE, MC, V.*

¢   **Kings Hotel.** This central hotel represents Loei's best value. An unassuming entrance leads into a modest five-floor, atrium-style complex, with a small square garden at its base. The rooms are clean and white, with functional wood furnishings; cheaper fan-cooled rooms are also available by way of a thigh-burning hike up to the fifth floor. Prices and cleanliness undercut the competition, making it a good deal downtown. ✉ *11/9–12 Chumsai Rd., 42000* ☎ *042/811701, 042/811783, or 042/811225* ⌨ *50 rooms* ⌂ *In-hotel: restaurant, laundry service, public Internet* ▭ *MC, V.*

¢   **Sugar Guesthouse.** This is the one and only guesthouse in Loei. Rooms are basic but clean, ranging from cheap fan rooms with steel-frame beds to bigger-fan and air-conditioned rooms with teak beds, chairs, and wardrobes. The owner speaks English and has set up the place for travelers' needs with motorbike and bicycle rental, a good breakfast menu to get the day rolling, and tour services to destinations in the province. If you're looking for a home away from home, this could be it. ✉ *4/1 Wisuttitep Soi 2 Rd., 42000* ☎ *042/812982 or 09/711–1975* ⌨ *8 rooms* ⌂ *In-hotel: laundry service* ▭ *No credit cards.*

Phu Kra Dueng National Park

★ ⓐ *70 km (42 mi) south of Loei.*

This was supposed to be Thailand's first national park, but lack of funding prevented that from happening. It wasn't until 1949 that government funds were finally allocated, and it took another 10 years before Phu Kra Dueng was finally granted national park status, becoming Thailand's second (after Korat's Khao Yai). Regardless of the slow start, it has become one of Thailand's most visited destinations.

The park consists of a lone, steep-sided mountain, which rises out of a flat plain that sprawls over 348 square km (134 square mi), and is crowned by a 60-square-km (23-square-mi) plateau. It takes four hours to hike the 5 km (3 mi) to the top, but there's a spectacular panorama at 4,265 feet above sea level waiting for you.

The mountaintop is usually covered in mist from October to February, when the temperature can drop as low as freezing. The summit, full of rich flora year-round, is mostly a combination of dense evergreen forest and equally dense pine forest, but from February onward color begins to saturate the park. Summer brings out the mountain's famed red-and-white rhododendrons and flowering grasses such as Pro Phu and Ya Khao Kam. In winter the park is ablaze with lush green mosses and ferns, set against the reddening of maple tree leaves. More than 276 animal species have been identified here, such as serows (a type of Asian goat), Asiatic elephants, tigers, bears, and boars, plus 171 species of birds including silver pheasants, black hawks, and red jungle fowl.

Main tourist attractions are well marked. Trails take you through forest vegetation and vast grasslands, and along streams to waterfalls, caves, and overhanging cliffs (perfect for taking in a sunrise or sunset). There's plenty to do, and the park is equally good for a day trip or extended exploration. The park headquarters at the base of the mountain has maps and information for you to plan your wanderings.

Accommodation, food, and conveniences are readily available from top to bottom. Most people bring their own tents (there's a B30 pitching fee). There are also larger, more expensive bungalow rooms from B1,200 to B3,600. The park is open from late September to early June, but ▪ TIP→ the crowds will come out in force from late October through mid-January, so unless you're bringing you own tent, be sure to contact the park headquarters to reserve accommodation as soon as possible.

Note that they stop letting visitors into the park at 2 PM—the climb to the top takes a long time and they don't want people tackling it in the dark. If you are already inside the park, however, you don't need to be worried about being ushered out.

You can reach the park by bus from Loei's bus terminal—buses cost B91. You have to get off at Pha Nok Khao junction and continue to the park by songthaew for another 20 km (12 mi); a songthaew generally costs B300 for up to six people. ✉ *Hwy. 201, Loei-Phu Kra Dueng Rd.* ⊕ *www.dnp.go.th/national_park.asp* ✉ B400 ⊙ *Late-Sept.–early June, daily 7–2.*

Chiang Khan

(18) *235 km (146 mi) east of Nong Khai, 43 km (26 mi) north of Loei.*

Travel north of Loei and soon you come to Chiang Khan, a village on the banks of the Mekong. Thanks to the old wooden houses along the river, the community retains much of its rural charm. On the eastern edge of town are scores of restaurants with seating areas facing the river and Laos. Downriver, a series of rapids tests the skills of the boatmen. From Chiang Khan the road turns south to Loei, the provincial capital, a major stop on bus routes in all directions.

Where to Stay

★ ¢ 🏨 **Chiang Khan Hill Resort.** On the banks of the Mekong, this resort commands a marvelous view of a series of rapids. You can also see across to the Laotian countryside, making this resort worth a trip in its own right. Rooms are in octagonal bungalows; the best are the ones overlooking the water. There's an excellent open-air restaurant where the deep-fried shrimp cakes are crispy and delicious and the *somtan* (relish) tingles with lime. The chicken dishes are made from free-range birds. ✉ *28/2 Ruamjai Naruemit Rd.* ☎ *042/821285 or 042/821414* 🛏 *50 rooms* ⚬ *In-room: refrigerator. In-hotel: restaurant, pool* ▭ *MC, V.*

¢ 🏨 **Loogmai Guesthouse.** A small French colonial port house is the setting for this elegant guesthouse. Stylish, minimalist studios have well-chosen, untreated, antique wooden furnishings. The owner, Somboon, is a local artist who exhibited his work in Germany for 25 years, and his influence is plain to see. The upstairs fan-cooled room with private bathroom and a view over the Mekong is the one to aim for and well worth booking in advance. ✉ *112 Mu 1, Soi 5, Chaikong Rd.* ☎ *09/210–0447* ✉ *loogmaiguest@thaimail.com* 🛏 *5 rooms* ⚬ *In-hotel: laundry facilities* ▭ *No credit cards.*

¢ 🏨 **Rimkong Pub & Guesthouse.** This is the most sociable and informative place in Chiang Khan. A converted wooden shophouse from the 1970s, Rimkong has simple, mattress-on-the-floor fan-cooled rooms next to the Mekong. The owner, Pascal from France, is the man to speak to for maps, information on sights of interest, and timetables for public transportation—ask to see the folder at the bar. ✉ *294, Soi 5, Chaikong Rd.* ☎ *042/821125* ⊕ *http://rimkhong.free.fr* 🛏 *6 rooms* ⚬ *In-hotel: restaurant, laundry facilities* ▭ *No credit cards.*

Nong Khai

(19) *51 km (32 mi) north of Udon Thani, 60 km (36 mi) east of Chiang Khan.*

Nong Khai is literally the end of the line—it's the country's northernmost railhead and bus terminus. To the east and west, the mighty Mekong meanders through largely uncharted territory, while across the river to the north lies Laos. The French influence that is still evident in the Laotian capital of Vientiane can also be seen in Nong Khai. The architecture of the town has noticeable Gallic touches, particularly the governor's residence on Meechai Road. Running parallel to Meechai Road is Rim Khong Road, lined by small guesthouses and restaurants. Laotian goods, mostly textiles, are cheap and plentiful at Nong Khai's lively night market.

One of the main draws to Nong Khai is access to Laos via the **Friendship Bridge.** The 1-km-long (½-mi-long) bridge, which opened in 1992, has brought Nong Khai and its province a boost in tourist traffic, which means you can find accommodations here that rival those of bigger towns. To cross into Laos, you must buy a visa for US$30. From the Laotian side it's a 25-km (15-mi) samlor ride to the immensely charming capital city of Laos, Vientiane.

Wat Po Chai is Nong Khai's best-known and most attractive temple, easily accessible by way of Prajak Road. It houses a revered gold Buddha image, Luang Pho Phra Sai, which was lost for many centuries after capsizing in a storm and falling to the muddy bottom of the Mekong. Its rediscovery, part of the local lore, is displayed in a number of beautiful murals seen spread over the *ubosot* (ordination hall) walls. 🎫 *Free ⊙ Daily 6–6.*

Thailand's strangest temple grounds are 5 km (3 mi) west of town on the Nong Khai–Phon Pisai Road at **Wat Khaek** (also called Sala Kaew Koo). The temple's gardens, created by an ecumenically minded monk, have an extraordinary collection of immense (and immensely bizarre) statues representing gods, goddesses, demons, and devils from many of the world's faiths, though the emphasis is on Hindu gods. 🎫 *B100 ⊙ Daily 6–6.*

Wat Noen Pranao is in a shaded forest, and makes for an interesting excursion. The central ubosot is the dominating structure, with its rich motifs and gold stenciling, but the aging wooden hall to its east and the small courtyard bungalows are also worth investigating. This is Nong Khai's leading meditative retreat and is serious business for those involved, who practice meditation and abstinence to heal their troubled souls. It's free to stay, including daily courses and meals, but donations are greatly appreciated. You can reach the center on the Nong Khai–Phon Pisai Road by songthaew, which costs around B50.

Where to Stay

$–$$ 🏨 **Mae Khong Royal.** The main attraction of this Western-style lodging is its large pool, which is a godsend in the hot summer season. The nearby terrace, cooled by breezes off the Mekong River, is also pleasant. Rooms have great views of the Friendship Bridge and Laos. The hotel's only disadvantage is its isolated location about 2 km (1 mi) outside town. ✉ *222 Jommanee Beach, 43000* ☎ *042/465777 up to 81 or 042/420024* 📠 *198 rooms* 👤 *In-room: refrigerator. In-hotel: 2 restaurants, room service, 2 bars, laundry service, public Internet* 🍽 *DC, MC, V.*

¢–$ 🏨 **Ruan Thai Guesthouse.** An ornate wooden house set in lush green gardens makes this one of the more attractive guesthouses along Rimkhong Road. The original house and additional two-story wooden chalets mean plenty of rooms and a range of prices. Rooms are comfortable, with cozy plaid bedding and chunky wooden furniture. Even though there are no views of the Mekong River, it's only a few feet away. ✉ *1126/2 Rimkhong Rd., 43000* ☎ *042/412519 or 09/186-7227* ⊕ *www.ruanthaihouse.com* 📠 *18 rooms* 👤 *In-hotel: bicycles, laundry service, public Internet* 🍽 *No credit cards.*

★ ¢ ▦ **Mut Mee Guesthouse.** A wonderful little oasis of charm and friendliness right on the banks of the Mekong River, this great find seems to be the heart of a seasonal community that includes artists; qualified yoga, fitness, and Reiki instructors; and many others. Rooms are scattered around a tropical garden and are stylishly decorated with terra-cotta tiles, stone-slab bathrooms, and antique four-poster beds. Steel-welded Buddha images add a nice touch to the window grates and local artwork hangs on the walls. The small pavilion restaurant and lounge serve up healthful dishes and juices. ✉ *1111/4 Kaeworawut Rd., 43000* ☎ *042/460717 or 01/261–2646* ⊕ *www.mutmee.net* ⌨ *27 rooms* ⌂ *In-hotel: restaurant, laundry service* ▭ *No credit cards.*

¢ ▦ **Pantawee Resort.** It's not really a resort, but this spacious complex on the banks of the Mekong River is certainly comfortable. It's also ideally located just west of the Friendship Bridge. ▧ TIP→ **Many of the inexpensive rooms have sweeping views of the river—ask for Room 5, which has a private terrace with access to the waterside restaurant and café.** The resort is a 15-minute bus ride from town. ✉ *210 Kaeworawut Rd., 43000* ☎ *042/411008* ⌨ *36 rooms* ⌂ *In-room: refrigerator. In-hotel: 2 restaurants* ▭ *No credit cards.*

Shopping

Village Weaver Handicrafts (✉ 1020 Prajak Rd. ☎ 042/422651 up to 53) is an inviting converted shophouse rich with woodwork and vibrant fabrics. It was established as an outlet for the Village Weaver Handicrafts Self-Help Project, which supports local women villagers in a network of about 50 villages, helping them earn personal income to counter the constant threat of poverty. The store has a small workshop at its rear where skilled seamstresses weave high-quality mudmee fabric. The center is open daily from 9 AM to 7 PM.

Udon Thani & Environs Essentials

Transportation

BY AIR
There are two major airports in this region, at Udon Thani and Khon Kaen, and both have several daily flights from Bangkok. The major carrier is Thai Airways, but a number of budget airlines, such as Air Asia, Nok Air, and Phuket Air, also service these routes and have offices at Udon Thani International Airport. Phuket also has a link between Chiang Mai and Udon Thani, with one flight per day on Sunday, Monday, Wednesday, and Friday.

🛧 Airlines **Air Asia** ☎ 042/224313 up to 15 in Udon Thani ⊕ www.airasia.com. **Nok Air** ☎ 042/348771, 042/348772 in Udon Thani ⊕ www.nokair.com. **Phuket Air** ☎ 042/224161, 042/224162 in Udon Thani ⊕ www.phuketairlines.com. **Thai Airways** ☎ 042/243222 in Udon Thani, 043/227701 in Khon Kaen ⊕ www.thaiair.com.

BY BUS
There are regular buses connecting Udon Thani to Khon Kaen, Nong Khai, Nakhon Phanom, and Loei, as well as far off Bangkok and Korat. Bangkok-bound buses, via Korat, are nine-hour trips departing every

night at 8 and 8:20. Fares are B330 for first-class air-conditioned buses or B490 for VIP buses. Further hourly connections to Khon Kaen from Udon Thani depart between 6 AM and 5 PM and cost B85 for first-class air-conditioned buses.

From Udon Thani, first-class air-conditioned buses run every half hour to Nong Khai (1½ hours) from Udon's bus terminals on Udon Dutsadi Road or at the more accessible station off Prajak Road. Buses cost B30, running throughout the day from 5:45 AM to 6 PM. Udon also has buses heading east to Nakhon Phanom and farther along the Mekong. It's 5 hours to Nakhon Phanom; buses leave between 5:30 AM and 11 AM, costing B122.

Getting to Loei from Nong Khai (four hours) means taking a fan-cooled bus. Buses depart daily from 5:40 AM to 10 AM and cost around B84. You can also connect to Phitsanulok from Loei, with buses running from 6 AM to 4 PM and costing B79 for fan-cooled or B161 for air-conditioning.

◪ Bus Stations **Khon Kaen** ⊠ Prachasamosorn Rd. (fan) and Ammart Rd. (air-conditioning) ☎ 042/611421. **Loei** ⊠ Maliwan Rd. ☎ 042/833586. **Nong Khai** ⊠ Prajak Rd. ☎ 042/411612. **Udon Thani** ⊠ Prajak Rd. ☎ 042/221489.

BY CAR

Roads are generally in good condition around Udon Thani. The fast, four-lane Highway 2 links Udon to Bangkok, making travel to Khon Kaen and Nong Khai also easy. Highway 22 through Sakhon Nakhon also provides links to Nakhon Phanom and the Mekong River towns, but narrow two-lane roads can be slow going. Loei's spacious 210 road offers easy access to and from Udon with the optional 211 road being smaller but more scenic as it follows the Mekong River route, swinging through Chiang Khan to Nong Khai. The 212 road follows the Mekong, connecting Nong Khai to Nakhon Phanom and Mukdahan.

Avis and Budget have branches at the Udon Thani Airport. OK Mom Travel and Narujee Car Rental are reliable local agencies.

◪ Agencies **Avis** ⊠ Udon Thani Airport ☎ 042/244770. **Budget** ⊠ Udon Thani Airport ☎ 042/246805. **Narujee Car Rent** ⊠ Kosa Rd., Khon Kaen ☎ 043/224220. **OK Mom Travel** ⊠ 345/9 Phosi Rd., Udon Thani ☎ 042/346673.

BY SAMLOR & SONGTHAEW

Motorized samlors and songthaews are the most common means of public transportation in the region, with the exception of Khon Kaen and Udon Thani, which have good public bus routes. Motorbike taxis and pedal samlors are widespread and available late into the evening.

BY TRAIN

Trains run three times daily from Bangkok's Hua Lamphong train station to Khon Kaen, Udon Thani, and Nong Khai, departing at 8:20 AM, 8 PM, and 8:45 PM. Travel times are 8 hours to Khon Kaen, 12 hours to Udon, and 13 hours to Nong Khai. Fares to Khon Kaen run from B200 for third class (fans) up to B1,000 for a first-class sleeper. The range for travel to Udon Thani is B200 to B1,200, and to Nong Khai, B200 to B1,200.

The Nong Khai sleeper departs from Bangkok at 7 PM to arrive at 7:10 AM and on the return trip leaves Nong Khai at 6:35 PM to be back in Bangkok at 6:10 AM.

Note that departure times are subject to change; always double-check the day before your trip.

Contacts & Resources

BANKS & EXCHANGING SERVICES

You'll have no difficulty finding banks with ATMs in all larger towns. Udon Thani is littered with banks, mainly found on Prajak Road. In Khon Kaen, you can find a glut on Srichan Road, and in Nong Khai on Meechai Road. Loei banks are clustered around Charoenrat Road.

EMERGENCIES

⚑ In Nong Khai **Police** ☎ 042/411020. **Nong Khai Provincial Hospital** ✉ Meechai Rd. ☎ 042/411504.
⚑ In Udon Thani **Police** ☎ 042/611333. **Wattana Hospital** ✉ Pho Niyom Rd. ☎ 042/465201 up to 8.

TOUR OPTIONS

Central and eastern Isan are well covered by Kannika Tours, Prayoon Transport Tours, and Thorsaeng Travel in Udon Thani.
⚑ Tour Companies **Kannika Tours** ✉ 36/9 Sisutha Rd., Udon Thani ☎ 042/240443. **Prayoon Transport Tours** ✉ 546/1 Phosi Rd., Udon Thani ☎ 042/221048. **Thorsaeng Travel** ✉ 546/1 Phosi Rd., Udon Thani ☎ 042/221048.

VISITOR INFORMATION

⚑ Tourist Authority of Thailand **Khon Kaen** ✉15/5 Prachasamosorn Rd. ☎043/244498 or 043/244499. **Loei Tourism Coordination Center** ✉ Charoenrat Rd. ☎ 042/812812. **Nong Khai** ✉ Thai-Laos Friendship Bridge Rd. ☎ 042/467844. **Udon Thani** ✉ 16/5 Mukmontri Rd. ☎ 042/325406.

Cambodia

Monks at tha Angkor Temple Complex just north of Siem Reap.

WORD OF MOUTH

"I found Angkor to be one of those rare places that was better than the hype. There were a lot of visitors, but our guide, Dara, was able to avoid the crowds most of the time. Angkor is so spread out that there are lots of ruins miles from the tour bus destinations where you can enjoy the natural area virtually alone. You can also visit Tonle Sap lake, and arrange to go off the beaten path to see more remote villages or the bird migration if you're there at the right time."

—Talb

WELCOME TO CAMBODIA

Water festival Phnom Penh.

TOP REASONS TO GO

★ **Angkor Temple Complex** Hands-down Southeast Asia's most magnificent archaeological treasure, Angkor has hundreds of ruins, many still hidden deep in the jungle.

★ **Education and enlightenment** You'll learn a heap about history, warfare and human tragedy, science, and archaeology.

★ **Off-the-Beaten-Track Beaches** Along the Gulf of Thailand lie some of Southeast Asia's most unspoiled beaches and unpolluted (for now) waters. You'll eat some of the best seafood of your life here.

★ **Philanthropy** Work with street kids, give blood, buy a cookie to support the arts—if you're looking to do good while you travel, you'll find plenty of interesting opportunities here.

★ **Southeast Asia's Rising Star** Though it doesn't yet have worldwide attention, Phnom Penh is one of the hippest cities in Southeast Asia.

1 Phnom Penh & Environs. You'll find it all in the capital—a palace and war monuments, great food and fine wine, and ample opportunities for people-watching along the breezy riverfront. It's an eye-opening place—a city that's come a long way in postwar recovery—and the stories its residents have to tell are both tragic and optimistic.

2 North of Phnom Penh. As you travel north, you'll see some of Asia's last remaining jungles where wildlife populations are actually increasing. Get a glimpse of the rare Irrawaddy dolphin at Kratie. There are still hill tribes in the far north in Ratanakkiri Province.

3 Siem Reap & Angkor Temple Complex. Angkor Wat is the largest religious structure ever built, and it's but one temple in a complex of hundreds. Siem Reap, a rapidly growing city, is the gateway to Angkor and other off-the-beaten-path excursions that await the adventuresome.

Water festival Phnom Penh.

THAILAND

Samrong

Batdambang

Trat

CHUOR PHNUM KRAVAN

Koh Chang

Koh Kut

Krong Kaoh Kong

Kaoh Kong

Kompong Som Bay

Gulf of Thailand

Sihanoukville

4

0   50 mi

0   50 km

Bayon Temple, Angkor Wat.

4 Southern Cambodia. The once-sleepy coast is perking up. Whether you stay at a high-end resort, in a hillside bungalow, or in an island hut, it remains a treat to see such beauty, yet untrammeled. Sihanoukville and Kep are beautiful seaside destinations.

LAOS

Anlong Veng

Preah Vihear

Stoeng Treng

Lumphat

Kong River

Srepok River

Angkor Temple Complex

Siem Reap **3**

Mekong River

Lake Tonle Sap

Kampong Thum

Senmonorom

Pouthisat

Kratie **2**

Kampong Chnang

Kampong Cham

1 PHNOM PENH

VIETNAM

Kampong Spoe

Tay Ninh

Svay Rieng

Takev

Kampot

Dao Phu Quoc

Fishing boat, Sihanouk.

GETTING ORIENTED

Cambodia is one of Southeast Asia's smallest countries—about the size of the state of Washington. The country is bordered by Thailand to the west and northwest, Laos to the northeast, and Vietnam to the east and southeast. In the south, Cambodia faces the Gulf of Thailand, which provides access to the Indian and Pacific oceans. The coastline here is small, largely undeveloped, and isolated by a low mountain range. Much of the country is a low-lying plain dominated by the region's largest lake, the Tonle Sap, and a network of waterways forming the start of the Mekong Delta. Its northern border with Thailand is a remarkable escarpment, rising from the plains to heights of up to 1,800 feet—a natural defensive border and the site of many ancient fortresses.

CAMBODIA PLANNER

Getting Around

Regular air service links Phnom Penh and Siem Reap to Bangkok and Vientiane and Phnom Penh to Pakse, Laos. Domestic flights run between Phnom Penh and Siem Reap and Phnom Penh and Ratanakkiri.

Cambodia has a comprehensive bus network, and bus travel is cheap. It's also generally the safest cross-country transportation, aside from flying (Cambodian taxi and share-truck drivers are notoriously dangerous).

Note that some bus companies advertise a direct Phnom Penh–Bangkok ticket, but that trip takes 20 hours on rough roads, so it's not recommended. A direct Bangkok–Siem Reap ticket, obtainable at all Bangkok travel agencies, costs about $15. The journey, over some rough roads, takes 10–12 hours. In Siem Reap, bus tickets to Bangkok are widely available, but the road from Siem Reap to the border is usually a slow-moving morass in the rainy season. Buses from Thailand also stop at Koh Kong; from there, you can take a minivan to Sihanoukville. Minivans travel between the Lao border and Stung Treng (about 2 hours), where you can catch a bus to Phnom Penh.

Within cities and for shorter journeys, motorcycle taxis (motos), tuk-tuks, and cyclos (pedal-powered trishaws) are the best ways of getting around. Motorcycle taxi drivers, known as *motodops*, will find you at every street corner.

How Much Can You Do?

Three days is barely enough to skim the surface. If you're strapped for time, you can indulge in Angkor, spending all three days there, and save the capital for your next trip—undoubtedly, you will want to return. Spend at least one day in a taxi or tuk-tuk (the open-air breeze lends a very different feel) exploring the Siem Reap countryside and a few of the outlying temples. If you can't fathom a trip to Cambodia without seeing its capital, spend the first day touring Phnom Penh's key sights—the Killing Fields, Tuol Sleng, the Royal Palace, and the National Museum—and head to Siem Reap early the next morning.

If You Have 5 Days

Five days offers a little more breathing room, though you'll still have a packed itinerary if you want to see more than Phnom Penh and Siem Reap. One option is spend two days in Phnom Penh, with a side trip on the second day, then three days in Siem Reap. If you're itching to dip your toes in the ocean, spend Day 1 in Phnom Penh, Day 2 in Sihanoukville, and Day 3 heading back to Phnom Penh. Catch a late flight to Siem Reap that night, or travel in the morning so you can spend the bulk of Days 4 and 5 at the temples.

If You Have 7 Days

Start in Phnom Penh, and be sure to get into the country-side. On Day 3, head to Sihanoukville—you should arrive in time to try the catch-of-the-day for dinner at a beach-side restaurant. On Day 4, catch a taxi to Kampot or Kep (a beautiful two- to three-hour drive) and spend the afternoon exploring. Return to Phnom Penh on Day 4 and either catch the next flight to Siem Reap that day or spend another evening in Phnom Penh. Devote Days 5, 6, and 7 to the temples, the surrounding area, or a side trip to Battambang or Prek Toal Biosphere Reserve.

TIP: Save Siem Reap for last so you can fully appreciate Phnom Penh's sites, as well as the country's complex history. By the time you get to Angkor, you'll be better prepared to put the site into context.

When to Go

Two seasons are affected by the monsoon winds. The northeastern monsoon blowing toward the coast ushers in the cool, dry season in November, which lasts through February, with temperatures between 65°F (18°C) and 80°F (27°C). December and January are the coolest months. It heats up to around 95°F (35°C) and higher in March and April, when the southwestern monsoon blows inland from the Gulf of Thailand, bringing downpours that last an hour or more. This rainy, humid season runs through October, with temperatures ranging from 80°F (27°C) to 95°F (35°C). The climate in Phnom Penh is always very humid. This is the way it's been for centuries, anyway. Thanks to climate change, Cambodia now experiences rainstorms in the dry season, cool temps in the hot season, and a lot of unpredictability. Bring your umbrella.

When planning your trip, remember Cambodia's festival-packed calendar. It's important to book in advance if you plan on visiting during mid-April's New Year celebrations or for the Water Festival in Phnom Penh in November. Strangely, the New Year is one of the best times to see the capital because the majority of Phnom Penh residents come from somewhere else—and they all go home for the holidays.

Boat Travel

Though the price of bus tickets has decreased, seeing Cambodia from the water is a worthwhile experience. From Phnom Penh, ferries called "bullet boats" travel along the Tonle Sap to reach Siem Reap and Angkor. As the name implies, these boats are fast and sometimes dangerous. The same boats also ply the ocean waters between Sihanoukville and Koh Kong. Watch the weather before booking, as the rainy season makes for extremely choppy waters. Buy your tickets from a tour operator, your hotel's concierge, or at the Phnom Penh port. For a more pleasant ride between Phnom Penh and Siem Reap, **Compagnie Fluviale Du Mekong** (✉ 30 St. 240, Phnom Penh ☎ 023/216070 ⊕ www.cfmekong.com) offers three-day river excursions.

Smaller ferries travel daily between Siem Reap's port and Battambang, on the Sangker River. Ask about water levels before booking a ticket; in dry season, the water can get so low the boat may get stuck for hours at a time.

Border Crossings

Every few months, it seems, another border crossing opens with a neighboring country. As of this writing, the following border points with Thailand were open: Koh Kong (Hat Lek), Pailin (Ban Pakard), Duan Lem (Ban Laem), Poipet (Aranyaprathet), O'Smach (Chong Jom), and Anlong Veng (Chong Sa Ngam). From Laos you can cross at Dom Kralor (Voeung Kam). Overland crossings through Poipet and Koh Kong are the most popular, but bear in mind that Cambodian roads remain arduous, particularly in the rainy season. Coming from Laos overland, the only way to continue into Cambodia is by boat or bus to Stung Treng, then on from there the following morning.

As of this writing, one-month tourist visas, which cost $20, are available at all border crossings listed above. Note, however, that if you want to cross into Laos from Cambodia, you'll need to secure your visa to Laos in advance, as they are not available at the border crossing. Border crossings are open daily 7:30–11:30 and 2–5.

All visitors must have a valid passport to enter Cambodia. One-month visas are given to tourists from most countries on arrival at the airports in Phnom Penh and Siem Reap; you'll need two passport photos and $20. Unfortunately, travelers report corruption at many border crossings. Cambodian authorities often will ask for a $1 fee at the Laos border, or for 1,000 Thai baht or more (well above the legal $20 fee for a tourist visa) at the Thailand crossings. Often, there's not much you can do to avoid this unless you speak Khmer.

7

Regional Cuisine Highlights

Cambodian cuisine is distinct from that of neighbors Thailand, Laos, and Vietnam, although some dishes are common throughout the region. Fish and rice are the mainstays, and some of the world's tastiest fish are to be had in Cambodia. The country has the benefit of a complex river system that feeds Southeast Asia's largest freshwater lake, plus a coastline famous for its shrimp and crab. Beyond all that, Cambodia's rice paddies grow some of the most succulent fish around. (Besides fish, Cambodians also eat a lot of pork, more so than beef, which tends to be tough.)

Be sure to try prahok, the Cambodian lifeblood: a stinky cheeselike fermented fish paste that nourishes the nation. Amok, too, is a sure delight. Done the old-fashioned way, it takes two days to make this fish-and-coconut concoction, which is steamed in a banana leaf.

Down south, Kampot Province grows world-renowned pepper. If you're coming from a northern climate, try a seafood dish with whole green peppercorns on the stalk. You won't find them (not fresh, anyway) in your home country.

Generally, the food in Cambodia is not as spicy as that of Thailand or Laos, but flavored heavily with herbs.

Tours & Packages

Tour companies are a dime a dozen in Cambodia. Hanuman Tourism Voyages (✉ 12, St. 310, Sangkat Tonle Bassac, Phnom Penh ☎ 023/218356 or 012/807657 ⊕ www.hanumantourism.com) puts its money into rural development projects, which is a real bonus. Birders will enjoy oSmoSe Conservation Ecotourism Education (✉ 0552, Group 12, Wat Bo Village, Siem Reap ☎ 012/832812 ⊕ http://jinja.apsara.org/osmose), which offers tours to the Prek Toal Biosphere Reserve, mainland Southeast Asia's most important waterbird nesting territory. Wild Asia (⊕ www.wildasia.net) has good information on responsible tourism in Asia. Do a search for Cambodia on the site to see a number of tour possibilities. On the coast, several dive companies have popped up in recent years; EcoSea Dive (☎ 012/654104 ⊕ www.ecosea.com) is a popular option.

More Information

It's now much easier to find concrete, useful information about Cambodia than it ever was before. For starters, read Andy Brouwer's blog, ⊕ http://andybrouwer. blogspot.com, and visit his Web site, ⊕ http://andy-brouwer.co.uk. Brouwer, a longtime traveler to Cambodia, has dedicated a good chunk of his life to informing people about the country and helping those in need. Likewise, Tales of Asia, w www.talesofasia.com, is an excellent source of information, with travelers' stories, road reports, and up-to-date information on overland travel.

Once you arrive, pick up a visitor's guide (separate editions for Phnom Penh, Siem Reap, and Sihanoukville), as well as any of the various Cambodia Pocket Guides. These are widely available free at airports, hotels, and restaurants, and they provide great up-to-the-minute information on traveling through Cambodia.

The Ministry of Tourism has some information on its Web site www.mot.gov.kh. Tourism Cambodia's site, www. tourismcambodia.com, has similar information, but has more detailed descriptions of top attractions.

Safety

Cambodia is safer than many people realize, but you still need to exercise caution. Most violence (and there's a lot of it) occurs against Cambodians. However, tourists have been mugged and sometimes killed in Phnom Penh and on the beaches of Sihanoukville. Keep most of your cash, valuables, and your passport in a hotel safe, and avoid walking on side streets after dark. Siem Reap has much less of a crime problem than the capital, but that's starting to change.

Be careful of taking a moto late at night. Moto theft is one of Cambodia's most widespread crimes, and the unfortunate driver often winds up dead.

Most Cambodians, including taxi and tuk-tuk drivers, are exceedingly friendly and their forwardness is often mistaken for suspicious activity. Generally, they're just curious (and hoping to get a fare), and mean no harm. But do use common sense. Avoid confrontations and arguments with locals, particularly in bars. And avoid heated confrontations with the military or police.

Land mines laid during the civil war have been removed from most major tourist destinations. Mines and UXO (unexploded ordinance) are a concern, however, if you go too far astray around off-the-beaten-track temples (in which case, you should travel with a knowledgeable guide). Although most tourists will never be in danger of stepping on a mine, as a general rule, never walk in uncharted territory in Cambodia, unless you know it's safe.

Cambodia has one of Asia's most atrocious road records. Accidents are common in the chaotic traffic of Phnom Penh and on the highways, where people drive like maniacs. The better the road, the scarier it is. Keep in mind that Cambodians do not have a widespread driving culture. Rules of the road are new concepts to the thousands of Khmers. Unfortunately, chauffeurs aren't much better; in fact, they're some of the worst drivers in the country. If you're hiring a driver, be very clear about what you want—slow, safe driving. Tell your driver you will not pay if he doesn't drive well.

Money Matters

The monetary unit in Cambodia is the riel, but the U.S. dollar is nearly as widely accepted (as well as the Thai baht in bordering provinces). Payment in dollars is required by many upper-end hotels, airlines, tour operators, and restaurants.

At this writing, the official exchange rate was approximately 4,000 riel to one U.S. dollar, 100 riel to the Thai baht, 3,590 riel to one Canadian dollar, 4,480 riel to one Australian dollar, and 7,545 riel to one British pound.

Because the riel and U.S. dollar operate as almost dual currencies, it's possible to change dollars to riel just about anywhere. Most every Cambodian market will change money (look for the glass cases with currency inside), and as of this writing, they give better exchange rates for Thai baht than you'll find in Thailand. Banks and businesses usually charge 2% to cash U.S. dollar traveler's checks.

ATMs are now available in Phnom Penh and Siem Reap (ANZ and Canadia banks have them), and Sihanoukville has one in town. Credit cards are accepted at major hotels, restaurants, and at some boutiques.

Restaurant prices are per person for a main course at dinner. Hotel prices are for a standard double room, excluding tax and service.

WHAT IT COSTS In U.S. Dollars

	$$$$	$$$	$$	$	¢
RESTAURANTS	over $16	$12–$16	$8–$12	$5–$8	under $5
HOTELS	over $150	$100–$150	$50–$100	$25–$50	under $25

PHNOM PENH & ENVIRONS

Updated by
Karen Coates

Cambodia's capital is also the country's commercial and political hub, a busy city amid rapid change. Over the past few years, the number of international hotels, large restaurants, sidewalk cafés, art galleries, boutiques, Internet cafés, and sophisticated nightclubs has increased dramatically. So has the city traffic: motorbikes, tuk-tuks, and cyclos (trishaw taxis) fight for space with cars and SUVs.

Phnom Penh is the natural gateway to anywhere in Cambodia: a slew of the north's accessible towns, far-off Ratanakkiri Province in the northeast, the beaches of Sihanoukville and Kep, and Kampot nearby in the south. Cambodia's roads have come a long way in recent years, but many remain potholed and difficult in the rainy season (particularly heading toward the Thai border). Roads heading out of the capital lead to day-trip destinations like the ruins of Tonle Bati and Phnom Chisor in the south, and the pagoda-topped hill of Udong and the Mekong island of Koh Dach in the north.

Phnom Penh

The capital of Cambodia, Phnom Penh is strategically positioned at the confluence of the Mekong, Tonle Sap, and Bassac rivers. The city's origins date to 1372, when a wealthy woman named Penh, who lived at the eastern side of a small hill near the Tonle Sap, is said to have found four Buddha statues hidden in a large tree drifting down the river. With the help of her neighbors, she built a hill (a *phnom*) with a temple on top, and invited Buddhist monks to settle on its western slope. In 1434 King Ponhea Yat established his capital on the same spot and constructed a brick pagoda on top of the hill. The capital was later moved twice, first to Lovek and later to Udong. In 1866 during the reign of King Norodom, the capital was moved back to Phnom Penh.

It was approximately during this time that France colonized Cambodia, and the French influence in the city is palpable—the legacy of a 90-year period that saw the construction of many colonial buildings, including the grandiose post office and railway station (both still standing, though the latter is threatened by potential development plans). Some of the era's art deco architecture remains, in varying degrees of disrepair. Much of Phnom Penh's era of modern development took place after independence in 1953, with the addition of tree-lined boulevards, large stretches of gardens, and the Independence Monument, built in 1958.

Today Phnom Penh has a population of about 2 million people. But during the Pol Pot regime's forced emigration of people from the cities, Phnom Penh had fewer than 1,000 residents. Buildings and roads deteriorated, and most side streets are still a mess. The main routes are now well paved, however, and the city's wats (temples) sport fresh coats of paint, as do many homes. This is a city on the rebound, and its vibrancy is in part due to the abundance of young people, many of whom were born after those war years. Its wide streets are filled with motorcycles, which weave about in a complex ballet, making it a thrilling achievement merely to cross the street (the best way is to screw up your courage and step straight into the flow, which should part for you as if by magic).

There are several wats and museums worth visiting, and the old city has some attractive colonial buildings scattered about, though many disappear as time goes on. The wide park that lines the waterfront between the Royal Palace and Wat Phnom is a great place for a sunset stroll, particularly on weekend evenings when it fills with Khmer families, as do the other parks around town (Hun Sen Park, the Vietnamese monument area, and the promenade near the monstrous new Naga Casino). On a breezy evening, you'll find hundreds of Khmers out flying kites.

> ## RESPONSIBLE TOURISM
>
> In the aftermath of Cambodia's civil war foreign aid groups and governments have poured billions of dollars into the country. Hundreds of nonprofit organizations are working toward a better Cambodia on all fronts: health, environment, safety, women's rights, human rights, children's rights, economy, education. Many nonprofits run hotels, restaurants, and travel agencies that give a chunk of their earnings to development projects and people in need. Do-good travel options are noted in this chapter's listings. It's possible to wine, dine, and shop your way through Cambodia, knowing your money is helping others.

What to See

Choeung Ek Memorial (the Killing Fields). In the mid- to late 1970s, thousands of Khmer Rouge prisoners who had been tortured at the infamous Tuol Sleng prison were taken to the extermination camp of Choeung Ek, for execution. Today the camp is a memorial, and the site consists of a monumental glass stupa built in 1989 and filled with 8,000 skulls, which were exhumed from mass graves nearby. It's an extremely disturbing sight: many of the skulls, which are grouped according to age and sex, bear the holes and slices from the blows that killed them. The site is at the end of a rough and dusty road, and can be reached in 30 minutes by motorbike, tuktuk, or car. ■ TIP➔ **Guides are available, but they are not necessary.** ✛ *15 km (9 mi) southwest of downtown Phnom Penh* ☎ *012/897046* 🎫 *$2* ⊙ *Daily 7–5.*

❹ **National Museum.** Within this splendid, rust-red colonial landmark are many archaeological treasures. Exhibits chronicle the various stages of Khmer cultural development, from the pre-Angkor periods of Fu Nan and Zhen La (5th to 8th century) to the Indravarman period (9th century), classical Angkor period (10th to 13th century), and post-Angkor period. Among the more than 5,000 artifacts and works of art are 19th-century dance costumes, royal barges, and palanquins. A palm-shaded central courtyard with lotus ponds houses the museum's showpiece: a sandstone statue of the Hindu god Yama, the Leper King, housed in a pavilion. Guides, who are usually waiting just inside the entrance, can add a lot to a visit here. ■ TIP➔ **This is Cambodia's only national museum, and it's the best place to view archaeological relics that have survived war, genocide, and widespread plundering.** ⊠ *Junction of Sts. 178 and 13, next to Royal Palace* ☎ *023/211755* 🎫 *$3* ⊙ *Daily 8–5.*

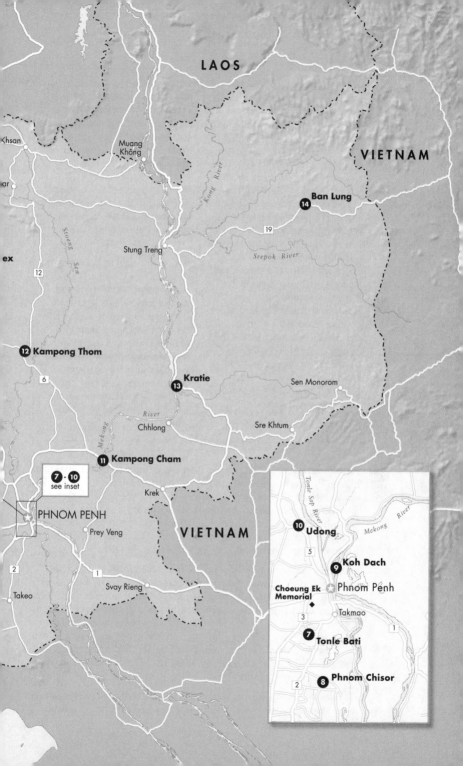

TOURING PHNOM PENH

Start your tour early, just as the sun rises over the Tonle Sap. Take a tuk-tuk to **Wat Phnom**; as you walk in the surrounding gardens, say hello to Sambo, Phnom Penh's only working elephant. She's a gentle creature, and she's had a hard life (someone cut off the end of her tail prior to the 2003 election). Then, climb the staircase and head for the temple, where King Ponhea Yat is venerated. After descending the hill, head east to the Tonle Sap and walk south along the riverfront promenade. Across the street, you are greeted by a plethora of breakfast options; pick the restaurant of your choice. After eating, return to the riverfront, where you have a fine view of the Chroy Changvar Peninsula. The cobbled riverside path leads you to **Wat Ounalom,** one of Phnom Penh's largest and oldest pagodas.

After visiting the wat, continue south on Sisowath Quay, past a busy strip of bars and restaurants, and on to a huge lawn in front of the cheerful yellow **Royal Palace.** On the grounds of the palace is the must-see **Silver Pagoda,** or Wat Preah Keo Morokat. Remember that the palace closes for lunch from 11 AM to 2 PM, so plan accordingly. On the northern side of the palace, a side street leads to the traditional-style **National Museum,** which is a very peaceful and quiet place to spend an hour or two.

By now you might be hungry again. As you exit the museum, head north on Street 13 to **Friends the Restaurant** for a light lunch and tasty drink. From there, catch a tuk-tuk to the **Tuol Sleng Genocide Museum,** which will require an hour or more with a clear head. It's a somber, sobering experience. If you can handle more, take a tuk-tuk from there to **Choeung Ek,** the Killing Fields, several kilometers outside town.

⑤ Phsar Thmei (Central Market). An inescapable sightseeing destination in Phnom Penh is the colonial-era Central Market, built in the late 1930s on land that was once a watery swamp. This wonderfully ornate building with a large dome retains some of the city's art deco style. The market's Khmer name, Phsar Thmei, translates as "new" market to distinguish it from Phnom Penh's original market, Phsar Chas, near the Tonle Sap River; it's popularly known as Central Market, however.

You enter the market through one of four great doors that face the directions of the compass. The main entrance, facing east, is lined with souvenir and textile merchants hawking everything from cheap T-shirts and postcards to expensive silks, handicrafts, and silverware. Other stalls sell electronic goods, mobile phones, watches, jewelry, household items, shoes, secondhand clothing, flowers, and just about anything else you can imagine. Money changers mingle with beggars and war veterans with disabilities asking for a few riel. ⊠ *Blvd. 128, Kampuchea Krom, at 76 St.* ☎ *No phone* ☉ *Daily 7–5.*

Phsar Tuol Tom Pong (Russian Market). This popular covered market earned its nickname in the 1980s, when the wives and daughters of Russian

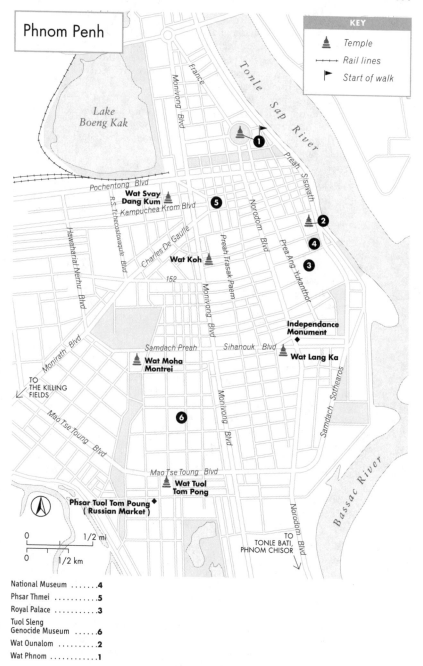

Phnom Penh

KEY

🛕 Temple

├─┼─┤ Rail lines

🚩 Start of walk

Lake Boeng Kak

Tonle Sap River

France

Monivong Blvd

Pochentong Blvd

Wat Svay Dang Kum

R.S. Tchecoslovaquie Blvd

Kampuchea Krom Blvd

Charles De Gaulle

Preah Trasak Paem

Wat Koh

152

Hawahariat Nerhu Blvd

Monivong Blvd

Norodom Blvd

Preah Sisovath

Preah Ang Yukanthor

Monirath Blvd

Samdach Preah

Sihanouk Blvd

Independance Monument ◆

Wat Lang Ka

Wat Moha Montrei

TO THE KILLING FIELDS ↙

Mao Tse Toung Blvd

Monivong Blvd

Samdach Sothearos

Mao Tse Toung Blvd

Wat Tuol Tom Pong

Phsar Tuol Tom Poung ◆
(Russian Market)

0 ____ 1/2 mi

0 ____ 1/2 km

Bassac River

Norodom Blvd

TO TONLE BATI, PHNOM CHISOR ↓

diplomats would often cruise the stalls on the lookout for curios and antiques. Today the market has a good selection of Cambodian handicrafts. Wood carvings and furniture abound, as do "spirit houses" used for offerings of food, flowers, and incense. Colorful straw mats and hats, as well as baskets, are in high demand. The market is the city's best source for art objects, including statues of the Buddha and Hindu gods, and you can also buy valuable old Indochinese coins and paper money printed during different times of Cambodia's turbulent modern history. A jumble of stalls concentrated at the market's south side sells CDs, videos, and electronics. It's also a great place to buy overstock clothes from Cambodia's numerous garment factories. ⊠ *South of Mao Tse Tung Blvd., between Sts. 155 and 163* 🕾 *No phone* ☉ *Daily 7–5.*

❸ Royal Palace. A walled complex that covers several blocks near the river, the official residence of current King Preah Norodom Sihamoni and former residence of King Sihanouk and Queen Monineath Sihanouk is a 1913 reconstruction of the timber palace built in 1866 by King Norodom. The residential areas of the palace are closed to the public, but within the pagoda-style compound are a number of structures worth visiting. These include Wat Preah Keo Morokat *(see below)*; the Throne Hall, with a tiered roof topped by a 200-foot-tall tower; and a pavilion donated by the Emperor Napoleon III and shipped from France to Cambodia. Guides can be hired at the entrance for $5. ⊠ *Sothearos between Sts. 184 and 240* 🕾 *No phone* 🎫 *$3, camera fee $2, video camera fee $5* ☉ *Daily 7:30–11 and 2–5.*

❻ Tuol Sleng Genocide Museum. This museum is a horrific reminder of the cruelty of which humans are capable. Once a neighborhood school, the building was seized by Pol Pot's Khmer Rouge and turned into a prison and interrogation center, the dreaded S-21. During the prison's four years of operation, some 14,000 Cambodians were tortured here; most were then taken to the infamous Killing Fields for execution. Many of the soldiers who did the torturing were children, some as young as 10—many may be walking the streets of Phnom Penh today. The four school buildings that made up S-21 have been left largely as they were when the Khmer Rouge left in January 1979. The prison kept extensive records and photos of the victims, and many of the documents are on display. Particularly chilling are the representations of torture scenes painted by S-21 survivor Vann Nath. ⊠ *At St. 113 (Boeng Keng Kang) and St. 350* 🕾 *012/927659* 🎫 *$2* ☉ *Daily 10–3.*

❷ Wat Ounalom. The 15th-century Wat Ounalom is now the center of Cambodian Buddhism. Until 1999 it housed the Institute Buddhique, which originally contained a large religious library destroyed by the Khmer Rouge in the 1970s. Wat Ounalom's main vihear, built in 1952 and still intact, has three floors; the top floor holds paintings illustrating the lives of the Buddha. The central feature of the complex is the large stupa, **Chetdai**, which dates to Angkorian times and is said to contain hair from one of the Buddha's eyebrows. Four niche rooms here hold priceless bronze sculptures of the Buddha. The sanctuary is dedicated to the Angkorian king Jayavarman VII (circa 1120–1215). In much more recent times, the wat served as a temporary sanctuary for monks fleeing cops and soldiers in postelection political riots. ⊠ *Riverfront, about 250 yards north of National Museum* ☎ *No phone* 🎫 *Free* ☉ *Daily 7–5.*

❶ **Wat Phnom.** According to legend, a wealthy woman named Penh found four statues of Buddha washed up on the banks of the river, and in 1372 she built this hill and commissioned this sanctuary to house them. It is this 90-foot knoll for which the city was named: Phnom Penh means "Hill of Penh." Sixty years later, King Ponhea Yat had a huge stupa built here to house his funeral ashes after his death. You approach the temple by a flight of steps flanked by bronze friezes of chariots in battle and heavenly *apsara* dancers. Inside the temple hall, the *vihear,* are some fine wall paintings depicting scenes from the Buddha's lives, and on the north side is a charming Chinese shrine. The bottom of the hill swarms with vendors selling everything from devotional candles and flowers to elephant rides. ⊠ *St. 96 and Norodom Blvd.* ☎ *No phone* 🎫 *$1* ☉ *Daily 7:30–6.*

★ **Wat Preah Keo Morokat** (Temple of the Emerald Buddha). Within the Royal Palace grounds is Phnom Penh's greatest attraction: the Temple of the Emerald Buddha, built in 1892–1902 and renovated in 1962. The temple is often referred to as the Silver Pagoda because of the 5,329 silver tiles—more than 5 tons of pure silver—that make up the floor in the main vihear. At the back of the vihear is the venerated **Preah Keo Morokat** (Emerald Buddha)—some say it's carved from jade, whereas others maintain that it's Baccarat crystal. In front of the altar is a 200-pound solid-gold Buddha studded with 2,086 diamonds. Displayed in a glass case are the golden offerings donated by Queen Kossomak Nearyreath (King Sihanouk's mother) in 1969; gifts received by the royal family over the years are stored in other glass cases. The gallery walls surrounding the temple compound, which serves as the royal graveyard, are covered with murals depicting scenes from the Indian epic, the *Ramayana.* Pride of place is given to a bronze statue of King Norodom on horseback, completed in Paris in 1875 and brought here in 1892. There's a nearby shrine dedicated to the sacred bull Nandi. ⊠ *Sothearos, between Sts. 240 and 184.* ☎ *No phone* 🎫 *Included in $3 admission to Royal Palace, $2 camera fee, $5 video camera fee* ☉ *Daily 7:30–11 and 2–5.*

Where to Stay & Eat

Phnom Penh is quickly becoming one of the top culinary cities in Asia. With delectable Khmer food at all levels, from street stalls to five-star establishments, plus an influx of international restaurants, you'll eat well every night in Phnom Penh. The country's colonial history means you'll find many French-inspired restaurants, too.

Times have changed on the hotel front as well. These days, the capital offers a plethora of accommodations for all budgets. Phnom Penh has several international-standard hotels, including the Raffles's refurbishment of a 1929 beauty. Clean and comfortable guesthouses have sprung up across the city, particularly in the Boeung Kak area. Most charge less than $10 a night. If you haven't found what you're looking for, wander the riverfront and its side streets. You're bound to discover something to your liking among the dozens upon dozens of options.

Cambodia Then and Now

THE KINGDOM OF CAMBODIA, encircled by Thailand, Laos, Vietnam, and the sea, is a land of striking extremes. Internationally, it's most well known for two contrasting chapters of its long history. The first is the Khmer empire, which in its heyday covered most of modern-day Southeast Asia. Today, the ruins of Angkor attest to the nation's immutable cultural heritage. The second chapter is the country's recent history and legacy of Khmer Rouge brutality, which left at least 1.7 million Cambodians dead. In 1993, the United Nations sponsored democratic elections that failed to honor the people's vote. Civil war continued until 1998, when another round of elections was held, and violent riots ensued in the aftermath. Cambodia's long-standing political turmoil—both on the battlefield and in much more subtle displays—continues to shape the nation's day-to-day workings. Through decades of war, a genocide, continued widespread government corruption, high rates of violence and mental illness, the provision of billions of dollars in international aid, and the disappearance of much of that money, Cambodia has suffered its demons. It remains one of the poorest, least developed countries in the world.

Yet Cambodians are an energetic and friendly people, whose quick smiles belie the inordinate suffering their nation continues to endure. Though practically destroyed by the regional conflict and homegrown repression of the 1970s, individual Cambodians have risen from those disasters. The streets of Phnom Penh are abuzz with a youthful vibrancy, and the tourism boomtown of Siem Reap, near the Angkor ruins, is full of construction sites.

More than half of Cambodia was once covered with forest, but the landscape has changed in recent decades thanks to ruthless and mercenary deforestation. The country is blessed with powerful waters: the Mekong and Tonle Sap rivers, and the Tonle Sap lake, which feeds 70% of the nation. The surrounding mountain ranges, protecting Cambodia's long river valleys, are home to hill tribes and some of the region's rarest wildlife species.

The three ranges of low mountains—the northern Dangkrek, the exotically named Elephant Mountains in the south, and the country's highest range, the Cardamoms, in the southwest—formed natural barriers against invasion and were used as fortresses during the war years. Among these ranges is a depression in the northwest of Cambodia connecting the country with the lowlands in Thailand; by allowing communication between the two countries, this geographic feature played an important part in the history of the Khmer nation. In eastern Cambodia, the land rises to a forested plateau that continues into the Annamite Cordillera, the backbone of neighboring Vietnam.

As the seat of the Khmer empire from the 9th to the 13th century, Cambodia developed a complex society based first on Hinduism and then on Buddhism. After the decline of the Khmers and the ascendancy of the Siamese, Cambodia was colonized by the French, who ruled from the mid-1860s until 1953. Shortly after the end of World War II, during which the

Japanese had occupied Cambodia, independence became the rallying cry for all of Indochina. Cambodia became a sovereign power with a monarchy ruled by King Norodom Sihanouk, who abdicated in favor of his father in 1955 and entered the public stage as a mercurial politician.

In the early 1970s, the destabilizing consequences of the Vietnam War sparked a horrible chain of events. The U.S. government secretly bombed Cambodia, arranged a coup to oust the king, and invaded parts of the country in an attempt to rout the Vietcong. Civil war ensued, and in 1975 the Khmer Rouge, led by French-educated Pol Pot, emerged as the victors. A regime of terror followed. Under a program of Mao Tse-tung–inspired reeducation centered on forced agricultural collectives, the cities were emptied and hundreds of thousands of civilians were tortured and executed. Hundreds of thousands more succumbed to starvation and disease. During the four years of Khmer Rouge rule, somewhere between 1 and 2 million Cambodians—almost one-third of the population—were killed.

By 1979, the country lay in ruins. Vietnam, unified under the Hanoi government, invaded the country in response to a series of cross-border attacks and massacres in the Mekong Delta by the Khmer Rouge. The invasion forced the Khmer Rouge into the hills bordering Thailand, where they remained entrenched and fighting for years. United Nations–brokered peace accords were signed in 1991. International mediation allowed the return of Norodom Sihanouk as king and the formation of a coalition government that included Khmer Rouge elements after parliamentary elections in 1993. But civil war continued.

In 1997 Second Prime Minister Hun Sen toppled First Prime Minister Norodom Ranariddh in a coup. During the following year's national elections, Hun Sen won a plurality and formed a new government, despite charges of election rigging. Pol Pot died in his mountain stronghold in April 1998, and the remaining Khmer Rouge elements lost any influence they still had. It has taken years for the United Nations and the Cambodian government to establish a tribunal that will bring to justice the few surviving key leaders of the Khmer Rouge regime. Proceedings began in 2007, but only one former Khmer Rouge leader (Duch, the infamous head of Tuol Sleng) is in jail; Ta Mok, the so-called "Butcher," was the only other Khmer Rouge leader to be imprisoned, but he died in 2006. The others remain free; many have blended with ease into current society, and some remain in the folds of the Cambodian government.

Foreign investment and the development of tourism have been very strong in recent years, but it remains to be seen whether domestic problems can truly be solved by Prime Minister Hun Sen and his hard-line rule.

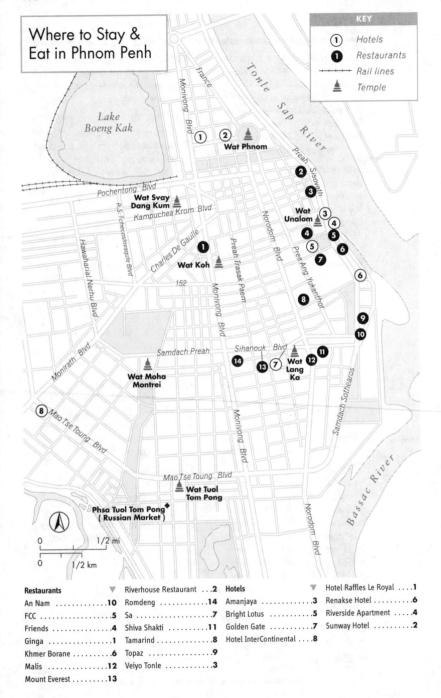

Where to Stay & Eat in Phnom Penh

KEY

① Hotels
❶ Restaurants
┼┼┼┼┼ Rail lines
🔺 Temple

Lake Boeng Kak

Tonle Sap River

Wat Phnom

Wat Svay Dang Kum

Wat Unalom

Wat Koh

Wat Moha Montrei

Wat Lang Ka

Wat Tuol Tom Pong

Phsa Tuol Tom Pong (Russian Market)

Bassac River

0   1/2 mi
0   1/2 km

◼ TIP→ When booking a hotel in Cambodia, always ask for the best price. Often, just asking for a discount will yield a rate that's half the listed price. If you're doing business in Cambodia, be sure to say so, as other discounts may apply.

$–$$ ╳ **Malis.** The Phnom Penh elite frequent this upscale traditional Khmer restaurant with outdoor seating. The long menu features lots of fish and seafood, soups and curries, and meats. The prices are right and the place is open all day, starting at 6 AM. ✉ *136 St. 41, Norodom Blvd.* ☎ *023/221022* ▭ *AE, MC, V.*

$–$$ ╳ **Topaz.** The first-class French specialties at this fine restaurant and the extensive wine list here make it a longtime Phnom Penh favorite. Though it no longer truly stands out in the city's growing restaurant scene, it is a reliable choice for a good, candle-lit meal. Note that Topaz is opens for lunch early around 11 AM, but closes again at 2 PM; dinner starts at 6 PM. ✉ *100–102 Sothearos* ☎ *023/211054* ▭ *AE, MC, V.*

¢–$$ ╳ **An Nam.** Delicious Vietnamese food is served at this air-conditioned restaurant near the Hong Kong Center. The cuisine is central Vietnamese; try the fresh shrimp spring rolls as a starter. ✉ *118 Sothearos* ☎ *023/212460* ▭ *AE, MC, V.*

¢–$$ ╳ **Riverhouse Restaurant.** The Riverhouse evokes a French bistro, with sidewalk seating and a daily set menu. It's on a corner across the street from the northern end of the waterfront park, with half the tables outside, behind a potted hedge, and half beneath the ceiling fans of the open-air dining room. The menu is eclectic, ranging from couscous to tagines to stewed rabbit. ◼ TIP→ **With a balcony overlooking the street and river, the upstairs evening bar is a great place for a drink or a game of pool.** It's a good idea to reserve ahead. ✉ *Sisowath Quay at 110th St.* ☎ *023/212302* ▭ *AE, MC, V.*

¢–$$ ╳ **Sa.** Restaurants in Phnom Penh don't get much more quaint than Sa, which is in a tiny old colonial building that overlooks the palace park. Sa serves elegant international dishes with Khmer touches, as well as tapas. ✉ *Royal Palace Esplanade* ☎ *012/901822* ▭ *No credit cards* ⊙ *Closed Sun.*

¢–$$ ╳ **Shiva Shakti.** Succulent samosas, vegetable *pakoras* (fritters), spicy lamb masala, chicken korma, and prawn *biryani* (with rice and vegetables) are among the dishes served at this small Indian restaurant, which is popular with expats. In the pleasant dining room, a statue of the elephant-headed Hindu god Ganesha stands by the door, and reproductions of Mogul art line the walls. There are also a few tables on the sidewalk. It's just east of the Independence Monument. ✉ *70E Sihanouk Blvd.* ☎ *012/813817* ▭ *AE, MC, V* ⊙ *Closed Mon.*

$ ╳ **FCC.** You don't have to be a journalist to join the international crowd gathered here. In fact, it's not really a Foreign Correspondents Club, though it does attract a fair expat following. People drop in as much for the atmosphere of the French colonial building and its river views as for the food, which is as eclectic as the diners. The beer is always cold and you can always grab a reliable burger or pizza. If you find it difficult to leave this pleasant corner of Phnom Penh, you're in luck: there are even rooms for overnight guests. ✉ *363 Sisowath Quay* ☎ *023/724014* ▭ *MC, V.*

$ ╳ **Ginga.** This Japanese spot is located on (unpleasantly) busy Monivong Boulevard, but patrons come here for the fresh sushi, not the locale. Along with the usual sushi bar items, Ginga serves great appetizers and plenty of sake and green tea. ⊠ *295 Monivong Blvd.* ☎ *023/217323* ▤ *MC, V.*

$ ✕ **Tamarind.** The Mediterranean comes east at this popular three-story bar-restaurant in the heart of arty Street 240. The menu extends from North African couscous specialties to Spanish tapas. The wine list is comprehensive and quite good. ⊠ *31 St. 240* ☎ *012/830139* ▤ *MC, V.*

¢–$ ✕ **Khmer Borane.** This casual, breezy riverfront café on the bottom floor of an old colonial-era building attracts a steady crowd. Try something from the extensive list of classic Khmer dishes; the pomelo salad and fish soup with lemon and herbs are both good choices. If those don't please your palate, Khmer Borane also offers a wide variety of Western dishes for reasonable prices. ⊠ *389 Sisowath Quay* ☎ *012/290092* ▤ *No credit cards.*

¢–$ ✕ **Mount Everest.** You'll find all the classic Indian and Nepalese dishes at Mount Everest, which has been consistently serving fantastic Indian food for years. Entrées can be ordered as spicy as you like them. ▤ TIP➔ The restaurant will deliver to your hotel for free. ⊠ *98A Sihanouk Blvd.* ☎ *023/213821* ▤ *No credit cards.*

★ ¢–$ ✕ **Romdeng.** Some of the country's tastiest provincial Khmer dishes are served at this gorgeously redesigned house in a residential area. The adventurous can try the three flavors of *prahok,* Cambodia's signature fermented fish paste, or even fried spiders. If those don't suit your tastes, Romdeng (which means "galangal" in Khmer) offers plenty of piquant soups, curries, salads, and meat dishes. Have a glass of palm wine to sip with the meal, and enjoy the paintings on the walls—artwork by former street kids. As part of the Mith Samlanh (Friends) group, your dollars will help the former street kids who have been trained to work here. ⊠ *21 St. 278* ☎ *092/219565* ▤ *No credit cards.*

★ ¢–$ ✕ **Veiyo Tonle.** This Khmer-owned and -operated nonprofit restaurant on the riverfront serves excellent traditional Khmer dishes, pizzas (39 varieties!), pastas, and more. Proceeds go toward an orphanage established by the owner. Visit on a Saturday or Monday night and watch the kids perform traditional dances. ⊠ *237 Sisowath Quay* ☎ *012/847419* ▤ *No credit cards.*

¢ ✕ **Friends the Restaurant.** Before Romdeng, there was Friends the Restaurant. This extremely popular nonprofit café near the National Museum serves a wide range of tapas treats, fruit juices, salads, and international dishes. Admire the colorful artwork, then visit the Friends store next door. ⊠ *215 St. 13* ☎ *012/802072* ⊕ *www.streetfriends.org* ▤ *No credit cards.*

★ $$$$ ✕▤ **Hotel Raffles Le Royal.** Phnom Penh's best hotel first opened in 1929, was practically destroyed during the Khmer Rouge years, and was meticulously restored by the

---

LOCAL EATS

For a local treat, try the afternoon **noodle shops** on Street 178 near the National Museum. These street-side eateries pack in the Khmer crowds, serving quick fried noodles and rice-flour-and-onion cakes. They're very popular among locals, and very cheap (less than a dollar per serving). You won't find the cleanest of restaurants here, but everything is well-cooked and you'll get a tasty snack with an eye for what it's like to eat Khmer-style. Don't get here before 4 PM.

Raffles group in 1996. A colonial landmark surrounded by gardens, Le Royal has an elegant lobby, a tranquil pool area shaded by massive trees, and various bars and restaurants that are a world apart from this slightly chaotic city—as are the prices. Guest rooms are furnished with fine Cambodian handicrafts in an elegant colonial and art deco style and overlook the pool or gardens. Suites in the main building include clawfoot tubs from the original 1929 hotel. The Elephant Bar is famous for its cocktails (and happy hour), and the sumptuous Restaurant Le Royal ($$$–$$$$) serves Khmer haute cuisine. ⊠ *92 Rukhak Vithei Daun Penh* ☎ *023/981888, 800/637–9477 in U.S., 800/6379–4771 in U.K.* ⊕ *www.raffles.com* ⌑ *170 rooms* ⌂ *In-room: safe, refrigerator, ethernet (some). In-hotel: 3 restaurants, bar, pool, gym, spa, laundry service, concierge, no-smoking rooms* ⊟ *AE, MC, V* ⧉ *BP, MAP.*

$$$$ 🏨 **Amanjaya.** With tasteful rosewood furnishings and silk textiles, the Amanjaya is the classiest hotel on the banks of the Tonle Sap River. This is an all-suites property and all suites have balconies with views of either the river or Wat Ounalom. In-room massage services are available. The price includes your choice of an American, Continental, or Asian breakfast. ⊠ *1 St. 154, Sisowath Quay* ☎ *023/214747* ⊕ *www.amanjaya.com* ⌑ *21 suites* ⌂ *In-room: safe, refrigerator, Wi-Fi. In-hotel: restaurant, room service, bar* ⊟ *AE, MC, V.*

$$$$ 🏨 **Hotel InterContinental.** One of Phnom Penh's finest hotels is on the far edge of town. For this reason, it may not be the first choice for many tourists. But the InterCon has long been a favorite of business travelers and tycoons requiring VIP treatment. Upper-level rooms offers sweeping views of the flat lands surrounding Phnom Penh. ▪ TIP→ **Check out the wineshop in the basement for a unique collection of bottles with prewar labels.** ⊠ *296 Blvd. Mao Tse Tung* ☎ *023/424888* ⊕ *www.intercontinental.com* ⌑ *372 rooms* ⌂ *In-room: safe, refrigerator, ethernet. In-hotel: 2 restaurants, bar, tennis courts, pool, gym, spa, laundry service, concierge, executive floor* ⊟ *AE, MC, V* ⧉ *BP.*

$$ 🏨 **Sunway Hotel.** This hotel near Wat Phnom and the U.S. Embassy is a primary choice among business travelers. Suites offer dinettes and kitchenettes. If you are traveling on business, be sure to ask for a corporate rate, especially if your business is located in Cambodia—prices drop dramatically. Leisure travelers will also enjoy good prices, which are especially good for the amount of amenities offered, as well as the hotel's convenient location. ⊠ *No. 1, St. 92* ☎ *023/430333* ⊕ *www.sunway.com.kh* ⌑ *138 rooms* ⌂ *In-room: safe, ethernet. In-hotel: restaurant, bar, gym, spa, laundry service, concierge* ⊟ *MC, V.*

★ **$** 🏨 **Renakse Hotel.** In a beautiful colonial-era building set amid jasmine-scented gardens across from the Royal Palace, the Renakse is a Phnom Penh landmark. A recent refurbishment gave the place new paint and new furniture while maintaining every old touch possible. The atmosphere here, evocative of colonial times, is exactly what many travelers to Southeast Asia hope to find but rarely do. Spend the extra money and book a spacious suite with a raised-platform sitting area (and silk Khmer-style pillows), a huge bathroom with shower and tub, and enormously high ceilings. Breakfast, included in the price, is served in a lovely lobby overlooking the gardens. ⊠ *Sothearos* ☎ *023/215701* ⌑ *30* rooms ♿ In-room: no a/c, refrigerator. In-hotel: laundry service ▭ MC, V ⍅Oⅼ BP.

$ 🖼 **Riverside Apartment.** Newly refurbished rooms are available for rent by night, week, or month. The rooms are immaculate and surprisingly stylish for a budget property; note that rooms in the back have no windows. An extra $10 per night will get you a room facing the river—one of the best riverside views you'll find. The Riverside is above the Sunny Internet Café, which makes up for the lack of Internet access in rooms. ✉ Nos. 351 and 353 Sisowath Quay ☎ 012/842036 ⍨ lek_sovanarith@yahoo.com ♿ ▭ No credit cards.

¢ 🖼 **Bright Lotus Guesthouse.** This centrally located guesthouse, across from the National Museum, is a pleasant and convenient option. Each floor has a balcony with a sitting area. Rooftop rooms offer wide views of the area. Corner rooms are bigger and brighter than the rest of the standard rooms. The restaurant offers tasty Khmer, Mediterranean, and American food at reasonable prices in a shaded area. ✉ 22 St. 178 ☎ 023/990446 or 012/676682 ⍨ sammy_lotus@hotmail.com ⌇ 12 rooms ♿ In-room: no a/c (some), refrigerator (some) ▭ No credit cards.

¢ 🖼 **Golden Gate Hotel.** Long popular with long-term and frequent visitors, the Golden Gate offers rooms by the night or by the month. The hotel is located in two separate buildings across the street from each other in a neighborhood with many nonprofit offices and expatriate homes. Laundry service is included in the room price. ✉ 9 St. 278, Sangkat Bengkengkang 1 ☎ 023/427618 or 012/737319 ♿ In-room: refrigerator. In-hotel: restaurant, laundry service, public Internet ▭ AE, MC, V.

Nightlife & the Arts

THE ARTS Various Phnom Penh theaters and restaurants offer programs of traditional music and dancing. Many of these shows are organized by nonprofit groups that help Cambodian orphans and disadvantaged kids. Siem Reap perhaps has more venues, but many there are run by for-profit companies in the tourism industry. ■ TIP→ **If you want to help local kids, catch a dance performance, such as those at the Veiyo Tonle restaurant (✉ 237 Sisowath Quay ☎ 012/847419). The nonprofit restaurant sponsors an orphanage, and twice a week the kids put on a beautiful show.**

Chaktomuk Theater (✉ Sisowath Quay, north of St. 240 ☎ 023/725119) hosts performances of traditional music and dance. The dates and times of shows are listed in the English-language newspaper *The Cambodia Daily*. Very authentic and aesthetically pleasing performances of traditional music and dance are presented every Friday and Saturday at 7:30 PM at the **Sovanna Phum Khmer Art Association** (✉ 111 360th St. ☎ 023/987564).

CLOSE UP

Cambodia's Festivals

LIKE MANY SOUTHEAST ASIAN NATIONS, Cambodia celebrates a lot of important festivals. Quite a few of them are closely tied to Buddhism, the country's predominant religion.

Khmer New Year: Celebrated at the same time as the Thai and Lao lunar new year, it's a new-moon festival spread over the three days following the winter rice harvest. People celebrate by cleaning and decorating their houses, making offerings at their home altars, going to Buddhist temples, and splashing lots and lots of water on each other. Be forewarned: Foreigners are fair game.

Bonn Om Touk: The Water Festival ushers in the fishing season and marks the "miraculous" reversal of the Tonle Sap waters. It's celebrated throughout the country: longboat river races are held, and an illuminated flotilla of *naga*, or dragon boats, adds to the festive atmosphere. The biggest races are held in Phnom Penh in front of the Royal Palace, where the King traditionally presides.

Chrat Preah Nongkol: The Royal Ploughing Ceremony, a celebration of the start of the summer planting season, is held in front of the Royal Palace in Phnom Penh in May. The impressive ceremony includes soothsaying rites meant to predict the outcomes for the year's rice harvest.

Meak Bochea: On the day of the full moon in February, this festival commemorates the Buddha's first sermon to 1,250 of his disciples. In the evening, Buddhists parade three times around their respective pagodas.

King Sihanouk's Birthday: The birthday of former King Norodom Sihanouk, born October 31, 1922, in Phnom Penh, is celebrated October 30–November 1; the whole nation joins in to honor him, and a grand fireworks display is held along the riverfront in Phnom Penh.

Pchum Ben (All Souls' Day): In mid-October, the spirits of deceased ancestors are honored according to Khmer tradition. People make special offerings at Buddhist temples to appease these spirits.

Visakha Bochea: This Buddhist festival, on the day of the full moon in May, celebrates the Buddha's birth, enlightenment, and death.

7

These days Phnom Penh has a number of remarkably good art and photo galleries to browse. **Le Popil Photo Gallery** (✉ 126 St. 19 ☎ 012/992750 ⊕ www.lepopil.com) exhibits photojournalism and art photography with a focus on Cambodia and the region. **Reyum** (✉ 47 St. 178 ☎ 023/217149), a gallery managed by the Institute of Arts and Cultures, offers exhibits on traditional Khmer art and architecture.

NIGHTLIFE Phnom Penh's nightlife now rivals that of Bangkok and in many cases exceeds it. What makes the nightlife here so great is how easy it is to get from place to place in this compact city. Most of the dusk-to-dawn nightspots are near the Tonle Sap riverside, along Street 240 and Street 51. Stroll around the riverfront and you'll be duly entertained. ⚠ **But always be careful after dark in Phnom Penh—robberies and violence are com-**

mon, and although foreigners aren't specifically targeted, they are certainly not exempt from the rise in crime.

With its American and Australian music, **Freebird** (⊠ 69 240th St. ☎ 012/810569) attracts an expat crowd.

The **Heart of Darkness** (⊠ 26 51st St. ☎ 023/231776) has undergone a full renovation. Gone are the legendary Conrad-inspired days of this popular haunt, but it continues to pack in the crowds.

Phnom Penh Internet Café Pub (⊠No. 219E Sisowath Quay ☎ 012/956292) is an Internet café, restaurant, and nightspot all in one. It offers great music and cocktails and happy-hour deals, as well as coffee and Khmer and Western food. The Wi-Fi and public computers are available at all times—you get 30 minutes of Internet time free with any drink order.

> ## ETIQUETTE & BEHAVIOR
>
> As elsewhere in Southeast Asia, confrontational behavior and displays of anger are considered bad manners, as is too much bare skin at a religious site. The foot is regarded as a base part of the body, so avoid pointing your foot at a person. You should also avoid touching someone on his or her head. Remove your shoes and hat before entering a temple or home. Public displays of affection should be avoided by all couples, gay or straight. It's polite to ask permission before taking a photo of someone, especially monks. Women should avoid any bodily contact with monks. That said, many Cambodian monks—unlike those in neighboring Thailand—will shake a woman's hand and initiate conversations.

Shopping

The city has many boutiques selling everything from fake antiques to fine jewelry. Prices are generally set at these boutiques, so you won't be able to bargain. The best are on streets 178 and 240.

The largest market in Phnom Penh is **Phsar Thmei** (⊠ Blvd. 128, Kampuchea Krom, at St. 76), popularly known as Central Market, an art deco–style structure in the center of the city that sells foodstuffs, household goods, fake antiques, and some silver and gold jewelry. You're expected to bargain—start off by offering half the named price and you'll probably end up paying about 70%. It's busiest in the morning. The **Phsar Tuol Tom Pong** (Russian Market ⊠ Adjacent to Wat Tuol Tom Pong, at Sts. 155 and 163 ☎ No phone) sells Cambodian handicrafts, wood carvings, baskets, electronics, clothes, and much more.

ANTIQUES & FINE ART **Bazar Art de Vivre** (⊠ 28 Sihanouk Blvd. ☎ 012/866178) includes some rare Chinese pieces among its eclectic collection of Asian art and antiques. **Couleurs d'Asie** (⊠ 19 St. 360 ☎ 012/902650) has regular exhibitions of Asian art and also many fine examples of local artists' work. **Le Lezard Bleu** (⊠ 61 St. 240 ☎ 023/986978) has a gallery of local artists' work and a collection of small antiques. **Lotus Pond** (⊠ 57 St. 178 ☎ 023/426782) has a good selection of fine Cambodian silks, carvings and statues, spirit houses, and small items of furniture.

LOCAL CRAFTS **Northeast Cambodia Souvenir Shop** (⊠ 52CE0 St. 240 ☎ 012/838350) sells cotton clothing and handicrafts made by the hill tribes of Ratanakkiri

Province, many of whom have little contact with the world beyond the forests they live in. **Rajana** (⊠ At 2 locations on St. 450 by the Russian Market ☎ 023/993642 ⊕ www.rajanacrafts.org) sells unique and interesting handicrafts, jewelry, silks, clothing, and knick-knacks. Proceeds go toward the Rajana Association, which trains local artisans. ■ TIP→ **Check out the old war-scrap necklaces and recycled spark-plug figurines.** There are locations in Sihanoukville and Siem Reap as well. **Roth Souvenir Shop** (⊠ 18 St. 178 ☎ 012/603484) is the

outlet for curios, handicrafts, and small decorative items. **Watthan Artisans Cambodia** (⊠ Wat Than Pagoda, 180 Norodom Blvd. ☎ 023/216321 ⊕ www.wac.khmerproducts.com), an organization worth supporting, features silks and other handicrafts made on-site by people with disabilities.

SILK **Kravanh House** (⊠ 13E St. 178 ☎ 012/756631) has one of the city's best selections of raw silk and silk products. **Sayon Silk Shop** (⊠ 40 St. 178 ☎ 012/859380) has an exquisite collection of silks and ready-made items.

Around Phnom Penh

Within easy reach to the south of Phnom Penh are the beaches of Tonle Bati, a small lake with a couple of temples nearby, and the lovely temple at Phnom Chisor. North of Phnom Penh are two easily accessible destinations: the river island of Koh Dach and the pilgrimage center of Udong.

To get to Tonle Bati or Phnom Chisor, take a bus to Takeo (departing Phnom Penh every hour). There's a Tonle Bati stop, but for Phnom Chisor, you'll have to get out at Prasat Neang Khmau, where you can hire a moto to take you up the hill. ■ TIP→ **Though the bus is dirt cheap, you can combine Tonle Bati and Phnom Chisor in one trip if you hire a car and driver.**

Tonle Bati

🅒 ❼ *33 km (20 mi) south of Phnom Penh.*

On weekends, Phnom Penh residents head for this small lake just a half hour's drive south on Highway 2. It has a beach with refreshment stalls and souvenir stands. Note that you'll encounter many beggars and children clamoring for attention here. The nearby, but more remote, **Ta Phrom,** a 12th-century temple built around the time of Siem Reap's Angkor Thom and Bayon, is less chaotic. The five-chambered laterite temple has several well-preserved Hindu and Buddhist bas-reliefs. Nearby is an attractive, smaller temple, **Yeah Peau.** Both temples are free and open to the public at all times. ■ TIP→ **About 11 km (7 mi) farther south is Phnom Tamao, Cambodia's leading zoo, but it's not worth a detour.**

Religion in Cambodia

AS IN NEIGHBORING THAILAND, LAOS, AND VIETNAM, Buddhism is the predominant religion in Cambodia. But animism and superstition continue to play strong roles in Khmer culture and society. Many people believe in powerful *neak ta*, or territorial guardian spirits. Spirit shrines are common in Khmer houses as well as on temple grounds and along roadsides. The Khmer Loeu hill tribes, who live in the remote mountain areas of Ratanakkiri and Mondulkiri provinces, and some tribes of the Cardamom Mountains are pure animists, believing in spirits living in trees, rocks, and water.

The main layer of Cambodian religion is a mix of Hinduism and Buddhism. These two religions reached the country from India about 2,000 years ago and played a pivotal role in the social and ideological life of the earliest kingdoms. Buddhism flourished in Cambodia in the 12th to 13th century, when King Jayavarman VII embraced Mahayana Buddhism. By the 15th century, influenced by Buddhist monks from Siam and Sri Lanka, most Cambodians practiced Theravada Buddhism.

Cambodian religious literature and royal classical dance draw on Hindu models, such as the *Reamker*, an ancient epic about an Indian prince searching for his abducted wife and fighting an evil king. Brahman priests still play an important role at court rituals.

Cambodia's Muslim Chams, who number a few hundred thousand, are the descendants of the Champa Kingdom that was based in what is today Vietnam. Many have lived in this area since the 15th century when they were forced from the original kingdom. The country's 60,000 Roman Catholics are mainly ethnic Vietnamese. A small Chinese minority follows Taoism.

Phnom Chisor

8 *55 km (34 mi) south of Phnom Penh.*

A trip to Phnom Chisor is worth the drive just for the view from the top of the hill of the same name. There's a road to the summit, but most visitors prefer the 20-minute walk to the top, where stunning vistas of the Cambodian countryside unfold. At the summit, the 11th-century temple, which is free and open to the public, is a Khmer masterpiece of laterite, brick, and sandstone.

Koh Dach

9 *30 km (19 mi) north of Phnom Penh.*

This Mekong River island is home to a handicrafts community of silk weavers, wood-carvers, potters, painters, and jewelry makers. To get there, cross the Tonle Sap at the Japanese Bridge and continue north on Route 6a. From there, take a ferry to the island; the route to the ferry terminal is obvious from 6a. Ferries leave roughly every half hour. Tuk-tuk and moto drivers will know where you want to go—just tell them your destination is Koh Dach. In all, the trip over to the island is pretty quick; most people spend about half a day on this excursion.

Udong

⑩ *45 km (28 mi) north of Phnom Penh.*

This small town served as the Khmer capital from the early 1600s until 1866, when King Norodom moved the capital south to Phnom Penh. Today it's an important pilgrimage destination for Cambodians paying homage to their former kings. You can join them on the climb to the pagoda-studded hilltop, site of the revered Vihear Prah Ath Roes assembly hall, which still bears the scars of local conflicts from the Khmer Rouge era.

Phnom Penh Essentials

Transportation

BY AIR

Thai International Airways flies twice daily from Bangkok to Phnom Penh, and Bangkok Airways has three flights a day. The trip takes about an hour and costs less than $200 round-trip. Siem Reap Airways and AirAsia also have service between Bangkok and Phnom Penh. Lao Airlines flies from Vientiane and Pakse in Laos to Phnom Penh. Siem Reap Airways, PMT Air, and Royal Khmer Airlines provide service between Cambodian cities.

AIRPORTS & TRANSFERS   Phnom Penh's modern Pochentong Airport is 10 km (6 mi) west of downtown. The international departure tax is $25, and the charge for domestic departures is $5–$15. A taxi from the airport to downtown Phnom Penh costs $7. ■ TIP→ **Motorcycles and tuk-tuks are cheaper than taxis (around $3), but it's a long, dusty ride, so you may prefer a taxi.**
🛈 Carriers **AirAsia** ☎ 023/356011 ⊕ www.airasia.com. **Bangkok Airways** ☎ 023/722545 ⊕ www.bangkokair.com. **Lao Airlines** ☎ 023/216563 ⊕ www.laoairlines.com. **PMT Air** ☎ 023/224714 ⊕ www.pmtair.com. **Royal Khmer Airlines** ☎ 023/994502 ⊕ www.royalkhmerairlines.com. **Siem Reap Airways** ☎ 023/720022 ⊕ www.siemreapairways.com. **Thai International Airways** ☎ 023/214359 ⊕ www.thaiair.com.

BY BOAT

Boats from Phnom Penh depart early in the morning from the municipal port on Sisowath Quay (at Street 84) to make the six-hour trip up the Tonle Sap to Chong Khneas, near Siem Reap and Angkor. The cost is about $25 one-way, although some travel agents offer lower prices. Tickets can be purchased at the port or through most hotels and travel agencies. Compagnie Fluviale du Mekong offers three-day luxury trips between Siem Reap and Phnom Penh. ⚠ **The "bullet boats" between Phnom Penh and Siem Reap can be dangerous, and during the dry season, when the water is very low, passengers may be required to switch boats in the middle of the journey. Given the high ticket prices, many travelers opt to take a bus to Siem Reap.**
🛈 **Compagnie Fluviale du Mekong** ✉ 30 St. 240 ☎ 023/216070 ⊕ www.cfmekong.com. **Phnom Penh port operators** ☎ 012/932328.

BY BUS

Phnom Penh has a half dozen or more private bus companies with regular service to all major Cambodian cities (check around, as some destination points change with the seasons and road conditions). Major bus stations include the Central Market, Sisowath Quay near the ferry port, and the Hua Lian station near the Olympic Stadium. Mekong Express charges a little more, but offers clean, comfortable, direct rides with tour guides and bathrooms on board all buses. Most long-distance bus tickets cost $3–$10, depending on the destination and distance.

GST Bus ⊠ Central Bus Station, Phnom Penh ☎ 012/895550. **Hua Lian** ⊠ Station near Olympic Stadium, Phnom Penh ☎ 012/376807. **Mekong Express** ⊠ 87E0 Sisowath Quay, Phnom Penh ☎ 023/427518 or 012/787839. **Neak Krorhorm** ⊠ 127 St. 108, Phnom Penh ☎ 023/219496.

BY CAR

A hired car with a driver costs about $40 a day, but settle on the price before setting off. You can arrange to hire a car with driver through any hotel. This is perhaps the easiest way to visit Tonle Bati and Phnom Chisor.

BY TAXI, MOTO & CYCLO

The most common forms of transportation are the moto (motorcycle taxi) and tuk-tuk. They cruise the streets in abundance, and gather outside hotels and restaurants—wherever you walk, you'll attract them. The standard fare for a short trip on a moto is 2,000–4,000 riel; tuk-tuks run a little higher. Foreigners will always pay more than locals, but the price is generally so cheap it's not worth arguing. Less-abundant cyclos (pedal trishaws) charge the same rates as tuk-tuks. Cruising taxis are nonexistent, but there are usually a couple parked outside large hotels, and the receptionist at any hotel can call one. Almost all drivers speak varying degrees of English, some of them fluently.

Contacts & Resources

BANKS & EXCHANGING SERVICES

Gone are the days when all transactions were conducted in cash and people kept their savings in secret stashes at home. In the cities at least, Cambodians are relying more and more on a Western banking system, and modern conveniences such as credit cards, money transfers, and ATMs have made life much easier for tourists. ANZ Royal Bank has several ATM machines throughout Phnom Penh and Siem Reap, as well as one in Sihanoukville. Canadia Bank also offers ATM services at the airport.

■ TIP→ **Keep in mind that Cambodian banking hours are shorter than in many Western countries. They generally open at 8 AM, but often close by 3 or 4. ATMs, however, are open 24 hours.**

Banks ACLEDA Bank (Western Union services) ⊠ 28 Mao Tse Tung, Phnom Penh ☎ 023/214634. **ANZ Royal Bank** ⊠ 100 Sihanouk, Phnom Penh ☎ 023/726900. **Canadia Bank** ⊠ 265-269 St. 214, Phnom Penh ☎ 023/215286.

EMERGENCIES

For medical emergencies, visit the International SOS Medical Clinic or Tropical & Travelers Medical Clinic. Bangkok Hospital also has an office in Phnom Penh and an international clinic in Siem Reap; the hospital can arrange for medical evacuations to their Bangkok hospital if necessary.

🏥 Hospitals **Bangkok Hospital Office** ✉ Hong Kong Center, Sothearos, Phnom Penh ☏ 023/219422. **International SOS Medical Clinic** ✉ 161 St. 51, Phnom Penh ☏ 023/216911 or 012/816911. **Tropical & Travelers Medical Clinic** ✉ 88 St. 108, Phnom Penh ☏ 023/366802 or 012/898981.

INTERNET, MAIL & SHIPPING

New Internet cafés are opening all the time in Phnom Penh, so you'll have no problem finding one. Prices run about 50¢ to $1 an hour. Wi-Fi is offered at some cafés.

📮 Post Office **Main Post Office** ✉ St. 13, 1 block east of Wat Phnom, Phnom Penh.

📦 Shipping Services **DHL** ✉ 353 St. 110 ☏ 023/427726. **FedEx** ✉ 701D Monivong ☏ 023/216712.

TOUR OPTIONS

Various companies arrange day tours of Phnom Penh and nearby sights; note, however, that guides can be hired right at the Royal Palace and National Museum. Hanuman Tourism Voyages offers an extensive list of tour possibilities, including guided trips outside the Phnom Penh area. The company puts its money back into development projects to help minorities in Cambodia's remote provinces. Exotissimo and Diethelm are reliable, popular tour companies offering standard excursions.

🎫 **Diethelm Travel** ✉ 65 240th St., Phnom Penh ☏ 023/219151 ⊕ www.diethelm-travel.com.

Exotissimo ✉ 46 Norodom, Phnom Penh ☏ 023/218948 ⊕ www.exotissimo.com.

Hanuman Tourism Voyages ✉ 12 St. 310, Phnom Penh ☏ 023/218356 ⊕ www.hanumantourism.com.

NORTH OF PHNOM PENH

If you're looking to go even farther afield, you can visit the ancient ruins of Kampong Thom or Kampong Cham; see highly endangered freshwater Irrawaddy dolphins at Kratie; or head to the remote and largely undeveloped provinces of Ratanakkiri or Mondulkiri, both of which offer trekking opportunities among hill tribes. The city of Battambang (Cambodia's second largest) may be closer to Siem Reap on the map, but Phnom Penh is the logical jumping-off point for a visit there. Note that many of these destinations are quite removed from one another or accessed via different routes, and thus can't be combined in one tour. ■ TIP→ Ratanakkiri is often inaccessible by road during the rainy season. Ask around first—your best bet may be flying there on PMT Air.

Kampong Cham

❶ *125 km (78 mi) northeast of Phnom Penh.*

Cambodia's third-largest city was also an ancient Khmer center of culture and power on the Mekong River, and it has a pre-Angkorian temple, **Wat Nokor,** which is free and open to the public at all times. Just outside town are the twin temple-topped hills, Phnom Pros and Phnom Srei. Ask a local to explain the interesting legend about their creation.

Where to Stay

¢   ☰ **Mekong Hotel.** A Japanese enterprise built this riverside hotel but kept to a high-eaved Cambodian style. The boat pier is close by and river-craft skippers tend to blast their horns early to announce their departure, so if you like to sleep late, book a room at the back. Rooms are large and smartly furnished in light woods and fabrics. ⊠ *River Rd.* ☎ *042/941536* ↝ *18 rooms* ♤ *In-room: refrigerator. In-hotel: restaurant, laundry service* ▭ *No credit cards.*

Kampong Thom

⑫   *160 km (99 mi) north of Phnom Penh.*

This provincial town, exactly halfway between Phnom Penh and Siem Reap, boasts ruins that are even older than those at Angkor. They are all that remain of the 7th-century Sambor Prei Kuk, the capital of Zhen La, a loose federation of city-states. The ruins, which are free and open to the public at all times, are near the Stung Sen River, 35 km (22 mi) northeast of Kampong Thom.

Kratie

★ ⑬   *350 km (217 mi) northeast of Phnom Penh.*

Kratie is famous for the colony of freshwater Irrawaddy dolphins that inhabit the Mekong River some 15 km (9 mi) north of town. ■ TIP→ **The dolphins are most active in the early morning and late afternoon.** Taxis and hired cars from Kratie charge about $10 for the journey to the stretch of river where the dolphins can be observed. You will likely have to hire a local boatman to take you to where the dolphins are, as they move up and down the river. Ferries from Phnom Penh no longer make the journey to Kratie, but regular bus service is offered by several companies.

Where to Stay

¢   ☰ **Santepheap Hotel.** Ask for a room with a river view at this relatively new hotel across the road from the boat pier. Rooms are simple, with little decoration, but comfortable enough, and the bathrooms are large, with tubs. ⊠ *River Rd., Kratie* ☎ *072/971537* ↝ *24 rooms* ♤ *In-room: no a/c (some), no TV (some). In-hotel: restaurant* ▭ *No credit cards.*

Ratanakkiri Province

Ban Lung is 635 km (394 mi) northeast of Phnom Penh.

Visiting this region makes you feel as if you've arrived at the end of the world. The government aims to turn Ratanakkiri and nearby Mondulkiri Province into ecotourism destinations—both provinces are mountainous and covered with dense jungle, and together they are home to 12 different Khmer Loeu ethnic-minority groups.

⑭ The provincial capital of Ratanakkiri is **Ban Lung**; it's best to fly here from Phnom Penh, though flights only run four times a week. Buses sometimes run between Phnom Penh and Ban Lung, and share taxis are always an option, unattractive as that option may be. It's an arduous drive. In Ban Lung you can hire a jeep (preferably with a driver-guide) or, if you're very adventurous, a motorcycle, to visit the fascinating destinations an hour or two away: the gem-mining area of **Bo Keo,** some 35 km (22 mi) to the east; mystical **Yeak Laom Lake,** deep in a volcanic crater and sacred to many of the Khmer Loeu hill tribes; and the beautiful **Virachey National Park,** 35 km (22 mi) to the northeast, with its the two-tiered Bu Sra Waterfall.

Where to Stay & Eat

$–$$ ✕🏠**Terres Rouge Lodge.** This handsome property on the edge of Ban Lung's Boeung Kan Siang Lake is the region's best. It's a traditional wooden Cambodian country house, decorated in traditional style, with antiques and local artifacts in the spacious rooms. The restaurant is also one of the best of the area. ⊠ *Boeung Kan Siang Lake, Ban Lung* ☎ *075/974051* ⟆ *14 rooms* ⚒ *In-room: refrigerator. In-hotel: restaurant, laundry service* ☐ *No credit cards.*

¢–$ ✕🏠**Yaklom Hill Lodge.** This popular lodge, which prides itself on an eco-friendly philosophy, offers 13 wooden cottages and a traditional hill tribe house in a jungle setting outside the city. Note that the cottages do not have hot water. The lodge arranges tours of the area, and the property itself allows you to enjoy nature—there are several terraces with outstanding views and a few short nature trails. Bicycles and motorcycles are available for rent. ⊠ *Outside Ban Lung* ☎ *011/725881* ⊕ *www. yaklom.com* ⟆ *14 rooms* ⚒ *In-room: no a/c, no phone, no TV. In-hotel: restaurant* ☐ *No credit cards.*

Battambang

⑮ *290 km (180 mi) northwest of Phnom Penh.*

Cambodia's second-largest city straddles the Sanker River in the center of the country's rice bowl. Dusty Battambang is bypassed by most visitors to Cambodia, but it's an interesting city to explore. ■ TIP→ **The French left their mark here with some fine old buildings, more than you'll find in most Cambodian cities these days.** Long before the French arrived, Battambang was an important Khmer city, and among its many temples is an 11th-century Angkorian temple, **Wat Ek Phnom.** The temple has some fine stone carvings in excellent condition. Outside the city is the 11th-century hilltop temple **Phnom Banan,** with five impressive towers. Both temples are free and open to the public at all times.

Perhaps most interesting of all is a mountain, **Phnom Sampeou,** which contains a temple and a group of "killing caves" used by the Khmer Rouge. In one, which contains the skeletal remains of some of the victims, you can stand on the dark floor and look to a hole in the cave ceiling with sunlight streaming through. The Khmer Rouge reportedly pushed their victims through that hole to their deaths on the rocks below.

Phsar Nath Market, like most local markets, is a decent place for souvenir-hunting. The market is known for its gems and Battambang's famous fruit, but it also sells everything from fresh produce to electronics imported from China. Some stalls sell textiles, but most of these are imported. ⊠ *On the Sangker River* ☎ *No phone* ⊗ *Daily 7–5.*

Where to Stay & Eat

$$ ✕⬚ **La Villa.** La Villa is perhaps the city's first boutique hotel. It's in a restored 1930s colonial house; rooms have an art deco feel and antique furnishings. ⊠*E. River Rd.* ☎*012/991801 or 012/858571* ✎*lavilla@online.com.kh* ⬚*6 rooms* ♿ *In-room: no a/c (some). In-hotel: restaurant, bar* ⊟ *No credit cards.*

$ ✕⬚ **Teo Hotel.** Teo is one of Battambang's best hotels, but it is on a busy main road, so insist on a room at the back. Rooms are reminiscent of French provincial auberges, with lots of fussy chintz and incongruous decorations. There are even floor-to-ceiling French windows. The garden restaurant serves Khmer, Thai, and Western dishes. ⊠ *3rd St., Svay Pro Commune* ☎ *012/857048* ⬚ *81 rooms* ♿ *In-hotel: restaurant* ⊟ *MC.*

North of Phnom Penh Essentials

Transportation

BY AIR

PMT Air flies four times a week between Phnom Penh and Ban Lung. 🖪 Carriers **PMT Air** ⊠ Regency Sq., Suite B9, Mao Tse Tung, Phnom Penh ☎ 023/224714 ⊕ www.pmtair.com.

BY BOAT

Boats from Phnom Penh make the six-hour trip on the Tonle Sap to Chong Khneas, near Siem Reap and Angkor. Ferries depart Phnom Penh from the municipal port on Sisowath Quay, at Street 84, early in the morning. The cost is about $25 one way. Tickets can be purchased at most hotels and travel agencies, or at the port. There's a daily boat from Battambang to Siem Reap, which takes three to four hours on the Tonle Sap lake and costs $15. ⚠ **In the dry season, the water level is often too low to travel this route. Boats often get stuck in the lake, turning a pleasant journey into a 10-hour ordeal.**
🖪 **Phnom Penh port operators** ☎ 012/932328.

BY BUS

Buses to outlying cities and towns leave from Phnom Penh's Central Market, the Hua Lian station near the Olympic Stadium, and on Sothearos road near the ferry port. Tickets can be purchased at the bus companies' offices or through most hotels and guesthouses. Several buses depart daily from Phnom Penh to Battambang (and in some cases, on to Poipet). The trip takes about five hours. Mekong Express and Neak Krorhorm provide bus services within the country.
🖪 **GST Bus** ⊠ Central Bus Station, Phnom Penh ☎ 012/895550.

Hua Lian ✉ Station near Olympic Stadium, Phnom Penh ☎ 012/376807.

Mekong Express ✉ 87E0 Sisowath Quay, Phnom Penh ☎ 023/427518 or 012/787839.

Neak Krorhorm ✉ 127 St. 108, Phnom Penh ☎ 023/219496.

BY CAR

A hired car with a driver costs about $40 a day, but settle on the price before setting off. Drivers are notoriously fast and dangerous. Tell him firmly and clearly that you want to go slowly and safely, or you will not pay.

BY TRAIN

Cambodia's decrepit once-a-week train is also an option; the journey takes up to 14 hours and attracts only the poorest of travelers. If you have the time, it's a great way to see the countryside and meet people. Tickets, a couple of dollars, can be purchased at the central train station in Phnom Penh.

Contacts & Resources

BANKS & EXCHANGING SERVICES

ANZ has quickly become the most popular bank among travelers, with two branches with ATMs in Battambang. Dollars and other currencies can be exchanged for riel at local markets (look for the glass cases with money inside).

SIEM REAP & ANGKOR TEMPLE COMPLEX

The temples of Angkor constitute one of the world's great ancient sites and Southeast Asia's most impressive archaeological treasure. The massive structures, surrounded by lush tropical forest, are comparable to the Mayan ruins of Central America—and far exceed them in size. Angkor Wat is the world's largest religious structure; so large, it's hard to describe its breadth to someone who hasn't seen it. And that's just one temple in a complex of hundreds.

The abundant statues and extensive bas-relief murals are as beautiful as those in the great temples of India, or as the art of the ancient Egyptians. These days, the complex is often overrun with tourists from the world over, arriving by the busload to gawk, sigh, contribute to a babble of collective admiration, and wander into each other's snapshots. But part of Angkor's beauty is its vastness. It's still possible to find a quiet nook or an empty alcove all to oneself.

Siem Reap (which means "Siam defeated," based on a 15th-century battle with Cambodia's neighbors to the west) was once a small, provincial town known only for

NIGHT FLIGHTS

Around sunset, the sky fills with thousands of large bats, which make their homes in the trees behind the Preah Ang Chek Preah Ang Chorm Shrine near the gardens in front of the Raffles.

the nearby Angkor ruins. The town stretches along both sides of the Siem Reap River, some 315 km (195 mi) northwest of Phnom Penh. In recent years, it has grown tremendously, becoming a tourism hub that's critical to the Cambodian economy. An international airport, about 6½ km (4 mi) outside town, works almost to capacity, with flights landing and taking off throughout the day.

Siem Reap

16 *315 km (195 mi) north of Phnom Penh.*

Siem Reap is turning into a thriving, bustling city with great shopping, dining, and nightlife options. There's still not much in the town itself to distract you from Angkor, but after a long day at the temples, you'll be happy to spend your evening strolling along the river, and dining at an outdoor table on a back alley in the hip old French quarter near Pub Street, which is closed to traffic in the evening.

True, construction sites are common eyesores and disrupters of the peace in this rapidly expanding town, but don't let that deter you from exploring Siem Reap. The Old Market area is a huge draw and the perfect place to shop for souvenirs. Many of the colonial buildings in the area were destroyed during the Khmer Rouge years, but many others have been restored and turned into delightful hotels and restaurants.

You could spend an entire afternoon in the Old Market area, wandering from shop to shop, café to café, gallery to gallery. It changes every month, with ever more delights in store. Long gone are the days when high-end souvenirs (the legal kind) came from Thailand. Today, numerous shops offer high-quality Cambodian silks, Kampot pepper and other Cambodian spices, and herbal soaps and toiletries made from natural Cambodian products.

No matter where you wander in the evening, you're likely to encounter a traditional dance performance; dozens of hotels and restaurants offer them nightly. For a full-blown affair, try the **Angkor Mondial Restaurant** (⊠ Pokambor Ave., Wat Bo Bridge ☎ 063/966875), where $12 gets you a Khmer buffet dinner and an apsara show.

Where to Stay & Eat

$$–$$$$ ✕ **Meric.** The best thing on offer at the Hotel de la Paix is its fine Khmer restaurant, named for the famous pepper that grows in Kampot Province. Here, you'll dine in style in the hotel's courtyard. Choose a traditional seven-course meal (set menu), with foods served on clay, stone, or banana leaf, and adorned with local herbs. A pungent ginger fish stew is a highlight. Portions are small, but the point is to savor each bite. ⊠ *Sivatha Rd.* ☎ *063/ 966000* ▭ *AE, MC, V.*

> **GOOD DEEDS**
>
> Not far from the Old Market on Achamen Street sits the **Angkor Hospital for Children** (☎ 012/725745 ⊕ www.fwab.org), providing pediatric care to more than 100,000 children each year. It was founded in 1999 by Japanese photographer Kenro Izu. Give blood, save a life.

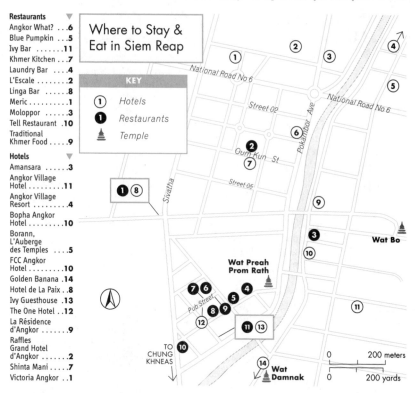

Restaurants ▼
Angkor What? ...**6**
Blue Pumpkin ...**5**
Ivy Bar **11**
Khmer Kitchen ...**7**
Laundry Bar **4**
L'Escale **2**
Linga Bar **8**
Meric **1**
Moloppor **3**
Tell Restaurant .**10**
Traditional
Khmer Food **9**

Hotels ▼
Amansara **3**
Angkor Village
Hotel **11**
Angkor Village
Resort **4**
Bopha Angkor
Hotel **10**
Borann,
L'Auberge
des Temples ...**5**
FCC Angkor
Hotel **10**
Golden Banana .**14**
Hotel de La Paix ..**8**
Ivy Guesthouse .**13**
The One Hotel ..**12**
La Résidence
d'Angkor **9**
Raffles
Grand Hotel
d'Angkor **2**
Shinta Mani **7**
Victoria Angkor ..**1**

Where to Stay & Eat in Siem Reap

KEY

① Hotels
❶ Restaurants
⛩ Temple

★ ¢–$$ ✕ **L'Escale des Arts & des Sens.** Siem Reap's dining scene raised several notches with the opening of this restaurant. Chef Didier Corlou, who hails from the Hotel Metropole in Hanoi, has a long, fine tradition of creating modern Indochinese culinary marvels. His menus are specific to the locale, which means you can try his favorite delights from the Tonle Sap, or beef prepared in seven ways (based on an old tiger recipe). You could return every night for a week and still not have sampled everything on offer. ⊠ *Oum Khum St.* ☎ *063/761442* ▱ *MC, V.*

¢–$ ✕ **Blue Pumpkin.** Don't miss this sleek Internet café, bakery, and restaurant near the Old Market. In addition to fresh-baked goods, the Blue Pumpkin serves up interesting salads, mild Asian dishes, and energizing fresh juices (try the Lolita). You could easily take a post-meal nap on the big white bed-couches upstairs. ⊠ *Old Market* ☎ *063/963574* ▱ *No credit cards.*

¢–$ ✕ **Tell Restaurant.** German dishes, as well as Khmer and Asian specialties, are served at this well-run restaurant. The portions of German pork knuckle and schnitzel are huge, and imported Bavarian wheat beer is an ideal accompaniment. ⊠ *374 Sivatha Rd.* ☎ *063/963289* ▱ *AE, MC, V.*

¢–$ ✕ **Traditional Khmer Food.** The name says it all—this Khmer-owned and -operated restaurant gives you a hearty introduction to real Khmer

A Rare Opportunity

A SOCIOLOGY STUDENT named Sok Chea recently interviewed tourists about their thoughts on Cambodian beggars. Overwhelmingly, the tourists said beggars made them feel bad and ruined their pleasant vacations. When Sok Chea asked beggars how they felt, living on the streets, asking for money, they poured out their sadness. They felt less than human; people walked by and never said hello.

Beggars will approach you in Cambodia. So will street kids selling bracelets and books. Occasionally you'll run into a scam, but generally these Cambodians have no choice. The bookseller is paying for school, the mother trying to feed her kids. Whether or not you give anything directly to beggars or street kids is your call, but be aware that many NGO workers who work with the homeless advise against giving handouts on the street. Instead, you should acknowledge the people that

greet you, politely decline, and make a donation to an organization that operates larger-scale programs to aid beggars and street kids.

There's a larger issue at play here than how to react to requests for money. Many Cambodians say that tourists don't understand the day-to-day realities of Cambodian life, especially in Siem Reap, where they can simply fly in, stay in a nice hotel, see the temples, and fly out—the whole time remaining somewhat insulated from the city and the country. Thus, many tuk-tuk drivers in Siem Reap try to take tourists to their home villages, just for a glimpse. Take the offer. The real Cambodian life is nothing like that seen from a tour bus window, and far from ruining a "pleasant" vacation, understanding the greater context of a country that's in tremendous transition will make every experience richer.

cooking. The bright little spot (painted in orange and purple) is along one of the back alleys near Pub Street. It serves a wide selection of Khmer soups, curries, and meat and vegetable dishes. ⊠ *Pub St. alley* ☎ *015/999909* ▭ *No credit cards.*

¢ ✕**Khmer Kitchen.** Like its neighbor, Traditional Khmer Food, this popular restaurant serves tasty Khmer dishes (and some Thai), but with modern interpretations. ⊠ *Pub St. area* ☎ *063/964154* ▭ *No credit cards.*

¢ ✕**Moloppor.** This pleasant Japanese-style café by the river offers good snacks, small plates, desserts, and drinks. Try a cashew nut shake—you'll want a second. Or try the sauna upstairs. ⊠ *E. River Rd.* ☎ *063/760257* ▭ *No credit cards.*

★ $$$$ ✕▦ **La Résidence d'Angkor.** Employing ancient Angkor style, this luxury retreat is packed into a central walled compound on the river. The guest rooms are stunning and spacious—subtle mixes of hardwoods, white walls and bedspreads, colorful pillows, and Khmer art. Sliding glass doors open onto balconies, and sliding wooden doors enclose long bathroom/dressing areas that have large round tubs at one end. The gardens, statues, and open-air bar are equally attractive. The restaurant ($$–$$$$), which serves an inventive mix of Asian and Western dishes, is one of the town's best. ⊠ *River Rd. (east side)* ☎ *063/963390* ⊕ *www.pansea. com* ⇆ *55 rooms* ♨ *In-room: safe, refrigerator. In-hotel: restaurant, bar, pool, laundry service, concierge, public Internet* ▭ *AE, MC, V.*

$$$$ ✕⌖ **Raffles Grand Hotel d'Angkor.** Built in 1932, this grande dame was restored and reopened a decade ago after nearly being destroyed by occupying Khmer Rouge guerillas. The Grand now ranks among the region's finest, and most expensive, hotels. It combines French sensibilities and Cambodian art with Oriental carpets and wicker furniture; rooms are large and elegant, with balconies that overlook the extensive gardens and blue-tile pool. Horticulture is something taken seriously at the Raffles: 60,000 square meters of greenery with flowers, shrubs, and local trees. ▪ TIP→ **The elegant Restaurant Le Grand is one of Siem Reap's finest; royal Khmer cuisine is offered nightly 6:30–10:30.** ⊠ *1 Vithei Charles de Gaulle* ☎ *063/963888* ⊕ *www.raffles-grandhoteldangkor.com* ⇆ *150 rooms* ♨ *In-room: safe, refrigerator, Wi-Fi. In-hotel: 3 restaurants, room service, bar, pool, gym, spa, laundry service, concierge, no-smoking rooms* ▭ *AE, MC, V* ⏸ *BP, MAP.*

$–$$ ✕⌖ **Bopha Angkor Hotel.** Across the street from the Siem Reap River's east bank is this small hotel offering quality Khmer cuisine and comfortable rooms at very competitive prices. The guest rooms have tile floors, wood ceilings, local handicrafts, and mosquito nets. They surround an attractive, open-air restaurant (¢–$$$) set amid gardens and small pools, where dinner is accompanied by live Cambodian traditional music. ▪ TIP→ **A delicious and affordable selection—from set meals to à la carte hot pots and fish dishes to tantalizing fresh juices and desserts—makes this a good dinner option even if you're staying elsewhere.** ⊠ *512 Vithei Acharsvar (River Rd., east side)* ☎ *063/964928* ⊕ *www.bopha-angkor.com* ⇆ *23 rooms* ♨ *In-room: refrigerator. In-hotel: restaurant, laundry service, public Internet* ▭ *MC, V* ⏸ *EP.*

¢ ✕⌖ **Ivy Guesthouse & Bar.** This charming corner spot in the Old Market area offers clean, comfortable rooms that retain the original colonial ambience of the building: high ceilings, green French doors opening onto balconies, and black-and-white tile floors. ▪ TIP→ **The restaurant (Western and Khmer) and bar downstairs have long been popular with expats and tourists.** ⊠ *Old Market* ☎ *012/800860* ⇆ *6 rooms* ♨ *In-room: no a/c (some) In-hotel: restaurant, room service, bar, laundry service, airport shuttle* ▭ *No credit cards.*

$$$$ ⌖ **Amansara.** There's the Amansara, and then there's every other hotel.
Fodor'sChoice   The Amansara is so good it doesn't need to advertise or even post an
★   English-language sign out front. This all-suites retreat is in what was once a guest villa of former King Norodom Sihanouk. It is clearly the sleekest of Siem Reap's resorts—it does the minimalist black-and-white and earth-tone decor, something of a trend these days among the city's hotels, just a little better than any other property. Pool suites include, as the name suggests, private plunge pools—not that you need one, because the resort has two others (one for lap swimming). Visit the jasmine-scented spa for a private treatment, followed by a few moments in a private relaxation room. The resort has shuttle service to the temples in private black tuk-tuks and offers cultural tours of the area. Note that although there are no TVs in the suites, they do have CD players.

✉ *Road to Angkor (behind the Tourism Department)* ☎ *063/760333* ⊕ *www.amanresorts.com* ⇨ *24 suites, 12 with private pools* ⌂ *In-room: safe, refrigerator, no TV, ethernet. In-hotel: restaurant, 2 pools, spa, bicycles, public Internet, concierge, laundry service* ▭ *AE, MC, V* |○| *EP.*

$$$$ ⊡ **Angkor Village Resort.** Love the Angkor Village Hotel concept, but looking for something quieter and farther out of the city? The hotel's sister resort, in a shady plot off the road to Angkor, offers bungalows in flowering gardens, linked by a brick walkway. Enjoy a soak in your room's large corner tub or a swim in the 200-meter pool. Rooms, all with four-poster beds, are decorated in fine Khmer style with chic modern touches like flat-screen TVs. ✉ *Phum Traeng (between Siem Reap town and Angkor Wat)* ☎ *063/963361* ⊕ *www.angkorvillage.com* ⇨ *80 bungalows* ⌂ *In-room: safe, refrigerator, ethernet. In-hotel: restaurant, bar, pool, spa, laundry service, airport shuttle* ▭ *AE, MC, V* |○| *BP.*

$$$$ ⊡ **Hotel de La Paix.** This much-hyped addition to the city offers boutique rooms in black and white. The hotel's internationally acclaimed design has incorporated all the amenities one would expect of a member of the Small Luxury Hotels of the World: spa suites with in-room massage facilities, terrazzo soaking tubs, preprogrammed iPods, DVD players, and a lot more. Unfortunately, the hotel is located on the dusty, noisy Sivutha Boulevard, with construction sites in all directions, though for some, this may actually accentuate the feeling of exclusive luxury. Here, you can sip a drink poolside or gaze out the windows of your swanky room, thankful you're not parching in the heat like the laundry hung on the neighbors' lines. ✉ *Sivutha Blvd.* ☎ *063/966000* ⊕ *www.hoteldelapaixangkor. com* ⇨ *107 rooms* ⌂ *In-room: safe, refrigerator, Wi-Fi. In-hotel: restaurant, bar, pool, gym, laundry service* ▭ *AE, MC, V.*

★ **$$$$** ⊡ **The One Hotel.** The One Hotel has but one room, but it's on the one street in town where you'd want to be. Across from the affiliated (and equally hip) Linga Bar is this unique option in a renovated colonial shophouse. Inside, you get sleek, modern design with all the trimmings, including an iPod and iBook. Open the balcony doors of your second-story suite, and watch over Siem Reap's new nightlife scene. Take the staircase to the rooftop and indulge in a private Jacuzzi and shower under the moonlight. A personal chef provides your meals. What more do you need, when The One does all this? ✉ *Pub St. area, across from Linga Bar* ☎ *012/755311* ⊕ *www.theonehotelangkor.com* ⇨ *1 room* ⌂ *In-room: safe, refrigerator, Wi-Fi. In-hotel: room service, laundry service, concierge, airport shuttle* ▭ *AE, MC, V.*

$$$$ ⊡ **Victoria Angkor Resort & Spa.** Situated just west of the Raffles botanical gardens is this splendid spread evocative of colonial times. Rooms employ lots of wood and rattan, and offer porches with pool or garden views. Enjoy a dip in the sunken pool, surrounded by a wooden deck and a stone wall. ✉ *Central Park* ☎ *063/760428* ⊕ *www.victoriahotels-asia.com* ⇨ *120 rooms, 10 suites* ⌂ *In-room: safe, refrigerator, ethernet. In-hotel: 2 restaurants, pool, spa, public Internet* ▭ *AE, MC, V* |○| *BP.*

★ **$$$-$$$$** ⊡ **Angkor Village Hotel.** A couple of blocks from the river, on a stone road in a green neighborhood, is this oasis of wooden buildings, gardens, and pools filled with lotus blossoms. It's a warm and welcoming place, from the airy teak lobby to the tasteful rooms, all designed like a traditional Khmer village. Standard rooms are small, so it's best to pay a little extra for superior rooms, which are bigger and brighter and overlook the water and greenery. All rooms have Khmer handicrafts. The open-air restaurant, set in the middle of a pond, serves French and Asian cuisine. ■ TIP→ **The cultural show performed in the hotel's gorgeous theater, designed like a temple, is a must-see.** ⊠ *Wat Bo Rd.* ☎ *063/ 963361* ⊕ *www.angkorvillage.com* ⇆ *49 rooms* ⌂ *In-room: safe, re-frigerator. In-hotel: restaurant, bar, pool, laundry service, concierge, pub-lic Internet, airport shuttle* ⊟ *AE, MC, V* ⃘⃘ *BP.*

★ **$$$–$$$$** ▦ **Shinta Mani.** When you spend your money here, you help enrich a young Cambodian's life. The resort, in a laid-back, tree-lined neighbor-hood, is the flagship of the Institute of Hospitality, which trains young Cam-bodians to work in the hotel and restaurant industry. Not only will you sleep and eat in style here, your money will also help support projects bring-ing clean water, transportation, and jobs to underprivileged communities. ■ TIP→ **The Shinta Mani's two deluxe rooms are modeled in style after those at the Hotel de la Paix, but cost a fraction of the price.** ⊠ *Oun Khum and 14th Sts.* ☎*063/761998* ⊕*www.shintamani.com* ⇆*18 rooms* ⌂*In-room: safe, refrigerator, Wi-Fi. In-hotel: restaurant, bar, pool, spa* ⊟ *AE, MC, V.*

$$$ ▦ **FCC Angkor Hotel.** Yet another in a line of resorts with black-and-white décor, the FCC Angkor takes a former French Consulate and turns it into an inviting respite along the river. Rooms and suites, done in min-imalist art deco design, wrap around an attractive pool and gardens. The hotel is far from the noise of the city. ⊠ *Pokambor Ave. (next to the Royal Palace)* ☎ *063/760280* ⊕ *www.fcccambodia.com* ⇆ *29 rooms, 2 suites* ⌂ *In-room: DVD, ethernet. In-hotel: restaurant, bar, pool, spa* ⊟ *MC, V* ⃘⃘ *CP.*

$ ▦ **Borann, l'Auberge des Temples.** The accommodations are attrac-tive and the rates low at this tran-quil, small hotel a couple of blocks east of the river. Khmer handicrafts and antiques fill the rooms, which have high ceilings and tile floors. Each one has a large porch or bal-cony overlooking a nicely planted yard, which holds a small pool and open-air thatched restaurant. Large bathrooms with stone floors have both a shower and the traditional Cambodian bathing option of scooping water out of a giant ce-ramic urn, which sounds archaic but is thoroughly refreshing after a hot day at the temples. ✛ *1½ blocks east of river, 1 block north of 6th St., behind La Noria hotel* ☎ *063/ 964740* ⊕*www.borann.com* ⇆*20 rooms* ⌂ *In-room: no a/c (some),*

7

THE BEST OF THE BEST

Reliable international chains have begun to open along the road to Angkor, and both the dusty airport road and the town's noisy thor-oughfares are clogged with upper-end accommodations. However, why settle for a lousy location? Siem Reap offers several superb options in the quaint and quiet river area, where lush gardens are the norm and birds and butterflies thrive. Booking a room in a high-price hotel in this quarter means that your view of the hotel pool won't include the neighbors' laun-dry line, and your view will delight you with natural splendor instead of traffic jams.

safe. In-hotel: restaurant, pool, laundry service ▭ *No credit cards* ⊚ *EP.*

$ ⊡ **Golden Banana Boutique Hotel/Golden Banana Bed & Breakfast.** When renovation of the new building was completed in summer of 2006, it made this gem of a getaway one of the best budget accommodations in the region. Each room at the hotel is a duplex—bedroom and bathroom downstairs, and a sitting room upstairs. The rooms are grouped around a refreshing pool. The original bed-and-breakfast still offers great budget accommodations, too, though with fewer amenities. Both properties emphasize that they are gay friendly, though the clientele is very mixed. ⊠ *Wat Damnak area* ☎ *012/654638* ⊕ *www.goldenbanana.info* ⌂ *In-room: safe, refrigerator, DVD, ethernet. In-hotel: restaurant, bar, pool, laundry service* ▭ *MC, V* ⊚ *BP.*

Nightlife

Most of Siem Reap's nightlife is concentrated around the Old Market, particularly on vibrant Pub Street, which has become very popular. Just wander around, and you're sure to find a hangout that fits your style. **Angkor What?** (⊠ Pub St. ☎ 012/490755) was one of the first nighttime establishments in the old quarter, and it still packs in the crowds until early morning. Write your name and your personal philosophy on the walls. The **Laundry Bar** (⊠ Old Market area ☎ 016/962026) is another favorite, popular for its music, which thumps until late. The **Linga Bar** (⊠ Pub St. alley ⊕ www.lingabar.com), across from the affiliated One Hotel, offers stylish cocktails (at stylish prices) in a funky setting.

Around Siem Reap

★ Be sure to visit the **Cambodia Land Mine Museum** (⊠ Off the road to Angkor ⊕ www.cambodialandminemuseum.org), established by Akira, a former child soldier who fought for the Khmer Rouge, the Vietnamese, and the Cambodian Army. Now, he dedicates his life to removing the land mines he and thousands of others laid across Cambodia. His museum is a must-see, an eye-opener that portrays a different picture of Cambodia from the glorious temples and five-star hotels. Any tuk-tuk or taxi driver can find the museum. When in the Old Market area, visit the Akira Mine Action Gallery for more information on land mines and ways to help land-mine victims go to college.

Tonle Sap

10 km (6 mi) south of Siem Reap.

Covering 2,600 square km (1,000 square mi) in the dry season, Cambodia's vast Tonle Sap is the biggest freshwater lake in Southeast Asia. Its unique annual cycle of flood expansion and retreat dictates Cambodia's rice production and supplies of fish. During the rainy season, the Mekong River backs into the Tonle Sap River, pushing waters into the lake, which quadruples in size. In the dry season as the Mekong lowers, and the Tonle Sap River reverses its direction, draining the lake. Boats make the river journey to the lake from Phnom Penh and Battambang, tying up at Chong Khneas, 12 km (7½ mi) south of Siem Reap. Two-hour tours of the lake, costing $6, set off from Chong Khneas.

Between Chong Khneas and Battambang is the **Prek Toal Biosphere Reserve,** which is mainland Southeast Asia's most important waterbird nesting site. It's a spectacular scene if you visit at the start of the dry season when water remains high and thousands of rare birds begin to nest. Visits can be booked through **oSmoSe Conservation Ecotourism Education** (✉ 0552, Group 12, Wat Bo Village, Siem Reap ☎ 012/832812 ⊕ http://jinja.apsara.org/osmose). Day tours and overnight stays at the Prek Toal Research Station can be arranged. Prices vary.

Kulen Mountain
50 km (31 mi) north of Siem Reap.

King Jayavarman II established this mountain retreat 50 km (31 mi) northeast of Siem Reap in AD 802, the year regarded as the start of the Angkor dynasty. The area is strewn with the ruins of Khmer temples from that time. The mountain was revered as holy, with a hallowed river and a waterfall. Admission to the area costs $20, and is not included in the ticket price to the Angkor Temple Complex.

Angkor Temple Complex

17 *6 km (4 mi) north of Siem Reap.*

Fodor'sChoice
★

The Khmer empire reached the zenith of its power, influence, and creativity from the 9th to the 13th century, when Angkor, the seat of the Khmer kings, was one of the largest capitals in Southeast Asia. Starting in the 15th century, the temples of Angkor's heyday were abandoned until their "discovery" in the early 1860s by French naturalist Henri Mouhot (the Cambodians living there sure knew about them). In all there are some 300 monuments reflecting Hindu and Buddhist influence scattered throughout the jungle, but only the largest have been excavated and only a few of those reconstructed. Most of these lie within a few miles of each other and can be seen in one day, though two or three days will allow you to better appreciate them.

Although the centuries have taken their toll on the temples—some of which still hide their beauty beneath a tangle of undergrowth—they miraculously survived the ravages of the Khmer Rouge years. Many of the monks living in the temples at this time were massacred, however. The Khmer Rouge mined the area, but the mines have been removed, and the temples are now perfectly safe to visit.

Most people visit the temples of Bayon and Baphuon, which face east, in the morning—the earlier you arrive, the better the light and the smaller the crowd—and west-facing Angkor Wat in the late afternoon, though this most famous of the temples can also be a stunning sight at sunrise. The woodland-surrounded Ta Prohm can be visited any time, though it is best photographed when cloudy, whereas the distant Banteay Srei is prettiest in the late-afternoon light.

Phnom Bakheng
One of the oldest Angkor structures, dating to the 9th century, the hilltop Bakheng temple was built in the center of the first royal city site, dedicated to the Hindu god Shiva. The temple, which resembles a five-

Hiring an Angkor Guide

A GUIDE CAN GREATLY ENRICH YOUR APPRECIATION of Angkor's temples, which are full of details you might miss on your own. Guides can be hired through the tourism office on Pokambor Avenue, across from the Raffles Grand Hotel d'Angkor; the office offers a list of guides who speak a variety of languages. But the best way to find a guide is through your hotel or guesthouse. Ask around. Most guides who work for tour companies (and the tourism office) are freelancers, and often when you book through a tour company, you'll pay a higher price. Find a young staffer at your hotel or guesthouse and tell him or her what you want— the type of tour, what you hope to learn from your guide, your particular interests in the temples.

Prices usually run around $20 a day, not including transportation, for a very well-informed guide fluent in your native language. That said, if you still feel more comfortable booking through a travel company, **Hanuman Tourism Voyages** (⌧ 12 St. 310, Sangkat Tonle Bassac, Phnom Penh ☎ 023/218356 or 012/807657) is an excellent choice. The company, which works throughout Indochina, has established a foundation to help eradicate poverty in Cambodia's hinterlands. Your tourist dollars will go toward wells, water filters, mosquito nets, and other items that can greatly improve a rural family's life. Neak Krorhorm Travel (⌧ 127 St. 108, Phnom Penh ☎ 023/219496) also arranges Angkor guides.

---

tiered pyramid, was constructed from rock hewn from the hill and faced with sandstone. Phnom Bakheng is perhaps the most popular sunset destination for Angkor visitors, as the view from the top affords a fine look at Angkor Wat and the surrounding area. Climb the stairs or take an elephant ride up.

Angkor Thom

Angkor Thom was a city in its own right, the last Angkorean capital, built by King Jayavarman VII in the late 12th century. At the height of Angkor Thom's prosperity in the 12th and 13th centuries, more than 1 million people lived within its walls, and it was the richest city in Southeast Asia. The Siamese destroyed the city in the 15th century, and it became an insignificant ghost town. The south gate, towering 65 feet and crowned by four characteristic Bodhisattva faces, is so monumental it appears to dominate the entire area.

A defensive wall and moat, 3 km long by 3 km wide (2 mi by 2 mi), surrounded the city, which was entered via bridges lined with massive stone guardians holding a mystical serpent. At its geographic center stands the 12th-century **Bayon**, a large, ornate Buddhist structure that rises into 54 small towers, most of which are topped with huge, strangely smiling faces. On the outer walls of the central sanctuary, and on some of the inner walls, are 1½ km (1 mi) of marvelous bas-relief murals depicting historic sea battles, scenes from daily life, and gods and mythical creatures performing legendary deeds.

CLOSE UP

The Angkor Circuits

There are stories of visitors who arrive in Siem Reap with the intention of seeing Angkor Wat, only to leave soon after in dismay after discovering that the wat is just one of many temples in an area covering several square miles.

Forget any idea of strolling casually from temple to temple—even a bicycle tour of the vast site is exhausting. There are two recommended circuits to gain an overview of the temples, the shortest 17 km (11 mi) and the longest 26 km (16 mi). If you have just one day, stick to the short circuit, which takes in Phnom Bakheng, the south gate of Angkor Thom, Bayon, Baphuon, the Elephant Terrace and the Terrace of the Leper King, and Ta Prohm, and ends with a visit to Angkor Wat itself to catch the sunset. If you have two days, take the longer route—do the shorter circuit on the first day, then tackle Preah Khan, Neak Pean, East Mebon, and Pre Rup (at sunset) on Day 2.

Just to the north of the Bayon is the slightly older **Baphuon,** built in the mid-11th century by King Udayadityavarman II (a small settlement was here before King Jayavarman VII built up the area in the late 12th century). A fine example of poor planning, the temple was erected on a hill without proper supports, so that when the earth shifted in the 16th century, it collapsed. Originally the temple was a Shiva sanctuary crowned with a copper-covered cupola. A magnificent reclining Buddha was added to the three-tiered temple pyramid in the 16th century. ■ TIP→ **The temple is undergoing reconstruction and is not open to the public; however, the exterior gate and elevated walkway are open.**

Elephant Terrace & the Terrace of the Leper King
Built at the end of the 12th century by King Jayavarman VII, the ornamental Elephant Terrace once formed the foundation of the royal audience hall. The gilded wooden palace that once stood here has long since disappeared. Stone-carved elephants and *garuda,* or giant eagle-people, adorn the 6½-foot-tall wall of the terrace, which abuts an empty field where troops used to parade before the Khmer monarchs. At the north end of the Elephant Terrace is the Terrace of the Leper King, named after a stone statue found here (and now housed in the National Museum). Precisely who the Leper King was and why he was so named remains uncertain, though several legends offer speculation.

Ta Prohm
Built in 1186 by the prolific King Jayavarman VII to honor his mother, Ta Prohm is a large Buddhist monastery of five enclosures that has been only partially restored. The eerie temple looks as it more or less did when Western adventurers and explorers rediscovered Angkor in the 19th century; many buildings have been reduced to piles of stone blocks, and giant tropical fig and silk-cotton trees grow on top of the walls. Stone inscriptions reveal that the complex originally had 566 stone dwellings, including 39 major sanctuaries, and was attended by 13 high priests,

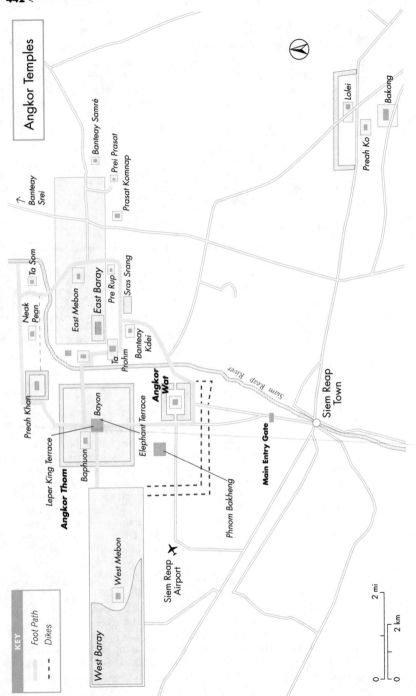

Angkor Temples

Banteay Srei

Banteay Samré

Prei Prasat

Prasat Kommap

Ta Som

Neak Pean

East Mebon

East Baray

Pre Rup

Sras Srang

Ta Prohm

Banteay Kdei

Preah Khan

Leper King Terrace

Bayon

Angkor Thom

Baphuon

Elephant Terrace

Angkor Wat

West Baray

West Mebon

Phnom Bakheng

Siem Reap Airport

Siem Reap River

Main Entry Gate

Siem Reap Town

Preah Ko

Lolei

Bakong

KEY

Foot Path

Dikes

2 mi

2 km

0

0

2,740 officials, 2,202 assistants, and 615 dancers, who were supported by 3,140 villages. Today you're likely to share it with a couple of hundred camera-toting tourists. Still, it's a gorgeous, magical spot, with thick knotted tree roots sprawled over half-tumbled walls, and flocks of parrots squawking in the branches high above.

Angkor Wat

The most impressive and best preserved of the Khmer temples is the one that gave the whole complex its name: Angkor Wat, the beautiful apotheosis of Khmer architecture, and the world's largest religious monument. It was built at the beginning of the 12th century by King Suryavarman II (reigned 1112–52), who dedicated it to the Hindu god Vishnu, making sure that its dimen-

> ### ANGKOR ESSENTIALS
>
> Admission to the complex, which opens from 5 AM to 6 PM, costs $20 for one day, $40 for three days, and $60 for a week. Bring a passport photo—you'll need one for your entrance ticket. Transport is a necessity, and most independent travelers hire a car and driver ($20–$25 per day) or tuk-tuk ($8–$12 per day), though bicycles ($3–$4 per day) and electric bicycles are available for those who can stand the heat and effort. (The latter have caused a bit of a ruckus lately among tuk-tuk drivers: So many tourists are opting for electric bikes that it's taking business away from the local drivers.)

sions were suitably grand for the divine patron. Those dimensions are staggering: the temple compound covers an area of 4,920 feet by 4,265 feet. The surrounding moat is 590 feet wide. A causeway leading to the huge western entrance is flanked by balustrades of giant serpents believed to represent cosmic fertility.

The centerpiece of the complex is the giant lotus bud formed by the five familiar beehivelike towers, which alone took 30 years to complete. Three of the towers appear in the white silhouette of Angkor Wat that is the central emblem of the Cambodian national flag, signifying the triple motto of nation, religion, and king.

Like all the other major monuments at Angkor, the 215-foot-high complex represents the Hindu/Buddhist universe. The central shrines symbolize Mt. Meru, the mythical home of the Hindu gods, and the moats represent the seven oceans that surround Mt. Meru. The three-tiered central pyramid itself rises in four concentric enclosures opening to the west, with terraces decorated with images of Hindu deities, many of which have lost their heads to looters. More impressive than the statues, towers, and the sheer size of the temple is the extensive bas-relief work that covers its walls, especially the scenes on its outer front wall depicting epic battles of Hindu mythology, an audience given by the king, and the creation of the world. On top of that, there are nearly 2,000 apsara—celestial female dancers—scattered throughout the temple complex. Two libraries flank the ancient Hindu temple.

Preah Khan

This former royal retreat was built in 1191 by King Jayavarman VII for his father, but it later became a Buddhist institution with more than 1,000 monks. The moated temple, near the north gate of Angkor Thom, is similar to Ta Prohm, but has only four enclosures. The temple houses a hall decorated with a bas-relief of heavenly apsara dancers, a two-story columnar building to keep the "sacred sword" (an important part of the royal regalia) of the kingdom, and a large lingam, or phallic symbol, representing Shiva. In the eastern part of the complex is a *baray,* one of the five huge reservoirs built to supply the growing Angkor Thom and irrigate its fields and plantations. The water was channeled from the Tonle Sap lake in an amazing feat of engineering.

Neak Pean

Sitting on an island in the middle of one of Angkor's barays, or water reservoirs, the temple of Neak Pean ("entwined serpent") is one of King Jayavarman VII's most unusual creations. He intended to create his own version of the sacred lake Anavatapta in the Himalayas, venerated for its powers of healing. From a large square reservoir, gargoyles channel water into four smaller square basin sanctuaries. The temple's central tower is dedicated to the Bodhisattva Avalokitesvara, depicted riding the fabulous horse Balaha along with people escaping a disastrous pestilence and seeking the healing waters of Anavatapta.

East Mebon

The temple of East Mebon was built on a baray island by King Rajendravarman in the 10th century and now sits high and dry in the empty reservoir known as the Eastern Baray. The pyramid-shaped temple, dedicated to Shiva, has all the characteristics of the temple mount construction so favored by the Khmer kings: in brick and laterite, with a 10-foot-high platform carrying five imposing towers arranged in a quincunx (one at each corner and one in the center of the ensemble). The sandstone lintels have been superbly carved and preserved, and monolithic elephants stand at the four corners of each enclosure.

Pre Rup

This grander version of the East Mebon temple is thought to have once been the center of the royal city of King Rajendravarman, who ordered its construction in 961. The five upper brick towers are adorned with fine stucco moldings. From the top of the highest platform there are sweeping views of the palm-studded countryside. If you want to avoid the crowds that gather at Angkor Wat and Phnom Bakheng at sunset but you still want a good view, this is the place to come.

Banteay Srei

★ If you have the time, extend your tour of Angkor to include the Banteay Srei (Citadel of Women), 38 km (24 mi) northeast of Siem Reap. The temple resembles a small fortress and it's dedicated to the Hindu goddess Sri (the Khmer version of this name was Srei, meaning "women"). This small but magnificent 10th-century temple contains fine sculptures of pink sandstone illustrating scenes from the Indian Reamker legend and gods and goddesses of the Hindu pantheon; they're surprisingly well preserved, having survived the war years. The temple achieved fame when the former French government minister and noted author and philosopher Andre Malraux was accused of plundering it during reconstruction work in the 1930s. ⚠ Admission is included in the Angkor ticket, but a tuk-tuk driver may charge an extra $20 to get here. The temple closes at 5 PM.

Roluos Temples

About 12 km (7½ mi) east of Siem Reap on Highway 6 is a group of three temples—**Preah Ko, Bakong,** and **Lolei**—all built in the 9th century, the formative period of the Khmer empire. The capital at that time was called Hariharalaya, when the two gods Shiva and Vishnu were both venerated; the temples were erected in their honor. A large water reservoir was fed from the Tonle Sap lake, via the Roluos River, and Lolei was then on an island. Admission to the site is included in the Angkor ticket.

Siem Reap & Angkor Temple Complex Essentials

Transportation

BY AIR

Bangkok Airways flies six times daily between Siem Reap and Bangkok. The flight takes about an hour and costs about $250 round-trip. Lao Air flies three times a week to Siem Reap from both Pakse and Vientiane. PMT, Royal Khmer Airlines, and Siem Reap Airways all fly between Phnom Penh and Siem Reap. Expect to pay about $80 one way, though prices can vary greatly. Siem Reap Airways has a few flights between Siem Reap and Luang Prabang in Laos.

AIRPORTS & TRANSFERS Siem Reap International Airport is 6 km (4 mi) northwest of town. The taxi fare to any hotel in Siem Reap is $5.

🏠 Carriers **Bangkok Airways** ☎ 023/722545 ⊕ www.bangkokair.com. **Lao Airlines** ☎ 023/216563 ⊕ www.laoairlines.com. **PMT Air** ☎ 063/760942 ⊕ www.pmtair.com. **Royal Khmer Airlines** ☎ 023/994502 ⊕ www.royalkhmerairlines.com. **Siem Reap Airways** ☎ 023/720022 ⊕ www.siemreapairways.com.

BY BOAT

The road to Phnom Penh was upgraded several years ago, but some tourists still prefer to try the six-hour boat trip on the Tonle Sap (the fare is about $20–$25). Several high-speed ferries depart Phnom Penh from the municipal port on Sisowath Quay, at Street 84, early in the morning. Three-day luxury riverboats are also available from Compagnie Fluviale du Mekong. The ferry port is at Chong Khneas, 12 km (7½ mi) south of Siem Reap.

🏠 **Compagnie Fluviale du Mekong** ✉ 30 St. 240, Phnom Penh ☎ 023/216070 ⊕ www.cfmekong.com.

Phnom Penh port operators ☎ 012/932328.

BY BUS

Buses from Phnom Penh to Siem Reap take about five hours via Skun and Kampong Thom on Highway 6. The fare is $4–$9, depending on which company you use. Regular long-distance bus service links Bangkok and Siem Reap via Sisaphon and Poipet. Neak Krorhorm Travel in Siem Reap can help you arrange bus trips.

🏠 **GST Bus** ✉ Central Bus Station, Phnom Penh ☎ 012/895550.

Mekong Express ✉ 87E0 Sisowath Quay, Phnom Penh ☎ 023/427518 or 012/787839.

Neak Krorhorm Travel ✉ 127 St. 108, Phnom Penh ☎ 023/219496.

BY CAR

The road to Siem Reap from Phnom Penh has greatly improved in recent years—which means it's even more dangerous than in the past. When they build a smooth road, fast drivers take full advantage of it. Cambodia's highway accident rate is atrocious, which is a good reason to take a bus rather than a taxi. Besides that, a bus (especially a Mekong Express bus) is much more comfortable than a shared taxi with a dozen other people, all their belongings, pets, motos, TVs, bicycles and anything else that fits. From Siem Reap, Highway 6 heads west out of town to Thailand. The road is often rough, especially in the rainy season.

BY MOTO & TUK-TUK

The number of tourists visiting Siem Reap has grown in recent years, but tuk-tuk and moto drivers have kept apace. They'll find you; you won't need to find them. They cost about $1–$2 for a trip within town, but be sure to settle on the fare before setting off. There are no cruising taxis, but hotels can order one.

Contacts & Resources

BANKS & EXCHANGING SERVICES

As in Phnom Penh, ATMs are dotted throughout Siem Reap now. ANZ is the most popular bank among travelers.

EMERGENCIES

Siem Reap has a few international clinics these days, and the Angkor Hospital for Children can provide some services to those in need. If a real emergency arises, transport to Bangkok is the best option.
🎬 Hospitals **Angkor Hospital for Children** ☎ 063/963409. **Jin Hua international Hospital** ✉ Airport Rd. ☎ 063/963299. **Ly Srey Vyna Clinic** ✉ Airport Rd. ☎ 063/965088. **Naga International Clinic** ✉ Airport Rd. ☎ 063/964500.

SIGHTSEEING TOURS

It's well worth spinning through the countryside around Siem Reap to get a feel for the way Cambodian farmers and fishermen live. Take a day to tour some of the out-lying temples, some of which are still covered by jungle growth; others are incorporated into village life. Naturalists won't be sorry with a trip to Prek Toal, to see the birdlife there. But timing is crucial: November or December is the best time to go, when the water level is high and the birds are nesting. If you prefer to stay closer to shore, shorter boat trips from Chong Khneas will take you to floating villages in the area. Most any guesthouse can arrange such trips, and tuk-tuk drivers can get you to your jumping-off point. For more structured itineraries, contact one of the travel companies listed below.
🎬 **Hanuman Tourism Voyages** ✉ 12 St. 310, Sangkat Tonle Bassac, Phnom Penh ☎ 023/218356 or 012/807657. **oSmoSe Conservation Ecotourism Education** ✉ 0552, Group 12, Wat Bo Village, Siem Reap ☎ 012/832812 ⊕ http://jinja.apsara.org/osmose.

SIHANOUKVILLE & SOUTHERN CAMBODIA

The beaches of Sihanoukville are quickly becoming a top Cambodian tourist destination (after Angkor, of course). Much of the country's stunning coastal areas remain relatively undiscovered, a natural draw for those who tire of the crowds on neighboring Thai islands. Sihanoukville lies some 230 km (143 mi) southwest of Phnom Penh, a four-hour bus ride from the capital.

The Road to the Coast

The four-hour bus journey from Phnom Penh to Sihanoukville along Highway 4—the only fully sealed, fully functional highway in the country—is an interesting one, winding through uplands, rice paddies, and orchards. Once you drive past Phnom Penh's Pochentong Airport and the prestigious Cambodia Golf & Country Club, and on through the area of Kompong Speu, the landscape turns rural, dotted with small villages where a major source of income seems to be the sale of firewood and charcoal. Somewhere around the entrance to Kirirom National Park all buses stop for refreshments at a roadside restaurant.

The halfway point of the journey lies at the top of the **Pich Nil mountain pass,** guarded by dozens of colorful spirit houses. These spirit houses were built for the legendary deity Yeah Mao, guardian of Sihanoukville and the coastal region. Legend has it that Yeah Mao was the wife of a village headman who worked in far-off Koh Kong, an island near today's border with Thailand. On a journey to visit him, Yeah Mao died when the boat transporting her sank in a storm—an all-too-believable story to anyone who has taken the boat from Sihanoukville to Koh Kong. Her spirit became the guardian of local villagers and fisherfolk.

At the small town of Chamcar Luang, a side road leads to the renowned smuggling port of Sre Ambel. The main highway threads along Ream National Park, with the **Elephant Mountains** as a backdrop. The sprawling Angkor Beer brewery heralds the outskirts of Sihanoukville and the journey's end.

Sihanoukville

⓲ *230 km (143 mi) southwest of Phnom Penh.*

A half a century ago, Cambodia's main port city, Sihanoukville, was a sleepy backwater called Kampong Som. Then, a series of world-shattering events overtook it and gave rise to the busy industrial center and coastal resort now prominent on every tourist map.

The French laid the foundations of Kampong Som back in the mid-1950s, before they lost control of the Mekong Delta and its ports following their retreat after the French-Indochina War. The town was renamed Sihanoukville in honor of the then king. A decade later, Sihanoukville received a further boost when it became an important transit post for weapons destined for American forces fighting in the Vietnam War. In

CLOSE UP

Khmer: A Few Key Phrases

A KNOWLEDGE OF FRENCH may get you somewhere in francophone Cambodia, but these days it's far easier to find English speakers. The Cambodian language, Khmer, belongs to the Mon-Khmer family of languages, enriched by Indian Pali and Sanskrit vocabulary. It has many similarities to Thai and Lao, a reminder of their years as vassal lands in the Khmer empire.

The following are some useful words and phrases:

Hello: joom reap soo-uh

Thank you: aw-koun

Yes: bah (male speaker), jah (female speaker)

No: aw-te

Excuse me: som-toh

Where?: ai nah?

How much?: t'lay pohn mahn?

Never mind: mun ay dtay

Zero: sohn

One: muay

Two: bpee

Three: bay

Four: buon

Five: bpram

Six: bpram muay

Seven: bpram pull

Eight: bpram bay

Nine: bpram buon

Ten: dop

Eleven: dop muay

Hundred: muay roi

Thousand: muay poan

Food: m'hohp

Water: dteuk

Expensive: t'lay nah

Morning: bprek

Night: youp

Today: tngay nee

Tomorrow: tngay sa-ik

Yesterday: mus'el mun

Bus: laan ch'nual

Ferry: salang

Village: pum

Island: koh

River: tonle

Doctor: bpet

Hospital: moonty bpet

Bank: tia-nia-kia

Post Office: praisinee

Toilet: baan tawp tdeuk

the mid-1970s, Sihanoukville itself came under American attack and suffered heavy casualties after Khmer Rouge forces captured the SS *Mayaguez,* a U.S. container ship.

Today Sihanoukville presents a relatively peaceful face to the world as Cambodia's seaside playground. It has seven primary tourist beaches, all easily accessible from downtown by motorbike taxi or even a rented bicycle. **Victory Beach** is named after the Vietnamese victory over the Khmer Rouge regime in 1979. The beach itself has a few hotels to offer, but the popular spot (for backpackers, especially) sits on a hill overlooking the beach. Known as Victory Hill, or Weather Station Hill, this area has grown from a small Khmer neighborhood 10 years ago to a bustling sprawl of guesthouses, cafés, pubs, and music dens, much like those in neighboring Thai islands.

Hawaii Beach, where the foundations of Sihanoukville were dug in the early 1950s, almost meets the promise of its name. It has one of Sihanoukville's longtime favorite seafood restaurants, the Hawaii Sea View Restaurant. Though accommodation on Hawaii Beach is not yet available, check back in the near future. Several construction sites were in the works at this writing.

Many locals prefer **Independence Beach,** also known as 7-Chann Beach, and on weekends and holidays its long narrow stretch of sand can get crowded. The beach is backed by a neglected little park, where vendors set up food and drink stalls. ■ TIP→ The historical Independence Hotel, for years abandoned during Cambodia's civil war, was under renovation at this writing. Check back: if and when it opens, its seven-story gleaming white presence on the Independence Hill is sure to be the attraction for miles around.

Some of the best swimming can be enjoyed at **Sokha Beach,** site of Cambodia's first international-class beach resort, the Sokha Beach Resort (owned and operated by the Cambodian oil giant, Sokimex Group). Budget beachcombers favor **Ochheuteal Beach** and neighboring **Serendipity Beach,** both of which offer inexpensive bungalows, in-the-sand dining, and plenty of activities for the young-at-heart.

The Sihanoukville coast is flanked by several islands (many untouristed and lightly populated by Khmer fishermen) accessible by boat. **Koh Rong Samlem, Koh Tas,** and **Koh Russei** are popular day-trip destinations for snorkeling and picnicking. ■ TIP→ Local guides also can arrange overnight stays in rustic bungalows on some of these islands.

Where to Stay & Eat

The most inexpensive guesthouses, restaurants, and other tourist services are on Victory (Weather Station) Hill, Serendipity Beach, and Ochheuteal Beach. Some of the lodgings in these areas are quite attractive, and a few restaurant gems sit amid the masses.

$$–$$$$ ╳ **Hawaii Sea View Restaurant.** You can practically dangle your feet in the surf as you tuck into giant prawns and crabs at this beach restaurant. The sunset alone is reason enough to grab a table, which the staff will set up for you right on the beach. ⊠ *Hawaii Beach* ☎ *012/513008* ▭ *MC, V.*

$–$$$ ╳ **La Paillote.** Tucked away in the sprawl of Weather Station Hill is this elegant open-air restaurant whose chef hails from Madagascar. La Paillote serves foie gras and a number of dishes employing distinctly European and imported ingredients; the accompanying wine list is good. ⊠ *Victory (Weather Station) Hill, between Papagayo and MASH* ☎ *012/ 633247* ▭ *No credit cards.*

¢ ╳ **Starfish Bakery & Café.** Proceeds from this delightful little garden café go toward the Starfish Project, which supports individuals and families in need. Try a shake or brownie, indulge in a massage, and learn about volunteering opportunities in Sihanoukville. The café has Internet access and a handicrafts shop upstairs. It's not the easiest of places to find—it's hidden down a dirt road behind the Samudera Market in town—but it's well worth the trek. It's open from 7 AM to 5 PM. ⊠ *On unmarked road off 7 Makara St.* ☏ *012/952011* ▤ *No credit cards.*

$$$ 🖫 **Sokha Beach Resort.** This is the top address in Sihanoukville, a first-class resort hotel with all the facilities required for a fun-filled beach holiday. The resort takes up 6 acres of landscaped gardens that lead directly to the beach. Rooms have tiled floors, wood and rattan furniture, and French doors leading to small balconies overlooking the pool and the beach. A playground and a special kid's menu at one of the restaurants makes this place family-friendly. ⊠ *Sokha Beach* ☏ *034/935999* ⊕ *www.sokhahotels.com* ⟿ *188 rooms* ◔ *In-room: safe, refrigerator. In-hotel: 2 restaurants, room service, 2 bars, 2 tennis courts, pool, gym, spa, beachfront, diving, water sports, laundry service, public Internet* ▤ *AE, MC, V* ⦿ *BP.*

$ 🖫 **House of Malibu.** Sihanoukville hotels don't get much more secluded than this. Perched on a hillside overlooking the rocky coastline of Serendipity and Sokha beaches are a handful of tastefully designed bungalows, accessible by a dirt road. Malibu sits away from the (growing) Serendipity crowd of budget accommodations. Each wood-and-thatch bungalow offers a private porch with views of the sea. A small sunbathing deck awaits you, right on the edge of the water. ⊠ *Group 14, Mondol 4, Sangkat 4, Khan Mitteapheap* ☏ *012/733334 or 016/770277* ◔ *In-room: no a/c (some), safe, refrigerator. In-hotel: restaurant, bar, laundry service* ▤ *No credit cards.*

$ 🖫 **New Beach Hotel.** This modern three-story concrete hotel offers basic, clean rooms that overlook the rocky shoreline of Victory Beach. Some rooms have fine views of the ships entering and exiting Sihanoukville Port. Deluxe rooms have Internet access. ⊠ *Victory Beach, opposite Customs office* ☏ *034/933822* ⊕ *www.newbeachhotel.com* ⟿ *38 rooms* ◔ *In-room: refrigerator. In-hotel: restaurant, public Internet* ▤ *No credit cards.*

¢–$ 🖫 **Orchidee Guesthouse.** This brick-and-stucco lodging is one of Sihanoukville's oldest and consistently popular choices. To keep up with the times it has recently added a pool and rooms with balconies in a new wing. It's one block, or an easy five-minute walk, from the beach. Rooms are perfectly clean; those in the new wing feature a bit of artwork. The small shrub-enclosed patio is pleasant, particularly in the evening. ⊠ *Ochheuteal Beach, 23 Tola St.* ☏ *016/867764 or 034/933639* ⊕ *www.orchidee-guesthouse.com* ⟿ *44 rooms* ◔ *In-room: refrigerator. In-hotel: restaurant, bar* ▤ *No credit cards.*

¢–$ 🖫 **Queen's Hill Resort.** If you're looking for a bungalow at an even better price than the House of Malibu, stay here. High on the hill between Ochheuteal and Otres beaches, the Queen's Hill Resort offers spectacular views and the chance to sleep to the sound of waves crashing below. Basic wooden bungalows with fans and mosquito nets have up to three beds each. Dine in solitude with your feet in the sand at the resort's restaurant on Otres Beach—for now, it's about the only thing on that beach. Note that the showers are cold water only. ✛ *Follow*

Ochheuteal Beach St. south over the small bridge and up the hill ☎ 011/ *937373* ⊕ *www.cambodia-beach.com* ⤳ *18 bungalows* ⌂ *In-room: no a/c. In-hotel: restaurant, bar* ▭ *No credit cards.*

¢ ⬚ **Small Hotel.** If you're looking for a budget hotel in Sihanoukville town that doesn't cater to bar girls and their clientele, this is it. Not only is the Small Hotel clean. It's also conveniently close to the bus station. A portion of your payment will go toward the nonprofit children's organization sponsored by the hotel's Swedish owner. ⊠ *Behind the Caltex station off Sopheakmongkol St.* ☎ 012/487888 or 016/567778 ⤳ *thesmallhotel@yahoo.com* ⌂ *In-room: no a/c (some), refrigerator. In-hotel: restaurant, bar, laundry service* ▭ *No credit cards.*

Sports & the Outdoors

Most hotels and guesthouses arrange boat trips, which include packed lunches, to the many offshore islands. Several companies offer diving and snorkeling; two of the most popular dive centers are: **EcoSea Dive** (⊠ Ekareach St. ☎ 012/654104 ⊕ www.ecosea.com), and Cambodia's first certified PADI dive center, **Scuba Nation Diving Center** (⊠ Weather Station Hill ☎ 012/715785 ⊕ www.divecambodia.com).

Kampot

⓳ *110 km (68 mi) east of Sihanoukville, 150 km (93 mi) south of Phnom Penh.*

This attractive riverside town at the foot of the Elephant Mountain range, not far from the sea, is known for its French colonial architecture remnants—and for salt and pepper. In the dry season, laborers can be seen along the highway to Kep, working long hours in the salt fields; pepper plantations are scattered around the province. Kampot is the departure point for trips to the seaside resort of Kep and Bokor Hill Station. The coastal road from Sihanoukville to Kampot is somewhat rough, but has spectacular views. To get here, take a taxi, or hire a car and driver through your hotel. Several spectacular limestone caves speckle the landscape from Kampot to Kep to the Vietnam border. Plan at least a morning or afternoon excursion to see the cave at Phnom Chhnork, which shelters a pre-Angkor-era ruin. You can arrange transport through any hotel or just ask a taxi or moto driver to take you.

35 kilometers (22 mi) west of Kampot is **Bokor Hill Station,** an early-20th-century, French-built retreat from the heat and humidity of the coast. It's now a collection of ruins, but it's worth visiting for the spectacular sea views from its 3,000-foot heights. Travel here is extremely rough in the rainy season.

Where to Stay & Eat

¢–$ ✕**Phnom Kamchay Thmey.** Cambodia's best seafood is found at local joints like this. The decor consists of plastic chairs and fluorescent lighting, but the beer is cold, the room is bright, the menu's extensive, and the food is delectable. Try the crab curry. ⊠ *Riverfront St.* ☎ *No phone* ▭ *No credit cards.*

¢–$ ✕ **Rusty Keyhole.** This is a great spot to watch the sunset as rush hour (three squeaky bikes, a stray dog, and a compact car) hits Kampot's riverfront street. The place has happy-hour specials, and serves standard pub food and nightly barbecues. ⊠ *Riverfront St.* ☎ *012/679607* ⊟ *No credit cards.*

¢ ✕ **Epic Arts Cafe.** Order a strong cup of Lao coffee, a banana cinnamon milk shake, or a slice of cake at this pleasant little nonprofit café on the edge of the Kampot lawn. ⊠ *Across from the abandoned market* ☎ *011/ 376968* ⊕ *www.epicarts.org.uk* ⊟ *No credit cards* ☽ *No dinner.*

¢ ▦ **Blissful Guesthouse.** This foreign-run guesthouse is cheap and friendly. The remodeled, two-story house has basic fan-cooled rooms (some with attached bathrooms), a pleasant garden, and a "chill out" TV room where you can trade tales with other travelers. The bar is popular and has great music. ⊠ *Across from Orchid Guesthouse, near Acleda Bank* ☎ *012/ 513024* ✎ *blissfulguesthouse@yahoo.com* ⚒ *In-room: no a/c. In-hotel: restaurant, bar* ⊟ *No credit cards.*

¢ ▦ **Bokor Mountain Lodge.** In a beautifully restored colonial building on the riverfront, this lodge offers a handful of rooms and a good view. ⊠ *Riverfront Rd. near the Rusty Keyhole* ☎ *033/932314* ⊕ *www. bokorlodge.com* ☞ *5 rooms* ⚒ *In-room: Wi-Fi. In-hotel: restaurant, bar, laundry facilities* ⊟ *No credit cards.*

¢ ▦ **Orchid Guesthouse.** This quiet but quaint little guesthouse on a neighborhood street offers bungalows and a patio in a pleasant garden setting. The staff is very friendly. ⊠ *Across from Acleda Bank and Blissful Guesthouse* ☎ *092/226996* ✎ *orchidguesthousekampot@yahoo.com* ⚒ *In-room: no a/c (some). In-hotel: restaurant, bar, bicycles* ⊟ *No credit cards.*

Kep

㉚ *25 km (mi) east of Kampot; 172 km (mi) south of Phnom Penh.*

You'll never find another seaside getaway quite like Kep. Twenty-five kilometers (16 mi) east of Kampot is this narrow pebble beach bordered by the ghostly villa ruins of the Khmer Rouge era. What once was the coastal playground of Cambodia's elite was destroyed in decades of war. Squatters have taken up residence in the old mansions, and ever so slowly investors are refurbishing what's salvageable. Someday soon, Kep will again bustle with activity—it's already the home of the most expensive hotel in the country. But first, Kep needs the basics, like electricity—if you see an electric light, it's powered by a car battery or a generator. Don't let the mention of squatters scare you away; Kep is not dangerous. When you arrive, moto drivers and tour guides are sure to find you. Not much traffic comes through Kep, so the locals know the bus schedule. They're sure to offer you a tour of the nearby pepper plantation. Take up the offer. Kep grows some of the world's best.

The beach in town is small but sandy. Offshore, **Rabbit Island** is an idyllic spot with nothing but a few huts, a few fishermen, and a few seaweed farmers in residence. You can hire a boat to take you there for $10. Sit in one of the beachside salas to enjoy the afternoon, or take a walk around the island. Hurry, though—a Vietnamese casino is planned for the island, and soon its calm will be lost forever.

Where to Stay & Eat

¢ ✗ **Thmor Da.** Situated in Kep's seafood market, this little restaurant in a string of several offers superb crab stir-frys and curries, shrimp with Kampot pepper, and a long list of other delectable options. Thmor Da has some of the cheapest, tastiest seafood you'll ever eat and a great waterfront location. ⊠ *Riverfront St.* ☎ *No phone* ▭ *No credit cards.*

¢ ✗▦ **Kep Seaside Guesthouse.** Rooms are very basic—fan-cooled and cold water only—at this hotel, but its waterfront location is hard to beat. All rooms have balconies. Enjoy a meal in one of the seaside cabanas, which offer some of Kep's best views—and some of its best seafood, too. The staff is exceptionally friendly. ✛ *Next to Knai Bang Chatt, not far from the seaside seafood market* ☎ *012/858571* ✎ *sengbunly@bnckh. com* ↩ *20 rooms* ⚸ *In-room: no a/c, no phone, no TV. In-hotel: restaurant* ▭ *No credit cards.*

$$$$
Fodor'sChoice
★
▦ **Knai Bang Chatt.** Kep's newest addition raises the bar not only for Kep, but perhaps on the hotel scene throughout Cambodia. This isn't a hotel per se, but a collection of waterfront villas. You can rent one house, all four houses, or just a single room. A two-night minimum stay is required. Pay extra and have the chef provide a daily menu of your choice. You'll also have help arranging trips to a nearby island, scheduling a spiritual visit with monks, or setting up fishing excursions with locals. A permanent staff of 14 and the participation of a host of local venues means that you can arrange anything from a massage to a tai chi class to a lecture on Cambodian history. ⊠ *Phum Thmey Sangkat Prey, Thom Khan Kep* ☎ *012/349742* ⊕ *www.knaibangchatt.com* ↩ *4 houses* ⚸ *In-hotel: pool, gym, laundry service, concierge, airport shuttle* ▭ *No credit cards.*

$ ▦ **Beach House.** A relative newcomer to the Kep scene, this hotel is perched on a hillside overlooking the sea. Rooms are clean and basic and have balconies. ⊠ *On beach road in central Kep* ☎ *012/240090* ⊕ *www. thebeachhousekep.com* ↩ *16 rooms* ⚸ *In-room: no TV. In-hotel: restaurant, bar, pool* ▭ *No credit cards.*

$ ▦ **Champey Inn.** What could easily be called a boutique hotel, the Champey Inn is a laid-back resort with stylish bungalows set in tropical gardens. Rooms are simply but attractively furnished with local dark woods. Power runs on a generator from 5 PM to 7 AM; there is no electricity in the guest rooms during the day. ⊠ *25 Ave. de la Plage* ☎ *012/ 501742* ✎ *champeyinn@mobitel.com.kh* ↩ *12 bungalows* ⚸ *In-hotel: restaurant, bar, pool* ▭ *No credit cards.*

Sihanoukville & Southern Cambodia Essentials

Transportation

BY AIR

The Sihanoukville airport has reopened after a long closure. At this writing, commercial flights between Siem Reap and Sihanoukville hadn't started up again, but were expected to soon.

BY BOAT

A daily ferry runs from Sihanoukville to the island of Koh Kong, near the Thai border. The boat departs Sihanoukville's port's passenger terminal at noon, and the trip takes four hours in good weather. A ticket costs $15, and you can make it across the Thai border before 5 PM to catch a bus via Trat to Bangkok. ⚠ During the stormy weather of the rainy season you may want to give this trip a miss, as the boat tosses madly in the waves for hours.

BY BUS

Air-conditioned buses from Phnom Penh to Sihanoukville run several times daily and take four hours. Buses depart from the Central Market or the Hua Lian station near Olympic Stadium. The journey costs $3. Sihanoukville's bus terminal is one block off Ekareach Street, where crowds of aggressive moto and taxi drivers meet incoming vehicles.

BY CAR

You can hire a private car and driver through your hotel or guesthouse for the trip to the coast from Phnom Penh. The price varies. However, the highway to Sihanoukville is one of the most dangerous in the country. Buses are almost as quick and often safer.

Contacts & Resources

BANKS & EXCHANGING SERVICES

ANZ has an ATM in the center of town on Ekareach Street in Sihanoukville. The Acleda Bank has Western Union services. Canadia Bank and Mekong Bank can advance money against a MasterCard; Union Commercial Bank can advance cash against a Visa card.

EMERGENCIES

🏥 Hospitals **International Peace Clinic** ✉ Ekareach Rd., Sihanoukville ☎ 012/794269. **Sihanouk Public Hospital** ✉ Ekareach Rd., Sihanoukville ☎ 034/93311.

Laos

A young girl bikes near Vang Vienne.

WORD OF MOUTH

"I am really glad that we were able to see Vientiane, even it was a brief visit. A lot of the buildings were somewhat dilapidated— it has the feel of an old colonial city that has seen better times. The layout of the city is very pleasant. I enjoyed walking along the banks of the Mekong in the evening, interacting with the extremely friendly Lao people."

—sallyho

WELCOME TO LAOS

TOP REASONS TO GO

★ **Natural Beauty.** It may not have the sheer variety of Thailand, but Laos is a beautiful country. Take a multiday trek or bike ride, or enjoy the scenic bus ride from Luang Prabang to Vang Vieng.

★ **Archaeological Wonders.** The country's most unusual attraction is the Plain of Jars, which has 5-ton stone-and-clay jars of mysterious origin. Wat Phu, pre-Angkor Khmer ruins, is Laos's most recent world heritage site.

★ **Buddhist Customs.** Observing or participating in morning alms in Luang Prabang is a magical experience; so, too, is sitting in a temple to chat with a novice monk, surrounded by the sounds of chanting and chiming bells.

★ **The Mekong.** The Mekong is the lifeline of Laos. You can travel down the mighty river and stop at one of 4,000 islands for a chance to spot freshwater dolphins.

Plain of Jars

1 **Vientiane & Environs.** Vientiane is a curiosity—more like a small market town than a national capital—but it has some fine temples, many French colonial buildings, and a riverside boulevard unmatched elsewhere in Laos. Vang Vieng, a short bus ride north, has beautiful mountains, waterfalls, and a laid-back, rural vibe.

Monks collecting morning alms.

2 **Luang Prabang & Northern Laos.** Luang Prabang is the country's major tourist destination, thanks to its royal palace (now a museum), temples, French colonial architecture, and the villagelike ambience it's managed to retain and refine. Hill tribes, Buddhist rituals, and Lao textiles are also major draws of the northern part of the country, as are trekking and river-rafting adventures.

3 Southern Laos. Few tourists venture to the far south of the country, but Pakse is an interesting town and a convenient base from which to explore ancient Khmer ruins, such as the fabulous Wat Phu. Fishing villages line the lower reaches of the Mekong River, a water wonderland with islands and countless waterfalls.

Along the Mekong River.

GETTING ORIENTED

Boxed in by China, Myanmar (Burma), Thailand, Cambodia, and Vietnam, Laos is geographically divided into three regions, each with its chief city: northern Laos and Luang Prabang, central Laos and Vientiane, southern Laos and Pakse. About 90% of Laos is mountainous, so once you leave Vientiane, Luang Prabang, and the southern lowlands, you're in true off-the-beaten-track territory. Luang Prabang is the best base for single or multiday trekking, biking, and river-rafting expeditions.

8

LAOS
PLANNER

Getting Around

Most of the country's mountainous terrain is impenetrable jungle, which is cut by rivers and ravines, and the only practical way of touring the country in anything less than a week is by plane. Even the country's main highway, linking Vientiane and Luang Prabang, is a difficult road to travel for much of the way. Fortunately, the national airline, Lao Airlines, runs frequent (and cheap) flights between Vientiane and provincial cities such as Luang Prabang, Savannakhet, and Pakse. There are daily flights to both Vientiane and Luang Prabang from Chiang Mai and Bangkok.

Although it's possible to enter Laos by car or motorbike and drive around on your own, it's not recommended, as driving conditions are difficult: nearly 90% of the country's 14,000 km (8,700 mi) of roads are unpaved, and road signs are often indecipherable. Security checkpoints are frequent on highways, a daunting prospect for foreign drivers. Chauffeur-driven cars can be hired for about $50 a day, and are a much better alternative.

A network of bus services covers almost the entire country. The favorite mode of transportation for most visitors, bus travel is cheap, but slow and not generally comfortable. "VIP" buses connect Vientiane, Luang Prabang, and Pakse, and are somewhat more comfortable than regular buses.

How Much Can You Do?

Most travelers confine their visit to just Vientiane and Luang Prabang, occasionally stopping in Vang Vieng for a day or two. You'll need a day apiece for each city, plus one day for travel between them. You can catch some of the country's highlights in three days, but see at least one week is necessary to really get to know the country. Five days is an absolute minimum if you plan to visit the Plain of Jars and some of the sights around Luang Prabang.

If You Have 5 Days Fly directly to Luang Prabang. Wake up early on Day 1 for morning alms and spend the day visiting the National Museum and several temples; spend the evening shopping at the night market. You can spend the next two days either taking several different day trips around Luang Prabang or embarking on a multiday trekking, biking, or rafting trip. On Day 4 head to Vang Vieng or fly directly to Vientiane for a day before flying out on Day 5.

If You Have 7 Days With seven days you can extend the five-day itinerary to include an extra day or two in Vang Vieng to visit the caves and swimming holes or flying to the Plain of Jars and overnighting in Phonesavanh.

Border Crossings

In addition to the three international airports in Vientiane, Luang Prabang, and Pakse, there are numerous land and river crossings into Laos. The busiest is the Friendship Bridge, which spans the Mekong River 29 km (12 mi) east of Vientiane; it connects to the Thai railhead of Nong Khai. Other border crossings from Thailand to Laos are: Chiang Khong to Huay Xai, in Bokeo Province (by ferry across the Mekong River); Nakhon Phanom to Tha Khek, in Khammuan Province; Mukdahan to Savannakhet, in Savannakhet Province; Chongmek to Vang Tao, in Champasak Province. You can cross into Laos from Cambodia at Voeung Kam, in Champasak Province; and from Boten, in Luang Nam Tha Province, into Mohan, in China's Yunnan Province.

All border crossings are open daily 8:30 AM–5 PM, except for the Friendship Bridge, which is open 6 AM–10 PM.

When to Go

Laos has a tropical climate with two distinct seasons: the dry season from November through April, and the rainy season from May to October. The dry season is cooler, making it the more comfortable time to tour Laos. During the rainy season, the days can get very hot and sticky; July and August register the highest rainfalls. Travel can be slower during the rains, but not impossible, as you often have the option of taking a boat. The country is greener and less crowded during the rains and prices are much lower.

The yearly average temperature is about 82°F (28°C), rising to a maximum of 100°F (38°C) during the rainy season. In many mountainous areas, however, temperatures can drop to 59°F (15°C) in winter; nights in these areas can be chilly, sometimes dropping to the freezing point. The average temperature in Vientiane in January is 66°F (19°C).

Another factor to consider when planning a visit to Laos is the country's busy festival calendar. Most *bun* (festivals) are connected with religion and the rice-farming cycle; they're timed according to the Buddhist lunar calendar. Vientiane and Luang Prabang can get very crowded during these festivals (such as the That Luang Festival in Vientiane in November), so it's advisable to book your hotel room early. Luang Prabang is experiencing a tourism boom, so it's a good idea to always reserve lodgings well in advance.

Boat Travel

Running north–south virtually the entire length of the country, the Mekong River is a natural highway. Because all main cities and virtually all tourist sights lie along the Mekong, boats offer an exotic but practical way to travel. "Express" boats, with noisy outboard motors, and more leisurely "slow" boats ply the river. The most popular water route is between Huay Xai (on the Thai border) and Luang Prabang. More adventurous travelers can board boats in Huay Xai for Xieng Kok in northern Luang Nam Tha Province, or negotiate with barge captains for a passage from Luang Prabang to Vientiane and even farther south. Two luxury vessels ply the Mekong. The *Wat Phu* (⊠ 23 Ban Anou, Haengboun Rd., Chanthaboury, Vientiane ☎ 021/215958 ⊕ www.asian-oasis.com) is moored at Pakse and is run by the Vientiane-based Indocruise Ltd. The *LuangSay* (⊠ Sakkarine Rd., Luang Prabang ☎ 071/252553) makes a twice-weekly run between Luang Prabang and Huay Xai.

Passports & Visas

All visitors to Laos (except for those coming in from some Association of Southeast Asian Nations countries) need a passport and visa. Some travelers obtain their visas at the embassy in Bangkok, but if you fly to Vientiane or Luang Prabang, you can get a visa upon arrival at the airport. Visas cost $30, and must be paid in cash (in U.S. dollars). You must have a passport photo with you. You can also get a visa at the Friendship Bridge in Nong Khai, in Chiang Khong (near Chiang Rai), and in Khon Kaen in northeastern Thailand, though the process can take anywhere from a few hours to a day. The same process takes one to two days in Bangkok, where you can pay a travel agency to do the footwork.

Tourist visas are good for 30 days and can be extended for another 15. Sometimes immigration officials want to see evidence of sufficient funds and an air ticket out of the country. Because the regulations tend to change without warning, it's advisable to check with the Lao embassy in your own country before setting out.

8

Tours & Packages

Tourism professionals in Thailand and Laos have been energetically pushing a joint cooperation program, making it considerably easier for visitors to Thailand to plan a side trip to Laos. Much of the Thai part of this program is based in Chiang Mai. Most travel agents in Chiang Mai can set you up with a tour to Laos for as little as $250 (including airfare). In Chiang Mai, **Nam Khong Travel** (⊠ 6 Chaiyaphoom Rd., Chiang Mai ☎ 053/874321) is the leading specialist in package tours to Laos.

Diethelm Travel (⊠ Kian Gwan II Bldg., 140/1 Wittayu (Wireless) Rd., Bangkok ☎ 02/255-9150 ⊕ www.diethelm-travel.com) is one of the oldest and most-respected travel agencies offering trips to Laos. **Journeys International** (⊠ 107 April Dr., Ann Arbor, MI 48103, U.S. ☎ 734/665-4407 or 800/255-8735 ⊕ www.journeys-intl.com). **Smiling Albino** (⊠ 2098/414 Ramkhamhaeng Soi 24/2, Bangkok ☎ 02/718-9561 or 07/035-0705 ⊕ www.smilingalbino.com) provides specialized tours that feature a broad range of activities, modes of transport, and venues; tours are led by foreign and local experts.

Money Matters

The currency is the Lao kip (LAK), which is a generally unstable currency and comes in relatively small notes (the largest denomination equals approximately $5). Hence, dollars are preferred and are almost always used to pay hotel and airline bills. All hotel rates are listed in U.S. dollars—some hotels even charge higher rates for guests who pay their bills in kip. The Thai baht is accepted in Vientiane, Luang Prabang, and border towns along the Mekong River. Kip cannot be changed back into a hard currency; however, it is useful to carry $20 or so in kip for making small purchases at markets, paying tuk-tuk drivers, etc. At this writing, the official exchange rate was 265 kip to the Thai baht, 10,500 kip to one U.S. dollar, 9,400 kip to one Canadian dollar, 8,000 kip to one Australian dollar, and 19,500 kip to one British pound.

At this writing, there was only one ATM in the country—at Vientiane's Banque Pour le Commerce Exterieur Lao (BCEL), one block south of Nam Phu Square on Pang Kham Road. Credit cards are accepted at the more expensive hotels and restaurants in Vientiane, Luang Prabang, and Pakse. In addition, banks in major tourist destinations will provide a cash advance on a MasterCard or Visa, typically for a 5% service charge. Finally, Western Union has a number of branches in the major cities. Look for the yellow sign next to a similar yellow Bank of Ayudya sign and at post offices.

WHAT IT COSTS In U.S. Dollars

	$$$$	$$$	$$	$	¢
RESTAURANTS	over $12	$9–$12	$6–$9	$3–$6	under $3
HOTELS	over $150	$100–$150	$50–$100	$25–$50	under $25

Regional Cuisine Highlights

It may not be as famous as Thai food, but Lao cuisine is often just as good; the two cuisines are similar, but Lao cooking is usually not as spicy. Chilies are often used as a condiment, but Lao cuisine also makes good use of ginger, lemongrass, coconut, tamarind, crushed peanuts, and fish paste. Because so much of the country is wilderness, there's usually game, such as venison or wild boar, on the menu. Fresh river prawns and fish—including the famous, massive Mekong catfish, the world's largest freshwater fish—are also standard fare, along with chicken, vegetables, and sticky rice.

More Information

Diethelm Travel (⌧ Setthathirat Rd. at Nam Phu Fountain Sq., Vientiane ☎ 021/213833, 021/215920, or 021/215128 ⌧ Sisavang Vong Rd., Luang Prabang ☎ 071/212277 ⊕ www.diethelm-travel.com) is your best source of travel information in Laos. Lao Youth Travel (⌧ 24 Fa Ngum Quay, Ban Mixay, Vientiane ☎ 021/240939 ⌧ 72 Sisavang Vong Rd., Ban Pakham, Luang Prabang ☎ 071/253340 ⊕ www.laoyouthtravel.com) is also helpful. The National Tourism Authority of the Lao People's Democratic Republic (⌧ BP 3556, Ave. Lan Xang, Vientiane ☎ 021/212248 or 021/250681 ⊕ www.MaeKhongcenter.comare caps OK in web?) has offices in Vientiane and all other provinces; they provide some printed materials, but little else. The private Web site ⊕ www.laos-hotels.com can provide information on the major hotels in the country.

Health

As in all of Southeast Asia, it's advisable to drink bottled water and avoid uncooked food (except for peeled fruit such as bananas). For minor stomach upsets, try bananas and boiled rice. Pharmacies are well stocked and often staffed with assistants who speak some English. Carry mosquito repellent at all times, and sleep under mosquito nets in rural areas. Before venturing into very remote, mountainous regions, it's advisable to be inoculated against malaria, typhoid, hepatitis, tetanus, and Japanese encephalitis. Note that AIDS is widespread in border areas.

Safety

Laos is fairly free of crime in tourist areas, though traveling by road puts you at a small risk of encountering highway thieves. Petty crime like pickpocketing is rare, but you should still be careful when visiting crowded fairs and markets. Never leave luggage unattended. Note that the penalties for possession of even small amounts of drugs are very severe. Also, inappropriate behavior between foreigners and Lao citizens is illegal. Prostitution is clearly illegal, but $500 fines can also be levied against foreigners for having sexual relations with Laotian citizens (where that line is drawn or how they prove such behavior is unknown, but even close dancing or public displays of affection can be seen as toeing the line).

In the countryside, trekkers should watch out for unexploded ordnance left over from the Vietnam War, especially in Xieng Khuang and Hua Phan provinces and in southern Laos (particularly near the former Ho Chi Minh Trail in Salavan, Attapeu, and Sekong provinces). Don't wander off well-traveled trails. Better yet, trek with a group led by a qualified guide. Be careful not to photograph anything that may have military significance, like airports or military installations.

8

VIENTIANE & ENVIRONS

Updated by
Trevor Ranges

Vientiane is not only the capital of Laos but also the logical gateway to the country, as it's far more accessible to the outside world than Luang Prabang. The city sits along the Mekong River, with Thailand just across the water. A 20-minute ride by taxi or even *tuk-tuk* (three-wheel motorbike) brings you to the Friendship Bridge, which links Laos and Thailand. Crossing the bridge is a mere formality. On the Thai side of the bridge is the riverside frontier town of Nong Khai, which has direct rail services to Bangkok and a bus terminus serving the Thai capital and most cities in eastern Isan. Many tourists choose this route from Thailand into Laos, although Vientiane is easily and cheaply reached by air from Bangkok, Chiang Mai, and most Southeast Asian cities.

Vientiane

Vientiane is the quietest Southeast Asian capital, with a pace as slow as the Mekong River, which flows along the edge of town. It doesn't have the kind of imposing sights you find in Bangkok, but neither does it have the air pollution and traffic jams. That's not to say that Vientiane isn't changing at all—though there are still many more bicycles and scooters than cars on its streets, several of the main thoroughfares are beginning to bustle. ⚠ Perpetual road and sidewalk construction makes getting around by bicycle or on foot a bit tricky at times.

The abundance of ugly cement-block buildings in urgent need of paint gives the town a superficially run-down appearance, but scattered among these eyesores are some remnants of elegant colonial French architecture. There are also dozens of temples—ornate, historic Buddhist structures that stand amid towering palms and flowering trees. First-time visitors often find Vientiane a drab, joyless city, but you only have to arrive in the midst of the weeklong That Luang Festival in November to be reminded that first impressions can be misleading.

What to See

❸ **Ho Phra Keo.** There's a good reason why Ho Phra Keo, one of the city's oldest and most impressive temples, has a name so similar to the wat in Bangkok's Grand Palace. The original Ho Phra Keo here was built by King Setthathirat in 1565 to house the Emerald Buddha, which he had taken from Chang Mai in Thailand. The king installed the sacred statue first in Luang Prabang and then in Vientiane at Ho Phra Keo, but the Buddha was recaptured by the Siamese army in 1778 and taken to Bangkok. The present temple was restored in 1936, and has become a national museum. On display are Buddha sculptures of different styles, some wonderful chiseled images of Khmer deities, and a fine collection of stone inscriptions. The masterpiece of the museum is a 16th-century lacquered door carved with Hindu images. ⊠ *Setthathirat Rd. at Mahosot St.* ☎ *No phone* 🖃 *2,000 kip* ⊙ *Daily 8–4.*

❶ **Nam Phu Square** (Fountain Square). An attractive square with a nice but nonfunctioning circular fountain in the middle, this is one of several reminders in the city of French colonial influence—reinforced further by

Etiquette & Behavior

LAOTIANS ARE GENERALLY GENTLE AND POLITE, and visitors should take their lead from them—avoiding any public display of anger or impolite behavior. Even showing affection in public is frowned upon.

Laotians traditionally greet others by pressing their palms together in a sort of prayer gesture known as a *nop*; it is also acceptable for men to shake hands. If you attempt a nop, remember that it's basically reserved for social greetings; don't greet a hotel or restaurant employee this way. The general greeting is *sabai di* ("good health"), invariably said with a smile.

Avoid touching or embracing a Laotian, and keep in mind that the head has spiritual significance; even patting a child affectionately on the head could be misinterpreted. Feet are considered "unclean," so when you sit, make sure your feet are not pointing directly at anyone, and never use your foot to point in any situation. Shoes must be removed before you enter a temple or private home, as well as some restaurants and offices.

Shorts and sleeveless tops should not be worn in temple compounds. When visiting a temple, be careful not to touch anything of spiritual significance, such as altars, Buddha images, or spirit houses. Ask permission from any individual before taking a photograph of him or her.

---

the presence on the square's perimeter of some very Gallic restaurants. Nam Phu Square is a convenient meeting or starting point as it is easy to find and is situated in the center of Vientiane's tourist area; restaurants, Internet cafés, travel agents, and massage parlors are all located in this area.

National Museum. A modern, well-laid-out, two-story building houses interesting geological and historical displays. Exhibits touch on Laos's royal history, its colonial years, and its struggle for liberation. The museum also highlights the country's 50 main ethnic groups and indigenous instruments. ⊠ *Sam Sen Tai Rd.* ☎ *021/212460, 021/212461, or 021/212462* 🖾 *5,000 kip* ☉ *Daily 8–noon and 1–4.*

Suan Wattanatham Bandapao (National Ethnic Cultural Park). The attraction at this park near the river is a model village of miniature Lao houses. Sculptures of Lao heroes dot the grounds, which also include a small zoo in one corner. This is a pleasant place to stroll and admire

THE RISE OF THE MOON CITY

Originally named Chanthaburi (City of the Moon), Vientiane was founded in the 16th century by King Setthathirat near a wide bend of the Mekong River, on the grounds of a Khmer fortress dating to the 9th to 13th century. In 1828 the Siamese army from Bangkok razed the city. But the old part of Vientiane is still an attractive settlement, where ancient temples that survived the Siamese attack, museums, and parks are all just a short distance from one another.

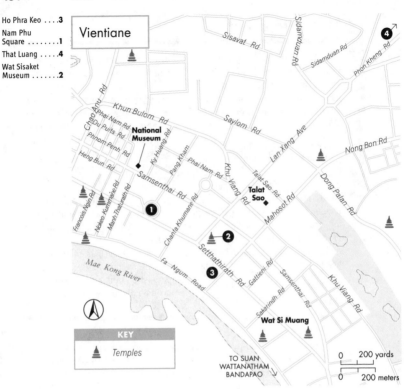

the sleek lines of the Friendship Bridge, just a short distance downstream. A string of restaurants lines the riverbank here. ⊠ *Km 20 on Tha Deua Rd.* ☎ *No phone* 🖼 *3,000 kip* 🕘 *Daily 8–6.*

Talat Sao (Morning Market). To truly immerse yourself in Vientiane, visit this vast indoor bazaar that is, despite its name, actually open all day. The bright, orderly emporium holds everything from handwoven fabrics and wooden Buddha figures to electric rice cookers and sneakers. Most of the shops cater to locals, but there's still plenty to interest travelers: handicrafts, intricate gold-and-silver work, jewelry, T-shirts, and bags and suitcases to accommodate all your extra purchases. Many products are imported from abroad. Fruits, confections, and noodle soups are sold at open-door stalls outside, where Vietnamese shoemakers also ply their trade. The market, which is near the main post office, is made up of three Lao-style buildings, each with two floors. The funding of the construction (1989–91) came mainly from the market traders themselves. A new market, next to the old buildings on the corner of the intersection, may be completed in the near future. As to whether tenants of the old Morning Market will move to the new site is unclear, but be aware that the original bazaar is in the older, traditionally designed, green-roofed buildings. ⊠ *Lane Xang Ave. at Khoun Boulom St.* ☎ *No phone* 🕘 *Daily 7–6.*

Laos's Festivals

LAOS HAS MANY FASCINATING FESTIVALS, quite a few of which are steeped in Buddhism. Be sure to book hotels in advance if you're planning on visiting during festival time, particularly in the big cities.

Bun Bang Fai: The Rocket Festival is held in the middle of May. Rockets are fired and prayers are said in the paddy fields to bring rain in time for the planting of the rice seedlings.

Bun Khao Padab Din: This is a special rice ceremony held in August (the exact date depends on the harvest schedule). People make offerings at local temples to keep alive the memory of spirits who have no relatives.

Bun Khao Salak: This is a similar rice ceremony in September (the exact date depends on the harvest schedule), wherein people visit local temples to make offerings to their ancestors. Boat races are held on the Mekong, especially in Luang Prabang and Khammuan Province.

Bun Ok Pansa: The day of the full moon in October marks the end of Buddhist Lent and is celebrated with donations to local temples. Candlelight processions are held, and colorful floats are set adrift on the Mekong River. The following day, boat races are held in Vientiane, Savannakhet, and Pakse.

Bun Pimai: Lao New Year takes place April 13–15. This is a water festival similar to Thailand's celebrated Songkran, when all the important Buddha images get a cleaning with scented water (and the general public gets wet in the bargain). The festivities are particularly lively in Luang Prabang.

Bun Visakhabucha (Buddha Day): On the day of the full moon in May, candlelight processions are held in temples to mark the birth, enlightenment, and death of the Buddha.

That Ing Hang Festival: This takes place in Savannakhet in December and lasts several days on the grounds of the ancient Wat That Inhang, just outside the city. There are performances of traditional Lao music and dance, sports contests, and a spectacular drumming competition.

That Luang Festival: This is a weeklong event in Vientiane in November, which ends with a grand fireworks display. Hundreds of monks gather to accept alms. The festival runs concurrently with an international trade fair showcasing the products of Laos and other countries of the Greater Mekong Subregion (GMS).

Wat Phu Festival: Also known as Makhabucha Day, this festival is held during the day of the first full moon in February at Wat Phu, near Champasak. A full schedule of events includes elephant races, buffalo fights, cockfights, and traditional Lao music-and-dance performances.

★ ❹ **That Luang.** The city's most sacred monument, this massive, 147-foot-high, gold-painted stupa is also the nation's most important cultural symbol, representing the unity of the Lao people. It was built by King Setthathirat in 1566 (and restored in 1953) to guard a relic of the Buddha's hair and to represent Mt. Meru, the holy mountain of Hindu mythol-

Laos: Then and Now

DESPITE ITS LIMITED INFRASTRUCTURE, Laos is a wonderful country to visit. The Laotians are some of the friendliest, gentlest people in Southeast Asia—devoutly Buddhist, and traditional in many ways. Not yet inured to countless visiting foreigners, locals volunteer assistance and a genuine welcome. And because this landlocked nation is so sparsely populated—fewer than 6 million people in an area larger than Great Britain—its mountainous countryside has not yet been deforested or overdeveloped. Laos has a rich culture and history, and though it's been a battleground many times in the past, it's a peaceful, stable country today.

Prehistoric remains show that the river valleys and lowland areas of Laos were settled as far back as 40,000 years ago, first by hunters and gatherers and later by more developed communities. The mysterious Plain of Jars—a stretch of land littered with ancient stone and clay jars at least 2,000 years old—indicates the early presence of a sophisticated society skilled in the manufacture of bronze and iron implements and ceramics. Starting in the 3rd century BC, cultural and trading links were forged with Chinese and Indian civilizations.

Between the 4th and 8th century, farming communities along the Mekong River began to organize themselves into communities called "Muang"—a term still used in both Laos and neighboring Thailand. This network of Muang gave rise in the mid-14th century to the first Lao monarchy, given the fanciful name of Lan Xang, or the "Kingdom of a Million Elephants," for the large herds of the pachyderms that roamed the land.

At the start of the 18th century, following fighting over the throne, the kingdom was partitioned into three realms: Luang Prabang, Vientiane, and Champasak. Throughout the latter part of the 18th century Laos was under the control of neighboring Siam. In the early 19th century Laos staged an uprising against the Siamese, but in 1828 an invading Siamese army under King Rama III sacked Vientiane and took firm control of most of Laos as a province of Siam. Siam maintained possession of Laos until the French established the Federation of French Indochina, which included Laos, Vietnam, and Cambodia, in 1893. In 1904 the Lao monarch Sisavang Vong set up court in Luang Prabang, but Laos remained part of French Indochina until 1949. For a brief period during World War II Laos was occupied by Japan, but reverted to French control at the end of the war. In 1953 the Lao PDR became an independent nation, which was confirmed by the passage of the Geneva Convention in 1954. The monarchy was finally dissolved in 1975, when the revolutionary group Pathet Lao, allied with North Vietnam's communist movement during the Vietnam War, seized power after a long guerrilla war.

During the Vietnam War, the U.S. Air Force, in a vain attempt to disrupt the Ho Chi Minh Trail, dropped more tons of bombs on Laos than were dropped on Germany during World War II. Since the end of the Vietnam War, the People's Democratic Party (formerly the Pathet Lao) has ruled the country, first on Marxist-Leninist lines and now on the basis of limited pro-market reforms. Overtures are being made to the outside, particularly to Thailand, Japan, and China, to assist in developing the country—not an easy task. The Friendship Bridge over the Mekong River connects Vientiane with Nong Khai in northeastern Thailand, making Laos more accessible to trade with neighboring countries.

Decentralization of the state-controlled economy began in 1986, resulting in a steady annual growth rate of around 6%. The country has continued to grow steadily: Vientiane, Luang Prabang, and Pakse have new airports; visitors from most countries can now get a visa upon arrival, and those from some ASEAN (Association of Southeast Asian Nations) countries need no visa at all. New hotels are constantly opening. Nonetheless, infrastructure in the country remains primitive in comparison to the rest of the world. Laos has no railways; communications technology and electricity are common only in more densely populated areas (cell phones outnumber landlines five to one), and only 9 of the country's 44 airports and airstrips are paved. The road from the current capital, Vientiane, to Laos's ancient capital, Luang Prabang, has been paved and upgraded—though it still takes eight hours to make the serpentine, 320-km (198-mi) journey north, and nearly 90% of the nation's roads are unpaved. The upgraded road running south from Vientiane can now accommodate tour buses going all the way to the Cambodian border. Other border crossings have also opened up, especially along the Vietnamese border.

A low standard of living (the GDP per-capita of $1,900 is one of the world's lowest, and 34% of the population lives below the poverty line) and a rugged landscape that hampers transportation and communication has long made the countryside of Laos a sleepy backwater. But Luang Prabang, boosted by its status as a World Heritage Site, has become a busy and relatively prosperous tourist hub. Vientiane, despite its new hotels and restaurants, remains one of the world's sleepiest capital cities.

Despite their relative poverty, Lao people are frank, friendly, and outwardly cheerful people. Although Laos certainly has far to go economically, it is currently a member of the ASEAN trade group, has Normal Trade Relations status with the United States, and receives assistance from the European Union to help it acquire WTO membership. Growing investment in Laos and expanding numbers of tourists to both the main tourist centers and more remote areas should continue to benefit the people of Laos.

8

ogy, the center and axis of the world. Surrounding the lotus-shaped stupa are 30 pinnacles on the third level and a cloistered square on the ground with stone statues of the Buddha. The complex is flanked by two brilliantly decorated temple halls, the survivors of four temples that originally surrounded the stupa. On the avenue outside the west gate stands a bronze statue of King Setthathirat erected in the 1960s by a pious general. ■ TIP→ **That Luang is the center of a major weeklong festival during November's full moon.** It's on the outskirts of town (a 10-minute songthaew ride from the center). The city's most important monument is a short *songthaew* ride away from the riverside area. Be sure to return to the riverbank in the late afternoon to experience one of Vientiane's most spectacular sights—sunset over the Mekong. ✉ *North end of That Luang Rd.* ☎ *No phone* 💳 *5,000 kip* ⊙ *Daily 8–4.*

Wat Si Muang. This wat, built in 1956, guards the original city pillar, a revered foundation stone dating to the 16th century. In a small park in front of the monastery stands a rare memorial to Laos's royal past: a large bronze statue of King Sisavang Vong. ✉ *Lan Xang Ave.* ☎ *No phone* 💳 *Free* ⊙ *Daily 7–5.*

② **Wat Sisaket Museum.** This interesting museum complex is made up of a crumbling temple and monastery compound across the road from Ho Phra Keo. Built in 1818 by King Anu, the temple survived the destruction of the city by the Siamese army in 1828. The monastery stands intact in its original form and is one of the most frequented in the city. Inside the main compound, the courtyard walls have hundreds of little niches and large shelves displaying 6,840 Buddha statues. Although it's in need of more work, the impressive temple hall underwent some restoration in 1938. The paintings that once covered its interior walls have largely been destroyed by the ravages of time, but the intricately carved wooden ceiling and doors are still intact. There's also an intriguing wooden library that stores palm-leaf manuscripts. ✉ *Setthathirat Rd. at Mahosot St.* ☎ *No phone* 💳 *5,000 kip* ⊙ *Daily 8–4.*

Xieng Khuan Buddha Park. The bizarre creation of an ecumenical monk, Luang Pa Bunleua Sulilat, who dreamed of a world religion embracing all faiths, this park is "peopled" by enormous Buddhist and Hindu sculptures spread among an attractive landscape of trees, shrubs, and flower gardens. Keep an eye out for the remarkable 165-foot-long sleeping Buddha. The park was laid out by the monk's followers in 1958 on the banks of the Mekong, opposite the Thai town of Nong Khai. ✉ *Km 27–28 on Tha Deua Rd.* ☎ *No phone* 💳 *5,000 kip* ⊙ *Daily 8–4:30.*

Where to Stay & Eat

$–$$ ✕ **Le Provençal.** A local family that lived in France for many years runs this little bistro behind Nam Phu Square. Chef Daniel's menu is almost exclusively French, although there's a hybrid pizza à la française. Try the beef-based terrine *du maison* to start, then sink your teeth into chicken niçoise, frogs' legs à la lyonnaise, or fillet of fish à la Provençale. Save room for such desserts as crème caramel and chocolate mousse. On sunny days, you can sit on the terrace overlooking the square. ✉ *73/1 Pang Kham Rd.* ☎ *021/219685* 🚫 *MC, V* ⊙ *No lunch Sun.*

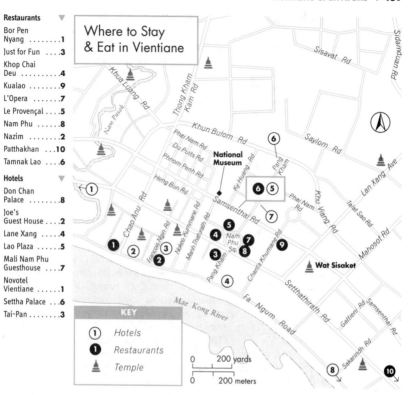

Where to Stay
& Eat in Vientiane

KEY

① Hotels

❶ Restaurants

▲ Temple

$–$$ ✕ **L'Opera.** Vientiane's best Italian restaurant serves authentic pastas, pizzas, and fresh salads. From a table at the small front terrace you can watch the action on Nam Phu Square. ⊠ *12 Nam Phu Fountain Sq.* ☎ *021/215099* ▭ *AE, MC, V.*

★ **$–$$** ✕ **Nam Phu.** A filet mignon as good as any you can find in Paris is one of the specialties at this very French restaurant on central Nam Phu Square. The dish, which comes with a blue-cheese sauce, is one of several savory creations on a menu also distinguished for its seafood and freshwater fish. There's an excellent wine list, with prices for bottles starting at a very reasonable $12. ⊠ *18–20 Nam Phu Fountain Sq.* ☎ *021/216248* ▭ *AE, MC, V.*

¢–$ ✕ **Just for Fun.** A cozy little café with indoor and outdoor seating, Just for Fun serves healthful and tasty Lao vegetarian and nonvegetarian food, a variety of freshly brewed teas, and homemade cakes and ice cream. The menu includes a message from the American National Cancer Institute on healthful eating habits, a practice that is well supported by simple, fresh dishes like *gaeng kou maknut* (a pineapple red curry). The restaurant also sells a small collection of Lao handbags and scarfs. ⊠ *Pang Kham Rd., opposite Lao Airline Office (just south of Nam Phu Fountain Sq.)* ☎ *021/213642* ▭ *No credit cards* ⊗ *Closed Sun.*

¢–$ ✕ **Khop Chai Deu.** A French colonial structure houses this very popular downtown restaurant and bar, which serves as an excellent meeting point for happy-hour cocktails or dinner. The long menu is crammed with Lao and international dishes, and a daily buffet is also served. ■ TIP→ **For a tasty introduction to traditional Lao cuisine, try the Lao Discovery, a set menu including** *laab,* **a semi-spicy salad;** *tom yam,* **a sour-chili-and-lemongrass fish soup;** *khao niaw,* **Lao sticky rice; and a glass of** *lao-lao* **(rice whiskey).** Draft beer is on tap, live music plays in the bar nightly, and the kitchen is open until 11 PM. ⊠ *54 Setthathirat Rd.* ☎ *021/223022* ▤ *MC, V.*

¢–$ ✕ **Kualao.** In a fading mansion one block southeast of Nam Phu Square, this is Vientiane's best Lao restaurant, despite its rather tacky decor. The food is quite good, and the vast menu ranges from *mok pa fork* (banana-leaf-wrapped steamed fish cooked with eggs, onions, and coconut milk) to *gaeng panaeng* (a thick red curry with chicken, pork, or beef). Servings are small, so most people order several entrées, or set menus with seven to nine dishes, plus dessert and coffee. Photos and English descriptions facilitate the ordering process. There's Lao folk dancing nightly from 7 to 9. ⊠ *111 Samsenthai Rd.* ☎ *021/215777* ▤ *MC, V.*

¢–$ ✕ **Nazim.** Mr. Nazim has opened Indian restaurants in Luang Prabang, Vang Vieng—and now in Vientiane. His Indian-style curries, served with *papadum* (crunchy lentil bread) and thick rounds of nan, are the real thing. Try for one of the few seats on the small terrace; in the evening, you can watch the sun set over the Mekong, which flows just across the road. ⊠ *335 Fa Ngum Quay* ☎ *021/223480* ▤ *V.*

¢–$ ✕ **Patthakhan.** Vientiane's largest Lao restaurant, on the edge of the city, is a new structure built in traditional style. The extensive menu is dominated by Lao dishes, but it also includes Thai, Chinese, and other Asian food. Freshly caught Mekong fish is a specialty. ⊠ *Km 4 on Tha Deua Rd.* ☎ *021/312480* ▤ *No credit cards.*

¢–$ ✕ **Tamnak Lao.** Classical Lao dances are performed every evening at this fine outdoor restaurant specializing in the cuisine of Luang Prabang. Many dishes, such as the *pla laab* (minced fish with herbs), are prepared with fish fresh from the Mekong River. Note that dinner service doesn't begin until 6. ⊠ *308 That Luang Rd., Ban Phon Xay* ☎ *021/413562* ▤ *No credit cards.*

★ $$$$ ▨ **Settha Palace.** This colonial landmark has been through a lot of changes: it was built by the French at the turn of the 19th century, converted into a hotel in the 1930s, and expropriated by the communist government in the 1970s. It became a hotel again in the late 1990s. Although it underwent extensive renovations—the marble floors and fixtures are new—the owners have respected the original design. Rooms have high ceilings, hardwood floors, Oriental rugs, and period pieces; the executive suite has a large and comfortable sitting room as well. All rooms have tall windows that overlook lush gardens surrounding a large pool. The lobby, decorated with fine antiques, is adjacent to a small bar and elegant restaurant, La Belle Epoque, which specializes in Lao and French cuisine. City tours are available via the hotel's London Taxi and wireless Internet is available throughout the hotel. ⊠ *6 Pang Kham Rd.* ☎ *021/217581 or 021/217582* ⊕ *www.setthapalace.com* ⇲ *29 rooms* △ *In-room: safe, refrigerator, Wi-Fi. In-hotel: restaurant, room service,* *bar, pool, laundry service, concierge, public Wi-Fi, no-smoking rooms* ▭ *AE, MC, V* ⦿ *BP.*

$$$–$$$$ ▦ **Don Chan Palace.** The tallest building in Laos, Don Chan Palace has spectacular views of Vientiane and of Thailand, across the Mekong River. Otherwise, it is a very typical four-star international hotel, geared mainly to corporate and diplomatic travelers—it has all the expected services and facilities, but very little character. ▪ TIP➜ Note that even if you don't choose to stay here, you might want to stop by to use the hotel's open-air fitness center and pool ($8 per day for nonguests), to take in the sunset view at the Sky Lounge, or to party at the popular nightclub. ⊠ *Unit 6, Piawat Village* ☏ *021/ 244288* ⦿ *www.donchanpalacelaopdr.com* ⟿ *240 rooms* ♿ *In-room: safe, Wi-Fi. In-hotel: 2 restaurants, room service, bar, pool, gym, spa, laundry service, concierge, no-smoking rooms* ▭ *AE, MC, V* ⦿ *BP.*

$$$ ▦ **Lao Plaza.** Something of a local landmark, Lao Plaza stands six stories tall in the center of town. The sleek exterior is a contrast to the old-fashioned comforts within: rooms are furnished with dark woods, shades of powder blue and soft rose, Oriental rugs, and some fussy, homey touches. ⊠ *63 Sam Sen Tai Rd.* ☏ *021/218800 or 021/218801* ⦿ *www.laoplazahotel.com* ⟿ *142 rooms* ♿ *In-room: safe. In-hotel: 2 restaurants, room service, bar, pool, gym, spa, laundry service, public Internet, airport shuttle, a/c, minibars, IDD phones, cable TV* ▭ *AE, MC, V.*

$$$ ▦ **Novotel Vientiane.** Although Vientiane's Novotel is just a five-minute drive from the airport, it has a pleasant location in front of Fa Ngum Park. The modern building, with a sweeping art nouveau facade, has all the usual Novotel comforts and facilities, including a dance club that is popular with locals. ⊠ *Unit 9, Sam Sen Tai Rd.* ☏ *021/213570* ⦿ *www.novotel.com* ⟿ *201 rooms* ♿ *In-hotel: 2 restaurants, bar, tennis court, pool, gym, laundry service* ▭ *AE, MC, V.*

$$ ▦ **Tai-Pan.** With a convenient location in the heart of town near the Mekong River, and comfort at competitive rates, this hotel is popular with business travelers. Rooms are spacious and have dark parquet floors. The ground floor holds the reception area, restaurant, and lounge, which are separated by potted plants and wooden dividers. Behind the building is a narrow garden and a small pool, a nice place to take advantage of the hotel's Wi-Fi. ⊠ *2–12 Francois Nginn Rd., Ban Mixay* ☏ *021/216906 up to 09* ⦿ *www.travelao.com* ⟿ *44 rooms* ♿ *In-hotel: restaurant, bar, pool, gym, laundry service, public Wi-Fi, no-smoking rooms* ▭ *AE, MC, V.*

$ ▦ **Lane Xang.** Once a government showpiece, the venerable old Lane Xang has come down in the world: the furnishings are worn, the ceilings need paint, and the bathrooms show the wear and tear of decades (though they're relatively large and clean). Many of the rooms were undergoing renovation at this writing, but if you don't mind the dog-eared appearance of the older rooms, you'll get a great deal, especially when you add in the complimentary breakfast, airport transfers, and nightly folk-dancing show in the Sa Long Xay restaurant. The best rooms overlook the Mekong, though they only come with two single beds. Back rooms overlook the hotel pool, which has a shaded terrace. ⊠ *1 Fa Ngum Quay* ☏ *021/214100 up to 07* ⦿ *www.lanexanghotel.com* ⟿ *109*

8

rooms, 12 suites ⟳ *In-hotel: 2 restaurants, bar, pool, spa, laundry service, public Internet* ⊟ *AE, DC, MC, V* ⊙ *BP.*

¢ ▦ **Joe's Guest House.** This is probably the cleanest and friendliest budget guesthouse along the river road. Rooms are very simple and plain, but have crisp, white bedding. Some rooms have shared baths. Larger rooms have air-conditioning and private baths. ⊠ *135/01 Fa Ngum Rd.* ☏ *021/ 241936* ✎ *joe_guesthouose@yahoo.com* ⤳ *14 rooms* ⟳ *In-room: no a/c (some). In-hotel: restaurant, bar, bicycles* ⊟ *No credit cards.*

★ ¢ ▦ **Mali Nam Phu Guesthouse.** This spotlessly clean, Vietnamese-run guesthouse is a short walk away from several restaurants and shopping areas. Rooms are comfortable, although simply furnished. A central garden courtyard offers a quiet place to relax after a day of sightseeing. ⊠ *114 Pang Kham Rd.* ☏ *021/215093 or 021/263297* ⊕ *www. malinamphu.com* ⤳ *40 rooms* ⟳ *In-room: no a/c. In-hotel: laundry service* ⊟ *MC, V.*

Nightlife & the Arts

The after-dark scene in Vientiane is very subdued, mostly confined to some of the more expensive hotels and a handful of bars and pubs along the Mekong River boulevard. Otherwise, entertainment in Vientiane means a cultural pursuit.

You can enjoy traditional Lao folk music and dancing on a Maeong River cruise aboard the **Lane Xang riverboat** (☏ 020/235–8123). The one-hour cruise is free to board and departs from the jetty at the western end of Fa Ngum Quay at 7:30 pm. Food and drink are available for purchase at reasonable rates. The **Laos Tradition Show** (⊠ National Theater, Manthaturat Rd. ☏ 021/242978) highlights traditional music and dance. It's staged by the Ministry of Information and Culture and takes place nightly at 8:30.

The **Daothong Night Club** (☏ 020/543120), on the Luang Prabang Road at Ban Nakham, has live music nightly. The Lane Xang hotel's **Snack Bar** (⊠ 1 Fa Ngum Quay ☏ 021/214100) is a popular haunt—a little shady, but interesting. Vientiane's most popular dance club, **Zeaza Disco** (⊠ Khun Bolom Rd., Ban Haysok ☏ 020/551–2858) caters to real night owls. You enter the club through a dragon's mouth. **Lunar 36,** a new disco at the Don Chan Palace Hotel, is the most recent edition to the Vientiane nightlife scene—it's the prime nightlife venue every night except Tuesday. There is a small cover charge. Believe it or not, the **bowling alley** on Khun Bolom Road, around the corner from Settha Palace, is a happening after-hours spot, serving food and drinks to a rowdy mix of locals, expats, and travelers until 5 AM.

Shopping

With crafts, jewelry, T-shirts, and more, the **Talat Sao** (Morning Market; ⊠ Lane Xang Ave. at Khoun Boulom St.) market should satisfy all your shopping needs.

If you're still looking for that something special and you can't find it at Talat Sao, try the **Small and Medium Enterprises Promotion Center** (SMEPC; ★ ⊠ Phokheng Rd. ☏ 021/416736). **Lao Handicraft Group** (⊠ Ban Thongphanthong ☏ 021/416267) also sells a wide selection of Lao crafts. Lao handwoven silk is world renowned, and you can find fine examples at **Maicome** (⊠ Ban Sokpaluang ☎ 021/312275) and **Phaeng Mai Silk Gallery** (⊠ Ban Nongbuathong Tai ☎ 021/243121). For wood carvings, head to **Humsinh Craft** (⊠ Ban Dong Miang ☎ 021/212329).

Nam Ngum Lake

⑤ *90 km (56 mi) north of Vientiane via Phonhong on Hwy. 13.*

Forested mountains surround this island-dotted reservoir lake, which is accessible by car from Vientiane. Floating restaurants here serve freshly caught lake fish, and there's a large hotel complex, the Dansavanh Nam Ngum Resort. Visitors who have built substantial amounts of time into their itineraries to explore Laos, may want to skip this trip as there are others that are far better. But those who only have a few days in the country will enjoy this side trip as a way to see a bit of Laos's countryside without having to travel too far from Vientiane.

Where to Stay

¢–$ 🏨 **Dansavanh Nam Ngum Resort.** Among the attractions at this ugly boxlike resort are a water theme park, a casino, and a golf course. The resort organizes treks in the countryside around the lake, and boat trips can be made to some of the islands for about $7 an hour. ⊠ *End of access Rd.* ☎ *021/217594* ⊕ *www.dansavanh.com* ↩ *166 rooms* ♨ *In-hotel: restaurant, bar, golf course, pool, gym, spa.*

Phu Khao Khouay

⑥ *40 km (25 mi) northeast of Vientiane on Hwy. 10.*

Phu Khao Khouay, or Buffalo Horn Mountain, lies in a national park—a dramatic area of sheer sandstone cliffs, river gorges, and the Ang Nam reservoir. The park's three rivers empty into the Mekong. The banks of the reservoir have several simple restaurants and refreshment stands. The park can be reached on Highway 10 (follow the signs from Ban Napheng).

Plain of Jars

★ **⑦** *390 km (242 mi) northeast of Vientiane, 96 km (60 mi) southeast of Luang Prabang.*

One of the world's major archaeological wonders, the Plain of Jars is also one of the world's most tantalizing mysteries. The broad, mountain-ringed plain northeast of Vientiane is littered with hundreds of ancient stone and clay jars, some estimated to weigh 5 or 6 tons. The jars are said to be at least 2,000 years old, but to this day, nobody knows who made them or why. They survived heavy bombing during the Vietnam War, and their sheer size has kept them out of the hands of antiquities hunters.

The jars are scattered over three main areas, but only the Ban Ang site is accessible and worth visiting. Here you can find some 300 jars dotting a windswept plateau about 12 km (7½ mi) from Phonesavanh, capital of Xieng Khuang Province. This is true Hmong territory: you pass

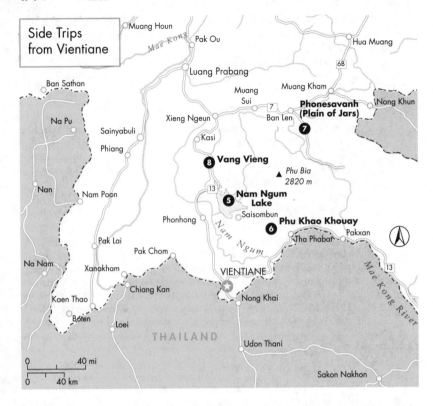

Side Trips from Vientiane

Hmong villages on the way from Phonesavanh to Ban Ang and on High-way 7, which leads east to the Vietnamese border at Nong Het. There's much of interest in this remote area along Highway 7, including hot mineral springs at Muang Kham. From Muang Kham, a road leads to Vieng Xay, which has more than 100 limestone caves, some of them used as hideouts by the revolutionary Pathet Lao during the war years.

Getting Here

A hard day's drive along Highway 7 from either Vientiane or Luang Prabang, the vast plain is difficult to reach. Travel operators in both cities, such as Diethelm Travel and Lao Youth Travel, offer these tours by road, but the most comfortable route is by air from Vientiane to the tiny airfield at Phonesavanh. Here, a couple of hotels have basic but adequate accommodations, and a taxi can be hired for around $25 for the 30-km (19-mi) journey to the edge of the plain.

Where to Stay

$ 🏨 **Vansana Plain of Jars.** On a hilltop overlooking Phonesavanh, this is the best hotel in the city. The guest rooms are comfortably furnished and have balconies, minibars, and TVs. ⊠ *Phonthan Rd., Phonesavanh* ☎ *61/213170 up to 75* ⊕ *www.vansanahotel-group.com* ⇗ *36 rooms* ⚬ *In-hotel: restaurant, laundry service* ⊟ *No credit cards* ⏐⊙⏐ *CP.*

Vang Vieng

★ ❽ *160 km (99 mi) north of Vientiane.*

The town of Vang Vieng was discovered in the mid-1990s by backpackers traveling between Vientiane and Luang Prabang on Highway 13. It's not only a convenient stopover, but also a town bordered by an attractive countryside, including the Nam Song River and a dramatic range of jagged limestone mountains. During the Vietnam War, the United States maintained an airstrip in the town center; the abandoned tarmac is now part of the bus terminal. A new airport is currently under construction and will soon be accommodating Vang Vieng's burgeoning upscale clientele. Today the town center is jam-packed with bars and backpacker hangouts, but you can escape the noise and the crowds by making for the river, which is lined with guesthouses and restaurants catering to both backpackers and those on a more flexible budget. The river is clean and good for swimming and kayaking, and the mountains beyond are riddled with caves and small pleasant swimming holes. River trips and caving expeditions are organized by every guesthouse and hotel. ⚠ **Note that the treks to the caves can be fairly arduous, and some are only accessible by motorbike.** The less-adventurous adventurer can rent an inner tube for $3 and float down the river for a few hours, starting at the riverside rope swing and ending at one of 10 island bars on the north end of town.

Where to Stay & Eat

$$ ✕🏠 **Villa Nam Song.** The Mediterranean-style rooms at this hotel have wooden floors and ceilings, yellow concrete walls, and wooden beds, desks, and chairs. The rooms are decent, but the view from the restaurant is the property's big allure; tables at La Verandah Restaurant and Terrace have great views across the river to the towering mountains in the distance. The restaurant serves Lao and international cuisine as well as French wines, and homemade ice cream and cakes. At this writing, a small spa was under construction to open at the end of 2007. ✉ *Unit 9, Ban Vieng Keo* ☎ *023/511016* ⊕ *www.villanamsong.com* ⇌ *16 rooms* ⚐ *In-hotel: restaurant* ▤ V ⦿ *BP.*

$ 🏠 **Elephant Crossing Hotel.** Every room at this modern four-story hotel has a river view, a balcony, hardwood floors, and wooden trim constructed of recycled bits of old Lao houses. The restaurant spills over onto the lawn and a patio alongside the river, where guests can sip complimentary tea and Lao coffee. A sauna and massage room are in the works. ■ **TIP➡ Dormi-**

VANG VIENG PADDLING ADVENTURE

Vang Vieng Paddling (✉ Sri Serang Rd. ☎ 020/5624783 ⊕ tipaddleadventure@hotmail.com) offers a unique way to travel from Vang Vieng to Vientiane. Departing at 9:30 AM, you are transported downstream, where you get in a kayak for the four-hour paddle to Vientiane, stopping for lunch and a 33-foot rock jump into the river. You're picked up riverside outside Vientiane around 4 PM, reunited with your luggage, and dropped off at Nam Phu Fountain Square in Vientiane around 5 PM. The one-way trip costs a reasonable $2.

---

tory-style rooms are also available, and are the best value in town. ☒ *Ban Viengkeo (Namsong Riverside)* ☎ *023/511232 or 020/560–2830* ⊕ *www.theelephantcrossinghotel.com* ⤳ *32 rooms* ⚿ *In-hotel: restaurant, public Wi-Fi* ☱ *MC, V.*

★ **$** ⊡ **Xayoh Ban Sabai Bungalows.** The chicest rooms in town are in traditional Lao-style thatch-roof bungalows that are raised on stilts. All bungalows have wooden floors, comfortable bedding, modern baths, and glass doors that open onto balconies with river views. The grounds have brick walkways and a pond, and they blend in harmoniously with the river habitat and pastoral fields and mountains across the water. The resort staff provide Laotian hospitality and friendly and competent service. The riverside restaurant has great view and Wi-Fi access from the hotel next door. Bungalow 14 has the best location—right beside the Nam Song River. ☒ *Sisavang Vong Rd.* ☎ *023/511088* ⊕ *www.xayohgroup.com* ⤳ *13 bungalows* ⚿ *In-hotel: restaurant, concierge* ☱ *MC, V.*

¢ ⊡ **Saixong Guest House.** Cheap. Riverside. Did we mention cheap? You won't find a better price ($4–$10) for a riverside location. Most rooms are ultrabasic but clean, and the location just can't be beat. The three rooms that face the river have extras like TVs and minibars; a few more rooms have air-conditioning. ■ TIP→ **Book in advance, especially if you want a river-view room—even in low season this place is normally full.** ☒ *Ban Sengsavang* ☎ *023/511130* ✉ *saysong1@yahoo.com* ⤳ *31 rooms* ⚿ *Inroom: no a/c (some), no TV (some). In-hotel: restaurant, laundry service, public Internet* ☱ *No credit cards.*

Vientiane & Environs Essentials

Transportation

BORDER CROSSINGS

Vientiane's border crossing to Thailand is 19 km (12 mi) east of the city at the Friendship Bridge, which spans the Mekong River. The taxi fare between the bridge and Vientiane is about $10 or B350 (the drivers prefer to be paid in dollars or baht rather than kip). Taxis, songthaews, and some tuk-tuks wait at the Lao side of the bridge to take you to Vientiane. A free shuttle-bus service runs across the bridge. On the Thai side of the bridge, taxis, songthaews, and tuk-tuks can take you into the border town of Nong Khai, 3 km (2 mi) away. The border is open 6 AM–10 PM. Buses from Vientiane Morning Market are the cheapest, most direct way to cross the border into Thailand.

BY AIR

Thai Airways International has daily flights from Bangkok to Vientiane. The national airline, Lao Airlines, has daily flights between Vientiane and Bangkok as well as five flights a week from Chiang Mai. All of these flights last about 80 minutes and cost $100 to $120, plus the departure tax from Thailand of B400 (approximately $10).

Lao Airlines also flies several times a day between Vientiane and Luang Prabang, plus four times weekly from Vientiane to Phonesavanh, a jumping-off point for visiting the Plain of Jars, and twice a week to Pakse, the gateway to the south.

⚠️ It should be noted that the U.S. Department of State advises U.S. citizens not to fly Lao Airlines over mountainous areas of Laos during bad weather owing to a history of aircraft crashes in those areas. Furthermore, they recommend flying only on aircraft that have been certified for international air routes, such as Boeing, Airbus, or ATR.

🛫 Airlines **Lao Airlines** ☎ 021/212050 up to 54 for international flights, 021/212057 or 021/212058 for domestic flights ⊕www.laoairlines.com. **Thai Airways International** ☎021/222527 up to 29 in Vientiane, 02/628-2000 in Bangkok ⊕ www.thaiair.com.

AIRPORTS & TRANSFERS
Vientiane's Wattay International Airport is about 4 km (2½ mi) from the city center. You can take a metered taxi from Wattay International Airport into the city for $10; obtain a taxi voucher from the kiosk in the arrivals hall. The ride to the city center takes about 15 minutes. If you don't have much luggage, consider a tuk-tuk, a more exciting and cheaper option at 2,000–4,000 kip. But it's not practical if you're traveling with heavy luggage.

🛫 **Wattay International Airport** ☎ 021/512028 or 021/512165.

BY BUS

Although there's city bus service in Vientiane, schedules and routes are confusing for first-time visitors, so it's best to stick to taxis, tuk-tuks, *samlors* (bicycle rickshaws), and songthaews. The city bus station is next to the Morning Market. Comfortable VIP buses depart here for Vang Vieng, as well as Pakse and southern Laos. For the overnight journey to Pakse, VIP buses leave Vientiane nightly at 8:30 PM and arrive in Pakse 11 hours later. VIP buses to Savannakhet also leave at 8:30 PM and arrive 6½ hours later. From the Morning Market you can also cross the border into Thailand; there are four daily departures to Nong Khai (1-hour trip) and five daily departures to Udon Thani (2-hour trip). ■ TIP→ In Udon Thani, you can catch budget Air Asia flights to Bangkok, a cheaper alternative than flying directly from Vientiane.

The bus terminal for trips to northern Laos is at Nong Duang Market. To Luang Prabang, local buses leave five times daily and take 11–12 hours; express buses leave three times daily and take 10 hours; and one VIP bus departs at 8 AM and arrives 8 hours later. Passengers to Vang Vieng can take the Luang Prabang VIP bus for the 2-hour journey or can take one of three local buses departing from the Morning Market bus station for a budget 5,000 kip.

🚌 **City bus station** ☎ 021/216507.

BY CAR

You can rent a car, either with or without a driver, for $25–$50 a day. Car rental companies are a fairly new enterprise in Laos, but one of the most reliable in Vientiane is Asia Vehicle Rental.

🚗 Agency **Asia Vehicle Rental** ✉ Sam Sen Tai Rd. ☎ 021/217493 or 021/223867 ⊕ www.laopdr.com.

BY TAXI, TUK-TUK, SONGTHAEW, OR SAMLOR

You can cover Vientiane on foot, but tuk-tuks (three-wheel motorbikes), songthaews (covered pickups with bench seating), samlors (bicycle rickshaws), and "jumbos" (motorcycle taxis) are cheap and easy to flag down. Buses are best avoided, as the routes and schedules can be confusing for first-time visitors. For any of these vehicles, be sure to negotiate the price before setting off; you can expect to pay about 2,000 kip for a ride within the city if you are a firm negotiator.

Taxis are available but must be reserved, which you can do through your hotel or at the Morning Market. For day trips outside the city, ask your hotel or guesthouse to book a car with a driver.

Contacts & Resources

BANKS & EXCHANGING SERVICES

Banks have better exchange rates than money changers or hotels. At this writing, there was one ATM in the country, at Vientiane's Banque Pour le Commerce Exterieur Lao (BCEL), one block south of Nam Phu Square on Pang Kham Road. Major credit cards are accepted in most hotels and many restaurants, but few shops. Most banks will allow you to get cash advance on credit cards for a fee. Western Union money transfer is available at Bank of Lao PDR on Nam Phou Square.

EMERGENCIES

The best clinic in the country is Mahosot Hospital International Clinic in Vientiane, though you should go here only if you're unable to obtain assistance through your hotel. The U.S. Embassy in Vientiane can be contacted at ☎ 021/267000 or 021/212581.

🏥 Hospital **Mahosot Hospital International Clinic** ✉ Fa Ngum Quay ☎ 021/214022.

HEALTH

As in all of Southeast Asia, it's advisable to drink bottled water (stay away from ice also) and avoid uncooked foods. Vientiane is malaria-free, but it's still advisable to use mosquito repellent. Drugstores are well stocked with medicine for minor ailments.

INTERNET, MAIL & SHIPPING

Internet cafés abound near Nam Phu Square in Vientiane. Wi-Fi service is available at a quickly expanding number of venues, including major hotels, such as Don Chan Palace, Settha Palace, and the Tai-Pan in Vientiane, and the Elephant Crossing Hotel in Vang Vieng.

The post office in Vientiane is at the corner of Lane Xang and Khoun Boulom streets and is open 8–4 daily. EMS and FedEX offices are located behind the post office along Khoun Boulom. The post office in Vang Vieng has recently moved, as the city has grown and split into "new" and "old" sections. Currently, the post office is located near the "new" market about 2½ km (1½ mi) north of the "old" touristy part of town.

TOURS & PACKAGES

Diethelm Travel arranges two- and three-day package tours of Vientiane. Costs range from $238 to $570 and include lodging. The company also has tours to the Plain of Jars, as does Lao Youth Travel.

🏢 **Diethelm Travel** ✉ Setthathirat Rd. at Nam Phu Fountain Sq. ☎ 021/213833, 021/

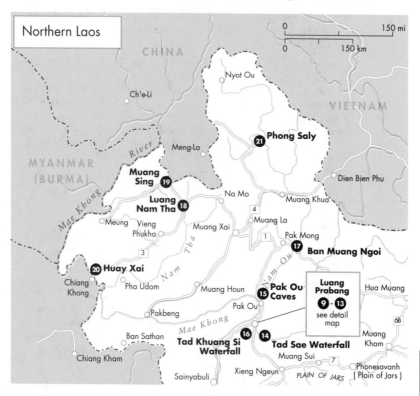

Northern Laos

215920, or 021/215128 ⊕ www.diethelm-travel.com. **Lao Youth Travel** ✉ 24 Fa Ngum Quay, Ban Mixay ☎ 021/240939 ⊕ www.laoyouthtravel.com.

LUANG PRABANG & NORTHERN LAOS

For all its popularity as a tourist destination, Luang Prabang remains one of the most remote cities in Southeast Asia. Although a highway now runs north to the Chinese border, the hinterland of Luang Prabang is mostly off-the-beaten-track territory, a mountainous region of impenetrable forests and deep river valleys. Despite Luang Prabang's air links to the rest of the country and the outside world, the Mekong River is still a preferred travel route. Passenger craft and freight barges ply the river's length as far as China in the north and near the Cambodian border in the south.

Luang Prabang

390 km (242 mi) north of Vientiane.

This is Laos's religious and artistic capital, and its combination of impressive natural surroundings, historic architecture, and friendly inhabitants make it one of the region's most pleasant towns. The city's abundance of ancient temples led UNESCO to declare it a World Heritage Site in 1995, and since then it's been bustling with construction and renovation activity.

Some 36 temples are scattered around town, making Luang Prabang a pleasant place to explore on a rented bicycle or on foot. But the charm of Luang Prabang is not exclusively architectural—just as pleasant are the people, who seem to spend as much time on the streets as they do in their homes. Children play on the sidewalks while matrons gossip in the shade, young women in traditional dress zip past on motor scooters, and Buddhist monks in saffron robes stroll by with black umbrellas, which protect their shaven heads from the tropical sun.

⚠ Despite scores of guesthouses, finding accommodation here can be a challenge in the peak season. And when you visit the main attractions, be prepared for crowds of tourists.

Touring Luang Prabang

Touring the city's major sights should take about half a day—longer if you climb Phu Si Hill, which has particularly lovely views at sunset. The evening bazaar on Sisavang Vong Road starts around 6 PM.

Start your tour of Luang Prabang at the pulsing heart of the city: the **Tribal Market** at the crossroads of Sisavang Vong Road and Setthathirat Road. From here, head northeast along Sisavang Vong Road, stopping on the left at one of the city's most beautiful temples, **Wat Mai.** Magnificent wood carvings and golden murals decorate the main pillars and portico entrance to the temple. Continue down Sisavang Vong Road to the compound of the **Royal Palace,** with its large bronze statue of King Sisavang Vong. On leaving the palace grounds by the main entrance, climb the staircase to **Phu Si Hill.** The climb is steep and takes about 15 minutes, but you'll be rewarded with an unforgettable view of Luang Prabang and the surrounding countryside.

Back in front of the Royal Palace, follow Sisavang Vong Road toward the confluence of the Mekong and Nam Khan rivers, where you can find another fascinating Luang Prabang temple, **Wat Xieng Thong.** Leaving the compound on the Mekong River side, walk back to the city center along the romantic waterside road, which is fronted by several French colonial houses and Lao traditional homes. Passing the port area behind the Royal Palace, continue on to the crossroads at Wat

A JACK OF ALL TRADES

L'etranger Books and Tea (✉ Ban Aphay, next to Hive Bar) has a little bit of everything for those in search of a sightseeing break. The first floor contains a collection of new and used books in a variety of languages for sale or for loan (2,000 kip per hour or 5,000 kip per day). Upstairs, 20 years of *National Geographic* magazines line the walls and patrons sip on tea, coffee, and smoothies or nibble on snacks while reclining on comfortable and chic floor pillows. In the evening, the place fills up for nightly DVD screenings. A gallery in an adjoining room on the second floor features local Lao artists.

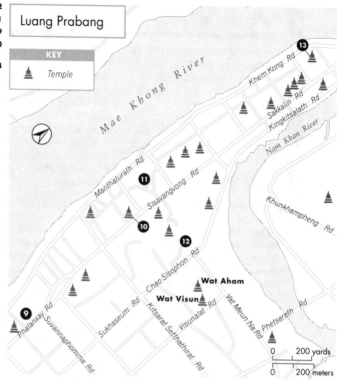

Phu Xay; turn right here to return to the Tribal Market. Every evening there's a local night bazaar, stretching from the Tribal Market to the Royal Palace on Sisavang Vong Road.

What to See

⑫ Phu Si Hill. Several shrines and temples and a golden stupa crown this forested hill, but the best reason to ascend its 328 steps is to enjoy the view from the summit: a panorama of Luang Prabang, the Nam Khan and Mekong rivers, and the surrounding mountains. It's a popular spot for watching the sunset (just be sure to bring insect repellent), but the view from atop old Phu Si is splendid at any hour. ■ TIP→ **If you're not up for the steep climb up the staircase, try the more enjoyable hike up the trail on the "back" side of the hill.** ☒ *Rathsavong Rd.* ☎ *No phone* ☜ *5,000 kip* ☉ *Daily 6–6.*

★ ⑪ Royal Palace. In a walled compound at the foot of Phu Si Hill stands this palace, the former home of the royal Savang family. Built at the beginning of the 20th century, the palace served as the royal residence until the Pathet Lao took over Laos in 1975 and exiled Crown Prince Savang Vatthana and his children to a remote region of the country (their fate has never been established). It still has the feel of a large family home—a maze of teak-floor rooms surprisingly modest in scale. The largest of

Religion in Laos

THE OVERWHELMING MAJORITY OF Laotians are Buddhists, yet, as in neighboring Thailand, spirit worship is widespread, blending easily with temple traditions and rituals. A common belief holds that supernatural spirits called *phi* have power over individual and community life.

Laotians believe that each person has 32 *khwan*, or individual spirits, which must be appeased and kept "bound" to the body. If one of the khwan leaves the body, sickness can result, and then a ceremony must be performed to reattach the errant spirit. In this ritual, which is known as *bai-si*, white threads are tied to the wrist of the ailing person in order to fasten the spirits. Apart from the khwan, there are countless other spirits inhabiting the home, gardens, orchards, fields, forests, mountains, rivers, and even individual rocks and trees.

Luang Prabang has a team of ancestral guardian spirits, the Pu Nyeu Na Nyeu, who are lodged in a special temple, Wat Aham. In the south, the fierce guardian spirits of Wat Phu are appeased every year with the sacrifice of a buffalo to guarantee an abundance of rain during the rice-growing season.

Despite the common belief in a spirit world, more than 90% of Laotians are officially Theravada Buddhists, a conservative nontheistic form of Buddhism said to be derived directly from the words of the Buddha. Buddhism arrived in Laos in the 3rd century BC by way of Ashoka, an Indian emperor who helped spread the religion. A later form of Buddhism, Mahayana, which arose in the 1st century AD, is also practiced in Laos, particularly in the cities. It differs from Theravada in that followers venerate the bodhisattvas. This northern school of Buddhism spread from India to Nepal, China, Korea, and Japan and is practiced by Vietnamese and Chinese alike in all the bigger towns of Laos. The Chinese in Laos also follow Taoism and Confucianism.

Buddhism in Laos is so interlaced with daily life that you have a good chance of witnessing its practices and rituals firsthand—from the early-morning sight of women giving alms to monks on their rounds through the neighborhood, to the evening routine of monks gathering for their temple recitations. If you visit temples on Buddhist holy days, which coincide with the new moon, you'll likely hear monks chanting texts of the Buddha's teachings.

Christianity is followed by a small minority of mostly French-educated, elite Laotians, although the faith also has adherents among hill tribe converts in areas that have been visited by foreign missionaries. Missionary activity has been curbed in recent years, however, as the Lao government forbids the dissemination of foreign religious materials.

Islam is practiced by a handful of Arab and Indian businesspeople in Vientiane. There are also some Muslims from Yunnan, China, called Chin Haw, in the northern part of Laos. More recently, a very small number of Cham refugees from Pol Pot's Cambodia (1975–79) took refuge in Vientiane, where they have established a mosque.

them is the **throne room,** with its gilded furniture, colorful mosaic-covered walls, and display cases filled with rare Buddha images, royal regalia, and other priceless artifacts.

The walls of the **king's reception room** are decorated with scenes of traditional Lao life painted in 1930 by the French artist Alex de Fautereau. The **queen's reception room** contains a collection of royal portraits by the Russian artist Ilya Glazunov. The room also has cabinets full of presents given to the royal couple by visiting heads of state; a model moon lander and a piece of moon rock from U.S. president Richard Nixon share shelf space with an exquisite Sevres tea set presented by French president Charles de Gaulle and fine porcelain teacups from Chinese leader Mao Tse-tung. Other exhibits in this eclectic collection include friezes removed from local temples, Khmer drums, and elephant tusks with carved images of the Buddha.

The museum's most prized exhibit is the **Pha Bang,** a gold image of the Buddha slightly less than 3 feet tall and weighing more than 100 pounds. Its history goes back to the 1st century, when it was cast in Sri Lanka; it was brought to Luang Prabang from Cambodia in 1353 as a gift to King Fa Ngum. This event is celebrated as the introduction of Buddhism as an official religion to Laos, and Pha Bang is venerated as the protector of the faith. An ornate temple called Ho Pha Bang, near the entrance to the palace compound, is being restored to house the image.

Tucked away behind the palace is a crumbling wooden garage that houses the royal fleet of aging automobiles. ■ TIP➜ **You'll need about two hours to work through the Royal Palace's maze of rooms.** ✉ *Sisavang Vong Rd. across from Phu Si Hill* ☎ *071/212470* ✇ *20,000 kip* ☉ *Weekdays 8:30–11 and 1–4.*

❾ **Tribal Market.** A hive of daily activity, this central covered market is usually packed with shoppers sifting through piles of produce and household goods, including textiles and Chinese-made items. Hill tribe people often shop here, particularly during cooler weather, when they journey into town to buy winter blankets and clothing. ✉ *Sisavang Vong Rd. at Setthathirat Rd.* ☉ *Daily 7–5.*

❿ **Wat Mai.** This small but lovely temple next to the Royal Palace compound dates from 1796. Its four-tier roof is characteristic of Luang Prabang's religious architecture, but more impressive are the magnificent wood carvings and gold-leaf murals on the main pillars and portico entrance to the temple. These intricate panels depict the last life of the Buddha, as well as various Asian animals. During the Bun Pimai festival (Lao New Year), the Pha Bang sacred Buddha image is carried from the Royal Palace compound to Wat Mai for ritual cleansing ceremonies. ✉ *Sisavang Vong Rd.* ☎ *No phone* ✇ *10,000 kip* ☉ *Daily 6–6.*

Wat Visun. The 16th-century Wat Visun and neighboring **Wat Aham** play a central role in Lao New Year celebrations, when ancestral masks, called *phu gneu gna gneu,* are taken from Wat Aham and displayed in public. Wat Visun was built in 1503, during the reign of King Visunalat, who had the temple named after himself. Within the compound is a large and

The Prabang Buddha

BUT FOR A FEW SIMPLE FACTS, the Prabang Buddha image, the namesake of Luang Prabang, is shrouded in mystery. This much *is* known: the Prabang image is approximately 33 inches tall and weighs 110 pounds. Both hands of the Buddha are raised in double *abhaya mudra* position (the meaning of which has predictably ambiguous symbolic interpretations, including dispelling fear, teaching reason, and offering protection, benevolence, and peace). Historically, the Prabang Buddha has been a symbol of religious and political authority, including the legitimate right to rule the kingdom of Laos. Beyond that, there is much speculation.

It is believed that the image was cast in bronze in Ceylon (Sri Lanka) between the 1st and 9th century, although it has also been suggested that it is made primarily of gold, with silver and bronze alloys. Regardless of its composition, the double-raised palms indicate a later construction (14th century), and a possibly Khmer origin.

Nonetheless, in 1359 the Prabang was given to Fa Ngum, the son-in-law of the Khmer king at Angkor, and brought to Muang Swa, which was subsequently renamed Luang Prabang, the capital of the newly formed kingdom of Lang Xang. The Prabang Buddha became a symbol of the legitimate rule of the king and a device for promoting Theravada Buddhism throughout Laos.

In 1563, the Prabang image was relocated, along with the seat of power, to the new capital city of Vientiane. In 1778, Siamese invaders ransacked Vientiane and made off with both the Prabang and Emerald Buddhas. The Prabang was returned to Laos in 1782 after political and social unrest in Siam was attributed to the image. Similar circumstances surrounded the subsequent capture and release of the Prabang by the Siamese in 1827 and 1867.

Following its return to Laos, the Prabang was housed in Wat Wisunalat, Luang Prabang's oldest temple, and then at Wat Mai. In 1963, during the reign of Sisavang Vatthana, Laos's final monarch, construction began on Haw Pha Bang, a temple to house the Prabang on the grounds of the palace.

However, in 1975 the communist Pathet Lao rose to power, absolved the monarchy, and installed a communist regime. The communist government, having little respect for any symbol of royalty *or* Buddhism, may have handed over the Prabang to Moscow in exchange for assistance from the Soviet Union. Other accounts of the image have it spirited away to Vientiane for safekeeping in a vault, where it may still reside today.

Regardless, there is a 33-inch-tall Buddha statue, real or replica, housed behind bars in an unassuming room beside the entrance to the Royal Palace Museum (until Haw Pha Bang is completed). On the third day of every Lao New Year (April 13–15), the image is ferried via chariot to Wat Mai, where it is cleansed with water by reverent Laotians.

In regards to its authenticity, a respectable and reliable source told me simply this, "People believe that it is real because the Prabang Buddha belongs in Luang Prabang."

–Trevor Ranges

unusual watermelon-shaped stupa called **That Makmo** (literally Watermelon Stupa). The 100-foot-high mound is actually a royal tomb, where many small precious Buddha statues were found when Chin Haw marauders destroyed the city in the late 19th century (these statues have since been moved to the Royal Palace). The temple hall was rebuilt in 1898 along the lines of the original wooden structure and now houses an impressive collection of Buddha statues, stone inscriptions, and other Buddhist art. ⊠ *Visunalat Rd.* ☎ *No phone* 🎫 *10,000 kip* ☉ *Daily 6–6.*

★ ⓭ **Wat Xieng Thong.** Luang Prabang's most important and impressive temple complex is Wat Xieng Thong, a collection of ancient buildings near the tip of the peninsula, where the Mekong and Nam Khan rivers meet. Constructed in 1559–60, the main temple is one of the few structures to have survived centuries of marauding Vietnamese, Chinese, and Siamese armies, and it's regarded as one of the region's best-preserved examples of Buddhist art and architecture. The intricate golden facades, colorful murals, sparkling glass mosaics, and low, sweeping roofs of the entire ensemble of buildings (which overlap to make complex patterns) all combine to create a feeling of harmony and peace.

The interior of the main temple has decorated wooden columns and a ceiling covered with wheels of dharma, representing the Buddha's teaching. The exterior is just as impressive thanks to mosaics of colored glass that were added at the beginning of 20th century. Several small **chapels** at the sides of the main hall are also covered with mosaics and contain various images of the Buddha. The bronze 16th-century reclining Buddha in one chapel was displayed in the 1931 Paris Exhibition. The mosaic on the back wall of that chapel commemorates the 2,500th anniversary of the Buddha's birth with a depiction of Lao village life. The chapel near the compound's east gate, with a gilded facade, contains the royal family's funeral statuary and urns, including a 40-foot-long wooden boat that was used as a hearse. ⊠ *Sisavang Vong Rd.* ☎ *071/212470* 🎫 *10,000 kip* ☉ *Daily 6–6.*

Where to Stay & Eat

New hotels are shooting up in Luang Prabang to accommodate the growing numbers of tourists. Many of the most attractive of them are in converted buildings dating from French colonial days, and two old favorites are former royal properties.

★ **$$–$$$$** ✕ **L'Elephant Restaurant Français.** When you can't face another serving of rice or spicy sauces, it's time to walk down the hill from the Villa

---

COOKING CLASSES

Restaurant **Tamnak Lao** (⇨ *below*) doesn't just serve tasty Laotian food, it also teaches you how to cook it yourself. The restaurant's school comprehensively explains Lao cuisine, cultural influences, and provides ingredients for 12 recipes. Full-day (from 10 to 6) classes of no more than eight students each are held daily. The restaurant at the hotel **Tum Tum Cheng** (⇨ *below*) now offers cooking classes. You can spend a half day learning one of their 150 recipes, some of which are adapted from the cookbook of Phia Sing, former chef to the Lao royal family.

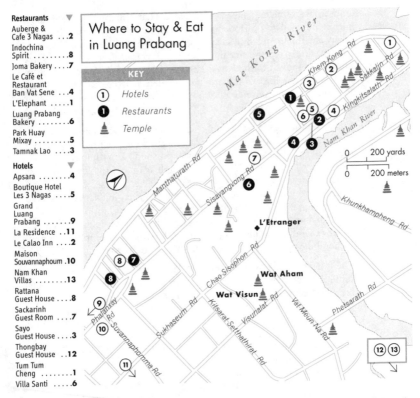

Santi to this pleasant corner restaurant. The menu is traditional French, with a bit of Lao influence, especially when it comes to the ingredients. Consider, for example, the *chevreuil au poivre vert* (local venison in a pepper sauce). There are always the three-course set meal and several daily specials, which usually include fish fresh from the Mekong. Seating is available in the bright, airy dining room or on the sidewalk, behind a barrier of plants. ⊠ *Ban Wat Nong* ☎ *071/252482* ▤ *MC, V* ☽ *No lunch weekdays.*

$$$ ✕ **Auberge & Cafe 3 Nagas.** Local buffalo meat with green-pepper sauce, and fillet of perch with mushrooms are two delicious specialties served at this stylish French restaurant under the same management as L'Elephant Restaurant Francais. It's opposite the Boutique Hotel Les 3 Nagas. ⊠ *Sakkalin Rd.* ☎ *071/253888* ▤ *MC, V.*

¢–$$ ✕ **Indochina Spirit.** For a hearty meal, head to this circa-1920s former residence of a royal physician, now an eclectic Thai-run restaurant where a selection of Lao specialties costs just $5. Start with an appetizer of Mekong seaweed, followed by the "Indochina" steak. Italian pastas and pizza are also on the menu, and delicious pancakes are served for breakfast. ⊠ *52 Ban Wat That* ☎ *071/252372* ▤ *MC, V.*

¢–$ ✕ **Joma Bakery Cafe.** Canadians run this cheap, friendly self-service restaurant, where an in-house bakery turns out delicious pastries, pizzas, salads, and French bread. The homemade soups are excellent. ✉ *Chao Fa Ngum Rd.* ☎ *071/252292* ▭ *No credit cards* ☉ *Closed Sun.*

¢–$ ✕ **Le Café et Restaurant Ban Vat Sene.** Sidewalk seating and a retractable brown-striped awning contribute to the traditional French café atmosphere here. Freshly made quiche, baguettes, and *grandes tartines* (large slices of homemade bread with various toppings) are the highlights of the menu. Across from Villa Santi on the northern end of town, the café is a relaxing place for a meal or simply a cup of coffee and some pastries. ■ TIP→ **A $6 purchase also buys you unlimited Wi-Fi access.** ✉ *Sakkalin Rd.* ☎ *071/252482* ▭ *MC, V.*

¢–$ ✕ **Luang Prabang Bakery.** It would be difficult not to eventually wander into Luang Prabang Bakery—it has a great central location and the most enticing atmosphere of the several outdoor-seating restaurants in this part of town. It certainly is a great spot for a cool drink and some prime people-watching. The restaurant also serves more than 20 different Laotian dishes, *jo mart len pak lae kout noi* (steamed fresh vegetables with a spicy grilled-tomato sauce), and you can also satisfy a craving for Western food with a tasty hamburger, a pizza, some pasta, or even a steak. The menu includes a variety of French and Australian wines. ✉ *Sisavangvong Rd.* ☎ *071/252499* ▭ *V.*

¢–$ ✕ **Park Huay Mixay.** Venison steak is recommended at this long-established pan-Asian restaurant, a favorite with locals. Start your meal, though, with a more conventional Lao dish, such as tom yam soup (with lemongrass, coriander, chilies, and chicken or fish), and end it with a glass of the local lao-lao (home-brewed rice whiskey). ✉ *75/6 Sothikuman Rd., Ban Xieng Muan* ☎ *071/212260 or 020/551–1496* ▭ *No credit cards.*

★ ¢–$ ✕ **Tamnak Lao.** If you're looking for excellent Laotian food, this is the place to start. Try a set menu to sample a variety of the country's cooking styles or order from the lengthy menu that includes *kaipan*, a crispy dried Mekong River plant covered with sesame seeds and served with a local chutney (the local equivalent of chips and salsa), and *orlam*, an eggplant "casserole" that can be compared to an exotic *gaeng kiew waan* (Thai green curry) and is a local favorite. You can even try venison, wild boar, or kangaroo steaks (the latter arguably not so traditional). ✉ *Sakkalin Rd.* ☎ *071/252525* ▭ *MC, V.*

$$$$ ✕⌂ **La Residence Phou Vao Hotel.** Its prime position on Kite Hill gives this sumptuous hotel the best views in town. Traditional Lao touches are everywhere and create a sense of exotic luxury in the rosewood-furnished rooms. In the evening, you can relax over cocktails at the Dok Chama Bar and soak in the restful garden surroundings. The restaurant ($$$$) is among Luang Prabang's best, serving authentic Lao food and rich French dishes. Seven different therapies are available at the spa; guests staying a full week can try a different treatment each day. ■ TIP→ **Nonguests can use the small but picturesque pool area, including the steam room, for $10 per day.** The hotel provides free shuttle service into town for its guests. ✉ *Phu Vao Hill* ☎ *071/212530 up to 33* ⊕ *www.pansea.com* ⇄ *34 rooms* ⌂ *In-room: safe, refrigerator. In-hotel: restaurant, bar, room service, pool, spa, laundry service, public Internet* ▭ *AE, MC, V.*

$$$–$$$$ ✕⌂ **Villa Santi.** This 19th-century royal residence in the heart of town was converted to a boutique hotel in 2001 by a local princess's son-in-

law, who also built a resort outside town. Rooms in both the resort and the two structures in town are decorated with rosewood furniture, handicrafts, and fine silks decorate the rooms. In town, the lovely garden courtyard doubles as the Elephant Garden Bar, and the Princess Restaurant, which has live folk music nightly and dancing Friday and Saturday, serves authentic "royal" Lao and Western cuisine; there are several nine-course set menus that are ideal samplers of Laotian food, like deep-fried lemongrass stuffed with minced pork and Lao egg dumpling soup. Five minutes from town, the resort offers some respite from the "bustle" of the city and features a 20-meter swimming pool. Free shuttle service allows those at the resort to visit the town, and those in town to chill out at the pool. The open-air terrace restaurant serves Lao and international cuisine. *Hotel:* ✉ *Sakkalin Rd.* ☎ *071/252157* ⊕ *www.villasantihotel.com* ➲ *25 rooms* ♿ *In-room: no phone, safe, refrigerator, no TV. In-hotel: restaurant, bar, room service, laundry service, concierge, airport shuttle, no-smoking rooms* ▭ *MC, V* ⅋ℂ *BP* ✉ *Resort:* ✉ *Nadeuay Rd.* ☎ *071/253470* ⊕ *www.villasantihotel. com* ➲ *52 rooms* ♿ *In-room: refrigerator. In-hotel: restaurant, pool, laundry service* ▭ *MC, V* ⅋ℂ *BP.*

$$$–$$$$

FodorsChoice

★

✕🄸 **Boutique Hotel Les 3 Nagas.** This turn-of-the-19th-century mansion stands under official UNESCO World Heritage Site protection, thanks in no small measure to the efforts of the French owner to retain its weathered but handsome colonial look. The wooden floors and clay tiles are original, and the large rooms are furnished with dark wood, silks, and homespun local fabrics (you can also buy these fabrics in the hotel shop, along with Lao teas, coffee, and spices). Some rooms have four-poster beds. Superior Room 6 has a balcony like that of the executive suite, ideal for watching the morning alms procession of local monks. The hotel's restaurant is one of the few in Luang Prabang serving exclusively vegetarian Lao dishes. ✉ *Sakkalin Rd., Ban Wat Nong* ☎ *071/253888* ⊕ *www.3nagas. com* ➲ *15 rooms* ♿ *In-room: safe, refrigerator, ethernet. In-hotel: restaurant, room service, laundry service* ▭ *MC, V* ⅋ℂ *BP.*

★ $$

✕🄸 **Apsara.** With its white facade and balustrades and its riverside location, this French-style *maison* would be at home in southern France; instead, it's the trendiest boutique hotel in Luang Prabang. ▪ TIP→ **The plush silk-adorned restaurant ($), with its terrace overlooking the Nam Khan River, is worth a visit, even if you're not staying the night (it claims to serve the driest martini in town).** The reasonably priced rooms have floor-to-ceiling windows that face east, so you can catch the sunrise over the nearby mountains. Rooms 1 through 5 on the second floor have the best river or mountain views. Under the same management is a pretty, city-center, three-bedroom, traditional wooden Lao house in secluded gardens that's ideal for families (they even have maid service!) and is available for $165–$210 per night. ✉ *Kingkitsarat Rd.* ☎ *071/212420* ⊕ *www.theapsara.com* ➲ *13 rooms, 1 3-bedroom house* ♿ *In-room: safe, refrigerator, Wi-Fi. In-hotel: restaurant, bar, laundry service, public Wi-Fi* ▭ *MC, V* ⅋ℂ *BP.*

★ $–$$

✕🄸 **Nam Khan Villas & El Gecko Restaurant.** Proprietors Graham and Caroline have successfully combined the atmosphere of traditional Laos with the comforts of the Western world; the resort is laid out like a local village, with meandering paths connecting reconstructed Laotian houses set amid local flora and overlooking the Nam Khan River. The Mediterranean-style, open-air El Gecko restaurant serves delectable European and Lao tapas (Caroline has 30 years' experience catering to an international clientele in Spain). Although a bit farther from town than the other major hotels, the resort is connected via a walking path to the Ban Phanom weaving village, and boat service ferries hotel and restaurant patrons to and from Luang Prabang. ✛ *Just before the New Bridge on the New Road leading to the airport, turn right onto a small dirt road. Follow the dirt road 100 meters; the hotel is on the right* ☎ *071/254631 or 020/777–1305* ⊕ *www.nkvresort.com* ⤴ *10 rooms* ⛌ *In-room: no a/c, no TV, no phone. In-hotel: restaurant, bar, bicycles* ▭ *No credit cards.*

★ $ ✕▥ **Tum Tum Cheng.** Although accommodations here don't rank among this town's best, the restaurant definitely does. The intimate spot on the northern end of town serves an inventive menu of Lao food, with such treats as Mekong catfish in a sweet ginger sauce and venison with mushrooms. Seating is available inside on cushions or on the garden terrace, but is limited, so reservations are essential in peak season. A newer version of the restaurant on the same road but closer to the center of town serves the same menu. Rooms are simple but sufficient—they're decorated with local handicrafts, but are short on amenities, and have rather basic bathrooms. The location, a stone's throw from Wat Xieng Thong, is perfect, and the owners, a Lao/Hungarian couple, are charming. ✉ *50/1 Ban Xieng Thong* ☎ *071/253224* ⤴ *10 rooms* ⛌ *In-room: no phone, no TV. In-hotel: restaurant, laundry service* ▭ *MC, V.*

$$$$ ▥ **Maison Souvannaphoum.** The once-run-down residence of Prince Souvannaphoum, prime minister in the 1960s, has been transformed into one of the top hotels in Luang Prabang. The colonial-style mansion contains the reception area, an open-air restaurant, a bar, and upstairs, the suites; guest rooms occupy a newer building alongside the main building. Rooms are large and bright, with small balconies overlooking tropical greenery. Ask for a room at the back, away from the busy street, for more peace and quiet, or opt for the prince's bedroom suite, which is spacious, elegant, and romantic. After Banyan Tree Hotels took over the resort in 2005, they opened the Angsana Spa in the hotel, which offers a variety of luxurious treatments but is unfortunately located alongside the main road out of town. ✉ *Chao Fa Ngum Rd.* ☎ *071/212200* ⤴ *24 rooms* ⛌ *In-room: refrigerator, Wi-Fi. In-hotel: restaurant, bar, pool, spa, laundry service* ▭ *MC, V* ⊙ *BP.*

$$$ ▥ **Grand Luang Prabang.** This Thai-owned hotel occupies the former residence of nationalist hero Prince Petsarath (1890–1959), whose villa stands amid the hotel's new (but traditionally designed) buildings. The hotel has an unmatched location on a bend of the Mekong River, and though guest rooms are set back a bit, most have river views. Rooms are spacious and have hardwood floors, white marble baths, and sliding glass doors that open onto large balconies. It's 4 km (2½ mi) from Luang Prabang, near the village of Xieng Keo; a shuttle provides regular transportation to town and the airport. In summer a boat ferries guests into town. ✉ *Ban Xieng Keo, Khet Sangkalok* ☎ *071/253851 up to 57* ⊕ *www.grandluangprabang.com* ⤴ *78 rooms* ⛌ *In-room: refrigerator. In-hotel: restaurant, bar, bicycles, laundry service, concierge, airport shuttle, no-smoking rooms* ▭ *AE, MC, V* ⊙ *BP.*

8

$$ ⊞ **Le Calao Inn.** Fronting the Mekong and just down the street from Wat Xieng Thong is this small hotel, which was resurrected from a ruined mansion built by a Portuguese merchant in 1904. Four guest rooms upstairs open onto a colonnaded veranda to views of the river and the hills beyond. The two rooms on the lower floor are larger—with three beds each—and have private terraces, but are a bit dark. The Buasavan Restaurant on the ground floor serves French and Asian fare. ■ TIP→ **Because of the hotel's small size and popularity, it's highly advisable to book ahead November–April.** ⊠ *Suvanna Kham Phong Rd.* ☎ *071/212100* ✑ *calaoinn@laotel.com* ➫ *6 rooms* ⚲ *In-room: no TV. In-hotel: restaurant, laundry service* ▣ *MC, V* ⦿ *BP.*

$ ⊞ **Sayo Guest House.** An elegant white colonial-style hotel with green shutters, Sayo Guest House is almost prototypical Luang Prabang style. Chic yet unpretentious, the hotel consists of rooms with river views, furnishings made from local wood, mosquito nets, and Lao comforters, the combined effect being old-world charm and a relaxed vibe. The second floor has hardwood floors, and rooms 1 and 2 have private balconies, ideal for lazy afternoon river-watching. ⊠ *Corner of Souvannakhamphong and Sisaleumsak Rds.* ☎ *071/252614* ⊕ *sayo@laotel.com* ➫ *20 rooms* ⚲ *In-room: refrigerator. In-hotel: laundry service* ▣ *No credit cards.*

¢ ⊞ **Rattana Guest House.** Family-run guesthouses are common in Luang Prabang, but this one certainly makes you feel right at home. The Rattana sisters Somsanith and Somporn, their mother, and their adopted daughter are extremely knowledgeable and helpful (one sister works for an established tour operator, the other is a doctor). Rooms are bright, clean, and comfortable. Rooms 101 and 102 have small balconies; note that 102 has a detached, though private, bath. There's no restaurant, but there is a breakfast room. ⊠ *Koksack St., 4/2 Ban What That* ☎ *071/252255* ➫ *12 rooms* ⚲ *In-room: no a/c (some)* ▣ *No credit cards.*

¢ ⊞ **Sackarinh Guest Room.** This friendly place in the center of town is the ideal Luang Prabang guesthouse—it's spotless and it's super cheap. Rooms are large and bright, but have shared baths. There is, of all things, a Scandanvian restaurant attached to the guesthouse, but you are so close to many good Lao restaurants that you'll probably want to skip it. ⊠ *Sisavang Vong Rd.* ☎ *071/254512 or 020/544-2001* ✑ *sackarinh_guestroom@hotmail. com* ➫ *8 rooms with private bath, 2 rooms with shared bath* ⚲ *In-room: no a/c, no TV (some), no phone* ▣ *No credit cards.*

★ ¢ ⊞ **Thongbay Guest House.** Thongbay is just outside town, but it's right on the Nam Khan River. The resort is a small village of well-built, comfortable, thatch huts with fans. Stone and tile bathrooms are clean and surprisingly stylish for such a rustic retreat. Every bungalow has a deck with floor pillows and chairs from which to look out over the river or the beautiful gardens. It's about a 10-minute ride into town on a bicycle, which the guesthouse has for rent. ✛ *On a small dirt road off 13 North Rd. near the new bridge* ☎ *071/253234* ⊕ *www.thongbay-guesthouses.com* ⚲ *In-room: refrigerator. In-hotel: restaurant, laundry service* ▣ *No credit cards.*

Nightlife & the Arts

Luang Prabang's nightlife is limited. Monday, Wednesday, and Saturday evenings at 6:30, the **Royal Ballet Theater Phralak-Phralam** (☎ 071/

253705) performs at the Royal Palace museum. The program includes local folk songs, a local *bai-si* ceremony, classical dances enacting episodes from the Indian *Ramayana* epic, and outdoor presentations of the music and dances of Lao minorities. Admission is $8.

Locals head to the nightclub **Muong Swa** (⊠ Phu Vao Rd.) for Lao-style folk and rock music. If you need a dancing partner, the waiters will find you one. Otherwise wait until the locals start line-dancing and simply get in line! When Muong Swa shuts down at 11:30 PM the party moves to **Dao Fa** (⊠ Across from Southern Bus Terminal), where Luang Prabang's young "nouveau riche" strut their stuff.

A number of bar-restaurants consisting of simple tables and chairs are set up on the hill above the Mekong River on Souvannakhamphong Road. On the other side of Phousi Hill are **Lao Lao Garden,** a casual, open air restaurant and bar, **L'etranger book store and café,** and the **Hive bar,** where young backpackers congregate within a dimly lit interior or around small outdoor "campfires" to mix, mingle, and share tales of the road. The three are located near the corner of Phou Si and Phommathay streets. **The Opium Den,** scheduled to open in September 2007, will feature Luang Prabang's first Western-style night club: downstairs, a stylish, chic wine/martini bar with a small stage for acoustic music; upstairs, a dance club occasionally featuring international DJs. It's one block beyond the new Talat Dara market.

Sports & the Outdoors

Many of the tour operators in town offer interesting rafting and kayaking trips, plus cycling expeditions. Several guesthouses and hotels rent bikes for about $1 a day.

The owner of **White Elephant Adventures** (⊠ Sisavang Vong Rd., opposite Luang Prabang Bakery ☎ 020/589–4394 or 030/514–0243 ⊕ www.white-elephant-adventures-laos.com), Derek, is as enthusiastic about sharing his adopted home country as he is about making sure each visitor's experiences are authentic and uncrowded and that the impact of these journeys on the local people and their environment is low. The tours are educational, led by local university students, and are constantly exploring new areas to provide a less touristy experience. Single- or multiday hiking, biking, and kayaking adventures are available for groups of two to six people.

Shopping

Luang Prabang has two principal markets where you can find a large selection of handicrafts: the Dala Central Market, on Setthathirat Road, and the Tribal Market, on Sisavang Vong Road. In the evening, most of Sisavang Vong Road turns into an open bazaar, similar to Thailand's night markets. It's a pleasant place to stroll, bargain with hawkers, and stop for a simple meal and a beer at one of many roadside stalls.

Locally worked silver is cheap and very attractive. You can find a good selection at **Thit Peng** (⊠ 48/2 Ban Wat That ☎ 071/212327).

Pathana Boupha (⊠ 29/4 Ban Visoun ☎ 071/212262) is an antiques and textile shop and museum. It claims to produce the costumes and ornaments for the Miss New Year pageant in Luang Prabang (a seemingly prestigious endeavor). It certainly does have a dizzying array of goods on display, many of which are not for sale. Shoppers *can*, however, select from textiles produced by a variety of different Laotian ethnic groups.

Tad Sae Waterfall

14 *15 km (9 mi) east of Luang Prabang.*

Accessible only by boat, this spectacular waterfall is best visited in the rainy season, when the rivers are high and their waters thunder over the cascade. The waterfall features multilevel limestone formations divided into three steps with big pools beneath them—don't forget your bathing suit. There are some old waterwheels here and a small, simple resort nearby.

The rainy-season route takes you from Luang Prabang (depart from the jetty on the river side of Wat Xieng Thong) up the Nam Khan River to its confluence with the Huay Sae River. On the way you pass the weaving village of Ban Phanom; the tomb of the French naturalist Henri Mouhot, who died in Luang Prabang in 1861; and the Xieng Lom Resort, with an elephant camp founded by a German benefactor, Markus Peschke. The other route to the waterfall follows Highway 13 south from Luang Prabang for 13 km (8 mi) to the turnoff to the pristine Lao Lum riverside village of Ban Aen. A boat can then be hired at Ban Aen for a short trip upstream to the waterfall. ■ TIP→ **An alternative way to see the falls and enjoy a day on the river is to do a kayaking day trip with one of the adventure-tour agencies based in Luang Prabang.** *8,000 kip.*

Pak Ou Caves

15 *25 km (16 mi) up the Maekong from Luang Prabang.*

Set in high limestone cliffs above the Mekong River, at the point where it meets the Nam Ou River from northern Laos, are two sacred caves filled with thousands of Buddha statues dating from the 16th century. The lower cave, **Tham Thing,** is accessible from the river by a stairway and has enough daylight to allow you to find your way around. The stairway continues to the upper cave, **Tham Phum,** for which you need a flashlight. The admission charge of 10,000 kip includes a flashlight and a guide.

Slow boats make the three-hour journey to the caves from Luang Prabang, many of them stopping at waterside villages for a perusal of the rich variety of local handicrafts, a nip of lao-lao, and perhaps a bowl of noodles. If you're in a hurry you can catch a speedboat from Luang Prabang to the caves—a noisy one-hour trip. An alternative route is by bus from the Northern Bus Terminal or by taxi to the town of Pak Ou, where boats ferry visitors across the river to the caves. Pak Ou has several passable restaurants.

Tad Khuang Si Waterfall

★ ⑯ *29 km (18 mi) south of Luang Prabang.*

A series of cascades surrounded by lush foliage, Tad Khuang Si is a popular spot with Lao and foreigners alike. Many visitors merely view the falls from the lower pool, where picnic tables and food vendors invite you to linger, but a steep path through the forest leads to pools above the falls that are the perfect spot for a swim. Tour operators and taxi drivers in Luang Prabang offer day trips for $25 that combine Tad Kuang Si with a visit to a Khamu tribal village nearby. The drive, past rice farms and small Lao Lum tribal villages, is half the adventure. The best time to visit the falls is between November and April, after the rainy season. The **Elephant Park Project** (☎ 071/252655 ⊕ www.laos-adventures.com), operated by Tiger Trail Tours, offers elephant-back trips to the waterfall, among other educational and ecotourism-related activities. 🎫 *15,000 kip.*

Ban Muang Ngoi

⑰ *150 km (93 mi) northeast of Luang Prabang.*

This picturesque river village sits on the eastern side of the Nam Ou River, which descends from Phong Saly Province in the north to meet the Maekong River opposite the famous Pak Ou Caves. The village, populated by Lao Lum, is surrounded by unusual limestone peaks. The journey here is an adventure in itself: a songthaew takes you from Luang Prabang's Northern Bus Terminal to a pier at Nong Khiaw, where boats continue on a one-hour trip upstream to the village.

Where to Stay

¢ 🏠 **Ning Ning Guesthouse.** Of the many guesthouses in Ban Muang Ngoi, this is among the best. It has five clean bungalows to rent for $5 a day. ⊠ *Ban Muang Ngoi* ☎ *No phone* 🛏 *5 bungalows* ♿ *In-room: no a/c, no phone, no TV* ⊟ *No credit cards* 🍽 *BP.*

Luang Nam Tha

⑱ *319 km (198 mi) north of Luang Prabang.*

The capital of Laos's northernmost province, Luang Nam Tha is the headquarters of the groundbreaking Nam Ha Ecotourism. The program, a model for Southeast Asia, actively encourages the involvement of local communities in the development and management of tourism policies. You can join a two- or three-day trek, organized through the Boat Landing Guesthouse, through the Nam Ha Protected Area, which shelters numerous animals, including elephants, tigers, and bears. Khamu, Akha, and Lanten Yao tribes live in the dense forest.

Where to Stay

$ 🏠 **Boat Landing Guesthouse.** Comfortable accommodations can be found in the timber-and-bamboo bungalows at this ecofriendly guesthouse run by an American. Rooms are furnished in rattan. The guesthouse organ-

8

izes two- and three-day treks into the Nam Ha Protected Area. ✉ *Ban Kone* ☎ *086/312398* 🖷 *086/12239* ⊕ *www.theboatlanding.laopdr. com* ⇲ *10 rooms* ⚂ *In-hotel: restaurant, bicycles* ⊟ *No credit cards* ⭐ *BP.*

Muang Sing

🔟 *60 km (37 mi) north of Luang Nam Tha.*

In the late 19th century, this mountain-ringed town on the Sing Mountain River was the seat of a Tai Lue prince, Chao Fa Silino; Muang Sing lost its regional prominence, however, when French colonial forces occupied the town and established a garrison here. Muang Sing is known for its market, which draws throngs of traditionally robed tribespeople. Shoppers from among the 20 different tribes living in the area, and even traders from China, visit the market to buy locally produced goods and handicrafts. The market is open daily 6 AM–9 AM.

River Journey to Huay Xai

🔟 *297 km (184 mi) up the Mekong from Luang Prabang.*

Growing rapidly in popularity is the 300-km (186-mi) Mekong River trip between Luang Prabang and Huay Xai, across the river from Chiang Khong in Thailand. It's a highly dramatic journey on what must qualify as one of the world's most spectacular stretches of river. Your boat ploughs through the rushing water and a constantly changing primeval scene of towering cliffs, huge mud flats and sandbanks, rocky islands, and riverbanks smothered in thick jungle, with the occasional patch of cultivated land, mulberry trees, bananas, and tiny garlic fields. There are no roads, just forest paths linking dusty settlements where the boats tie up for refreshment stops.

The only village of note is a halfway station, Pakbeng, which has a few guesthouses and a general store along its one main street. ■ TIP→ **Once you arrive in Huay Xai (which has little of interest in itself), a good way to return to Thailand is to cross the river to Chiang Khong and then take a bus to Chiang Rai, 60 km (37 mi) inland.**

There are two main ways to make the journey to Huay Xai from Luang Prabang: either by regular "slow" boat, which holds about 50 passengers, or by speedboat, which seats about 4. The regular boat takes 12 hours or more over the course of two days. The night is spent at Pakbeng in very basic lodgings—guesthouses with cold water and limited electricity. The speedboats make the journey between Luang Prabang and Huay Xai in 6 hours. ⚠ **Speedboats, although thrilling for the first hour, become extremely uncomfortable after the novelty wears off.** The seats are hard and uncomfortable, the engine noise is deafening (earplugs are advised), and the wind and spray can be chilling. Bring a warm, waterproof windbreaker, and be sure to get a life jacket and crash helmet with a visor from the boat driver. Another option is to journey to Pakbeng by speedboat, overnight at the village, and continue the following day by either speedboat or regular boat. For the regular boat, the fare is about

$10 per person; the speedboat is $30 per person. Slow boats and speedboats depart daily.

Much more comfortable than the regular boat and speedboat, but far more expensive, is the *LuangSay* luxury boat, which is specially designed for leisurely river travel. The river cruise includes accommodation in Pakbeng at the very comfortable LuangSay Lodge. The *LuangSay* departs from Luang Prabang every Wednesday and Saturday, and returns from Huay Xai every Monday and Friday (and Thursday November–April). The cruise costs $130. Contact **LuangSay Cruises** (✉ Sakkarine Rd., Luang Prabang ☎ 071/252553 ⊕ www.asian-oasis.com).

Where to Stay

PAKBENG   ▢ **LuangSay Lodge.** This comfortable lodging sits on the riverbank amid
$$ lush green hills. ✉ *Pakbeng* ☎ *020/670177, 021/215958 in Luang Prabang, 071/252553 in Vientiane* ⊕ *www.asian-oasis.com* ✑ *19 rooms* ⌂ *In-room: no a/c* ▭ *No credit cards.*

HUAY XAI   ▢ **Keo Udomphon Hotel.** This old town house is more comfortable than
¢   its outside appearance might lead you to believe. Rooms are furnished in an eclectic mix of styles, but are bright and clean. ✉ *Saikang Rd., Huay Xai* ☎ *084/211504* ✑ *20 rooms* ⌂ *In-hotel: restaurant* ▭ *No credit cards.*

Phong Saly

㉑ *425 km (264 mi) north of Luang Prabang.*

If you're looking for off-the-beaten-track "soft" adventure, head for the provincial capital Phong Saly, in the far north of Laos. It's a hill station and market town nearly 5,000 feet above sea level in the country's most spectacular mountain range, Phu Fa. Trekking through this land of forest-covered mountains and rushing rivers may be as close as you'll ever get to the thrill of exploring virgin territory; ■ TIP➜ **you can arrange for a guide (a must) through any of the hotels or guesthouses in town.** There are about 25 different ethnic groups in the area, and the local **tribal museum** offers a fascinating look into their lives and culture. Among the exhibits is a kaleidoscopic display of tribal costumes. ☎ *No phone* ✑ *1,000 kip* ⊗ *Weekdays 7:30–11:30 and 1:30–4:30.*

The journey to Phong Saly is quite an adventure; a bus from Luang Prabang's Northern Bus Terminal takes you the 115 km (71 mi) to Udom Xay, where you have to hire a car to continue, via the towns of Bun Sin Xay and Bun Nua. From Bun Nua it's an additional 40 km (25 mi) to Phong Saly via a side road that branches off Highway 13. Note that it's possible to catch a flight from Udom Xay or Bun Nua to Vientiane—a good option if the journey back to Luang Prabang seems too daunting.

Where to Stay

PHONG SALY   ▢ **Phu Fa.** Formerly the Chinese consulate, this forbidding building in
¢   an industrial compound is now a government-run hotel. You're unlikely to want to linger in the rooms, but some have stunning views of the surrounding countryside. ✉ *Phong Saly* ☎ *088/210031* ✑ *24 rooms* ⌂ *In-room: no a/c. In-hotel: restaurant* ▭ *No credit cards.*

Linda Guesthouse. This is a good choice if you're overnighting in
¢ Udom Xay on the way to Phong Saly. All rooms have hot showers, a
luxury in this neck of the woods. ⊠ *Udom Xay* ☎ *081/312147* ✈ *17
rooms* ⑆ *In-room: no a/c (some)* ▭ *No credit cards.*

Luang Prabang & Northern Laos Essentials

Transportation

BY AIR

Direct flights to Luang Prabang from neighboring Thailand originate
in both Chiang Mai and Bangkok. Lao Airlines operates a thrice-weekly
service from Bangkok to Luang Prabang and five flights weekly from
Chiang Mai to Luang Prabang. Bangkok Airways flies direct twice daily
from Bangkok to Luang Prabang.

Lao Airlines has several flights a day between Vientiane and Luang Prabang, plus three weekly flights from Vientiane to Huay Xai. Lao Airlines has three flights a week to Vientiane from Udom Xay, which is on
the route from Luang Prabang to Phong Saly.

Bangkok Airways also has daily connecting service from Luang Prabang
to Koh Samui, Phuket, Krabi, and Trat (Koh Chang), all via Bangkok,
and a nonstop flight to Siam Riep in Cambodia.
🚩 Carriers **Bangkok Airways** ☎ 071/253334 in Luang Prabang, 02/265-5555 in
Bangkok ⊕ www.bangkokair.com. **Lao Airlines** ☎ 071/212172 in Luang Prabang, 021/
212016 in Vientiane, 02/236-9821 in Bangkok ⊕ www.laoairlines.com.

Luang Prabang International Airport is 4 km (2½ mi) northeast of the
city. The taxi ride to the city center costs $5.
🚩 Airport **Luang Prabang International Airport** ☎ 071/212173 or 071/212856.

BY BIKE

Biking is one of the best ways to visit all of the interesting sights within
Luang Prabang. At many guesthouses and hotels you can rent a bicycle for about $1 for 12 hours.

BY BOAT & FERRY

There are several interesting destinations in northern Laos that are accessible from Luang Prabang by boat, including the Tad Saefall Waterfall, the Pak Ou Caves, and Huay Xai. In Luang Prabang you can find
a boat for hire just about anywhere along the entire length of the road
bordering the Mekong River; the main jetty is on the river side of Wat
Xieng Thong.

The slow boats to Huay Xai depart from the river side of Wat Xieng
Thong; the speedboats to Huay Xai depart from a pier on the northern
outskirts of the city.

Adventurous travelers can board boats in Huay Xai for Xieng Kok in
northern Luang Nam Tha Province, or negotiate with barge captains
for a passage from Luang Prabang to Vientiane and even farther south.
The port office in Huay Xai is the place to find obliging skippers, who

demand $10–$20 for a place on deck as far as Luang Prabang, and $50 or more for the longer upstream trip to Chinese ports.

BY BUS

Luang Prabang's bus service is basically a fleet of songthaews; a short trip within town costs about $1.

There are two bus terminals with service out of town: one serving northern Laos and the other, Vientiane and the south. VIP buses to Vang Vieng and on to Vientiane leave three times daily, cost around $10, and take approximately six and nine hours, respectively. A minivan to Vang Vieng can be arranged at any travel agency; the trip costs the same as a VIP bus, but only takes five hours. The public bus to Phonesavanh (Plain of Jars) costs 85,000 kip and takes eight hours.

For quick border runs to Thailand, a public bus leaves at 9 AM for the three-hour trip to Sayaburi (40,000 kip), where a newly opened border crossing allows access to Nan Province in Thailand. (Check that the border crossing is officially open for foreigners before making the trip!)

Buses from the Northern Bus Terminal take you part way to Ban Muang Ngoi and Phong Saly. You can also catch a bus from this terminal to Luang Nam Tha and change to a bus to Muang Sing.

BY CAR

Although you can drive from Vientiane to Luang Prabang, it takes seven to eight hours to make the 242-km (150-mi) trip along the meandering, but paved, road up into the mountains. Driving on your own is probably not the best idea as the roads are harrowing and accidents will invariably be considered your fault. If you wish to travel by car, hiring a driver is safer and more enjoyable.

BY TAXI, TUK-TUK & SONGTHAEW

You can cover Luang Prabang on foot or by bicycle. The few taxis in town must be booked through your hotel or guesthouse. Tuk-tuks and songthaews make up Luang Prabang's public transport system. They cruise all the streets and are easy to flag down. Plan on paying around $1–$2 for a trip within the city.

Depending on the destination, you can take a car, taxi, bus, or, in some cases, boat, to travel outside Luang Prabang.

Contacts & Resources

BANKS & EXCHANGING SERVICES

There are no ATMs in Luang Prabang or northern Laos, so make sure you have enough kip or dollars to cover your visit; you can, however, change money at Luang Prabang's Lan Xiang Bank, on Sisavang Vong Road, or at the Lao Development Bank, which is open daily from 8:30 to 3:30. Major credit cards are accepted in most hotels and many restaurants, but few shops. There is a Western Union office at the post office on the corner of Fa Ngum and Setthathirath roads in the center of town.

CLOSE UP

Lao: A Few Key Phrases

THE OFFICIAL LANGUAGE IS LAO, part of the extensive Tai family of languages of Southeast Asia spoken from Vietnam in the east to India in the west. Spoken Lao is very similar to the Northern Thai language, as well as local dialects in the Shan states in Myanmar and Sipsongbanna in China. Lao is tonal, meaning a word can have several meanings according to the tone in which it's spoken.

In tourist hotels, the staff generally speaks some English. You can find a smattering of English speakers in shops and restaurants. A few old-timers know some French.

Here are a few common and useful words:

Hello: sabai di (pronounced sa-bye dee)

Thank you: khop chai deu (pronounced cop chi dew; use khop cheu neu in northern Laos)

Yes: heu (pronounced like deux) *or* thia

No: bo

Where?: iu sai (pronounced you sai)?

How much?: to dai (pronounced taw dai)?

Zero: sun (pronounced soon)

One: neung

Two: song

Three: sam

Four: si

Five: ha

Six: hok

Seven: tiet (pronounced tee-yet)

Eight: pet

Nine: kao

Ten: sip

Twenty: sao (rhymes with cow. Different from Thai "yee sip")

Hundred: neung loi

Thousand: neung phan

To have fun: muan

To eat: kin khao (pronounced kin cow)

To drink: kin nam

Water: nam

Rice: khao

Expensive: peng

Bus: lot me (pronounced lot may)

House: ban

Road: thanon

Village: ban

Island: don

River: mae nam (pronounced may nam)

Doctor: mao (pronounced mow)

Hospital: hong mo (pronounced hong maw)

Post Office: paisani

Hotel: hong hem

Toilet: hong nam

EMERGENCIES

For medical and police emergencies, use the services of your hotel or guesthouse. They will be able to summon a doctor or official quickly. Otherwise, consult the International Clinic in Luang Prabang.

🏥 **Hospital International Clinic** ✉ Ban Thongchaloen, Luang Prabang ☎ 071/252048.

INTERNET, MAIL & SHIPPING

The Luang Prabang post office is on the corner of Fa Ngum and Setthathirath roads in the center of town. EMS delivery is available there, as is Western Union money transfer. The post office (zip 06000) is open daily 8–noon and 1–3:30.

There are many Internet cafés along Sisavang Vong Road, and Wi-Fi is increasingly available at nicer restaurants and hotels, including Maison Souvannaphoum and Le Café Ban Vat Sene.

TOUR OPTIONS

Diethelm Travel is the major tour operator in Luang Prabang and the most reliable. The company offers "stopovers" of three to four days, which cost $321–$781; these include tours of Luang Prabang, plus excursions to outlying villages, waterfalls, and the Pak Ou Caves. Tours to the Plain of Jars are available through Diethelm Travel, as well as Lao Youth Travel. For single or multi-day hiking, biking, and kayaking adventures, White Elephant Adventures gives tours for groups of two to six people. Smiling Albino provides specialized tours of the region that feature a broad range of activities, modes of transport, and venues, led by foreign and local experts in the region.

🚩 **Diethelm Travel** ✉ Sisavang Vong Rd., Luang Prabang ☎ 071/212277 ⊕ www.diethelmtravel.com. **Lao Youth Travel** ✉ 72 Sisavang Vong Rd., Ban Pakham ☎ 071/253340 ⊕ www.laoyouthtravel.com.

Smiling Albino ✉ 2098/414 Ramkhamhaeng, Soi 24/2., Bangkok, Thailand ☎ 02/718-9561 or 07/035-0705 ⊕ www.smilingalbino.com. **White Elephant Adventures** ✉ Sisavang Vong Rd., Luang Prabang ☎ 020/589-4394 or 030/514-0243 ⊕ www.white-elephant-adventures-laos.com.

SOUTHERN LAOS

In some ways, Laos is really two countries: the south and north are as different as two sides of a coin. The mountainous north was for centuries virtually isolated from the more accessible south, where lowlands, the broad Mekong valley, and high plateaus were easier to traverse and settle. The south does have its mountains, however: notably the Annamite range, called Phu Luang, home of the aboriginal Mon-Khmer ethnic groups who lived here long before Lao farmers and traders arrived from northern Laos and China. The Lao were followed by French colonists, who built the cities of Pakxan, Tha Khek, Savannakhet, and Pakse. Although the French influence is still tangible, the southern Lao cling tenaciously to their old traditions, making the south a fascinating destination.

Pakse is the regional capital and has an international airport with daily flights to Vientiane, as well as Phnom Penh and Siem Reap in neighbor-

Southern Laos

ing Cambodia. There's also overnight bus service to Pakse from Vientiane, plus good local service in the area.

The Road South of Vientiane

Highway 13 out of Vientiane penetrates as far as the deep south of Laos and the Cambodian border, a distance of 835 km (518 mi). It's paved all the way. The first stop of interest, about 80 km (50 mi) southeast of Vientiane, is the pilgrimage temple complex **Wat Phrabat,** which has a revered footprint in stone said to be that of the Buddha.

❷ Pakxan, 150 km (93 mi) south of Vientiane, in Bolikhamxay Province, is a former French colonial outpost, a Mekong River port, and now the center of the Lao Christian community. Traveling south of Pakxan, Highway 13 crosses the Nam Kading River, for which the protected forested NBCA (National Biodiversity Conservation Area Nam Kading) is named. About 90 km (56 mi) south of Pakxan, Highway 13 meets Highway 8, which leads via Lak Sao to Nam Pho on the Vietnamese border. From here the road leads to the Vietnamese coastal city of Vinh and other areas of north Vietnam.

❸ Tha Khek, 350 km (217 mi) south of Vientiane, in Khammuan Province, is a bustling Mekong River port, with some of its ancient city wall still intact. It's surrounded by stunning countryside and karst (limestone caverns and sinkholes). There are some spectacular limestone caves in the area—notably **Tham Khong Lor.** This cave is more than 6½ km (4 mi) long and is so large that the Nam Hin Bun River runs through it. Opposite Tha Khek is Thailand's provincial capital of Nakhon Phanom. Ferries ply the waters between the two cities.

Where to Stay

¢ 🖼 **Phudoi Hotel.** This is a very basic but reliable lodging choice in Tha Khek. Note that only cold water is available. ⊠ *13 Kouvolavong St., Ban Phonsanam, Tha Khek* ☎ *051/212048* 🛏 *12 rooms* ⚴ *In-room: no a/c (some)* ☱ *No credit cards.*

Savannakhet

㉔ *470 km (290 mi) south of Vientiane.*

A former French colonial provincial center, the pleasant riverside town of Savannakhet is today the urban hub of a vast rice-growing plain. It's distinguished by some fine examples of French colonial architecture. The Thai town of Mukdahan (⇨ Chapter 6, Isan) lies just across the Mekong River and is accessible by ferry or by crossing the second of three bridges connecting Thailand and Laos. The bridge, one of several established to create an East-West Economic Corridor connecting the Vietnamese port of Da Nang with Laos, Thailand, and Myanmar (Burma), also greatly facilitates tourist travel between Thailand and Laos. Eight to twelve buses shuttle passengers the 10 mi in either directions; buses depart daily 7 AM to 5:30 PM, stopping briefy at the border, where passengers must pay a B10 fee. There is no visa service provided at either checkpoint.

One of Savannakhet's curiosities is a **dinosaur museum,** which displays fossils discovered in the area. ⊠ *Khantaburi Rd.* ☎ *No phone* 🎟 *1,000 kip* 🕙 *Weekdays 8–11:30 and 1–3:30.*

Pakse

㉕ *205 km (127 mi) south of Savannakhet, 675 km (420 mi) south of Vientiane.*

Pakse is a former French colonial stronghold, linked now by a bridge with neighboring Thailand. It plays a central role in an ambitious regional plan to create an "Emerald Triangle"—a trade and tourism community grouping Laos, Thailand, and Cambodia. The city is also the starting point for tours to the Khmer ruins at Wat Phu, and the Boloven Plateau, which straddles the southern provinces of Saravan, Sekon, Attapeu, and Champasak. The volcanic soil of the plateau makes the vast region ideal for agriculture: it's the source of much of the country's prized coffee, tea, and spices. Despite its beauty and central role in the Lao economy, the plateau has virtually no tourist infrastructure and is very much off-the-beaten-track territory.

Pakse's **Historical Heritage Museum** displays stonework from the famous Wat Phu in Champasak, handicrafts from the Boloven Plateau ethnic groups, and locally made musical instruments. ⊠ *Hwy. 13* ☎ *No phone* 🎟 *3,000 kip* 🕙 *Daily 8–11:30 and 1–4.*

$ ×▦ **Champa Residence Hotel.** Five handsome traditional-style houses make up this comfortable hotel complex near Pakse's evening market and the Historical Heritage Museum. Rooms have terraces overlooking the leafy grounds. ⊠ *Champasak Rd.* ☎ *031/212120* ✎ *champare@lao-tel.com* ↰ *45 rooms* ♿ *In-room: safe, refrigerator. In-hotel: restaurant, bar, laundry service* ▤ *MC, V.*

$ ▦ **Pakse Hotel.** Fully renovated in 2004, this central hotel now offers international standards of comfort and service. Its rooftop terrace is a pleasant evening retreat, with a fine view of the town and surrounding countryside. ⊠ *Rd. 5, Ban Vat Luang* ☎ *031/212131* ✎ *info@pakse-hotel.com* ↰ *65 rooms* ♿ *In-room: refrigerator. In-hotel: restaurant, bar, laundry service* ▤ *AE, MC, V.*

¢–$ ▦ **Champasak Palace.** On the banks of the Seddon River on the town's out-skirts, this former residence of a local prince is impressive but scarcely pala-tial. It's a vast four-story complex with flanking wings and pagodalike eaves. Rooms are royally large and comfortably furnished, with an antique here and there. ⊠ *Ban Prabaht* ☎ *031/212263 or 031/212779* ⊕ *www. champasak-palace-hotel.com* ↰ *90 rooms* ♿ *In-room: refrigerator. In-hotel: restaurant, bar, laundry service, public Internet* ▤ *AE, MC, V.*

Champasak

㉖ *40 km (25 mi) south of Pakse.*

In the early 18th century, the kingdom of Laos was partitioned into three realms: Luang Prabang, Vientiane, and Champasak. During the 18th and 19th centuries this small village on the west bank of the Mekong River was the royal center of a wide area of what is today Thailand and Cambodia. ■ TIP→ **Every February, at the time of the full moon, the village holds a nationally renowned festival that includes elephant racing, cockfight-ing, concerts, and lots of drinking and dancing.**

★ **Wat Phu** sits impressively on heights above the Mekong River, about 6½ km (4 mi) south of Champasak, looking back on a centuries-old his-tory that won it UNESCO recognition as a World Heritage Site. Wat Phu predates Cambodia's Angkor Wat—Wat Phu's hilltop site was cho-sen by Khmer Hindus in the 6th century AD, probably because of a nearby spring of fresh water. Construction of the wat continued into the 13th century, at which point it finally became a Buddhist temple. Much of the original Hindu sculpture remains unchanged, however, including rep-resentations on the temple's lintels of the Hindu gods Vishnu, Shiva, and Kala. The staircase is particularly beautiful, its protective *nagas* (mys-tical serpents) decorated with plumeria, the national flower of Laos. Many of the temple's treasures, including pre–Angkor era inscriptions, are pre-served in an archaeology museum that is part of the complex. ☎ *No phone* ☑ *30,000 kip* ⊙ *Daily 8–4:30.*

Si Phan Don

★ **㉗** *80 km (50 mi) south of Champasak, 120 km (74 mi) south of Pakse.*

If you've made it as far south as Champasak, then a visit to the Si Phan Don area—celebrated for its 4,000 Mekong River islands and freshwater dolphins—is a must. *Don* means island, and two of them in particular are worth visiting: Don Khong and the similarly named Don Khon, both of which are accessible by boat.

Don Khong is the largest island in the area, inhabited by a community of fisherfolk living in small villages amid ancient Buddhist temples.

You can hike to the spectacular Liphi waterfall on the island known as **Don Khon.** A second stunning waterfall, Khon Phapeng, is just east of Don Khon on the mainland. Also on Don Khon are the remains of a former French-built railway (you can also see them on another island, Don Det).

Downstream of Don Khon, at the border between Laos and Cambodia, **freshwater dolphins** frolic in a protected area of the Mekong. Boat trips to view the dolphins set off from Veun Kham and Don Khon.

Where to Stay & Eat

$ ╳⌂ **Villa Muong Khong Hotel.** At this little residence on the island of Don Khon, you live alongside local Lao fisherfolk. Not surprisingly, Mekong fish figures prominently at the hotel's open-air restaurant (¢–$). ✉ *Don Khong Island* ☎ *031/213011* ✍ *xbtrvlmk@laotel.com* ⚓ *32 bungalows* ⚒ *In-room: no phone. In-hotel: restaurant, bar* ▭ *No credit cards.*

Southern Laos Essentials

Transportation

BORDER CROSSINGS

There are border crossings between Laos and Thailand at Tha Khek in Khammuan Province; Savannakhet in Savannakhet Province; and Vang Tao (a land crossing) in Champasak Province. Border crossings are open 8:30–5.

BY AIR

There's one Lao Airlines flight a day from Vientiane to Pakse, sometimes routed via Savannakhet.

There's also one Lao Airlines flight between Pakse and Cambodia from Siem Reap. Flights depart every Wednesday, Friday, and Sunday morning. The price of a one-way ticket is $68.

✈ Carrier **Lao Airlines** ☎ 031/212252 in Pakse.

AIRPORTS & TRANSFERS A taxi from Pakse International Airport to the city center costs $5.

✈ **Pakse International Airport** ☎ 032/212844.

BY BOAT & FERRY

Ferries crisscross the Mekong River along its entire length. The main ferry crossings into neighboring Thailand are at Tha Khek and Savannakhet; the one-way fare is about $1.

A luxurious double-deck houseboat, the *Wat Phu*, operated by Indocruise Ltd., plies the southern length of the Mekong between Pakse and Si Phan Don. The cruises, which last three days and two nights, depart from Pakse every Wednesday and Saturday.

Indocruise Ltd. ⊠ 23 Ban Anou, Haengboun Rd., Chanthaboury, Vientiane ☎ 021/215958 📠 021/215958 ⊕ www.asian-oasis.com.

BY BUS

Efficient local bus service connects all the towns of the south. From Pakse, buses depart from the central bus station (Km 8 on the road east of Pakse) for local destinations such as Savannakhet and Champasak.

Buses from Pakse to Vientiane and the north depart from a terminal at Km 7 on Highway 13 (running north of Pakse).

BY CAR

Highway 13, the main north–south route, penetrates the deep south as far as the Cambodian border. It's fully paved, but once you get off the highway and onto minor roads, driving conditions get difficult. This is particularly true of the Boloven Plateau region. Therefore, we recommend that you hire a driver if you want to travel around the region by car.

BY TAXI, TUK-TUK & SONGTHAEW

The easiest way to travel around the area is to hire a car and driver or use the bus system. Taxis must be booked by your hotel, but tuk-tuks and songthaews cruise the streets of every town and are easy to flag down and rarely cost more than a dollar or two for a short trip within town.

Contacts & Resources

BANKS & EXCHANGING SERVICES

There are no ATMs in the south, but all banks change money and traveler's checks. Nevertheless, make sure you travel with enough cash (in dollars or kip) to cover your likely expenses. Credit cards are accepted at major hotels and some restaurants, but few shops. Look for yellow Western Union signs outside post offices and banks in larger towns and cities.

Western Union ☎ 31/212168 Pakse, 41/212226 Savannakhet.

EMERGENCIES

Pakse's Provincial Hospital can handle emergencies.

Hospital Provincial Hospital ⊠ Ban Pakse, Pakse ☎ 031/212018.

TOUR OPTIONS

Diethelm Travel runs tours of southern Laos (originating in Pakse) that last between a half day and two days. The half-day tour to the Boloven Plateau, ethnic villages, and a tea-and-coffee plantation costs $44. An overnight excursion by boat to Champasak, Wat Phu, and Don Khong costs $331. Diethelm Travel has an office in Pakse, but it's best to book the tours through the Vientiane office.

Diethelm Travel ⊠ Ban Tha Luang, Pakse ☎ 031/251941 ⊠ Setthathirat Rd. at Nam Phu Fountain Sq., Vientiane ☎ 021/213833, 021/215920, or 021/215128 ⊕ www.diethelm-travel.com.

UNDERSTANDING
THAILAND

A BUDDHIST NATION

INTRODUCTION TO THAI ARCHITECTURE

VOCABULARY

MENU GUIDE

A BUDDHIST NATION

RELIGION PLAYS A PROFOUND AND HIGH-PROFILE ROLE in day-to-day Thai life. Almost 95% of the population is Buddhist (4% of the population is Muslim, the remaining 1% is shared by Taoism, Confucianism, Hinduism, and Christianity); the country has 400,000 monks and novices, and there are more than 30,000 wats (temples) throughout the land. Buddhism is present on the national flag, denoted by the white bar as one of the foundations of nationhood, alongside the monarchy (blue) and the people (red). Thai monarchs are required to be Buddhist: King Rama IV spent 27 years as a forest monk before ascending the throne in 1851. In Bangkok, intricate golden temple rooftops gleam like fairy glitter amid the gray concrete. Images of the Buddha adorn cafés, gas stations, shops, and bars, and many local artists paint according to religious themes. Each morning people rise early to give alms to monks, who are required to beg for food and other essentials.

Origins

There are two main branches of Buddhism in Asia: Theravada, found today in Thailand, Myanmar (Burma), and Sri Lanka; and Mahayana, which spread northward from India to China, Korea, Vietnam, and Japan. The Mahayana movement emerged from Theravada, the original teachings of the Buddha, in the 1st century. Its main departure was the introduction of *bodhisattvas*, embodiments of enlightened ones who had chosen to stay on earth to help ease suffering. It's a less austere doctrine and therefore more accessible than Theravada, which stresses devotion to study and meditation. Theravada arrived in Thailand via Sri Lanka, and has been the country's official religion since the founding of the nation at Sukhothai in the 13th century. It was written into the constitution as the state religion of modern Thailand in 1997.

The origins of both forms of Buddhism lie in the life of the Indian prince Siddhartha Gautama (563 BC–483 BC). Gautama taught that there are three aspects to existence: *dukkha* (stress, misery), *anicca* (impermanence), and *anatta* (the absence of self). He maintained that it's the unfulfilled desire for status, self-worth, and material possessions that creates dukkha and that it's pointless to desire such things because anicca dictates that everything is impermanent and cannot be possessed. Therefore, if we can learn to curb desire and cultivate detachment, we will cease to be unhappy.

Gautama devised the Middle Way to achieve this state, based on the triple pillars of wisdom, morality, and concentration. Within wisdom are the concepts of Right Understanding, where you are able to determine and understand dukkha and its causes, and Right Thought, where you develop a resistance to anger, ill will, cruel or aggressive thoughts and acts—and to all things that cause dukkha. Within morality are Right Speech (refraining from telling lies, using abusive language, or engaging in idle chatter), Right Action (refraining from harming or killing others, stealing, and engaging in sexual misconduct), and Right Livelihood (earning a living in an honest, peaceful, and righteous way). Within concentration are the facets of Right Effort (using your energy to fuel positive things like discipline, honesty, and kindness, and to work toward abandoning old counterproductive ways), Right Mindfulness (acquiring an acute awareness of one's words, thoughts, and actions), and Right Concentration (total focus on positive things or "pure thoughts,").

The ultimate goal of Buddhism is to reach enlightenment or Nirvana, which is basically the cessation of struggle—this happens when you have successfully let go of all desire (and by definition, all suffering). This also signals the end to the cycle of reincarnation, a concept all Buddhists believe in.

Despite the overwhelming presence of Buddhism, the Thai religious psyche is complicated by the absorption of Hindu deities, superstition, and ancient animist beliefs. The precepts of Buddhism developed within Hinduism, and Thailand retains many Hindu religious elements—the famous Erawan Shrine in Bangkok is a site of homage to Brahma.

Practice & Rituals

Thai children learn Buddhist teachings (Dhamma) in school, and most males will at some time ordain as a *bhikku* (monk). Some only do this for a few days, but many join the monkhood for three months at the beginning of the yearly Rains Retreat (a religious retreat, sometimes referred to as Buddhist Lent, when monks are required to remain in their wats for the duration of the rainy season) in July, which is marked by major festivals, such as the Candle Parade, in Nakhon Ratchasima. Joining the monkhood, even for a short time, is such an important event that employers grant time off work for the purpose. Women wanting to devote their lives to Buddhism may become white-robed nuns, known as *mae chi*. However, women are not allowed to be officially ordained, but a growing feminist lobby increasingly questions their lower status.

Although Thais don't really visit temples on a regular basis, wats are the center of community life, particularly up-country, and serve many functions, such as schools, meeting halls, and hospitals (monks are traditional healers, originators of the herbal remedies that now form the basis for New Age spa treatments). The country's most important temples are associated with royalty, revered monks, or religious icons thought to be close to the Buddha. Temples often have the most ornate gilt work and statuary, so they tend to become tourist attractions.

Alongside spiritual guidance and funeral rites, monks provide ceremonies in houses and businesses to bring good fortune, and will even bless vehicles to keep drivers safe from accidents.

All Buddhists believe in reincarnation (a concept inherited from Hinduism) and the goal of Nirvana, which is the end of the cycle of rebirth. Advancement along the cycle is, in part, achieved through good deeds called *tham boon* (merit making). These deeds result in good karma, something striven for daily to either atone for bad deeds or to build credit for a better future life. Tham boon can be accomplished by small gestures such as placing a candle at a place of worship or wai-ing (bowing) toward a significant shrine or statue. At fairs and markets anyone can make merit by releasing caged birds offered by vendors specifically for the purpose. Larger deeds might involve a lifetime's devotion to monastic life—or a large cash donation to a worthy cause. Families can attain merit by sending their sons to study as a novice monk.

Modern Concerns

Many Thai commentators believe that a rapidly modernizing Thailand is eroding traditional Buddhist values. Greater personal wealth has brought billowing consumerism to the middle classes, while younger generations are progressively more Westernized through education abroad, satellite TV, and the Internet. The concern is that, as material rewards begin to overshadow the temporal, Thais may be less inclined toward religion; this is borne out to some extent by a slight decrease in the number of wats, although other factors, such as greater migration to cities, also play a part.

However, despite undeniable changes in Thailand's economic and cultural condition, the country is adapting, rather than abandoning, its heritage. Buddhism remains hugely manifest in all aspects and sectors of society and the religion continues as the dominant influence on the unique national psyche.

—Howard Richardson

INTRODUCTION TO THAI ARCHITECTURE

THOUGH REAL ARCHITECTURE BUFFS are few and far between, you'd be hard pressed to find a visitor to Thailand who doesn't spend at least a little time staring in slack-jawed amazement at the country's glittering wats and ornate palaces—and the elegant sculptures of the mythical beasts that protect them. As befitting this spiritual nation, most of the fanfare is saved for religious structures, but you can find plenty to admire in the much simpler lines of the traditional houses of the Central Plains and Northern Thailand.

Wats

Wat is the Thai name for what can range from a simple ordination hall for monks and nuns to a huge sprawling complex comprising libraries, bell towers, and meditation rooms. Usually the focal point for a community, it's not unusual for a wat to also be the grounds for village fetes and festivals. Although most wats you come across symbolize some aspect of Theravada Buddhism, examples of other architectural styles are relatively easy to find: Khmer ruins dot the Isan countryside to the east, while Northern Thailand is littered with Burmese-style temples.

Wats are erected as acts of merit—allowing the donor to improve his karma and perhaps be reborn as a higher being—or in memory of great events. You can tell much about a wat's origin by its name. A wat *luang* (royal wat) for example, was constructed or restored by royals and may have the words *rat, raja,* or *racha* in its name (e.g., Ratburana or Rajapradit). The word *phra* may indicate that a wat contains an image of the Buddha. Wats that contain an important relic of the Buddha have the words *maha* (great) and *that* (relic) in their names. Thailand's nine major wat mahathats are in Chiang Rai, Chai Nat, Sukhothai, Phisanulk, Ayutthaya, Bangkok, Yasothon, Phetchaburi, and Nakhon Si Thammarat.

Thai wats, especially in the later periods, were seldom planned as entire units, so they often appear disjointed and crowded. To appreciate a wat's beauty you often have to look at its individual buildings.

Perhaps the most recognizable feature of a wat, and certainly a useful landmark when hunting them down, is the towering conelike *chedi*. Originally used to hold relics of the Buddha (hair, bones, or even nails), chedis can now be built by anyone with enough cash, to house their ashes. At the base of the chedi you can find three platforms representing hell, earth, and heaven, while the 33 Buddhist heavens are symbolized at the top of the tallest spire by a number of rings.

The main buildings of a wat are the *bot,* which contains a Buddha image and functions as congregation and ordination hall for the monks, and the *viharn,* which serves a similar function, but will hold the most important Buddha image. Standard bot and viharn roofs will feature three steeply curved levels featuring red, gold, and green tiles; the outer walls range from highly decorated to simply whitewashed.

Other noticeable features include the *mondop, prang,* and *ho trai.* Usually square with a pyramid-shaped roof, the mondop is reminiscent of Indian temple architecture and serves as a kind of storeroom for holy artifacts, books, and ceremonial objects. The prang is a tall tower similar to the chedi, which came to Thailand by way of the Khmer empire and is used to store images of the Buddha. Easily identifiable by its stilts or raised platform, the ho trai is a library for holy scriptures.

Roofs, which are covered in glazed clay tiles or wooden shakes, generally consist of three overlapping sections, with the lower roof set at gentle slopes, increasing to a topmost roof with a pitch of 60 degrees. Eave brackets in the form of a *naga* (snakes believed to control the irrigation waters of rice fields) with its head at the bottom often support the lower edges of the roofs. Along the eaves of many roofs are a row of small brass bells with clappers attached to thin brass pieces shaped like Bodhi tree leaves.

During the early Ayutthaya period (1350–1767), wat interiors were illuminated by the light passing through vertical slits in the walls (wider, more elaborate windows would have compromised the strength of the walls and, thus, the integrity of the structure). In the Bangkok period (1767–1932), the slits were replaced by proper windows set below wide lintels that supported the upper portions of the brick walls. There are usually five, seven, or nine windows on a side in accordance with the Thai preference for odd numbers. The entrance doors are in the end wall facing the Buddha image; narrower doors may flank the entrance door.

Principal building materials have varied with the ages. Khmer and Lopburi architects built in stone and laterite; Sukhothai and Lanna builders worked with laterite and brick. Ayutthaya and Bangkok architects opted for brick cemented by mortar and covered with one or more coats of stucco (made of lime, sand, and, often, rice husks). In early construction, walls were often several feet thick; when binding materials and construction techniques improved they became thinner.

The mid-13th century saw an enormous wave of men entering the monkhood as the Kingdom of Sukhothai adopted Hinayana Buddhism as its official religion. Consequently there was a need for bigger monasteries. Due to the lack of quality stone and brick available, wood became the building material of choice, marking a shift away from the exclusively stone structures of the Khmer period.

Sculpture

The Thai image of the Buddha usually features markedly long ears weighed down by heavy earrings in reference to his royal background, and is caste in bronze and covered in gold leaf by followers. Typically depicted seated or standing, less common images are reclining Buddhas, acknowledging his impending death, and walking Buddhas, which were favored during the Sukhothai period (13th to 15th century). Statues from the Lanna period of the 13th to 15th century and the present Ratanakosin era feature eyes fashioned from colored gems or enamel, while the Lopburi period of the 10th to 13th century favored metal.

A collection of 32 Pali *lakshanas,* descriptions used to identify future incarnations of the Buddha, popularly serve as a kind of blueprint for reproductions. The lakshanas include reference to wedge-shape heels, long fingers and toes of equal length, legs like an antelope, arms long enough that he could touch either knee without bending, skin so smooth that dust wouldn't adhere to it, a body as thick as a banyan tree, long eyelashes like those of a cow, 40 teeth, a hairy white mole between his eyebrows, deep blue eyes, and an *ushnisha* (protuberance) atop his head—either a turban, a topknot, or a bump on his skull.

Palaces

Although King Bhumibol currently uses Chitlada Palace when in Bangkok, the Chakri Dynasty monarchs who preceded him used the showpiece Grand Palace as their official residence. Shots of the palace with its gleaming spires floodlighted up at night fill every postcard stand, and it's arguably Bangkok's single most important tourist attraction.

Built in 1782 when King Rama I chose Bangkok as Siam's new capital, the Grand Palace is the only remaining example of early Ratanakosin architecture—Ramas II and III chose not to initiate any large-scale construction projects in the face of economic hardship. A primarily functional collection of buildings, the compound contains the Royal Thai Decorations and Coin Pavilion, the Museum of Fine Art, and the Weapons Museum.

Also worth checking out while in the capital is what is believed to be the world's largest golden teak-wood building. The three-story Vimanmek Palace was moved from Chonburi in the east to Bangkok's Dusit Palace and contains jewelry and gifts given as presents from around the world.

Rama IV led the revival of palace construction in the second half of the 19th century, overseeing the building of several royal getaways. Perhaps the most impressive of these getaways is Phra Nakhon Khiri in the southern town of Phetchaburi. Known locally as Khao Wang, the palace sits atop a mountain with wonderful panoramic views. Sharing its mountain home are various wat, halls, and thousands of macaque monkeys. Klai Kangwon in nearby Hua Hin is still used as a seaside getaway for the royal family and as a base when they visit southern provinces. Built in 1926 by Rama VI, the two-story concrete palace's name translates as Far From Worries and was built in the style of European chateaux.

Houses

Look around many Thai towns and you can see that this is a swiftly modernizing country: whitewashed apartment blocks, everything-under-one-roof shopping malls, and glass-fronted fast-food outlets are testaments to a growing economy and general rush to get ahead (as well as to the disappearance of Thailand's forests, which once provided cheap and sturdy building materials). However, peer a little closer and you will find Thailand's heritage staring right back at you.

Traditional Thai houses are usually very simple and essentially boil down to three basic components: stilts, a deck, and a sloping roof. Heavy, annual monsoon rains all over the country necessitate that living quarters be raised on stilts to escape flooding; in the dry season the space under the house is typically used as storage for farming equipment or other machinery. The deck of the house is essentially the living room—it's where you can find families eating, cooking, and just plain relaxing.

As with wats, it's often the roofs of houses that are the most interesting. Lanna-style (Northern Thailand) roofs, usually thatched or tiled, are thought to have evolved from the Thai people's roots in Southern China, where steeply pitched roofs would have been needed to combat heavy snows. Although there's no real chance of a snowball fight in Thailand, the gradient and overhang allows for quick runoff of the rains and welcome shade from the sun.

These basics are fairly uniform throughout the country, with a few small adjustments to accommodate different climates. For example, roofs are steepest in areas with more intense weather patterns, like the Central Plains, and Northern Thai houses have smaller windows to preserve heat better.

VOCABULARY

Thai has several distinct forms for different social levels. The most common one is the street language, which is used in everyday situations. If you want to be polite, add "khrup" (men) or "kah" (women) to the end of your sentence. For the word "I," men should use "phom" and women should use "deeshan."

Note that the "h" is silent when combined with most other consonants (th, ph, kh, etc.). Double vowels indicate long vowel sounds (uu=oo, as in food), except for "aa," which is pronounced "ah."

Basics

Hello/goodbye.	Sa-wa-dee-khrup/kah.
How are you?	Sa-bai-dee-mai khrup/kah.
I'm fine.	Sa-bai-dee khrup/kah.
I'm very well.	Dee-mark khrup/kah.
I'm so so.	Sa-bai sa-bai.
What's your name?	Khun-chue-ar-rai khrup/kah?
My name is Joe.	Phom-chue Joe khrup.
My name is Alice.	Deeshan chue Alice kah.
It's nice to meet you.	Yin-dee-tee dai ruu jak khun khrup/kah.
Excuse me.	Khor thod khrup/kah.
I'm sorry.	Phom sia jai khrup (M)/Deeshan sia chy kah (F).
It's okay/It doesn't matter.	Mai pen rai khrup/kah.
Yes.	Chai khrup/kah.
No.	Mai chai khrup/kah.
Please.	Karoona.
Thank you.	Khop-khun-khrup/kah.
You're welcome.	Mai pen rai khrup/kah.

Getting Around

How do I get to . . .	Phom/chan ja pai . . . (name of the place) . . . dai yang-ngai khrup/kah?
. . . the train station? . . . the post office? . . . the tourist office? . . . the hospital?	sa-ta-nee rod-fai pai-sa-nee sam-nak-ngan tong-teow rong-pha-ya-barn
Does this bus go to?	Rod-khan-nee bpai-nai khrup/ka?

Where is . . .?	Yoo tee-nai khrup/ka?
. . . the bathroom?	hong nam
. . . the subway?	sa-ta-nee rot-fai-tai-din
. . . the bank?	ta-na-kahn
. . . the hotel?	rong ram
. . . the store?	rarn
. . . the market?	talaat
Left	sai
Right	kwah
Straight ahead	trong-pai
Is it far?	Klai mai khrup/kah?

Useful Phrases

Do you speak English?	Khun pood pa-sa ung-grid dai mai khrup/kah?
I don't speak Thai.	Phom/chan pood pa-sa Thai mai dai khrup/kah.
I don't understand.	Phom/chan mai cao jai khrup/kah.
I don't know.	Phom/chan mai roo khrup/kah.
I'm American/British.	Phom/chan pen American/Ung-grid khrup/kah.
I'm sick.	Phom/chan mai sa-bai khrup/kah.
Please call a doctor.	Choo-ay re-ak mor doo-ay khrup/kah.
Do you have any rooms?	Khun-mee hawng-mai khrup/kah?
How much does it cost?	Tao rai khrup/kah?
Too expensive.	pa-eng gern-pai
It's beautiful.	soo-ay.
When?	Muah-rai khrup/kah?
Where?	Tee-nai khrup/kah?
Help!	Choo-ay doo-ay!
Stop!	Yoot!

Numbers

1	nueng	7	jet
2	song	8	bpaet
3	sam	9	gao
4	see	10	sib
5	hah	11	sib-et
6	hok	12	sib-song

13	sib-sam	40	see-sib
14	sib-see	50	hah-sib
15	sib-hah	60	hok-sib
16	sib-hok	70	jet-sib
17	sib-jet	80	bpaet-sib
18	sib-bpaet	90	gao-sib
19	sib-gao	100	nueng-roy
20	yee-sib	101	nueng-roy-nung
21	yee-sib-et	200	song-roy
30	sam-sib	1000	nueng-pan

Days and Time

Today	wannee
Tomorrow	proong nee
Yesterday	muah-waan-nee
Morning	thawn-chao
Afternoon	thawn bai
Night	thorn muet
What time is it?	gee-mong-laew khrup/kah?
It's 2:00	song mong.
It's 4:00	see mong.
It's 2:30	song moang sarm-sip na-tee.
It's 2:45	song moang see-sip hah na-tee.
Monday	wan-jun
Tuesday	wan-ung-kan
Wednesday	wan-poot
Thursday	wan-phra-roo-hud
Friday	wan-sook
Saturday	wan-sao
Sunday	wan-ar-teet
January	Mok-ka-ra-kom
February	Goom-pha-parn
March	Mee-na-kom
April	May-sar-yon
May	Prus-sa-pa-kom
June	Me-tu-na-yon

July	Ga-rak-ga-da-kom
August	Sing-ha-kom
September	Gun-ya-yon
October	Thu-la-kom
November	Prus-sa-ji-ga-yon
December	Tan-wa-kom

MENU GUIDE

The first term you should file away is "aroi," which means delicious. You'll no doubt use that one again and again whether you're dining at food stalls or upscale restaurants. When someone asks "Aroi mai?" that's your cue to practice your Thai—most likely your answer will be a re-sounding "aroi mak" (It's very delicious).

Another useful word is "Kaw," which simply means "Could I have . . .?" However, the most important phrase to remember may be "Gin ped dai mai?" or "Can you eat spicy food?" Answer this one wrong and you might have a five-alarm fire in your mouth. You can answer with a basic "dai" (can), "mai dai" (cannot), or "dai nit noi" (a little). Most restaurants will tone down dishes for foreigners, but if you're visiting a food stall or if you're nervous, you can ask your server "Ped mai?" (Is it spicy?) or specify that you would like your food "mai ped" (not spicy), "ped nit noi khrup/kah" (a little spicy), or if you have very resilient taste buds, "ped ped" (very spicy). Don't be surprised if the latter request is met with some laughter—and if all Thai eyes are on you when you take your first bite. Remember, water won't put out the fire; you'll need to eat something sweet.

food	a-harn
breakfast	a-harn chao
lunch	a-harn klang wan
dinner	a-harn yen
eat here	gin tee nee khrup/kah
take away	kaw glub baan khrup/kah
The check, please	Check bin khrup/kah
More, please	Kaw eek noi khrup/kah
Another please	Kaw eek an khrup/ka
A table for two, please	Kaw toh song tee khrup/kah
vegetarian	gin jay
spicy	ped
Is it spicy?	Ped mai?
not spicy	mai ped
a little spicy	ped nit noi khrup/kah
very spicy	ped ped
steamed	nueng
stir-fried	pad
stir-fried with ginger	pad king
stir-fried hot and spicy	pad ped
grilled (use *phao* instead when referring to seafood)	ping

deep-fried	tawd
boiled	thom

Utensils

spoon	chawn
fork	sorm
plate	jarn
glass	gaew
knife	meed
napkin	par ched park
cup	tuay
chopsticks	tha-geab

Basic Ingredients

rice	kao
steamed rice	kao suay
fried rice	kao pad
sticky rice	kao niao
rice with curry sauce	kao gaeng
rice porridge (usually for breakfast)	joke
noodles	kuay theow
egg noodles	ba mee
egg	kai
vegetables	pak
meat	nua
pork	moo
chicken	gai
roast duck	bped
beef	nua (same as meat)
fish	pla
prawns	gung
squid	pla muek
crab	bpu
vegetarian	jay
galanga (herb)	ka
ginger	king

lemongrass	ta krai
garlic	kratiam
fish sauce	nam pla
soy sauce	see-ew
chili paste (spicy dips usually accompanied by various vegetables)	nam prik
satay sauce (peanut base sauce made of crushed peanuts, coconut milk, chili, and curry)	satay

Beverages

Thai iced tea (*cha yen*) is Thai black tea mixed with cinnamon, vanilla, star anise, and food coloring. It's usually served cold, but you might see a hot version being enjoyed at the end of a meal. It's very sweet. Don't buy these from food stalls that are working off a block of ice—there's a good chance that the ice isn't purified.

ice	nam kang
iced coffee	ga-fare-yen
coffee with milk	ga-fare sai noom
whiskey	wis-gee
tea	nam charr
plain water	nam plao
soda water	nam soda
a sweet drink brewed from lemongrass	nam takrai
vodka	what gaa
gin	gin

Appetizers

spring rolls	por pia tawd
panfried rice noodles	mee krob
spicy raw papaya salad	som tam
spicy beef salad	yum nua

Meat & Seafood

chicken fried with cashew nuts	gai pad med mamuang himmapan
spicy chicken with basil	gai ka-prao
grilled chicken	gai yang
curry soup	gaeng ga-ree
green curry soup	gaeng keow wan

mild yellow curry soup	gaeng massaman
red curry soup	gaeng ped
hot and sour curry	kaeng som
minced meat with chilies and lime juice	larb
spicy salad	yum
panfried rice noodles	pad tai
soup made with coconut cream, chicken, lemongrass, and chilies	tom ka gai
lemongrass soup with shrimp and mushrooms	tom yum kung

Fruit

banana	gluay
tamarind	ma karm
papaya	ma la gore
mango	ma muang
coconut	ma prao
mangosteen	mung kood
mandarin orange	som
pomegranateň	tub tim

Desserts

dessert	ka nom
mango with sticky rice	kao niao ma muang
grilled bananas	gluay bping
coconut pudding	ka nom krog
rice based dessert cooked in coconut milk	kao larm

Thailand
Essentials

PLANNING TOOLS, EXPERT INSIGHT,
GREAT CONTACTS

There are planners, and there are those who fly by the seat of their pants. We happily place ourselves among the planners. Our writers and editors try to anticipate all the issues you may face before and during any journey, and then they do their research. This section is the product of their efforts. Use it to get excited about your trip to Thailand, to inform your travel planning, or to guide you on the road should the seat of your pants start to feel threadbare.

GETTING STARTED

We're really proud of our Web site: Fodors.com is a great place to begin any journey. Scan Travel Wire for suggested itineraries, travel deals, restaurant and hotel openings, and other up-to-the-minute info. Check out Booking to research prices and book plane tickets, hotel rooms, rental cars, and vacation packages. Head to Talk for on-the-ground pointers from travelers who frequent our message boards. You can also link to loads of other travel-related resources.

▌ RESOURCES

ONLINE TRAVEL TOOLS

All About Thailand Other sites worth checking out are: www.tat.or.th, www.amazingsiam.com, www.thailand-travelsearch.com, and www.nectec.or.th for more information on Thailand.

Currency Conversion **Google** ⊕ www.google.com does currency conversion. Just type in the amount you want to convert and an explanation of how you want it converted (e.g., "14 Swiss francs in dollars"), and then voilà. **Oanda.com** ⊕ www.oanda.com also allows you to print out a handy table with the current day's conversion rates. **XE.com** ⊕ www.xe.com is a good currency conversion Web site.

Safety **Transportation Security Administration** (TSA) ⊕ www.tsa.gov.

Time Zones **Timeanddate.com** ⊕ www.timeanddate.com/worldclock can help you figure out the correct time anywhere.

Weather **Accuweather.com** ⊕ www.accuweather.com is an independent weather-forecasting service with good coverage of hurricanes. **Weather.com** ⊕ www.weather.com is the Web site for the Weather Channel.

Other Resources **CIA World Factbook** ⊕ www.odci.gov/cia/publications/factbook/index.html has profiles of every country in the world. It's a good source if you need some quick facts and figures.

Visitor Information **Tourism Authority of Thailand** ☎ 212/219-7447 in New York, 213/461-9814 in Los Angeles ⊕ www.tourismthailand.org.

▌ THINGS TO CONSIDER

GOVERNMENT ADVISORIES

As different countries have different world views, look at travel advisories from a range of governments to get more of a sense of what's going on out there. And be sure to parse the language carefully. For example, a warning to "avoid all travel" carries more weight than one urging you to "avoid nonessential travel," and both are much stronger than a plea to "exercise caution." A U.S. government travel warning is more permanent (though not necessarily more serious) than a so-called public announcement, which carries an expiration date.

▌ TIP→ **Consider registering online with the State Department (https://travelregistration.state.gov/ibrs/), so the government will know to look for you should a crisis occur in the country you're visiting.**

The U.S. Department of State's Web site has more than just travel warnings and advisories. The consular information sheets issued for every country have general safety tips, entry requirements (though be sure to verify these with the country's embassy), and other useful details.

The military coup that ousted Prime Minister Thaksin Shinawatra seemed to be proceeding without incident until several bombings occurred in Bangkok on January 1, 2007, killing three people. At this writing, no one is sure who is responsible for

> ### WORD OF MOUTH
>
> After your trip, be sure to rate the places you visited and share your experiences and travel tips with us and other Fodorites in Travel Ratings and Talk on www.fodors.com.

the New Year's bombings, though it doesn't seem to be related to the separatist fighting in the south, which by default may indicate it was the work of supporters of the former government unhappy with the military junta running the country. While day-to-day life remains calm and unaffected by these events, there are obvious dangerous undertones to the political situation in Thailand. The best advice is to stay informed about local developments as best you can and determine if the possible dangers make you too uneasy to travel or stay in Thailand. The *Bangkok Post* (⊕ www.bangkokpost.net) and *The Nation* (⊕ www.nationmultimedia.com) are the best sources of local news.

You should not travel in the four southern provinces closest to the Malaysian border: Yala, Pattani, Songkhla, and Narathiwat. A low-grade, three-year insurgency there has led to the deaths of more than 1,700, with another 2,500 injured from bombings, drive-by shootings, executions, and machete attacks. Although the insurgents originally targeted government institutions and officials, they have also begun bombing tourist centers, shopping malls, and the airport at Hat Yai. A Canadian woman was killed and an Australian man injured in a bombing in Hat Yai in September 2006—the first Western tourists hit in the attacks.

Unfortunately, the Thai government's heavy-handed and often equally violent reactions have been widely seen as adding gas to the fire. The government and army were so wrapped up in a military crackdown that it took them well over a year to clearly identify the insurgents and their goal of an independent Islamic state. As of this writing, there is no end in sight to the violence, though it has remained contained to the four southernmost provinces. **General Information & Warnings U.S. Department of State** ⊕ www.travel.state.gov.

GEAR

Light cotton or other natural-fiber clothing is appropriate for Thailand; drip-dry is an especially good idea, because the tropical sun and high humidity encourage frequent changes of clothing. Avoid delicate fabrics because you may have difficulty getting them laundered. A sweater is welcome on cool evenings or in overly air-conditioned restaurants, buses, and trains.

Despite the usual association of silk and the tropics, it is quite impractical if you venture out of air-conditioned places. Unlike cotton or linen, silk soaks up sweat and clings to the body in a most uncomfortable (and occasionally embarrassing) manner.

The paths leading to temples can be rough, so bring a sturdy pair of walking shoes. Slip-ons are preferable to lace-up shoes, as they must be removed before you enter shrines and temples.

Bring a hat and UV-protection sunglasses and use them. The tropical sun is powerful and its effects long-lasting and painful.

If you feel you have forgotten a fashion necessity, don't worry. Thailand has a huge range of clothing options at good prices.

PASSPORTS & VISAS

U.S. citizens—even infants—need only a valid passport and an onward ticket to enter Thailand for stays of up to 30 days. The onward ticket is hardly ever checked.

The Immigration Division offices in Bangkok and Chiang Mai issue Thai visa extensions. If you overstay by a day or two, don't worry; you'll pay a B500 fine for each day overstayed as you go through immigration on departure.

Tourist visas can be extended one month at a time, at the discretion of the immigration office where you apply. The fee is B1,900. You must apply in person; expect the process to take one day.

PASSPORTS

A passport verifies both your identity and nationality—a great reason to have one. Another reason is that you need a pass-

PACKING 101

Why do some people travel with a convoy of huge suitcases yet never have a thing to wear? How do others pack a duffle with a week's worth of outfits *and* supplies for every contingency? We realize that packing is a matter of style, but there's a lot to be said for traveling light. These tips help fight the battle of the bulging bag.

MAKE A LIST. In a recent Fodor's survey, 29% of respondents said they make lists (and often pack) a week before a trip. You can use your list to pack and to repack at the end of your trip. It can also serve as record of the contents of your suitcase—in case it disappears in transit.

THINK IT THROUGH. What's the weather like? Is this a business trip? A cruise? Going abroad? In some places dress may be more or less conservative than you're used to. As you create your itinerary, note outfits next to each activity (don't forget accessories).

EDIT YOUR WARDROBE. Plan to wear everything twice (better yet, thrice) and to do laundry along the way. Stick to one basic look—urban chic, sporty casual, etc. Build around one or two neutrals and an accent (e.g., black, white, and olive green). Women can freshen looks by changing scarves or jewelry. For a week's trip, you can look smashing with three bottoms, four or five tops, a sweater, and a jacket.

BE PRACTICAL. Put comfortable shoes atop your list. (Did we need to say this?) Pack lightweight, wrinkle-resistent, compact, washable items. (Or this?) Stack and roll clothes, so they'll wrinkle less. Unless you're on a guided tour or a cruise, select luggage you can readily carry. Porters, like good butlers, are hard to find these days.

CHECK WEIGHT AND SIZE LIMITATIONS. In the United States you may be charged extra for checked bags weighing more than 50 pounds. Abroad some airlines don't allow you to check bags over 60 to 70 pounds, or they charge outrageous fees for every excess pound—or bag. Carry-on size limitations can be stringent, too.

CHECK CARRY-ON RESTRICTIONS. Research restrictions with the TSA. Rules vary abroad, so check them with your airline if you're traveling overseas on a foreign carrier. Consider packing all but essentials (travel documents, prescription meds, wallet) in checked luggage. This leads to a "pack only what you can afford to lose" approach that might help you streamline.

RETHINK VALUABLES. On U.S. flights, airlines are liable for only about $2,800 per person for bags. On international flights, the liability limit is around $635 per bag. But items like computers, cameras, and jewelry aren't covered, and as gadgetry can go on and off the list of carry-on no-no's, you can't count on keeping things safe by keeping them close. Although comprehensive travel policies may cover luggage, the liability limit is often a pittance. Your home-owner's policy may cover you sufficiently when you travel—or not.

LOCK IT UP. If you must pack valuables, use TSA-approved locks (about $10) that can be unlocked by all U.S. security personnel.

TAG IT. Always tag your luggage; use your business address if you don't want people to know your home address. Put the same information (and a copy of your itinerary) inside your luggage, too.

REPORT PROBLEMS IMMEDIATELY. If your bags—or things in them—are damaged or go astray, file a written claim with your airline *before leaving the airport*. If the airline is at fault, it may give you money for essentials until your luggage arrives. Most lost bags are found within 48 hours, so alert the airline to your whereabouts for two or three days. If your bag was opened for security reasons in the States and something is missing, file a claim with the TSA.

port now more than ever. At this writing, U.S. citizens must have a passport when traveling by air between the United States and several destinations for which other forms of identification (e.g., a driver's license and a birth certificate) were once sufficient. These destinations include Mexico, Canada, Bermuda, and all countries in Central America and the Caribbean (except the territories of Puerto Rico and the U.S. Virgin Islands). Soon enough you'll need a passport when traveling between the United States and such destinations by land and sea, too.

U.S. passports are valid for 10 years. You must apply in person if you're getting a passport for the first time; if your previous passport was lost, stolen, or damaged; or if your previous passport has expired and was issued more than 15 years ago or when you were under 16. All children under 18 must appear in person to apply for or renew a passport. Both parents must accompany any child under 14 (or send a notarized statement with their permission) and provide proof of their relationship to the child.

■ TIP→ Before your trip, make two copies of your passport's data page (one for someone at home and another for you to carry separately). Or scan the page and e-mail it to someone at home and/or yourself.

There are 13 regional passport offices, as well as 7,000 passport acceptance facilities in post offices, public libraries, and other governmental offices. If you're renewing a passport, you can do so by mail. Forms are available at passport acceptance facilities and online.

The cost to apply for a new passport is $97 for adults, $82 for children under 16; renewals are $67. Allow six weeks for processing, both for first-time passports and renewals. For an expediting fee of $60 you can reduce this time to about two weeks. If your trip is less than two weeks away, you can get a passport even more rapidly by going to a passport office with the necessary documentation. Private expediters can get things done in as little as 48 hours, but charge hefty fees for their services.

VISAS

A visa is essentially formal permission to enter a country. Visas allow countries to keep track of you and other visitors—and generate revenue (from application fees). You *always* need a visa to enter a foreign country; however, many countries routinely issue tourist visas on arrival, particularly to U.S. citizens. When your passport is stamped or scanned in the immigration line, you're actually being issued a visa. Sometimes you have to stand in a separate line and pay a small fee to get your stamp before going through immigration, but you can still do this at the airport on arrival.

Getting a visa isn't always that easy. Some countries require that you arrange for one in advance of your trip. There's usually—but not always—a fee involved, and said fee may be nominal ($10 or less) or substantial ($100 or more).

If you must apply for a visa in advance, you can usually do it in person or by mail. When you apply by mail, you send your passport to a designated consulate, where your passport will be examined and the visa issued. Expediters—usually the same ones who handle expedited passport applications—can do all the work of obtaining your visa for you; however, there's always an additional cost (often more than $50 per visa).

Most visas limit you to a single trip—basically during the actual dates of your planned vacation. Other visas allow you to visit as many times as you wish for a specific period of time. Remember that requirements change, sometimes at the drop of a hat, and the burden is on you to make sure that you have the appropriate visas. Otherwise, you'll be turned away at the airport or, worse, deported after you arrive in the country. No company or travel insurer gives refunds if your travel

Trip Insurance Resources

INSURANCE COMPARISON SITES		
Insure My Trip.com		www.insuremytrip.com
Square Mouth.com		www.quotetravelinsurance.com
COMPREHENSIVE TRAVEL INSURERS		
Access America	866/807-3982	www.accessamerica.com
CSA Travel Protection	800/873-9855	www.csatravelprotection.com
HTH Worldwide	610/254-8700 or 888/243-2358	www.hthworldwide.com
Travelex Insurance	888/457-4602	www.travelex-insurance.com
Travel Guard International	715/345-0505 or 800/826-4919	www.travelguard.com
Travel Insured International	800/243-3174	www.travelinsured.com
MEDICAL-ONLY INSURERS		
International Medical Group	800/628-4664	www.imglobal.com
International SOS	215/942-8000 or 713/521-7611	www.internationalsos.com
Wallach & Company	800/237-6615 or 504/687-3166	www.wallach.com

plans are disrupted because you didn't have the correct visa.

Citizens of the U.S. need visas only if they wish to stay in Thailand for more than 30 days. Currently, the fee for tourism visas is $25 per entry, with each entry granting you a stay of up to 60 days. Be sure to apply for the correct amount of entries; for example, if you plan to leave Thailand to go to Laos on a side trip, you'll need to apply for two entries (the first being when you arrive in Thailand and the second being when you reenter Thailand from Laos).

Visa Extensions Bangkok Immigration ✉ Soi Suan Phlu, Sathorn Rd., Bangkok ☎ 02/287-3101. **Chiang Mai Immigration** ✉ Thanon Mahidon (near the airport), Chiang Mai ☎ 053/277510.

U.S. Passport Information U.S. Department of State ☎ 877/487-2778 ⊕ http://travel.state.gov/passport.

U.S. Passport & Visa Expediters A. Briggs Passport & Visa Expeditors ☎ 800/806-0581 or 202/464-3000 ⊕ www.abriggs.com. **American Passport Express** ☎ 800/455-5166 or 603/559-9888 ⊕ www.americanpassport.com. **Passport Express** ☎ 800/362-8196 or 401/272-4612 ⊕ www.

passportexpress.com. **Travel Document Systems** ☎ 800/874-5100 or 202/638-3800 ⊕ www.traveldocs.com. **Travel the World Visas** ☎ 866/886-8472 or 301/495-7700 ⊕ www.world-visa.com.

SHOTS & MEDICATIONS

Although Thailand does not require or suggest vaccinations before traveling, we make the following recommendations:

Tetanus and polio vaccinations should be up-to-date, and you should be immunized against (or immune to) measles, mumps, and rubella. ■ TIP→ **Do not leave home without a hepatitis A vaccination.**

Malaria and dengue fever are also possible (though remote) risks as you move out of the main tourist areas, so make sure to get fever and nausea checked out by a doctor as soon as possible. To repeat what is noted above, the Thai Ministry of Public Health does not recommend taking antimalarial drugs for normal visits to Thailand, as the disease is rare and many strains are already drug resistant. Get in touch with a local travelers' health clinic or the CDC's International Travelers Hotline if you still have concerns about malaria risks.

According to the U.S. government's National Centers for Disease Control (CDC) there's also a risk of hepatitis B, rabies, and Japanese encephalitis in rural areas of Thailand. In most urban or easily accessible areas you need not worry. However, if you plan to visit remote regions or stay for more than six weeks, check with the CDC's International Travelers Hotline.

For more information *see* Health *under* On the Ground in Thailand, *below.*

Health Warnings **National Centers for Disease Control & Prevention** (CDC) ☎ 877/ 394–8747 international travelers' health line ⊕ www.cdc.gov/travel. **World Health Organization** (WHO) ⊕ www.who.int.

TRIP INSURANCE

What kind of coverage do you honestly need? Do you even need trip insurance at all? Take a deep breath and read on.

We believe that comprehensive trip insurance is especially valuable if you're booking a very expensive or complicated trip (particularly to an isolated region) or if you're booking far in advance. Who knows what could happen six months down the road? But whether or not you get insurance has more to do with how comfortable you are assuming all that risk yourself.

Comprehensive travel policies typically cover trip-cancellation and interruption, letting you cancel or cut your trip short because of a personal emergency, illness, or, in some cases, acts of terrorism in your destination. Such policies also cover evacuation and medical care. Some also cover you for trip delays because of bad weather or mechanical problems as well as for lost or delayed baggage. Another type of coverage to look for is financial default— that is, when your trip is disrupted because a tour operator, airline, or cruise line goes out of business. Generally you must buy this when you book your trip or shortly thereafter, and it's only available to you if your operator isn't on a list of excluded companies.

If you're going abroad, consider buying medical-only coverage at the very least. Neither Medicare nor some private insurers cover medical expenses anywhere outside of the United States besides Mexico and Canada (including time aboard a cruise ship, even if it leaves from a U.S. port). Medical-only policies typically reimburse you for medical care (excluding that related to pre-existing conditions) and hospitalization abroad, and provide for evacuation. You still have to pay the bills and await reimbursement from the insurer, though.

■ TIP→ **Thailand has very low medical costs for what is usually very good care. If you do get sick or become injured here, the resulting bills are very unlikely to bankrupt you. Some larger hospitals do accept some foreign insurance plans. You will need to check to see if and under what circumstances.**

Expect comprehensive travel insurance policies to cost about 4% to 7% of the total price of your trip (it's more like 12% if you're over age 70). A medical-only policy may or may not be cheaper than a comprehensive policy. Always read the fine print of your policy to make sure that you are covered for the risks that are of most concern to you. Compare several policies to make sure you're getting the best price and range of coverage available.

■ TIP→ **OK. You know you can save a bundle on trips to warm-weather destinations by traveling in rainy season. But there's also a chance that a severe storm will disrupt your plans. The solution? Look for hotels and resorts that offer storm/hurricane guarantees. Although they rarely allow refunds, most guarantees do let you rebook later if a storm strikes.**

BOOKING YOUR TRIP

Unless your cousin is a travel agent, you're probably among the millions of people who make most of their travel arrangements online.

But have you ever wondered just what the differences are between all those Web sites? Is it truly better to book directly on an airline or hotel Web site? And when does a real live travel agent come in handy?

ONLINE

You really have to shop around. A travel wholesaler such as Hotels.com or Hotel-Club.net can be a source of good rates, as can discounters such as Hotwire or Priceline, particularly if you can bid for your hotel room or airfare. Indeed, such sites sometimes have deals that are unavailable elsewhere. They do, however, tend to work only with hotel chains (which makes them just plain useless for getting hotel reservations outside of major cities) or big airlines (so that often leaves out upstarts like jetBlue and some foreign carriers like Air India).

Also, with discounters and wholesalers you must generally prepay, and everything is nonrefundable. Before you fork over the dough, check the terms and conditions so you know what a given company will do for you if there's a problem and what you'll have to deal with on your own.

TIP→ To be absolutely sure everything was processed correctly, confirm reservations made through online travel agents, discounters, and wholesalers directly with your hotel before leaving home.

Booking engines like Expedia, Travelocity, and Orbitz are actually travel agents, albeit high-volume, online ones. And airline travel packagers like American Airlines Vacations and Virgin Vacations—well, they're travel agents, too. But they may still not work with all the world's hotels.

An aggregator site will search many sites and pull the best prices for airfares, ho-

tels, and rental cars from them. Most compare the major travel-booking sites such as Expedia, Travelocity, and Orbitz; some also look at airline Web sites, though rarely the sites of smaller budget airlines.

WITH A TRAVEL AGENT

If you use an agent—brick-and-mortar or virtual—you'll pay a fee for the service. And know that the service you get from some online agents isn't comprehensive. For example Expedia and Travelocity don't search for prices on budget airlines like jetBlue or small foreign carriers. That said, some agents (online or not) *do* have access to fares that are difficult to find otherwise, and the savings can more than make up for any surcharge.

TIP→ Remember that Expedia, Travelocity, and Orbitz are travel agents, not just booking engines. To resolve any problems with a reservation made through these companies, contact them first.

A top-notch agent planning your trip to Thailand will be able to get you a package trip that's not available to you directly, an air pass, or a complicated itinerary including several overseas flights. What's more, travel agents that specialize in a destination may have exclusive access to certain deals and insider information on things such as charter flights. Agents who specialize in types of travelers (senior citizens, gays and lesbians, naturists) or types of trips (cruises, luxury travel, safaris) can also be invaluable. And complain about the surcharges all you like, but when things don't work out the way you'd hoped, it's nice to have an agent to put things right. Agent Resources **American Society of Travel Agents** ☎ 703/739-2782 ⊕ www.travelsense. org.

ACCOMMODATIONS

Nearly every town offers accommodation. In smaller towns hotels may be fairly

Online Booking Resources

AGGREGATORS		
Kayak	www.kayak.com	looks at cruises and vacation packages.
Mobissimo	www.mobissimo.com	
Qixo	www.qixo.com	compares cruises, vacation packages, and even travel insurance
Sidestep	www.sidestep.com	compares vacation packages and lists travel deals
Travelgrove	www.travelgrove.com	compares cruises and vacation packages

BOOKING ENGINES		
Cheap Tickets	www.cheaptickets.com	discounter.
Expedia	www.expedia.com	large online agency that charges a booking fee for airline tickets.
Hotwire	www.hotwire.com	discounter.
lastminute.com	www.lastminute.com	specializes in last-minute travel; the main site is for the U.K., but it has a link to a U.S. site.
Luxury Link	www.luxurylink.com	has auctions (surprisingly good deals) as well as offers on the high-end side of travel.
Onetravel.com	www.onetravel.com	discounter for hotels, car rentals, airfares, and packages.
Orbitz	www.orbitz.com	charges a booking fee for airline tickets, but gives a clear breakdown of fees and taxes before you book.
Priceline.com	www.priceline.com	discounter that also allows bidding.
Travel.com	www.travel.com	allows you to compare its rates with those of other booking engines.
Travelocity	www.travelocity.com	charges a booking fee for airline tickets, but promises good problem resolution.

ONLINE ACCOMMODATIONS		
Asia Hotels	www.asia-hotels.com	good selection of mid- to top-end hotels.
Hotelbook.com	www.hotelbook.com	focuses on independent hotels worldwide.
Hotel Club	www.hotelclub.net	good for major cities worldwide.
Hotels.com	www.hotels.com	big Expedia-owned wholesaler that offers rooms in hotels all over the world.

OTHER RESOURCES		
Bidding For Travel	www.biddingfortravel.com	good place to figure out what you can get and for how much before you start bidding on, say, Priceline.

10 WAYS TO SAVE

1. Join "frequent guest" programs. You may get preferential treatment in room choice and/or upgrades in your favorite chains.

2. Call direct. You can sometimes get a better price if you call a hotel's local toll-free number (if available) rather than a central reservations number.

3. Check online. Check hotel Web sites, as not all chains are represented on all travel sites.

4. Look for specials. Always inquire about packages and corporate rates.

5. Look for price guarantees. For overseas trips, look for guaranteed rates. With your rate locked in you won't pay more, even if the price goes up in the local currency.

6. Look for weekend deals at business hotels. High-end chains catering to business travelers are often busy only on weekdays; to fill rooms they often drop rates dramatically on weekends.

7. Ask about taxes. Verify whether local hotel taxes are included in quoted rates. In some places taxes can add 20% or more to your bill.

8. Read the fine print. Watch for add-ons, including resort fees, energy surcharges, and "convenience" fees for such things as unlimited local phone service you won't use or a free newspaper in a language you can't read.

9. Know when to go. If your destination's high season is December through April and you're trying to book, say, in late April, you might save money by changing your dates by a week or two. Ask when rates go down, though: if your dates straddle peak and non-peak seasons, a property may still charge peak-season rates for the entire stay.

10. Weigh your options (we can't say this enough). Weigh transportation times and costs against the savings of staying in a hotel that's cheaper because it's out of the way.

simple, but they will usually be clean and certainly inexpensive. In major cities or resort areas there are hotels to fit all price categories. At the high end, Thai luxury hotels are among the best in the world. Service is generally superb—polite and efficient—and most of the staff speak English. At the other end of the scale, the lodging is simple and basic—a room with little more than a bed. The least expensive places may have Asian toilets (squat type with no seat) and a fan rather than air-conditioning.

Many hotels have restaurants and offer room service throughout most of the day and night. Many will also be happy to make travel arrangements for you—for which they receive commissions. Be sure to use hotel safe-deposit boxes if they are offered.

During the peak tourist season, hotels are often fully booked and charge peak rates. At special times, such as December 30–January 2 and Chinese New Year (in January or February, depending on the year), rates climb even higher, and hotel reservations are difficult to obtain on short notice. Weekday rates at some resorts are often lower, and virtually all hotels will discount their rooms if they are not fully booked. Don't be reticent about asking for a special rate. Though it may feel awkward to haggle over what are usually set prices in Western hotels, this practice is perfectly normal in Thailand. Breakfast is rarely included in the room tariff. Hotel rates tend to be lower if you reserve through a travel agent in Thailand. The agent receives a reduced room rate from the hotel and passes some of this discount on to you.

The lodgings we list are the cream of the crop in each price category. We always list the facilities that are available, but we don't specify whether they cost extra; when pricing accommodations, always ask what's included and what costs extra.

Most hotels and other lodgings require you to give your credit-card details before they will confirm your reservation. If you don't feel comfortable e-mailing this information, ask if you can fax it (some places even prefer faxes). However you book, get confirmation in writing and have a copy of it handy when you check in.

Be sure you understand the hotel's cancellation policy. Some places allow you to cancel without any kind of penalty—even if you prepaid to secure a discounted rate—if you cancel at least 24 hours in advance. Others require you to cancel a week in advance or penalize you the cost of one night. Small inns and B&Bs are most likely to require you to cancel far in advance. Most hotels allow children under a certain age to stay in their parents' room at no extra charge; find out the cutoff age.

■ TIP➔ **Assume that hotels operate on the European Plan (EP, no meals) unless we specify that they use the Breakfast Plan (BP, with full breakfast), Continental Plan (CP, Continental breakfast), Full American Plan (FAP, all meals), Modified American Plan (MAP, breakfast and dinner) or are all-inclusive (AI, all meals and most activities).**

APARTMENT & HOUSE RENTALS

It is possible to rent apartments or houses for longer stays in most places in Thailand. Bangkok, Chiang Mai, Phuket, and Pattaya in particular have large expat and long-term tourist communities. Also, many hotels and guesthouses are willing to offer greatly reduced rates for long-term guests. Agents are available in all big cities and are used to helping foreigners. Often, they will be the only way to find an affordable place quickly in a city like Bangkok. The *Bangkok Post, Chiang Mai CityLife* magazine, *Chiang Mai Mail, Phuket Gazette,* and *Pattaya Mail* are all good places to begin looking for agents or places for rent.

BED & BREAKFASTS

Bed-and-breakfasts are not common, though a few do exist. The trend simply hasn't taken off. What you can find, though, are tiny family-run hotels or guesthouses off the beaten track. These are some of the nicest places to stay, and if they're not exactly B&Bs, they do offer some of the same charms and experiences. Reservation Services **Bed & Breakfast.com** ☎ 512/322-2710 or 800/462-2632 ⊕ www. bedandbreakfast.com also sends out an online newsletter. **Bed & Breakfast Inns Online** ☎ 615/868-1946 or 800/215-7365 ⊕ www. bbonline.com. **BnB Finder.com** ☎ 212/432-7693 or 888/547-8226 ⊕ www.bnbfinder.com.

HOME EXCHANGES

With a direct home exchange you stay in someone else's home while they stay in yours.

Exchange Clubs **Home Exchange.com** ☎ 800/877-8723 ⊕ www.homeexchange. com; $59.95 for a 1-year online listing. **HomeLink International** ☎ 800/638-3841 ⊕ www. homelink.org; $90 yearly for Web-only membership; $140 includes Web access and two

Online Booking Resources

CONTACTS		
At Home Abroad	212/421-9165	www.athomeabroadinc.com
Barclay International Group	516/364-0064 or 800/845-6636	www.barclayweb.com
Vacation Home Rentals Worldwide	201/767-9393 or 800/633-3284	www.vhrww.com
Villanet	206/417-3444 or 800/964-1891	www.rentavilla.com
Villas & Apartments Abroad	212/213-6435 or 800/433-3020	www.vaanyc.com
Villas International	415/499-9490 or 800/221-2260	www.villasintl.com
Villas of Distinction	707/778-1800 or 800/289-0900	www.villasofdistinction.com
Wimco	800/449-1553	www.wimco.com

catalogs. **Intervac U.S.** ☎ 800/756–4663 ⊕ www.intervacus.com; $78.88 for Web-only membership; $126 includes Web access and a catalog.

HOSTELS

Hostels offer bare-bones lodging at low, low prices—often in shared dorm rooms with shared baths—to people of all ages, though the primary market is young travelers, especially students. Most hostels serve breakfast; dinner and/or shared cooking facilities may also be available. In some hostels you aren't allowed to be in your room during the day, and there may be a curfew at night. Nevertheless, hostels provide a sense of community, with public rooms where travelers often gather to share stories. Many hostels are affiliated with Hostelling International (HI), an umbrella group of hostel associations with some 4,500 member properties in more than 70 countries. Other hostels are completely independent and may be nothing more than a really cheap hotel.

Membership in any HI association, open to travelers of all ages, allows you to stay in HI-affiliated hostels at member rates. One-year membership is about $28 for adults; hostels charge about $10–$30 per night. Members have priority if the hostel is full; they're also eligible for discounts around the world, even on rail and bus travel in some countries.

There aren't as many hostels in Thailand as you'd think because budget guesthouses

are so cheap, common, and clean (usually). That said, Bangkok has a few hostels where you can grab a cheap dorm bed for less than B100, or if you're willing to pay a bit more, decent private rooms can be had for similar prices to regular guesthouses. You can also find hostels in most other destinations in Thailand, such as Chiang Mai, Hua Hin, and Phuket. For more information, check out the official Thai Youth Hostels Association Web site or the Thailand page of Hostels.com, which has great up-to-date information. There are also YMCAs in Bangkok, Chiang Mai, and Chiang Rai.

Hostelling International–USA ☎ 301/495–1240 ⊕ www.hiusa.org. **Hostels.com** ⊕ www.hostels.com. **Thai Youth Hostels Association** ☎ 02/628-7413 ⊕ www.tyha.org.

HOTELS

Thailand has an official government hotel star rating system, though there is little sign of it in recent years. It seems hotels were rated when new, but were rarely, if ever, reevaluated. Don't place much faith in these designations as signs of quality, but they can be used as a guide to amenities (one star=not many; five stars=all the bells and whistles). A better guide is room price and the hotel's date of construction or last major renovation.

You can often get a deal by booking mid- to upper-range hotel rooms through Thai travel agents. They get a deeply discounted rate, part of which they then pass on to you. Finally, you should always ask if there is a discount, or if the price quoted is the hotel's best price. It is an expected and normal part of hotel business in Asia, a part of the local bargaining and haggling culture. Often it will get you nothing, but it can occasionally save you up to 50% if you catch a manager in the right mood and with a bunch of empty rooms. Give it a whirl. The worst they can say is "no."

Expect any room costing more than the equivalent of US$20 a night to come with hot water, air-conditioning, and a TV. Southeast Asian hotels traditionally have two twin beds. Make sure to ask for one big bed if that is your preference, though this may end up being two twins pushed together. All hotels listed have private bath unless otherwise noted.

Thai cities are noisy. Rooms facing away from the road are often quieter, more so those higher up. Keep in mind, though, that less expensive hotels don't have elevators. If you prefer to sleep without air-conditioning, cooled by a fan and an open window, be prepared to be awakened by roosters very early every morning, no matter where you are. They are the sound track to all Southeast Asian mornings.

▌ AIRLINE TICKETS

International tickets may be either electronic or paper. With an e-ticket the only thing you receive is an e-mailed receipt citing your itinerary and reservation and ticket numbers. The greatest advantage of an e-ticket is that if you lose your receipt, you can simply print out another copy. You usually pay a surcharge (up to $50) to get a paper ticket, if you can get one at all.

The sole advantage of a paper ticket is that it may be easier to endorse over to another airline if your flight is canceled and the airline with which you booked can't accommodate you on another flight.

▌ TIP➔ Discount air passes that let you travel economically in a country or region must often be purchased before you leave home. In some cases you can only get them through a travel agent.

Independent travelers should check out "Circle Pacific" fares. The pricing and routing of these tickets depend on the arrangements that the airline has with the local carriers of the region. The tickets must be purchased at least 7 to 14 days in advance. You usually can add on extra stopovers, including Australian and South Pacific destinations, for a nominal charge. Several airlines work together to offer "Around the World" fares, but you must follow a specific routing itinerary and can-

10 WAYS TO SAVE

1. Nonrefundable is best. If saving money is more important than flexibility, then non-refundable tickets work. Just remember that you'll pay dearly (as much as $100) if you change your plans.

2. Comparison shop. Web sites and travel agents can have different arrangements with the airlines and offer different prices for exactly the same flights.

3. Beware those prices. Many airline Web sites—and most ads—show prices *without* taxes and surcharges. Don't buy until you know the full price.

4. Stay loyal. Stick with one or two frequent-flier programs. You'll rack up free trips faster and you'll accumulate more quickly the perks that make trips easier. On some airlines these include a special reservations number, early boarding, access to upgrades, and more roomy economy-class seating.

5. Watch those ticketing fees. Surcharges are usually added when you buy your ticket anywhere but on an airline Web site. (That includes by phone—even if you call the airline directly—and paper tickets regardless of how you book).

6. Check early and often. Start looking for cheap fares up to a year in advance. Keep looking until you find a price you like.

7. Don't work alone. Some Web sites have tracking features that will e-mail you immediately when good deals are posted.

8. Jump on the good deals. Waiting even a few minutes might mean paying more.

9. Be flexible. Look for departures on Tuesday, Wednesday, and Thursday, typically the cheapest days to travel. And check on prices for departures at different times and to and from alternative airports.

10. Weigh your options. What you get can be as important as what you save. A cheaper flight might have a long layover, or it might land at a secondary airport, where your ground transportation costs might be higher.

not backtrack. "Around the World" itineraries usually include a couple of Asian destinations before continuing through Africa and Europe.

Thai Airways has a pass that entitles you to fly to any three cities within Thailand for a discount, but this may no longer be such a good deal because low-cost carriers now fly many domestic routes alongside Thai Airlines and can be much cheaper. You also have the option of purchasing additional discount coupons if you need to add on a few more flights. Unfortunately, this deal is only available if you purchase your round-trip international ticket through Thai Airways.

Bangkok Airways offers a Discovery Air Pass, a coupon system for purchasing flights around the region, either on Bangkok Airways, Lao Airways, or Siem Reap Airways International (a re-branded Bangkok Airways carrier).
Air Pass Info **Bangkok Airways Discovery Air Pass** ☎ 02/265–5555 in Bangkok ⊕ www.bangkokair.com/discoveryairpass/. **Cathay Pacific All Asia Pass** ☎ 800/233–2742 ⊕ www.cathaypacific.com. **Thai Airlines** ☎ 800/864–8331 in the U.S. ⊕ www.thaiairlines.com.

∎ RENTAL CARS

When you reserve a car, ask about cancellation penalties, taxes, drop-off charges (if you're planning to pick up the car in one city and leave it in another), and surcharges (for being under or over a certain age, for additional drivers, or for driving across state or country borders or beyond a specific distance from your point of rental). All these things can add substantially to your costs. Request car seats and extras such as GPS when you book.

Cars are available for rent in Bangkok and in major tourist destinations. However, the additional cost of hiring a driver is small and the peace of mind great. If a foreigner is involved in an automobile accident, he or she—not the Thai—is likely to be judged at fault, no matter who hit whom or who was driving.

Rates in Thailand begin at $40 a day for an economy car with unlimited mileage. This includes neither tax, which is 7% on car rentals, nor the collision damage waiver. It's better to make your car-rental reservations when you arrive in Thailand, as you can usually secure a discount.

In smaller towns and cities, consider renting a jeep or motorcycle, popular and convenient ways to get around. Smaller 100cc–125cc motorcycles cost only a few dollars a day. Dirt bikes and bigger road bikes, 250cc and above, start at $20 per day. Do be aware that motorcycles skid easily on wet or gravel roads. On Koh Samui, a sign posts the year's count of foreigners who never made it home from their vacations because of such accidents!

You must have an International Driver's Permit (IDP) to drive or rent a car in Thailand. IDP's are not difficult to obtain, and having one in your wallet may save you from unwanted headaches if you do have to deal with local authorities. Check the AAA Web site for more info as well as for IDPs ($10) themselves.

CAR-RENTAL INSURANCE

Everyone who rents a car wonders whether the insurance that the rental companies offer is worth the expense. No one—including us—has a simple answer. It all depends on how much regular insurance you have, how comfortable you are with risk, and whether or not money is an issue.

If you own a car, your personal auto insurance may cover a rental to some degree, though not all policies protect you abroad; always read your policy's fine print. If you don't have auto insurance, then seriously consider buying the collision- or loss-damage waiver (CDW or LDW) from the car-rental company, which eliminates your liability for damage to the car. Some credit cards offer CDW coverage, but it's usually supplemental to your own insurance and rarely covers SUVs, minivans, luxury models, and the like. If your coverage is secondary, you may still be liable

GETTING STARTED / BOOKING YOUR TRIP / TRANSPORTATION / ON THE GROUND

Car Rental Resources

AUTOMOBILE ASSOCIATIONS		
U.S.: American Automobile Association AAA	315/797-5000 regional organizations	www.aaa.com state and
National Automobile Club	650/294-7000 California residents only	www.thenac.com
MAJOR AGENCIES		
Alamo	800/522-9696	www.alamo.com
Avis	800/331-1084	www.avis.com
Budget	800/472-3325	www.budget.com
Hertz	800/654-3001	www.hertz.com
National Car Rental	800/227-7368	www.nationalcar.com

for loss-of-use costs from the car-rental company. But no credit-card insurance is valid unless you use that card for *all* transactions, from reserving to paying the final bill. All companies exclude car rental in some countries, so be sure to find out about the destination to which you are traveling.

■ TIP→ Diners Club offers primary CDW coverage on all rentals reserved and paid for with the card. This means that Diners Club's company—not your own car insurance—pays in case of an accident. It *doesn't* mean your car-insurance company won't raise your rates once it discovers you had an accident.

You may be required to purchase CDW coverage or car-rental companies may in-clude it in quoted rates. Ask your rental company about issues like these. In most cases it's cheaper to add a supplemental CDW plan to your comprehensive travel-insurance policy (⇨ Trip Insurance *under* Things to Consider *in* Getting Started, *above*) than to purchase it from a rental company. That said, you don't want to pay for a supplement if you're required to buy insurance from the rental company.

■ TIP→ You can decline the insurance from the rental company and purchase it through a third-party provider such as Travel Guard (⊕ www.travelguard.com)—$9 per day for $35,000 of coverage. That's sometimes just under half the price of the CDW offered by some car-rental companies.

TRANSPORTATION

▎ BY AIR

Bangkok is 17 hours from San Francisco, 18 hours from Seattle and Vancouver, 20 hours from Chicago, 22 hours from New York, and 10 hours from Sydney. Add more time for stopovers and connections, especially if you're using more than one carrier. Thai Airways' new direct flights between Bangkok and New York and Bangkok and Los Angeles are 16½ and 14½ hours respectively, far and away the quickest trips available.

On popular tourist routes during peak holiday times, domestic flights in Thailand are often fully booked. Make sure you have reservations, and make them well in advance of your travel date. Be sure to reconfirm your return flight when you arrive in Thailand.

Airlines & Airports **Airline and Airport Links.com** ⊕ www.airlineandairportlinks.com has links to many of the world's airlines and airports.

Airline Security Issues **Transportation Security Administration** ⊕ www.tsa.gov has answers for almost every question that might come up.

AIRPORTS

Bangkok remains Thailand's gateway to the world. The look of that gateway changed very recently with the opening of the new international Suvarnabhumi Airport, 30 km (18 mi) southeast of town, which is a huge improvement over the old Don Muang International Airport. Unfortunately, the new airport is not any closer to the city than the old one—it lies far from downtown and as of yet does not have any decent public transportation links. The government promises eventual subway and light-rail connections.

At Chiang Mai International Airport, work hurries along to finish a large new terminal to handle the recent sharp increases in national and regional air traffic. The airport lies on the edge of town, and taxi service to most hotels costs a flat B120 (about $3).

Perhaps Thailand's third-busiest airport (especially in high season) is the one at Phuket, a major link to the Southern Beaches region, particularly the islands of the Andaman Coast.

Bangkok Airways owns and runs the airports in Sukhothai, Trat, and Koh Samui. They have the only flights to these destinations, which can be expensive in high season. You also have to use the airport transport options they offer.

Airport Information **Airports of Thailand** ⊕ www.airportthai.co.th has information on the country's major airports, though much of it is in Thai. **Suvarnabhumi Airport** ⊕ www.suvarnabhumiairport.com.

GROUND TRANSPORTATION

Free shuttle buses run from the airport to a public bus stand, where you can catch a bus into the city.

Meter taxis run between the airport and town and charge a B50 airport fee on top of the meter charge. Taxis in town will often try to set a high flat fee to take you to the airport, though this is theoretically illegal. If you do talk a taxi driver into charging by the meter, expect a long, scenic trip to the airport.

Thai Airways offers a B1,000 limousine service that takes you by Mercedes to most major hotels in town.

Many who travel regularly in and out of Bangkok plan their flights to leave and arrive outside of rush hours. A trip to Suvarnabhumi from the main hotel strip along Sukhumvit Road can take as little as 25 minutes if traffic is moving. A trip from the Khao San Road area can take two hours or more during a bad evening rush hour.

▎ TIP➔ It helps to have a hotel brochure or an address in Thai for the driver. Also, stop at one of the ATMs in the arrival hall and get some baht before leaving the airport so you can pay your taxi driver.

FLIGHTS

Bangkok is one of Asia's—and the world's—largest air hubs, with flights to most corners of the globe and service from nearly all of the world's major carriers, plus dozens of minor carriers. Most flights from the United States stop in Hong Kong, Tokyo, or Taipei on the way to Bangkok, though Thai Airways now offers a direct flight from New York.

Northwest Airlines and Japan Airlines (JAL) are both major carriers with hubs in the United States and offer daily flights from six U.S. cities. JAL is one of the best options around with a flight time of 17 hours from Dallas including a stopover at Narita airport, Tokyo. East Coast travelers departing from New York or Washington D.C. could also consider using British Airways or Virgin Atlantic/Thai Airways via London or Singapore Airlines from Newark via Amsterdam. From the West Coast, Thai Airways has good connections from Los Angeles, San Francisco, and Seattle. Cathay Pacific often has good fares from San Francisco.

■ TIP➜ **Many Asian airlines (Thai Airways, Singapore Airlines, Cathay Pacific, Malaysian Airlines) are rated among the best in the world for their service.** They often have more-comfortable seats, better food selections, and more entertainment options than do most U.S.-based carriers. Many Asian airlines also allow you to change your bookings for free (or for a nominal charge) if done a week in advance. Lastly, tickets purchased from these carriers are generally no more expensive than those offered by U.S. carriers. And the extra creature comforts these airlines provide can leave you a little less frazzled when you reach your destination, ensuring that you don't spend your entire vacation recovering from the trip over.

Chiang Mai, Thailand's second-biggest city, is slowly becoming an important regional destination and offers direct flights to Hong Kong, Singapore, Tokyo, Taipei, various points in China, Luang Prabang in Laos, and on-again off-again flights to Bangladesh, Myanmar (Burma), and the Maldives.

For now, Bangkok Airways offers the only flights between Bangkok and Siem Reap, Cambodia (home of Angkor Wat), and charge monopoly prices for the service. However, several budget airlines now fly regional international routes, making short country-hopping excursions far more feasible than ever before.

Airline Contacts Asiana Airlines ☎ 800/227-4262 ⊕ http://us.flyasiana.com. **British Airways** ☎ 800/247-9297 ⊕ www.britishairways.com. **Cathay Pacific** ☎ 800/233-2742 ⊕ www.cathaypacific.com. **China Airlines** ☎ 800/227-5118 ⊕ www.china-airlines.com. **Continental Airlines** ☎ 800/523-3273 for U.S. and Mexico reservations, 800/231-0856 for international reservations ⊕ www.continental.com. **Delta Airlines** ☎ 800/221-1212 for U.S. reservations, 800/241-4141 for international reservations ⊕ www.delta.com. **EVA Air** ☎ 800/695-1188 ⊕ www.evaair.com. **Japan Airlines** ☎ 800/525-3663 ⊕ www.jal.com. **Korean Air** ☎ 800/438-5000 ⊕ www.koreanair.com. **Malaysia Airlines** ☎ 800/552-9264 ⊕ http://us.malaysiaairlines.com. **Northwest Airlines** ☎ 800/225-2525 ⊕ www.nwa.com. **Singapore Airlines** ☎ 800/742-3333 ⊕ www.singaporeair.com. **Thai Airways** ☎ 800/426-5204 ⊕ www.thaiair.com. **United Airlines** ☎ 800/864-8331 for U.S. reservations, 800/538-2929 for international reservations ⊕ www.united.com.

Regional Carriers AirAsia ☎ 02/515-9999 in Thailand, 603/8660-4343 from all other countries ⊕ www.airasia.com. **Bangkok Airways** ☎ 02/265-5555 in Thailand ⊕ www.bangkokair.com. **JetStar Asia** ☎ 02/267-5125 in Thailand, 800/611-2957 from other countries ⊕ www.jetstar.com. **Lao Airlines** ☎ 21/212-057 in Laos ⊕ www.laoairlines.com. **Silk Airlines** ☎ 053/904985 in Thailand ⊕ www.silkair.com. **Tiger Airlines** ☎ 02/975-5333 in Thailand ⊕ www.tigerairways.com.

AIR TRAVEL WITHIN THAILAND

Thai Airways has by far the largest network of any airline in Thailand and connects all major and many minor destinations across the country. Bangkok Airways, which bills itself as a luxury boutique airline with comfy seats and good food, flies many major routes and has sole service routes to Koh Samui, Trat, and Sukhothai—they built the airports there. Both airlines fly a mix of larger jet aircrafts and smaller turbo-props. For the last few years, buying tickets on the Thai Airways Web site was an act suitable only for sadists; as of this writing, it is still easier *and cheaper* to go to a travel agent to get Thai Airways tickets. The Web sites of the other airlines noted here generally work well for online bookings.

Three budget airlines now fly routes in Thailand, and have dramatically dropped the cost of travel: Nok Air (a subsidiary of Thai Airlines, and the more expensive of the three), Thai Air Asia, and Orient Thai Airlines (under its One-Two-GO moniker). With all three, book online to get the cheapest fares. You can phone in bookings for a small extra charge, but you can't guarantee you'll get an English-speaking operator on the phone. Tickets can also be purchased at airports served by the airlines—the most expensive option. Thai Air Asia has a network of "agents," often found in minimarts in major towns and cities; they can usually get you a ticket for the best available online price if you are unable to buy it yourself.

As with all low-cost carriers, you save money by dealing with the fewest number of people and buying your tickets as far in advance as you feel comfortable. They keep their prices low by offering no or added-cost services (like food). They charge less for flights at odd hours, generally park on the tarmac and bus you to a terminal, and change their schedules based on the availability of cheap landing and take-off times. Nok and Orient Thai keep pretty constant flight schedules and fares. Air Asia seems to change their flight times and routes every couple of months, if not more often—they also tend to be cheapest. Although flights anywhere tend to run late later in the day, low-cost flights tend to be the latest. Keep this in mind if you have to make an international connection.

Air Asia ☎ 02/515-9999 ⊕ www.airasia.com. **Bangkok Airways** ☎ 02/265-5555 ⊕ www.bangkokair.com. **Nok Air** ⊕ www.nokair.com. **One-Two-GO (part of Orient Thai Airways)** ⊕ www.fly12go.com/en/main.shtml. **Thai Airways** ☎ 02/232-8000 ⊕ www.thaiairlines.com.

▌ BY BUS

Thai buses are cheap, faster than trains, and reach every corner of the country. There are usually two to three buses a day on most routes and several (or even hourly) daily buses on popular routes between major towns. Most buses leave in the morning, with a few other runs spaced out in the afternoon and evening. On long routes, buses will leave in the evening for overnight trips. Overnight buses are very popular with Thais, but they do crash with disturbing regularity—many foreign expats avoid them.

If you're setting out on a long bus journey, it's worth inquiring about on-board entertainment—14 hours on a bus with continuous karaoke VCDs blasting out old pop hits can be torturous. Be aware that air-conditioned buses are always so cold that you'll want to bring an extra sweater. On local buses, space at the back soon fills up with all kinds of oversize luggage that will take up your legroom, so it's best to sit toward the middle or front.

Bangkok has three main bus stations, serving routes to the north (Mo Chit), south (Southern Terminal), and east (Ekamai). Chiang Mai has one major terminal. All have telephone information lines, but the operators rarely speak English.

▌ TIP→ **Avoid taking private bus company trips from the Kao San Road area.** The buses are not as comfortable as public buses, they take longer, and they usually try to trap you at an affiliated hotel once you reach your destination. There have also been many reports of rip-offs, scams, and luggage thefts on these buses over the years. It is simply not worth the risk.

There are, generally speaking, three classes of bus service: cheap, no-frills locals on short routes that stop at every road crossing and for anyone who waves them down; second- and first-class buses on specific routes that have air-conditioning, toilets (sometimes), and loud chop-socky movies (too often); and VIP buses that provide nonstop service between major bus stations, and feature comfortable seats, drinks, snacks (sometimes), frigid air-conditioning, and movies (usually starring either Steven Segal or Jean-Claude Van Damme).

Many travel agents will have general bus schedules, but you will normally need to go to the station to get exact times and fares. Sometimes agents can get tickets for you, but unless you are booking a long-distance VIP bus trip, the agent fee can be more than the cost of the ticket itself. Thais usually just head to the bus station and get their tickets an hour before they plan to leave. You may want to go a day early and buy your ticket in advance just to make sure you get one.

All fares are paid in cash. Larger bus terminals often have ATMs if you forget to bring money with you.

▌ BY CAR

Driving in Thailand has its ups and downs. The major roads in Thailand tend to be congested, and street signs are often only in Thai. But the limited number of roads and the straightforward layout of cities combine to make navigation relatively easy. The exception, of course, is Bangkok. Don't even think about negotiating that tangled mass of traffic-clogged streets in a rental vehicle.

The main rule to remember is that traffic laws are routinely disregarded. Bigger vehicles have the unspoken right of way, motorcyclists seem to think they are invincible, and bicyclists often don't look around them. Few Thai drivers go anywhere anymore without a cell phone stuck to one ear. ■ TIP→ Drive *very* carefully, as those around you generally won't.

Police checkpoints are common, especially near international borders and in the restive south. You must stop for them (don't even think of doing otherwise), but you will most likely be waved through.

GASOLINE
A liter of gasoline costs approximately B30. Many gas stations stay open 24 hours and have clean toilet facilities and minimarts. As you get farther away from developed areas, roadside stalls sell gasoline from bottles or tanks.

PARKING
You can park on most streets; no-parking areas are marked either with red-and-white bars on the curb or with circular blue signs with a red "don't" stroke through the middle. The less urban the area, the more likely locals will double- and triple-park to be as close as possible to their destination. Thai traffic police do "boot" cars and motorcycles that are improperly parked, though only when they feel like it. The ticketing officer usually leaves a sheet of paper with a contact number to call; once you call, he returns, you pay your fine (often subject to negotiation), and he removes the boot.

In cities, the larger hotels, restaurants, and department stores have garages or parking lots. Rates vary, but count on B10 or more an hour. If you purchase anything, parking is free, but you must have your ticket validated.

ROAD CONDITIONS
Thai highways and town roads are generally quite good. Byways and rural roads range from good to indescribably bad. In rainy season, expect rural dirt roads to be impassable bogs.

■ TIP→ Leafy twigs and branches lying on a road are not decorations but warnings that something ahead is amiss, anything from a pothole to a smashup. Slow down and proceed with caution.

Thai traffic signs will be familiar to all international drivers, though most roads are marked in Thai. Fortunately, larger roads, highways, and tourist attractions often have English signs, too. Signs aren't always clear, so you may find yourself asking for directions quite often.

If you have a choice, don't drive at night. Those motorists out after dark drive like maniacs. Also beware of oxcarts, cows, dogs, small children, and people on bikes joining the traffic fray anywhere in the country at any time, day or night.

ROADSIDE EMERGENCIES

Should you run into any problems, you can contact the Tourist Police at their hotline number, 1155.

RULES OF THE ROAD

As in the United Kingdom, drive on the left side of the road, even if the locals don't. Speed limits are 60 kph (37 mph) in cities, 90 kph (56 mph) outside, and 130 kph (81 mph) on expressways, not that anyone pays much heed. If you're renting a motorcycle, remember that it's the law to always wear a helmet. Traffic police have really been cracking down on riders without helmets in recent years, though, somewhat strangely, only during daylight hours. If you're caught breaking traffic laws, you officially have to report to the police station to pay a large fine. In reality, an on-the-spot fine of B100 or B200 can usually be paid. Never presume to have the right of way in Thailand and always expect the other driver to do exactly what you think they should not.

▌ BY MOTORCYCLE

Many people rent small motorcycles to get around the country or on the islands. A Thai city is not a place to learn how to drive a motorcycle. Phuket in particular is unforgiving to novices—don't think of driving one around there unless you are

experienced. Motorcycle wrecks are common, so always wear a helmet, shoes, a shirt, and long pants, even if the locals rarely seem to.

Two-wheeled vacations are a growing segment of Thai tourism, especially in the north. Generally, people rent bikes in Chiang Mai for tours along the twisty roads through the Lanna and Golden Triangle countryside, and sometimes across the border into Laos as well. With Thailand's crazy traffic, this is not a good option for first-time tourists to the area. That said, Golden Triangle Rider has a fantastic Web site, www.gt-rider.com, on biking in the area, with information on rentals and routes.

▌ BY SAMLOR

For short trips, these bicycle rickshaws are a quaint, inexpensive form of transport, but they become expensive for long trips. ▌TIP→ Fares are negotiable, so be very clear about what price is agreed upon. Drivers have a tendency to create misunderstandings leading to a nasty scene at the end of the trip, which may partially explain their declining popularity and presence.

▌ BY SONGTHAEW

With a name that literally means "two rows," these pickup trucks have a couple of wooden benches in the back. They operate in towns outside Bangkok. Drivers generally wait until they are at least half full before departing. If you jump in a songthaew that already has people in it, a short trip usually costs between B10 and B20. However, they will be dropping off other customers before getting to you, so, if you're in a hurry, ask if they can take you solo for extra.

Chiang Mai's songthaew drivers deserve special note. They are notorious maniacs, racing around town, cutting off other drivers while swerving in and out of traffic to snatch fares from the curb. For years, the "songthaew mafia" simultaneously managed to keep regular meter taxis from working in town, thwart various plans for public bus service, and keep local government from enacting any sort of law that would limit the swarms of red trucks on the street. Furthermore, many drivers are openly contemptuous of their tourist passengers. Thankfully, this behavior seems limited to Chiang Mai.

▌ BY TAXI

Most Thai taxis now have meters installed, and these are the ones tourists should take. Taxis waiting at hotels are more likely to demand a high flat fare than those flagged down on the street. ▌TIP➜ **Never enter any taxi until the price has been established or the driver agrees to use the meter.** Most taxi drivers do not speak English, but all understand the finger count. One finger means B10, two is for B20, and so on. Whenever possible, ask at your hotel front desk what the approximate fare should be. If you flag down a meter taxi and the driver refuses to use the meter, you can try to negotiate a better fare, or simply get another taxi. If you negotiate too much, he will simply take you on a long route to jack the price back up.

▌ BY TRAIN

Trains are a great way to get around Thailand. They are inexpensive, generally punctual, and they're more comfortable and safer than buses (though slower). They go to (or close to) most of the country's biggest tourist areas, and many go through areas where major roads don't venture. The State Railway of Thailand has four lines, all of which terminate in Bangkok. Hualamphong is Bangkok's main terminal; you can book tickets for any route in the country there. (Chiang Mai's station is another major hub, where you can also buy tickets for any route.)

The Northern Line connects Bangkok with Chiang Mai, passing through Ayutthaya, Phitsanulok, and Sukhothai. The Northeastern Line travels up to Nong Khai, on the Laotian border (across from Vientiane), and has a branch that goes east to Ubon Ratchathani. The Southern Line goes all the way south through Surat Thani (the stop for Koh Samui) to the Malaysian border and on to Kuala Lumpur and Singapore, a journey that takes 37 hours. The Eastern line splits and goes to both Pattaya and Aranyaprathet on the Cambodian border. A short line also connects Bangkok with Nam Tok to the west, passing through Kanchanaburi and the bridge over the River Kwai along the way. (There's no train to Phuket, though you can go as far as Surat Thani and change to a scheduled bus service.)

To save money, look into rail passes. But be aware that if you don't plan to cover many miles, you may come out ahead by buying individual tickets.

Many travelers assume that rail passes guarantee them seats on the trains they wish to ride. Not so. You need to book seats ahead even if you're using a rail pass; seat reservations are required on some trains and are a good idea on trains that may be crowded—particularly in summer on popular routes. You'll also need a reservation if you purchase overnight sleeping accommodations.

Local trains are generally pretty slow and can get crowded, but you'll never be lonely! Most travel agencies have information on train schedules. For a small fee, many will book your tickets, saving you a trip to the station.

Most trains offer second- or third-class tickets, and some overnight trains to the north (Chiang Mai) and to the south offer first-class sleeping cabins. Second-class cars have comfy padded bench seats and most are air-conditioned. Third-class cars have hard benches and no air-conditioning. First-class cars have nice individual cabins for two to four people, but they are increasingly rare. Cheap air flights between first-class destinations have really cut the number of first-class passengers and there often aren't enough to justify running the car. Couchettes, with sheets and curtains for privacy, are available in second class.

Second-class tickets are about half the price of first-class, and since the couchettes are surprisingly comfortable, most Western travelers choose these. You also have a choice of air-conditioned or fan-cooled cars in second-class sleepers. The air-conditioning tends to be freezing and leaves you dehydrated. Sleeping next to an open train window can leave you deaf and covered in soot. It's your choice. If you have the chance, it can be romantic (well, sort of) to splurge and take a first-class overnight cabin. You'd be hard-pressed to find a first-class sleeper cabin this cheap anywhere else in the world.

Meals are served in attached dining cars and at your seat in second and first classes.

■ TIP➔ **Do not leave valuables unguarded on any train.**

The State Railway of Thailand's rather basic Web site has timetables, routes, available seats, and other information, but no way to book tickets. The British-based Web site Seat 61 has everything you ever wanted to know about train travel in Thailand (and every other country with trains) including photos, timetables, detailed coach descriptions, and how to go about booking a ticket through a travel agent.

The State Railway of Thailand offers two types of rail passes. Both are valid for 20 days of unlimited travel on all trains in either second or third class. The **Blue Pass** costs B1,100 and does not include supplementary charges such as air-conditioning and berths; for B3,000, the **Red Pass** does. To put the cost in perspective, you would need to take three overnight sleeper trains between Bangkok and Chiang Mai (at about B700 each) to get your money's worth on a B2,000 pass. That's a lot of train travel, but if it's going to be your primary mode of travel, it may save you some money.

Train schedules in English are available from travel agents and from major railway stations.

An air-conditioned, second-class couchette, for example, for the 14-hour journey from Bangkok to Chiang Mai is B671 for the lower bunk, B761 for the upper; a first class cabin is B1,233.

Tickets may be bought in cash at railway stations. Most travel agencies can also sell tickets in advance, saving you a trip to the station. Reservations are strongly advised for all long-distance trains especially if you want a sleeper on the Bangkok–to–Chiang Mai trip. **Chiang Mai Railway Station** ☎ 053/244795. **Hualamphong Railway Station** ☎ 02/223-3762 or 02/223-0341. **Seat 61** ⊕ www.seat61.com/Thailand.htm. **The State of the Railway of Thailand** ⊕ www.railway.co.th/english.

■ BY TUK-TUK

So-called because of their flatulent sound, these three-wheel cabs can be slightly less expensive than taxis and are, because of their maneuverability, sometimes a more rapid form of travel through congested traffic. All tuk-tuk operators drive as if chased by hellhounds. Tuk-tuks are not very comfortable, require hard bargaining skills, are noisy, are very polluting, are very difficult to see out of if you are more than 4 feet tall, and subject you to the polluted air they create, so they're best used for short journeys, if at all. They are fun to take once, mildly amusing the second time, and fully unpleasant by the third.

If a tuk-tuk driver rolls up and offers to drive you to the other side of Bangkok for B20, think twice before accepting, because you will definitely be getting more than you bargained for. By dragging you along to his friend's gem store, tailor's shop, or handicraft showroom, he'll usually get a petrol voucher as commission. He'll tell you that all you need to do to help him put rice on his family's table is take a five-minute look around. Sometimes that's accurate, but sometimes you'll find it difficult to leave without buying something. It can be fun at times to go along with it all and watch everybody play out their little roles, but other times you really just want a ride to your chosen destination. Either way you end up paying for it.

ON THE GROUND IN THAILAND

▌ COMMUNICATIONS

INTERNET

Only the largest hotels offer in-room Internet connections: they vary greatly and are often surprisingly inconvenient, expensive, or nonexistent. It is not uncommon for a hotel to claim to have complimentary Internet access, but in reality, you must buy a local dial-up Internet plan which you then connect to via the hotel's phone (incurring extra costs from the hotel in the process). Reliable Wi-Fi connections are very uncommon. Those hotels or businesses that have them tend to have them in one location, such as the lobby. Fortunately, many hotels have business centers that provide Internet access.

Phone and network (ethernet) connectors are the same as in the United States. Outside of large hotels and business centers, the electrical supply can be temperamental. Surging and dipping power supplies are normal, and power outages are not unheard of.

Even the smallest towns have Internet shops, though speeds can be slow and connections temperamental. Shops used to dealing with foreigners will often allow you to connect a laptop. The standard price in a tourist area is B1 per minute, while shops aimed at locals can be as cheap as B20 per hour. Larger hotels and resorts usually charge more—sometimes a lot more—so make sure to ask in advance.

Be forewarned that it's quite common to find Internet shops packed with schoolkids playing linked-up computer games, so either check your e-mail when school's in session or have a backup plan in case your location is too full or chaotic.

Cybercafes ⊕ www.cybercafes.com lists over 4,000 Internet cafés worldwide.

PHONES

The country code for Thailand is 66. When dialing a Thailand number from abroad, drop the initial 0 from the local area code.

To call Cambodia from overseas, dial the country code, 855, and then the area code, omitting the first "0." The code for Phnom Penh is 023; for Siem Reap it's 063. Unfortunately, Cambodia's international lines are frequently jammed; booking and requesting information through Web sites is consequently the best option. Almost all Internet shops offer overseas calling, which runs about 25¢–50¢ a minute. This is the most popular way to make such calls.

To call Laos from overseas, dial the country code, 856, and then the area code, omitting the first 0. The outgoing international code is 00, but IDD phones are rare. If you have to make an international call from Laos, use your hotel's switchboard. This is a good idea even for local calls, as there are few pay phones.

CALLING WITHIN THAILAND

There are three major phone companies and at least four cell phone operators. Pay phones are available throughout the country, and they generally work, though long-distance calls can only be made on phones that accept both B1 and B5 coins.

Many hotels and guesthouses use cruddy third-party pay phones, which rarely work well but make extra money for the hotel. Avoid them if you can.

If you wish to receive assistance for an overseas call, dial 100/233-2771. For local telephone inquiries, dial 100/183, but you will need to speak Thai. In Bangkok, you can dial 13 for an English-speaking operator.

CALLING OUTSIDE THAILAND

The country code for the United States is 1.

LOCAL DO'S & TABOOS

King Bhumibol Adulyadej has ruled Thailand for 60 years, and is revered by his people. Any insult against him is an insult against the national religion and patrimony. Lighthearted remarks or comparisons to any other person living or dead are also taboo. If you don't have something nice to say about the king, don't say anything at all.

Buddhism forms the root of nearly all Thai manners and customs. To live modestly and without emotional extremes, known as having a "cool heart," or "*wan jai*," is the ultimate day-to-day goal. This takes many forms visible to the visitor. Thais don't walk quickly, they don't eat quickly, and they are not always punctual, as being in a hurry shows an obvious lack of calm. The kingdom's most famous phrase is "*mai pen rai*," which can be translated as "don't worry," or "never mind," or "I don't care." Try to leave space in any itinerary for mai pen rai time, as something slow and unavoidable will invariably happen.

The long lunch hour is a holdover from when Thailand was primarily a country of rice farmers, and everyone napped during the hottest hours of the day. It also promotes a cool heart, and is much more sanook than eating at your desk while working.

Some general social tips: Do not step over a seated person's legs. Don't point your feet at anyone; keep them on the floor, and take care not to show the soles of your feet (as the lowest part of the body, they are seen by Buddhists as the least holy). Never touch a person's head, even a child's (as the highest part of the body, the head is considered by Buddhists to be the most sacred), and avoid touching a monk if you're a woman. When possible do not give or receive anything with your left hand; use your right hand and support it lightly at the elbow with your left hand to show greater respect. Superstitious Thais also don't like anything done in twos, a number associated with death. Hence, you should buy three mangoes, not two; stairways have odd numbers of stairs; and people rarely want to have their photo taken if there are only two people.

One of the most surprising (and often misunderstood) aspects of Thai culture to first-time visitors is the "lady boy." These men act, dress, and make themselves up to look—often quite convincingly—like women. Many are found in districts catering to salacious foreign visitors, but this doesn't mean they are sex workers or gay. In fact, many Thais refer to them as a "third sex," Thai men with feminine characteristics and mannerisms, more so than most women. You may hear them referred to as "katoey," but that is a derogatory term—they prefer to be called "lady boy."

Displays of anger, raised voices, or even very direct speech are considered bad form.

When visiting temples, dress modestly. Don't wear shorts, short skirts, or tank tops. If you show up improperly attired, some temples have wraps you can borrow. Others will not let you enter. Remove your shoes before entering the temple and don't point your toes at any image of the Buddha, as it's considered sacrilegious. It's worth dressing modestly even outside temple grounds. At the beach Thais will often go swimming wearing jeans and T-shirts, so walking around a city center with your midriff (or worse) hanging out is not really the way to endear yourself to the locals.

Proper respect of religious sites is the most important form of courtesy to practice. Something that a foreigner might think is funny, such as sitting on the lap of a Buddha statue for a photo, could be deeply offensive to a Thai. As with the king, never disparage Buddhism to a Thai.

To make overseas calls, you can use either your hotel switchboard—Chiang Mai and Bangkok have direct dialing—or the overseas telephone facilities at the central post office and telecommunications building. You'll find one in all towns. In Bangkok, the overseas telephone center, next to the general post office, is open 24 hours; up-country, the facilities' hours may vary, but they usually open at 8 AM and some stay open until 10 PM. Some locations in Bangkok have AT&T USADirect phones, which connect you with an AT&T operator.

The cheapest—and often easiest—way to call internationally is on the Internet. Any Internet shop should be able to set you up. You can also start a Skype (or similar) account before leaving home, and use it on the road. It is an increasingly popular option among frequent travelers.

Access Codes AT&T USADirect ☎ 0019-991-1111, 800/222-0300 for other areas. **MCI WorldPhone** ☎ 001-999-1-2001 not from pay phones, 800/444-3333 for other areas. **Sprint International Access** ☎ 001-999-13-877, 800/877-4646 for other areas.

MOBILE PHONES

If you have a GSM cell phone and your operator allows it, your phone may work in Thailand, though the roaming charges can be deadly. Many use their cell phones to send and receive text messages, a cheap way to write home.

■ TIP➔ **If you travel internationally frequently, save one of your old mobile phones or buy a cheap one on the Internet; ask your cell phone company to unlock it for you, and take it with you as a travel phone, buying a new SIM card with pay-as-you-go service in each destination.**

Alternately, if you have a GSM phone (and it has not been locked to one number by your phone company), you can buy a SIM card (the chip that keeps your phone number and account) in Thailand for about B800 at one of the ubiquitous cell phone kiosks, pop it into your phone, and have a local number while visiting.

Then buy phone cards in B200 to B500 denominations and pay for calls as you go, generally B3–B10 a minute depending on the time of day and number you are calling. International calls will run about B40 a minute.

Cellular Abroad ☎ 800/287-5072 ⊕ www. cellularabroad.com rents and sells GMS phones and sells SIM cards that work in many countries. **Mobal** ☎ 888/888-9162 ⊕ www. mobalrental.com rents mobiles and sells GSM phones (starting at $49) that will operate in 140 countries. Per-call rates vary throughout the world. **Planet Fone** ☎ 888/988-4777 ⊕ www.planetfone.com rents cell phones, but the per-minute rates are expensive.

▮ CUSTOMS & DUTIES

THAILAND

Customs checks upon entering Thailand are quite rare, and they're straightforward when they do happen. The country worries more about people smuggling opium across borders than they do about an extra bottle of wine or your new camera. That said, if you're bringing any foreign-made equipment from home, such as cameras, it's wise to carry the original receipt with you or register it with U.S. Customs before you leave (Form 4457). Otherwise, you may end up paying duty on your return.

One liter of wine or liquor, 200 cigarettes or 250 grams of smoking tobacco, and all personal effects may be brought into Thailand duty-free. Visitors may bring in and leave with any amount of foreign currency; you cannot leave with more than B50,000 without obtaining a permit. Narcotics, pornographic materials, protected wild animals and wild animal parts, and firearms are strictly prohibited.

Many tourists dream of Thailand as a tropical paradise floating on a cloud of marijuana smoke—not so. Narcotics are strictly illegal and jail terms for the transporting or possession of even the smallest amounts are extremely harsh.

If you purchase any Buddha images (originals or reproductions), artifacts, or true antiques and want to take them home, you need to get a certificate from the Fine Arts Department. Taking unregistered or unauthorized antiques out of the country is a major offence to the culture-conscious Thais. If you get a particularly good reproduction of an antique, get a letter or certificate from the seller saying it is a reproduction, or risk losing it on your way out of the country. Art or antiques requiring export permits must be taken to one of the museums listed below at least five days before the departure date. You will have to fill out an application and provide two photographs—front and side views—of the object as well as a photocopy of your passport information page. **Antiques Permits Chiang Mai National Museum** ☎ 053/221308. **National Museum–Bangkok** ☎ 02/224-1370 or 02/224-1333. **Songkhla National Museum** ☎ 074/31172.

CAMBODIA

You are allowed to bring into Cambodia 200 cigarettes, 50 cigars, or ½ pound of tobacco, and 946 milliliters of liquor. You are not allowed to bring in local currency.

You are not allowed to take out local currency, nor are you allowed to remove Angkor antiquities. The export of other antiques or religious objects requires a permit. Contact your embassy for assistance in obtaining one before laying out money on an expensive purchase.

LAOS

Tourists are allowed to bring into Laos 1 quart of spirits and 200 cigarettes, 50 cigars, or ½ pound of tobacco. Bringing in or taking out local currency is prohibited, as is the export of antiques and religious artifacts without a permit.

Note that the dissemination of foreign religious and political materials is forbidden, and you should refrain from bringing such materials into the country. **U.S. Information U.S. Customs and Border Protection** ⊕ www.cbp.gov.

▌ EATING OUT

Thais know that eating out can be cheaper than eating in, and that inexpensive restaurants often serve food that's as good as, and sometimes better than, the fare at fancy places. That's why you see so many Thai families gathered around vendor carts or crowded around tables at a town's night market. As tempting as it might be to jump straight in and feast on street-side goodies, it's worth remembering that your stomach may need some time to adapt. When you do try the food stalls, try not to choose dishes that may have been sitting out for hours and add extra spices in moderation. Water is usually provided free and most places have some bottles of Fanta and Coke.

Thai food is eaten with a fork and spoon; the spoon held in the right hand and the fork is used like a plow to push food into the spoon. Chopsticks are used only for Chinese food, such as noodle dishes. After you have finished eating, place your fork and spoon on the plate at the 5:25 position; otherwise the server will assume you would like another helping. For information on food-related health issues, *see* Health *below.*

MEALS & MEALTIMES

Thai cuisine's distinctive flavor comes particularly from the use of fresh Thai basil, lemongrass, tamarind, lime, and citrus leaves. And though some Thai food is fiery hot from garlic and chilies, an equal number of dishes serve the spices on the side so that you can adjust the incendiary level. Thais use *nam pla,* a fish sauce, instead of salt.

If you're not sure what to order, start with some staples such as *tom yam kung,* which is prawn and lemongrass soup with mushrooms, then move on to *pad thai,* which is fried noodles with tofu, vegetables, eggs, and peanuts. Wash it down with a Singha, a tasty Thai beer.

Restaurants tend to open in late morning and serve food until 9 or 10 in the evening.

Street vendors can be found in most places 24 hours a day. Unless otherwise noted, the restaurants listed in this guide are open daily for lunch and dinner.

PAYING

Expect to pay for most meals in cash. Larger hotels and fancy restaurants in metropolitan areas accept some major credit cards, but they will often charge an extra 2%–4% for the convenience. If you are at the restaurant of the hotel where you are staying, you can generally just add the bill to your room and leave a cash tip if you desire. Street vendors and small, local restaurants only accept cash.

For guidelines on tipping *see* Tipping *below*.

RESERVATIONS & DRESS

Generally, reservations are not necessary at Thai restaurants, and even then are only accepted at the most expensive and popular ones.

Because Thailand has a hot climate, jackets and ties are rarely worn at dinner except in expensive restaurants, usually in the big hotels. We mention dress when men are required to wear a jacket or tie.

WINES, BEER & SPIRITS

Singha, Tiger, and Heineken are at the top end of Thailand's beer market, while Chang, Leo, and a host of other new brands fight it out for the budget drinkers. It's also becoming more common to find imports such as Guinness, Corona, and Budweiser lining the shelves of cosmopolitan bars.

If you want to drink like the hip locals, you won't be bothering with beer. Grab a bottle of whiskey (Chivas Regal, Johnnie Walker, or the very affordable 100 Pipers) to mix with cola or soda.

Rice whiskey, which tastes sweet and has a whopping 35% alcohol content, is another favorite throughout Thailand. It tastes and mixes more like rum than whiskey, really. Mekong and Sam Song are by far the most popular rice whiskeys,

---

WORD OF MOUTH

Was the service stellar or not up to snuff? Did the food give you shivers of delight or leave you cold? Did the prices and portions make you happy or sad? Rate restaurants and write your own reviews in Travel Ratings or start a discussion about your favorite places in Travel Talk on www.fodors.com. Your comments might even appear in our books. Yes, you, too, can be a correspondent!

---

but you will also see labels such as Kwangthong, Hong Thong, Hong Ngoen, Hong Yok, and Hong Tho. Thais mix their rice whiskey with soda water, though it goes great with Coke, too.

Thailand is not a wine-drinking country, and the foreign tipples on offer are expensive and mediocre. Thirty years ago, the king first brought up the idea of growing grapes for wine and fruit through his Royal Projects Foundation. Now, both fruit- and grape-based wines are made in various places up-country. Their quality generally does not match international offerings (they tend to taste better if you don't think of them as wines, as such), but some are quite pleasant. International markets often carry them, and they can occasionally be found on the menus of larger restaurants.

■ ECOTOURISM

Unfortunately, Thailand's tourism boom has had many negative effects on Thai culture and resources; problems range from the overwhelming presence of sex tourism to water pollution to the transformation of hill tribe villages into veritable theme parks. Though these problems are far-reaching and difficult to reign in, there are a few simple things you can do to ensure that, at the very least, you're not contributing to the morass.

■ TIP→ **Don't litter.** Garbage is now a common sight on Thailand's once-pristine beaches. Many places lack the resources and infrastructure to continually mount litter patrols, so pay the extra few baht to buy water in glass bottles that can be recycled. If you travel (or plan to travel) regularly in the developing world, consider buying a hand-pump style water purifier, available at many sporting goods stores. You can make your own clean water wherever you go, and reuse your water bottles at the same time.

■ TIP→ **Don't disturb animal and plant life.** Whether you're trekking through a forest or snorkeling along a reef, be as unobtrusive to the environment as possible. Don't remove plant life or coral for souvenirs—what may look like it won't be missed might in fact be rare or sacred to a community or essential to the survival of an ecosystem. Don't feed fish or animals—period; though they'll probably eat it, trying to digest inappropriate foods could harm or kill them. Just because your boat driver waves you on doesn't mean you're not doing something harmful.

■ TIP→ **Respect local customs.** Though this may seem more an issue of etiquette than ecotourism, demonstrating basic respect for and interest in a culture is part and parcel of sustainable tourism. True, Thais seem to be exceedingly tolerant of Western behavior but tourists' ever-present ignorance of even the most basic Thai customs does have lasting negative effects on the communities they encounter. Take the time to learn about major cultural sticking points (especially those related to Buddhism) and be patient and respectful when misunderstandings occur.

Tour agencies increasingly try to be ecofriendly, particularly on jungle treks in Northern Thailand. This is especially true in Chiang Mai and Chiang Rai, where many people enjoy elephant rides into the mountains. However, ecotourism has not blossomed here as much as it has in other regions of the world, so it may be hard to find a company that is truly ecofriendly. Before booking a tour, ask tough questions about what the company does to preserve the environment and help local villages. Responsible Ecological Social Tours Project (REST) arranges remote village tours (with possible homestays) and ensures that 70% of the profits of each trip goes directly to the community. Their Web site (www.ecotour.in.th) is a good place to start for a different perspective on hill tribe village visits.

ANIMAL RIGHTS

The elephant, revered for its strength, courage, and intelligence, has a long history in Thailand. These gentle giants were used to haul timber, including the teak pillars used in royal palaces and temples. In recent years, however, mechanization has made the domesticated elephant obsolete, and elephant trainers have come to rely on the tourist industry as their only source of income. To make sure they are not mistreated, the group Friends of the Asian Elephant monitors the treatment of elephants used in shows and treks. If you are going on an elephant-back trek and have concerns, check out how various companies treat their animals. Find out, for example, how many hours the elephants are worked each day and whether you'll be riding in the afternoon heat.

Friends of the Asian Elephant ✉ 350 Moo 8, Ram-Indra Rd., Soi 61, Tharaeng, Bangkhen, Bangkok 10230 ☎🖷 02/945-7124 ⊕ www.elephant.tnet.co.th.

▌ ELECTRICITY

The electrical current in Thailand is 220 volts, 50 cycles alternating current (AC); wall outlets take either two flat prongs, like outlets in the United States, or continental-type plugs, with two round prongs, or sometimes both. Plug adapters are cheap and can be found without great difficulty in tourist areas and electrical shops. Outlets outside expensive international hotels are rarely grounded, so use caution when plugging in delicate electronic equipment like laptops.

In both Cambodia and Laos, the electrical current is 220 volts AC, 50 Hz. In Laos, outside of Vientiane and Luang Prabang, electricity is spotty, and even in Luang Prabang there are frequent late-afternoon outages in hot weather.

Consider making a small investment in a universal adapter, which has several types of plugs in one lightweight, compact unit. Most laptops and mobile phone chargers are dual voltage (i.e., they operate equally well on 110 and 220 volts), so require only an adapter. These days the same is true of small appliances such as hair dryers. Always check labels and manufacturer instructions to be sure. Don't use 110-volt outlets marked FOR SHAVERS ONLY for high-wattage appliances such as hair-dryers. **Steve Kropla's Help for World Traveler's** ⊕ www.kropla.com has information on electrical and telephone plugs around the world. **Walkabout Travel Gear** ⊕ www. walkabouttravelgear.com has a good coverage of electricity under "adapters."

EMERGENCIES

Thais are generally quite helpful, so you should get assistance from locals if you need it. The Tourist Police will help you in case of a robbery or rip-off. The Tourist Police hotline is ☎ 1155.

Many hotels can refer you to an English-speaking doctor. Major cities in Thailand have some of Southeast Asia's best hospitals, and the country is quickly becoming a "medical holiday" destination (i.e., a cost-effective place to have plastic surgery, dental work, etc., done). However, if you are still wary about treating serious health problems in Thailand, you can fly cheaply to Singapore for the best medical care in the region.

Most nations maintain diplomatic relations with Thailand and have embassies in Bangkok; a few have consulates also in Chiang Mai. Should you need to apply for a visa to another country, the consulate hours are usually 8–noon daily.

In Bangkok **U.S. Embassy** ⊠ 120–122 Wittayu (Wireless Rd.) ☎ 02/205-4000.

In Chiang Mai **U.S. Consulate** ⊠ 387 Wichayanom Rd. ☎ 053/252629.

In Phnom Penh, Cambodia **U.S. Embassy** ⊠ Corner of Sts. 96 and 51, behind Wat Phnom, Phnom Penh ☎ 023/728000.

In Vientiane, Laos **U.S. Embassy** ⊠ BP 114, rue Bartholomé, Vientiane ☎ 21/267000 or 021/212581.

General Emergency Contacts **Police** ☎ 191. **Tourist Police** ☎ 1155.

HEALTH

The most common vacation sickness in Thailand is traveler's diarrhea. You can take some solace in knowing that it is also the most common affliction of the locals. It generally comes from eating contaminated food, be it fruit, veggies, unclean water, or badly prepared or stored foods—really anything. It can also be triggered by a change in diet. Generally speaking, watch what you eat. Avoid ice (unless you know it comes from clean water), uncooked and undercooked foods, and unpasteurized milk and milk products. ■ TIP→ **Drink only bottled water or water that has been boiled for at least 20 minutes, even when brushing your teeth.** The water served in pitchers at small restaurants or in hotel rooms is generally safe, as it is either boiled or from a larger bottle of purified water, though if you have any suspicions about its origins, it's best to go with your gut feeling.

The best way to treat "Bangkok belly" is to wait for it to pass. Take Pepto-Bismol to help ease your discomfort and if you must travel, take Imodium (known generically as loperamide) which will immobilize your lower gut and everything in it. It doesn't cure the problem, but simply postpones it until a more convenient time. Note that if you have a serious stomach sickness, taking Imodium can occasionally intensify the problem, leading to massive debilitating fever and sickness. If at any time you get a high fever with stomach sickness, find a doctor.

Also, if you have frequent, watery diarrhea for more than two days, see a doctor for diagnosis and treatment. Days of sickness can leave you seriously dehydrated and weak in the tropics.

In any case, drink plenty of purified water or tea—chamomile is a good choice. In severe cases, rehydrate yourself with a salt-sugar solution (½ teaspoon salt and 4 tablespoons sugar per quart of water) or rehydration salts, available at any pharmacy.

For information on travel insurance, shots and medications, and medical-assistance companies *see* Shots & Medications *under* Things to Consider *in* Before You Go, *above*.

SPECIFIC ISSUES IN THAILAND

The avian flu crisis that ripped through Southeast Asia at the start of the 21st century had a devastating impact on Thailand. Poultry farmers went out of business, tourists stayed away, and each week brought news of a new species found to be infected (including isolated cases of humans contracting the virus). As of this writing, the worry has died down as human cases continue to be exceedingly rare. Of course, that doesn't mean it won't flare up again. Note, however, that all cases have occurred in rural areas outside the tourist track, and infections mainly were among people who dealt with large numbers of dead birds.

Malaria and dengue fever are more common than bird flu. Thankfully, they are still quite rare where tourists go. Malarial mosquitoes generally fly from dusk to dawn, while dengue carriers do the opposite: both are most numerous during the rainy season, as they breed in stagnant water.

The best advice for both diseases is to not get either in the first place. To that end, wear light-color clothing and some form of insect repellent (preferably containing DEET) on any exposed skin when out and about in the mornings and evenings, especially during the rainy season. Make sure that hotel rooms have air-conditioning, mosquito nets over the bed or good screens over windows, or some combination thereof. You can also use a bug spray (available everywhere) in your room before heading out to dinner, and return to a bug-free room.

Dengue fever tends to appear with a sudden high fever, sweating, headache, joint and muscle pain (where it got the name "breakbone fever"), and nausea. A rash of red spots on the chest is a telltale sign. Malaria offers a raft of symptoms, including fever, chills, headache, sweating, diarrhea, and abdominal pain. A key sign is the recurrent nature of the symptoms, coming in waves every day or two.

Find a doctor immediately if you think you may have either disease—don't wait until you return home. In Thailand, the test for both is quick and accurate and the doctors are much more accustomed to treating these diseases than are doctors in the United States. Left untreated, both diseases can quickly become serious, possibly fatal. Even when properly treated, dengue has a long recovery period, leaving the victim debilitated for weeks, sometimes months.

Due to the rise in drug-resistant strains of malaria, the Ministry of Public Health says, "Chemoprophylaxis (use of preventive drugs) is not recommended for the general population. Personal protection using mosquito repellents and bed nets is strongly recommended." There is no preventive treatment for dengue, but, once infected and diagnosed, the treatment is straightforward and effective.

On a sad note, the recent puppy fad among urban Thais has led to an explosion of abandoned dogs, often left at the outskirts of towns or at temples. Thais see spaying, neutering, and putting dogs to sleep as un-Buddhist, so they leave the unwanted pets with monks who take care of the unwanted souls. Rabies does exist in Thailand, so be very careful when approaching unknown dogs. If you are bitten, Thai hospitals are very efficient and ready with rabies vaccines.

Be aware that a high percentage of sex workers in Thailand are HIV positive, and unprotected sex is extremely risky.

Do not fly within 24 hours of scuba diving.

OVER-THE-COUNTER REMEDIES

Thailand has nearly every drug known to the Western world, and many that aren't. All are readily available at pharmacies throughout the country. They are also often cheaper than in the United States and many prescription drugs don't require the prescriptions and doctor visits needed at home.

HOURS OF OPERATION

Thai business hours generally follow the 9–5 model, though the smaller the business, the more eclectic the hours. Nearly all businesses either close or slow to a halt during lunch hour—don't expect to accomplish anything important at this time. Many tourist businesses in the north and on the beaches and islands in the south often shut down outside the main tourist seasons of November through January and June through August.

Thai and foreign banks are open weekdays 8:30–3:30, except for public holidays. Most commercial concerns in Bangkok operate on a five-day week and are open 8–5. Government offices are generally open weekdays 8:30–4:30, with a noon–1 lunch break. Generally speaking, avoid visiting any sort of office during the Thai lunch hour—or bring a book to pass the time.

Gas stations in Thailand are usually open at least 8–8 daily; many, particularly those on the highways, are open 24 hours a day. Twenty-four hour minimart-style gas stations are growing in popularity. Many also have fast-food restaurants and convenience stores.

Each museum keeps its own hours and may select a different day of the week to close (though it's usually Monday); it's best to call before visiting.

Temples are generally open to visitors from 7 or 8 in the morning to 5 or 6 PM, but in truth they don't really have set hours. If a compound has gates, they open at dawn to allow the monks to do their rounds. Outside of major tourist sights like Wat Po in Bangkok, few temples appear to have fixed closing times.

Most pharmacies are open daily 9–9. You'll find a few 24-hour pharmacies in tourist areas.

Most small stores are open daily 8–8, whereas department and chain stores are usually open from 10 until 10.

HOLIDAYS

Thailand: New Year's Day (January 1); Chinese New Year (February 7, 2008 and January 26, 2009); Magha Puja (on the full moon of the third lunar month); Chakri Day (April 6); Songkran (April 13–15); Coronation Day (May 5); Visakha Puja, May (on the full moon of the sixth lunar month); Queen's Birthday (August 12); King's Birthday (December 5). Government offices, banks, commercial concerns, and department stores are usually closed on these days, but smaller shops stay open.

Cambodia: New Year's Day (January 1), Victory Day (January 7), Meak Bochea Day (February), International Women's Day (March 8), Cambodian New Year (mid-April, depending on the lunar cycle), Labor Day (May 1), Visak Bochea (the Buddha's Birthday; early May), King Sihamoni's birthday (May 13–15), Royal Ploughing Ceremony (May), International Children's Day (June 1), Queen's birthday (June 18), Pchum Ben (September), Constitution Day (September 24), Anniversary of Paris Peace Agreement (October 23), Sihanouk's birthday (October 31), Independence Day (November 9), Water Festival (November), Human Rights Day (December 10).

Laos: New Year's Day (January 1); Army Day (January 24); International Women Day (March 8); Lao New Year (Water Festival, April 13–15); Labor Day (May 1); National Day (December 2).

LANGUAGE

Thai is the country's national language. It has five tones, which makes it confusing to most foreigners. Thankfully, Thais tend to be patient with people trying to speak their language, and will often guess what you are trying to say, even if it's badly mispronounced. In polite conversation, a male speaker will use the word "krup" to end a sentence or to acknowledge what someone has said. Female speakers use "ka." It's easy to speak a few words, such as "sawahdee krup" or "sawahdee ka" (good day) and "khop khun krup" or "khop khun ka" (thank you).

With the exception of taxi drivers, Thais working with travelers in the resort and tourist areas of Thailand generally speak sufficient English to permit basic communication. If you find yourself truly unable to communicate something important to a Thai, he or she will often start grabbing people from the street at random to see if they speak English to help you out.

▌ MAIL

Thailand's mail service is generally reliable and efficient. It is a good idea—and cheap—to send all packages registered mail. Major hotels provide basic postal services. If something must get to its destination quickly, send it via FedEx, UPS, or DHL, which have branches in the major tourist centers. Bangkok's central general post office on Charoen Krung (New Road) is open weekdays 8–6, weekends and public holidays 9–1. Up-country post offices close at 4:30 PM.

Letter, packet, and parcel rates are low— B27 for a letter to the United States, B17 for a letter to Europe. Allow at least 10 days for your mail to arrive. For speedier delivery, major post offices offer overseas express mail service (EMS), though if you are sending anything more than a letter, FedEx, UPS, and DHL are only slightly more expensive and much faster. A sea, air, and land service (SAL) is available for less urgent mail at a much cheaper rate. Note it can take up to three months for packages to reach their destination by this method.

Post offices in major towns are often quite crowded. Never go to a post office over the lunch hour unless you bring a book and a mountain of patience.

You may have mail sent to you "poste restante" at the following address: Poste Restante, General Post Office, Bangkok, Thailand. There's a B1 charge for each piece collected. Thais write their last name first, so be sure to have your last name written in capital letters and underlined.

SHIPPING PACKAGES

Did you find a painting you can't live without? A new lamp for the front hallway? Well, you can easily ship it home. Most shops catering to tourists will offer to pack and arrange shipping to any destination on the globe, usually at very reasonable rates. Shipping can easily cost as much or more than your newfound treasure, though. Although thousands of people have had no problems shipping things around the globe via the Thai Post, on a recent trip to a post office in Chiang Mai, a resident saw a car-size pile of mauled boxes, no longer on their way to their Western owners, most with missing or illegible labels. Ouch. If your new handpainted footstool positively has to make it home, consider paying the extra money to send it by an international courier like DHL, Federal Express, or UPS. If you want to ship a larger piece, most furniture and antiques stores offer freight shipping and associated customs services.

"Overnight" shipping time from Thailand to the United States is actually two working days. Expect to pay B800 to B1,000 for an "overnight" letter.

Parcels are easy to send from Thailand via Thai Post. Parcel rates vary by weight, country of destination, and shipping style (air or surface). Expect to pay between B700 and B1,100 for a kilo package and then an additional B300 to B350 per added kilo.

Express Services **DHL Worldwide** ⊠ 22nd fl., Grand Amarin Tower, Phetburi Tat Mai, Bangkok ☎ 02/207-0600. **Federal Express** ⊠ 8th fl., Green Tower, Rama IV, Bangkok ☎ 02/367-3222. **UPS** ⊠ 16/1 Sukhumvit Soi 44/1, Bangkok ☎ 02/712-3300.

■ MONEY

It's possible to live and travel quite inexpensively if you do as Thais do—eat in small, neighborhood restaurants, use buses, and stay at non-air-conditioned hotels. Traveling this way, two people could easily get by on $30 a day or less. Once you start enjoying a little luxury, prices jump drastically. For example, a sleeper berth on the train from Bangkok to Chiang Mai runs roughly B700. A flight on a discount airline will run B1,600. But the former takes at least 12 hours, the latter, 1½ hours.

Prices are higher in resort areas catering to foreign tourists, and Bangkok is more expensive than other Thai cities.

Imported items are heavily taxed, but you didn't come to Thailand to drink French champagne, did you?

Prices throughout this guide are given for adults. Substantially reduced fees are almost always available for children, students, and senior citizens.

ATMS & BANKS

Your own bank will probably charge a fee for using ATMs abroad; the foreign bank you use may also charge a fee. Nevertheless, you'll usually get a better rate of exchange at an ATM than you will at a currency-exchange office or even when changing money in a bank. And extracting funds as you need them is a safer option than carrying around a large amount of cash.

■ TIP→ **PIN numbers with more than four digits are not recognized at ATMs in many countries. If yours has five or more, remember to change it before you leave.**

Thankfully, over the last few years, ATMs have sprouted like mushrooms around the country. Only smaller towns don't yet have them, and even that is changing. Most ATMs accept foreign bank cards; all pay in baht. As of this writing, most Thai ATMs do not charge any extra fees, but your home bank may well add extra fees for using a foreign bank and/or converting foreign currency. Do contact your bank and ask about this before leaving to avoid any nasty billing surprises. Some Thai ATMs take Cirrus, some take Plus, some take both.

CREDIT CARDS

Throughout this guide, the following abbreviations are used: **AE**, American Express; **D**, Discover; **DC**, Diners Club; **MC**, MasterCard; and **V**, Visa.

It's a good idea to inform your credit-card company before you travel, especially if you're going abroad and don't travel internationally very often. Otherwise, the credit-card company might put a hold on your card owing to unusual activity—not a good thing halfway through your trip. Record all your credit-card numbers—as well as the phone numbers to call if your cards are lost or stolen—in a safe place, so you're prepared should something go wrong. Both MasterCard and Visa have general numbers you can call (collect if you're abroad) if your card is lost, but you're better off calling the number of your issuing bank, since MasterCard and Visa usually just transfer you to your bank; your bank's number is usually printed on your card.

If you plan to use your credit card for cash advances, you'll need to apply for a PIN at least two weeks before your trip. Although it's usually cheaper (and safer) to use a credit card abroad for large purchases (so you can cancel payments or be reimbursed if there's a problem), note that some credit-card companies *and* the banks that issue them add substantial percentages to all foreign transactions, whether they're in a foreign currency or not. Check on these fees before leaving home, so there won't be any surprises when you get the bill.

■ TIP→ **Before you charge something, ask the merchant whether or not he or she plans to do a dynamic currency conversion (DCC). In such a transaction the credit-card *processor* (shop, restaurant, or hotel, not Visa or MasterCard) converts the currency and charges you in dollars. In most cases you'll pay the merchant a 3% fee for this service in addition to**

WORST-CASE SCENARIO

All your money and credit cards have just been stolen. In these days of real-time transactions, this isn't a predicament that should destroy your vacation. First, report the theft of the credit cards. Then get any traveler's checks you were carrying replaced. This can usually be done almost immediately, provided that you kept a record of the serial numbers separate from the checks themselves. If you bank at a large international bank like Citibank or HSBC, go to the closest branch; if you know your account number, chances are you can get a new ATM card and withdraw money right away. **Western Union** (☎ 800/325-6000 ⊕ www.westernunion. com) sends money almost anywhere. Have someone back home order a transfer online, over the phone, or at one of the company's offices, which is the cheapest option. The U.S. State Department's **Overseas Citizens Services** (☎ 202/647-5225) can wire money to any U.S. consulate or embassy abroad for a fee of $30. Just have someone back home wire money or send a money order or cashier's check to the state department, which will then disburse the funds as soon as the next working day after it receives them.

any credit-card company and issuing-bank foreign-transaction surcharges.

Dynamic currency conversion programs are becoming increasingly widespread. Merchants who participate in them are supposed to ask whether you want to be charged in dollars or the local currency, but they don't always do so. And even if they do offer you a choice, they may well avoid mentioning the additional surcharges. The good news is that you *do* have a choice. And if this practice really gets your goat, you can avoid it entirely thanks to American Express; with its cards, DCC simply isn't an option.

Credit cards are almost always accepted at upper-end hotels, resorts, boutique

stores, and shopping malls, and that list is slowly expanding. Expect to pay a 2%–5% service charge. It is illegal, but that's what everyone does.

Reporting Lost Cards American Express ☎ 800/992-3404 in the U.S. or 336/393-1111 collect from abroad ⊕ www.americanexpress. com. **Diners Club** ☎ 800/234-6377 in the U.S. or 303/799-1504 collect from abroad ⊕ www.dinersclub.com. **MasterCard** ☎ 800/622-7747 in the U.S. or 636/722-7111 collect from abroad ⊕ www.mastercard.com. **Visa** ☎ 800/847-2911 in the U.S. or 410/581-9994 collect from abroad ⊕ www.visa.com.

CURRENCY & EXCHANGE

The basic unit of currency is the baht. There are 100 satang to one baht. There are six different bills, each a different color: B10, brown; B20, green; B50, blue; B100, red; B500, purple; and B1,000, beige. Coins in use are 25 satang, 50 satang, B1, B2, B5, and B10. The B10 coin has a gold-color center surrounded by silver.

Major hotels will convert traveler's checks and major currencies into baht, though exchange rates are better at banks and authorized money changers. The rate tends to be better in any larger city than up-country and is better in Thailand than in the United States.

At this writing, B33 = US$1.

■ TIP→ Even if a currency-exchange booth has a sign promising no commission, rest assured that there's some kind of huge, hidden fee. (Oh . . . that's right. The sign didn't say no *fee*.). And as for rates, you're almost always better off getting foreign currency at an ATM or exchanging money at a bank.

TRAVELER'S CHECKS & CARDS

Some consider this the currency of the cave man, and it's true that fewer establishments accept traveler's checks these days. Nevertheless, they're a cheap and secure way to carry extra money, particularly on trips to urban areas. Both Citibank (under the Visa brand) and American Express issue traveler's checks in the United

States, but Amex is better known and more widely accepted; you can also avoid hefty surcharges by cashing Amex checks at Amex offices. Whatever you do, keep track of all the serial numbers in case the checks are lost or stolen.

Traveler's checks are slowly fading in popularity as ATMs become more common. Banks and money changers tend to charge 2%–5% to change traveler's checks. However, you may want to bring a few with you as emergency money, in case you lose your ATM card or misplace your other money. If you don't use them on vacation, you can always use them when you return home.

American Express now offers a stored-value card called a Travelers Cheque Card, which you can use wherever American Express credit cards are accepted, including ATMs. The card can carry a minimum of $300 and a maximum of $2,700, and it's a very safe way to carry your funds. Although you can get replacement funds in 24 hours if your card is lost or stolen, it doesn't really strike us as a very good deal. In addition to a high initial cost ($14.95 to set up the card, plus $5 each time you "reload"), you still have to pay a 2% fee for each purchase in a foreign currency (similar to that of any credit card). Further, each time you use the card in an ATM you pay a transaction fee of $2.50 on top of the 2% transaction fee for the conversion—add it all up and it can be considerably more than you would pay when simply using your own ATM card. Regular traveler's checks are just as secure and cost less.

American Express ☎ 888/412-6945 in the U.S., 801/945-9450 collect outside of the U.S. to add value or speak to customer service ⊕ www.americanexpress.com.

▌RESTROOMS

Western-style facilities are usually available, although you still may find squat toilets in older buildings. For the uninitiated, squat toilets can be something of a puzzle. You will doubtless find a method that works best for you, but here's a general guide: squat down with feet on either side of the basin and use one hand to keep your clothes out of the way and the other for balance or, if you're really good, holding your newspaper. The Thai version of a bidet is either a hose or a big tank of water with a bowl. If you've had the foresight to bring tissues with you, throw the used paper into the basket alongside the basin. Finally, pour bowls of water into the toilet to flush it—and after thoroughly washing your hands, give yourself a pat on the back. With the exception of the plusher hotels and restaurants, plumbing in most buildings is archaic, so resist the temptation to flush your paper unless you want to be remembered as the foreigner who ruined the toilet.

Find a Loo **The Bathroom Diaries** ⊕ www. thebathroomdiaries.com is flush with unsanitized info on restrooms the world over—each one located, reviewed, and rated.

▌SAFETY

Thailand is a safe country, but normal precautions should be followed: be careful late at night, watch your valuables in crowded areas, and lock your hotel rooms securely. Thai crooks generally try to relieve you of cash through crimes of convenience or negligence, not violence. That said, every year a few tourists are attacked and/or killed after running into the wrong people at the wrong time, generally either in Bangkok or in the Southern Beaches region. Be careful when out and about in dark places or on lonely beaches late at night.

Thailand offers many adventurous ways to spend your days, few of which include the safety provisions demanded in Western countries. Motorcycle wrecks are a common way to cut a vacation tragically short.

Beaches almost never have lifeguards, but that doesn't mean they don't have undertows or other dangers. In 2006 a young

Dutch woman was killed when the bamboo raft she was on capsized in a river in Northern Thailand and she drowned. It's a good idea to exercise more caution when doing things here than you normally do at home.

Credit card scams—from stealing your card to swiping it several times when you use it at stores—are a frequent problem. Don't leave your wallet behind when you go trekking and make sure you keep an eye on the card when you give it to a salesperson.

■ TIP➔ A great little invention is the metal doorknob cup that can be found at Thai hardware shops. It covers your doorknob and locks in place with a padlock, keeping anyone from using a spare key or even twisting the knob to get into your room. A good B300 investment, it's usable anywhere.

A fad for puppies has led to older dogs being dumped after a few months around temples and on the outskirts of towns in the north. Beware of dogs in these areas. Rabies exists in Thailand, and local dogs are rarely trained and are certainly unused to the scent of foreigners.

It's never wise to become involved in a brawl, and it's particularly foolish to do this in Thailand because: a) many of the locals are accomplished martial artists and/or are carrying weapons, and b) as a foreigner, you will likely be deemed at fault, even if you weren't.

Thailand's most famous danger comes from the ocean. The Asian tsunami hit the Andaman coast in December 2004 and killed more than 5,300 people in Thailand. Reports from the areas hit show that many people could have been saved if they had known how to recognize the signs of an impending tsunami, or if a tsunami evacuation plan had been in place. A tour operator in Phuket town felt the initial earthquake and tried to warn hotels on the coast, to no avail. Furthermore, people on the beach that lived to tell the tale said that all of the water raced away from the beach, leaving several hundred meters of bare ocean floor in a very short time. Unfortunately, almost no one knew this meant a tsunami was on the way.

Tsunamis are rare and very unpredictable. Thankfully, it's highly unlikely to experience one while on vacation. But it also pays to be prepared. If you plan to stay in a beach resort, ask if they have a tsunami plan in place, and ask what it is. If you feel an earthquake, prepare to leave any waterside area. ■ TIP➔ Pay attention to the ocean: if you see all of the water race off the beach, evacuate immediately and head for high ground. A tsunami could be only minutes away. Remember, a tsunami is a series of waves that could go on for hours. Do not assume it is over after the first wave.

Guesthouses also offer commission for customers brought in by drivers, so be wary of anyone telling you that the place where you booked a room has burned down overnight or is suddenly full. Smile and be courteous, but be firm about where you want to go. If the driver doesn't immediately take you where you want to go, get out and get another taxi.

Two-tier pricing—one price for Thais, another for foreigners—is the norm in Thailand, and although it's up to you to determine how to deal with this, getting angry rarely achieves results.

Watch out for scams while shopping. Bait and switch is common, as is trying to pass off reproductions as authentic antiques. True antique and artifact vendors will gladly help you finish the necessary government paperwork to take your purchase home. Keep in mind that authentic Thai or other Southeast Asian antiques in Thailand are usually stunningly expensive. Thais, Chinese, Malaysians, and Singaporeans are all fanatical collectors themselves, and pay as much as any Western buyer. If you think you're getting a super deal on a Thai antique, think twice.

Foreign women in Thailand get quite a few stares, and Thai women as often as Thai men will be eager to chat and become your friend. Although there's no doubt that attitudes are changing, traditional Thai women dress and act modestly, so loud or overly confident behavior from a foreign woman can be a shock to both men and women alike. It's also worth noting that Thai men often see foreign women as something exotic. If you're being subjected to unwelcome attention, be firm, but try to stay calm—"losing face" is a big concern among Thai men and embarrassing them (even if it's deserved) can have ugly repercussions.

▮ TIP→ **Distribute your cash, credit cards, IDs, and other valuables between a deep front pocket, an inside jacket or vest pocket, and a hidden money pouch. Don't reach for the money pouch once you're in public.**

▮ TAXES

A 10% Value Added Tax (V.A.T.) is built into the price of all goods and services, including restaurant meals. You can reclaim some of this tax on souvenirs and other high-price items purchased at stores that are part of the V.A.T. refund program at the airport upon leaving the country. You cannot claim the V.A.T. refund when leaving Thailand by land at a border crossing. Shops that offer this refund will have a sign displayed; be sure to ask shopkeepers to fill out the necessary forms and make sure you keep your receipts. You'll have to fill out additional forms at the airport.

V.A.T. refund guidelines are particular. The goods must be purchased from stores displaying the V.A.T. REFUND FOR TOURISTS sign. Purchases at each shop you visit must total more than B2,000 before they can fill out the necessary forms. The total amount claimed for refund upon leaving the coun-

try cannot be less than B5,000. You must depart the country from an international airport, where you finish claiming your refund at the V.A.T. Refund Counter—allow an extra hour at the airport for this process. You cannot claim V.A.T. refunds for gemstones.

For refunds less than B10,000, you can receive the money in cash at the airport, or have it wired to a bank account or to a credit card for a B100 fee. Refunds over B10,000 are paid either to a bank account or credit card for a B100 fee.

▮ TIME

Thailand is 7 hours ahead of Greenwich Mean Time. It's 12 hours ahead of New York, 15 hours ahead of Los Angeles, 7 hours ahead of London, and 3 hours behind Sydney.

▮ TIPPING

Tipping is not a local custom, but it is expected of foreigners, especially at larger hotels and restaurants and for taxi rides. If you feel the service has been less than stellar, you are under no obligation to leave a tip, especially with crabby cabbies.

In Thailand, tips are generally given for good service, except when a price has been negotiated in advance. If you hire a private driver for an excursion, do tip him. With metered taxis in Bangkok, however, the custom is to round the fare up to the nearest B5. Hotel porters expect at least a B20 tip, and hotel staff who have given good personal service are usually tipped. A 10% tip is appreciated at a restaurant when no service charge has been added to the bill.

EFFECTIVE COMPLAINING

Things don't always go right when you're traveling, and when you encounter a problem or service that isn't up to snuff, you should complain. But there are good and bad ways to do so.

TAKE A DEEP BREATH. This is always a good strategy, especially when you are aggravated about something. Just inhale, and exhale, and remember that you're on vacation. We know it's hard for Type A people to leave it all behind, but for your own peace of mind, it's worth a try.

COMPLAIN IN PERSON WHEN IT'S SERIOUS. In a hotel, serious problems are usually better dealt with in person, at the front desk; if it's something quick, you can phone.

COMPLAIN EARLY RATHER THAN LATE. Whenever you don't get what you paid for (the type of hotel room you booked or the airline seat you pre-reserved) or when it's something timely (the people next door are making too much noise), try to resolve the problem sooner rather than later. It's always going to be harder to deal with a problem or get something taken off your bill after the fact.

BE WILLING TO ESCALATE, BUT DON'T BE HASTY. Try to deal with the person at the front desk of your hotel or with your waiter in a restaurant before asking to speak to a supervisor or manager. Not only is this polite, but when the person directly serving you can fix the problem, you'll more likely get what you want quicker.

SAY WHAT YOU WANT, AND BE REASONABLE. When things fall apart, be clear about what kind of compensation you expect. Don't leave it to the hotel or restaurant or airline to suggest what they're willing to do for you. That said, the compensation you request must be in line with the problem. You're unlikely to get a free meal because your steak was undercooked or a free hotel stay if your bathroom was dirty.

CHOOSE YOUR BATTLES. You're more likely to get what you want if you limit your complaints to one or two specific things that really matter rather than a litany of wrongs.

DON'T BE OBNOXIOUS. There's nothing that will stop your progress dead in its tracks as readily as an insistent "Don't you know who I am?" or "So what are you going to do about it?" Raising your voice will rarely get a better result.

NICE COUNTS. This doesn't mean you shouldn't be clear that you are displeased. Passive isn't good, either. When it comes right down to it, though, you'll attract more flies with sugar than with vinegar.

DO IT IN WRITING. If you discover a billing error or some other problem after the fact, write a concise letter to the appropriate customer-service representative. Keep it to one page, and as with any complaint, state clearly and reasonably what you want them to do about the problem. Don't give a detailed trip report or list a litany of problems.

INDEX

PHOTO CREDITS

NOTES

NOTES

NOTES

NOTES

NOTES

NOTES

ABOUT OUR WRITERS

Karen Coates, who updated the Essentials chapter and the Cambodia chapter, has covered Southeast Asia since 1998, starting with a gig as an editor at the *Cambodia Daily.* She is a correspondent for *Gourmet Magazine* and writes regularly for newspapers, magazines, and journals in the United States and Asia. She is the author of *Cambodia Now: Life in the Wake of War,* and also keeps a food blog at www.ramblingspoon.com/blog.

Mick Elmore tackled the sights and lodging sections of the Bangkok chapter and the Around Bangkok chapter, which includes Kanchanaburi, where he has lived since early 2006. He arrived in Bangkok in 1991, after a five-month journey from Melbourne, Australia, and has called different places in Thailand and Cambodia home ever since. A freelance journalist since 1984, he writes for several magazines and wire services. Mick's a Fodor's veteran, covering destinations as far flung as Indonesia and Colombia, as well as Thailand (for several editions).

Robin Goldstein traveled many, many miles for this edition, covering Bangkok, the Central Plains, Isan, and the Eastern Gulf of the beaches region. Fortunately he's an old pro, having written for more than 30 different guidebooks; he's covered destinations for Fodor's ranging from Argentina to Hong Kong. He currently resides in Austin, Texas, where he is the editor-in-chief of the Fearless Critic series of restaurant guides, making far more use of his culinary training than of his law degree.

Six years after moving from the Islands of Aloha to the Land of Smiles, **Trevor Ranges** is still spending his free time exploring Thai beaches and islands. Following the credo: "I suffer so that you don't have to," Trevor searches out luxurious resorts, charming beach bungalows, and savory restaurants that are not only postcard perfect, but provide the friendliest Thai service. In between sojourns around Southeast Asia, he writes for various magazines and a collaborative Web project, www.thailandroad.com. This edition, he also tackled the Laos chapter.

Robert Tilley is a veteran Fodor's writer and researcher. He masterminded the first Gold Guide to Germany in 1988 and updated it regularly until 1999, when he left Europe for Asia. From his current base in Chiang Mai, Northern Thailand, he writes for several regional and international publications and is working on his third book. He updated the Northern Thailand chapter.